Historical Dictionary of Women's Education in the United States

Edited by
LINDA EISENMANN

Greenwood Press
Westport, Connecticut • London

Library of Congress Cataloging-in-Publication Data

Historical dictionary of women's education in the United States /
   edited by Linda Eisenmann.
       p.   cm.
   Includes bibliographical references (p.).
   ISBN 0–313–29323–6 (alk. paper)
     1. Women—Education—United States—History—Encyclopedias.
   I. Eisenmann, Linda, 1952–   .
   LC1752.H57   1998
   371.822—dc21   97–32966

British Library Cataloguing in Publication Data is available.

Library of Congress Catalog Card Number: 97–32966
ISBN: 0–313–29323–6

First published in 1998

Greenwood Press, 88 Post Road West, Westport, CT 06881
An imprint of Greenwood Publishing Group, Inc.

Printed in the United States of America

The paper used in this book complies with the
Permanent Paper Standard issued by the National
Information Standards Organization (Z39.48–1984).

10 9 8 7 6 5 4 3 2 1

Contents

Preface

The *Historical Dictionary of Women's Education in the United States* is a concise reference tool for researchers, scholars, teachers, students, and laypersons interested in examining significant events, ideas, movements, institutions, and people concerned with the history of women's education in the United States from the colonial period to the present. More an encyclopedia than a dictionary, the book discusses the history of women's education in America through a series of 245 original entries contributed by 104 scholars from the United States and abroad. Each entry defines a subject and explores its significance to women's educational history. When presenting a wide-ranging topic like a biography or a historical movement, the entry emphasizes the particular contributions to education.

Creating a reference book may be, by nature, a conservative activity. That is, the editor is capturing the state of knowledge at a particular point in time and ''conserving'' it for future use. However, the editor can also hope to alert readers to areas where knowledge is newly growing, where interpretations are changing or contested, and where research is underdeveloped. Selecting entries to cover this range, especially in burgeoning fields like women's history and educational history, poses true intellectual challenges and may, on occasion, present inconsistencies in coverage. For example, *Dictionary* readers will find an essay on deaf education for women but not one for visually impaired women. Such a discrepancy results because a historian of the hearing-impaired has recently treated the issue of women's education, making an up-to-date scholarly analysis readily available. Similar discrepancies may appear throughout the volume, although by using the index readers can find coverage of topics that did not receive a separate alphabetical entry. For instance, working-class women do not have a separate entry, but their issues receive good coverage in the entries on Hull-House, labor colleges, the Women's Trade Union League, and labor unions.

Several criteria guided selection of topics. First, the volume tries to represent the geographic, racial, and socioeconomic diversity of schooling for girls and women throughout the various eras of U.S. history. Here, too, coverage varies depending on the availability of solid scholarship. Many of the entries treat the history of white women and girls, an accurate representation of the bulk of scholarship in educational history. However, a wider array of ethnic and class perspectives increasingly informs historical studies, providing better coverage of Native American women, immigrants, and students at nonprestigious institutions. African American women, for example, have received considerable historical attention in recent years, so the number of entries on their efforts is relatively full; however, the histories of both Hispanic American women and Asian American women in U.S. schools are only beginning to receive sustained attention. There, single entries examine the issues through a historiographic approach.

A second selection criterion was the inclusion of both formal and informal educational settings, since women's history has demonstrated that the full picture of women's participation in American life involves traditional institutions as well as alternate routes. Thus, schools and colleges, school founders and leaders, and educational movements are included; but less traditional sources of women's education also appear, such as suffrage organizations, women's clubs, advocacy groups, and popular writers. Comprehensive entries on movements or themes such as female literacy, teaching, or the Progressive Era provide good sources for an overall presentation on women's roles and educational opportunities.

Third, the number of biographies is minimized in favor of issues, events, and themes that cover the range of women's education in a topical format. The *Dictionary*, therefore, provides a wider context for understanding individual accomplishments, and readers are urged to consult the cross-referenced topics.

Cross-references, indicated in the text by **boldface** with an asterisk (*), will expand information about any particular subject. For example, some entries, such as Mount Holyoke Female Seminary, have a narrowly defined scope. However, the reader should also turn to entries on seminaries, academies, teaching, common schools, and separate spheres to complement and extend understanding of this particular institution. Each entry also provides a short bibliography directing readers to good sources on each topic as well as related issues. A selected bibliography at the end of the volume provides a list of the strongest general sources on women's educational history. Finally, the introduction to the *Dictionary* and the appendix, "Timeline of Women's Educational History in the United States," both can help readers put this particular educational history into a wider perspective.

Numerous scholars, including the more than one hundred *Dictionary* contributors, offered sound advice on the inclusion of topics and the availability of scholarly work. In particular, I am grateful to two colleagues who served as advisers to the entire project. Professor Barbara Beatty of Wellesley College, an expert in the histories of preschool education and teacher education, and Professor Sally Schwager of the Harvard Graduate School of Education, a scholar in women's educational history with a particular interest in secondary schooling, provided invaluable guidance. In addition, a group of able research assistants, each of whom is a student of women's education, provided scholarly as well as administrative support to the project. I thank Sarah Burley, Amelia Kaplan, Renée Sbaschnig, Kimberley Dolphin, Karen Philipps, Christine Brown, and Heather Sullivan. I learned a great deal from each scholar's contributions and suggestions; however, as editor, I assume responsibility for editorial decisions or omissions.

Introduction

The story of women's education in the United States is a continuous effort to move from the periphery to the mainstream in both formal institutions and informal opportunities. Because their needs seemed different and insignificant, and their very intelligence was questioned, females were seldom welcomed into schools or colleges. In response, they developed a two-pronged approach of separatism. While never abandoning the effort to open traditional educational doors, women created their own separate institutions. Thus, women's colleges and **normal schools*** for teacher training paralleled the older or better-known colleges and universities that trained men for business and the professions. Simultaneously, women used the **separate spheres*** of influence that had been designated for them since colonial times, taking advantage of the informal power ceded to them in domestic, familial, and religious arenas. There they created and educated themselves through nonschool opportunities and associations to become better mothers and community leaders. Organizations as diverse as the **Girl Scouts**,* the **National Council of Negro Women**,* the **General Federation of Women's Clubs**,* and the **National College Equal Suffrage League*** provided women opportunities to expand both their knowledge and skill.

A full story of women's educational history winds through both recognized and little-known leaders and settings and is not always a tale of continuous progress. Although some measures show steady improvement—for example, the **female literacy*** rate or graduation from schools and colleges—other issues recur with disturbing frequency, such as the continued push for full support of women's institutions and the ongoing battle for access and equity. The 1990s are demonstrating renewed struggles around **affirmative action**,* family values, and welfare, all issues that recur in the history of women's push for educational parity.

COLONIAL AND REPUBLICAN ERAS (1600s TO EARLY 1800s)

Both the colonial era and the early years of the new nation were marked by a lack of consistent educational institutions for either men or women. No system existed to provide schooling for boys and girls; most education was rudimentary and held in women's homes (**dame schools***) or makeshift **district schools**.* Teachers taught the basics of arithmetic and the alphabet. More important was religious training offered by whatever sectarian group dominated a town or settlement. Character formation constituted a prime goal of early education, and both girls and boys used the Bible as a basic text.

Women played a key role in spreading and strengthening religious values within both the family and the community. The **Great Awakening*** was a series of religious revivals that swept the eastern seaboard from 1700 through 1750. With its emphasis on personal conversion and public testimony for both men and women, the movement allowed females the chance to influence others in their religious activities and choices. Some women led prayer groups and spoke publicly or wrote about their conversions. This enhanced role for women in formal churches was an entering wedge that they used over many decades to strengthen their public role and their demands for adequate education.

Late eighteenth-century leaders recognized women's influence on the family as a significant way to foster the values of a newly independent Republic. Early advocates for women like **Abigail Adams**,* **Judith Sargent Murray**,* and Mercy Otis Warren pushed for women's role and women's rights in the new nation. Adams reminded her husband to "remember the ladies" in crafting laws that would enhance their participation; influenced by Enlightenment thought, Murray called for stronger educational opportunities that would allow women to exercise their political and moral reasoning. Although such direct calls did not always produce widespread change, the matching of women's familial role with the needs of the new nation did. The notion of "**Republican mother-hood**,"* a modern term for the belief that women could influence the next generation's citizens, propelled the opening of formal education for girls. Although a somewhat limited way of asserting women's educational rights, the notion nonetheless justified women's need for schooling and influenced creation of stronger formal opportunities.

The sporadic availability of education in the early Republic led to vastly different educational achievement for women and men, depending on region of the country, urban or rural setting, social class, and gender. The rudimentary literacy rate in New England in 1675 reached about 45 percent for women and 70 percent for men; by 1790, the gender gap had closed, with 80 percent of women literate and slightly more for men. In the South and West, the figures diverged more significantly.

EARLY NINETEENTH CENTURY (1820–1860)

The decades preceding the Civil War showed significant advances in formal education for both genders, but they also reveal a vastly different story for the nation's white and black women. White women, who were beneficiaries of the legacy of Republican motherhood, found new justifications for their demands for education, while black women—the vast majority slaves in the South—found continued prohibitions against their formal schooling.

The concept of Republican motherhood rested on women's primary authority within the home. In colonial times, women and men had generally worked side by side in a domestic economy; certainly labor was divided, but both parents often produced their work from the homesite. With the antebellum rise in urbanization and industrialization, women's domestic role heightened as men were increasingly called into an economic sphere beyond the home. Although scholars are beginning to question the strength of the "separate spheres" ideology in actual practice, this powerful notion nonetheless limited female access to education. The market economy demanded increased skills from men but not from the majority of women.

However, the same ideology that had encouraged women's education for instructing their nascent Republican citizen-sons took on a new aspect in the hands of female educational leaders. A strong group of institution builders including Sarah Pierce, **Emma Willard**,* **Catharine Beecher**,* **Mary Lyon**,* and **Zilpah Polly Grant Banister*** borrowed this ideology to assert a strong need for women's education. Women's domestic authority stemmed from belief in their moral superiority, a notion that had been enhanced by women's role in the First and **Second Great Awakenings**.* As men moved further into the economic and political spheres, women were expected to sustain the purity of the home. An ideology of **"true womanhood"*** appeared in the **prescriptive literature*** of the antebellum era, exhorting women to be pure, pious, submissive, and domestic. As women developed these qualities, they asserted themselves as the community's moral leaders. What Willard, Beecher, and others recognized in this division of authority was a keen opportunity for women to move more publicly into the role of educating children. If women could lay claim to being more pure and pious than men, then surely they should be the formal teachers of children as well as their informal guides within the family.

The opportunity for women to assume public roles as teachers was enhanced in the mid-1800s by the growth of the **common schools**.* Starting in Massachusetts and Connecticut through the efforts of **Horace Mann**,* Henry Barnard, and others, local public schooling was organized and systemized for the first time. The casual outlines of district schooling were being replaced by early efforts to standardize curriculum, attendance, and teacher qualifications. Girls as well as boys increasingly entered elementary schools, raising the need for additional teachers.

Teaching,* like schooling, had been haphazard work before the growth of common schooling. Men—often college students with a need to earn their tuition money—served as teachers whether or not their skills or inclinations suited the job. Yet women had been recognized, at least within the home, as the proper guardians of youngsters. With formal training to strengthen their own academic skills, they could make better—even professional—teachers.

The **academies*** and **seminaries*** founded for young women in the early 1800s did not have the sole purpose of training teachers. Some institutions like **Litchfield Female Academy*** sought to provide solid academic training for pupils, sometimes in conjunction with **ornamental education**,* offering needlepoint, sewing, and music instruction in an integrated curriculum. But the schools created by Willard, Lyon, and Beecher pursued a new direction with their clear focus on preparing good Christian teachers. The seeds of women's collegiate education, which would not flower for several decades, were planted in these seminaries.

Parallel with this push for formal schooling, many women pursued informal educational opportunities in the widespread antebellum reform movement. French observer Alexis de Tocqueville had identified Americans' propensity for creating organizations to advance their communal interests, and the antebellum era saw women leading many efforts. The women's rights movement coalesced at the 1848 **Seneca Falls*** Convention when a group of women and men issued a call for women's equality in its **Declaration of Sentiments**,* a document modeled on the Declaration of Independence. **Abolitionism**,* an organized push for elimination of **slavery**,* attracted radical women and men throughout the North. Christian women with an interest in advancing their faith appealed to the **Board of Foreign Missions*** to send them abroad. Each of these movements educated its participants and allowed women to influence others through public advocacy.

Antebellum African American women enjoyed few such opportunities for either formal or informal education. Of the 4.5 million blacks in the United States in 1860, 4 million were slaves, all in the South. Although initially schooling of slaves had not been prohibited, over time laws declared that slaves could not be educated. Punishments for those who learned to read or write were severe; nonetheless, clandestine **moonlight schools*** and other informal efforts managed to allow about 5 percent of slaves to become literate. Although some records show free blacks in the North and the South receiving academy education, many free blacks were effectively denied education as well.

MID–LATE NINETEENTH CENTURY (1860–1890)

The latter half of the nineteenth century produced huge advances in formalized educational opportunities for women of all backgrounds. In an era of institution building, several efforts began as firm bases for women's ongoing educational involvement. Collegiate education opened to women, both through separate **women's colleges*** and, more reluctantly, in coeducational universities. Normal schools thrived as providers of **teacher education*** to women nationwide. **High schools**,* although not mass institutions until after 1900, began to serve a portion of the population. Common schooling spread throughout the country, formalizing its systems and its goals. With Emancipation, educational institutions for African Americans burgeoned, from elementary schools to colleges and training institutes. Education for Native Americans grew, although its purpose of assimilating Indians into white culture often defeated the self-determination of native people.

Oberlin College* in Ohio generally wins distinction as the first true college to open to women, welcoming its first female students in 1837. Oberlin further staked its radical claim by inviting African American students into its coeducational setting and, for years, trained most of the nation's prominent black women educators. Collegiate education remained limited for women until the establishment in 1865 of **Vassar College**,* the first of the so-called **Seven Sisters*** women's colleges. By 1894, **Wellesley**,* **Bryn Mawr**,* **Radcliffe**,* **Barnard**,* and **Smith Colleges*** had opened specifically for women, and **Mount Holyoke Female Seminary*** had converted to collegiate status. These seven institutions soon took the lead in offering strong classical curricula to women and in providing most of the professorial jobs open to women.

Coeducation,* although customary in the common schools, proceeded cautiously at colleges and universities. In the late 1860s and 1870s, with a push from the federal **Morrill Land-Grant Act**,* state universities began to serve a wider population than had small sectarian private colleges throughout the country. Not all universities chose to open as coeducational, but the insistence of female taxpayers about the public nature of these schools encouraged universities such as Iowa, Wisconsin, and Kansas to serve women as well as men. The shunting of women into "ladies" or **normal departments**,* however, revealed the lack of enthusiasm that often greeted widespread coeducation.

Normal schools were not officially women's institutions, but in practice, women far outnumbered men at these teacher-training schools. Often less rigorous and with shorter degree programs than colleges, normal schools allowed students to strengthen their own educations and to gain valuable marketable skills as teachers. Although usually headed by men, some normal schools had female presidents, or preceptresses, and offered another avenue for women to test their leadership skills.

High schools, a late-century innovation sandwiched between normal schools and colleges, did not attract a steady clientele until after the turn of the twentieth century. Before then, high schools generally drew boys and some girls who planned to attend college but still less than 7 percent of the age group. When these institutions took on a more comprehensive nature after 1900, offering general and **vocational education*** along with English and classical programs, they would prove to be greater draws to women than men, a development of considerable consternation to educational planners.

Common schooling was successful first in New England where systematization proved easiest. The older district system of education disappeared in Massachusetts by 1882. By the turn of the century, the South and Midwest strengthened local and state systems of schooling, although regional differences, frequently exacerbated by racial issues, made implementation variable. Nonetheless, the common schools served girls in numbers equal to boys, offering solid literacy training for females, as well as providing the single largest opportunity for women to work as teachers.

Emancipated blacks in the South—or **freedmen**,* as they were known—were not welcomed enthusiastically into the growing common school systems. The first schools for newly freed slaves were missionary efforts by the **American Missionary Association*** and the Freedmen's Bureau, a federal agency that provided basic needs as well as schools. The educational demands of this population were huge, spanning children to adults. Night schools, Sunday schools, and common schools were created, with both local and northern teachers serving crowded schools and classrooms. Women constituted three-quarters of these teachers, and about one-eighth of teachers were African Americans.

Although advanced education for African Americans lagged behind white schooling for several decades, the first black colleges and training institutions began in this era. Many African Americans had been trained at Oberlin or elsewhere and created their own institutions to help spread educational opportunities among black Americans. **Anna Julia Cooper**,* **Fanny Jackson Coppin**,* **Nannie Helen Burroughs**,* and others joined the better-known Booker T. Washington and W.E.B. Du Bois as educational leaders of African Americans. While the two men vied for philosophical prominence in educating black Americans—Washington arguing for mass industrial and vocational training, and Du Bois for liberal education of a professional ''talented tenth''—the women generally negotiated an educational practice that served both the vocational and the professional needs of the African American population. **Bethune-Cookman College**,* **Spelman College**,* the **Institute for Colored Youth**,* and **Howard University*** all served African American women pushing for a share of educational opportunity.

Native Americans were subject to policies of assimilation throughout the nineteenth century; the government-sanctioned goal was to blend Indians into the white population, with education as one strong means. The **Bureau of Indian Affairs*** (BIA) held primary responsibility for ''civilizing'' native people through schooling, and it contracted with missionary groups to provide basic education for Indians. This system proved ineffective, however, and after the 1880s, the BIA ran its own Indian schools, usually boarding institutions like **Carlisle Indian School*** that took Indian children from their homes and educated them at some distance. Returning to reservations, these Indians fit neither their old way of life nor the new style pushed on them in the schools. The domestic arts program created by the women of the **Field Matron Program***

of the 1890s was similarly unsuccessful in substituting Euro-American values, as many Indians resisted efforts to obliterate their traditional life.

By 1900, an array of educational options served girls and women throughout the country, sometimes in mainstream schooling, but just as often in separate institutions that treated white women, black women, and Indian women as groups with different needs. Although resources and opportunities rarely equaled those of men, most of these late-century institutions provided strong bases for women's subsequent activity.

PROGRESSIVE ERA (1890–1920s)

Progressive Era* reformers recognized that government and other public institutions could play a large role in ameliorating the vast changes Americans were experiencing as immigration, urbanization, and industrialization buffeted their lives. Institutions of all types grew: Businesses consolidated and expanded, school systems formalized, government agencies proliferated, professions coalesced, and civic organizations burgeoned. Women, some college trained but all civic minded, assumed leadership roles in many Progressive movements.

In terms of access, the late Progressive Era marked a high point for women students' participation in collegiate life, not reached again until the 1980s. In 1920, women constituted 47 percent of all college students; in the elementary schools, female students matched their proportion of the general population, and in the high schools, they exceeded it. As women moved through college, they sought postgraduate and professional opportunities, only to find that graduate schools and the professions were not as welcoming as undergraduate institutions. In law and **medical education**,* women were generally excluded from formal educational opportunities. Interestingly, both of these professions began with apprenticeship as the primary training mode; when law and medical schools cornered the market on professional training after the turn of the twentieth century, women were effectively excluded. Many women, for example, had trained at all-female medical colleges. These separate institutions lost out, however, in the profession's move to upgrade qualifications and training. Thus, the percentage of women physicians dropped between 1910 (6 percent) and 1930 (4 percent); in law, women were still only 2 percent of all lawyers by 1930. Other professional areas—sometimes derogated as **semiprofessions***—drew women and became, effectively, female areas. In **librarianship**,* nursing, and **social work**,* women represented two-thirds or more of all practitioners by the 1930s, although men frequently held the most visible managerial and leadership roles.

Teaching, too, rapidly experienced **feminization**.* By 1880, 80 percent of schoolteachers were women, and large percentages of college and normal school graduates pursued teaching as a career. In keeping with Progressive Era tendencies to build systems and bureaucracies, the schools established hierarchies of authority that usually found men as superintendents and principals, and women as classroom teachers. To strengthen the voice of women teachers under this arrangement, unions began to flourish after 1900. Some, notably the **Chicago Teachers' Federation*** (CTF), were led by strong women for several decades. **Margaret Haley*** and Catherine Goggin not only headed the CTF; they also supported the candidacy of **Ella Flagg Young*** as the nation's first female superintendent of a major urban school system (Chicago, 1909–1915) and as first female president of the nation's largest educators' organization, the National Education Association (1910). Besides **teacher unions**,* which were primarily an urban effort, women also exercised authority in more rural areas as **county superintendents*** who supervised schools, certified teachers, and apportioned state funds. Nationwide, women constituted one-quarter of county superintendents during the Progressive Era but held more than half of these posts in some western states.

Besides these formal opportunities for women to pursue and lead education, the Progressive Era was marked by an amazing array of informal educational efforts, many crafted and sustained by women. The **suffrage*** movement, which won women's right to vote in 1920, spawned several national organizations with women as leaders and advocates. The **settlement house movement**,* made most prominent by **Jane Addams**'s* Chicago-based **Hull-House**,* brought educated women to underserved city populations with educational, health, and legal advocacy. **Kindergartens*** began as child-centered efforts by a group of middle-class women reformers who saw early education of children both as a way to enhance the lives of youth and their families and as a vocational opportunity for women. A notion of government's efficacy in improving people's lives highlighted the Progressive Era; besides economic agencies like the Federal Trade Commission and the Interstate Commerce Commission, family-oriented agencies including the **Women's Bureau*** and the Children's Bureau emerged with women as both clients and leaders. The huge sweep of the **women's club movement*** at the turn of the century exemplified women's involvement in civic, educational, and literary affairs. White and black middle-class women took responsibility for improving local civic life, as well as their own educations. Many of these efforts in **social housekeeping*** allowed women an informal authority in civic affairs that was ultimately formalized when movements like kindergartens, public health, and protective labor legislation became institutionalized contributions to public life.

Working-class women were not merely recipients of services during the Progressive Era. Through grassroots efforts by working women and men, many **labor colleges*** flourished during the century's early decades. Organizations like Brookwood Labor College in New York and Commonwealth College in Arkansas were cofounded by women who sought to raise consciousness and train leaders in the workers' movement. The **Women's Trade Union League*** supported a Training School for Women Organizers in Chicago. Even some traditional colleges joined the workers' education movement; the **Bryn Mawr Summer School for Women Workers*** shared its elite setting with women factory workers for two decades. Through these efforts, the Progressive Era stands as one of the nation's strongest in building institutions that would sustain educational services throughout the twentieth century.

MODERN ERA (1940s–1990s)

The Great Depression of the 1930s helped end the institutional growth of the Progressive Era, although recovery from that disturbance and from World War II in the 1940s and 1950s fueled another round of change for women and for education. Many of the professional and educational advances women had made during the war years evaporated in the 1950s, when women's percentage as college students (30 percent in 1950) and professionals diminished. Nonetheless, the **G. I. Bill*** of Rights—which served women in the same proportion as their membership in the wartime military (3 percent)—began to change the country's notion of the clientele that could benefit from collegiate study, and colleges themselves began a period of enormous growth and change.

The modern era affected women's education through changes in three arenas: cultural, legal, and educational. Culturally, the civil rights and feminist movements hit their strides in the 1950s and 1960s, expanding women's sense of entitlement to equal services, opportunities, and treatment. In many ways, the civil rights movement, which preceded the 1960s rejuvenation of feminism, was a training ground for women leaders, teaching them techniques, arguments, and approaches to fostering equity. The feminist movement, often regarded as a white middle-class women's effort, expanded women's options formally and informally. The **Commission on the Status of Women**,* for example, highlighted concerns for women nationwide and created a blueprint for attacking inequities.

Legal changes followed the increase in cultural awareness of women's issues. **Title VII of the Civil Rights Act*** (1964), **Title IX of the Education Amendments of 1972**,* and the **Women's Educational Equity Act*** (1974) created legal support for changes that women pushed in education and employment. Protections around **sexual harassment*** and affirmative action proved more controversial, setting precedents that remain disputed after two decades.

Educationally, new formats and opportunities expanded to serve women's new demands. **Reentry programs*** for women returning to school and college after raising families pushed institutions to create expanded counseling and financial aid services; likewise, new delivery systems enhanced continuing education efforts. Community colleges exploded in numbers after the 1960s; women and minority students often used these institutions as their initial entry to higher education and constituted more than half of those student populations. In traditional colleges and universities, **women's studies*** and **women's centers*** gave institutional form to increased interest in women's issues. These innovations were not without critics, however, who regarded these research focuses as less serious and less scholarly than more long-standing fields.

Nearing the turn of the twenty-first century, American women's education has undoubtedly made enormous progress. Rudimentary female literacy is nearly universal, girls graduate from high school at slightly higher rates than boys, women constitute more than half of all college students, law and medical schools graduate at least one-third women, and women have moved into the mainstream in many fields. Yet such statistics that demonstrate unquestionable positive growth should not disguise pockets of continuing concern, difference, and dispute. Although, for example, basic literacy is solid, "functional illiteracy," which measures skills adults need to reach their full potential, remains at more than 20 percent of the adult American population, many of whom are women living in poverty. The nature of poverty itself is being questioned, with issues about who deserves government aid and under what circumstances forcing re-examination of decisions that had experienced increasing support for several decades. Single women who are mothers of young children, a vulnerable group in terms of education and other needs, will be especially affected by these changes. Title IX and affirmative action have increased financial support for women's programs, but a new version of the **"backlash"*** that challenged women's educational success in the first decades of this century is asking whether these formal supports have gone too far. As a new century turns, many issues related to women's education are up for reargument, although women's advocates will be able to respond from a base of unprecedented formal and informal support.

abolitionism. Abolitionism is the fervent pre–Civil War reform movement that opposed both **slavery*** and gradual abolition and called for immediate emancipation of slaves. Rooted in the evangelical enthusiasm of the **Second Great Awakening**,* the abolitionist crusade used moral suasion to seek repentance not only of slaveholding southerners but also of complacent northerners. Abolitionists were predominantly white, native-born, Evangelical Protestant members of the upwardly mobile middle class, although free blacks had fought slavery and racism even earlier. The movement was particularly strong in cities and towns swept by the free market economy because northerners concerned with the social turmoil and moral disorder that plagued their own communities made the sin of slavery the target of moral regeneration.

Among reformers, women were most apt to carry the antislavery message. As mothers, they seemed entitled to fight the "peculiar institution" that destroyed families. Moreover, while the ideology of **separate spheres*** excluded the majority of women from the booming cash economy, it nonetheless granted them moral superiority. Women also entered the public sphere when praying aloud and repenting with men during revivals.

William Lloyd Garrison led the way in recognizing the importance of women to the abolitionist cause. His radical newspaper, *The Liberator* (1831–1866), included a "Ladies' Department," seeking the sympathy of women readers. The abolitionist press was both educational medium and recruiting tool for new activists. Beginning with the founding of the all-male New England Anti-Slavery Society in 1832, followed in 1833 by the Boston Female Anti-Slavery Society (BFASS), the Philadelphia Female Anti-Slavery Society (PFASS), and the American Anti-Slavery Society (AASS), such groups quickly proliferated. By 1838 the AASS claimed a membership of 250,000 and over 1,300 local societies. The work of women as successful fund-raisers, primarily through annual antislavery fairs, provided financial support. Lydia Maria Child, author of *An*

Appeal in Favor of That Class of Americans Called Africans (1833), organized the first antislavery fair in 1834 in Boston. Fairs featured needlework of female sewing circles as well as antislavery gift books such as *The Liberty Bell* (1839–1858), edited by Maria Weston Chapman, bringing thousands of dollars.

Nonetheless, women's contributions went far beyond financial support of male leadership. Female activity ranged from petitioning Congress or joining a society to writing antislavery tracts and speaking on lecture circuits. Although abolitionist women worked within separate female organizations and often circulated sex-separated petitions, not all women agreed on the propriety of such public activity. The result was concentration of female activism in the Garrisonian wing of the movement. In contrast, moderate abolitionists, including conservative women, and most ministers found it unladylike for female speakers to address promiscuous assemblies of men and women and believed that women's influence should be confined to the home.

However, a small number of women, particularly **Quakers**,* took to the podium. The 1837 lecture tour of southerners Angelina and Sarah Grimké in New England and New York served to galvanize movement support [see **Charlotte Forten Grimké***]. Wherever they spoke, more petitions were signed, and new female societies were organized. Petitioning, lecturing, and organizing were closely interrelated.

The spread of abolitionism was further tied to antebellum women's interest in education. **Teaching*** was the most common occupation of working women who joined the movement. The prime movers of the Boston society, Chapman and Child, were teachers. Members also included African American teachers: Susan Paul taught in the Smith School, and Julia Williams, herself a pupil of **Prudence Crandall**,* became a teacher in Martha and Lucy Ball's school for black girls. Similarly, Philadelphia members included Sarah Mapps Douglass, a well-known free black and teacher, whose school for black women received funding from PFASS in return for its use as a meeting place. The dual goal of abolitionism and self-improvement was pursued by black female literary societies such as Boston's Afric-American Female Intelligence Society and Philadelphia's Female Minervian Association. Black abolitionists trusted that education produced **race uplift*** and would diminish white prejudice.

One teacher and militant abolitionist was Abby Kelley of Massachusetts. Unfunded by any society and facing intimations of immorality, young Kelley traveled alone to speak in rural New England where she met lukewarm abolitionists and violent anti-abolitionist mobs. Her Quaker background helped her master the art of quotations and unrehearsed public lectures, which she delivered in schoolhouses when barred from speaking in churches. Her eloquence energized the movement as far as Ohio, where her visits to **Oberlin College*** impressed students, including **Lucy Stone**.* Detractors, however, coined the term "Abby Kelleyism" to describe women who transgressed gender boundaries.

By 1840 the "woman question" regarding female participation, public speaking, and voting rights led to irreconcilable divisions between Garrisonians and their opponents. When in 1840 Kelley was elected by a substantial majority as the first woman on the AASS executive committee, 300 dissenting men walked out and formed the all-male American and Foreign Anti-Slavery Society. The next month, at the World Anti-Slavery Convention in London, women's participation was again debated. British abolitionists who disapproved resolved to seat women behind a curtain. Among those hidden were Lucretia Mott and Elizabeth Cady Stanton, who began thinking about a women's rights convention, leading to **Seneca Falls*** eight years later.

After the 1840 split in the movement and the shift from moral reform to politics, female participation declined. Whereas female activities yielded to male control of antislavery organizations, the less controversial antislavery fairs reached their peak in the 1850s. They succeeded in bringing a larger audience to abolitionist speakers and raising more money without recruiting new members. Women continued to engage in writing and editing, and Harriet Beecher Stowe's best-selling, sentimental novel *Uncle Tom's Cabin* (1852) reaffirmed the importance of women's influence, albeit limited to the private sphere. Nonetheless, radical abolitionism of the 1830s provided antebellum women with practical training in political activism, paving the way for the women's rights movement beyond 1850.

There was also a legacy of tension between white and black activists. Black abolitionist Frederick Douglass attended the Seneca Falls convention. Yet racial prejudice persisted in the white women's movement, directly addressed by Sojourner Truth's eloquent plea for political inclusion, "Ar'n't I a Woman," at the 1851 convention in Akron, Ohio.

Ultimately, unity broke down over strategy during the 1860s. Not all abolitionists kept alliance with the Republican Party, whose priority was black male **suffrage**.* While Lucy Stone and her husband Henry Blackwell agreed to postpone woman suffrage in order to ensure passage of the Fourteenth and Fifteenth Amendments, Susan B. Anthony and Stanton broke with Republican abolitionists and fought for enfranchisement of women.

Bibliography: Ronald G. Walters, *The Antislavery Appeal: American Abolitionism after 1830* (1978); Karen Sanchez-Eppler, "Bodily Bonds: The Intersecting Rhetorics of Feminism and Abolition," *Representations*, 24 (Fall 1988): 28–59; Dorothy Sterling, *Ahead of Her Time: Abby Kelley and the Politics of Antislavery* (1991); Shirley J. Yee, *Black Women Abolitionists: A Study in Activism, 1828–1860* (1992); Debra Gold Hansen, *Strained Sisterhood: Gender and Class in the Boston Female Anti-Slavery Society* (1993); Jean Fagan Yellin and John C. Van Horne, eds., *The Abolitionist Sisterhood: Women's Political Culture in Antebellum America* (1994).

Isabelle Lehuu

academies. Academies were the first form of higher education for American women. They began in the mid-eighteenth century and flourished in the decades immediately following the American Revolution. In the antebellum era the term *seminary** was used more frequently, although there are no clear defining features distinguishing the two. The earliest female academies include the Ursuline Convent school in New Orleans (1727) and the Bethlehem Female Seminary in Pennsylvania (1749).

In the colonial era, families who wanted and could afford education for girls beyond a few years in a public school might send their daughters to a **venture school**.* These schools sprang up in cities, mostly in the Northeast, and tended to be short-lived. Men, women, or couples might advertise instruction in a foreign language, dance, music, or art. A student might take dance at one school, French at another, and lessons in embroidery at a third. Few schools offered a coherent program of study, and few offered highly academic subjects.

Academies, in contrast, were more institutionalized. Many academies built separate facilities, rather than holding school in the dining room of a house, as Sarah Pierce did when she opened her famous **Litchfield Female Academy**.* Academies increasingly incorporated and adopted boards of trustees. The more serious academies offered certificates or diplomas when a student completed an outlined course of study, an approach that became much more common in the nineteenth-century seminary movement.

Academies varied widely, sometimes offering ''ornamental'' subjects of music, painting, and embroidery, and sometimes more academic subjects similar to men's academies, teaching literature, grammar, rhetoric, and some arithmetic. Many combined ornamental with academic subjects. **Ornamental education*** was relatively short-lived, and it may have been a type of female training, just as men trained for specific occupations. But ornamental education was neither functional nor accessible to more than a wealthy few.

Women who wanted to pursue education had to confront several issues that men did not. One was why they needed advanced education at all. People assumed that some men needed education to become ministers, lawyers, doctors, or other professionals. Women, on the other hand, were expected to become wives and mothers; the classical curriculum of Latin, Greek, and mathematics seemed of little use. Yet women had powerful influence on men as mothers, wives, and sisters, and they needed an education to use their influence well. Benjamin Rush, a Revolutionary War surgeon and proponent of public schools after the war, argued that because ''the opinions and conduct of men are often regulated by the women'' (Rush, p. 22), women needed a sound education to help shape virtuous and patriotic citizens [see **"Republican motherhood"***].

A related issue was fear that education would ''unsex'' women and unfit them for domestic roles. Proponents replied that education would better fit women for their domestic duties. Wives and mothers needed the common sense and reasoning skills that academies could teach. Attention to serious study would make them more sensible and would counter the deleterious effects of novel reading. In addition, an educated woman would make a better companion. **Abigail Adams*** thought that a ''well-informed woman . . . is more capable of performing the relative duties of life, and of engaging and retaining the affections of a man of understanding, than one whose intellectual endowments rise not above the common level'' (quoted in Norton, p. 265).

Early proponents of female education cited other practical purposes. Rush and Noah Webster urged academies to teach English grammar, handwriting, and bookkeeping so that women could help their husbands or fathers run businesses or so that, if widowed, women could manage their own estates. Rush recommended that women study geography and history, and perhaps astronomy and natural philosophy, believing that these subjects would prevent superstition, reflecting Enlightenment beliefs in the importance of science. Finally, virtually everyone agreed that academies should provide instruction in Christian principles.

A second challenge to women, after establishing a need for education, was the all-too-common belief that women simply were not as smart as men and not capable of the same type of education. **Judith Sargent Murray*** contested this in her 1790 essay "On the Equality of the Sexes." She argued that men's superiority in reason and judgment stemmed only from differences in training. "If an opportunity of acquiring knowledge hath been denied us," Murray wrote, "the inferiority of our sex cannot fairly be deduced from thence."

The two most well-known early academies were Miss Pierce's Litchfield Female Academy, and the **Young Ladies' Academy of Philadelphia**.* Pierce's school for young ladies was founded in 1792 in Litchfield, Connecticut; by 1810 women attended from throughout the eastern seaboard. Pierce wanted to "vindicate the equality of female intellect" and to cultivate the abilities of memory, imagination, and reason in her students. Further, one of the notable features of the school was its proximity to a law school for men; the many marriages between students enhanced the academy's popularity.

Another type of academy was the Young Ladies' Academy of Philadelphia. Founded in the 1780s, its curriculum mirrored that of the Academy of Philadelphia for boys, which Benjamin Franklin helped establish. Both sets of students studied reading, writing, arithmetic, grammar, composition, rhetoric, and geography.

Academies developed earlier in the North than in the South. One reason is that the South was more devastated by the Revolutionary War and therefore had fewer resources available for education. Wealthy southern families often sent their children north for schooling.

Academies of the mid- to late-eighteenth and early nineteenth centuries represent a bridge from the inconsistent, highly variable, and seldom academic education offered in venture schools in the colonial era to the more rigorous and organized schooling in seminaries of the nineteenth century. Seminaries, in turn, helped pave the way for the **women's college*** movement.

Bibliography: Benjamin Rush, *A Plan for the Establishment of Public Schools and the Diffusion of Knowledge in Pennsylvania; To which Are Added Thoughts Upon the Mode of Education Proper in a Republic* (1786); Thomas Woody, *A History of Women's Ed-*

ucation in the United States (1929); Linda K. Kerber, *Women of the Republic: Intellect and Ideology in Revolutionary America* (1980); Mary Beth Norton, *Liberty's Daughters: The Revolutionary Experience of American Women, 1750–1800* (1980); Barbara Miller Solomon, *In the Company of Educated Women: A History of Women and Higher Education in America* (1985); Nancy Beadie, "Emma Willard's Idea Put to the Test: The Consequences of State Support of Female Education in New York, 1819–67," *History of Education Quarterly*, 33, no. 4 (Winter 1993): 543–562; Doris J. Malkmus, "Female Academies in the Early Republic" (master's thesis, University of Oregon, 1993).

Margaret A. Nash

Adams, Abigail Smith. Abigail Smith Adams (1744–1818) was an early champion of women's education in the United States whose influence mounted posthumously with publication of her prolific correspondence. Selections of her letters, particularly those to her husband John Adams, second president of the United States, were first published in 1840 and grew enormously popular through frequent reprinting. Evident in her letters was Adams's belief in the equality of the male and female intellect and in the need for expanded educational opportunities for women, ideas that resonated with the burgeoning mid-nineteenth-century feminist movement. However, her fundamentally conservative nature rejected the idea of a social order or political system that treated the sexes alike. Close friends with Thomas Jefferson, John Jay, and other Revolutionary leaders, Adams used her connections to stay abreast of and to influence current events and political thought. She pushed but did not overstep the bounds of womanly conduct prescribed by eighteenth-century society and to future generations stood as one of the premier examples of a traditional woman able to find both public and private fulfillment.

Adams was born in Weymouth, Massachusetts, where her father, Reverend William Smith, served as Congregational minister for almost fifty years. Her mother, Elizabeth Quincy, a descendant of prominent Puritan families of the Bay Colony, bore three other children, Mary in 1741, William in 1746, and Betsey in 1750. Though their brother attended the local school, Adams and her sisters were educated at home, first by their mother, who taught them letters and numbers in addition to the household managerial skills then considered the most essential components of a woman's education. Unlike most fathers of his day, Reverend Smith tutored his daughters in advanced reading and encouraged them to explore his library. Adams eventually became one of the best-read women of the era. In her adolescence, she studied the works of Shakespeare, Milton, Dryden, Pope, and other literary figures and attempted to teach herself French. Later she read treatises on ancient and modern history, political theory, theology, and other subjects traditionally reserved for masculine audiences.

In 1764, Abigail married John Adams, a Boston lawyer from nearby Braintree who was unusually appreciative of his wife's intellect. Their first decade of marriage was peaceful compared to the times that lay ahead. Abigail bore four children who survived infancy, Abby in 1765, John Quincy (later the sixth president of the United States) in 1767, Charles in 1770, and Thomas Boylston in 1772. John became increasingly embroiled in politics and eventually moved to Philadelphia as a delegate to the first Constitutional Congress in 1774, leaving Abigail in Braintree to oversee the family farm and finances. The next ten years were characterized by prolonged absences of her husband; John worked in Congress and then served in succession as diplomat to France, Holland, and England, and these lengthy separations compelled Abigail to become a prolific correspondent. The difficulty of raising children alone confirmed her opinion that advancing women's education would create more learned mothers and thus promote better **early childhood education**,* which would in turn benefit future generations [see **"Republican motherhood"**].

A letter to John written early in 1776 contains a rare chiding that constitutes her most frequently quoted passage: "I desire you would Remember the Ladies, and be more generous and favorable to them than your ancestors. Do not put such unlimited power into the hands of the Husbands. Remember all Men would be tyrants if they could." Although this excerpt is often cited as a demand for women's **suffrage**,* it was likely intended as a denunciation of the British common law practice recognizing absolute power of husbands over wives. Adams never set down her opinions in formal writing, which she considered an unfeminine pursuit, but she valued acquaintances with learned women of her day who did publish their ideas, including Mercy Otis Warren and Catharine Macaulay. Still, Adams's generally conservative attitude led to frequent disagreement with more radical contemporaries such as Mary Wollstonecraft.

In August 1779, Abigail and John were reunited in London, remaining together abroad until 1788. Upon their return to the United States, John served two terms as vice president under George Washington from 1789 to 1797 and one term as president from 1797 to 1801, when he and Abigail became the first residents of the Washington, D.C., White House. Throughout John's political career, Abigail remained his most intimate and trusted adviser, and their ardent Federalist convictions overlapped so much that disagreements between them were very rare. In 1801 John retired from politics, and the couple returned to a new home in Quincy, Massachusetts. Despite the death of two children, the remaining seventeen years of Abigail's life were rewarding, particularly because of her eldest son's successful political career. She contracted typhoid fever in the fall of 1818 and died a few days short of her seventy-fourth birthday.

Bibliography: Lyman H. Butterfield, ed., *Adams Family Correspondence*, 6 vols. (1963, 1973, 1993); Charles W. Akers, *Abigail Adams: An American Woman* (1980); Lynne Withey, *Dearest Friend: A Life of Abigail Adams* (1981); Edith Belle Gelles, *Portia: The World of Abigail Adams* (1992); Rosemary Skinner Keller, *Patriotism and the Female Sex: Abigail Adams and the American Revolution* (1994). See also Adams's surviving letters at the Massachusetts Historical Society, Boston, Massachusetts.

Baird Jarman

Addams, Jane. Jane Addams (1860–1935), a pioneer of the **settlement house movement*** in the United States, founded Chicago's **Hull-House*** in an effort to bridge the gap between the rich and the poor via access to education in both practical skills and the fine arts. Herself a member of the first generation of college women, Addams devoted her life to the creation of a community in which her ideals of open-minded, free expression; experience-based education; and human solidarity could flourish.

The eighth of nine children of whom four survived to maturity, Addams was born on September 6, 1860, in Cedarville, Illinois. Her mother, Sarah Weber, died when she was two, which likely contributed to Addams's intense devotion to her father William, a prosperous community leader, state senator, and fervent believer in **abolitionism**.* When Addams was seven, her father married Anna Haldeman, an energetic, highly intelligent woman who did much to foster Addams's education, particularly in literature and music.

Motivated initially to pursue a career in medicine, Addams planned to attend **Smith College*** in Massachusetts; she acceded to her father's wishes, however, and attended the more local **Rockford Female Seminary*** in Illinois, as had her two older sisters before her. A zealous student with demonstrable leadership skills, Addams graduated first in her class and played an important role in Rockford's evolution into a degree-granting institution during her tenure there.

Her beloved father's death immediately after the completion of her degree in 1881 sent Addams into a severe depression, leading her to seek medical care from rest cure advocate S. Weir Mitchell and to take two trips abroad. It was on the second of these trips that Addams visited London's Toynbee Hall, an early British example of the settlement house, and thereby conceived the philanthropic project that was to become her life's work.

With her traveling companion and former Rockford classmate Ellen Gates Starr, Addams returned to the United States within the year (1889) determined to find a place that could serve as a home for educated women—thus providing an alternative to the traditional career of wife, mother, and homemaker—in a neighborhood whose residents would benefit from exposure to high culture. Charles Hull's dilapidated former mansion at Halsted and Polk Streets, a rare survivor of the Great Chicago Fire, seemed just the place. An ever-growing immigrant community surrounded Hull-House and quickly became the raison d'être for both its facilities and the talents of the seventy-plus women who came to call it home.

Initially, Addams and Starr rented only the second floor of the building from Charles Hull's cousin and business partner, Helen Culver, in 1891. A philanthropist herself, Culver was instrumental in helping the pair finance the rapid, exponential growth of Hull-House into a charitable cultural and educational community complex. By 1907, Hull-House covered an entire city block, with thirteen buildings devoted to dormitory-style housing for single women, meeting rooms for **labor unions**,* nursery facilities for the children of working mothers, and the salon where the Hull-House Players put on performances about important women in history and where significant thinkers like John Dewey came to participate in spirited discussions of social issues.

In accordance with her British compatriots who served as the inspiration for Hull-House, Addams was greatly influenced by John Ruskin and considered aesthetics and justice intimately related. Like Hull-House visitor Dewey, she located a pragmatic function in education and thus included sewing classes and courses in **home economics*** in the Hull-House program along with music classes and invigorating physical activity on the first public playground in the city.

This playground—eventually taken over by the city—was but one of a long series of 'firsts for Addams and Hull-House. Ever mindful of the unique needs of the immigrant population that constituted their neighbors, Addams and the Hull-House residents offered the first citizenship preparation classes in the city, the first college extension courses (in conjunction with the **University of Chicago***), and the first group work school. Conscious of the dire conditions under which their neighbors were forced to live and work, Addams, Florence Kelley, Julia Lathrop, and Grace Abbott, among others, boldly undertook the first investigations of truancy, children's reading, working conditions in factories, urban sanitation, and tenement conditions in Chicago. Addams served on the Chicago Board of Education from 1905 to 1908, and largely as a result of her efforts, the city developed its first compulsory education law and the first juvenile court in the world. Hull-House also provided a forum for some of the first organized women's labor unions, including the Women Shirt Makers, Women Cloak Makers, and the Chicago **Women's Trade Union League**.*

Powerfully committed to the advancement of marginalized members of society, Addams served as the first vice president of the **National American Woman Suffrage Association*** (1911–1914), presided at the International Congress of Women at the Hague (1915), and helped found the American Civil Liberties Union (1920). When she was named the first woman recipient of the Nobel Peace Prize in 1931, Addams promptly turned over the monetary portion of the award to the Women's International League for Peace and Freedom (WILPF), another organization that she helped create.

World peace became a central focus of Addams's energies in the last thirty years of her life. She organized the Women's Peace Party (1915) and founded WILPF in 1919, serving as its president for a decade [see **peace education***]. Amid strident opposition from those who supported the United States' entry into World War I, Addams staunchly opposed the war. Ever a popular public figure, Addams was nevertheless bitterly attacked for her opposition to the conflict, and this experience provided the material for one of her better-known works, *Peace and Bread in Time of War* (1922).

A tireless speaker and writer, Addams traveled widely throughout her years in residence at Hull-House, urging progressive reform to combat the social ills created by rapid industrialization. In fact, Addams's work at Hull-House pro-

vided the genius behind much **Progressive Era*** reform; an early and spirited
supporter of woman's **suffrage**,* Addams seconded Theodore Roosevelt's presidential nomination at the Progressive Party convention in 1912. She published
a staggering array of articles during her lifetime, but probably her most enduring
contribution to the literary world is her autobiography, *Twenty Years at Hull-
House* (1910). The clearest, most methodical articulation of her social philosophy, the book's popularity and significance surpass even that of its companion
volume, *The Second Twenty Years at Hull-House* (1930).

By the late 1920s Addams's health was in serious decline. She persisted
through a major surgery in 1931 and a heart attack in 1933 with her work at
Hull-House, committed to facing the new problems posed by the onset of the
Great Depression. On May 21, 1935, she succumbed to intestinal cancer in a
Chicago hospital. She is buried in her hometown of Cedarville, Illinois.

Bibliography: Daniel Levine, *Jane Addams and the Liberal Tradition* (1971); Allen F.
Davis, *American Heroine: The Life and Legend of Jane Addams* (1973); Mary Jo Deegan,
Jane Addams and the Men of the Chicago School (1988); Jean Bethke Elshtain, "A
Return to Hull House: Reflections on Jane Addams," in Jean Bethke Elshtain, ed., *Power
Trips and Other Journeys: Essays in Feminism as Civic Discourse* (1990); Maura Sul-
livan, "Social Work's Legacy of Peace: Echoes from the Early Twentieth Century,"
Social Work, 38 (September 1993): 513–520.

Regina Buccola

affirmative action. Affirmative action can be defined generally as any steps
taken to remedy current or past discrimination against certain groups of people.
It exists in two main areas of opportunity: higher education and employment.
Affirmative action plans can be required by law for certain organizations, court
ordered in a discrimination suit, mandated in a union contract or consent decree,
or developed voluntarily by an organization.

The idea of affirmative action developed in the early 1960s as the civil rights
movement was in full force, pressuring the government to take action against
widespread discrimination. President John Kennedy responded in 1961 with Executive Order 10925 which urged federal contractors to "take affirmative-
action" to hire more minorities. Later, the Civil Rights Act of 1964 prohibited
discrimination on the basis of race, color, sex, religion, and national origin in
several areas. Two sections concern affirmative action: **Title VII**,* which applies
to employment, and Title IX, which applies to education. In 1965, President
Lyndon Johnson issued Executive Order 11246, which prohibits discrimination
along the same categories as Title VII; however, the order went further to require
federal contractors of certain sizes to adopt "goals and timetables" to achieve
proportional representation, thus promoting affirmative action plans. Executive
Order 11375 added "sex" to the categories protected by such orders. Affirmative action was the first antidiscrimination policy that explained to organizations "what to do" rather that "what not to do."

Affirmative action plans are intended to prevent discrimination in two forms as defined by Title VII. *Disparate treatment* occurs when people of a certain race, religion, sex, color, or national origin intentionally are not hired on the basis of those qualities. The only exception for such discrimination is a bona fide occupational qualification. For example, a Chinese restaurant legitimately may hire only employees of Asian background to enhance the atmosphere of the restaurant. A second form of discrimination is *adverse impact*. While no intentional discrimination exists with this form, some type of selection system results in elimination of more people of a certain group. Adverse impact is legally defended only by demonstrating the validity of the selection system.

Affirmative action was conceived to provide equality of opportunity to un-derrepresented groups. Following the spirit and language of Title VII and the Thirteenth, Fourteenth, and Fifteenth Amendments, it aimed to create a color-blind society where racial, ethnic, or other attributes and resources were not considered in decisions. The concept evolved from equality of opportunity to equality of results. In this approach, racial and sexual attributes are considered when hiring or admitting applicants but not for discriminatory purposes. The goal is to create a racial or sexual balance within the school or workplace, even when some preferential treatment is in order to amend for past discrimination against certain groups. Justice Thurgood Marshall wrote in 1974 that equality of opportunity to reach one's potential as a citizen is tied to everyone's having an equal start in life.

Within institutions of higher education and companies, four types of affir-mative action are used separately and in combination: (1) recruiting underrepre-sented groups; (2) changing management/administration attitudes and prejudices toward certain groups; (3) removing discriminatory obstacles; and (4) giving preferential treatment to certain groups. The fourth type is the most controversial because it conflicts with standards of fair employment, whereby employment decisions are not affected by illegal discrimination. Affirmative action, for the purpose of creating a balance, requires that employment decisions be made, at least in part, on the basis of characteristics such as race or sex.

Developing an affirmative action program begins with a utilization analysis to compare how many minorities and women are working or participating in certain capacities in the organization versus an estimate of the number of qual-ified minorities and women available in the local applicant pool. The analysis allows the organization to find areas or departments where there is underutili-zation. From the results, the organization establishes "goals and timetables" to achieve equal employment opportunities for minorities and women. The only requirement is that the organization make a "good-faith effort." The goals are not meant to be rigid quotas but reasonable targets. Federal contractors are required by law to develop this plan and present supporting documentation of good-faith efforts to the Office of Federal Contract Compliance in the Depart-ment of Labor.

Implementing an affirmative action plan requires careful consideration of puz-zling questions. A salient issue is what constitutes minority status and how individuals define themselves. Current standards consider only certain races, ethnic groups, and females because they have suffered past discrimination; however, some feel that economic status should also be a consideration in affirmative action programs.

During the Reagan administration, the use of **quotas*** in affirmative action plans was debated. Quotas, which require a set number of minorities and women in each job group or educational program, have been decried as discriminatory against white males, a form of reverse discrimination. In reality, Executive Order 11246 does not require a quota system, and quotas were court ordered only in situations of extreme discrimination. In response to the quota backlash of the 1980s, the Civil Rights Act of 1990 made quotas an illegal method of affirmative action.

Since passage of Title VII and Executive Order 11246, racial and gender imbalances in organizations have decreased but not been eliminated. Additionally, some feel that the affirmative action movement has harmed certain protected groups by causing minorities and women to doubt their own abilities and qualifications because "they were only accepted because of affirmative action." Likewise, some argue that affirmative action places underqualified women and minorities into situations where they are destined to fail. Regardless of affirmative action, some areas of employment remain undiversified because of reasons unaccounted for by plan officers. For example, some careers and jobs have a very restricted, self-selected minority job market.

Despite the controversy that affirmative action generates, statistics show that it has made a difference for women and minorities. Between 1980 and 1990, the proportion of all managers who are white women grew by about one-third, from 27 to 35 percent, and the proportion who are women of color more than doubled, 3 to 7 percent (National Council for Research on Women, p. 6). In 1996, 55.1 percent of the total college enrollment was female. Most colleges and universities support affirmative action goals for what they consider compelling educational, social, and moral reasons.

Since the 1980s, considerable challenge has occurred over the concept of "an equal start." The Supreme Court has heard several cases concerning affirmative action and reverse discrimination, and its rulings have been perplexing. In 1995, the Court let stand a lower court ruling in *Podberesky v. Kirwan* that the University of Maryland's minority scholarship program violated the Fourteenth Amendment equal protection clause. It also held in *Adarand Constructors v. Pena* that race-based affirmative action programs are constitutional only if they are "narrowly tailored measures that further compelling government interests." In other words, preferential treatment must withstand the courts' "strict scrutiny."

Cities and states have also reacted to the growing political discomfort with preferential racial and gender treatment in both workplaces and higher education. Richmond, Virginia, suspended its affirmative action program in 1987. In 1996 the University of California Board of Regents voted to end affirmative action in admission, hiring, and contracting at all state campuses by 1997. Later in 1996, the state's voters enacted Proposition 209, which abolished affirmative action in all areas of state and local government. In collegiate admissions, the pendulum has swung from the 1978 Supreme Court *Bakke* decision, which expressly approved the use of race as a factor in admissions, to the 1996 *Hopwood* decision by a lower federal court, which struck down the University of Texas's affirmative action program in admissions.

At the end of the twentieth century, the concept of affirmative action is no longer accepted as a guiding principle, and the debate has become increasingly strident. The problems that originally propelled the legislation have not disappeared, however, and the country continues to ask to what extent government is responsible for guaranteeing equal rights in a nation where issues of race, class, and gender are volatile.

Bibliography: W. E. Block and M. A. Walker, eds., *Discrimination, Affirmative Action & Equal Opportunity* (1981); Mariam K. Chamberlain, *Women in Academe: Progress and Prospects* (1988); Donald Altschiller, ed., *Affirmative Action* (1991); J. Ledvinka and V. G. Scarpello, *Federal Regulation of Personnel and Human Resource Management* (1991); Paul Burstein, ed., *Equal Employment Opportunity* (1994); National Council for Research on Women, *Affirmative Action: Beyond the Glass Ceiling and the Sticky Floor* (1996).

Brenda Lamb and Deborah Elwell Arfken

African American sororities. Greek-letter societies for African American college and university women began around the turn of the twentieth century. Within twenty years, four national Greek-letter sororities were founded by a generation of young black women, the majority of whom were daughters and granddaughters of former slaves. Three of those sororities were organized at **Howard University**,* the first black institution of higher education to offer courses of study consistent with curricula of the most prestigious American universities. At Howard, the founding of Alpha Kappa Alpha (AKA) sorority in 1908 was followed by Delta Sigma Theta in 1913 and, finally, with Zeta Phi Beta in 1920. Sigma Gamma Rho, founded in 1922 at Butler University in Indianapolis, was the only African American sorority to be founded in a predominantly white private women's school.

These four **sororities*** are similar to their white counterparts in demanding high academic attainment, stressing the importance of performing charitable civic duties, imparting secret rituals, and engaging in social activities. However, they differ in owing their existence in no small part to the theory of **race uplift**,* the predominant social construct of the emerging black middle class of the early 1900s. Racial uplift was widely advanced by W. E. B. Du Bois in his essay ''The Talented Tenth'' (1903) and championed by black women's civic and social organizations. These newly organized women were inspired by the challenge to ''lift as we climb,'' doing their part to eradicate the illiteracy and poverty that restricted the black masses.

It seems no coincidence that the founding of sororities occurred during the first quarter of the century, arguably the most progressive era in African American history until the civil rights movement at midcentury. The AKAs, Deltas, Zetas, and Sigmas, as they are known in casual parlance, flowered in a literary and social milieu unknown by previous generations of their ancestors in America, an environment that likely fostered their commitment to race uplift. Sorority founders would have been inspired by both Booker T. Washington's *Up from Slavery* and the alternate philosophies of Du Bois's *Souls of Black Folk*. They would have been encouraged by the founding in 1909 of the **National Association for the Advancement of Colored People**,* an organization determined to gain denied civil rights through the courts. After 1911, they would have read its literary magazine, *The Crisis*, edited by Du Bois, which focused on evidence of racial advancement across the country. Their role models dedicated to race uplift in a number of settings and methods would have been social activists **Mary Church Terrell*** and Ida B. Wells and writers Langston Hughes, Countee Cullen, and Zora Neale Hurston.

Although these sorority women were inspired by the same role models, each organization created a unique niche in its charge to serve the community. The AKAs promoted the arts and culture in an effort to foster race pride. The Deltas sponsored political activism, eagerly supporting the **suffrage*** movement. Zeta Phi Beta, organized as a sister organization to the Phi Beta Sigma fraternity at Howard, focused its efforts on academic achievement. Sigma Gamma Rho initially extended membership to elementary or secondary education majors, with the goal of providing professional development for new teachers.

By the 1990s, with over 335,000 members in 2,300 undergraduate and graduate chapters, both nationally and internationally, these four sororities continued to transcend the frequent unfortunate image of being solely frivolous. By becoming powerful forces in voter registration and the civil rights movement of the 1960s, by providing millions in college scholarships, by founding literacy and pregnancy prevention and health collaboratives, each sorority has, through a united sisterhood, accepted the century's long challenge of racial uplift.

Bibliography: Marjorie Parker, *Alpha Kappa Alpha, 1908–1958* (1958); Ola Adams, *Zeta Phi Beta Sorority (1920–1930)* (1965); Pearl Schwartz White, *Behind These Doors a Legacy: The History of Sigma Gamma Rho Sorority* (1974); Paula Giddings, *In Search of Sisterhood; Delta Sigma Theta and the Challenge of the Black Sorority Movement* (1988); Darlene Clark Hine, ed., *Black Women in America: An Historical Encyclopedia*, 2 vols. (1993).

Brenda Williams Mercomes

American Association of University Women. The American Association of University Women (AAUW) is a national organization dedicated to promoting education and equality for women and girls. Members must be graduates of colleges and universities recognized by the association. Headquartered in Washington, D.C., the AAUW also has branch organizations throughout the United

States. In 1995, membership numbered 150,000. Through current projects such as the Initiative for Educational Equity and the long-standing graduate fellowship program, the AAUW has been a major force in seeking to improve and expand the educational opportunities available to American women throughout their entire lives, while at the same time promoting a supportive institutional environment.

The AAUW was established in 1921 from a merger between the **Association of Collegiate Alumnae*** (ACA), a national body founded in 1881, and the Southern Association of College Women (SACW), a smaller, regionally based group formed in 1903. Both the ACA and the SACW sought to improve and expand opportunities available to women in higher education. The ACA in particular had a long history of significant contributions to the cause of equity in education, the professions, and public life throughout the United States, while the SACW focused on problems unique to women's education in the South. With time, however, the need for two separate organizations became less apparent. When the International Federation of University Women was formed in 1920, with membership restricted to one association from each nation, the ACA and the SACW decided to join forces.

The AAUW thus constituted a new entity in name only; in spirit, it represented a continuation of the aims and ideals of its predecessors, especially the ACA. The reorganization did, however, bring about changes in the association's structure and leadership designed to broaden its focus on education and equity for women throughout the United States and the rest of the world. A new Committee on Educational Policy was formed, responsible for establishing the AAUW's annual educational agenda. This committee also nominated candidates for the office of educational secretary, a full-time staff position created to provide oversight of the association's various education-related programs. Other committees newly formed or reorganized included the Committee on Standards, responsible for monitoring conditions for women in the nation's colleges and universities; the Committee on the Economic and Legal Status of Women, which conducted investigations into subjects such as the earning capacity of college women and the relation between women's professional lives and domestic responsibilities; the Committee on Legislation, which sponsored various legal measures involving the welfare and education of women and children; and the Committee on International Relations, responsible for fulfilling the association's commitments to the International Federation of University Women. By 1929, the growing size and complexity of the organization prompted the appointment of a general director to serve as the association's full-time administrative head.

One of the most important tasks carried out by the AAUW's national organization involved evaluating the status of women in the nation's colleges and universities. Throughout the 1930s in particular, when women's programs suffered a lack of funds, the AAUW's accreditation process played a critical role in assuring the maintenance of high standards for women's higher education. Colleges and universities desiring inclusion on the AAUW's roster of recognized

institutions had to meet criteria in regard to admission and graduation requirements designed to ensure that men and women obtained the same quality of
education. Institutions were expected to provide adequate classrooms, dormitories, and extracurricular facilities for women students. **Vocational education,***
especially as geared toward women's traditional roles, was discouraged in favor
of a liberal arts curriculum. In addition, the number, status, and salaries of
women faculty and administrators were considered, along with the representation
of women on the boards of trustees. In numerous instances, the prestige associated with inclusion on the AAUW's list acted as a positive inducement to the
improvement of conditions for women on campus.

Although the AAUW discontinued its accreditation program in 1949, opting
instead to accept women graduates of colleges or universities approved by one
of the nation's six regional accreditation agencies, the association remained dedicated to serving the needs of women students, faculty, and staff. Establishment
in the late 1970s of the AAUW's Legal Advocacy Fund, which recognizes
innovative attempts to improve conditions for women in academe and also provides financial assistance to individuals charging discrimination or **sexual harassment,*** represents a continuation of this commitment.

Another important function of the national organization has been to administer
the AAUW's fellowship program. Established in 1889 under the auspices of the
ACA, the fellowships provide funds for women to pursue graduate education
and scholarly research, both in the United States and abroad. The international
fellowship program, established in 1917, enables women from other countries
to study in the United States. Financed primarily through members' contributions, the fellowship program has grown steadily. Beginning with small sums
of $500 or $1,000 awarded annually to one or two women, by 1929 the association awarded nearly a dozen grants totaling $14,000. By the mid-1950s, when
the AAUW voted to establish a separate tax-exempt foundation, annual donations from members exceeded $200,000 and provided for over seventy fellow-
ships. In 1995 the AAUW Educational Foundation awarded nearly $2.5 million
to 264 women. By the mid-1990s, more than 6,500 individuals from 110 countries had received fellowships and grants.

When the ACA initiated the fellowship program before the turn of the century,
no other organization provided support for women to pursue graduate study.
The AAUW thus inherited a tradition of leadership in funding women's educational aspirations. In more recent times, the AAUW Educational Foundation
has sought to broaden its scope, both in terms of individuals who benefit from
grants and the fields of endeavor grant recipients are encouraged to pursue. In
1962, for example, the Educational Foundation instituted its College Faculty
Program, aimed at encouraging mature women to return to school in order to
pursue academic careers. Also in 1962 the foundation made its first grant to an
African American, thereby signaling a new commitment to promoting education
for minority women. This resolve was reinforced in 1969 with the establishment
of the Coretta Scott King Project, intended to foster the study of African Amer-

ican history and nonviolent change. Having abandoned its exclusive emphasis on the liberal arts, the AAUW by the 1970s was using its fellowship program to enable women to enter such traditionally male-dominated fields as medicine, law, dentistry, veterinary medicine, architecture, and business administration [see **medical education**,* **semiprofessions***].

A later project, the Eleanor Roosevelt Fund, seeks to extend the AAUW's influence even further by focusing on equity issues in the education of girls from early childhood through **high school**.* Inaugurated in 1988, the fund provides fellowships for public school teachers, especially those in math or science, with a demonstrated commitment to equality in the classroom. The fund also sponsors research initiatives, including two landmark studies, *The AAUW Report: How Schools Shortchange Girls* (1992) and *Hostile Hallways: The AAUW Survey on Sexual Harassment in America's Schools* (1993). Finally, under the auspices of the AAUW's Initiative for Educational Equity, the fund provides resources, lobbying, leadership, and recognition for community-school partnership projects designed to establish models of gender-fair teaching in public schools across the country.

While the national association organizes and oversees these programs, much of the impact of the AAUW occurs at the local level, through the efforts of more than 1,750 branch organizations. Membership in AAUW branches has grown and changed over the years, reflecting shifts in American society, as well as the evolution of the AAUW itself. In the 1930s, for example, when only about 10 percent of young women attended college, AAUW branches provided more than 35,000 university graduates, many of whom also possessed advanced degrees and pursued careers, with a means to achieve professional recognition and form lasting and supportive friendships with other educated women, as well as take an active role in influencing the political process in favor of women's rights. Throughout the 1950s, by contrast, although AAUW membership continued to grow quite rapidly, reaching nearly 144,000 by the end of the decade, a greater percentage of the association's members were housewives and mothers. Branch organizations, meanwhile, tended to adopt a lower political profile, concentrating on community service projects and **continuing education*** for their members. Both changes reflected the era's emphasis on domesticity and conformity. By the 1960s the situation had shifted again, with membership becoming somewhat more diverse and grass roots activism in favor of equal rights and other women's issues enjoying a resurgence. Again, both changes mirrored developments among college graduates and society at large. Throughout the early 1970s, with membership continuing to grow, the AAUW and its branch organizations worked increasingly with other women's groups such as the **League of Women Voters*** and the **National Organization for Women*** in support of measures including **Title IX*** and the Equal Rights Amendment.

By the 1980s, the AAUW began to face new challenges associated with its own success. As women achieved some level of recognition and equality in many fields, the role of organizations like the AAUW came into question, leading to a potential decline in membership and loss of effectiveness. In response, the AAUW refocused its energies, renewing the association's historical commitment to specific issues involving education through projects like the Roosevelt Fund and the Initiative for Educational Equity. In working toward these goals, AAUW members put their own educations to practical use for the benefit of other women. Such has been the association's purpose from the beginning. [See also **women college presidents**,* **women's colleges**.*]

Bibliography: *AAUW Journal* (1921–present); Marion Talbot and Lois Kimball Mathews Rosenberry, *The History of the American Association of University Women, 1881– 1931* (1931); Susan Levine, *Degrees of Equality: The American Association of University Women and the Challenge of Twentieth-Century Feminism* (1995).

Sarah V. Barnes

American Missionary Association. The American Missionary Association (AMA) was the most significant of the many missionary societies engaged in the training and education of African Americans in the mid-nineteenth century. The AMA was founded in 1846, formed by a merger of the Union Missionary Society, the Committee for West Indian Missions, and the Western Evangelical Missionary Society. The organization was staunchly antislavery, its leadership including the evangelical abolitionists Lewis Tappan, Simeon S. Jocelyn, and George Whipple. The association's original mission in the South was oriented more toward **abolitionism*** than education. During the Civil War the AMA began to concentrate on education and religious instruction, particularly among the freedmen, and it provided an opportunity for women teachers to use their skills in service of an ideal [see **freedmen's teachers***].

One of the most notable AMA teachers was Mary S. Peake of Norfolk, Virginia, the daughter of a free black mother and a European father. Her school in Hampton, Virginia, established in 1861, signaled the first step in the AMA's efforts to educate southern blacks. Other significant teachers included Mary Bailey, who founded a school at Fortress Monroe in Virginia; Rachel Crane Mather, who established a school in Beaufort, South Carolina, in 1868 and remained there for thirty-six years; Mary F. Wells, of the Trinity School in Athens, Alabama; and Esther W. Douglass, who taught black children for thirty years in four different states.

The association's teachers were predominantly well educated, white, and female; most were from New England and the Midwest. Many were experienced teachers, although some had no **teaching*** experience or training at all. They overcame many obstacles—hostility from southern whites, poor living conditions, disease, lack of funds, the indifference of the Union Army to their cause, the perceived indifference of President Abraham Lincoln to the plight of the freedmen, and bickering among the association's leaders. Few women held leadership positions. As in society in general, women primarily served as productive, resourceful, hardworking subordinates in the AMA.

For almost a century, colleges founded by the AMA provided the best educational opportunities for southern blacks. The AMA chartered seven institutions of higher learning between 1866 and 1869: **Fisk University**,* Atlanta University, Straight (now Dillard) University, Talladega College, Tougaloo College, **Hampton Institute**,* and Berea College. All except Berea, which was interracial, were founded explicitly to serve African Americans. The AMA was also instrumental in founding **Howard University**,* with the association paying the salary of its first teacher and dominating the university's initial board of trustees.

The AMA was not without flaws. It has been criticized for its paternalistic attitude toward the freedmen, failing to recognize the desire of African Americans for self-determination. In its initial forays into the South, the association failed to gauge the intense power of racial prejudice. Mission schools were often ridiculed as being unrealistic in curriculum and in appraisal of the freedmen's needs; colleges were dismissed as mere vocational schools. By 1880, overcome by increasing northern weariness with "black problems" and incessant money problems, the "great crusade" for the integration of African Americans into society had lost its impetus. There is little doubt, however, that the AMA was successful in its mission of training and educating freedmen, providing relief to scores of families, and assisting in the transition from **slavery*** to freedom.

The AMA continued with its missionary and educational endeavors after Reconstruction, albeit on a smaller scale. The association exists in the 1990s as part of the United Church Board for Homeland Ministries.

Bibliography: Augustus F. Beard, *A Crusade of Brotherhood: A History of the American Missionary Association* (1909); Robert C. Morris, *Reading, 'Riting, and Reconstruction: The Education of Freedmen in the South, 1861–1870* (1981); Joe M. Richardson, *Christian Reconstruction: The American Missionary Association and Southern Blacks, 1861–1890* (1986); Jacqueline Jones, *Soldiers of Light and Love: Northern Teachers and Georgia Blacks, 1865–1873* (1992). See also the American Missionary Association Archives, Amistad Research Center, New Orleans.

Joseph E. Weber

Antin, Mary. Mary Antin (1881–1949) was a Jewish Russian immigrant whose autobiography *The Promised Land* (1912) glorified the American public schools for helping her become an American. Although born in the Russian Pale during Jewish persecutions, Antin's earliest years were happy in her comparatively well-to-do family. Her unusually progressive parents gave her more schooling than was typical for Jewish girls in the Pale. After her family fell upon hard times, her father immigrated to Boston, and the rest of the family followed three years later when Antin was eleven.

Her Yiddish account of her journey to the United States was translated into English by Antin two years after her arrival. *From Plotzk to Boston* was published in 1899. This feat symbolized her rapid progress in mastering the English language, American ways, and Boston's public schools. Four months after her father proudly enrolled her in the first grade at the local school, Antin wrote an

English essay, "Snow," that was published in an educational journal. Within a few years of her arrival, Antin graduated first in her grammar school class. She also became a devoted patron of Boston's public libraries. Proud of her academic accomplishments, despite their extreme poverty, Antin's parents allowed her to attend the **Girls' Latin School*** with the hope that she would go to college and thereafter improve the family's fortunes. Although isolated from her wealthier and more sophisticated classmates, Antin continued her academic success in **high school**.*

Antin's autobiography ends with her high school years. In 1901, she married a non-Jewish German American professor, William Grabau, who took a position at Columbia University. Antin took classes at Teachers College and **Barnard College*** but never a degree. Antin had one daughter. In New York, she met Josephine Lazarus, the poet Emma Lazarus's sister, who encouraged her literary aspirations. Josephine's death spurred Antin to write *The Promised Land*, which was first published as a series of articles in the *Atlantic Monthly*. As the personification of the successfully Americanized immigrant, Antin became a prominent figure on the lecture circuit.

Coming from a world that persecuted her because of her religion and further limited her horizons because of her sex, it is not surprising that Antin so eagerly shed her foreign language, dress, and manners to become American. Devoted to the democratic ideals embedded in the Declaration of Independence, she responded to national efforts to restrict immigration by writing an impassioned defense of open immigration, *They Who Knock at Our Gates* (1914). Here, she praised the public schools for their role in Americanizing immigrants.

During World War I, Antin disappeared from the public eye due to poor health and family problems caused by her husband's rejection of anti-German sentiments aroused by the war. In 1920, without Antin, he immigrated to China where he died in 1946. Long a thoroughly secularized Jew, the threat from Hitler inspired her to write "House of the One Father" (in *Common Ground*, 1941), an article that showed her solidarity with all Jews. She died after a long illness in 1949.

Bibliography: Mary Antin, *They Who Knock at Our Gates: A Complete Gospel of Immigration* (1914); Antin, *The Promised Land*, with a forward by Oscar Handlin (1969); William A. Proefriedt, "The Education of Mary Antin," *Journal of Ethnic Studies*, 17 (Winter 1990): 81–100.

Maureen A. Reynolds

Asian American women's education. A comprehensive history of Asian American women's education has yet to be written. Although scattered work exists on specific incidents and movements, several factors inhibit the creation of a wider history. First, much work on the history of Asian Americans is fairly recent and attempts to counter an early focus solely on discrimination against Asian Americans. As historian Sucheng Chan notes of the Chinese, for example:

"Virtually all the major monographs in Chinese American history written by non-Chinese authors before 1985 dealt with the anti-Chinese movement.... Only in recent years have white scholars told their stories from a more Chinese-centered perspective" that also emphasizes the role of culture and family life (p. xiv). Second, a considerable amount of scholarship on education focuses on current concerns rather than history. Specifically, much work addresses perceptions of Asian Americans as a "model minority" who do not need special services or, worse, threaten the opportunities available to other Americans. A third factor working against a synthetic history is recognition that the term *Asian American* not only covers people from more than twenty different national backgrounds but also conflates the study of groups spanning generations of experience in the United States with that of recent immigrants and refugees. The immigration experience, as well as the educational and economic backgrounds of these various groups, makes comparison of their history a challenge. Finally, the Asian American women's studies movement is still young and has yet to focus much attention on educational history.

The term *Asian American* needs closer definition. Recently, it is often amended to *Asian Pacific Americans* to connote the inclusion of Pacific Islanders, although many people see this as a bureaucratic convenience that combines people of too wide a geographic and cultural base. An advisory group for the California State University system provides one useful clarification of a term that identifies at least 3 percent of the U.S. population: "Asian/Pacific Americans are defined as immigrants, refugees, and the U.S.-born descendants of immigrants from Asia, including Pakistan and the countries lying east of it in South Asia, Southeast Asia, East Asia and the Pacific Islands" (quoted in Nakanishi and Nishida, p. xii).

Immigrants from just a few countries provided the bulk of the initial Asian American population. Chinese and Japanese, who immigrated in the 1800s, and Filipinos, who increased after U.S. acquisition of the Philippines, constituted the largest ethnic groups of Asian Americans before 1970. Over the decades, their children created a large concentration of native-born Asian Americans. In the 1970s, a new influx of foreign-born Asians changed the mix. A first wave of Southeast Asian refugees came in 1975, constituting generally well-educated and urban Vietnamese. A second group began to arrive later in the decade, consisting of poorer refugees from Laos, Cambodia, and Vietnam. The numbers of Koreans and Asian Indians grew during this period as well. By the 1980 census, only 28 percent of Japanese Americans were foreign born, while 91 percent of Vietnamese had been born abroad. Obviously, both the educational needs and histories of these groups vary widely.

The Chinese were the first group to emigrate in large numbers, arriving in the United States following the 1849 Gold Rush in California. Because Chinese were recruited as laborers, the immigrant population tended to be men who came unmarried or who left families behind in China. Most planned to secure their fortunes and return home. In 1900, only about 5 percent of the Chinese population in the United States was female; as late as 1920, only 12 percent. With so few Chinese families, the issue of their formal, public education was considered insignificant by white citizens for several decades. Chinese beliefs about the importance of women to home life also muted interest in girls' education. A reform movement in China in 1898 increased awareness of educating girls, although the rationale generally presumed that educated girls would make better mothers, much like the **Republican motherhood*** beliefs in early America.

In much of California, schooling initially was provided through two private venues. First were missionary schools founded by Christian missionary groups eager to convert the Chinese; their efforts focused on teaching English as well as Christian doctrine. A second source of education were Chinese language schools fostered by a number of Chinese benevolent associations for the purpose of sustaining Chinese language and culture among immigrants and the children. These institutions hired Chinese teachers and followed a curriculum similar to what children would find in their parents' homeland. After public schooling became available in California, these schools became supplements to traditional schooling.

In 1884 a well-documented challenge occurred to the exclusion of Chinese American students from the public schools of San Francisco. Joseph and Mary Tape precipitated a crisis by demanding that their eight-year-old daughter Mamie, born in the United States, be admitted to her local elementary school. The principal denied entrance on the grounds that city school policy prohibited Chinese students from attending public schools. By law, the state legislature followed a ''separate but equal'' principle in segregating Chinese students; by practice, especially in San Francisco, Chinese children were regularly blocked from attendance at any public school. The Tape protest resulted in the quick creation of a Chinese-only school. The school ultimately thrived, although integrated schools became more common by the 1910s. Elsewhere in California and in other states like Hawaii where the Chinese American population was more dispersed, children attended ''mixed'' schools.

The Tapes' challenge occurred during a time of increased nationwide anti-Chinese sentiment. In 1882, the Chinese Exclusion Law suspended the immigration of laborers and was followed by a series of additional acts and court interpretations that further limited not only immigration rights but also reentry opportunities for Chinese men and women who attempted to return to the United States. During the six decades of restricted immigration (1882–1943), women's opportunities were affected by ongoing attempts first to define the female Chinese immigrant population as undesirable prostitutes and later by connecting a woman's immigration and citizenship status to that of her husband. Chinese immigrants, like all Asians, were prohibited from becoming American citizens.

Japanese immigration followed the Chinese movement by several decades. Only in the 1880s did Japan lift restrictions on out-migration, eventually allowing tens of thousands of Japanese women and men to leave Japan for work abroad. Many Japanese settled in Hawaii, where they often began as plantation laborers. Many, however, emigrated to California, which held over half the mainland Japanese American population by 1910. Like the Chinese immigrants, many Japanese hoped to return home, and they sent money back to their families in Japan. Many of the Japanese possessed more skills than the earlier immigrants, partly because of Japan's strong public education system. Female Japanese immigrants averaged two to five years of education; male immigrants, four to six.

Nevertheless, the Japanese inherited much of the discrimination that had been aimed at the Chinese, for similar racial and economic reasons. A high-profile segregation challenge around a ten-year-old Japanese student in San Francisco initially followed the same progress as the Tapes' experience. However, the Japanese rallied around the *Aoki v. Deane* court case, bringing pressure from the local community, from Japan, and from the Japanese ambassador to the United States. A Gentlemen's Agreement signed by Japan and the United States settled the issue in 1907 whereby the school segregation policy was withdrawn in return for immigration agreements favored by Japan.

Some roots of the "model minority" viewpoint may have begun with subsequent Japanese involvement in public schooling. Nisei (second-generation Japanese Americans) children succeeded very well in educational attainment and achievement throughout the first decades of the twentieth century. Discrimination did not end, however, and the forced relocation to internment camps of all Americans of Japanese ancestry in 1942 demonstrates the height of this prejudice, often directed at citizens with long roots in the country. Camp schools aimed at a normal public school curriculum for girls and boys, but the situation itself was hardly a normal experience.

Differences in immigration history often produce different experiences and challenges for Asian American schoolchildren. Whereas children of "older" groups are often assimilated, newer arrivals can face language, cultural, and socioeconomic challenges. Refugee children face particular adjustment concerns, depending on their resettlement experience, family composition, and economic opportunities.

As expected given the difference in immigration histories, the newer Asian immigrants lag behind more established groups in high school completion and participation in higher education. The 1980 census, for example, demonstrated that only 22 percent of Hmong students and 43 percent of Cambodians finished high school, while 80 percent of Japanese Americans did so. Gender differences also appear in high school experience. Overall, 79 percent of Asian American men and 71 percent of women finished high school. Within certain groups, the differences are more pronounced. Ninety percent of Korean American men but only 70 percent of women finished; for Vietnamese Americans, 71 percent and 54 percent. Interpretation of these gender differences requires a deeper understanding of dynamics governing gender relations in Asian American families.

Asian Americans are turning increasingly to higher education, constituting 4 percent of all college students by 1988. Between 1976 and 1988 the number of

Asian American women students doubled. Yet women lag behind men in masters and doctoral studies, and they prefer different fields of study. Women study business, education, and health, whereas men choose business, engineering, and computer science.

Increased interest in Asian American studies combined with the maturation of women's history is producing a wider number of works on Asian American women's history. Stronger attention to the lived experience of these groups—rather than the earlier focus on instances of discrimination—should establish the study of women's educational history as an important facet of Asian American history.

Bibliography: Thomas James, *Exile Within: The Schooling of Japanese Americans 1942–1945* (1987); Sucheng Chan, ed., *Entry Denied: Exclusion and the Chinese Community in America, 1882–1943* (1991); Ronald Takaki, *A Different Mirror: A History of Multicultural America* (1993); Eileen Tamura, *Americanization, Acculturation, and Ethnic Identity: The Nisei Generation in Hawaii* (1993); Don T. Nakanishi and Tina Yamano Nishida, eds., *The Asian American Educational Experience: A Source Book for Teachers and Students* (1995).

Linda Eisenmann

Association of Collegiate Alumnae. The Association of Collegiate Alumnae (ACA) (1881–1921) was the first national organization of women graduates of colleges and universities, with a purpose "to unite alumnae of different institutions for practical educational work." To be eligible for membership, women had to have earned an approved degree from a college or university recognized by the ACA. Through the activities of the association's national committees, as well as local branches established throughout the United States, the ACA sought to achieve equality and expand opportunities for women in education, the professions, and public life. The ACA merged with the Southern Association of College Women in 1921 to create the still-extant **American Association of University Women*** (AAUW).

The preliminary organizational meeting for the Association of Collegiate Alumnae took place in Boston on November 28, 1881. At the instigation of **Marion Talbot,*** a recent graduate of Boston University, seventeen women representing eight institutions—including **Vassar,*** **Smith,*** **Wellesley,*** and **Oberlin*** Colleges, Boston University, Cornell University, and the Universities of Michigan and Wisconsin—met to consider how college women like themselves could best put their degrees to good use. In an era when few women pursued higher education (only 2 percent of the age group) and those who did found few opportunities open to them upon graduation, Talbot and her friends sought a means of overcoming the limitations and the isolation they faced. Their solution was to form a national association of collegiate alumnae who would work together, using the knowledge and skills they had gained as college graduates in order to improve the situation for other women.

At a second meeting, held on January 14, 1882, sixty-five women representing the same eight institutions gathered to adopt a constitution and elect officers. **Alice Freeman Palmer**,* who was then president of Wellesley College and went on to become the first **dean of women*** at the **University of Chicago**,* served as one of the ACA's first directors and was twice elected president. Talbot, who succeeded Palmer as dean of women at Chicago, served as the ACA's first secretary and was also later chosen as president. In general, officers of the association possessed advanced degrees, usually the Ph.D., and, like Palmer and Talbot, held important administrative positions in the nation's **women's colleges*** and **coeducational*** universities. Over the years, the leadership of the ACA thus represented some of the most academically and professionally accomplished women in the country.

Membership in the association grew quickly, from 356 in 1884 to over 2,000 by the turn of the century and nearly 16,000 in 1920. Likewise, the number of institutions recognized by the ACA increased from the original 8 to 15 in 1890, 24 in 1910, and 147 by 1920. To be included on the ACA's approved list, colleges and universities had to meet certain criteria in regard to curriculum, faculty, facilities, and endowment that assured that female graduates received a liberal education equal in quality to that received by male graduates of the same or similar institutions and comparable to that provided by the other colleges and universities already on the association's roster. In addition, the status of women in academic and administrative positions and on the institution's board of trustees was taken into account. As the prestige of the association grew, its role as an accrediting agency enabled the ACA to exert considerable influence over the development of higher education for women in the United States. Only later did organizations such as the Association of American Universities and the Carnegie Foundation for the Advancement of Teaching begin to exercise a similar standardizing function for higher education in general.

By the early years of the twentieth century, several of the ACA's national committees worked together to coordinate the association's efforts to monitor and improve the quality of higher education for women. Other activities on the national level included the work of the Committee on Educational Legislation, which oversaw lobbying efforts on behalf of measures affecting elementary and secondary as well as higher education, and the work of committees studying such diverse subjects as vocational opportunities for college women and child development. Notable research projects sponsored by the ACA included the association's report, issued in 1885, regarding the effects of higher education on women's health, and a further study conducted at the turn of the century surveying the health and marital status of over 3,000 alumnae in comparison to their sisters and female cousins who had not attended college. These reports were significant rebuttals to contemporary claims that higher education was deleterious to women [see *Sex in Education**].

On the local level, most ACA members belonged to branch organizations, which, in addition to providing a social focus and an opportunity for **continuing education**,* also undertook various research and civic service projects commensurate with the goals of the national association. The Washington, D.C., branch, for example, conducted a detailed study of the status of female federal civil service employees, while the San Francisco branch secured the appointment of the first woman member of the city's board of education and the first woman regent of the University of California. ACA branches throughout the country helped establish libraries, theaters, **nursery schools**,* and playgrounds in their local communities.

One of the most important activities undertaken by local branches was to encourage young women to pursue higher education. In addition to sponsoring college fairs and teas for high school seniors, branches offered numerous college scholarships and loans. On the national level, the ACA in the late 1880s and early 1890s established the first fellowships available to women to pursue **graduate education**,* both in the United States and abroad. By 1920, eighty-one such fellowships had been awarded, funded primarily out of members' dues. With few other resources available to support women's graduate work, the ACA played a crucial role in enabling women to obtain advanced degrees and in encouraging other funding agencies to follow its example.

By the second decade of the twentieth century, the ideals underlying the Association of Collegiate Alumnae were beginning to have an impact internationally, leading not only to the formation of ACA branches overseas but also to the establishment in England of a similar body, the British Federation of University Women (BFUW). Responding to the new spirit of internationalism following World War I, the ACA and the BFUW together sponsored the creation in 1920 of the International Federation of University Women (IFUW), an organization composed of representatives of newly formed university women's groups from around the globe. The federation worked to encourage educational exchanges between member nations and to further the cause of equity for women worldwide.

The formation of the IFUW also acted as a catalyst for important changes within the ACA itself. Since 1903 the Southern Association of College Women (SACW), a sister organization of the ACA, had focused on the special challenges of improving educational standards for women in the American South. By the time of the establishment of the IFUW, however, the need for a separate regional organization was becoming less significant, and since only one group from each country could belong to the IFUW, the ACA and the SACW decided in 1921 to join forces to form a single entity, the American Association of University Women.

Although the official existence of the Association of Collegiate Alumnae thus ended, its aims and ideals lived on in the programs of the AAUW. As the first national organization committed to furthering women's educational opportunities and improving the status of women in academic and professional life, the ACA made a significant and lasting contribution to the history of women's education.

Bibliography: Marion Talbot and Lois Kimball Mathews Rosenberry, *The History of the American Association of University Women, 1881–1931* (1931); Roberta Frankfort, *Collegiate Women: Domesticity and Career in Turn-of-the-Century America* (1977); Rosalind Rosenberg, *Beyond Separate Spheres: Intellectual Roots of Modern Feminism* (1982); Susan Levine, *Degrees of Equality: The American Association of University Women and the Challenge of Twentieth-Century Feminism* (1995).

Sarah V. Barnes

Association of Deans of Women and Advisers to Girls in Negro Schools.
The Association of Deans of Women and Advisers to Girls in Negro Schools was the primary professional society for African American women employed in the growing field of student personnel work between 1935 and 1954. The organization originated through the vision of **Lucy Diggs Slowe**,* Dean of Women at **Howard University**,* president of the **National Association of College Women*** (NACW), and chair of its Standards Committee. In March 1929, Slowe invited advisers of girls and **deans of women*** from African American institutions across the country to a conference in Washington, D.C., where representatives of ten public schools and colleges identified and discussed common problems of African American women students, administrators, and faculty. They concluded that institutions not only refused to provide students with adequate campus housing and extracurricular opportunities but also failed to appoint a representative number of women as trustees and administrators or to compensate adequately advisers of girls and deans of women.

Slowe and her colleagues relished the opportunity to meet, and between 1929 and 1935, the Conference of Deans of Women and Advisers to Girls in Negro Schools and Colleges met at the annual convention of the NACW. In 1935, the organization became independent and elected Slowe its first president. Following Slowe's untimely death in 1937, the conference nearly disbanded. However, at its annual meeting at **Tuskegee Institute*** in 1938, members adopted a new constitution and a new name—the Association of Deans of Women and Advisers to Girls in Negro Schools.

The association's mission was threefold: to foster communication within the profession, to enhance the professional status of advisers to girls and of deans of women, and to disseminate the most effective methods for counseling female students in **high schools*** and colleges. Crucial to the organization's survival was Georgia M. Teale, Dean of Women at **Wilberforce University**,* who was elected president.

Between 1939 and 1945, the association met annually at colleges and universities across the South. The postwar period, however, brought great change. In 1946, for the first time, the association held its annual meeting with the National Association of Personnel Deans and Advisers of Men in Negro Institutions, at Dillard University in New Orleans. In 1954, the two organizations merged, forming the National Association of Personnel Workers (NAPW). Consonant with the superior strength of the women's organization, several of its members assumed major leadership roles in the NAPW, serving as the first president, secretary, and chairs of many committees.

The founding of the Association of Deans of Women and Advisers to Girls in Negro Schools coincided with a middle-class preoccupation with authority that characterized a wide spectrum of traditional and emerging professions in the United States between 1880 and 1930. Not surprisingly, deans of women initially organized along racial lines. White deans made two attempts to establish professional societies. In 1903, under the leadership of **Marion Talbot**,* Dean of Women at the **University of Chicago**,* a group founded the Conference of Deans of Women and Advisors in State Universities, a loosely organized body that met biennially until 1922, when it merged with the **National Association of Deans of Women*** (NADW). In July 1916, at Columbia's Teachers College, graduate students and faculty members established the NADW, the primary professional society for white deans of women. During its early years, a few African American women, including Lucy Slowe, joined, but for decades, their numbers remained small.

The most persistently frustrating issue for African American members was the problem of adequate accommodations at the annual meeting of the NADW. Despite the efforts of an activist white minority, this remained an almost insurmountable problem, no matter where the NADW met. Within this context, the Association of Deans of Women and Advisers to Girls in Negro Schools flourished as an independent professional organization.

The Association of Deans of Women and Advisers to Girls in Negro Schools served its constituents in a variety of ways. Not only did it foster a national professional network for advisers and deans, but it also provided one of the few opportunities African American deans had for training and for encountering role models. Most important, it offered African American women in the profession a national platform from which to articulate their vision of secondary and higher education for black women.

Bibliography: Mary M. Carter, "The Educational Activities of the National Association of College Women, 1923–1960" (master's thesis, Howard University, 1962); Hilda A. Davis and Patricia Bell-Scott, "The Association of Deans of Women and Advisers to Girls in Negro Schools, 1929–1954: A Brief Oral History," *Sage* (Summer 1989); Davis and Bell-Scott, "Association of Deans of Women and Advisers to Girls in Negro Schools," in Darlene Clark Hine, ed., *Black Women in America: An Historical Encyclopedia* (1993).

Carolyn Terry Bashaw

B

"backlash." Within the context of women's history, *backlash* is a term scholars use to describe a powerful social or cultural counterassault on women's rights. Backlash can be defined as an effort to minimize and retract advances that feminism has won for women. Backlashes have subsided and resurfaced periodically, always triggered by the presumption that women have made inroads into areas of activity hitherto reserved to men. Backlash manifests itself through the media of popular culture—novels, magazines, newspaper editorials, and films—and in scholarly writings of academics, government officials, and even "liberated" women. To date, the most detailed treatment of this social and cultural phenomenon in the United States is Susan Faludi's *Backlash: The Undeclared War against American Women* (1991).

The themes of backlash have recurred throughout recent history. For example, in *Education for Equality: Women's Rights Periodicals and Women's Higher Education, 1849–1920* (1989), Patricia Smith Butcher describes how leaders of the mid-nineteenth-century American "woman movement" such as Elizabeth Cady Stanton and Susan B. Anthony sought to promote **suffrage*** and other rights for women, including higher education, equal employment, and marital and property rights. By the end of the century, however, a cultural backlash prompted a proliferation of warnings by scholars, religious leaders, medical experts, and journalists who argued that educated women were "feminizing" American society in harmful ways. Opponents of feminism claimed that it was responsible for creating a "man shortage" in various occupations, promoting an "infertility epidemic" among educated women [see **race suicide***], causing "female burnout," and destroying the "values of hearth and home." Rosalind Rosenberg argues that at least one of these themes can be traced to antiquity: the notion that woman's mind is limited by her body.

Whereas the rhetoric of backlash is disseminated openly through various media, its influence in promoting discriminatory practices against women is far more subtle. The introduction of **coeducation*** in North American and British nineteenth-century colleges and universities provides a useful example of a public backlash against women in higher education, described by Elizabeth Seymour Eshback in *The Higher Education of Women in England and America, 1865–1920* (1993). Fearful of impending **feminization*** at Stanford University, in 1899 Mrs. Leland Stanford established an enrollment limit of 500 women. Despite such actions, however, economic factors ensured that women's position as college students was never significantly threatened. In *"Equally in View": The University of California, Its Women, and the Schools* (1995), Geraldine Jonçich Clifford argues that women's enrollments allowed struggling, undersubscribed colleges to remain open during financially difficult periods. Additionally, admission of female students allowed institutions to more than double enrollments in what were perceived as more traditionally feminine fields: classical, literary, or English majors—fields of declining popularity among males.

Nevertheless, the societal backlash did have a noticeable effect in more covert ways. As evidenced in private correspondence, male professors and administrators took steps to restrict women's presence on the faculty and to reserve specific areas of the curriculum for males. For example, Tolley (1996) has documented efforts by faculty in colleges, universities, and secondary schools to hire men in preference to women when filling science positions during the early twentieth century [see **"sex repulsion"***].

Scholars have analyzed the effects of backlash on women's vocational opportunities. In *Doctors Wanted, No Women Need Apply: Sexual Barriers in the Medical Profession, 1835–1975* (1977), Mary Roth Walsh shows that medical schools set **quotas*** on female students just after 1910, reinforced by hospitals' refusals to accept female interns [see **medical education***]. In physics and chemistry, women encountered formidable barriers in hiring practices when prominent scientists preferred to hire young men rather than women, a phenomenon amply documented by Margaret Rossiter in *Women Scientists in America: Struggles and Strategies to 1940* (1982).

In education, late nineteenth-century women faced growing vocal opposition to their increasingly visible role as schoolteachers. In the United States and Canada, industrialization, construction of railroads, and migration of pioneers westward created so many employment opportunities for men that schools could no longer attract male teachers to stem the feminization of schools. Given their relatively limited employment opportunities, women continued to fill the growing number of **teaching*** positions. School boards in a number of states reacted by restricting the number of females in teaching and administrative positions, described by Jane Bernard Powers in *The "Girl Question" in Education: Vocational Education for Young Women in the Progressive Era* (1992).

Historians generally have addressed the subject of backlash using gender as the primary category of analysis. Ethnicity and social class have played minimal roles in scholarly discourse. As a result, experiences of African American, Latina, Asian, and Native American women during periods of cultural and societal backlash have yet to be described in satisfactory detail. One exception is *Black Women in Higher Education: An Anthology of Essays, Studies, and Documents* (1992), in which Elizabeth L. Ihle notes that African American women faced twin obstacles of racism and sexism in their persistent efforts for self-empowerment through college and university education in the late nineteenth and early twentieth centuries. In addition to expanding our understanding of the intersection of ethnicity and gender, we should also seek a clearer picture of the relation of gender and social class within the context of backlash. Tyack and Hansot note that many nineteenth-century women who argued most vehemently against the advances of feminism hailed from the middle and upper classes.

Finally, when using gender as a category of analysis, many scholars appear to view the male-dominated status quo as fixed, whereas recent scholarship suggests that during periods of societal backlash, cultural images of maleness undergo significant transformation. For instance, in *American Manhood* (1993), E. Anthony Rotundo traces a changing standard of masculinity that coincides with periods of backlash against women at the close of the nineteenth century. More research can expand our understanding of backlash as a phenomenon that affects the identity construction of both sexes.

Bibliography: Rosalind Rosenberg, *Beyond Separate Spheres: Intellectual Roots of Modern Feminism* (1982); David Tyack and Elisabeth Hansot, *Learning Together: A History of Coeducation in American Public Schools* (1990); Susan Faludi, *Backlash: The Undeclared War against American Women* (1991); James C. Albisetti, "The Feminization of Teaching in the Nineteenth Century: A Comparative Perspective," *History of Education*, 22 (September 1993): 253–263; Kimberley Tolley, "The Science Education of American Girls, 1784–1932" (Ed.D. diss., University of California, Berkeley, 1996).

Kimberley Tolley

Banister, Zilpah Polly Grant. Zilpah Polly Grant Banister (usually referred to historically as Zilpah Grant) (1794–1874) is, along with **Emma Willard**,* **Catharine Beecher**,* and **Mary Lyon**,* one of the nineteenth-century pioneers of women's education in the United States. She is not as well known as her close friend and colleague Lyon because the school that Grant founded, Ipswich Seminary, never achieved the fame of Lyon's **Mount Holyoke Female Seminary**.* Grant's legacy included her joint work with Lyon, her work as founder of Derry and Ipswich Seminaries, and her early contributions to the art of **teaching**.*

Grant was born into a farm family in South Norfolk, Connecticut, on May 30, 1794. Grant had little formal early schooling but by all accounts was able to learn quickly and well; this, combined with the strong religious education she received from her pious mother, made her an excellent nineteenth-century teacher. She began her teaching career at age fourteen and taught in various **district schools*** in East Norfolk. In these brief stints in a variety of schools, Grant developed her ideas on education.

Grant drew lessons from her personal religious experience, her quest for perfection, and various mentors that she encountered during her twelve years of teaching. She created a plan where the Bible was the center of all teaching, not just for instruction in history and religion. Early in her career, she insisted that all students must demonstrate progress and that this could only be done in an orderly classroom. Order came from various sources but primarily from use of the Bible in history, geography, and logic. Order also came from the organization of topics taught. Students would be expected to have a level of knowledge to progress in reading, spelling, arithmetic, geography, and English grammar. In later years at Ipswich, she added music, science, and calisthenics. The day always began with Bible reading and ended with reflection on what had been accomplished by both teacher and students. Reflection was her means of motivation as she practiced neither competition nor emulation in helping students achieve her goals of increasing their self-control and doing their best.

After teaching in district schools, Grant continued her educational work in various **seminaries**.* From 1820 to 1837 Grant worked in Byfield Female Seminary with Reverend Joseph Emerson. Then she became preceptress of Adams Female Academy in Derry, New Hampshire, and finally moved on to Ipswich Seminary in Massachusetts. At these early forms of **women's colleges*** she continued to practice her special brand of education based upon her strong tie to religion and the Bible, and she tried to convince **common school*** advocates that this approach would work there as well.

Grant promoted her ideas on education in several ways. More than 1,675 students attended the schools at Derry and Ipswich during her tenure. Four hundred of these became teachers in New England, and 88 were teachers in poor areas of the West and South. Twenty-one went on to become foreign missionaries. Grant continued her friendship and correspondence with Mary Lyon until the latter's death in 1849 and undoubtedly influenced many more young women through her correspondences. After her retirement in 1837 Grant toured colleges and seminaries to recruit teachers for the West, and in 1856, she promoted her educational ideas with a pamphlet entitled *Hints on Education*.

A new career began for Grant when she married in 1841. As the third wife of William Bostwick Banister, an attorney and state senator, she was afforded the wealth and leisure that permitted her to become a philanthropist. She founded the General Charitable Society of Newburyport and served on the board of managers of Catharine Beecher's American Women's Educational Association. She continued charitable work, her Bible class, and writing letters to friends and former students until her death on December 3, 1874. She had spent her entire life dedicated to education and betterment of society. Historians have sometimes found it difficult to separate Grant's ideas from those of Mary Lyon. Fame may have eluded Grant, but her legacy became a permanent part of women's education through her joint work with Lyon and her training of many students.

Bibliography: Rev. John P. Cowles, ''Miss Z. P. Grant—Mrs. William B. Banister: Memoir,'' *American Journal of Education*, 50 (September 1880): 611–624; Lucinda T. Guilford, *The Uses of a Life: Memorials of Mrs. Z. P. Grant Banister* (1885); Harriet Webster Marr, ''Study of Zilpah Polly Grant Banister, Noted Educator of Ipswich Seminary,'' *Essex Institute Historical Collections* (October 1953): 348–364; Rita S. Saslaw, ''Zilpah Polly Grant Banister,'' in Maxine Schwartz Seller, ed., *Women Educators in the United States, 1820–1993: A Bio-Bibliographic Sourcebook* (1994).

Rita S. Saslaw

Bank Street College of Education. Bank Street College of Education was founded as the Bureau of Educational Experiments (BEE) in 1916 by **Lucy Sprague Mitchell*** and Harriet Johnson, educators who pioneered in **early childhood education*** during the **Progressive Era.*** In the BEE's Nursery School and in Caroline Pratt's Play School, the founders pursued a shared dream: to study the growth needs and patterns of children in a school setting rather than an experimental laboratory in order to determine the best kinds of children's learning environments. Of progressive, reformist temperament, Mitchell and Johnson sought to bring together experimental schooling and child research to establish a scientific basis for practice, using the knowledge gained to reform public education. Much of the work and development of the institution that grew out of this vision was guided, directed, and financed by Mitchell for the next forty years.

Mitchell, influenced by her childhood heroine, settlement leader **Jane Addams**,* brought to this vision of an interacting relationship between theory and practice an equally collaborative vision for organizing her institution. BEE, renamed Bank Street College in 1950, was distinguished by a strong collaborative emphasis that was echoed in its political commitment to democratic humanism. It was led and administered by a roundtable of women, the Working Council, which functioned collectively. Steadfastly refusing the hierarchical position of president throughout her forty years at Bank Street, Mitchell encouraged ''joint thinking'' and the ''cooperative method.'' Bank Street thus presented women an alternative model of professionalism at a time when professions were dominated by men and organized along bureaucratic, hierarchical lines, and when education was characterized by many female teachers subordinated to a few male supervisors. At Bank Street, women collaboratively set direction and crafted policy.

In 1919 Harriet Johnson opened the BEE's Nursery School, probably the first in the country for children under three, which became part of a network of private, experimental schools founded by women progressives in New York City. The nursery school was unique in being both an experiment in education and a setting for research by science specialists, foreshadowing the growth of child study institutes in the 1920s. Johnson reported on the program in her book *The Children of the ''Nursery School''* (1929).

In 1930, located in its new quarters at 69 Bank Street in Greenwich Village, Mitchell and Johnson initiated BEE's innovative Cooperative School for Teachers (CST). With its mission to educate ''modern'' teachers for ''modern'' schools, CST went forward on two unusual premises: that in order to become teachers of children, students need to have child experiences and that understanding the growth needs and patterns of children is more important than methods used or subjects taught. These premises of **teacher education*** generated Bank Street's characteristic emphasis on child development and experiential learning for teachers, which continues today.

CST offered students, in much the same way BEE offered professionals, an alternative model, in this case for teacher education, one conceived and carried out by women committed to the importance in the developing teacher of empathy and understanding of the child experience. Equally important was the integration, through an ongoing seminar called Advisement, of the personal with the professional selves. And, unlike the careerism that focused many teacher education programs on preparing school administrators and professors of education, CST focused exclusively on the female sphere of classroom teaching and eschewed academic trappings until 1952, when it offered its first M.S. degree.

Today, Bank Street College, on the Upper West Side of New York City, continues these strands of its early work in its demonstration/laboratory school of 450 children ages three through thirteen and its highly regarded Graduate School of Education. Bank Street has also been active in educational reform since the 1940s through staff development work in public schools across the country and community and educational projects with special needs populations. A publisher of materials for children, teachers, and professionals, Bank Street introduced the first multicultural basal readers in the 1960s and the first word processor for children in the 1980s. Although no longer the female enclave it once was, the overwhelming majority of students and faculty in the graduate school are women.

Rather than spawning a major philosophical or pedagogical school of thought, or developing replicable models on a significant scale, Bank Street's influence resides in its direct impact on its students—children and adults in its two schools and participants in its staff development projects—and in fanning out that impact on children who are taught by Bank Street–educated teachers and teachers who are supervised by Bank Street–educated school leaders. Through its practice, and to a lesser extent its scholarship, Bank Street has been successful in keeping alive a set of distinctive ideas about teaching and learning in a value system of democratic humanism. It is through Bank Street and a small number of like-minded institutions that the ideals of progressive education in the best sense have continued to thrive. [See also **child study movement**,* **early childhood teacher education**.*]

Bibliography: Lucy Sprague Mitchell, *Two Lives: The Story of Wesley Clair Mitchell and Me* (1952); Joyce Antler, *Lucy Sprague Mitchell: The Making of a Modern Woman* (1987); Joan Cenedella, *The Bureau of Educational Experiments: A Study in Progressive Education* (1996).

Joan Cenedella

Barnard College. Barnard College, founded in 1889 as the coordinate women's institution to Columbia University, long provided the most rigorous liberal arts education for women in New York City. Created at a time when no other classical education was available to women in the city, Barnard built its reputation as a strong institution that matched Columbia's rigor. Over time, Barnard enhanced its connection with the increasingly strong group of **women's colleges*** known as the **Seven Sisters**,* aiming for a more national student body and offering an array of undergraduate and graduate opportunities. In 1983, when Columbia University adopted **coeducation**,* Barnard remained a women's institution, still closely allied with Columbia but sustaining an identity of its own.

Like **Radcliffe College*** with Harvard University and Pembroke College with Brown, Barnard opened as a **coordinate college*** with Columbia when the well-established men's institution rejected full coeducation. Although successive Columbia presidents F. A. P. Barnard and Seth Low favored higher education for women, support for opening the university's full resources to females was not unanimous. Yet, like women in other cities, New York's women sought the prestige of the male institution where so many of their fathers, brothers, or neighbors had studied. Early on, some Columbia professors consented to offer private tutoring to women, allowing them to study for and take the same examinations that granted Columbia's men the bachelor's degree. This measure was barely satisfactory, however, and, under the vigorous leadership of Annie Nathan Meyer, a committee of advocates for women's education persuaded Columbia's trustees to approve a female ''annex.''

Meyer, the young wife of a New York City physician who had used the tutorial system for one year before her marriage, secured the support of several influential New Yorkers on her committee. With their money and influence providing the base support for a women's college, Barnard was created with a single building on Madison Avenue, thirty-six students, and the services of certain Columbia faculty members. Ella Weed, who simultaneously served as head of a prestigious girls' school, joined Meyer in creating Barnard College and became its de facto dean as well as a trustee. With Meyer's steady involvement, Weed maintained strong entrance standards for Barnard students, striving to match the curriculum and requirements of Columbia rather than adhering to the work of other women's colleges.

One characteristic differentiated Barnard from both Radcliffe and Pembroke: Barnard hired some of its own faculty to supplement the teaching provided by Columbia professors. Along with some of the women's colleges, like **Wellesley**,* which recruited female faculty members, Barnard thus provided one of the few opportunities for early women college graduates to teach the liberal arts.

Barnard generally enjoyed more active support from its brother institution than did Radcliffe and worked over time to sustain a mutually satisfactory relationship. When many of Columbia's graduate departments refused to open their courses to women students, for example, President Low circumvented the system by hiring three new male scholars at Barnard with money that he contributed anonymously. These men, desirable colleagues to the male institution, agreed to offer courses in Columbia's graduate departments for an exchange of time to Barnard. As historian Helen Horowitz explains the transaction: "Once Barnard had something to offer, barriers to Columbia began to give way" (p. 137).

Barnard also benefitted from propitious philanthropy, especially in its first few decades. In a tight market like New York City, both buildings and land were needed to establish Barnard's security. Just before 1900, three large gifts enabled the erection of the first three Barnard buildings: Milbank, Brinckerhoff, and Fiske Halls. Simultaneously, Barnard's relationship with Columbia reached firmer ground when Barnard Dean Emily Smith Putnam and Columbia President Low in 1900 negotiated an arrangement that served both institutions for two decades. Barnard became the equal of Columbia College within the "federated" system of the university; Columbia's president became both Barnard's president and a member of its trustee board; Barnard would be run by a dean, with the advice and support of both the president and the faculty. Further, student access to both library and classroom facilities was eased and expanded.

With new buildings, enhanced philanthropic support, and the invigorated leadership of new dean Virginia Gildersleeve, Barnard began to expand its role as both a commuter institution for New York City women and a strong, national liberal arts college. Gildersleeve worked more smoothly than had her predecessor Laura Gill with Columbia president Nicholas Murray Butler, a man of strong opinions and firm actions. An alumna of both Barnard and Columbia, Gildersleeve persuaded Butler over time to open the university's graduate and professional schools to women, and she negotiated a more solid faculty arrangement whereby Barnard's graduate teachers held appointments at Columbia [see **graduate education***].

In the 1910s and 1920s, Gildersleeve began to foresee a more diverse student body and a more national scope to Barnard's mission. Although its college life differed greatly from that at the "country" women's colleges like **Smith*** and Wellesley, Barnard sustained an active urban milieu for its students. In some ways, Barnard already served a more diverse group than did most of the other women's schools. As a commuter school, women of more modest backgrounds could attend classes without the expense of boarding away from home. In addition, Barnard served a larger proportion of Jewish students than did the other Seven Sisters. Although Barnard never established a **quota*** on Jewish students, as did many other institutions, its move in the 1920s to draw students from far beyond New York was an attempt to widen its geographic appeal. Some irony exists in Barnard's efforts, given the prominence of Jewish supporters like Annie Nathan Meyer and philanthropist Jacob Schiff in sustaining the college's early decades.

Gildersleeve eased Barnard into closer relations with the other eastern women's colleges, seeing a benefit for Barnard complementary to its connection with Columbia. She was instrumental in creating the Seven College Conference in 1926, an informal organization that soon gave rise to the name Seven Sisters. Through this connection, Barnard joined **Bryn Mawr**,* Wellesley, Smith,

Mount Holyoke,* **Vassar**,* and Radcliffe in a beneficial arrangement for raising funds and support for women's education.

By the 1990s, Barnard had weathered the decision by Columbia University to make its undergraduate student body coeducational. Resisting suggestions to merge, Barnard sustained its role as a separate women's institution that, as one of the Seven Sisters, had long provided rigorous education for women.

Bibliography: Marian Churchill White, *A History of Barnard College* (1954); Helen Lefkowitz Horowitz, *Alma Mater: Design and Experience in the Women's Colleges from Their Nineteenth-Century Beginnings to the 1930s* (1984); Lynn D. Gordon, "Annie Nathan Meyer and Barnard College: Mission and Identity in Women's Higher Education, 1889–1950," *History of Education Quarterly*, 26, no. 4 (Winter 1986): 503–522; Bette Weneck, "Social and Cultural Stratification in Women's Higher Education: Barnard College and Teachers College," *History of Education Quarterly*, 31, no. 1 (Spring 1991): 1–25; Andrea Walton, "Women at Columbia: Power and Empowerment in the Lives of Six Scholars" (Ph.D. diss., Columbia University, 1995).

Linda Eisenmann

Beecher, Catharine. Catharine Esther Beecher (1800–1878), author, educator, and publicist for women's education, was founder of **Hartford Female Seminary**,* Western Female Institute, and Milwaukee Female College. An important voice in the nineteenth-century women's movement, she espoused ideals that embraced the religious and intellectual fervor of the eastern establishment. She is considered by some historians to be the founder of modern **home economics**.*

Born on September 6, 1800, in East Hampton, Long Island, Beecher was the eldest of nine children. Her father, Lyman Beecher, was an important Presbyterian clergyman, politically active as a Federalist (in their decline) and as a Whig (in their emergence). A leading light in nineteenth-century evangelism, Lyman Beecher was an early proponent of the antislavery movement [see **abolitionism***]. Catharine's early education was conducted at home, structured largely by her mother. Roxanna Beecher was a protean individual; she played guitar, spoke fluent French, was renowned for her paintings and drawings, and was interested in chemistry to the point of recreating experiments in her kitchen. Catharine probably studied in the private school for girls that her mother kept in their home after 1805. Beecher always regarded this home schooling, including housekeeping, cooking, sewing, and lessons in morality, as her true education.

In 1810 the family moved to Litchfield, Connecticut, and Beecher enrolled at Sarah Pierce's **Litchfield Female Academy**.* Pierce was a pioneer in women's education, and many of Beecher's ideas regarding education came from her. During Beecher's years at the academy, the focus was more on "social" than practical learning, although about the time Beecher left school Pierce brought in her nephew, John Brace, to improve the quality of learning. Brace, a graduate of Williams College and a future principal of Hartford Female Seminary, brought an expanded science program, including chemistry, astronomy, and botany.

On her mother's death in 1815 Beecher left Sarah Pierce's, spending the next few years helping out in her father's household, writing poetry and short stories, and **teaching*** occasionally at the female academy. In 1821 she took a teaching job in New London, Connecticut, where she met and became engaged to Alexander Fisher, professor of natural philosophy at Yale College. The next year amid wedding preparations, Fisher drowned in a shipwreck off the coast of Ireland, leaving Beecher to contemplate her future alone.

With $2,000 from Fisher's estate, and moral support from her father, Beecher decided to open a school for young women in Hartford. Support for a girls' school there was strong, owing to the closing of Lydia Sigourney's school for young ladies in 1819. In May 1823, Catharine and her younger sister Mary opened an academy on Main Street over a harness shop. The first year they had fifteen students, offering geography, grammar, rhetoric, science, and literature, as well as music and drawing. Latin was offered, with Catharine studying the language with her brother in the evenings, keeping one step ahead of her students. Within a year the school had over seventy students and had added a boarding department. The staff was expanded to seven including Catharine's aunt Esther Foote and sister Harriet Beecher (later, Stowe).

Beecher stayed at the seminary until 1831, refining her philosophy of education through practical experience. Believing that women deserved and required the same educational opportunities as men, she set out to structure women's education along similar lines. Eschewing the "social" basis of women's education and the emphasis on rote learning, Beecher devised a strong curriculum that compares favorably with today's learning approaches. She experimented with organizational structure, creating a system of evaluating and grouping students of similar academic background and experience, and establishing teaching assistants, with older students hearing recitations of younger ones. During her Hartford years, Beecher began to compile her ideas for publication, gaining success and national prominence with "Female Education" (1827), *Suggestions Respecting Improvements in Education* (1829), and *The Elements of Mental and Moral Philosophy* (1831).

In 1831, Beecher resigned and moved to Cincinnati, Ohio, where her father had recently taken a position at a theological seminary. Hoping to duplicate her success in Hartford, Catharine opened Western Female Institute with Harriet in 1833. Catharine prospered in Ohio, continuing her writings and teaching moral philosophy at area girls' schools, using her own book as a text. During her Ohio years, she published *Arithmetic Simplified* (1832), *The Lyceum Arithmetic* (1835), *An Essay on the Education of Female Teachers* (1835), and *An Essay on Slavery and Abolitionism, with Reference to the Duty of American Females* (1837). The antislavery tract was not well received in Cincinnati, and Western Female Institute ran into financial problems and was forced to close in 1837.

The next several years Beecher supported herself with her writings. Her most famous centered around the role of women in American society: *Treatise on Domestic Economy for the Use of Young Ladies at Home and at School* (1845), *The Duty of American Women to Their Country* (1845), *Principles of Domestic Science; As Applied to the Duties and Pleasures of the Home* (1870), *Woman's Profession as Mother and Educator with Views in Opposition to Woman Suffrage* (1872, with Harriet Beecher Stowe), and *The New Housekeeper's Manual* (1873). In these she encouraged women to take as much control of their lives as they could within the larger context of their roles as wives and mothers, a view representing the position of conservative feminists of her era. The position is well defined in the tract opposing **suffrage*** (1872); rather than proposing antifeminist views, the authors argue that the solution to the wrongs women had suffered in society was not to be found at the polls. Rather, the Beechers urged women to ''unite and establish their economic independence and insist that their domestic labor be granted the dignity and respect accorded to male labor outside the home.''

Beecher's third attempt at a school for young women was a college, Milwaukee Female Seminary (later Milwaukee Normal School), opened in 1850. Beecher raised several thousand dollars for the school, hoping to build a ''cottage'' on campus to house a department of domestic economy, but when the trustees balked, she disassociated herself with the school and returned to writing.

In her final years, Beecher continued to work for improvements in women's education, publishing the autobiographical *Educational Reminiscences and Suggestions* (1874). Declining health caused her to seek a ''water cure'' in Elmira, New York, where she moved in 1877, living with her brother Edward and his family. She died of a stroke in her sleep on May 12, 1878. [See also **academies,*** **seminaries.***]

Bibliography: Mary Kingsbury Talcott, ''Historical Sketch of the Seminary,'' in *Hartford Female Seminary Reunion* (1892); Emily Noyes Vanderpoel, *The Chronicles of a Pioneer School* (1903); Katherine Kish Sklar, *Catharine Beecher: A Study in American Domesticity* (1973); Daniel Walker Howe, *The Political Culture of the American Whigs* (1984); Joan Hedrick, *Harriet Beecher Stowe* (1994).

Thomas Ratliff

Bennett College. Bennett College, along with **Spelman College,*** is one of two continuing African American **women's colleges*** in the United States. It originated in 1873 as a day school in the basement of St. Matthew's Methodist Episcopal Church in Greensboro, North Carolina, under the direction of W. J. Parker. The Freedmen's Aid Society of the Methodist Episcopal Church assumed responsibility for the school in 1874, appointing Rev. Edward O. Thayer as its second principal. The school was named Bennett Seminary in honor of Lyman Bennett of Troy, New York, whose $10,000 donation helped purchase land for a campus and construction of the first building, Bennett Hall.

Bennett Seminary began offering college-level courses in 1879 and, in 1889, was chartered by North Carolina as a college. The renamed Bennett College's first president was Rev. Charles N. Grandison, who was not only the first African American to direct the institution but also the first black president of any school established by the Freedmen's Aid Society.

The college's principal aims were the same as most of the schools established for former slaves in the South during Reconstruction, namely, to provide elementary education and religious instruction, to produce black teachers to meet the growing demand created by the freedmen's schools, and to provide collegiate training. However, like most black schools of the era, only a small minority of students were in the collegiate division, and the overwhelming majority of Bennett graduates during its first fifty years pursued **teaching**.*

While Bennett was **coeducational*** from its inception, women were always prominent in the student body, in part because of early interest shown by the Woman's Home Missionary Society of the Methodist Episcopal Church. The Society established Kent Home in 1896, an industrial training and domestic arts program designed to "teach girls and young ladies how to make a perfect Christian home." The education of women to meet changing demands of family life, church leadership, and community activism was the principal mission of the society. It had long contemplated establishing a black women's college; however, the pressing need to educate African Americans of both sexes following Emancipation argued against establishment of single-sex institutions. In the social ferment of the post–World War I era, the society saw a need and opportunity for an African American women's college. Therefore, the society entered a partnership with the Board of Education for Negroes (formerly the Freedmen's Aid Society) of the Methodist Episcopal Church to change Bennett to Bennett College for Women.

David Dallas Jones, an Atlanta businessman active in the Methodist Church, the YMCA, and the Atlanta Inter-racial Commission, was selected as the first president, a post he held for thirty years. During Jones's tenure Bennett grew from 10 collegiate students in 1926 to 356 in 1940, composed of students from around the nation rather than just North Carolina, a change denoting the institution's growing national reputation. Despite the depression, Jones's fund-raising ability financed a remarkably successful building program during the 1930s.

Bennett College for Women sought to integrate its educational program with the social experience of college life, producing a "community of purposeful living experiences." In practice this meant continuation of **teacher education*** and preparation for homemaking (the latter reflected in the annual Homemaking Institute Week, an event that attracted national attention) but also a well-rounded liberal arts education that prepared graduates for professions other than teaching, as well as providing the means and desire to solve social problems. As befits a religiously affiliated institution, there was a strong emphasis on moral conduct. However, the college's strict code of behavior was also meant to "distinguish the Bennett Girl and to help her demand respect for Negro womanhood in the South" (Bennett Blue Book, 1844–1846). This desire to counteract negative stereotypes of both the intellectual ability and moral rectitude of black women perpetuated even stricter social regulations than those of southern white women's colleges. As a result, for many years dating was strictly regulated, visits to Greensboro discouraged, riding in automobiles prohibited, and formal attire mandated for off-campus outings.

Following the incapacitation of Jones in October 1955, Dr. Willa B. Player was named president. A Bennett faculty member since 1930 and vice president of instruction since 1952, Player was only the second African American woman, after **Mary McLeod Bethune**,* to serve as president of a higher education institution and the first woman to lead a college for African American women. She continued to solidify Bennett's academic reputation, and in 1957 Bennett was one of the first African American colleges admitted to the Southern Association of Colleges and Schools. Dr. Isaac H. Miller, Jr., succeeded Player in 1966, followed by a second African American woman, Gloria Randle Scott, in 1987.

This tradition of female leadership distinguishes Bennett from other historically black colleges, as does its single-sex status. It was a pioneer in providing black women with a college experience that went beyond vocational training and preparation for marriage. [See also **American Missionary Association**,* **freedmen's teachers**,* **slavery**,* **women college presidents**.*]

Bibliography: Willa B. Player, "A Statement of the Philosophy of Bennett College," *Bennett College Bulletin*, 20 (August 1948): 1–23; Virginia Ann Sutton, "The Early History of Bennett College, Greensboro, North Carolina" (master's thesis, Wake Forest University, 1969); James P. Brawley, *Two Centuries of Methodist Concern: Bondage, Freedom and Education of Black People* (1974).

Patrick F. Callahan

Bethune, Mary McLeod. Mary McLeod Bethune (1875–1955) spent her life promoting social reforms and greater educational opportunity for African Americans, especially through her work as a school founder and member of Franklin Roosevelt's New Deal cabinet. She was born Mary Jane McLeod near Mayesville, South Carolina, to Samuel and Patsy, both slaves. At age seven, Bethune began her education at Emma Wilson's mission school for black children at Mayesville Trinity Presbyterian Church. She studied reading, writing, arithmetic, and the Bible. Bethune graduated in 1886 and the following year was awarded a scholarship to Scotia Seminary (Barber-Scotia College) for black women in Concord, North Carolina. Believing she wanted to be a missionary to Africa, Bethune enrolled at Moody Bible Institute in Chicago in 1894.

In 1895, Bethune graduated from Moody but was denied her dream of being a missionary by the Presbyterian Board of Missions. In the following year, she taught eighth grade to black children at Haines Institute in Augusta, Georgia. **Lucy Laney**,* who began the institute in 1873, fueled Bethune's imagination about what she should accomplish, suggesting that Bethune could realize her life goal of educating black children just as easily in America as by missionary work in Africa. In 1897 Bethune was transferred to the Kindell Institute in Sumter, South Carolina, by the Presbyterian board. There she met Albertus Bethune; they married in May 1898 and had one son.

On October 4, 1904, Bethune realized her dream of educating black children when she opened the Daytona Normal and Industrial Institute for Negro Girls in Daytona, Florida. The school's curriculum was similar to **Tuskegee Institute**'s* where students were educated in academic subjects and industrial skills such as sewing and agriculture. The curriculum also included the concept of black pride. Students learned, for instance, about the black Haitian King Henri Christophe as an illustration of success. In 1908 Bethune changed the name of the school to the Daytona Educational Industrial Training School to recognize the growing number of boys who attended. That year she began a series of national tours that continued throughout her life. Bethune met noted individuals such as John D. Rockefeller, Andrew Carnegie, James Gamble, and others who financially aided her school. In 1923 Bethune merged Daytona with Cookman Institute for Boys (now **Bethune-Cookman College***).

Bethune's career of advancing education for African Americans evolved as her interest in civil rights grew. Torn between the educational philosophies of Booker T. Washington and W. E. B. Du Bois, Bethune advocated the rights of all citizens to receive an education. She was president of the Florida Federation of Colored Women (1917), president of the **National Association of Colored Women*** (1924), founded the Southeastern Federation of Colored Women (1920), and served on the National Commission for Child Welfare and the President's Commission on Home Building and Home Ownership (1929). In 1935 Bethune formed the **National Council of Negro Women*** to help focus attention on common social problems facing blacks.

Bethune's national prominence grew even stronger when she assumed the position of administrator of the Office of Minority Affairs (1935) in the Roosevelt administration, becoming the first black woman to serve as chief of a federal agency. Collaborating with such New Dealers as Robert Weaver, Lawrence Oxley, and Frank Horne, Bethune was an active member of the ''Black Cabinet'' or ''Black Brain Trust,'' a group that formed a conduit between the federal government and African Americans by which citizens were informed of federal programs. In 1936 she was appointed director of Negro Affairs for the **National Youth Administration*** and used the position to inform Americans of the need of educating blacks. In 1940, Bethune was elected vice president of the **National Association for the Advancement of Colored People*** (NAACP). She campaigned for racial acceptance, including the integration of medical personnel at hospitals.

In 1942 Bethune's wartime leadership and activity induced her to resign the presidency of Bethune-Cookman. She helped establish the Civilian Pilot Training Program at Tuskegee Institute and served as adviser to the Secretary of War on selection of officer candidates for the Women's Army Auxiliary. She was on the board of directors of the Woman's Voluntary Service and was a general in the Woman's Army for National Defense. In 1943 Roosevelt appointed her as special adviser on black issues.

In the postwar years, Bethune visited Haiti and traveled widely in Europe and Africa. In 1951 President Harry Truman appointed her to the Committee of Twelve for National Defense; she was instrumental in advising him of the necessity of desegregating the military. Bethune contributed her talents to many civil rights organizations. The most significant include the Mary McLeod Bethune Foundation, the National Urban League, the Association of American Colleges, the General Conference of the Methodist Church, Hadassah (the Women's Zionist Organization of America), and the **League of Women Voters**.* In 1985, with her son Albert in attendance, the United States honored Mary McLeod Bethune with a stamp bearing her likeness. She died in Daytona Beach, Florida, on May 18, 1955.

Bibliography: LaVere Anderson, *Mary McLeod Bethune: Teacher with a Dream* (1976); Beth Wilson, *Giants for Justice: Bethune, Randolph & King* (1978); Milton Meltzer, *Mary McLeod Bethune: Voice of Black Hope* (1987).

William E. Segall and Anna V. Wilson

Bethune-Cookman College. Bethune-Cookman College is a historically black, coeducational, liberal arts college notable as the sole surviving college founded by an African American woman and as the enduring legacy of a truly remarkable African American woman, **Mary McLeod Bethune**.* Bethune, daughter of exslaves, rose from a life of rural poverty in South Carolina to become one of the most prominent African American women of her time, a nationally recognized educator, and the only female member of President Franklin Roosevelt's informal black cabinet. Inspired by her Christian faith and motivated by a commitment to women's education and racial progress, Bethune moved to Daytona Beach, Florida, in 1904 to establish the Daytona Educational and Industrial Training School for Negro Girls. The school was started in near-legendary fashion in a rented shack with only $1.50, five little girls, and abundant faith in God. Heavily influenced by Emma Jane Wilson, who founded Mayesville Educational and Industrial Institute, **Lucy Laney**,* founder of Haines Institute, and the head-heart-hands philosophy of her alma mater, Scotia Seminary, Bethune's curriculum emphasized basic academic skills and religious precepts combined with training in traditional women's vocations.

Bethune's dynamic personality helped secure funding from the many rich northern philanthropists who maintained winter residences in Daytona Beach, most notably James N. Gamble, son of the founder of Procter and Gamble. Changing its name to Daytona Normal and Industrial Institute for Negro Girls, Bethune expanded the educational program to include **high school***–level preparation for **teaching*** and nursing, building a hospital to facilitate the latter. She also purchased a farm to provide a source of income and a place for agricultural **vocational education**.*

In 1923 the institute merged with the all-male Cookman Institute of Jacksonville, Florida. Cookman was founded in 1872 by Rev. Samuel B. Darnell, its first president, with the financial backing of the Freedmen's Aid Society of the Methodist Episcopal Church. Dedicated to primary education and preparation for the ministry, the school prospered until Darnell's departure in 1894. The next two decades were marked by stagnant or declining enrollment and uncertain finances. Therefore, the Board of Education for Negroes of the Methodist Episcopal Church agreed to relocate to Daytona Beach and merge with Bethune's institute to form Daytona-Cookman Collegiate Institute. The name was changed to Bethune-Cookman College in 1929 to reflect its development into a junior college. Bethune served as president, and the church provided stable financial support, which proved essential to the college's survival during the depression. Although **coeducational**,* the majority of graduates were women, most becoming teachers in Florida's segregated school system. In 1941 the college added a third year to its **teacher education*** program and in 1942 became a four-year college, awarding its first bachelor degrees in 1943.

During this period the college benefitted from Bethune's national prominence. However, her service in the **National Youth Administration*** and as president of the **National Council of Negro Women*** reduced her to a part-time college president. The conflicting responsibilities contributed to a decline in her health, forcing her to resign as president in December 1942, although she continued as president emerita until her death in 1955. Bethune was succeeded by James A. Colston, who in turn was replaced by Richard V. Moore in 1947. During his twenty-eight-year tenure, Moore stabilized the college's finances and presided over a period of sustained growth in enrollment and academic reputation.

The college's history illustrates both the evolution of Bethune's educational philosophy and changing societal views on the education of African American women. Bethune was originally imbued with turn-of-the-century ideals of domesticity and **racial uplift*** through education, which she translated into an educational program emphasizing vocational training in a religious context. However, Bethune eventually strove to make her school a liberal arts college to foster the intellectual development of African American women and promote racial and gender equality, a mission it continues to pursue.

Bibliography: James P. Brawley, *Two Centuries of Methodist Concern: Bondage, Freedom and Education of Black People* (1974); Audrey Thomas McCluskey, "Mary McLeod Bethune and the Education of Black Girls in the South, 1904–1923" (Ph.D. diss., Indiana University, 1991); Sheila Y. Fleming, *Bethune-Cookman College, 1904–1994* (1995).

Patrick F. Callahan

Blanton, Annie Webb. Annie Webb Blanton (1870–1945), who served as Texas state superintendent of public instruction and a longtime faculty member at the University of Texas, was the first woman elected to statewide public office in

Texas and founder of the Delta Kappa Gamma Society for women educators. Her influence included both Texas and the nation because of her service in national organizations.

Blanton was born on August 19, 1870, in Houston, to Thomas Lindsay and Eugenia (Webb) Blanton. She attended public schools in Houston and La Grange and, after graduation from La Grange High School in 1886, began her long **teaching*** career in a rural school in Fayette County, Texas. In 1888, she moved to Austin, where she taught both elementary and secondary school and attended the University of Texas, graduating in 1899.

Two years later, Blanton joined the English faculty at North Texas Normal College (now the University of North Texas) in Denton, where she taught until 1918. In 1916, she was the first woman elected president of the Texas State Teachers' Association (TSTA). Her outspoken advocacy for equal rights for women and her authorship of a popular school grammar textbook series launched Blanton into this role as leader of the largest teacher's organization in Texas [see **teacher unions***].

Following her TSTA presidency, Blanton was elected Texas' superintendent of public instruction in November 1918. Governor William P. Hobby, instrumental in obtaining **suffrage*** for Texas women in February 1918, supported Blanton in a sharply contested Democratic primary campaign against the incumbent and another man. Blanton served two two-year terms as superintendent of public instruction. Her notable accomplishments included establishing a system for the state to provide free textbooks to all public school pupils, substantially revising teacher certification laws, raising teacher salaries, and numerous efforts to improve rural education for large numbers of Texas schoolchildren. Additionally, Blanton's prominence as elected leader of Texas schools fostered a variety of advances for women in education.

After a second term as superintendent, Blanton stood unsuccessfully for election to the U.S. House of Representatives. She returned to the University of Texas to continue her studies. After receiving a master's degree in 1923, she taught in the university education department until 1926. She spent a year at Cornell University, where she obtained the Ph.D. (1927). She then returned to the University of Texas in 1927 and served as a professor of education for the remainder of her career. During her university tenure, she designed and directed the first elementary **teacher education*** program.

In addition to her influential textbook series, Blanton's books included *Review Outline and Exercises in English Grammar* (1903), *A Handbook of Information as to Education in Texas* (1922), *Advanced English Grammar* (1928), and *The Child of the Texas One-Teacher School* (1936).

One of her major accomplishments was founding the Delta Kappa Gamma Society in 1929. This honorary society for women teachers swiftly spread to all states and many foreign countries. By 1988, it claimed an international membership of 162,000.

Additionally, during her state superintendency, Blanton served as vice president of the National Education Association in 1917, 1919, and 1921. The needs of rural schools and improvement of elementary education remained Blanton's primary concerns throughout her career.

A Methodist, Blanton never married and died in Austin, on October 2, 1945. Public schools in Austin, Dallas, and Odessa bear her name, as does a women's dormitory on the campus of the University of Texas at Austin.

Bibliography: Eunah Temple Holden, *Our Heritage in the Delta Kappa Gamma Society* (1960; rpt. 1970); Debbie Mauldin Cottrell, *Pioneer Women Educator: The Progressive Spirit of Annie Webb Blanton* (1994).

Matthew D. Davis and O. L. Davis, Jr.

Blow, Susan. Susan Elizabeth Blow (1843–1926) founded the first public **kindergarten*** in the United States and was instrumental in training kindergarten educators and in disseminating the educational ideas of Friedrich Froebel. Blow was born into the distinguished Presbyterian family of Minerva (Grimsely) and Henry Taylor Blow and raised in Carondelet, a suburb of St. Louis. She was educated initially as one of two girls in the local boys' school, then in a school for girls established by her father, and finally for two years at Miss Haines' School in New York City. As a young woman, Blow was bookish, scholarly, and unconventional and spent much of her time reading Calvinist theologians, social commentators, and poets, as well as envisioning a vocation, much to her family's chagrin. In 1869–1870 she lived in Brazil, where her father was U.S. minister, and later traveled to Europe. In Germany she learned of Froebel's educational beliefs and visited kindergartens there, noting methodologies and collecting materials.

When she returned to Missouri in 1871, Blow met with St. Louis Superintendent of Public Schools William Torrey Harris about incorporating kindergartens into the public school system. Historians differ on whether Blow or Harris conceived the original idea. Regardless, Harris, familiar with kindergarten education, supported the idea on the condition that Blow be formally trained. She then enrolled for one year at the New York Institute for Kindergartners, established by noted Froebelian Maria Kraus-Boelte. In 1873, Blow returned to establish the first public kindergarten at the Des Peres School in Carondelet, and the following year she opened a school to prepare kindergarten educators. From this school emerged a number of women who established kindergartens and training schools throughout the country [see **early childhood education,*** **early childhood teacher education***].

As challenges to her authority increased and her health decreased, Blow left Missouri in 1889 for Cazenovia, New York, and Boston, placing herself under the care of numerologist Dr. James Jackson Putnam. Her health regained, Blow entered the second phase of her career as the leading American spokesperson for orthodox Froebelian philosophy and methodology. In 1894 she wrote five volumes for Harris's International Education Series explaining her views. She lectured throughout the Midwest and East to kindergarten associations and was an influential member of the International Kindergarten Union (IKU) until her death. From 1905 to 1909 she was a lecturer at Teachers College, Columbia University, and it was there that Blow, coteaching with the younger Deweyan kindergartner **Patty Smith Hill**,* defended Froebelian educational philosophy in the face of the Progressive education movement.

From the beginning, William Torrey Harris was an intellectual mentor for Blow, and together they studied the works of Froebel, Hegel, Dante, and Goethe. Yet interest in Hegelian philosophy and her religious beliefs were often at odds, though both were major forces in Blow's dedication to kindergarten education. It was not until late in her career, as she struggled to formulate ''contemporary kindergarten thought'' with members of the Advisory Committee of the IKU, that Blow was able to unite her religious and educational beliefs into a coherent educational philosophy. When still in Missouri, Blow had translated Froebel's *Mother Play* for use in her training school, since no translation then existed. However, Blow's translation of Froebel was literal and did not consider the impact of Darwinism and the evolution of human development. Consequently, her educational theory was at odds with those progressive educators who used child psychology and the scientific method in formulating their ideas. Nevertheless, Blow's contribution to educational history is profound, for much of her belief in Froebel's *Gliedganzes* (the unity of the whole through the relation of its parts) correlates to reform Darwinists' belief in the relationship between the individual and society.

Blow's teaching encouraged women to develop intellectual curiosity and a foundation of spiritual values fundamental to the stability and direction of kindergarten education. Like few members of her generation, Susan Blow established institutions that extended educational and professional opportunities to women. Like many female institution builders of the era, Blow offered women a type of education that prepared them to nurture children and thus perhaps did more to professionalize motherhood than to extend the boundaries of women's sphere of influence.

Bibliography: Susan Blow, *Systematic Education* (1894); Susan Blow, *Letters to a Mother on the Philosophy of Froebel* (1899); Susan Blow, *Kindergarten Education* (1900); Agnes Snyder, *Dauntless Women in Childhood Education, 1856–1931* (1972); Michael S. Shapiro, *Child's Garden: The Kindergarten Movement from Froebel to Dewey* (1983); Sorca M. O'Connor, ''Mothering in Public: The Division of Organized Child Care in the Kindergarten and Day Nursery, St. Louis, 1886–1920,'' *Early Childhood Research Quarterly*, 10 (1995): 63–80.

Deborah M. De Simone

Board of Foreign Missions. The American Board of Commissioners for Foreign Missions (ABCFM) was founded in Massachusetts in the early nineteenth century to support American Protestant missionary activities, both at home and abroad. Initially, women could serve only as wives of male missionaries, but over time they were accepted into missionary service and by 1880 constituted 57 percent of the missionary force.

The board originated in June 1810, when four male students at Andover Theological Seminary presented a plan to go abroad as missionaries to the General Association of Massachusetts Proper, a newly organized group of Congregational ministers. The General Association approved the purpose of the men, who had been inspired by a British model to serve overseas, and recommended that a foreign missionary board be organized to send Americans to a number of sites. Nine men were elected to the board, which was responsible for working out the details of ABCFM's organization. A Prudential, or executive committee, was created to develop and implement policies, and a secretary and treasurer were elected. Thus, the missionary movement in the United States traces its origins to the ABCFM, for a half-century the largest agency sending workers abroad.

Although the history of missionary activities in North America dates from English settlements at Jamestown, missionary work grew systematically and rapidly after establishment of the ABCFM. This expansion coincided with a nationwide grassroots religious revival movement among American Protestant Christians known as the **Second Great Awakening**.* One immediate result of this movement was renewed piety and religious fervor, some of which was channeled in support of foreign missions. The board emphasized compassion for nonbelievers who lived in non-Christian lands, and it turned toward Asia as its initial field of endeavor. The first mission was sent to Burma in 1812, but finding the country closed, they settled in India and then Ceylon. These small missions were located in places where the British had already prepared the way, so the ABCFM looked closer to home to make a mark.

The most promising field for a distinctly American mission was Hawaii, as New Englanders were familiar with the islands located in the middle of Pacific trade routes. Twenty-one individuals, including two teachers, a physician, and two ordained ministers, were sent by the ABCFM in 1819 to spread Christianity and to educate the native Hawaiians. Although conditions were difficult for mission members, by 1824 almost fifty native Hawaiians were employed as teachers throughout the islands, thousands of students had begun to learn to read, and over a hundred individuals chose to be baptized as Christians. Due to its early success, a mission remained in the islands until the 1850s.

In addition to Hawaii, the ABCFM sent missions to Native Americans. A mission was sent to the Cherokees in Tennessee in 1817 and to the Choctaw nation in Mississippi the following year. Efforts continued until the 1880s. The early missions established schools to encourage English as a primary language, to introduce methods of religious training, and to promote Christianity. Under missionary direction, these schools were organized following the philosophy of English reformer Joseph Lancaster, whose method was a bureaucratically organized system of mass education relying on monitorial instruction. Large numbers of students of various ages were sorted into smaller groups and assigned a monitor, usually an older or more advanced student, who facilitated learning through simultaneous instruction rather than individual recitation. This pedagogical method was ideally suited for mission work as it greatly reduced the number of teachers [see **Bureau of Indian Affairs***].

Although early missions were staffed by both men and women, the board had originally decided that only ordained ministers (all men) were eligible as missionaries. To ensure a steady supply of prospective missionaries, the board created the Foreign Mission School in Cornwall, Connecticut, in 1817 to educate men for this task.

There were no special qualifications necessary for missionary work; however, the Prudential Committee screened candidates carefully. Good health and education were important, and, until the 1830s, married status was unofficially required. Therefore, in the beginning decades, single men were highly encouraged to marry prior to departure, and many women married because it was almost the only way they could serve in the field.

Work in new fields, both at home and abroad, continued throughout the century, with missions to the Pacific Northwest of the United States, the Middle East, Southeast Asia, China, Japan, and Africa. However, as the need for missionaries increased dramatically, the board reversed its earlier decision and began to send hundreds of unmarried women abroad as assistant missionaries beginning in the 1830s.

While the Board's Foreign Mission School and denominational colleges were training young men for the ministry and missionary work, new avenues of education also opened for evangelically minded women. For example, **Mount Holyoke Female Seminary**,* founded by **Mary Lyon*** in 1837, developed a model for women's evangelical education. Mount Holyoke's stated purpose was "to cultivate the missionary spirit among its pupils; the feeling that they should live for God, and do something as teachers, or in such other ways as Providence may direct."

Although advanced education was certainly valued, missionary work was thought to draw upon women's supposedly "special" abilities to nurture and take care of others as well as their "inherent" piety and desire to serve God. Women served in many areas—education, medicine, fund-raising, and evangelism—although they seemed to favor "women's work," a nineteenth-century phrase for an array of women-centered missionary activities such as teaching sewing or infant health care classes, providing music, conducting home visitations, and leading prayer and Bible study [see **separate spheres***].

As more and more women became involved in missionary work, the ABCFM and later individual denominations formed separate women's foreign missionary societies between 1868 and 1888. The Women's Board of Missions, for example, was formed in 1868 in Boston as an auxiliary society of the ABCFM to support, publicize, and supervise women missionaries. The Women's Board's stated purpose was "to co-operate with the American Board in its . . . labor for the benefit of women and children in heathen lands, to disseminate missionary intelligence and increase missionary spirit among Christian women at home and to train children to interest and participation in the work.'' The Women's Board published a journal, *Life and Light for Heathen Women*, which was shared by a second separate ABCFM–affiliated board, the Women's Board of the Interior, formed the same year in Chicago. Other ABCFM Congregationalist–affiliated women's boards were also created, but eventually women of other Protestant denominations withdrew to form their own denominational societies with separate publications.

Although women made up more than half of the missionary force by the late 1880s, those serving in the field for the ABCFM did not gain full status with male missionaries until 1900. Nevertheless, there are over one hundred institutions still operating worldwide, including colleges, theological seminaries, hospitals, **kindergartens**,* schools, and philanthropic organizations, which were founded or inspired by missionaries of the American Board of Commissioners for Foreign Missions.

Bibliography: William Ellsworth Strong, *The Story of the American Board* (1969); Samuel C. Bartlett, *Historical Sketches of the Missions of the American Board* (1972); Mary Zwiep, *Pilgrim Path: The First Company of Women Missionaries to Hawaii* (1991). See also ABCFM mission papers, candidate files, papers of the Women's Board of Missions, and related materials in the Houghton Library, Harvard University, Cambridge, Massachusetts.

Elizabeth K. Eder

Board of National Popular Education. The Board of National Popular Education recruited and trained single women teachers from New England and upper New York State to teach and sometimes start schools in the West during the decade following 1847. The National Board offered unusual opportunities for women teachers in the Northeast, where competition lowered salaries and often made positions difficult to find, to teach in the West, where there was a shortage of schools and teachers. Nearly 600 women took advantage of the National Board's offer and journeyed to teach in schools in the Mississippi Valley; a few traveled across the Isthmus of Panama to teach in Oregon and California. Although the National Board expected the **pioneer women teachers*** to stay in the West for a minimum of two years, a study of their lives revealed that two-thirds became permanent settlers in the West.

The National Board was organized in Cleveland, Ohio, by a group of men who were city leaders and ministers. They searched for communities needing teachers or ready to start schools. A Boston group, the Ladies' Society for the Promotion of Education at the West, merged with the National Board in 1852 after sponsoring 109 teachers.

Catharine Beecher* was the board's first general agent. She prepared sixty-eight teachers in the first two classes in Albany, New York, and Hartford, Connecticut, before turning over administration of the program to William Slade, a recent governor of Vermont. Using prestige earned as governor, he was able to recruit a spring and fall class of twenty to twenty-five women each year. The prospective pioneer teachers met for a six-week institute at Hartford where they were supervised by Nancy Swift. Swift, former principal of the Middlebury (Vermont) Female Seminary, had been a pioneer teacher in Huntsville, Alabama, and corresponded with the teachers after they reached their western schools.

The teachers often found they had entered an entrepreneurial West. Schools opened and closed regularly; when public funds ran out, public schools closed or reverted to subscription schools [see **venture schools***]. Western society was constantly changing, and most teachers moved at least once and found new positions; several moved two or three times in the brief span that their letters reveal. A new self-confidence was expressed by many. Asenath Hammond, who had lived with a minister in Eliot, Maine, after both her parents died, was surprised at her success in Indiana: "I never thought I was anything of a teacher until I came here and here they think I am almost perfection" (Kaufman, p. 33).

Although committed to the National Board's goals of bringing education and Protestant evangelical religious values to the West, the pioneer teachers are particularly significant because they journeyed West as single women seeking wider opportunities for themselves at a time when women were perceived as tied to their families. They used **teaching,*** one of the few acceptable professions for women in the mid-nineteenth century, as a means of mobility and of enhancing their life chances.

Bibliography: Kathryn Kish Sklar, *Catharine Beecher: A Study in American Domesticity* (1973); Polly Welts Kaufman, *Women Teachers on the Frontier* (1984). Papers for the Board of National Popular Education in the Connecticut Historical Society include printed annual reports, applications of the pioneer teachers, teachers' letters written from the West to Nancy Swift, and a diary of pioneer teacher Arozina Perkins.

Polly Welts Kaufman

boarding around. Boarding out or boarding around defined the living accommodations of nineteenth-century local, single schoolteachers, especially in the widespread **district schools***: Teachers lived with various families of children in their schools. Depending on the district, a teacher might move frequently from family to family, staying for only a week or two at a time, or she might "board out" with a family for the entire school term. Occasionally, families charged the teacher for meals and use of a bedroom, although some schools included this in a teacher's salary. Teachers depended on the families for almost everything, including companionship, laundry services, food, and sometimes transportation to and from school.

Teachers wrote about their boarding around experiences with extremely mixed reactions. The most vocal complaints detailed in teachers' diaries were registered toward particular housing accommodations. One teacher in Washington territory was asked if some setting hens could be kept in the bedroom where she was to stay, as skunks were after the eggs. The teacher agreed, only to be kept awake all night "by the hens turning over the eggs so as to hatch evenly on all sides" (Bowden, p. 37). Even more sleep was lost when the little chicks finally hatched and entered the world chirping and peeping. Mollie Dorsey Sanford wrote of her experience boarding around near Nebraska City in the 1850s. She found the sleeping quarters with their "festive bedbugs" holding "high carnival" over her weary body the whole night very tiresome. And the food was intolerable: Meals consisted of cold, bland everything—greens, pork, even the cornbread. The beverage served with dinner was a concoction of "warm creek water, vinegar and brown sugar" (Sanford, p. 87). Although she stayed with a nice family the following week, Sanford's "digestive organs" were in such a state that she refused to teach until her accommodations were changed.

The North Dakota family who boarded Agnes Olson "spoke more Danish than English," and the schoolteacher's attempts to speak Danish "threw the folks into fits of laughter" (Feidler, p. 129). LaRoy Bobzien boarded out with a German family and was fed the "finest home-prepared foods washed down with superb natural spring water coffee" (Feidler, p. 128). The couple, a retired blacksmith and his wife, included the teacher in their games of "pitch" (cards) each evening with neighbors occasionally dropping by.

Some teachers found the contact with families awkward, while others used the experience to better understand a student's home life. Boarding around was eventually stopped with changes in individual accommodation needs of teachers, certainly after World War II when female teachers in many areas were allowed to marry. The situation demonstrates, however, the degree to which early teachers were poorly paid as well as subject to the scrutiny of the local populace. [See also **teaching**.*]

Bibliography: A. B. Bowden, *Early Schools of Washington Territory* (1935); M. D. Sanford, *Mollie: The Journal of Mollie Dorsey Sanford in Nebraska and Colorado Territories, 1857–1866* (1959); M. M. Feidler, *In Retrospect: Teaching in North Dakota, Recollections of Retired Teachers* (1976); P. Stock, *Better Than Rubies: A History of Women's Education* (1978).

Andrea Wyman

Boston marriages. *Boston marriage* is the late nineteenth-century term given to the practice of two adult women living together in a companionate relationship. Although found all over the country, such pairings were most common in New England, most likely due to the proximity of several **women's colleges*** and, consequently, the generous concentration of female college graduates in the population. The term is generally applied only to college-educated, middle-class or upper-middle-class white women, who lived together openly within the community. Same-sex partnerships among working-class women took a different form, often involving one partner passing as a man to hide the nature of the relationship.

Most documented cases of Boston marriages indicate that the women were

typically financially independent from men, either through their own career efforts or inheritance. These relationships were known to be monogamous, long-
term life choices for women and generally not "phases" or short-lived
arrangements during periods of transition from college to marriage.

The increase in the frequency and popularity of romantic friendships in the
latter half of the nineteenth century was due to a coincidence of two important
social factors in women's history. The rigidly enforced social arrangement that
obligated middle-class women and men to act within **separate spheres*** made
casual friendships or working partnerships between the genders difficult. At the
same time, the growth of women's participation in higher education gave women
a sense of their intellectual and professional potential and newly found economic
autonomy. In general, nineteenth-century women were socialized to depend
upon and revere female friendships and remain loyal to them until death. Homo-
social, single-sex networks helped women develop self-esteem and inner security.

The first few generations of women to participate in higher education challenged many preconceived notions of what was appropriate or even healthy for
women. These women took their roles as pioneers seriously; they were accomplished students with aspirations of a career. At women's colleges, the students
existed in a female-dominated environment, while students at coeducational universities established female enclaves on their campuses. The colleges supported
such separatism for the most part, fearing fraternization among young men and
women [see **feminization***].

College life was conducive to forming romantic friendships for other reasons
as well. Most of the students were from similar class and ethnic backgrounds,
and they possessed considerable leisure time. Colleges also tolerated the practice
of **smashing**,* where one female student formally courted, dated, and established a romantic friendship with another. Smashing or spooning was especially
common at women's colleges where many social events, including dances, were
limited to women. Students could also look to their faculty as role models. As
historian Patricia Palmieri discovered, dual female households were so common
among **Wellesley College*** faculty that they were referred to as "Wellesley
marriages."

Some women may have chosen this path feeling it was the only option available, but the vast majority considered a woman life partner a desirable choice.
Having grown up socialized to treasure women's friendships and women's values, the letters and diaries of participants in Boston marriages indicate that they
had found "kindred spirits" and discovered the full satisfactions of family life
in their living arrangements.

Stating that a Boston marriage fulfilled the same role for these women as a
heterosexual marriage did for others inevitably raises the question of sexuality.
Is the term *lesbian*, as it is currently understood, an appropriate label? The
answer is not simple. What is clear from the evidence is that the emotional
bonds between the women were real, strong, and quite passionate. There is

ample evidence, especially from sex surveys conducted around World War I, to suggest that the women were affectionate and physical, including hugging, kissing, and cuddling, but evidence of genital sex is much more obscure.

According to a 1918 survey by Katherine Bement Davis, 50 percent of the unmarried and 30 percent of the married women admitted to having intense emotional relationships with women. Yet the women involved were probably not lesbians in the full sense of the term as is understood now and would probably be shocked to learn that today they would be thought of as homosexual. The closest historians likely can come to assessing the realities of these women's lives is to recognize the tremendous variation in individual sexual practice, falling somewhere along what poet Adrienne Rich refers to as the "lesbian continuum."

Beginning in the second decade of the twentieth century and continuing through the 1920s, the way society came to view Boston marriages changed dramatically. One reason was the increasing sexual liberalism of the flapper era. **Coeducation*** served to encourage more freedom for students, and social restrictions governing male/female relations relaxed. Educated Americans became aware of the work of Sigmund Freud and various sexologists who now labeled same-sex relationships as deviant, inverted, perverse, and even pathological. The innocence with which Boston marriages had been viewed was lost. Those women who persisted in relationships revealed that they did so only with a sense of shame or guilt.

Boston marriages served an interesting purpose during an era when it was far more acceptable for women to be in relationships with other women than with men. They gave women an opportunity to express their romantic and perhaps sexual selves apart from procreation and the freedom to enjoy a work life unfettered by the traditional demands placed on women. As Jessie Taft said in her 1916 book *The Women's Movement*, "Everywhere we find the unmarried women turning to other women, building up with them a real home, finding in them the sympathy and understanding, the bond of similar standards and values, as well as the same aesthetic and intellectual interests, that are often difficult of realization in a husband, especially here in America where business crowds out culture" (pp. 10–11).

Bibliography: Jessie Taft, *The Women's Movement from the Point of View of Social Consciousness* (1916); Lillian Faderman, *Surpassing the Love of Men: Romantic Friendship and Love between Women from the Renaissance to the Present* (1981); Carroll Smith-Rosenberg, "The Female World of Love and Ritual: Relations between Women in Nineteenth-Century America," in Carroll Smith-Rosenberg, ed., *Disorderly Conduct: Visions of Gender in Victorian America* (1985); John D'Emilio and Estelle B. Freedman, *Intimate Matters: A History of Sexuality in America* (1988); Faderman, *Odd Girls and Twilight Lovers: A History of Lesbian Life in the Twentieth Century* (1991); Patricia Ann Palmieri, *In Adamless Eden: The Community of Women Faculty at Wellesley* (1995).

Jana Nidiffer

Breckinridge, Sophonisba. Author, lawyer, educator, social worker, researcher, and reformer, Sophonisba Preston Breckinridge (1866–1948) was a major influence in the development of **social work*** as an academic discipline. Breckinridge was born in Lexington, Kentucky, to William Campbell Preston Breckinridge and Issa Desha. Her early schoolwork completed in Lexington, she graduated from **Wellesley College*** in 1888. After teaching **high school*** mathematics in Washington, D.C., while her father served as a congressman, Breckinridge returned with her father to Lexington and studied in his law office, becoming the first woman admitted to the Kentucky bar in 1895.

Frustrated by lack of opportunities for a woman in law, Breckinridge moved to Illinois to work for **Marion Talbot**,* **dean of women*** at the **University of Chicago**,* and began graduate study in political science. In 1901 she received the Ph.D., the first woman awarded that degree in political science. She subsequently entered law school and in 1904 became the first woman to receive a law degree from the University of Chicago. Breckinridge then began **teaching*** economic and legal courses in the university's Department of Household Administration [see **home economics***].

Between 1905 and 1907 Breckinridge's publication of two articles about legal issues regarding the employment of women led to her involvement with the **Women's Trade Union League**,* an invitation to live with other female reform leaders at **Hull-House**,* and an opportunity to teach in the Chicago School of Civics and Philanthropy, founded to train social workers. She soon became dean and head of the research department. Among her publications were two books written with colleague Edith Abbott, *The Delinquent Child and the Home* (1912) and *Truancy and Non-Attendance in the Chicago Schools* (1917). These works centered on the negative impact of urban environment on family life. She also authored several books on women's rights and family welfare and was a founder of the *Social Service Review* and an editor for over twenty years.

As an activist and reformer, Breckinridge campaigned for a federal child labor law, for protection for immigrants, and for equal rights for blacks and women. Heavily involved in the **suffrage*** movement, she was equally concerned with economic equality for women as reflected in her support of women's trade unions and her work as a lawyer helping to draft bills to regulate women's wages and hours of employment. Breckinridge also became involved in the peace movement, helping organize the Women's Peace Party in 1915 and serving as secretary [see **peace education***].

Although her influence was widespread, Breckinridge's greatest contribution was to the discipline of social work. Primarily through her efforts, the Chicago School of Civics and Philanthropy became the Graduate School of Social Service Administration at the University of Chicago. Along with Edith Abbott, Breckinridge helped shape the program by stressing the need for both a strong academic component and a commitment to public social service.

After holding several administrative and professorial positions, she was named Samuel Deutsch Professor of Public Welfare Administration in 1929 and retained that title until retiring in 1933. Despite retirement, Breckinridge continued teaching until 1942 and maintained an active schedule until shortly before her death in Chicago at age eighty-two of a perforated ulcer and arteriosclerosis.

Bibliography: "Sophonisba Preston Breckinridge," in *The National Cyclopaedia of American Biography* (1967); Christopher Lasch, "Sophonisba Preston Breckinridge," in Edward T. James, Janet Wilson James, and Paul S. Boyer, eds., *Notable American Women, 1607–1950* (1971); Robyn Muncy, "Gender and Professionalization in the Origins of the U.S. Welfare State: The Careers of Sophonisba Breckinridge and Edith Abbott, 1890–1935," *Journal of Policy History*, 2 (1990): 290–315. Breckinridge's papers are in the Library of Congress.

Verbie Lovorn Prevost

Brown, Charlotte Hawkins. Charlotte Hawkins Brown (1883?–1961) founded and for fifty years directed the Palmer Memorial Institute, a nationally recognized preparatory school for African Americans in Sedalia, North Carolina. Born in Henderson, North Carolina, to Caroline Frances Hawkins and an unidentified father, Brown was named Lottie Hawkins but renamed herself Charlotte Eugenia Hawkins prior to her high school graduation. During Brown's childhood her family moved to Cambridge, Massachusetts, where Brown was an exceptional student first at Allston Grammar School and then Cambridge English High School.

In a chance encounter Brown so greatly impressed **Alice Freeman Palmer,*** second president of **Wellesley College,*** with her intelligence and eagerness to learn that Palmer later volunteered to provide financial support for Brown to attend the two-year State **Normal School*** at Salem, Massachusetts. Brown enrolled in fall 1900 but at the beginning of her second year was recruited to teach at Bethany Institute in the small community of Sedalia. A run-down church served as the school for her first class of fifteen. When financial difficulties caused the **American Missionary Association*** to close the school the following year, Brown was offered a position in another location, but local African Americans urged her to start her own school in Sedalia.

Brown returned to New England to discuss her plans with Palmer, who agreed to help raise funds. Brown remained in New England for the summer, raising funds herself by giving recitations and recitals. When she returned to Sedalia in the fall, the community gave her fifteen acres of land for a school, and the Bethany Congregational minister provided an old blacksmith shop, which she turned into classrooms. She established a board of trustees composed entirely of African Americans and in October opened the Alice Freeman Palmer Institute, named in honor of her mentor and benefactor. Brown added "Memorial" after Palmer's death that fall.

Palmer Memorial Institute grew steadily, with Brown running the school, **teaching,*** and raising money for new buildings and other needs. Faculty increased, as did offerings in both academic courses and agricultural and **vocational education.*** With biracial support and nationwide fund-raising efforts, Brown built Palmer into a highly successful school, offering rural African Americans the opportunity for college preparatory training. Palmer's first accredited **high school*** class graduated in 1922.

While devoting herself to developing Palmer, Brown also continued her own education. In addition to receiving a diploma from Salem Normal, she studied at Harvard, Wellesley, and Simmons Colleges. During 1909 at summer school at Harvard, she met Edward Sumner Brown, whom she married two years later. He taught at Palmer for a year but then left to teach in South Carolina, and the marriage ended in divorce in 1915. Charlotte Hawkins Brown had no children, but she took responsibility for rearing three nieces and four cousins, all of whom graduated from Palmer and pursued additional education.

In addition to promoting equality for African Americans through education, Brown also fought racial discrimination by bringing lawsuits, speaking about her experiences, writing, and encouraging interracial contacts. Brown's most famous story was "Mammy: An Appeal to the Heart of the South" (1919). *The Correct Thing to Do, to Say, to Wear* (1940) established her reputation as the "First Lady of Social Graces." Brown was the first African American appointed to the **Young Women's Christian Association*** national board, the first African American woman member of the Twentieth Century Club of Boston, and a founding member of the **National Council of Negro Women**.* In 1946 she was a delegate to the International Congress of Women.

In 1952 Brown retired as president of Palmer but continued as vice president of the board and director of finances until death from heart failure in 1961 in Greensboro, North Carolina. Ten years later Palmer Institute closed because of financial difficulties, but in 1987 the former campus was designated a state historic site. Through establishment of Palmer Memorial Institute and her leadership for fifty years, Charlotte Hawkins Brown profoundly affected many lives, including more than a thousand young African American graduates of Palmer.

Bibliography: Constance Marteena, *The Lengthening Shadow of a Woman* (1977); Sandra N. Smith and Earle H. West, "Charlotte Hawkins Brown," in Darlene Clark Hine, ed., *Black Women in American History: The Twentieth Century* (1990); Diana Silcox-Jarrett, *Charlotte Hawkins Brown: One Woman's Dream* (1996). The major collection of Brown's papers is at the Schlesinger Library, Radcliffe College, Cambridge, Massachusetts.

Verbie Lovorn Prevost

Bryn Mawr College. Chronologically sixth of the so-called **Seven Sister*** colleges (**Mount Holyoke**,* 1837; **Vassar**,* 1865; **Smith**,* 1875; **Wellesley**,* 1875; **Radcliffe**,* 1879; Bryn Mawr, 1885; and **Barnard**,* 1889), Bryn Mawr College, like the others, was founded to fulfill the vision of an education for women equivalent to men's. With their roots in earlier, religiously oriented female **seminaries**,* these nineteenth-century northeastern **women's colleges*** pioneered in offering women a liberal arts course of study. Though originally taking cues from its predecessors, especially Smith, Bryn Mawr soon pulled away from the influence of the female seminary and its moral discipline and became a leader in putting academic rigor at the center of women's education.

Bryn Mawr was founded by Joseph Taylor, an Orthodox **Quaker*** physician and businessman who bequeathed his fortune to establish a female Haverford College. Though he envisioned the preparation of Quaker teachers, Taylor emphasized the usefulness of liberal arts–educated mothers. This purpose was not so very different from those that animated the foundings of the earlier sister institutions: A liberal arts training for women would better prepare them for the distinctive female sphere they would enter—childrearing, wifely duties, and before marriage (or in its absence), **teaching**.* The vision, then, was at once bold—that women should have an education equivalent to men's—and conservative—that such an education would better prepare them for their traditional, female roles.

Bryn Mawr's departure from the seminarian influence of its predecessors was achieved by **M. Carey Thomas**,* its first dean and second president. Though a professed Quaker, and from a highly respected Quaker family, Thomas was, in fact, not particularly devout, and the gap between Taylor's vision and hers was great. Thomas, having graduated from Cornell University, pursued graduate work at Johns Hopkins, and received her Ph.D. summa cum laude in philology from the University of Zurich, was familiar with male university education, and it became the model she held up for Bryn Mawr. As she visited the major eastern colleges for men and women, she was dismayed by what she found: students unprepared for college study and even some women teachers at Wellesley, Smith, and Mount Holyoke who had never had a single college course themselves.

Thomas was determined that Bryn Mawr would be different, and she set about creating a college for women that incorporated the best aspects of its sisters but with the standards, curriculum, scholarship, and devotion to original inquiry that characterized the best universities for men. Bryn Mawr would offer women the highest standards of university training in the United States. To achieve this ambitious goal, Thomas recruited faculty largely from among young, male, German-educated scholars. Teaching time was limited to encourage the scholarship that Thomas believed must support teaching, and a graduate school was added. Standards for college admission were high: To matriculate, students first presented a comprehensive preparatory course, including Latin and Greek, and then passed a rigorous set of examinations modeled on the exam at Harvard. At the same time, appreciating the uniqueness of the sister colleges, Thomas took pains to create at Bryn Mawr a female community where women's influence prevailed. She achieved this largely through her own influence as dean and later president and through her careful selection of female resident supervisors who were much more involved with students than the teachers, male and female, who engaged in no supervision or oversight of students.

Over time, Bryn Mawr fulfilled much of Thomas's vision. It attracted the brightest and best-trained scholars, including Woodrow Wilson, sociologist Franklin Henry Giddings, historian Charles McLean, geneticist Edmund Wilson, and later Thomas Hunt Morgan. Upper-class students elected their courses in two groups of related specialties, a precursor of the major. Bryn Mawr students were prepared for graduate work and careers, and the graduate school became a leader in training scholars, irrespective of gender. By offering women scholarship of the highest standards and the graduate fellowships and training that were elsewhere denied them, Bryn Mawr represented a major breakthrough in the history of women's education in America.

Like four of its sister women's colleges, Bryn Mawr ceased in the 1970s to be an exclusively women's academic community; though not officially **coeducational**,* its close ties and academic cooperation with Haverford have brought men to the campus and placed women at Haverford, and students at both schools may major at either college.

Bibliography: Helen Lefkowitz Horowitz, *Alma Mater: Design and Experience in the Women's Colleges from Their Nineteenth-Century Beginnings to the 1930s* (1984); Barbara Miller Solomon, *In the Company of Educated Women: A History of Women and Higher Education in America* (1985); Horowitz, *The Power and Passion of M. Carey Thomas* (1994).

Joan Cenedella

Bryn Mawr Summer School for Women Workers. The Bryn Mawr Summer School for Women Workers in Industry (1921–1938) was founded in 1921 as a result of efforts by **Bryn Mawr College*** educators **M. Carey Thomas,*** Susan M. Kingsbury, and Hilda W. Smith. Between 1921 and 1938, over sixteen women wage earners enrolled in the school's eight-week sessions. Students attended classes, listened to lectures, participated in discussions, and visited local factories and labor meetings. Built around core classes in English and economics, the curriculum was designed to give workers a better understanding of the industrial world, as well as the courage and tools with which to change it. School director Hilda Smith proudly called this radical program ''an experiment station in workers' education.''

As president of Bryn Mawr College, M. Carey Thomas envisioned a school that would house working women for the summer, offer classes in the humanities and social sciences, and produce well-informed advocates of ''industrial justice and international peace.'' At Thomas's request, Susan Kingsbury (director of Bryn Mawr's Carola Woerishoffer Graduate Department of Social Economy) drafted a plan for the administration, financing, and curriculum of the school. Together with their colleague Smith, Thomas and Kingsbury consulted and gained the support of a group of women trade unionists, including Mary Anderson, chief of the **Women's Bureau*** of the United States Department of Labor, and Rose Schneidermann, head of the New York **Women's Trade Union League*** [see **labor unions***].

In December 1920, Bryn Mawr's Alumnae Association voted unanimously in favor of the Summer School; the following January, college directors and faculty approved the plan. Representatives from industry, the college administration, and alumnae formed a joint administrative committee to govern the school, which was eventually enlarged to provide a number of industrial workers equal to that of the college and alumnae members combined. Smith was appointed first director of the Summer School, a position she held until 1933.

The Bryn Mawr Summer School used experimental teaching methods, dispensing with student desks and replacing them with trestle tables to facilitate discussion. Frequently classes were held outside. Dedicated to "a broad spirit of impartial inquiry" and demonstrating its radical roots, the school was designed to provide women workers with "a fuller education in order that they may . . . help in the coming social reconstruction." Students with at least three years of industrial wage-earning experience and an eighth-grade education were recruited from throughout the United States by district committees, in cooperation with the **Young Women's Christian Association*** (YWCA), industrial firms, trade unions, and later the Summer School Alumnae Association. By recruiting a representative student body, the school hoped to help all workers. Beginning in 1926, the school admitted black students. Tuition was $250, paid largely by scholarships funded by the district committees, trade unions, **women's clubs**,* the YWCA, and other sources.

Bryn Mawr undergraduates often assisted the summer students as they settled into life on campus. All Summer School students attended classes in English (both literature and composition) and economics; electives included public speaking, general science, and drama. Classroom work was balanced with trips to museums and historical sites, as well as recreational activities, including baseball, "corrective gymnastics," and rhythmic dancing. The flexible curriculum and small classes were designed to avoid academic rigidity while teaching the social sciences and fostering active citizenship. The Summer School employed a largely female instructional staff, all hired from outside the regular Bryn Mawr faculty.

In addition to instructors and tutors, the Summer School employed two librarians from the college's staff as members of the faculty. The librarians gave students tours of the stacks and reading rooms as well as the Summer School's own book collection, taught them how to use the card catalog and other reference materials, and assisted them in gathering information for papers, talks, and projects. The library also served as an important meeting place for students attending poetry readings, creative writing sessions, and discussions of labor journalism. These efforts bore fruit in the school magazine, a collection of articles, essays, and short stories published in two or three issues during the summer under the direction of a student editor.

One of the tenets of the Bryn Mawr Summer School was that students learned by experience and community involvement; as a result, attendance at union meetings, legislative hearings, and strikes was considered vitally important fieldwork for women workers. Increasingly, however, these activities led to unfavorable publicity for both the Summer School and the college. In 1934, Bryn Mawr recommended that such outside activities by students and faculty be discontinued; the following year, the school withdrew from the campus and met instead at Mount Ivy, New York. While an agreement was reached that allowed the original policy encouraging fieldwork to be maintained, some associated with the Summer School felt that such activism would eventually be restricted by the increasingly conservative Bryn Mawr faculty. In a climate of fiscal and ideological restraint, the school's financial support diminished. The last summer sessions were held at Bryn Mawr in 1938.

A cooperative effort of feminists, unionists, and educators, the Bryn Mawr Summer School provided unprecedented educational opportunities for working women. From 1921 to 1938, this progressive program trained women to lead "the rapid advance towards industrial peace," introduced them to the rewards of learning, and paved the way for educational and labor reform. [See also **Progressive Era.***]

Bibliography: Hilda Worthington Smith, *Women Workers at the Bryn Mawr Summer School* (1929); Eleanor G. Coit, "Six Little Schools at Bryn Mawr," *American Teacher*, 15 (February 1931): 18–22; Florence Hemley Schneider, *Patterns of Workers' Education: The Story of the Bryn Mawr Summer School* (1941); Edith Finch, *Carey Thomas of Bryn Mawr* (1947); Rita Heller, "From Blue Collars to Bluestockings: Women at the Bryn Mawr School for Women Workers," in Joyce Kornbluh and Mary Frederickson, eds., *Sisterhood and Solidarity: Workers' Education for Women, 1914–1984* (1984). The School of Management and Labor Relations at Rutgers University holds unprocessed Bryn Mawr Summer School papers.

Jennifer Davis McDaid

Bureau of Indian Affairs. The Bureau of Indian Affairs (BIA) is a division of the federal government of the United States responsible for assimilation of native peoples into mainstream "American" life, generally through the use of schools. The BIA was founded in 1824 as a division of the War Department and was originally charged with negotiating treaties, "subduing" Indian populations when necessary, and implementing policies aimed at "civilizing" the Indians. In 1849, the BIA (then known as the Office of Indian Affairs) was transferred to the Interior Department. After the majority of Indian tribes were confined to reservations by the 1870s, the BIA's principal duty was to manage the Indian population with the ultimate goal of "assimilation," that is, educating the Indians so that they would gradually blend into the general "American" populace.

Initially, the BIA contracted with missionary groups to establish and run day schools on the reservations, allotting certain reservations to each of the major Christian denominations. Native women in these schools were trained in the Euro-American "domestic arts" of sewing, cooking, and cleaning. Reading and writing, while part of the curriculum, were not emphasized. Christian doctrine stressing women's subordination to men in both the private and public spheres was an important curricular component [see **separate spheres***]. Native peoples often refused to abandon their religious beliefs and send their children to the schools; ultimately, mission schools were not successful because missionaries had no authority to force native children to attend.

Recognizing the failure of the mission system, the BIA in the 1880s ceased contracting its schools to missionaries. In fact, many educators were concerned about the day schools on reservations, believing that by allowing native children to live at home under their parents' influence, children were not sufficiently indoctrinated in Western, Christian values. The BIA proposed separating children from parents to ensure their eventual acculturation as Americans.

Thus, the BIA began to establish its own series of Indian schools with a particular emphasis on off-reservation boarding schools. The majority of Indian children who attended school between the 1880s and the 1930s attended such boarding schools. Although ostensibly secular institutions, these schools always included some form of religious (usually Protestant) instruction. The premier boarding school, serving as a model, was the **Carlisle Indian School*** founded in Pennsylvania in 1879. Notable BIA off-reservation schools included Chilocco Indian School, Oklahoma; Chemawa Indian School, Oregon; Haskell Institute, Kansas; Sherman Institute, California; Albuquerque Indian School, New Mexico; and Phoenix Indian School, Arizona.

In BIA day and boarding schools, all native knowledge was vigorously suppressed. Native children were not allowed to speak their own language, practice their native religion, wear traditional clothing, or create indigenous arts and crafts. The curriculum was highly gendered and segregated by sex. Native girls were typically trained to become domestic servants, although by the 1910s, a few schools provided courses for girls to become nurses, teachers, or secretaries. A few exceptional students became professionals, such as Susan LaFlesche Picotte who became a doctor after graduating from **Hampton Institute*** (unique for educating African Americans and Indians in the same school). Native boys were trained as farmers, blacksmiths, and shoemakers.

The schools were enormously unpopular with native people, and many native children were taken from their homes without parental consent. Native people were suspicious of BIA boarding schools for a variety of reasons. First, separating children from parents was a horrifying prospect to most Indians. Second, reports of rampant disease and death in the schools reached the reservations; children often left for boarding school never to be seen again. Third, native children were kept at the school for long periods of time—frequently years—making it impossible for children to be initiated into tribal society as young adults. Without such initiation, children were unable to become full members of the tribe (which, of course, was intentional by the educators). For a native girl, separation from home might mean never having a puberty ceremony and thus never being fully integrated into her community as a woman.

In 1928, the Meriam Report, a government-authorized study of the BIA, stated that its boarding schools suffered from chronic problems including inadequate funding and staffing, overcrowding, poor facilities, bad nutrition, poor health care, and inappropriate curriculum. The report recommended closing some of the boarding schools, improving standards at others, and opening more day schools on the reservations. During the next four decades, most of these recommendations were ignored by the BIA. In 1969, the Kennedy Report—based on Senate investigations of the BIA system led by Senator Robert Kennedy and concluded by Senator Edward Kennedy—found many of the same failings in the BIA school system. The main thrust of the Kennedy recommendations was to give native people more control over their children's education. As a result of this report and native people's own political action for change, many tribes established reservation schools funded by the BIA but administered locally by tribal officials. Central components of these schools' curricula include tribal history and language instruction. In 1978, the Tribally Controlled Community College Assistance Act was passed by Congress, setting out guidelines for the creation of tribal community colleges funded, in part, by the BIA. In the mid-1990s, there were 106 BIA elementary and secondary schools, 60 tribally controlled elementary and secondary schools, and 24 tribally controlled community colleges. [See also **Board of Foreign Missions**.*]

Bibliography: Ardy Bowker, *Sisters in the Blood: The Education of Women in Native America* (1993); David DeJong, *Promises of the Past: A History of Indian Education in the United States* (1993); Valerie Sherer Mathes, "Susan LaFlesche Picotte, M.D.: Nineteenth Century Physician and Reformer," *Great Plains Quarterly*, 13 (Summer 1993): 172–186; K. Tsianina Lomawaima, *They Called It Prairie Light: The Story of Chilocco Indian School* (1994); David Wallace Adams, *Education for Extinction: American Indians and the Boarding School Experience, 1875–1928* (1995).

Jo Ann Woodsum

Burroughs, Nannie Helen. Nannie Helen Burroughs (1879–1961) was a forceful proponent for women's education and a founder and longtime head of the National Training School for Women and Girls in Washington, D.C. Through both formal education and informal advocacy, she enhanced opportunities for black women, especially those of the working class. She was born in Culpepper, Virginia, where she lived until age five. She and her mother later moved to Washington, D.C., where Burroughs graduated from the city's colored high school in 1896.

Trained as a secretary, Burroughs lived in Louisville, Kentucky, from 1900 to 1909. She was employed as a bookkeeper and editorial secretary for the Foreign Mission Board of the National Baptist Convention [see **Board of Foreign Missions***]. Burroughs, along with the Baptist women's society in Louisville, helped organize a women's industrial club that taught domestic science and secretarial courses. She was also one of the founders of the Women's Convention, an auxiliary to the National Baptist Convention USA. Burroughs served as corresponding secretary from 1900 to 1947 and as president of the convention from 1947 until her death.

The idea of establishing an industrial school for girls had been Burroughs's dream since childhood. She imagined that it was "going to be the national dream realized [and] a million women in our churches will make us have it." With the help of the Women's Convention, Burroughs's dream became a reality. In

1909, the National Training School for Women and Girls was founded, and Burroughs became its first president. The school's motto, "Work. Support thyself. To thine own powers appeal," affirmed Burroughs's and the convention's commitment to address issues of the working poor and employment options for black women. Their goal was to "professionalize" jobs that were understood as menial and believed to require little, if any, skill or training. The group chose an industrial school to highlight the importance and necessity of domestic and manual training for women.

Students attending the National Training School received a general education in academic subjects as well as a trade in a specific vocation that they could enter upon graduation. Courses included homemaking, housekeeping, household administration, interior decorating, and home nursing. The dormitory housed students from all over the United States, Africa, and the Caribbean. In its first year, the school boasted 11 students; twenty-five years later, 2,000 attended. In 1934, it was renamed the National Trade School for Women and operated until Burroughs's death in 1961. The board of trustees reestablished the school in 1964 for elementary students and renamed it Nannie Helen Burroughs School.

Burroughs's dream was representative of her commitment to the growth and welfare of black women, as observed in her involvement in both formal and informal means of education. She was an active member of the **National Association of Colored Women*** and founder of the National Association of Wage Earners Union. Unlike most **labor unions*** that focused on activities and discussions about trade or union ideas, Burroughs's forums primarily considered educational issues that discussed human equality and dignity for black women.

Burroughs's writings also reflect her continued support and commitment to struggles of black women. Her ideas and suggestions are described in articles such as "No Color But Character" (*The Voice*, July 1904) and *The Worker*, a quarterly publication by the Baptist Woman's Auxiliary, of which she was editor.

Nannie Helen Burroughs was a leader for the rights and education of African American women. She died of natural causes in Washington, D.C., in May 1961. [See also **race uplift**.*]

Bibliography: William Pickens, *Nannie Burroughs and the School of the 3B's* (1921); Evelyn Brooks Higginbotham, *Righteous Discontent: The Women's Movement in the Black Baptist Church, 1880–1920* (1993). See also Burroughs's papers in the Library of Congress.

Vanessa Allen-Brown

C

Carlisle Indian School. Carlisle Indian School in Carlisle, Pennsylvania, was founded in 1879 by Richard Pratt, who believed that the best way to civilize the Indian was to "immerse him in civilization and keep him there until well soaked." Pratt, a career army officer with extensive experience in the Indian wars, vigorously campaigned for off-reservation boarding schools.

Pratt first implemented his ideas of Indian education at Fort Marion, Florida, where he was in charge of Cheyenne, Kiowa, and Comanche prisoners of war. Pratt established an experimental school with these prisoners as students. He sought to prove the educability of Indian people, a point many nineteenth-century Euro-Americans doubted. Pratt's education of the prisoners focused on trade skills such as carpentry, blacksmithing, and shoemaking. He proclaimed his experiment with the prisoners a complete success.

Based on this success in Florida, Pratt traveled to Washington, D.C., to garner support for a school far from the reservations in the West where most Indians resided by that point, where Indian children could be brought for complete immersion in "civilization." With approval from the Interior Department (responsible for overseeing Indian Affairs), Pratt founded a boarding school for Indian children in abandoned cavalry barracks in Carlisle. Carlisle was the first, and perhaps the most famous, of the off-reservation boarding schools established by the U.S. Office (later **Bureau) of Indian Affairs**.*

During the school's first year, Pratt enrolled more than 200 students representing over a dozen tribes. He ran the school for twenty-four years; by 1903, the population had risen to 1,200 students.

Pratt constantly publicized Indian education at Carlisle as a means to raise funds to sustain the school and recruit new students. A famous series of "before and after" photographs was particularly successful in furthering these goals. Indian children were photographed upon their arrival at Carlisle. The children were then stripped of their traditional clothing, their hair was cut, and they were bathed and dressed in "civilized" or Euro-American clothing. This photo-graphic transformation was emblematic of the effects of Carlisle education on native children: "savage" one day, "civilized" the next. Their new identities as "civilized" persons were sealed when they were forced to choose Euro-American names from a long list on the blackboard.

Pratt organized Carlisle along military lines. Students were drilled and marched on a daily basis. Their time was strictly regimented; students spent half the day in the classroom, half working at various trades. The academic curric-ulum emphasized English-language skills as well as history and mathematics. The "trades" or industrial curriculum emphasized domestic skills for girls and farming for boys. Children were not allowed to speak their native languages or practice native singing, dancing, or religion. Punishment for breaking these rules was severe, ranging from corporal punishment to solitary confinement.

At Carlisle, the outing was a cornerstone of Pratt's plan of education. Instead of returning home for the summer, students were placed with Euro-American farming families for three months and, in some cases, for up to three years after graduation. Here they could experience firsthand the responsibilities and benefits of Euro-American family life and work. The outing was acknowledged as a strong and effective part of Pratt's educational strategy and was adopted at other off-reservation schools. Pratt believed that placing native children with Euro-American families would continue the process of acculturation begun in the school environment.

Carlisle's prestige declined after Pratt's retirement and was finally closed in 1918. The school endures as a potent symbol of the U.S. government's failed attempt to erase native cultural values and traditions.

Bibliography: Lonna Malmsheimer, " 'Imitation White Man': Images of Transformation at the Carlisle Indian School," *Studies in Visual Communication,* 11 (Fall 1985); 54–75; Richard Henry Pratt, *Battlefield and Classroom: Four Decades with the American Indian, 1867–1904* (1987); David Wallace Adams, *Education for Extinction: American Indians and the Boarding School Experience, 1875–1928* (1995).

Jo Ann Woodsum

Catholic colleges. A Catholic college or university is an institution that asserts the Catholic faith, each in its own way, so that in every discipline it is concerned about unity with Catholic faith and doctrine. Although the earliest Catholic col-leges in the United States were all male, Catholic **women's colleges*** were founded beginning in 1895 and have, in fact, often provided strong female com-munities for their religious leaders and students.

Today, almost all colleges and universities worldwide have been influenced from the European model, established around the year 1200 to train churchmen in the north (Paris and Oxford) and lawyers in the south (Bologna). In the nineteenth century, church authority greatly influenced higher education in both Europe and America, as those who authorized, taught in, and attended these universities were Catholic. Catholic institutions were founded in America to educate Catholic students (many of them newly arrived immigrants), partly as sources of recruitment for the clergy but mainly to care intellectually for people who still faced prejudice elsewhere in American higher education.

The first Roman Catholic institution of higher learning in the United States was Georgetown University, in Washington, D.C., established for men by the Jesuit order in 1789. St. Louis University, founded in 1818 (the oldest institution of higher learning west of the Mississippi), and Fordham University (the Bronx, New York), established in 1841 and conducted by the Jesuits, were two other early and influential Catholic institutions.

In addition to this Catholic influence, there have been other motivating factors in the organizational and ideological construct of Catholic colleges and universities, including most prominently the need to provide more advanced religious formation for Catholic youth who proceed to college. This was of particular significance during the nineteenth century, when the newly secularized universities moved away from religion and religious influences.

A third factor encouraging the establishment of Catholic colleges was the preservation and cultivation of the sacred sciences, viewed as vitally important by Pope Gregory XVI (reigned 1831–1846). Gregory wrote in a letter to the bishops of Belgium in 1833: "[I]n fulfillment of the apostolic office entrusted to them, it is most of all the duty of the Roman Pontiffs to preserve the Catholic faith and keep the deposit of its holy doctrine integral and undefiled, it must also be the prerogative to govern instruction in the sacred disciplines which are publicly taught in universities."

While scholars are not in unilateral agreement regarding any standardized set of norms that identify the nature and characteristics of a Catholic university, there is at least consensus that an institution's activities should be consistent with the mission of the Church, that it should be concerned with religious education, and that a Catholic institution of higher learning must in some way be dependent upon the authority of the Church. While greatly influenced by the Catholic Church, Catholic colleges and universities have nonetheless achieved a great deal of autonomy from ecclesiastical control. Institutional autonomy and an increased dedication to all organizational functions have enabled Catholic colleges and universities gradually to assume a more prominent place among mainstream American institutions of higher education.

The Association of Catholic Colleges and Universities observed in 1980, "In the United States, experience demonstrates that the purposes of Catholic Higher Education can best be served by implicit recognition of the Catholic nature of the institutions by the local church or churches."

A strong foundation in the arts and sciences curriculum intended to clarify, refine, and deepen the art of critical thinking within the context of Catholic values is a common thread for Catholic colleges and universities. Along these same lines, the Catholic university seeks to develop critical intelligence among (though not exclusively among) its own members. Thus, the Catholic university has a special vocation, grounded in faith, to develop the kind of critical intelligence necessary for effective service to the world.

The first Catholic women's college was the College of Notre Dame of Maryland, established by the sisters of Notre Dame in 1895. During the first two decades of the twentieth century, the Catholic Church adamantly opposed **suffrage*** and only reluctantly supported higher education for women. Their major fear was that educated women would choose careers over marriage and thus threaten the existence of the Catholic family. Nevertheless, other Catholic colleges for women were founded shortly after Notre Dame: St. Mary's (Indiana), 1894; Trinity College (Washington, D.C.), 1897; and the College of New Rochelle, 1904.

The Church held that the only model for a woman should be Mary, Mother of God, submissive, obedient, serving others. Both suffrage and higher education were seen as threats to a stable society and to a Catholic home. Although religious women have never had the authority, the power, or the opportunity of religious men, they established their own communities, in many ways models of a feminist world. The nuns who founded colleges had great expectations for higher education for women. They argued for quality education in the belief that such education would provide greater opportunity for women. Catholic women's colleges were committed to a liberal arts education for women.

In the mid-1990s, there are approximately 235 Catholic colleges and universities in the United States. Now, as in the early history of Catholic higher education, the Catholic environment breeds a sense of commitment to service and fosters a genuine concern for the poor and needy of society. [See also **Catholic education**,* **Catholic teaching orders**,* **Newman clubs**.*]

Bibliography: Mary J. Oates, ed., *Higher Education for Catholic Women: An Historical Anthology* (1987); James Jerome Conn, *Catholic Universities in the United States and Ecclesiastical Authority* (1991); Mary Lou Anderson, ''Catholic Women's Colleges and Feminism: A Case Study of Four Catholic Women's Colleges'' (Ph.D. diss., University of Massachusetts, Amherst, 1992); Philip Gleason, *What Made Catholic Identity a Problem?* (1994); Theodore M. Hesburgh, ed., *The Challenge and Promise of a Catholic University* (1994).

Gerald L. Willis

Catholic education. Between the first half of the nineteenth century and the middle of the twentieth, Catholic schools played a central role in American education. A wide variety of institutions, from primary schools through colleges, instructed millions of young Americans, many of whom might not otherwise have enjoyed the benefits of formal education. Girls and young women made up about half of the pupils; although the vast majority were Catholics, significant numbers also had Protestant backgrounds. Furthermore, Catholic schools gave thousands of women, most notably Catholic sisters, the opportunity to pursue careers as teachers with a high degree of autonomy.

Scattered efforts at Catholic schooling had existed in various forms since the early seventeenth century, particularly in the French and Spanish territories and the Catholic colony of Maryland. After the American Revolution, the liberalization of religious laws and practices permitted Catholic education to take firmer root. Among the first testimonies to that expansion was the Catholic free school of New York City, established in 1800 and within six years enrolling 220 pupils, the second largest denominational school of the city. By the 1840s, however, a massive immigration of Catholic Europeans was under way that would alter completely the American educational landscape of the next one hundred years. In 1820 Catholics in the United States comprised less than 200,000, or 2 percent of the country's inhabitants; but by 1840 their number had risen to 663,000 (3.9 percent), by 1850 to 1,606,000 (7 percent), and 1860 to 3.5 million (11 percent). In 1900 the number had reached over 12 million, or 17 percent of the total U.S. population. The multiplication of Catholic schools tracked this explosive immigration. From a modest 200-plus schools in 1840, this number had, by 1900, increased to about 4,600, with approximately 1 million registered pupils. In accord with the working-class and urban nature of Catholic immigration, these schools were concentrated in the cities of the Northeast and Midwest with additional high representation in California and the states bordering the west bank of the Mississippi (excluding Arkansas).

The girls and young women who attended Catholic institutions came from a large variety of cultural backgrounds. Members of the German and Irish exodus that was in full swing by the 1840s made up the bulk until the 1880s, when they were joined, and soon overtaken, by the new Catholic immigration from Southern and Eastern Europe, most notably Italians, Poles, Czechs, Slovaks, and Lithuanians. Further, French Canadians from Quebec had been streaming into New England's mill towns by the hundreds of thousands since the end of the Civil War. Between one-third and one-half of these new Americans enrolled their children in the quickly growing network of free parochial schools, the pillars of Catholic education.

After a sporadic beginning in the 1830s, these schools came into their own with the widespread formation of Catholic and mainly national parishes during the 1840s through 1860s, until exploding in the 1880s, when around 400,000 boys and girls were registered. By 1900, the number of parochial schools had risen to 3,811, and by 1910 to 4,845, with 1,237,000 students in attendance— 6.3 percent of the entire school-going population in the United States. Ethnic patterns of Catholic education were firmly established. In 1914, 95 percent of German parishes had schools, as did the large majority of French Canadian parishes, 71 percent of Polish parishes, about half of Czech and Irish parishes, 48 percent of Slovak parishes, 29 percent of Lithuanian, and roughly one-fifth of Italian parishes. In 1920, parochial school enrollment nationwide hovered around 1.7 million.

Education within the parish sought to provide a buffer against the cultural onslaught of the public schools. Public education endeavored the fastest possible assimilation of newcomers into American society and as such pursued a strongly

Protestant and monolingual curriculum. By contrast, parochial schools protected the immigrants' religion and in foreign-speaking neighborhoods were bilingual. Apart from these distinct features, Catholic parish schools differed little from public institutions. Both systems had similar curricula, they shared many textbooks, and importantly, the Catholic texts in use by the late nineteenth century endorsed the same civic and "American" values as their "Protestant" counterparts. As if to prove their compatibility with public schools, Catholic schools occasionally secured public funding and became an integrated part of the state system (as occurred in Lowell, Massachusetts, from 1831 until 1852, or in Poughkeepsie, New York, between 1873 and 1898). Though claims that the quality of instruction was better in public institutions were frequent, significant variation applied according to the educational backgrounds of the Catholic sisters who operated most schools. Thus, Polish sisters were often recruited with only a rudimentary preparation due to the fast increase of Polish parishes after the 1890s, while well-established **Catholic teaching orders*** like the German School Sisters of Notre Dame ranked among the best of American educators. By 1900, most parish schools had four or five grades, some six through eight, and larger establishments such as Chicago, Cincinnati, New York, Pennsylvania, and New England, featured high school courses in many instances; these latter had been added to prepare women for entrance into **normal school**.* By 1910, as in the public system, the typical curriculum encompassed eight grades.

Throughout the growth of the parochial school system, the Catholic female academy was an option for daughters of the financially better situated. Dating from the close of the eighteenth century, the academy was tuition based and offered elementary as well as secondary-level courses. The **academies*** were founded and staffed by Catholic sisters and increased rapidly from the 1830s onward, numbering over 660 by the turn of the century. Interestingly, they maintained a significant Protestant clientele. Sisters also established "free schools," which filled a significant void particularly before the large-scale creation of parochial and public schools.

The importance of the Catholic parochial school system cannot be overestimated. By offering instruction in English as well as the languages of the various ethnic groups, parochial schools absorbed the shock of transition for hundreds of thousands of new arrivals and allowed them to hold on to their heritage while they adapted to American culture. Moreover, in the absence of Catholic schools, countless young Americans would have remained without structured and formalized academic training as well as the opportunity to enter the labor market on a competitive basis. Many parents would have refused to send their children to public schools and expose them to what they considered alien cultural and religious doctrines. As for women, the successes of parochial schools as springboards toward economic independence were particularly apparent in the formidable numbers of those who started careers as teachers. In New York City, Irish women made up 22 percent of all schoolteachers in 1870, and 29 percent or 2,000 of the 7,000 instructors in the first decade of the twentieth.

In the late 1890s the Catholic Church moved toward institutionalizing higher education for women. Many academies already had collegiate departments, but the first of the **Catholic colleges*** for women—Notre Dame of Maryland—was established in 1896, followed a year later by Trinity College in Washington, D.C. Conducted, again, by female orders, Notre Dame had evolved from an academy, while Trinity was a new foundation. Both establishment patterns were common. The better among Catholic female colleges would soon commit themselves to progressive liberal arts curricula. Separate **high schools*** for women were also being started. The organization in 1900 of four high school ''centers'' in Philadelphia, each with a two-year course, marked the beginning.

Between World War I and the mid-1960s, Catholic schooling continued to expand significantly. The number of **women's colleges*** increased from 14 in 1915 to 37 in 1925 and 116 by 1955. Catholic schools overall doubled and enrollments tripled; during the peak decade of 1950 through 1960, elementary education increased by 171 percent, compared with 142 percent for public schools. In 1965, 4.5 million children or 12 percent of all elementary pupils attended parish schools. Thereafter, a sharp drop in students, schools, and the religious teaching force occurred following the general secularization of American society.

A significant question, and one raised incessantly by American Protestants for at least the first fifty years of the expansion of Catholic education, is whether a separate system encouraged ideological segregation of Catholics and immigrants from American society. Catholics claimed at the time what has been proven by hindsight, that Catholic schooling facilitated the assimilation of its constituents into the larger society because it was ''American'' in spirit and permitted initiation into the new culture to proceed gradually and with less pain. Catholic schools thus served, beyond their education function, the equally important purpose of easing the cultural transition to their new homeland for millions of Americans while not retarding, much rather hastening, the general process of integration.

Bibliography: James A. Burns, *The Growth and Development of the Catholic School System in the United States* (1912); Michael F. Perko, S.J., ed., *Enlightening the Next Generation: Catholics and Their Schools: 1830–1980* (1988); Jay P. Dolan, *The American Catholic Experience: A History from Colonial Times to the Present* (1992); Timothy Walch, *Parish School: American Catholic Parochial Education from Colonial Times to the Present* (1996).

Nikola Baumgarten

Catholic teaching orders. Catholic religious sisters belong to the unsung heroes in American history. During the nineteenth century, the period of their greatest increase, they created a network of schools in the United States that soon

spanned the entire country and collectively served America's students in all their
cultural and social diversity. They thus realized, long before the public schools,
the principle of universal education, which Americans considered a pillar of
their democratic state. In addition to building their own institutions, these nuns
administered and staffed the vast majority of America's Catholic parish schools,
thus playing a central role in the establishment and expansion of the Catholic
parochial school system.

Spurred on by the explosive Catholic immigration of the post-1830s, the number of women "religious" in the United States mushroomed from under 40 in
1810 to more than 40,000 by 1900. They constituted 119 religious communities,
12 being established between 1790 and 1829 (these were joined by the French
Ursulines from New Orleans after the Louisiana Purchase in 1803), 39 between
1830 and 1860, and 67 during the remaining forty years. Twenty-eight were
American, the first dating from 1809 when Elizabeth Seton established her soon-
flourishing Sisters of Charity in Emmitsburg, Maryland; 8 were Canadian; and
the remaining 83 European. Missions originated on the East Coast as well as in
the Midwest and South; Maryland, Kentucky, Louisiana, Massachusetts, and
Missouri were among the earliest states with original foundations.

The majority of religious orders conducted schools, either as their main employment or in addition to charitable works such as nursing or establishing
orphanages. Congregations founded explicitly for the purpose of **teaching*** included the well-known French Society of the Sacred Heart and the German
School Sisters of Notre Dame, which, with 3,786 members in twenty-seven
houses, was the largest order in 1910. Sisters instructed the poor and the well-
to-do, Catholics and Protestants, native English speakers as well as innumerable
ethnic groups; many of these constituencies were often hosted in a single classroom. The nuns' involvement with a population that represented the United
States in all its cultural breadth was unmatched until at least 1860 when the
public schools, whose pronounced purpose was to embrace all of America's
youth, had become more inclusive. Initially, the public schools bore a distinct
Protestant character with predominantly monolingual curricula and therefore
failed to accommodate the bulk of Catholic immigrants. The Catholic teaching
sisters, by contrast, taught mostly in the languages of their ethnic constituents
(in this they were often aided by their own ethnicity) as well as in English, and
in their religiously mixed schools, they held true to their pledge not to interfere
with their pupils' faiths.

The poorer students were taught chiefly in "free schools," which, next to the
girls, often admitted boys up to age ten or twelve in separate classes and offered
a basic elementary curriculum of reading, writing, arithmetic, geography, history, and religion. In newly settled areas these free schools frequently represented the only educational opportunity for families without means. Thus, the
Society of the Sacred Heart is noted for having founded the first free school
west of the Mississippi, in Florissant, Missouri, in 1818. Little is known about
the student composition of the free schools, but many were probably religiously

and ethnically diverse. The Florissant School of the Sacred Heart embraced native French and English speakers who were taught in their respective languages. Various orders instructed African Americans, including the two black Catholic communities in operation before the turn of the century—the Oblate Sisters of Providence in Baltimore and the Sisters of the Holy Family in New Orleans. After the widespread advent of Catholic parochial education in the 1840s and 1850s, the sisters' free instruction moved increasingly into the parishes [see **Catholic education***].

Sisters also built **academies,*** often alongside free schools, for a paying clientele. Throughout the antebellum period the curricula of these institutions were compatible with those of the best secular academies, and their high quality of instruction and multilingual courses, coupled with an emphasis on raising virtuous young women, attracted the most prestigious families regardless of ethnic background. Moreover, the academies stood out for their interdenominational character; at least until the Civil War, they typically maintained a significant Protestant clientele. Many academies also enjoyed the respect of the highest (Protestant) statesmen; thus James Madison during his presidency officiated at commencement exercises of the Visitation Academy at Georgetown, and Henry Clay in 1825 distributed diplomas at the first commencement of Nazareth Academy in Kentucky. By 1900, Catholic nuns had instructed thousands of children in their free schools (exact numbers are not available), established 663 girls' academies (which in 1900 enrolled over 56,000 students), and were staffing the majority of America's 3,811 Catholic parish schools.

In the course of their school building, the sisters encountered more hurdles than the average educator. In the general absence of European-type Catholic sponsors, poverty and grueling work schedules were almost a given during the early phases of establishment. Frequently, nuns had to assert their autonomy vis-à-vis male members of the Church hierarchy who attempted to interfere with the rules of their orders or to appropriate the sisters' services without consent. Language problems and varying social expectations made it difficult for many foreign orders to communicate with their students' parents, while the formidable cultural discrepancies between religious life and the American environment constantly challenged the courage and endurance of most communities. The religious dress or "habit," cloister regulations, and a class system within congregations that distinguished between lay and choir sisters, not to mention the Catholic nature of the orders, were all received in the United States with skepticism if not outright hostility or violence. During the nativist decades of the 1830s and 1850s, defamatory publications fanned suspicions about sinister activities behind convent walls, and various antebellum states passed convent inspection laws with the intent to rescue women supposedly held against their will. In the worst instances the sisters became victims of arson by nativist mobs, as happened in the legendary 1834 burning of the Ursuline academy in Charlestown, Massachusetts.

Internally, the rule of cloister severely hampered the sisters. As a result, com-

munities adapted their behavior to the exigencies of their new environment before altering their constitutions; or they split away from their European
motherhouses if these were unprepared to grant the necessary leeway for change.
In this respect, indigenous orders had an easier initiation as they issued less
restrictive rules. The pioneering decades of convent building made obvious the
crucial importance of adjustment: Of the six European communities established
between 1790 and 1829, five failed within a few years. By contrast, all six
American foundations from the same period survived. One can only surmise in
how many ways the varied challenges that confronted the teaching sisters fostered an independence and self-awareness rare for nineteenth-century women.
The role of female orders as emancipators of women and the impact of these
women on the girls they taught are fascinating questions that await further exploration.

Bibliography: Mary Ewens, *The Role of the Nun in Nineteenth Century America* (1978);
Eileen Mary Brewer, *Nuns and the Education of American Catholic Women, 1860–1920*
(1987); Barbara Misner, "Highly Respectable and Accomplished Ladies," in Barbara
Misner, ed., *Catholic Women Religious in America, 1790–1850* (1988); Margaret Susan
Thompson, "Sisterhood and Power: Class, Culture, and Ethnicity in the American Con-
vent," *Colby Library Quarterly*, 25 (September 1989): 149–175; Nikola Baumgarten,
"Education and Democracy in Frontier St. Louis: The Society of the Sacred Heart,"
History of Education Quarterly, 34 (Summer 1994): 171–192; Baumgarten, "Beyond
the Walls: Women Religious in American Life," *U.S. Catholic Historian* (special issue,
Winter 1996).

Nikola Baumgarten

Chautauqua movement. The Chautauqua movement is the name given to one
of the widest-ranging experiments in American popular education in the nineteenth century. Created as a summer camp to encourage better teaching of Sunday school, the movement grew over several decades to include correspondence
courses, reading clubs, and other types of adult education. The correspondence
program was especially appealing to women; two-thirds of participants were
female. The movement eventually included the "mother assembly," other local
permanent assemblies, correspondence education courses, and "tent" Chautauquas.

   The "mother" Chautauqua was founded as the National Sunday School Assembly in 1874 by Lewis Miller, an Akron, Ohio, businessman, and Rev. John
Heyl Vincent, a Methodist minister and later bishop, who helped launch the
International Sunday School Lessons Series. Miller and Vincent chose a spot at
Fair Point on New York's Lake Chautauqua that had been the site of a Methodist
camp meeting because they were convinced that education was more important
than religious revival and that, with growing leisure time, people would come
to a summer camp in order to learn to teach Sunday school more effectively.
Response was overwhelming.

   In his book *The Chautauqua Movement*, Vincent described the movement as a series of concentric circles, or steps, on a mountain that included a range of educational activities: training for Sunday school teachers, lectures and news-papers, summer school courses, and other educational endeavors at Chautauqua such as the School of Languages, the School of Theology, and the Chautauqua College of Liberal Arts, chartered by New York State. In addition to the mother assembly, the other permanent or "sister assemblies" included Bayside in Ohio, Monteagle in Tennessee, and Boulder Chautauqua in Colorado. By 1900 there were about fifty sister assemblies across the United States, at least twelve of which still exist. These sister Chautauquas shared some programming with the mother assembly.

For a short time, traveling, or "tent," chautauquas also appeared, offering education opportunities but, more important, "culture" and entertainment; how-ever, there were never any financial or programmatic ties between the Chautau-qua Assembly and the tent chautauquas. In fact, a 1903 court case ruled that these traveling shows were not to capitalize the "c" in their titles. They dis-appeared around the onset of the depression.

The Chautauqua Literary and Scientific Circle (CLSC) became the heart of Chautauqua's correspondence education for adults. The CLSC claims to be the oldest continuing book club in the United States and was a pioneer in adult education and correspondence education. The CLSC was founded in 1878, de-signed as a "people's college" allowing adults to study at home. The CLSC provided up to twelve books a year in its first three years, then settled into a pattern of four to six books per year written expressly for the CLSC and a monthly magazine, *The Chautauquan*. Vincent, credited with the idea behind the CLSC, hoped that 100 people would sign up for the course; almost 8,000 did in its first year, and at least 1,700 completed the program four years later, receiving a diploma on Recognition Day, an event like college graduation.

The CLSC had many rituals based on those of traditional colleges. Each class chose a name, a flower or symbol, and a motto, sometimes a song, and later a class cheer. Each class made a banner for the Recognition Day parade, and girls in white dresses threw flowers in the graduates' path. Graduate courses also existed in disciplines, including geology, history, and temperance. These ad-vanced levels of reading were rewarded with seals for diplomas and entrance into more select groups of readers. A person who read the whole Bible received a special gold seal. Eventually an alumni association was formed and a head-quarters built to store the banners and other class memorabilia.

Women were the main students of the CLSC. Usually twenty to forty years old, women constituted two-thirds of the 500,000 readers before 1914 and two-thirds of the graduates (about 35,000) from 1882 to 1914. They found that the CLSC provided three components necessary for a profitable adult education course: It was inexpensive, easily accessible, and provided materials of interest to the students. The low cost included the books and the monthly magazine, which could be ordered for under $2, later $4, per year. The materials concen-trated on a classic liberal arts education, giving students an overview of history and culture in Greece, Rome, England, France, Germany, and Italy, as well as some scientific knowledge about geology and household management and travelogues about exotic places in the United States and abroad. Access was simple because the books and magazines came via mail; there was a stable clerical staff headed by Kate Kimball, who served the organization from 1878 to her death in 1917. Readings were written for an adult audience with little spare time and could be done in about forty minutes a day; the magazine was useful, providing many helps for students, such as minidictionaries and sample meeting plans for local CLSC circles.

It was in the local circles that most members found the support and fellowship to keep reading for four years. Like other book clubs and **women's study clubs*** of the era, the CLSC provided a chance for women and men to discuss ideas and to support each other in their reading. At one time there were 10,000 local circles, and in many large cities, like Brooklyn, New York, the smaller circles joined a Union CLSC, which provided activities for members [see also **reading circles***].

Another reason for success of the CLSC was its connection with a recognized and reliable source of authority. The Chautauqua movement was a by-product of the Sunday school movement, and its leaders overlapped in many of the institutions that made up the Protestant educational ecology—Sunday schools, revivals, denominational camps, colleges, journals, and the Woman's Christian Temperance Union and other social reform movements [see **temperance movement***].

Even as the CLSC made a great impact on the lives of adults, especially women, who had no time or money for traditional college, it struggled with a reputation for being superficial. Despite efforts by Vincent, William Rainey Harper (president of the **University of Chicago***), and other advisers to dispel this charge, the CLSC soon took a backseat to other forms of adult education. By 1914 the University of Chicago and many land-grant colleges were providing women with opportunities for **continuing education*** and regular college degrees. The CLSC was also increasingly unable to compete with the growing bureaucratization and professionalization of society. The trend toward professionalization left amateur movements like the Sunday school and the CLSC behind.

Bibliography: John Heyl Vincent, *The Chautauqua Movement* (1886); Theodore Morrison, *Chautauqua* (1974); Robert Lynn and Elliott Wright, *The Big Little School*, 2nd ed. (1980); Alfred L. Irwin, *Three Taps of the Gavel*, 3rd ed. (1987); Anne M. Boylan, *Sunday School* (1988). The main archives of the Chautauqua Assembly and the CLSC are in Smith Memorial Library and the CLSC Alumni Hall, Chautauqua, New York.

Mary Lee Talbot

Chicago Teachers' Federation. Founded in 1897 to defend a recently enacted pension system, the Chicago Teachers' Federation (CTF) was one of the first

teacher unions* organized specifically to work for improved material benefits for teachers. Throughout its history (1897–1968), CTF worked to secure pensions and tenure, to increase wages, to involve teachers in school decisionmaking, and to promote teacher professionalism through organization. CTF supported democracy in the schools and lobbied against centralization of power in administrative hands and other administrative reforms.

Composed primarily of female grade and elementary teachers, CTF set an example of white-collar unionism that was emulated by teachers in other cities and women workers in general. From its inception, CTF excluded administrators and fought the city's school administration and elected officials to secure material benefits for members. CTF became involved with school, municipal, and state politics to secure its goals, as well as other progressive reforms, such as child labor laws and municipal ownership of utilities. These efforts brought CTF into affiliation with labor and civic associations. CTF was also instrumental in founding numerous local and national teacher organizations and in challenging male-dominated groups like the National Education Association (NEA). Yet even though CTF tactics appeared militant, its members never struck. By 1900, CTF secured a pension system and a pay increase, defeated a number of educational administrative reform bills, and grew in membership to 3,300.

Between 1897 and 1916, CTF was Chicago's most influential teacher organization. Up to half of Chicago's teachers were members, and by 1913 CTF was the largest teacher organization in the country. CTF was led by **Margaret Haley*** and Catherine Goggin during its most influential years, Haley serving as business representative and Goggin as president. Both women maintained their positions until their deaths (Haley in 1939 and Goggin in 1916). While Haley and Goggin believed they were the voice of teachers, they nonetheless ran the CTF in a bureaucratic manner.

The CTF's 1899–1902 battle with the city's large, tax-dodging corporations brought CTF and Haley into national prominence and spawned numerous similar organizations across the country. In 1898, Chicago's Board of Education voted a $50-per-year pay increase to teachers, but upon the recommendation of **University of Chicago*** President William Rainey Harper, the board decided that the city's tax structure could not support the raise. Harper angered CTF leaders and members by recommending that only men teachers receive the raise and by insinuating that incompetents in the school system were generally found among women grade teachers. Haley and CTF sued the city's utility corporations for not paying taxes and thereby creating the monetary shortage. In 1901, the Illinois Supreme Court decided in favor of CTF in the tax suit, bringing an extra $250,000 into the school board's coffers. Still, the board refused to pay teachers and instead tried to use the funds for school maintenance bills. CTF again went to court, winning a decision that forced the board to deliver the pay increase with the newly acquired tax monies.

While Chicago's female teachers did not yet have the vote, they were involved with municipal politics through CTF. For example, during the tax fight, members secured neighborhood audiences for hearing tax assessment information, posted leaflets, voluntarily contributed to the cost of CTF campaigns, and distributed pamphlets in various public places. Women teachers also collected signatures for city-wide referenda on municipal ownership of utilities. According to Haley, the fight against the corporations and Harper's plan to enact ninety-nine-year land leases on school properties (thereby diminishing school income) led women teachers to protest gender inequities in pay and to advance **suffrage*** in Chicago.

During the tax fight, Haley and Goggin recognized that without the vote teachers would have little influence on Chicago's elected officials. They therefore persuaded Chicago's teachers to allow CTF to affiliate with the Chicago Federation of Labor. CTF never affiliated with the national American Federation of Labor, though, because feminists Goggin and Haley developed an antipathy for Samuel Gompers. With the help of the **labor union**'s* male constituency, CTF lobbied and defeated state legislative bills that favored school administrators, centralization, and **vocational education**.* CTF also helped elect Edward J. Dunne (the judge who ruled in its favor in the tax fight) as mayor in 1905. Dunne, in turn, appointed a teacher-friendly school board, with three of seven members women. CTF leaders also worked closely with **Ella Flagg Young*** during her superintendency of the Chicago school system.

CTF was successful in maneuvering its leaders into positions of national prominence within various organizations. By gaining control of the Illinois delegation to the NEA, CTF was able to elect Ella Flagg Young as the first female president of the NEA in 1910 and to effect the removal of college president Nicholas Murray Butler. CTF aided in establishing the NEA's Department of Classroom Teachers in 1913 and in maintaining teacher voter participation at NEA conventions, thereby bringing women's issues to the fore. CTF was also involved in organizing the League of Teachers' Associations, which had sixty-two clubs nationwide by 1915. CTF, as the largest affiliating union, was named Local Number 1 of the American Federation of Teachers (AFT) in 1916.

By 1917, though, CTF disassociated itself from the AFT due to pressure from Chicago's school board. The board had enacted the Loeb Rule, which prohibited teachers from membership in any trade union or organization employing business agents. According to these stipulations, the Loeb Rule would have prohibited teachers from membership in even professional organizations, such as the NEA or the Illinois State Teachers' Association. Under the rule, thirty-eight CTF members were fired. CTF abandoned its affiliations with AFT, the Chicago Federation of Labor, and the **Women's Trade Union League*** to get the teachers reinstated. With the Loeb Rule, CTF membership dropped by half, and it began to lose influence. Although the Rule was rescinded in 1922, CTF did not attempt reaffiliation with labor unions.

Haley's unwillingness to cooperate with other teacher organizations that emerged after 1916 and her continual references to her past triumphs alienated younger teachers, and by the late 1920s, other teacher organizations in Chicago replaced CTF as the voice of teachers. In 1968, CTF was formally disbanded. During its most influential years (1899–1915), CTF stood as an example of teacher initiative in winning pay increases, tenure, pensions, and a voice in school decisionmaking. [See also **feminization**,* **teaching**.*]

Bibliography: Robert Louis Reid, "The Professionalization of Public School Teachers: The Chicago Experience, 1895–1920" (Ph.D. diss., Northwestern University, 1968); Margaret A. Haley, *Battleground: The Autobiography of Margaret A. Haley*, Robert L. Reid, ed. (1982); Wayne J. Urban, *Why Teachers Organized* (1982); Julia Wrigley, *Class Politics and Public Schools: Chicago, 1900–1950* (1982); Marjorie Murphy, *Blackboard Unions: The AFT and the NEA, 1900–1980* (1990). The papers of the Chicago Teachers' Federation are held at the Chicago Historical Society.

Laurie Moses Hines

child study movement. The child study movement of the late nineteenth century was a pioneering effort, involving academics and thousands of teachers and mothers, to study children and create data about their growth and development. Child study grew in part out of the **kindergarten movement*** of the mid-1800s, spawned by the writings of German educator Friedrich Froebel. Froebel's work inspired the establishment of American kindergartens and gave rise to a fascination with the processes of "natural" development. An outgrowth of a number of progressive social movements, child study was seen by its proponents as an arena for the scientific study of children from which would be derived a science of schooling and childrearing, which would, in turn, improve society.

Child study came into its own in the 1890s under the intellectual leadership of G. Stanley Hall, who pioneered the experimental study of the child using the questionnaire method of data gathering. As founding president of Clark University (1888), Hall hoped to make his institution the center of a new kind of popular, populist psychology, linking academe and schools. Hall believed that the differences between children and adults were developmentally based and that development was governed by internal growth processes rather than parental and cultural influences. First and foremost, then, those in charge of the young should first prevent harm and otherwise stand aside. For parents (mothers) this meant giving children freedom rather than insisting that they meet adult standards. For teachers, it meant adjusting curriculum to the natural interests and needs of children; that is, the school should fit the child rather than the other way around. The child study movement, in Hall's view, held the promise of modernizing education and childrearing in conformity with the principles of natural human development as determined by science.

Hall enlisted **women's clubs**,* which flourished in the 1890s for the middle and upper middle class, as vehicles for gathering data for scientists at Clark, who in turn analyzed and published findings, which the women then disseminated and put into practice. Thus, typical for the era, women did the practical work, and men the theoretical. With the advent of child study, women across the country convened regularly to discuss every conceivable aspect of children's development. Many of these women believed that the mother's role was crucial to preserving the inborn goodness of the child, and they were enthusiastic supporters of the kindergarten movement.

In 1891, Hall founded *Pedagogical Seminary*, the journal of child study through which he distributed the questionnaires and published findings. In 1892, he began a series of summer institutes at Clark that attracted kindergarten teachers from around the country [see **teacher institutes***]. Some of the major leaders of the kindergarten crusade attended these sessions. In fact, child study at Clark was conceived as research by and for teachers. Part of Hall's less obvious agenda was to unearth and perhaps correct the problems—impediments to natural development—that kindergartens, like parents, could pose for the developing child. Hall was wildly popular with teachers, who flocked to his lecture tours throughout the country.

The currents of child study and Hall's ideas flowed into the work of the **National Congress of Mothers**,* founded in 1897 when Alice McClellan Birney, an avid student of the ideas of Froebel and Hall, and Phoebe Apperson Hearst called a national assembly of mothers in Washington, D.C. The response was overwhelming, some 2,000 attending where only a few hundred had been expected. For its first twenty-five years, this growing and influential organization, later renamed the National Congress of Parents and Teachers (precursor of the Parent-Teacher Association, or PTA), remained dedicated to Hall's psychology. The work of the National Congress and, indirectly, of many other child-saving and child-welfare agencies was part of a vast network of mostly women social reformers with ancestry in the child study movement. Hall's work contributed to the concept of a **separate sphere*** of action for women.

Popular as Hall was with teachers and mothers, his ideas and the child study enterprise were roundly criticized by psychologists Edward L. Thorndike, Hugo Munsterberg, and other of Hall's peers for its inexact methodology, which relied on amateurs as data gatherers, and for its sentimentalization of the child. Hall's vision for an educational psychology, as Siegel and White have suggested, lacked an adequate method. That said, child study, in its struggle to discover the general in the actual, to count and measure, and to bring order and meaning to the understanding of human development, is the precursor of subsequent child study and child development. Hall's biographer has suggested that the movement stimulated interest in educational reform and the scientific study of the child and that, eventually, a great deal of Hall's vision, albeit transformed, found its way into later efforts of science and education. [See also **early childhood education**,* **early childhood teacher education**,* **Sidonie Matzner Gruenberg**,* **Progressive Era**.*]

Bibliography: Lawrence Cremin, *The Transformation of the School: Progressivism in American Education, 1876–1957* (1964); Dorothy Ross, *G. Stanley Hall: The Psychologist as Prophet* (1972); Alexander W. Siegel and Sheldon H. White, ''The Child Study Movement: Early Growth and Development of the Symbolized Child,'' *Advances in Child Development and Behavior*, 17 (1982): 234–280; Barbara Beatty, *Preschool Education in America: The Culture of Young Children from the Colonial Era to the Present* (1995).

Joan Cenedella

chilly classroom climate. *Chilly classroom climate* is a widely used term derived from the title of a 1982 landmark study, "The Classroom Climate: A Chilly One for Women?" The study argued that women students in higher education experience significant educational disadvantages that impede their personal, academic, and professional development. Published by the Project on the Status and Education of Women, an education advocacy organization for women directed by Bernice Sandler, the well-documented twenty-two-page report discussed behaviors of faculty and other university practices, both overt and inadvertent, that silence and discourage women students.

Researchers have shown how differential treatment of women in the classroom creates a climate that reinforces low self-esteem and increases a student's doubts about her abilities. For example, women's remarks may be ignored or devalued in classroom discussions in comparison to men's. Such behaviors also affect the experiences and opportunities of women graduate students, women in traditionally male fields (engineering, architecture, medicine) [see **medical education***], and minority/Third World students. The project's report also offered extensive recommendations for improving the classroom climate for women students, for example, asking faculty to attend more closely to their classroom questioning. Such ideas have been used widely by women's groups and faculty committees on campuses to advance the equal treatment of women.

Recent research and interviews with women students, faculty, and **women's studies*** majors indicate that the climate for women has improved as a result of several factors. **Affirmative action*** has increased the number of women faculty on campuses. And as feminist perspectives have been integrated into the curriculum, women faculty and students find more receptivity to and recognition of women's voices. On the other hand, in many coeducational classrooms in the 1990s, women students still report prejudicial attitudes. In addition, there is more overt antifeminism expressed in recent years in response to the increased prominence of feminist perspectives in the academy. [See also **women's centers**.*]

Bibliography: Roberta M. Hall and Bernice Sandler, "The Classroom Climate: A Chilly One for Women?" (1982); Donna L. Shavlik, Judith Touchton, and Carol Pearson, *Educating the Majority: Women Challenge Tradition in Higher Education* (1989); "Teaching Faculty to Be Better Teachers," Project on the Status and Education of Women (1992); Sara M. Deats and Lagretta T. Lenker, eds., *Gender and Academe: Feminist Pedagogy and Politics* (1994); Frances A. Maher and Mary Kay Thompson Tetreault, *The Feminist Classroom: An Inside Look at How Professors and Students Are Transforming Higher Education for a Diverse Society* (1994).

Ann Froines

Clarke, Edward H. Edward Hammond Clarke (1820–1877), a noted Boston physician who specialized in disorders of the eyes and nerves, gained significance in the history of women's education for publication of his *Sex in Education**; *Or, A Fair Chance for the Girls* (1873), which argued that the push to educate girls and young women in the same manner as boys had created a flood of nervous disorders and gynecological problems for women.

A Harvard College graduate of 1841, Clarke moved to Philadelphia due to illness and took his medical studies there, graduating in 1846. He joined the Harvard Medical School faculty in 1855 and for a time in the late 1800s had the largest medical practice in the city of Boston. He married Sarah Loring Loud of Plymouth, Massachusetts, in 1852.

Clarke was renowned for his skill in the use of various drugs and his talent as a diagnostician. He wrote several books, including *Observations on Polypus of the Ear* (1869), *Physiological and Therapeutical Action of Potassium and Bromide of Ammonium* (1871), and *The Building of a Brain* (1874). His most noteworthy, however, was *Sex in Education*.

In that book, Clarke argued that women were physiologically unsuited to rigorous intellectual pursuits and study. He warned that women forced to compete with men in **high schools*** and college could seriously damage their capacity to reproduce as the blood supply necessary for cerebral activity would starve the uterus and ovaries. He offered vivid examples and explanations for women's difficulties:

I once saw, in the streets of Coblent, a woman and a donkey yoked to the same cart, while a man with a whip in his hand, drove the team. . . . The sight symbolized the physical force and infamous degradation of the lower classes in Europe. . . . A human girl, yoked with a donkey and dragging a cart, is an exhibition of monstrous muscular and aborted brain development. An American girl, yoked with a dictionary, and laboring with the *catamenia*, is an exhibition of monstrous brain and aborted ovarian development. (pp. 178–179)

Clarke's book touched a sensitive chord at a time when many young women were advancing themselves through high school and considering college education. *Sex in Education* became a best-seller, as seventeen editions were published; Clarke even addressed the National Education Association in 1874 on the topic. Although Clarke died at age fifty-seven in 1877, his book fanned controversy for years. When the fledgling **Association of Collegiate Alumnae*** (later the **American Association of University Women***) was chartered in Boston in 1883, one of its first efforts was to sponsor research studies and produce brochures repudiating Clarke's arguments and supporting women's higher education. For several decades, this group and others continued studies to demonstrate that educated women were healthy and normal.

Bibliography: Barbara Miller Solomon, *In the Company of Educated Women: A History of Women and Higher Education in America* (1985); Sue Zschoche, ''Dr. Clarke Revisited: Science, True Womanhood, and Female Collegiate Education,'' *History of Education Quarterly*, 29, no. 4 (1989): 545–569.

Robert A. Schwartz

coed. *Coed*, short for **coeducation,*** is a term for a female student at a coeducational college or university. The term came into common usage during the second half of the nineteenth century, when female students broke attendance barriers at several previously all-male universities. There was no corresponding term for males; the term *coed* was a constant reminder that women were second-class citizens in university communities.

While women gained admission to some small liberal arts colleges beginning in the 1830s, it was not until the 1870s that a sizable number of universities—most of them state run—admitted women. Many did so reluctantly, and the first women students faced ostracism and sometimes open hostility. At the Universities of Michigan, Wisconsin, and California, as well as many other institutions, male students and faculty members called female students "coeds" rather than students, implying that men were the only legitimate students. Women were often segregated into "Ladies' Courses," **normal departments**,* or **home economics*** departments and restricted from using campus libraries and gymnasiums or even walking in certain areas. Extracurricular activities in these early years were for men only—no coeds were allowed.

By the 1890s and during the early decades of the twentieth century, some of the most stringent restrictions were lifted, but women remained less than full participants in mainstream university life. Still unwelcome in men's extracurricular activities, women started their own **student government*** associations and **sororities**.* They negotiated with men for the right to produce one issue of a magazine or publish a small section in the yearbook, often with "coed" in the title. The unofficial message of life on coeducational campuses remained that education of women was less important than education of men. This pattern of gender separation began to erode slowly by the 1920s, but the term *coed* remained as a subtle reminder that women were not quite equal to men on university campuses.

Bibliography: Florence Howe, *Myths of Coeducation: Selected Essays, 1964–1983* (1984); Barbara Miller Solomon, *In the Company of Educated Women: A History of Women and Higher Education in America* (1985); Helen Lefkowitz Horowitz, *Campus Life: Undergraduate Cultures from the End of the Eighteenth Century to the Present* (1987); Lynn D. Gordon, *Gender and Higher Education in the Progressive Era* (1990).

Christine A. Ogren

coeducation. Coeducation is the instruction of girls and boys, or women and men, in the same school, once known as "mixed schools." For much of the history of the United States most women have received their education in such institutions. However, this simple statement hides a considerable amount of variation in practice and controversy that continues to the present.

The earliest coeducational schools were colonial **dame schools*** where women taught young girls and boys rudiments of education. Beyond that, boys would advance to school taught by men, with a few eventually going on to college. Girls might attend summer schools or private school if their parents had the means. Local control of schools meant that the level of public education open to young women varied considerably. A study of schools in eighteenth-century Massachusetts found that local factors played an important role. In Northampton, for example, elite families controlled funds and used them to support advanced education for their sons, while their daughters went to private schools. In Sutton, where control was more diverse, there was more interest in universal education at a lower level.

In the early Republic, calls for educated mothers to raise responsible citizen-sons [see **"Republican motherhood"***] and the influence of the **Second Great Awakening*** (with its emphasis on the individual's relationship to God) gave strength to the movement to educate young women. Also growing out of re-publican ideals was the **common school*** movement of the mid-nineteenth cen-tury with its vision of providing a like education to all for the greater good of the country. The resulting schools were overwhelmingly rural, coeducational, and subject to local control. The demand for teachers could not be filled by men, and training women as teachers became an important function of the grow-ing number of **academies*** and **seminaries**,* which tended to be coeducational in rural areas and single-sex in urban areas, especially eastern cities. An im-portant exception was the South where private, sex-segregated schools were the norm.

Many academies were founded by religious groups, and those tended to be coeducational; seminaries founded specifically for women (outside the South) were often started by individuals. The influence of some, including Sarah Pierce, Joseph Emerson and his students **Mary Lyon*** and **Zilpah Polly Grant Ban-ister**,* plus **Emma Willard*** and **Catharine Beecher**,* extended beyond their seminaries to the many schools (single-sex and coeducational) where their stu-dents subsequently taught. A few academies and seminaries evolved into col-leges, often retaining their coeducational or single-sex nature.

Before the Civil War, **Oberlin College*** (1833), Genesee College (1849), New York Central College (1849), Antioch (1953), Alfred University (1857), and scores of other small colleges in the Midwest were coeducational. Metaphors of the family and women's role within the church, and in some cases in the **temperance movement*** and the efforts for **abolitionism**,* made coeducation a possible notion in rural New York and the Midwest. Yet coeducation varied among the schools. Oberlin and Genesee offered a separate, seminary-level course for women while allowing women access to the men's collegiate course. Antioch and abolitionist New York Central carefully circumscribed the activities of women students outside class. In an attempt to value women's culture, Alfred chose to create a college course for women, while encouraging them to take whatever subjects they wished, filling most classes with men and women while expanding the definition of women's sphere.

The first major arguments about coeducation came in the middle of the nine-teenth century as urban educational leaders tried to create a unified system from city schools that had previously treated girls in a variety of ways—excluding them, teaching them separately within the same building, or teaching them in classrooms with boys. Concerns included the propriety of mixing the sexes in classrooms with a variety of social classes and ethnic groups, the need to compete with private schools (most of which were single-sex), and pedagogical questions about what girls should be taught and how they should be disciplined. Despite questions, most systems outside the South adopted coeducation in their elementary schools and in their **high schools**.*

According to Tyack and Hansot, "Educators found it expedient to mix the sexes as a way of achieving better classification of students by subject as well as by age and proficiency" (p. 137). Urban schools replaced male teachers with cheaper female teachers but also segregated jobs by sex, with men in positions of authority and the female graduates of urban high schools providing a large pool of potential teachers.

In the 1870s a new round of attacks on coeducation was led by Dr. **Edward H. Clarke*** of Harvard Medical School and G. Stanley Hall, president of Clark University, who believed that coeducation was harmful to the health of adolescent girls, especially their reproductive organs. Other opponents of coeducation worried about its role in taking women out of their proper **separate sphere*** as wives and mothers.

The influence of the women's rights movement before the Civil War led to postwar increases in women's labor market participation, including training as doctors and tackling many urban problems as reformers [see **medical education***]. Women's rights advocates had long advocated coeducation as the best way of ensuring that women received a quality education, and they began to press their demands. At the college level, new **women's colleges*** such as **Vassar*** claimed to provide an education equivalent to the elite men's colleges, but there were also demands that women be admitted to colleges for men. Established eastern men's colleges were largely successful in keeping women out, but many state universities were more vulnerable. Some schools solved the problem by establishing **coordinate colleges**,* separate women's colleges connected to all-male institutions of higher education. However, even when women gained admittance to large universities, they were outnumbered at first by male students and often faced hostility from students and male faculty. Lynn Gordon has found that in the **Progressive Era*** women students (with help from female faculty and administrators) banded together to create their own organizations and culture on coeducational campuses, noting: "College women's separatism was not only a response to exclusion from men's colleges and men's campus activities but also a positive statement about gender distinctiveness" (p. 4).

In both college and high school, female students excelled academically, putting to rest any arguments about their ability to learn but raising new concerns about the effect on boys. By the end of the century Hall and others were voicing concerns about the **feminization*** of education. Girls had higher rates of graduation from high school since it prepared them for **teaching**,* while boys dropped out in pursuit of other opportunities. Adding to this concern was the active role women played in **teacher unions*** and the arguments of male teachers that older boys should be taught by men who would receive higher wages for this labor. To solve this problem, schools added sports and **vocational education*** tracks (shop and mechanics for boys and **home economics*** for girls), providing male-only space in coeducational institutions.

In the late 1960s feminists began to raise questions about the quality of education girls and women were receiving in coeducational schools at all levels. Studies found that teachers did not treat boys and girls equally, textbooks reinforced gender stereotypes, and girls were being shortchanged. Other research suggested that graduates of women's colleges fared better than those of coeducational colleges. Studies also looked at the **chilly classroom climate*** for women faculty members. All these studies have their critics who argue that other factors such as self-selection and family background play a role; that **women's centers*** and **women's studies*** programs can support women on coeducational campuses; and that it is important to look at who holds power over the educational process, not simply whether the school is coeducational.

Recent debates about coeducation are taking place at all levels. In 1990, Mills College students successfully reversed that college's decision to admit men. There have been court cases against both the Citadel Military College of South Carolina and Virginia Military Institute to force them to admit women students. Several schools are experimenting with all-girl sections in mathematics and the sciences, while others have created all-male programs for African American boys with mostly male African American teachers in hopes of preventing dropouts and providing good role models.

The studies are far from conclusive when comparing the benefits of coeducation to single-sex environments, in large part because there are so many variables, including the quality and nature of the program and teachers, outside influences such as peers and parents, and the students themselves. Another issue is defining both a good outcome and the best ways to measure it. The debate goes hand in hand with that over the nature of gender differences. While some would celebrate difference and stress the importance of women's values and culture, others see dangers, especially if society uses ''male'' models as the measuring stick. It seems likely that debates about coeducation will be longstanding.

Bibliography: Barbara Miller Solomon, *In the Company of Educated Women: A History of Women and Higher Education in America* (1985); Carol Lasser, ed., *Educating Men and Women Together: Coeducation in a Changing World* (1987); Carol S. Pearson, Donna L. Shavlik, and Judith G. Touchton, *Educating the Majority: Women Challenge Tradition in Higher Education* (1989); Lynn D. Gordon, *Gender and Higher Education in the Progressive Era* (1990); David Tyack and Elisabeth Hansot, *Learning Together: A History of Coeducation in American Public Schools* (1990).

Kathryn M. Kerns

College of St. Catherine. After decades of hope, planning, and struggle, the College of St. Catherine—the first Catholic women's college in Minnesota—

opened its doors to seven students in St. Paul in 1905. The Sisters of St. Joseph of Carondelet (CSJs) who founded the college had been working in education, social service, and health care in Minnesota since arriving from their motherhouse in St. Louis in 1851. The creation of the college was to be the crowning achievement for the religious community that had established the first Catholic elementary school and preparatory academy for girls in St. Paul—and now the first **women's college**.*

Although higher education for Catholic women was being hotly debated throughout the United States, Archbishop John Ireland, a vocal proponent of women's education, began planning and collaborating with his sister, Mother Seraphine Ireland, the CSJ provincial superior, about creating a college for Catholic women in Minnesota. The arguments for and against higher education for Catholic women mirrored debates that had taken place in the Protestant mainstream decades earlier. But eventually even conservative Catholics realized that young Catholic women had begun attending secular colleges; therefore, Catholic women's colleges had to be created to protect Catholic girls from "Protestant perspectives and radical feminist sentiments" (Oates, n.p.).

Financial setbacks delayed plans for the college through the 1890s, but in 1900 Archbishop Ireland signed over rights to his book *The Church and the Modern Society*, and the CSJs peddled the book door to door, netting $60,000. In 1902, a $20,000 donation from Hugh Derham, a wealthy farmer, provided the necessary money for the college's first building (Derham Hall) and scholarship money. Fund-raising was paired with recruiting trips as far away as Wyoming and Montana to secure monies and students for the new college. Yet even with the sisters' exhaustive efforts, for the first few years St. Catherine's functioned only as a junior college since students either ended their education in one or two years or completed it at the University of Minnesota. However, in 1911 two students returned for their junior year, and the college finally had its first graduating class in 1913.

From the beginning the sisters aspired to create a high-quality institution. Besides their vigilance and hard work in raising funds, in 1903, in a highly unusual move for Catholic sisterhoods, the CSJs sent two sisters to tour European institutions of higher learning for women. On this fact-finding mission, Srs. Hyacinth Werden and Bridget Bohen kept a diary and extensive notes. Their favorite European institution, St. Anna Stift, the Catholic Sisters College of Munster in Westphalia, Germany, became the model for St. Catherine's.

European and **graduate education*** became the standard for the growing faculty at St. Catherine's when a dynamic and high-powered sister, Antonia McHugh, became the first dean in 1914. Educated at the **University of Chicago**,* she immediately began moving St. Catherine's from obscurity to recognition as a high-quality liberal arts college for women. After it received North Central accreditation in 1916, recruitment brochures boasted that this endorsement placed St. Catherine's "educationally on a par with **Vassar**,* **Wellesley**,* and **Smith**.*" Although this was more rhetoric than reality at the time, Sister

Antonia laid the foundation for the future as she built the faculty. With the continued encouragement of the archbishop, Sister Antonia insisted that young sisters be sent for advanced degrees to secular institutions throughout the United States and Europe. By the late 1920s a number of sisters had received doctorates or done advanced graduate work at the Universities of Minnesota, Chicago, or Columbia and in European institutions in London, Paris, Munich, Madrid, and Rome. University graduate study was unusual for women generally, but for nuns who strove to avoid pride and singularity, Sister Antonia's approach to higher education at times challenged and contradicted the more self-effacing role deemed appropriate for religious women.

Continuing to build the program and utilizing her connections with former professors and alumni at Minnesota and Chicago, Sister Antonia, as dean and later president of St. Catherine's (1929–1937), garnered funding from the Rockefeller, Carnegie, and National Science Foundations. In 1937, the college became the first Catholic institution in the United States to secure a Phi Beta Kappa chapter.

The College of St. Catherine continued its outreach to the secular world. By midcentury, the college had over 1,400 students, fifty-five CSJ faculty, and fifty-three lay faculty. Students were recruited from all states and many foreign countries. Fulbright scholarships and other prestigious awards recognized both outstanding faculty and students.

Unlike many colleges in the 1970s, when the local Catholic male college became **coeducational**,* St. Catherine's decided to stay the course and keep its single-sex policy. In an effort to achieve greater diversity in age and ethnicity, the college acquired the downtown campus of St. Mary Junior College in 1985. By the mid-1990s, St. Catherine's boasted over 3,400 students on both campuses, making it one of the largest private colleges for women and one of the largest **Catholic colleges*** for women in the United States. [See also **Catholic teaching orders.***]

Bibliography: Helen Angela Hurley, *On Good Ground: The Story of the Sisters of St. Joseph in St. Paul* (1951); Karen Kennelly, "The Dynamic Sister Antonia and the College of St. Catherine," *Ramsey County History*, 14 (Fall–Winter 1978): 3–18; Mary J. Oates, ed., *Higher Education for Catholic Women: An Historical Anthology* (1987); Rosalie Ryan and John Christine Wolkerstorfer, *More Than a Dream: Eighty-five Years at the College of St. Catherine* (1992). See also the Archives of the College of St. Catherine and the Provincial Archives of the Sisters of St. Joseph of Carondelet, St. Paul, Minnesota.

Carol K. Coburn

colonial schooling. During the colonial period, education was more a bastion of social stratification than an equalizer of the public. Regardless of the settlement, the character and the extent of education varied markedly depending on social standing, gender, and race. Generally, girls received rudimentary but not advanced education, unless they came from wealthy homes. By the end of the colonial period, a climate more favorable to female education had developed.

Long before the settlement of Jamestown and Plymouth, the Spanish colonized Florida and significant portions of the Southwest. Catholic mission schools were the first European American educational institutions. First erected in the early sixteenth century, these schools were established to spread the Catholic faith, to make Spanish citizens of the Indians, and to promote the economic development of the mission village. Priests served as teachers, paid not by the Church but by the state. They instructed boys in Catholic doctrine, in reading and writing of the Spanish language, and in the values and customs of Spain. They also taught music, art, and other practical skills: pottery, carpentry, agriculture, masonry, hide tanning, and wine making. The achievements of these schools varied regionally, but some were responsible for significant levels of literacy and for sophisticated agricultural and industrial practices. The mission schools in New Mexico, in particular, experienced high levels of achievement [see **Hispanic American women's education***].

Education for Spanish American women consisted of religious and domestic instruction: catechism, cooking, sewing, spinning, and weaving. A few women, however, had the desire and opportunity to participate in life outside the home and chose a convent setting. Providing women safety and sustenance, convents legitimated women's pursuit of education. The spiritual demands of a nun's life necessitated intellectual training. Hers was a life of comprehensive reading, critical reflection, and devotional/confessional composition. For the most part, the intellectual products of these nuns remained within the walls of the cloister. Occasionally, however, their poems, songs, plays, and theological treatises gained life and popularity in the local communities. One nun, in particular, whose work brought her acclaim was Sor Juana Ines de la Cruz (1648–1695), known for her theological and literary compositions.

For over two centuries, the convent was an elite institution providing quality education to a limited few. Indian women, as well as women of mixed blood, were not welcome. Admission required a significant dowry, a price that severely limited participation by women from the lower economic strata. Not until the close of the eighteenth century were broader educational opportunities provided for women in the Spanish settlements.

Like the Spanish, French missionaries of the Catholic Church promoted schools for the Christianization of the Indians and for the edification of those faithful to the state. They were much less successful than the Spanish, however, in establishing educational institutions. Outside of Quebec and Montreal, education in French territory was sporadic and of minimal consequence.

One exception, however, was the Ursuline school for girls in New Orleans, the only French American school to survive to the national period. Opened in 1727, the school operated both a day school and a boarding school. The day school was open free of charge to girls of all races and social standing. Ursuline nuns taught reading, writing, catechism, basic arithmetic, sewing, and other do-

mestic skills. In a pedagogical approach similar to that promoted later by Joseph
Lancaster in England, the nuns used older, more advanced students as monitors
and tutors to younger girls. Unlike the day school, the boarding school required
tuition, and its students were from affluent families. In addition to day school
instruction, boarders received an education in cultural refinement. Many of these
girls married French and Spanish officers and officials, thereby joining the upper
echelon of New Orleans society [see **Catholic education,** * **Catholic teaching
orders** *].

The English colonists arrived with the notion that education was fundamentally a private matter, a concern of the family, not the state. In the southern
colonies there was little reason to change this approach to education, and a
variety of school settings developed. Education in the South began at home with
parents teaching their children the alphabet and the rudiments of religious faith.
Dame schools * were prevalent, as mothers opened their homes to neighborhood
children, instructing them in the alphabet, prayers, and basic arithmetic. Angli-
can priests taught the basics for a fee in parish schools. Enclaves of Catholics,
Quakers, * Presbyterians, and **Moravians** * operated denominational schools to
improve literacy and to inculcate specific sectarian beliefs. Farmers occasionally
united and erected schools in old fields. In the larger, more commercial communities, private **venture schools** * provided fee-based elementary instruction.
For those who could not afford tuition, missionary societies such as the Society
for the Propagation of the Gospel opened charity schools, and about a dozen
localities operated free community schools.

In the South, two options existed for advanced secondary education: tutors
and private venture schools. Home tutorials offered classical instruction in Latin
and Greek and prepared boys for collegiate study at home, usually at William
and Mary College, and abroad. Tutors were most common among the planter
elite. Private venture schools were market driven: They taught whatever subjects
people would pay to learn, and they held class at times most convenient for
students. Advanced study in rural private venture schools was classically oriented; in urban schools, it was much broader. In addition to the classics, urban
schools offered numerous practical courses: navigation, algebra, surveying, and
fortification. There were too few urban centers and urban schools, however, to
significantly impact southern education or to significantly alter the role education
played in the social order.

Race greatly affected educational opportunities. After the outbreak of hostility, very few institutions were constructed for Indian education. African Americans received little, if any, instruction. Social standing was also a crucial factor
in educational attainment. Secondary education was available only for affluent
children whose families could afford tuition and were not dependent upon the
labor of their children.

Gender also affected educational opportunities. Southern women usually received elementary instruction, and **coeducation** * was not uncommon in dame
schools, old field schools, denominational schools, and free schools. Secondary

education, however, was limited to daughters of the elite. These girls had access to tutors and private schools. All women, however, were prohibited from collegiate education.

Although elite women had opportunities for secondary education, their course of studies differed from that of elite boys. Since classical education played a large role in maintaining prominence, power, and prestige, usually preparing boys for the ministry and other leadership roles, elite women did not receive classical instruction. Rather, they received lessons in **ornamental education*** and social refinement: music, dance, needlework, art, horseback riding, and French. Institutions that provided such education were forerunners of female **academies*** and **seminaries.***

The colonization of New England differed from southern colonization in that the motive for immigration was primarily religious, not economic. Rather than a dispersed agrarian settlement, New England colonization progressed around the establishment of towns. Religious motivation and town settlement greatly affected the character of New England education. Theology prompted state involvement in education, and the population density enabled legislative enforcement.

In order to preserve the religious experiment, the Massachusetts Bay Colony in 1642 compelled parents to provide rudimentary instruction of reading, religion, and the laws of the state. If parents were negligent, the state was authorized to remove the child and place him with more diligent guardians. In 1647, the colony legislated towns with fifty or more households to provide schools for reading and writing, and towns with one hundred or more to provide secondary grammar schools. Of the New England colonies, all but Rhode Island legislated compulsory education.

On the one hand, public education in New England countered upper-class advantage: Regardless of wealth, children were taught to read and write. On the other hand, New England education was socially conservative. Puritan theology upheld a hierarchical view of society and demanded conformity to its social arrangement. To a certain extent, New England education—with its religious instruction—preserved distinctions of class and status.

Yet New Englanders were much more receptive to the education of African Americans than were southerners. They allowed, and even encouraged, elementary instruction of slaves. Secondary education and collegiate instruction, however, were not open to those of the African race [see **slavery***]. Indians, on the other hand, were allowed access to elementary, secondary, and higher education.

Coeducation was not an overwhelmingly popular practice. Women, however, were not denied basic instruction. Towns that did object to coeducation generally offered girls instruction at times and places separate from boys. Girls were provided an elementary public education, but they were not allowed to attend the public Latin grammar schools, and except for tutorials and private schools, women were excluded from secondary instruction. As in the South, only privileged girls received instruction beyond basic literacy. Among the most notable

New England women to procure advanced education are Phillis Wheatley, Mercy Otis Warren, and **Abigail Adams**.* Wheatley is exceptional not only because of her gender but also because of her race. She was a slave whose wealthy master nurtured her education.

The middle colonies were characterized by national and religious diversity. Quakers, Anglicans, Dutch Reformed, Presbyterians, Baptists, Puritans, and German Pietists established institutions of worship and Christian nurture. Most settlements maintained denominational schools where they provided rudimentary instruction in reading, writing, and sectarian doctrine. The multiplicity of religious institutions produced a general atmosphere of toleration but also precluded systematization of education.

Elementary education was generally provided to all members of religious communities regardless of ability to pay. Girls were frequently included in sectarian schools. The Quakers, in particular, provided free instruction for boys and girls, blacks and Indians. Most sects, however, viewed advanced education as unnecessary or even harmful to women.

Secondary education for women was limited to private venture schools in larger commercial cities like New York and Philadelphia. The curriculum of these schools ranged from the rudiments of reading to the niceties of needlepoint and the rigors of the classics. Opportunity for such advanced instruction depended on wealth and occasionally on sectarian belief. Perhaps the most notable secondary institution for girls was the Moravian school established in Bethlehem, Pennsylvania, in 1749.

From beginning to end, colonial society was marked by spheres of activity in which the proper roles of women and men were sharply defined. The concept of womanhood, however, changed. Originally, women were considered morally and intellectually inferior, but by the close of the era, they were considered morally equal, if not superior. With character formation such a crucial component of colonial education, it eventually became acceptable for women to teach, and the opening of the **teaching*** profession subsequently created a need for increased educational opportunities. Thus, by end of the colonial era, the climate toward female participation in education had grown considerably more favorable. [See also **female literacy**.*]

Bibliography: Thomas Woody, *A History of Women's Education in the United States* (1929); Harold Buetow, *Of Singular Benefit: The Story of Catholic Education in the United States* (1970); Lawrence Cremin, *American Education: The Colonial Experience* (1970); Sheldon Cohen, *A History of Colonial Education (1607–1776)* (1974); Asuncion Lavrin, "Women and Religion in Spanish America," in Rosemary Radford Reuther and Rosemary Skinner Keller, ed., *Women and Religion in America: The Colonial and Revolutionary Period* (1983); Wayne Urban and Jennings Wagoner, Jr., *American Education* (1995).

Benjamin D. Burks

commercial education. As the nation's industrial production rose at the end of the nineteenth century, so did the need for trained men and women in commercial fields. Such training was previously the aim of private business colleges; however, with the growth of young people attending public **high schools**,* businesses and community members, in keeping with the aim of public schooling, soon asked for this practical training in those schools. High schools, modeling private business schools, trained students to become competitive with business college graduates. Significantly for women, training in commercial courses opened the doors to secretarial and clerical positions for high school–trained commercial education students. Such courses proved extremely popular with female students. By the late-1920s, close to 20 percent of high school students, the majority of them girls, were enrolled in commercial education classes. Generally, commercial education classes appealed more to girls than did other **vocational education*** programs.

The **Smith-Hughes Act**,* also known as the Vocational Education Act, signed into law by President Woodrow Wilson on February 23, 1917, established vocational education programs that provided funds for agricultural, industrial, and **home economics*** course work to be taught in public schools. With federal aid offered by this act, commercial education took on new significance.

In Section 6 of the Smith-Hughes Act, the Federal Board for Vocational Education required: "To make, or cause to have made, studies, investigations and reports with particular reference to their use in aiding the State in the establishment of vocational schools and classes and in giving instruction . . . in commerce and commercial pursuits."

With encouragement from the business world, government approval, and financial aid, schools now designed training programs that students would have had to pursue elsewhere had they not been offered in public school. Early course work included accounting, shorthand, typing, and office machines (depending on the needs and budget of the district); later programs sought to work with other departments on campuses to include subjects like business math, business English, and others. The ultimate purpose of these articulated programs was to develop a student ready to enter the business world and gain employment while simultaneously fulfilling high school graduation requirements. Cooperative programs at many schools allowed students to attend school part-time and gain credit for working the other part of the day, enabling them to step into full-time positions upon high school graduation.

In recent years, the fast growth in technology has prohibited many commercial programs from maintaining programs that fill employers' requirements. On the one hand, school budgets have difficulty in keeping up with the expensive equipment required to train commercial students for the workplace; on the other, due to modern technology, many offices have downsized their need for trained employees other than those with university business degrees. Schools have also been accused of tracking students, mainly minorities and women, into commercial and vocational programs, thereby limiting those students' future options.

Bibliography: National Society for Vocational Education, *Commercial Education, Federal Aid, Recent Developments, Retail Selling Education* (1919); W. B. Miksell, "A Study of the Aims of Commercial Education in Public Schools; To Determine the Main

Objectives for the Commercial Courses of Such Schools'' (master's thesis, University of California, 1923); John L. Rury, *Education and Women's Work: Female Schooling and the Division of Labor in Urban America, 1870–1930* (1991); Jane Bernard Powers, *The "Girl Question" in Education: Vocational Education for Young Women in the Progressive Era* (1992).

Susan Clark Studer

Commission on the Status of Women. In December 1961, President John F. Kennedy created a Commission on the Status of Women at the urging of Esther Peterson, director of the U.S. **Women's Bureau*** and Assistant Secretary of Labor in Kennedy's administration. Agitation for such a group had begun as early as 1947 when supporters of protective labor legislation for women feared enactment of the Equal Rights Amendment. Eleanor Roosevelt was the first chairperson of the Commission until her death in 1962. Its final report, *American Women*, was issued in October 1963, with two clearly stated assumptions: (1) The nuclear family was vital to the stability of American society, and (2) women's primary function was that of wife and mother. The Commission also believed that obstacles to women's full participation in society must be removed. Yet it projected women's participation within gendered boundaries: Women's "natural abilities" to nurture and communicate could best meet societal needs through their education for and employment as nurses, teachers, secretaries, and social workers.

The Commission consisted of seven technical committees: civil and political rights, education, federal employment, private employment, protective labor legislation, social insurance and taxes, and the home and community. The Committee on Education, twelve of whose fifteen members were women, was composed primarily of university faculty and administrators and professional educators. Their recommendations to the larger group reflected the overall assumptions of the Commission. The Education Committee believed that special attention should be given to the "culturally deprived" (defined as African American and poor women) but that, in general, education should match each woman's intellectual and vocational potentialities and prepare her to fulfill home and family responsibilities. It urged creation of special programs that would prepare women to work in fields with urgent social needs (**teaching**,* nursing, **social work**,* and to a lesser degree, science). Some of the Education Committee's recommendations dealt with states' control of educational policies, for instance, suggesting that states develop reciprocal teaching certification and pension plans so that mobility of married women would not mean the loss to society of able teachers. The Committee also urged flexibility in providing education at all levels so that women's primary function as mothers could be performed while they continued their education.

Of the Committee's ten recommendations, the Commission adopted three: enhanced vocational training, increased counseling, and education for home responsibilities. First, the Commission recommended that more means of acquiring

basic education and literacy skills or **continuing education*** at post–high school
levels should be devised and attention paid to **vocational education**.* The Commission reasoned that after raising families women have approximately thirty to
forty years to contribute to society through paid or volunteer work. The majority
of the Commission's educational recommendations centered around counseling.
Schools were urged to begin counseling girls before they reached **high school***
and continue through high school and beyond. The Commission suggested counseling for women workers changing jobs, reentering the job market, or being
displaced from their current posts. Women who simply wanted to make constructive use of leisure should also receive counseling. In light of this strengthened role for counseling, the Commission recommended that states raise
standards for counseling certification, and train and put more counselors into
schools. Women, with their presumed inherent ability to listen to others, were
considered best suited for such jobs. The third recommendation stressed the
importance of education for home and family, with references to women's need
to make sound consumer choices, provide healthy meals, and create a proper
home environment. Passing references to sex education did not reflect the Education Committee's recommendation for thorough education on sexual reproduction and family planning.

The overall Commission did not officially include most of the Committee on
Education's recommendations, although some were mentioned in the discussion
section of the final report. While the Commission made only general statements
about education for women, the Committee on Education had made specific
suggestions for programs and policy changes, especially about the need for flexibility in higher education. The Committee recommended that colleges relax
women's admission and graduation requirements to better fit the average
woman's lifestyle. Suggestions included dropping requirements for on-campus
residency and physical education for the mature (i.e., married) woman student;
credit for knowledge and experience acquired outside the classroom; development of courses to build study habits in women returning to education after
raising a family; better guidance to handle the mature woman's problems of
returning to school and a second career; courses for home study through use of
media; and more part-time study and increased flexibility so that women could
pursue college while still fulfilling home obligations [see **reentry programs***].

The Committee on Education saw the new community college as a prime
means for women to meet these goals. Community colleges were believed to
be more adaptable to women's special needs, offering flexible times for classes,
being closer to a person's home, and offering both liberal and technical education. The community college was the answer for poor and disadvantaged girls
and could act as a stepping-stone to four-year institutions. The Committee also
saw the community college as an ideal job site for women academics.

The Committee on Education saw the Commission's work as the beginning
of research on women. It suggested that a program in the Office of Education
be established for surveying, summarizing, and disseminating research on

women's education. While the Commission did not officially make such a recommendation, numerous states initiated their own commissions on the status of
women after *American Women* appeared in 1963. That same year, **Betty Friedan*** published *The Feminine Mystique.** The Commission on the Status of
Women, by encouraging women to continue their education and move into the
labor force, advocated some of Friedan's more radical ideas but did so within
the confines of traditional thought about women's primary place in the home
and her role as nurturer.

Bibliography: Judith Hole and Ellen Levine, *Rebirth of Feminism* (1971); Cynthia E.
Harrison, "A 'New Frontier' for Women: The Public Policy of the Kennedy Adminis-
tration," *Journal of American History*, 67 (December 1980): 630–646; Harrison, *On
Account of Sex: The Politics of Women's Issues, 1945–1968* (1988).

Laurie Moses Hines

common schools. The term *common school* most often refers to the public
school system that became organized in the United States after about 1830. They
were called common schools because they were available to every child, with
the expense of schooling supported by the public (partly by a school fund but
mostly by town taxes). In the 1830s, one-third of the children in the United
States aged five to nineteen were attending some sort of school: town, district,
or private. The **district schools*** had been supported by local taxation or the
state and governed by a prudential committeeman, elected by people of the
district. Common schools built upon this system of town and district schools
from the eighteenth century and became the public school system of today. A
court decision of 1872 in Kalamazoo, Michigan, interpreted the new term as
covering all public schooling through higher education that was supported by
taxes and open on a common basis to all.

In 1655 a court decision in Hartford, Connecticut, required the state to educate
its children: sons to read and write, daughters to read and sew. By 1657, Massachusetts School Law required reading and writing to be taught in schools. But
for the most part, females in New England were excluded from town schools
until after the Revolutionary War; they were taught at home to read. In 1789
Boston city schools admitted girls, but only from April to October. Throughout
the 1700s, girls were expected to learn to read and sew and generally were
educated only until age twelve.

In the early nineteenth century, district schools were organized into winter
and summer terms, with winter term beginning the week after Thanksgiving and
continuing for twelve, fourteen, or sixteen weeks. Winter terms were taught by
a man and ran Monday through Saturday. Summer term began the first Monday
of May, taught by a woman addressed as "Marm." Mostly younger children
came in summer, as the older boys were working in the fields. There were no
books for these youngest students. Sewing was taught in summer, and schools
were closed every other Saturday. These district schools were one-room schools

holding twenty-five to thirty pupils. Most of the students left at age fifteen, which was the end of schooling for most girls. Boys could then proceed to study at an academy or with the local minister to prepare for college.

By the 1820s, a system of common schools began to be organized by educational reformers in New England, who believed that state-supported schooling would become the training ground for building a nation of educated and morally correct citizens. Moral training became a standard feature in the curriculum of the common school, which was to be a classroom, a family room, and a church building all in one. Influencing this drive toward an organized system was Victorian culture with its need for literacy among all people, its push for economic self-improvement, and its desire for nation building through education and moral reform. Educational reformers viewed the common school as the major instrument of cultural intervention in the local communities and the nation, and by the middle of the nineteenth century, the common schools had become the main means of raising literacy in the United States. But the literacy promoted in the schools was a specific literacy bound by moral training, as well as a general mastery of reading.

By the 1830s, **Horace Mann*** and Henry Barnard emerged as the two major spokesmen for the common school. Mann became president of the Massachusetts Senate in 1837 and aided in the enactment of a bill to establish a state board of education, which he then headed as Secretary of Education, becoming the most prominent national spokesman for the common school movement. Mann began a nationwide campaign to educate people about public education, believing that common schools should provide knowledge, moral elevation, and the basis for sound citizenship. Massachusetts law also required that its schools be kept by competent teachers, which furthered the push by Mann and James G. Carter for **normal schools**,* the start of state-supported **teacher education**.*

Yet the education of girls was still supported for national reasons. It was the belief of many in eighteenth-century society that girls needed to be educated in order to be good mothers for future sons of the Republic [see **"Republican motherhood"***]. Henry Barnard believed that a woman's world was only a domestic world and that her education and her access to books should enable her to discharge maternal and domestic duties and to render herself an enlightened companion for an intelligent man. Barnard, an assessor of schools in Connecticut and Rhode Island and editor of the *American Journal of Education* from 1855 to 1881, believed that the common schools would rejuvenate society, increase the general wealth of the nation, decrease crime and other social problems, and teach all citizens to participate in the democratic nation. In 1867 Barnard became the first U.S. Commissioner of Education. As such, he objected to the low pay of female teachers and pushed for women to be hired to teach winter as well as summer schools, believing that women were teachers by nature.

By the time of the abolishment of the district system in Massachusetts in 1882, the common school movement was well established, providing girls with an education through the age of fifteen and also supporting state normal schools with their female teachers and role models for girls in common schools. Compulsory school attendance became law in Massachusetts in 1852. By 1875, the school year contained three terms: winter, twelve weeks; spring, ten weeks; and fall, ten weeks. Female teachers were now the norm, often picked from the neighborhood but usually educated as teachers, paid between $5 and $6 per week. Saturday classes were eliminated. After the railroads and villages grew, school sessions were extended to ten or eleven months and **teaching*** became more a vocation than a passing job. By 1888, 63 percent of all teachers in the United States were women, and in the cities, 90.4 percent were women.

In the nineteenth-century South, where the widespread plantations made district schools difficult, daughters of the wealthy were educated by tutors. Those of the poor were educated by the churches or philanthropists or through apprenticeships. Prior to the Civil War, the African American population in the North was educated, often in separate schools (such as the African School built in Nantucket, Massachusetts, in 1825) but rarely at all in the South. After the war, when teachers traveled South to build schools during Reconstruction, common schools built for African Americans were, by law, separate but equal [see **American Missionary Association***]. In general, common schools were slower to reach the South.

Common schools were the beginning of the nation's first widespread opportunity for educating females. As a basis for the twentieth-century public school system, they provided instruction in basic literacy while socializing the young in moral and civic duties. [See also **female literacy.***]

Bibliography: George H. Martin, *The Evolution of the Massachusetts Public School System: A Historical Sketch* (1923); John S. Brubacher, ed., *Henry Barnard on Education* (1931); Lee Soltow and Edward Stevens, *The Rise of Literacy and the Common School in the United States: A Socioeconomic Analysis to 1870* (1981); George Willis, William H. Schubert, Robert V. Bullough, Jr., Craig Kridel, and John T. Holton, eds., *The American Curriculum: A Documentary History* (1993); Stanley William Rothstein, *Schooling the Poor: A Social Inquiry into the American Educational Experience* (1994).

Joan F. Pengilly

consciousness-raising. *Consciousness-raising* describes the process of discussion, self-education, and expansion of awareness in which women share personal experiences. The term generally connotes the process by which the 1960s feminist movement spread among women. Consciousness-raising (CR) groups were developed by radical feminists in the late 1960s; members of New York Radical Women wrote some of the first descriptions of the processes of CR sessions. In the groups, women came to understand that what they had previously viewed as personal concerns were, in fact, social and political problems related to women's relative powerlessness in society. That women themselves should be authorities on their own experience, instead of psychologists and other social scientists, was an important assumption of consciousness-raising. Some feminists believed that all strategies for the women's movement should develop from

CR groups. The groups also helped create a sense of solidarity or sisterhood among women. Eventually, the broader women's movement and some **women's studies*** courses embraced as central concepts the ideas that ''the personal is political'' and that women's experience provides an authority of its own. [See also **Betty Friedan**.*]

Bibliography: Jo Freeman, *The Politics of Women's Liberation* (1975); Alix Kates Shulman, ''Sex and Power: Sexual Bases of Radical Feminism,'' *SIGNS*, 5 (Summer 1980): 580–604; Hester Eisenstein, *Contemporary Feminist Thought* (1983); Alice Echols, *Daring to Be Bad: Radical Feminism in America 1967–1975* (1989).

Ann Froines

continuing education. The term *continuing education of women* refers to both credit and noncredit curricular offerings and includes both degree-granting and non-degree-granting programs. Beginning in the late 1950s and growing rapidly in subsequent decades, various continuing education programs offered adult women opportunities for traditional and nontraditional courses in a range of school settings. These programs have been instrumental in equalizing and enhancing women's educational progress.

Specific terms associated with continuing education of women are *adult education, continuing education, recurrent education, lifelong learning*, **reentry programs**,* and *nontraditional students*. Astin suggests the following distinctions in terminology:

Adult Education refers to vocational and avocational courses defined specifically for adults and offered by secondary schools and community agencies. *Continuing Education* refers to educational programs developed to help adults upgrade their education and occupational skills and offered in a postsecondary setting. *Recurrent* and *lifelong learning* are more global terms referring not so much to specific and limited programs and courses as to the concept of regular and repeated opportunities throughout the individual's lifetime, to return to education either to train for new skills and better jobs or to learn for leaning's sake. . . . Recurrent education is primarily the European term. Lifelong learning is its American equivalent. (p. 47)

Further, reentry students are those who dropped out of secondary and postsecondary education because of their financial and work-life situations but have returned to school to complete their education. Nontraditional students are non-residential, usually part-time, and over age twenty-four.

The importance of continuing education of women became apparent in the 1940s and 1950s when women's entry into the workforce was critical for the defense needs of the nation. During World War II and the Korean War, women proved to the country and to themselves that they, too, could perform in an environment once relegated to the male sphere. In 1951, the American Council on Education (ACE) sponsored a meeting entitled ''Women in the Defense Decade,'' the first major conference that distinctly identified the higher education of women as a council concern. In doing so, it recognized that continuing education of women was as valid as that of men. In 1953, ACE formed the Commission on the Education of Women. Less than six years later, this commission presented data that began to challenge traditional understanding of the role of women and higher education. The commission's two publications, *How Fare American Women?* (1959) and *The Span of a Woman's Life and Learning* (1960), confronted the notion that a liberal arts curriculum or a **home economics*** track was sufficient for women pursuing postsecondary education. Shortly after circulation of these studies, the first continuing education programs for women emerged. These eventually became institutionalized through the development of courses, centers, and programs scattered throughout campuses in the United States.

In the early 1970s, less than ten years later, nearly 500 such programs existed. These centers offered a variety of services, including preadmission counseling, academic advising and individual vocational assessment, employment information, noncredit seminars, small discussion groups, and workshops on building self-esteem and self-awareness. With the help of such efforts, career choices for women were broadened, and the means for gaining entrance into the workforce expanded.

Rather than take the established path to a baccalaureate degree, older women began to reenter academe through back doors and via new delivery systems such as community colleges, distance learning centers, apprentice schools, certificate programs, and business colleges. Traditional four-year colleges and universities, recognizing a new population for their services, soon joined forces in providing the necessary preparation that enabled women to break through male political and economic citadels. Such programs promoted the goals of equal access to education for all women, the legitimacy of women and **women's studies*** in mainstream academic disciplines, entry into all-male undergraduate schools, greater rates of admission into professional schools, and expanded theories about "women as women" (for example, the notion of "women's ways of knowing" popularized by Clinchy, Tarule, and Goldberger). In the 1970s and early 1980s, academic journals and research publications were replete with articles describing these initiatives.

In 1976, Astin found that the typical participant in continuing education was a thirty-six-year-old white Protestant woman from a middle-class background, married to a business executive or a professional, with two or three school-age children. In the mid-1990s, this profile was considerably altered. The palette of changing cultural attitudes, the social status of women, and the **feminization*** of poverty in the late 1980s and 1990s has created a vastly different portrait. Women are more diverse in need and in educational goals than their predecessors of the 1970s. Typical women enrolled in the continuing education programs of the 1990s are often younger, concerned with the obligations of wife and/or mother of young children, and simultaneously juggling the time constraints of a career or part-time job. They are usually nonresidential, part-time students working toward a certificate or degree to further their employment opportunities and improve their life situations. In these later lecture halls and university class-rooms, older women are sitting next to the traditional age eighteen- to twenty-four-year-old college student fulfilling educational goals that were not open to them in their earlier years. Others may be retooling for a second or third career change.

Access to postsecondary education restricted by gender is no longer a legal issue. The 1968 civil rights legislation prohibiting discrimination on the basis of gender eliminated overt barriers that impeded women's educational access. The 1996 Supreme Court decision against the all-male, state-supported Virginia Military Institute closed the final door on discrimination at public higher education institutions. Legally, gender discrimination is prohibited at all public institutions of higher education in the United States, but some cultural attitudes that limit women's options remain ingrained in American society. In reality, doors to many campuses are inaccessible to most women from low-income or poverty-level families. Odds are high that a poor woman, even one who graduates from high school, will not attend college.

Recognizing the need to eradicate the effects of poverty on the equality of American women and education, continuing education programs for women are beginning to recognize and concentrate on young "at-risk" women who are, or may be, potential high school or college "dropouts." Federally funded school, college, and university partnership programs such as TRIO, the McNair program, Upward Bound, and Educational Opportunity Centers meet the needs of low-income, disadvantaged adults. Both private philanthropy and community groups are working toward promoting equality in education for all women through intervention programs, financial aid, and special mentoring programs. Yet these programs are just the tip of the iceberg in addressing widespread need. Continuing education needs to signify not just a program but a process that begins in infancy and lasts throughout a woman's lifetime, a process intertwined and dependent upon the dignity and economic equality of opportunities for all people.

Bibliography: Helen S. Astin, *Some Action of Her Own: The Adult Woman and Higher Education* (1976); J. K. Rice and S. Meyer, "Continuing Education for Women," in S. B. Meyer and P. M. Cunningham, eds., *Handbook of Adult and Continuing Education* (1989); Renuka Mishra, "Concretizing Concepts: Continuing Education Strategies for Women," *Convergence*, 27 (1994): 126–137; Helen LoRe, "Budget Study," *Working Women* (September 1995); U.S. Department of Education, Division of Student Services, *Federal TRIO Programs and the School, College and University Partnership Programs* (February 1996); C. R. Stimpson, "Women's Studies and Its Discontents," *Dissent*, 43 (Winter 1996): 67–75.

Delrina M. Clarin

Cooper, Anna Julia. Anna Julia Haywood Cooper (1858–1964) was an African American educator, lecturer, and writer who devoted her life to improvement of education for her race, especially females. Born in Raleigh, North Carolina, to Hannah Stanley, a slave, and her owner, George Washington Haywood, Cooper attended Saint Augustine's Normal School and Collegiate Institute, an Episcopal school founded to train teachers for African Americans. Cooper rapidly distinguished herself, and when she protested the exclusion of women from advanced courses, she was allowed to take Greek. Completing her studies in 1877, she married a former teacher, George A. C. Cooper, and also became a teacher at Saint Augustine's. Cooper's husband, who was preparing for the ministry, died only two years later, and Cooper remained single for the rest of her life.

In 1881 Cooper entered **Oberlin College*** where she elected to follow the rigorous "gentleman's program," earning her A.B. in 1884. After teaching modern languages at **Wilberforce University*** for a year, Cooper returned to Saint Augustine's to teach mathematics, Latin, and Greek. In 1887, she received a master's in mathematics from Oberlin and accepted a position at the Preparatory High School for Colored Youth in Washington, D.C. This institution, which became M Street High School in 1891 and Paul Laurence Dunbar High School in 1916, provided the base for most of Cooper's career as an educator.

In 1902 Cooper became principal of M Street, the only school in the nation to offer both **vocational education*** and a college preparatory curriculum for African Americans. Under Cooper's leadership, the school's reputation for academic excellence grew, and graduates were admitted with scholarships to some of the nation's most prestigious universities, including Harvard and Yale. In 1906, however, conflicts with the board of education, reportedly over their attempts to dilute the academic curriculum of African American schools, led to her dismissal. Cooper spent the next four years chairing the language department at Lincoln University in Jefferson City, Missouri, but in 1910 returned to M Street School to teach Latin and remained there until her retirement in 1930.

In addition to **teaching**,* Cooper established a reputation as writer and lecturer. In 1892 her collection of essays, *A Voice from the South: By a Black Woman of the South*, attracted favorable critical reviews and widespread attention. Cooper had already achieved recognition for her writing in *The Southland*, a journal for African Americans with a large readership. She lectured on women's rights and education throughout the world before such groups as the American Conference on Education, Women's Congress, and the first Pan-African conference. Her numerous honors included membership in the American Negro Academy (founded 1897), the first woman so honored.

Though busy as teacher, lecturer, writer, and advocate for equal opportunities, Cooper determined to continue her own education. During the summers of 1911–1913 she studied at the Guilde International in Paris and 1914–1917 at Columbia University. Having successfully completed all course requirements for the Ph.D. at Columbia, Cooper began plans to meet the one-year residency requirement and complete her research for an edition of *Pélerinage de Charlemagne* (published in 1925) when she suddenly became guardian of five great-nephews and great-nieces on the death of their mother. Her dreams for the Ph.D.

resurfaced in 1923 when she applied to the Sorbonne, which agreed to accept her Columbia credits. After completing a dissertation in French on French attitudes toward **slavery*** between 1789 and 1848, Cooper was awarded her Ph.D. in 1925 from the Sorbonne, the fourth African American woman to earn the doctorate.

Following her retirement from secondary school teaching in 1930, Cooper became the second president of Frelinghuysen University, a nontraditional educational institution for working African Americans. Frelinghuysen had no facilities, endowment, or accreditation, and Cooper spent a decade in tireless work without salary as president and two additional years as registrar. Despite all her efforts, even opening her home for school use, Cooper was unable to get the necessary support to rescue Frelinghuysen, which closed in 1961.

Cooper spent the latter years of her life quietly in her Washington, D.C., home, writing when health permitted. She died in her sleep in 1964, having lived over a century and devoting her life to the education of African Americans.

Bibliography: Sharon Harley, ''Anna J. Cooper: A Voice for Black Women,'' in *The Afro-American Woman: Struggles and Images* (1978); Louise Daniel Hutchinson, *Anna J. Cooper, a Voice from the South* (1981); Leona C. Gabel, *From Slavery to the Sorbonne and Beyond: The Life and Writings of Anna J. Cooper* (1982); Karen Baker-Fletcher, *A Singing Something: Womanist Reflections on Anna Julia Cooper* (1994). Cooper's papers are in the Moorland-Spingarn Research Center, Howard University.

Verbie Lovorn Prevost

coordinate colleges. Coordinate colleges are separate, all-female institutions connected by governance, faculty, finances, or admissions to older, all-male colleges or universities. Examples include **Radcliffe College**,* in its relationship to Harvard University; **Barnard College**,* in its relationship to Columbia University; and Sophie Newcomb College, in its relationship to Tulane University.

Most coordinate colleges were established around the turn of the twentieth century, usually as an entering wedge into male institutions, particularly in the eastern United States. The tradition of educating college men and women separately generally did not transfer to the Midwest or West, where the paucity of collegiate opportunities made separate institutions infeasible and inefficient. The same was true of African American colleges, although some scholars have suggested that white founders of black colleges may have avoided the issue of sex-segregated training because of racial stereotypes and finances.

In the East, however, many well-established men's schools resisted the entreaties and demands of local women for the same education that was open to their brothers and male neighbors. In many cases, including Radcliffe, Barnard, and Pembroke (at Brown University), local politics would accept the grafting of a women's school onto the male institution but would not support complete **coeducation**.*

Most coordinate colleges were created by the sustained support of organized advocacy groups, usually led by local women with some connection to the male college (e.g., the Society for the Collegiate Instruction of Women, which incorporated Radcliffe). These groups raised money and awareness in their communities; many sustained both the fiscal and physical needs of the coordinate colleges for several decades.

Some schools shared faculty but had separate classroom meetings for men and women. A few, like Barnard, had their own women's faculty. All had separate facilities, which invariably suffered in comparison to the men's.

Over time, the nature of the coordinate relationship changed from school to school, generally assuming a more coeducational character. Some women's schools, like Jackson at Tufts and Flora Stone Mather at Case Western Reserve, eventually merged into the male university. Others continued to maintain a separate existence, but with much closer ties to the male neighbor (e.g., modern Radcliffe and Barnard).

The coordinate colleges represent a potent example of female institution building in the twentieth century, even as they demonstrate resistance to providing equal resources to women. Their history also mirrors the changes in American student populations over the course of the century.

Bibliography: Helen Lefkowitz Horowitz, *Alma Mater: Design and Experience in the Women's Colleges from Their Nineteenth-Century Beginnings to the 1930s* (1984); Barbara Miller Solomon, *In the Company of Educated Women: A History of Women and Higher Education in America* (1985); Polly Welts Kaufman, ed., *The Search for Equity: Women at Brown University, 1891–1991* (1991).

Linda Eisenmann

Coppin, Fanny Jackson. Fanny Jackson Coppin (1837–1913), an influential African American educator who headed Philadelphia's **Institute for Colored Youth*** for twenty-six years, was born a slave in the District of Columbia. Her hereditary slave status did not reflect that of her entire family. Several members were free, and Coppin's freedom was purchased by an aunt, Sarah Orr Clark, for $125 when Coppin was ten or twelve years old. Coppin was liberated from **slavery*** but not from labor. She lived with an aunt in New Bedford, Massachusetts, where she was sent out to board and work, limiting her schooling. At fourteen, she relocated with another aunt to Newport, Rhode Island, to give Coppin "a better chance at school."

In her *Reminiscences of School Life and Hints on Teaching* (1913), Coppin claimed that her desire for education was internal, but she was likely influenced by several factors. First, she was somewhat an elite slave, being light-skinned and mulatto, and born in the cosmopolitan District of Columbia. Several family members also pushed for her freedom and education. Finally, in New England, Coppin found African Americans occupying diverse occupations, many having used education as a key to progress.

In Newport, Coppin attended the local segregated public school while employed in the home of George and Elizabeth Calvert. She prepared for the entrance examination of the Rhode Island Normal School in Bristol. She passed its course without incident and set her sights on **Oberlin College*** in Ohio.

Oberlin was unusual as the nation's first college to admit both women and African Americans. Founded by liberal Congregationalists, Oberlin nonetheless carefully negotiated its cultural and social constructs to accommodate African Americans. Blacks did not serve on the college faculty, nor did black students live with white roommates. Oberlin admitted Coppin in 1860 to the Ladies Department, where she prepared for admission to the baccalaureate program the next year. At Oberlin, Coppin lived in an idyllic state for an African American woman in the 1860s, although not without some tensions. For example, with all her preparation, Coppin never recited in class, feeling that the "honor of the whole African race was on my shoulders." Yet she also felt comfortable enough to claim that she "had been so long in Oberlin that I had forgotten about my color."

During the Civil War, many male students left for army service, and by 1864, women constituted the majority of Oberlin's student population. With this shift, Coppin apparently gained an opportunity to shine among her peers. She came to the attention of the faculty and was invited to teach in the preparatory program, making her Oberlin's first African American faculty member. Her **normal school*** training and love of teaching seemed to enhance her success; she proved popular, and her classes grew. Yet Coppin felt obligated "to teach my people." Observing the migration to Oberlin of many African Americans fleeing the war-torn South, Coppin opened an evening school for African Americans, mostly adult learners. With her visibility in the preparatory school and her creative leadership in the evening program, Coppin gained valuable attention for Oberlin and herself.

Within a year, Oberlin received a request for a "colored woman who could teach Greek, Latin, and higher mathematics" at the Institute for Colored Youth. In 1865, Coppin moved to Philadelphia, home of strong **abolitionism**,* the antislavery and pro-education **Quakers**,* and a diverse African American population. One group of elite blacks had developed the African Methodist Episcopal Church and served as a voice for black interests in the city. Another population of newly freed African Americans was moving to Philadelphia, increasing the need for adult education.

The institute began in 1832 by Quaker Richard Humphreys, who wanted to educate African American boys for mechanical arts, trade, and agriculture. The school's early rural version failed but reopened in Philadelphia and by 1862 housed an evening program for boys and a day school. When Coppin joined the faculty in 1865, there was a preparatory program and a classical **high school**.* The Quakers strongly supported Coppin's appointment as a teacher and subsequently principal of the institute, in keeping with their long-standing ideological commitment to the education of women.

Coppin taught successfully for ten years and was named principal in 1875. She brought new strength to the entire institution. Under her leadership, the institute enhanced its preparatory program, strengthened its high school curriculum, and stiffened entrance requirements. Coppin also developed a normal school that allowed African American women and men to become teachers, and she established a field experience for teacher-student placement in the preparatory school.

With industrial education rising in American cities, Coppin introduced classes for women in cooking and sewing. Many women from this program became caterers, business owners, and managers. For male students, she pushed an industrial arts component. The institute's managers, however, were slow in supporting Coppin's effort to expand the school in this way. Believing in the need for such training, Coppin took her message to church meetings and newspapers, keeping her crusade in the public eye until the program opened in 1889.

By offering both industrial training and classical work, Coppin negotiated an educational program that responded to both of the era's philosophies: the self-help industrial model of Booker T. Washington and the educated elite of W.E.B. Du Bois. Coppin wanted equal opportunity for blacks to pursue whatever course suited them. She encouraged some students to join the elite and become engineers, doctors, lawyers, and teachers. But she also embraced Washington's design to help the masses of African Americans who pursued economic development through labor.

In reconciling these two philosophies, Coppin might be a called a "womanist" educational leader, following Alice Walker's conception of that term. Coppin proved herself responsible for her own education, leading her to reshape her vision of herself as an African American woman. She was committed to her people, demonstrated through her flexibility working with the black elite, the working class, and the poor, realizing that no single educational strategy could support all educational needs. Coppin also promoted the needs of African Americans, even when they clashed with the Quaker directors of the Institute for Colored Youth.

At age forty-four, Coppin married Levi Jenkins Coppin, a minister in the African Methodist Episcopal Church. Coppin did not leave her institute post when she married, and Reverend Coppin moved to Philadelphia to be with her. Because of illness, Coppin retired in 1902. She and her husband spent a year in South Africa but returned because of her continuing poor health. She spent her last eight years confined to her Philadelphia home and died there in 1913.

Fanny Jackson Coppin is perhaps less known than other African American educators because she published little and spent considerable time wrestling to get her plans and ideas accepted. However, she may have been one of the strongest educational leaders of her time, creating a system and a school to serve the people she felt called to help. Coppin State College in Baltimore, Maryland, has been named for her.

Bibliography: Linda M. Perkins, "Fanny Jackson Coppin and the Institute for Colored Youth: A Model of Nineteenth Century Black Female Educational and Community Leadership, 1837–1902" (Ph.D. diss., University of Illinois, 1978); Perkins, "Heed Life's

Demands: The Educational Philosophy of Fanny Jackson Coppin," *Journal of Negro Education*, 51 (1982): 181–190; Julie Winch, *Philadelphia's Black Elite: Activism, Accommodation and the Struggle for Autonomy, 1787–1848* (1988).

Imani-Sheila Newsome-McLaughlin

county superintendents. By the mid-1850s, need for connection between widely dispersed **district schools*** and emerging state and local organizational systems was becoming apparent. In response, states increasingly created the county superintendency, a supervisory position that provided a direct link between growing state bureaucracies and local initiatives. Over time, women fared well in these positions, especially in states with elected rather than appointed superintendents. By 1930, women held a quarter of county superintendent posts.

Methods of selecting county superintendents—election or appointment, popular vote or committee—differed and even changed over time, depending on the evolving school organization within individual states. By 1879, thirty-eight states and four territories had created a county superintendency. Once established, however, the office was not necessarily permanent; in some cases, it was abolished and then reestablished. No states or territories had legal educational requirements for the position in 1879, though a few stipulated that the county superintendent should be a competent teacher. As late as 1930, only four states had laws requiring superintendents to be college or **normal school*** graduates, and fourteen states required only a teaching certificate. Nonetheless, over time, requirements were raised, and by 1950, twelve states required county superintendents to have completed at least five years of college training.

Despite variations in the selection process, county superintendents' duties and responsibilities were remarkably consistent from state to state. In the nineteenth century, most states required superintendents to keep records and make reports on schools within their area, apportion state monies, settle disputes between and within districts, certify teachers and oversee their work through visitation and observation, and encourage districts to improve school facilities.

The twentieth-century rise of professionalization and expertise expanded the duties and expectations of county superintendents. School supervision became a major issue as educators sought ways to enhance standardization and teacher skills. In response, the county superintendency became more focused on teacher supervision and instruction. A 1932 national study of county superintendents presented a composite picture of the average superintendent who exercised "general supervision" over at least eighty-four schools, three-quarters of which were one-teacher schools and/or young teacher schools with students in eight grades. Five of the eighty-four schools had two or three teachers and five were consolidated, four had both elementary and high school departments, and four were strictly **high schools.*** The superintendents' eighty-four schools were dispersed over a 1,500-square-mile area, many on small, unfinished roads, most in the "open country." Half of the supervised teachers changed districts each year, and one-quarter had no prior **teaching*** experience. This composite described the supervisory aspects of an average superintendency but did not mention the job's extensive clerical and administrative aspects.

Popular election predominated as the most common method of superintendent selection and was probably the most criticized aspect of the office. In 1922, a majority of states still elected superintendents by popular vote. Superintendents' accountability to the electorate led to persistent criticism of their work for nearly a century. Foremost educational authority Ellwood Cubberley stated in 1922 that "the blighting influence of party politics in the county and the personal politics and jealousies in the districts alike combine to lay a heavy hand on rural educational progress" (Cubberley, 1922, p. 317). As late as 1949, twenty of forty-four states reported the use of popular vote, and among those, legal qualifications for the office ranged from no professional experience to graduate work in education. As a result of this survey, the Council of State Governments charged that the "most serious deterrents to the exercise of continuing and effective educational leadership are the election of superintendents by popular-vote."

Prior to 1900, women made up a small percentage of county superintendents, as they simultaneously grew to become a majority of **common school*** teachers. In Wisconsin, for example, women ran for election as county superintendents a decade before they were legally allowed to vote on school issues. Women comprised approximately 15 percent of Wisconsin superintendents in 1891. Nationally, women could vote in school elections in only twenty-four states by 1910 [see **suffrage***]. Nonetheless, between 1900 and 1930 women constituted 25 percent of all county superintendents, a number that then began to decline. Women's overall numbers rose from 276 in 1900 to 857 in 1922. A 1928 national survey revealed that women held the majority of county superintendent positions in thirteen states, all west of the Mississippi River. Montana claimed the highest number of women superintendents, 92. Of the twenty-five states selecting county superintendents by popular election, women comprised 43 percent, while states with appointed superintendents averaged 80 percent men. Eighty-five percent of all superintendents reporting were between the ages of thirty and sixty, with less than 6 percent under thirty. The same study found the median years of education among county superintendents was 19.9, with 43 percent holding college degrees.

The county superintendency still functioned in all states except Delaware and Nevada by 1950, with over 3,300 superintendents overall. Soon thereafter, however, school district reorganization and consolidation eliminated the county superintendency across the country. And though it meant losing their own positions, many superintendents aided the process in hopes of building a better educational system.

Bibliography: Ellwood Cubberley, *Rural Life and Education* (1922); Cubberley, *Public School Administration* (1929); Julian E. Butterworth, *The County Superintendency in the United States*, Bulletin #6 (1932); Council of State Governments, *The Forty-eight State School Systems* (1949); Wayne Fuller, *The Old Country School* (1982); David Tyack and

Elizabeth Hansot, *Managers of Virtue* (1982); Kathleen Weiler, "Women and Rural School Reform: California, 1900–1940," *History of Education Quarterly*, 34 (Spring 1994): 25–47.

Dina L. Stephens

Crandall, Prudence. Prudence Crandall (1803–1890), a proponent of education for young black females, devoted her life to this cause and to women's **suffrage.*** Born in Hopkinton, Rhode Island, Crandall received a "guarded," carefully supervised **Quaker*** education at the finest coeducational boarding school of the time, New England Yearly Meeting School, or Brown Seminary, located on property belonging to abolitionist [see **abolitionism***] Moses Brown.

In 1831 Crandall was appointed director of the new Canterbury Female Seminary in Canterbury, Connecticut, at a time of popularity for colonization societies, which advocated sending blacks to settle the new country of Liberia. Soon after Crandall moved into the handsome school building, she opened the school to twenty white female students. Sarah Harris, a young black woman and daughter of a free black farmer, asked to attend but live at home. Knowing that the woman was associated with the agent for *The Liberator*, a nationally influential liberal newspaper, Crandall agreed. Soon after, the local Episcopal minister's wife expressed her strong disapproval, stating that white parents would withdraw their daughters from the school.

Crandall consulted with William Lloyd Garrison, editor of *The Liberator*, and other prominent abolitionist leaders. With their support, she advertised for a completely new student body. In 1833, when the school became the High School for Young Colored Ladies and Misses with twenty girls enrolled from Providence, Boston, and Philadelphia, a major controversy erupted. Fearful that educated black girls would remain in Canterbury where they might contribute to an increase in crime and marry white men, the town asked Crandall to move her school away from the town center. Upon her refusal, the state legislature passed the Black Law on May 24, 1833, forbidding anyone from running an educational institution for noninhabitants of Connecticut. By restricting their freedom of movement and residence, the law implied that blacks were not citizens.

Crandall tried to concentrate on teaching the girls the basics of reading, writing, and arithmetic laced with religious principles, but continuing harassment interrupted the lessons. Despite several arrests, Crandall remained free, thanks to efforts of abolitionists who argued the wickedness of the law. She refused to abandon the school, declaring, "I have put my hand to the plough, and I will never, no never, look back." However, when the school was ravaged and the students traumatized by numerous assaults and a fire, Crandall closed her school and moved to New York and later to Illinois.

Crandall was among the first women actively involved in shaping the abolitionist movement at a time when most women were relegated to the traditional role of fund-raising for the cause. The ramifications of her stand in Canterbury strengthened the movement; citizens realized that the Colonization Society actually protected the institution of **slavery**.* Moreover, they were confronted with difficult questions: What was the intention of the framers of the Constitution? Were persons of color equal to whites? Were they citizens? The controversy was covered extensively in *The Liberator*, and a new weekly, *The Unionist*, was created expressly to distribute throughout New England news of Crandall's trials, the Black Law, and the national implications of the controversy. As a result of her unswerving stand, the United States and England were alerted to the need to educate black children.

For the remainder of her life, Crandall remained an outspoken abolitionist and fervent advocate of women's rights, frequently lecturing on peace, temperance, and suffrage [see **peace education**,* **temperance movement***]. In 1885 the citizens of Canterbury successfully requested the Connecticut legislature to make reparation to Crandall for the ''cruel outrage'' committed against her and expunge her criminal conviction. One nineteenth-century historian epitomized her contribution to history: ''Miss Crandall did not succeed in teaching many colored girls but she educated the people of Windham County'' (Fuller, p. 96).

Bibliography: Elizabeth Yates, *Prudence Crandall: A Woman of Courage* (1955); Edmund Fuller, *Prudence Crandall: An Incident of Racism in Nineteenth-Century Connecticut* (1971); Susan Strane, *A Whole-Souled Woman: Prudence Crandall and the Education of Black Women* (1990).

Deborah Elwell Arfken

D

Dalton Plan. The Dalton Plan, a progressive, child-centered approach to learning, was created by educator Helen Parkhurst, who popularized its use at the Dalton School in New York City, beginning in 1919. Parkhurst was born in Durand, Wisconsin (1887), and she received her B.S. degree in 1907 from the River Falls Normal School at Wisconsin State College. Following graduation, she taught from 1909 to 1910 at the Edison School in Tacoma, Washington, where she began to develop the Dalton Plan.

It is likely that Parkhurst was influenced by contemporaries Frederic Burk and Carleton Washburne, the latter founder of the "individual system" in Winnetka, Illinois, which permitted students to progress through their studies at their own pace. By 1910, Parkhurst called her idea the Laboratory Plan and emphasized the laboratory, or "lab," as her students and faculty later came to call it, as her creation. Lab was one of the focal points of the early plan, which would be developed more fully in subsequent years.

It is probably around 1915–1916 that Parkhurst began her relationship with Mrs. W. Murray Crane, the woman who eventually would provide Parkhurst the financial support she needed to found her own school. In 1919, with the encouragement and financial support of Mrs. Crane, Parkhurst opened her own school in New York City. Originally called the Children's University School, it was renamed the Dalton School in 1920; this was a compromise, as Parkhurst wanted to name the school after her benefactor, who declined the honor in favor of the name of the town where the Crane family originated. Her plan was also renamed the Dalton Plan in keeping with the new name of the school. The school's original site was a brownstone on West 74th Street. In 1929, the school moved to the present site of the middle school and **high school*** at 108 East 89th Street. By 1997, the lower school was on East 91st Street.

Parkhurst's early educational efforts attracted considerable attention. John Dewey frequently visited the school. Evelyn Dewey published *The Dalton Lab-*

oratory Plan in 1922. Parkhurst's own book, *Education on the Dalton Plan*, published in 1927, was translated into fourteen languages within six months of publication and eventually into fifty-eight languages. In the 1920s and 1930s, she traveled to England, Japan, Russia, China, Chile, Denmark, and Germany to lecture on the plan. Dalton schools were founded in England, the Netherlands, and Japan.

Based on a synthesis of the works of Dewey, **Maria Montessori**,* and Washburne, the Dalton Plan had three objectives: to connect students' studies to their needs and interests, to help students develop a sense of responsibility toward others, and to promote both independence and community. Three parts of the plan helped accomplish these goals: House, where students were organized into small communities; Laboratory, where students met individually with teachers on their studies; and Assignment, which provided each student with an individually planned and paced set of studies.

The guiding principles of the Dalton Plan were freedom and cooperation. By *freedom*, Parkhurst wanted the child to work on a task from its inception to its completion, free from the interruptions of the structure of the traditional school. To this end, Parkhurst abolished bells, for she was also cognizant of the fact that students acquire knowledge at their own rate and that they must have time to learn thoroughly. As Parkhurst stated, "Freedom is taking one's own time. To take someone else's time is slavery."

By *cooperation*, Parkhurst meant the interaction of children in groups. Like John Dewey, she was interested in preparing students to live in a democratic society; thus, she attempted to create a school in which there would be maximum cooperation and interaction between student and student, students and teachers. In September, students would be confronted with the year's work in each subject. They would be required to discuss their plans of action with their teachers, for it was essential to Parkhurst that both parties perceive their tasks. Later, students might discuss their plans with fellow students; they might modify their plans on peer recommendations; they might even abandon their plans and start over. Students would have participated, nevertheless, in planning their studies with both faculty and peers, interacting with the community in a spirit of cooperation.

In addition to planning, cooperation could be achieved through student activities and the first component of the Dalton Plan, House. Parkhurst conceived of House as an arrangement of students of mixed ages in advisory groups, meeting four times per week for a total period of ninety minutes with a teacher-adviser. House meetings might consist of students planning their work with their advisers, discussing problems of scheduling appointments with teachers, or perhaps a group assembly in order to discharge their responsibility to the rest of the community. House discussions might approach the more personal level, too. Student attitudes, habits, and experiences might be considered by the group as having a definite bearing on community life within the school. Thus, House would foster the spirit of cooperation among students; however, it would also serve to develop the qualities of independence and social awareness.

The second component of the Dalton Plan was Assignment, which developed out of a contract system. At the beginning of the Dalton School, the curriculum was divided into ''jobs'' encompassing twenty-day time periods. Students ''contracted'' for their tasks and signed a contract to the effect. Students' tasks appeared as the assignment, ''an outline of the contract job with all its parts.''

The plan's third component was Lab, large blocks of time set aside each morning to free the children and to assist their growth in independence and responsibility. Each teacher had a lab, and students would be expected to utilize the resources of their teachers to help them fulfill their contracts. Lab could either be a group or individual experience; lab rooms were stocked with both textbooks and ''adult books'' to facilitate learning.

Flexibility was the keystone of the plan. Conferences, or meetings between students and teachers, were called as needed. Classes met, too, as needed, and consisted of grade meetings to discuss problems common to that age group. The school during Parkhurst's time exuded a quality of informality, spur-of-the-moment decisionmaking, enormous energy, high-level engagement on the part of both faculty and students, and the element of surprise.

Helen Parkhurst founded a school with a particular philosophy, a special environment where teachers had lab rooms and classrooms, and educational jargon indigenous to the institution. But perhaps Parkhurst's greatest contribution to education was her emphasis on process rather than product. She believed that she was creating an environment in her school that would prepare her students for life.

Although the Dalton School of the mid-1990s has become a less progressive, elite college preparatory school, vestiges of the Dalton Plan remain, particularly House, Lab, and Assignment. Recently, efforts have been made to connect its new emphasis on technology to the Dalton Plan and to call it the Dalton Technology Plan.

Bibliography: Evelyn Dewey, *The Dalton Laboratory Plan* (1922); Helen Parkhurst, *Education on the Dalton Plan* (1927); Susan F. Semel, *The Dalton School: The Transformation of a Progressive School* (1992).

Susan F. Semel

dame schools. ''Schoolmothering'' young children accounts for the earliest form of the words *school mother, school marm,* and *school dame.* Women, many believed, were the most patient for **teaching*** young children and were, conveniently, located in the home. Educational histories refer to women's home-based institutions as dame schools, and town records before the Revolutionary War document widowed or unmarried older women accepting a few pence per week for instructing children in their homes. Women who took on the role of dame schoolteachers did so either out of sheer monetary need or the goodness of their hearts.

In the late 1600s, Hepzibah Pyncheon's life demonstrated the experience of a typical dame schoolteacher. She sold gingerbread and tape from her cottage and displayed a sign in the window announcing "School Kept Here" (*Harper's*). Seated beside the hearth, dame school scholars recited the alphabet, practiced writing letters, or gave recitations while "the knitting needle of the schooldame could be dignified by the pompous name of fescue, a pointer, a something of that nature, a straw, a pine, a quill, a skewer of wood, was always used to direct children's eyes to letter or word" (Earle, p. 122). Pay for schooling such students was handled through monetary remuneration or possibly bartering food or services. The payment of one dame schoolteacher was explained: "In Flushing [New York] Elizabeth Cowperthwait was reckoned with in 1681 for 'schooling and diet for children'; and in 1683 she received for thirty weeks' school, of 'Martha Johanna,' a scarlet Petticoat, a truly typical Dutch payment" (Earle, p. 35).

Dame teachers flourished when groups like the **Quakers**,* long-standing supporters of women's education, maintained that women should hold equal social, political, and religious positions with men. Quaker meetings established programs for rural Quaker mothers to teach grammar to their daughters. Anthony Benezet, a Philadelphia Quaker and founder of the movement, stressed the need for mothers to first teach themselves, then their own daughters.

By the time the Constitution was signed, women were thought not to be appropriate instructors for the formal teaching done in school; thus, men reigned briefly as teachers of America's one-room schools. If women were allowed to teach, they were restricted to the very youngest children. Yet historical circumstances provided opportunities such that women ultimately assumed the helm of America's rural classrooms, and by the late nineteenth century, more than three-quarters of teachers were women. [See also **feminization**.*]

Bibliography: "The School Mistress," *Harper's New Monthly Magazine* (September 1878): 607–611; A. M. Earle, *Child Life in Colonial Days* (1899); E. G. Dexter, *A History of Education in the United States* (1904); Thomas Woody, *A History of Women's Education in the United States*, 2 vols. (1929); J. Jensen, "Not Only Ours But Others: The Quaker Teaching Daughters of the Mid-Atlantic, 1790–1850," *History of Education Quarterly*, 24 (1984): 3–19; Andrea Wyman, *Rural Women Teachers in the United States: A Sourcebook* (1996).

Andrea Wyman

Day, Dorothy. Dorothy Day (1897–1980), together with Peter Maurin, was cofounder of the Catholic Worker movement. The movement, created in 1933, remains a social justice effort by Catholics to treat the poor with grace and dignity.

Dorothy Day did not have an especially religious upbringing; her family was loosely affiliated with the Episcopal tradition. Day was more strongly influenced by her family's economic life. Her father, John, a newspaper columnist, traveled frequently from paper to paper, and the family moved from Brooklyn to Berkeley to Chicago and back again. Their economic condition fluctuated wildly. Sometimes they owned a house, while at others they crowded into a tenement flat. Entering college, Day was introduced to the Haymarket Anarchists, to socialist Eugene Debbs, and to author Fyodor Dostoevski. She began to embrace a radical perspective and increasingly viewed religious devotion as an excuse for political apathy. Too many Christians, in Day's view, were content to do nothing about social injustice.

In 1917, Day went to work in New York City for the socialist paper *The Call* and later for *The Masses* and *The Liberator*. She lived in Greenwich Village and counted playwright Eugene O'Neill among her friends. She also pursued a disastrous affair that ended in unintended pregnancy and subsequent abortion. Feeling her life was becoming a shambles, she entered a quick marriage in 1920 to a man who could take her away; the couple went to Europe. When they returned, Day left him and moved to Chicago, where she roomed with two Catholic friends whose ideas began to impress her. After moving to New Orleans in 1923, she unexpectedly found herself attending mass at a cathedral in Jackson Square.

When the publishers of a novel she had written sold the movie rights to a Hollywood producer, Day realized an unexpected windfall of $5,000. With this, she bought a small bungalow on Staten Island in 1924 and entered into a common law marriage with Forster Batterham. Day recalled their life on the Island as happy. She was surprised to find herself praying more and more. Religion, particularly Catholicism, was becoming an important part of her life, a fact that created conflict with Batterham. In June 1926, Day discovered to her joy that she was pregnant. Batterham was not as happy. Tension increased as Day's intention to have the child baptized became clear. Their daughter, Tamar, was born in March 1927. True to her word, Day brought Tamar to a Catholic church to be baptized. By year's end, Day had followed her daughter into the Church. Her embrace of Catholicism ended her relationship with Batterham.

For the next five years, Day supported herself through writing, while she studied her adopted faith and tried to find a way to integrate it with her earlier radical beliefs. She wanted both to apply her faith to the cause of social justice and to serve her church. The usual methods for laypeople—Catholic charities, hospitals, and orphanages—seemed too impersonal. People could work in a Catholic hospital in the day yet return to their middle-class lives in the evening. Such efforts never addressed the underlying structure of social and economic injustice. Frustrated, Day continued to pray that she would find a way to best use her talents to serve the poor. She received an answer in December 1932 when she met Peter Maurin.

Maurin was a French Catholic immigrant from a large, poor family. He wanted to start a radical Catholic newspaper to bring his ideas about social justice to a wider audience. Together they started *The Catholic Worker*; its first issue appeared in New York City on May 1, 1933. Maurin showed Day how Catholic social teaching could be brought to bear on social issues. Their philosophy was anarchist, pacifist, and personalist. *The Worker*, as both paper and movement, emphasized daily practice of the Church's spiritual and corporal works of mercy. (Traditionally, the spiritual works of mercy include: instruct the ignorant, counsel the doubtful, admonish sinners, bear wrongs patiently, forgive offenses, comfort the afflicted, and pray for the dead. The corporal works of mercy are: feed the hungry, give drink to the thirsty, clothe the naked, shelter the homeless, visit the sick, ransom the captive, and bury the dead.) Maurin envisioned performance of the works in what he called "houses of hospitality" in urban settings offering food, shelter, and hospitality to the poor. Maurin also hoped to establish farming communes to restore an agrarian sensibility. Eventually, both houses and farms were created, but in the long run, the houses succeeded to a much greater degree, and the current movement remains a largely urban one. The first house of hospitality was opened in New York City on December 11, 1934; the first farm in spring 1935 on Staten Island.

The personalism of the Catholic Worker called for greeting the poor as ambassadors of Christ and treating them with grace and dignity. Importantly, Day stressed that one should do this work directly by living with the poor in voluntary poverty. The houses of hospitality were not shelters; they were the homes of workers opened to the poor. Nor, Day stressed, could the works of mercy be performed through an impersonal bureaucracy. "Creating a new society within the shell of the old," in Maurin's words, required personal action, personal responsibility, and personal sacrifice. As Day reminded people, love in action is a harsh and dreadful thing, but she believed that such action was what the gospels called believers to undertake.

Maurin died in 1949, but his death was not the end of the Catholic Worker movement. While Day had always emphasized her debt to Maurin, the movement's survival and public presence had always depended much more heavily on the force of Day's voice and the power of her charisma. Day guided the movement with a combination of orthodoxy toward Church dogma and radicalism toward social issues.

As Day led the movement, its mission grew, attracting people from sociologist Michael Harrington and Trappist monk Thomas Merton to activist Cesar Chavez. As Harrington suggested, *The Worker* was as far left as one could get without leaving the Catholic Church. Day's pacifism prompted her to speak out against the atomic bomb, the draft, air raid drills, the Korean and Vietnam Wars, and nuclear arms. Resistance to the military-industrial complex through rallies and protests, burning draft cards, and other acts of civil disobedience became part of the Catholic Worker mission as another way of performing the spiritual works of mercy and a potent way to call attention to misapplication of national wealth and resources.

The movement provided a powerful education for its members. Since the majority of Workers have been white, educated people with middle-class backgrounds, the choice to live in voluntary poverty becomes deeply personal and countercultural as they struggle with how to be with the poor in a way that is not patronizing. They struggle with seeing the poor as people and not as problems. As one woman in the movement explained, "It's not a social service agency, it's a home, and we open up our home to people who are in need. We offer hospitality and no one really understands what that means. We don't claim to be social workers here. We claim to be people" (Gayle Catinella, quoted in Troester, p. 171).

That powerful claim raises an important distinction between the Catholic Worker movement and **settlement house movement**.* The Catholic Worker hopes that its presence, its witness, and its service will help people and that in time some might change. The poor are their guests and not their clients. Catholic Workers live in uncertainty and hope. For women so educated, their own lives would never be the same.

Bibliography: Dorothy Day, *The Long Loneliness* (1952); William Miller, *Dorothy Day: A Biography* (1982); Mel Piehl, *Breaking Bread: The Catholic Worker and the Origin of Catholic Radicalism in America* (1982); June O'Connor, *The Moral Vision of Dorothy Day: A Feminist Perspective* (1991); Rosalie Riegle Troester, ed., *Voices from the Catholic Worker* (1993).

R.A.R. Edwards

deaf education. Deaf education in the United States traces its formal roots to 1817, when the American School for the Deaf opened in Hartford, Connecticut. Earlier, wealthy Americans sent their deaf children abroad to be educated, usually to Great Britain. The British system was dominated by the Braidwood family who educated deaf children using the oral method, that is, by teaching speech and lip-reading skills. The Braidwoods had made one unsuccessful attempt to open a school in the United States in 1811 in Virginia, but the effort failed, largely due to the hopeless alcoholism of John Braidwood, Jr. Without an American alternative, deaf children from families without means remained largely uneducated.

The impetus to open an American school for the deaf came from Mason Fitch Cogswell, a successful doctor well connected to the Hartford elite. His daughter Alice became deaf following a childhood illness. Cogswell did not want to send her abroad, but he did want her to be educated. In 1811, he convinced the Congregational Church in Connecticut to conduct a survey of deaf people in the state; census results revealed 84 deaf people. Using this figure, Cogswell estimated there were 400 deaf people in New England and 2,000 in the United States. He immediately saw the need to establish an American school. As he pursued this goal, he made arrangements for Alice's education in Hartford. She entered a school run by Lydia Sigourney, the popular poet and Hartford resident, in the fall of 1814.

Sigourney was fascinated by Alice and her deafness. She wrote several poems about Alice and about deafness in general that presented a highly sentimental and romantic view of deafness, imagining the deaf as people who communed with God in their silence so directly that there was no need for language. This overly romantic view, a tendency on the part of hearing people to view deafness as a state of grace, was fairly common in the early nineteenth century. However, it was not a view shared by deaf people, who recalled their lives before education as times of isolation and ignorance, not holiness and grace.

In spite of seeing Alice as an icon instead of a person, Sigourney did her best to educate and integrate her into the class of hearing girls. Alice gained some very basic skills in English; her sentences, though choppy, were understandable. Describing her neighborhood in Hartford in 1815, Alice wrote, ''Many candles in windows. Shine bright on snow. Houses most beautiful.''

While Alice was entering school, Thomas Hopkins Gallaudet, a family friend of the Cogswells, was graduating from Andover Theological Seminary. Upon graduation, he, too, spent time with Alice as a teacher. A minister and deeply pious Christian, Gallaudet viewed deaf education as a missionary effort, a way to bring Christianity to the deaf intellect and soul. Gallaudet dedicated himself to deaf education, and Cogswell convinced him in 1815 to go to Europe on a fact-finding mission.

There Gallaudet met Scottish philosopher Dugald Stewart, a thinker in the school of Scottish common sense and a strong critic of oral education. Stewart advised Gallaudet to travel to Paris to learn more about their manual method of teaching the deaf using sign language. Deaf students emerged from school bilingual, knowing both sign language and French, which they could read and write fluently. Gallaudet, who had read and admired Stewart's work at Andover, headed for Paris, to the National Institution for Deaf-Mutes. There Gallaudet realized that he would never learn all he needed to know about the French system in a short trip. He asked a teacher, the deaf Frenchman Laurent Clerc, to return with him to Hartford. Clerc agreed, and together the two set American deaf education on a manualist path that would facilitate the growth of American Sign Language (ASL) and the growth of American deaf culture.

Throughout much of the nineteenth century the manual method flourished across the country as other states followed Connecticut's lead and established their own residential schools for the deaf. Clerc and Gallaudet created a system that encouraged bilingualism and biculturalism for deaf students and hearing teachers alike. All were expected to become fluent in both ASL and English. Deaf students were expected to read and write English to become literate; they were not expected to speak. Hearing teachers were expected to learn ASL from their deaf students and to avoid the use of signs that were not used colloquially among students. In this way, all were expected to participate in the deaf cultural life of the school by using ASL correctly and to participate in the wider cultural life of America, by reading and writing the common language, English. A certain vision of cultural pluralism emerged from these educators wherein deaf people did not have to give up their language or their culture to be active American citizens.

Both men married deaf women, Gallaudet marrying Sophia Fowler and Clerc marrying Eliza Boardman. The hearing children of both couples grew up in bilingual, bicultural households. By their examples, these couples demonstrated a way that deaf and hearing people could share a common life, a way that did not hinge on eradicating the cultural deafness of the deaf partner. Neither woman was forced to try to pass as hearing; neither viewed her deafness as an obstacle to becoming a wife or mother or as a defect to avoid passing on to a child. They were deaf women, deaf wives, deaf mothers.

By the end of the nineteenth century, all of this would change. A vision of cultural pluralism hinging on sharing a public culture based in the written word, a vision that could comfortably include both deaf and hearing people, would no longer satisfy an increasingly xenophobic culture. Assimilating huge numbers of new immigrants meant Americanizing those immigrants, which in turn meant requiring them to speak English exclusively. It was no longer acceptable for immigrants to be bilingual, speaking one language in private and English in public. It had to be English only and English always.

Deaf education had to be brought in line with this new vision. By continuing to use ASL, deaf people appeared to be engaging in the behavior of foreigners, and hearing parents of deaf children did not want those children viewed in such a light. The oral method displaced the manual method in schools for the deaf nationwide. ASL, once the language of instruction, was banished from the classroom in favor of a pure oral approach that focused on acquiring speech and lip-reading skills. In this way, deaf people would be made over in the image of hearing people, acting and communicating in the same way. Hearing teachers of the deaf no longer learned ASL; they worked to suppress it. Alexander Graham Bell, the biggest proponent of the oral method, worried publicly in 1883 about the possible "formation of a deaf variety of the human race." He believed that the use of ASL encouraged deaf people to associate with and marry one another. If they spoke English, they would associate with and marry hearing people, thus preventing the birth of a deaf race. Bell regretted that laws could not be passed forbidding deaf people from marrying each other. He settled for urging friends and family of deaf people to pressure them to marry hearing spouses and for convincing schools for the deaf to abandon the manual method in favor of the oral approach. ASL, in his view, was part of the problem for deaf people, not part of the solution.

Bell practiced what he preached. He married Mabel Hubbard, a deaf woman educated at the Clarke School for the Deaf, an oral school in Northampton, Massachusetts. Hubbard did not know ASL. She refused to associate with other deaf people, going so far as to refuse to acknowledge them in public. She did her best to pass as a hearing person, and her husband praised her by telling her how well she succeeded.

Oralism dominated twentieth-century deaf education. Not until the 1970s was pure oralism abandoned in favor of the philosophy of total communication. Total communication meant using speech and sign, whatever worked best to teach deaf children, in the classroom. The method usually resulted in hearing teachers speaking and signing simultaneously. However, this meant that they were not using ASL, since ASL is a language with a grammar very different from English. These hearing teachers did not respect ASL as had teachers of the early nineteenth century; total communication advocates raided ASL for its signs to put them in English word order. A hearing style of sign language was let back in the classrooms. English only was still the message, only now deaf students were to sign English as well as read and write it. In the 1980s a few schools tried the bold experiment of using ASL as the language of instruction. These schools still number only a handful.

The majority of teachers during the years of the oral method's ascendancy were hearing women. During the manual method's control of deaf education, roughly 1817 to 1867, teachers were mostly hearing men. Some have argued that the women were more committed to academic achievement for deaf children and more intent on seeing them integrated into hearing society than the men were. But the rise of women in the profession cannot be explained simply in these terms. Hearing women were cost-effective; they were paid considerably less than male teachers. And the hearing women of the oralist camp were just as committed as their male counterparts to a vision of cultural hegemony that did not allow for cultural deafness or for ASL. Male teachers of the older manual method had also wanted deaf people integrated into predominantly hearing society; they simply had not seen the acquisition of speech as the key to that inclusion. Rather, manualists had seen literacy as the most important thing, and deaf people had agreed with them. Deaf women did not favor oral education and did not appreciate the efforts of hearing teachers in this area. Deaf women, like deaf men, supported manual education and ASL. They favored a vision of cultural pluralism that did not require them to pass as hearing to be accepted. Mabel Hubbard Bell was not a role model for deaf women; but for hearing teachers, she was the deaf woman they wanted their deaf students to become. Deaf women and hearing women viewed both education and life from strikingly different vantage points.

Bibliography: Margaret Winzer, "Talking Deaf Mutes: The Special Role of Women in the Methodological Conflict Regarding the Deaf, 1867–1900," *Atlantis*, 6 (1981): 123–133; Harlan Lane, *When the Mind Hears: A History of the Deaf* (1984); Mabs Holcomb and Sharon Wood, *Deaf Women: A Parade through the Decades* (1989); Douglas C. Baynton, " 'A Silent Exile on This Earth': The Metaphorical Construction of Deafness in the Nineteenth Century," *American Quarterly*, 44 (June 1992): 216–243; Phyllis Valentine, "Thomas Hopkins Gallaudet: Benevolent Paternalism and the Origins of the American Asylum," in John Vickrey Van Cleve, ed., *Deaf History Unveiled* (1993); Douglas C. Baynton, *Forbidden Signs: American Culture and the Campaign against Sign Language* (1996).

R.A.R. Edwards

deans of women. Deans of women were virtually ubiquitous on coeducational college campuses from the turn of the century until the 1960s. In the early years, they were often the first senior women administrators on their campuses, and they played a vital role in opening academic and social opportunities for women. The position of dean of women also played an interesting historical role by being the first systemic administrative response by higher education to cope with a new, and essentially unwelcome, population.

The foremothers of twentieth-century deans were the mid-nineteenth-century dormitory matrons hired at **Oberlin*** and Antioch Colleges by presidents wary of **coeducation**.* The matrons lived in the women's residence halls and were charged with seeing to the physical and moral well-being of students. By the 1870s coeducation was common in a new type of institution—the midwestern state university, whose growth was largely precipitated by the **Morrill Land-Grant Act of 1862**.* Most state universities patterned themselves after the American perception of the German university and paid scant attention to the out-of-classroom needs of students, male or female. As such, they provided little or no campus housing, so no matron was needed.

The laissez-faire attitude held by campus officials at state universities began to wane in the 1890s. Responding to social and parental pressure, universities began building dormitories. Renewed criticism of coeducation and fears of relaxing social standards caused presidents to worry anew about the moral propriety of men and women students mixing freely on campus. In response, President William Rainey Harper of the **University of Chicago*** hired **Alice Freeman Palmer**,* former president of **Wellesley College**,* to be the dean of women, to look after all the needs of women on campus, and to supervise dormitory matrons. Palmer planned to be in Chicago only a few months a year and brought **Marion Talbot*** as her assistant. Following Palmer's premature death, Talbot assumed the full duties of dean. Within a few years, Chicago's example was widely emulated.

Within two decades of Talbot's arrival in 1892, most state universities and smaller colleges, especially the **normal schools*** for teacher training, hired a dean or an adviser to women. Undoubtedly, some of these deans viewed their roles as limited to chaperoning, but there was a cadre of women who had a broader vision. These deans were aware of the inequities on coeducational campuses where women were kept on the margins of campus life. This collection of deans was composed of highly educated, ambitious women, many of whom aspired to faculty positions. Unfortunately, there were few opportunities for women to obtain faculty jobs, except at **women's colleges**.* So women accepted posts that were faculty hybrids, simultaneously academic and administrative. It was not surprising, given the collective talent and ambition of this cadre, that they strove to remake the position of matron into the profession of dean of women.

Marion Talbot was a pioneer who imposed her vision on the nascent profession. Talbot was devoted to ensuring that the women students enjoyed the full advantages of the university. She believed that women were as intellectually capable as men but that they were also unique, requiring a distinct community. This view of women's educational needs became the new profession's foundation: Securing parity in academic opportunity and building a distinct social community became the raison d'être of the new deans.

Talbot also organized the first professional conference. Eighteen women arrived in Chicago in November 1903, most representing midwestern institutions. Like Talbot, the majority held faculty appointments in addition to their work as deans. Not surprisingly, their first substantive concern was housing, but they discussed other topics as well. The deans then voted to meet two years hence and passed a series of resolutions summing up the collective opinions of the group. When the deans met in Chicago in December 1905, the gathering was convened as "The Conference of Deans and Advisors of Women in State Universities." With the exception of **Lucy Sprague** (later **Mitchell***) from the University of California, the early leadership of the new profession was securely in the hands of women working in the midwestern, public university sector.

The biennial conferences aided the individual women in their daily jobs by recommending standards of practice and facilitating communication among one another. Deans regularly published in educational journals, made connections to other professional women in education (especially the **Association of Collegiate Alumnae***), and became more scientific, using techniques and language associated with scientific research. In 1911, Dean Gertrude Martin of Cornell conducted and distributed the first statistical research project on the work of deans. This intellectual activity, Lucy Sprague said, saved the profession from the "bog of discipline and decorum." In 1915 Lois Mathews (University of Wisconsin, 1912–1918) wrote the profession's first book, *The Dean of Women*. Both pragmatic and ideological, it reportedly sat on the desk of every dean of women until well into the 1930s. Mathews, the first female associate professor at Wisconsin, emphasized the academic component of the dean's job and believed that all deans should hold faculty appointments.

The years immediately preceding World War I were active for deans of women and the newer position of dean of men. Some deans, especially in smaller universities and colleges, questioned the need for dual faculty appointments; they chose instead to emphasize the counseling, guidance, and regulatory nature of their work. A few women with this point of view were studying for a master's degree at Teachers College in the summer of 1916. With Kathryn Sisson Phillips as first president, they formed the **National Association of Deans of Women*** (NADW). While there was some overlap among the new NADW members and those women who attended the early conferences, the preponderance of NADW women represented a new guard. The NADW quickly became the professional organization for all deans and placed very little emphasis on the importance of faculty rank.

Deans of men were appointed on coeducational campuses after the dean of women, occasionally as the result of the female dean's prompting. Some men's colleges had adult men to look after the students before 1900, but they were not usually called dean of men until later in the twentieth century. The duties of the dean of men were not unlike those of dean of women, although there was rarely the same moral overtone to their responsibilities. Deans of men formed their own professional organization, the National Association of Deans of Men (NADAM) in 1919.

By the 1920s, deans of women had many of the trappings of a profession and a critical mass of practitioners. The *Educational Directory* of 1925 indicated that there were 302 deans of women across the country. In addition to a professional organization and literature, there were courses of study dedicated to training deans; programs at Teachers College and Indiana University were followed by others soon thereafter. The leadership of the new profession was firmly in the hands of the NADW, which for the first twenty-five years was led almost exclusively by women whose background included a degree from an eastern women's college, a position in a prestigious midwestern university, a diploma from the Teachers College preparation program, or some combination of the three. Race was an additional common characteristic: The leadership of new profession was comprised solely of white women.

In response to the NADW's practice of holding its annual conference in "restricted" hotels—meaning those that would neither serve nor rent rooms to African American women—**Lucy Diggs Slowe*** of **Howard University**,* the first African American member of NADW, formed a parallel organization. She gathered her peers to a Conference of Deans and Advisors of Women at Howard's campus in 1929. The conference became an organization in its own right in 1935, the **Association of Deans of Women and Advisers to Girls in Negro Schools.*** Slowe provided its leadership from the first conference in 1929 until her death in 1937.

Between the 1920s and early 1940s, deans of women performed many functions currently associated with a modern dean of students. As a profession, deans of women and men were absorbed with developments in intelligence and vocational testing and improving the status of the profession on campus. The professional association concentrated much of its efforts on defining what precisely were the duties and benefits of deans of women.

By the mid-1940s, there was a growing concern, however, that some of the deans' work was being eclipsed by other professionals. In 1946, Sarah Blanding wrote of a particularly disturbing trend. She noticed that colleges were increasingly placing men, often the dean of men, in charge of counseling and guidance and reducing the dean of women to a "secondary officer."

There were two trends in personnel administration that exacerbated during the 1950s and 1960s, the phenomenon Blanding adumbrated in 1946. The first was the proliferation of specialties within the field of student affairs. The second trend was the change in campus organizational structure that accompanied the growth in student personnel jobs. Early deans of women and men on coeducational campuses typically held equivalent positions on the organizational chart.

A survey conducted in 1936 found that 86 percent of deans of women still reported to the president, but by 1962, less than 30 percent. One of the first women presidents of the American College Personnel Association, Elizabeth Greenleaf, summed up the situation in 1968: "During the past few years, there has been a major reorganization of student personnel positions on campus after campus. When this takes place, most often a major problem is how to reassign the Dean of Women. She is left either as Director of Women's Education . . . or she is given an undefined job as a general administrator. Rarely are women in our profession given a real functional responsibility" (p. 225).

The name changes in the organizations for both deans of women and men reflected the preeminence of men in student affairs. NADW became the National Association of Women Deans and Counselors in 1956, the National Association of Women Deans, Administrators, and Counselors (NAWDAC) in 1973, and the National Association of Women in Education (NAWE) in 1991. In 1951, NADAM became the National Association of Student Personnel Administrators (NASPA), considered by many to be the premier student affairs professional organization.

By the late 1970s, there were relatively few deans of women on public co-educational campuses, and the model of chief student affairs officer in charge of a staff of various subspecialists was prevalent. As the 1990s approached, less than 20 percent of the chief student affairs officers were women. However, if the original vision of the pioneering deans of women is being carried into the next century, perhaps it is by the female heads of **women's studies*** programs or **women's centers**,* rather than deans of students. For many of these professionals, who often hold faculty positions, their missions are to secure parity in academic opportunity and build a women's community—a raison d'être not unlike Marion Talbot's and Lois Mathews's.

Bibliography: Ruth A. Merrill and Helen D. Bragdon, *The Vocation of Dean* (Press and Publicity Committee of the National Association of Deans of Women, 1926); Marion Talbot, *More Than Lore: Reminiscences of Marion Talbot* (1936); Lulu Holmes, *A History of the Position of Dean of Women in a Selected Group of Co-educational Colleges and Universities in the United States* (1939); Sarah M. Sturtevant, Ruth Strang, and Margaret Kim, *Trends in Student Personnel Work as Represented in the Positions of Dean of Women and Deans of Girls in Colleges and Universities, Normal Schools, Teachers Colleges, and High Schools* (1940); Elizabeth Greenleaf, "How Others See Us: ACPA Presidential Address," *Journal of College Student Personnel*, 9 (July 1968): 225; Karen Anderson, "Brickbats and Roses: Lucy Diggs Slowe, 1883–1937," in G. J. Clifford, ed., *Lone Voyagers: Academic Women in Coeducational Institutions, 1870–1937* (1989); Ellen Fitzpatrick, "For the 'Women of the University': Marion Talbot, 1858–1948," in G. J. Clifford, ed., *Lone Voyagers: Academic Women in Coeducational Institutions, 1870–1937* (1989); Jana Nidiffer, "From Matron to Maven: A New Role and New Professional Identity for Deans of Women, 1892 to 1916," *Mid-Western Educational Researcher: Special Issue on Midwestern History*, 8 (Fall 1995): 17–24.

Jana Nidiffer

Declaration of Sentiments. The Declaration of Sentiments is the document that emerged from the first Women's Rights Convention in the United States, convened in **Seneca Falls**,* New York, on July 19–20, 1848. The immediate cause for the convention was the frustration of Elizabeth Cady Stanton with life in Seneca Falls. Together with her husband, Henry, Stanton had moved from Boston to the upstate New York village in 1847. Elizabeth Cady Stanton found the sudden shrinkage of her life back to strict domestic boundaries in an isolated town stifling. Her situation led her to focus her attention once more on the condition of women generally. Visiting friends Lucretia Mott, Martha C. Wright (Mott's sister), Jane Hunt, and Mary Ann McClintock in nearby Waterloo, on the afternoon of July 13, 1848, Stanton issued both complaints and a call to action. The convention was called on only a week's notice, an announcement appearing in the *Seneca County Courier*. The group called for a Women's Rights Convention to meet in the Wesleyan Chapel in Seneca Falls "to discuss the social, civil, and religious conditions and rights of woman."

The group wanted to prepare a statement outlining the future course of the women's rights movement, but the effort floundered with too many ideas and no organizing principle. Finally, Stanton hit upon the idea of using the Declaration of Independence as a model; so was born the Declaration of Sentiments. It opens: "We hold these truths to be self-evident: that all men and women are created equal." Substituting "man" for "King George," Stanton outlined women's grievances: Man has framed divorce laws to favor himself; man has stripped woman of a separate legal existence in marriage; man has kept woman in a subordinate position in both church and state; man has denied woman a higher education; man has denied woman the franchise; in short, man has usurped the power of God by claiming a right to assign woman to the sphere of life that best suits him. Stanton concluded by saying, "We insist that [women] have immediate admission to all the rights and privileges which belong to them as citizens of these United States." She admitted that women's rights activists faced "no small amount of misconception, misrepresentation, and ridicule" but urged supporters to "use every instrumentality within our power to effect our object." One hundred people, sixty-eight women and thirty-two men, affixed their signatures to the final document. One, Charlotte Woodward Pierce, lived to cast a vote in the presidential election of 1920.

The Women's Rights National Convention did not appear in a vacuum, and it did not emerge simply around a kitchen table. The antebellum years were awash in reform movements, movements in which women were heavily invested, such as **temperance*** and **abolitionism**.* It was through these steps into the public sphere that many women came to recognize themselves as members of a marginalized group and to chafe against restrictions that society placed in their way. The Declaration represents the first organized statement of this emerging understanding.

Reaction to the Declaration was overwhelmingly negative. Newspapers reprinted it in order to mock it, but Stanton was happy for the free publicity. Women's rights entered the public arena in a way that could not be denied or ignored. The issue would fracture other reform efforts; abolitionists would split over it, some factions convinced that women should wait their turn and press for rights after those of Africans, free and slave, had been secured. Others refused to separate the issues, seeing both causes as linked by a commitment to emancipation, broadly defined. After the Declaration, the "woman question" was one society could no longer avoid answering.

Bibliography: Carroll Smith-Rosenberg, "Beauty, the Beast, and the Militant Woman: A Case Study in Sex Roles and Social Stress in Jacksonian America," *American Quarterly*, 23 (1971): 562–584; Miriam Gurko, *The Ladies of Seneca Falls: The Birth of the Woman's Rights Movement* (1974); Lois W. Banner, *Elizabeth Cady Stanton: A Radical for Woman's Rights* (1980); "The Seneca Falls Declaration of Sentiments and Resolutions," in Daniel J. Boorstin, ed., *An American Primer* (1985); Robert H. Abzug, *Cosmos Crumbling: American Reform and the Religious Imagination* (1994).

R.A.R. Edwards

Denison House. Denison House, a Boston settlement house sponsored by the College Settlements Association, opened in late 1892. **Wellesley College*** faculty members Vida Dutton Scudder and Katharine Coman played prominent roles in its creation. Although she never resided there, Scudder remained actively involved with Denison House throughout its first two decades. Emily Greene Balch, a **Bryn Mawr College*** graduate and a future leading pacifist, was Denison House's first headworker, or resident in charge of programs. A year later, Helena Dudley, another Bryn Mawr graduate, became headworker, serving until her socialist politics prompted her resignation in 1912. Her critical role in Denison House history was commemorated with the Helena Dudley Memorial Foundation established in the 1930s to sponsor conferences and educational work on industrial and international issues at the house.

Following the financial Panic of 1893, Denison House became active in the labor movement. In 1894, working out of the house, the Federal Labor Union helped organize 800 female garment workers. The settlement house's commitment to such activities constantly threatened its support from wealthy donors. Besides forcing Dudley's resignation, this situation caused Scudder, a Christian Socialist, to cease involvement with Denison House and the **settlement house movement*** in the same period.

Denison House's most noted educational activities were associated with the Circolo Italo-Americano (Italian-American Circle) established in the early 1900s. Although Italians were moving into the house's previously Irish neighborhood, Scudder's fascination with Italian culture and Saints Catherine of Siena and Francis of Assisi also played a role in the Circolo's birth. Scudder directed Denison House's Italian Department, which offered Italian language and history classes for Americans. The Circolo's evening meetings featured Italian songs, recitations, and political talks, while its Sunday afternoon lectures and concerts emphasized American issues and ideals.

During its prime, Denison House maintained a close relationship with Wellesley College. Wellesley students participated in settlement classes for children and adults and gave entertainments for the house's neighbors. Students no doubt decided to become **social workers*** after first working there. Not only did Wellesley students visit Denison House, but the house's neighbors also visited Wellesley, sometimes attending campus lectures. The Circolo's spring and summer fiestas were held on the Wellesley campus. During the settlement house movement's heyday before World War I, colleges and particularly their female students, faculty, and alumnae often fostered relationships with settlement houses like those between Denison House and Wellesley College.

Bibliography: Vida Dutton Scudder, *On Journey* (1937); Mary Jo Deegan, "Sociology at Wellesley College: 1900–1919," *Journal of the History of Sociology*, 5 (Spring 1983): 91–115; Mina Carson, *Settlement Folk: Social Thought and the American Settlement Movement, 1885–1930* (1990).

Maureen A. Reynolds

design school movement. Design schools, which sprang up in seven industrial northeastern cities in the 1850s and 1860s, were the first American institutions devoted to women's professional art education. Sponsored and encouraged by business leaders in Philadelphia, Boston, New York, Baltimore, and smaller cities, design schools gave women unprecedented access to highly paid craft skills. By the close of the nineteenth century, these schools had helped professionalize the work of women as art teachers and practicing artists.

In order to gain access to art training and rationalize paid work as genteel, nineteenth-century women artists and their supporters argued that the female mind and hand were suited by nature for artistic pursuits. The schools provided contacts with potential employers, who were often board members, and protective spaces for women to perform freelance contract work. Aimed at native-born white women seeking genteel yet well-paid work, these schools attracted a range of women between their midteens and midforties in age, most of whom enjoyed some family economic support for their educational endeavors.

The inspiration for this significant innovation in American women's education was London's Female School of Design, founded in 1842 and directed until 1857 by artist Fanny Whitaker McIan. McIan's school was originally part of the South Kensington government art school system (now the Royal College of Art).

Although early American design schools closely followed the British curricular model, they were private institutions. The first American design school, founded in 1848 by philanthropist Sarah Worthington King Peter, was Philadelphia's School of Design for Women (now Moore College of Art and Design). Sarah Josepha Hale, an advocate of women's educational advancement, dem-

onstrated her faith in its importance by serving as a board member from 1853
to 1859. As editor of **Godey's Lady's Book**,* Hale published promotional pieces
praising design education as a significant innovation for women on a par with
medical schools and typographical training. Male board members included
wealthy art collectors like locomotive manufacturer Joseph Harrison and banker
James Claghorn and a few artists with ties to the business community, like
engraver John Sartain. Through the later nineteenth century, the Philadelphia
School of Design for Women, directed from 1886 to 1920 by Emily Sartain,
provided a curricular model for other women's art schools and trained art teachers for all educational levels from elementary schools to universities.

The initial success of the Philadelphia school inspired similar undertakings in
Boston, New York, and Baltimore. In 1851, Boston abolitionist Ednah Dow
Littlehale Cheney organized the New England School of Design for Women,
explicitly modeled on Philadelphia's design school, with such illustrious board
members as James Russell Lowell and Julia Ward Howe. After Cheney left in
1853, the banker and art collector Samuel Gray Ward and other board members
successfully lobbied for state subsidies for the newly incorporated school. Nevertheless, the original Boston design school had disappeared by 1861. In 1870,
Charles Callahan Perkins, a founder of the Boston Museum of Fine Arts, led
the effort to recruit British-trained Walter Smith to direct art education, now
mandated for public schools under the new Massachusetts Drawing Act. By
1873 Smith had established the Massachusetts Normal School of Art to train art
teachers, designers, and illustrators. Although the school was open to men,
women filled the majority of places until after 1900. National prominence came
quickly, with Smith's publication of *Art Education, Scholastic and Industrial*
(1872); this work described methods of art education in the United States, Great
Britain, and Europe and listed the major American design schools of Boston,
Philadelphia, and New York.

Following closely in the path of Philadelphia and Boston, the New York
School of Design for Women was founded in 1852 by Mary Morris Hamilton,
a philanthropist and art collector. The school flourished for four years as an
autonomous enterprise, until Peter Cooper offered to incorporate the women's
design school as a separate unit into the new Cooper Institute for the Advancement of Science and Art, due to open in 1859. Also inspired by Philadelphia's
example, the Maryland Institute for the Promotion of the Mechanic Arts in
Baltimore established a female department in its design school in 1854.

Following the Civil War, design schools appeared in smaller industrial cities.
In Pennsylvania, Pittsburgh, Wilkes-Barre, and Scranton between 1866 and 1868
established "daughter" schools of the Philadelphia School of Design for
Women in consultation with its principal textile designer Thomas W. Braidwood. Available evidence indicates that these Pennsylvania institutions resembled the Philadelphia model in goals, curriculum, and the character of their
supporters. Although the Wilkes-Barre and Scranton schools were short-lived,

the Pittsburgh School of Design for Women flourished until 1902, when it was absorbed by the new Carnegie Institute of Technology.

Although women reformers initially conceived design schools as charitable ventures to aid destitute women, male industrialists and business leaders financially supported these ventures because they expected practical benefits from cooperation between art and industry. Local manufacturers, to compete with well-designed European imports, needed relatively low-paid but technically skilled designers for calicos, wallpaper, carpeting, and other household materials. Women art students accepted such contract work; their pay undercut male rates but gave them higher remuneration than other women's work such as sewing or elementary **teaching**.*

Besides contributing funds to operate the schools, business sponsorship influenced design schools to train students in fashionable styles for textile and wallpaper manufacturers and in engraving techniques for magazine and newspaper illustration. Such technical design courses were balanced by training for art education, reflecting the equally important needs of the public school system. Public schools needed these teachers, in turn, so that they could offer industrial arts classes and thus help prepare future workers and consumers for their adult roles.

The largest design schools offered three curriculum tracks: normal art, with basic drawing techniques for teachers; technical design for commercial work; and the fine arts track, focused on portrait and landscape painting. Normal art graduates qualified as art supervisors in public schools and as art instructors in general **normal schools**.* Graduates from the technical course found careers in manufacturing and retail sales of household furnishings, clothing, and accessories; while fine arts graduates aspired to illustrating books and magazines, as well as to self-expression through painting and sculpture.

The design school movement predated, then overlapped with, the Arts and Crafts movement. Arts and Crafts schools established in the 1870s to 1890s offered some of the same courses as the earlier schools of ''practical design'' and have been conflated with them in the historical literature. However, women in the Arts and Crafts movement were far less likely than design school graduates to support themselves with their art. The 1850s type of charitable women's design schools served as a model for some institutions even after the more fashionable Arts and Crafts model became dominant. In 1892, for example, philanthropist Ellen Dunlap Hopkins opened the New York School of Applied Design for Women in order to offer less fortunate women the means to self-respect and independence.

By 1890, Emily Sartain of Philadelphia, from her position as principal of the largest all-female art school in the country, had established herself as an authority on art and professional training for women in art-related fields. She represented professional women in art education as a speaker at the Chicago **World's Columbian Exposition*** (1893) and in the Professional Section of the

International Congress of Women (London, 1899); she was also one of three American delegates to the first international conference on art education in Paris in 1900.

As Sartain's career illustrates, art schools conferred professional status in a cultural field once dominated by men. Women artists used formal schooling to counter the accusation of amateurism frequently leveled at them. Nineteenth-century design schools were the first institutions to offer professional certification for women in such careers as art education, fabric design, or magazine illustration; hence, the schools opened unprecedented paths to female economic independence.

Bibliography: Diana Korzenik, "The Art Education of Working Women 1873–1903," in Alicia Faxon and Sylvia Moore, eds., *Pilgrims and Pioneers: New England Women in the Arts* (1987); Kathleen McCarthy, *Women's Culture: American Philanthropy and Art* (1991); Nina de Angeli Walls, "Art and Industry in Philadelphia: Origins of the Philadelphia School of Design for Women, 1848–1876," *Pennsylvania Magazine of History and Biography*, 117 (July 1993): 179–199; Walls, "Educating Women for Art and Commerce: The Philadelphia School of Design, 1848–1932," *History of Education Quarterly*, 34 (Fall 1994): 329–355; F. Graeme Chalmers, "Fanny McIan and London's Female School of Design, 1842–57," *Woman's Art Journal*, 16 (Fall 1995–Winter 1996): 3–9.

Nina de Angeli Walls

Dewey, Harriet Alice Chipman. As cofounder of the **University of Chicago*** Elementary School and as a teacher educator, Harriet Alice Chipman Dewey (1858–1927) encouraged educational experiences for girls that would expand rather than limit their experiences. Throughout her life, Dewey continually sought to enlarge her own horizons through education and advocated equal educational opportunities for girls and women. As a women's **suffrage*** activist, she was a leader in organizing education efforts of the National Woman Suffrage Association, particularly to educate young college and African American women. As an international spokeswoman, she met with women in China and Japan to encourage their activism and lobbied their leaders for educational reform that would include girls and women.

Alice Dewey was born in Fenton, Michigan, and raised by her maternal grandparents. As a young woman, she graduated in music from a local Baptist seminary and taught music in a nearby village, but it was her deep interest in philosophy that led her to the University of Michigan in 1882. While at Michigan, she was a charter member of the University Philosophical Society and a member of the Samovar Club, an informal student-faculty group whose members read and discussed literature. Unlike other social **sororities*** or fraternities, the club ignored the social class of its members upon acceptance; this policy suited Dewey, a lifelong supporter of both social and educational egalitarianism. During her junior year, she met John Dewey, who had come to Michigan to teach.

She took several courses with him, helping design at least one. In 1886, soon after Alice received her bachelor's degree, they married.

Throughout their lives, Alice and John Dewey worked together in intellectual endeavors, educational projects, and the parenting of seven children. John's interest and work in education were heavily influenced by his relationship with Alice and their mutual role as parents. They spent considerable time observing and studying their own children and developing a philosophy of education based on these observations.

At Alice Dewey's urging, in 1896 they founded The University Elementary School, otherwise known as "The Laboratory School" and "The Dewey School" at the University of Chicago where John now taught as professor of philosophy, pedagogy, and psychology. The school had sixteen pupils and two full-time teachers in its first year; eight years later, in its final year, it had 140 students, twenty-three teachers, and ten assistants. The students ranged in age from four through fifteen. Alice Dewey was both principal and Director of English at the school.

The Lab School is often cited as a prominent example of progressive education in practice, and it gave the Deweys an opportunity to test their ideas about educational methods. Alice was particularly interested in what she could learn about educational methods relating to girls and women since she was "inclined all the time to think of their bearings on the larger question of **co-education***" (letter to W. T. Harris, April 9, 1904).

Unlike common practice at the time, students at the school did not spend the majority of their time memorizing and reciting lessons. Rather, they engaged in a variety of experiences, most of them immediately practical, meaningful, and active. There was no differentiation in activities of girls and boys; for example, both used saws in the carpenter shop, cooked lunch, made looms, and subsequently used them to weave. In spring 1900, the older children put their knowledge and ability to use in successfully planning and building a house.

In 1904, the Deweys moved to New York City, where John assumed a teaching position at Columbia University. While in New York, Alice taught **teacher education*** classes at the School of Liberal Arts and Sciences. She encouraged teachers to become astute observers of children and then use what they learned about children's ways of thinking to create new ways of teaching. She believed that growth of intelligence was directly correlated with number of opportunities for meaningful engagement in a variety of experiences, but to be meaningful, experiences must connect with the child's current ways of thinking. She explained, "[N]o teacher has ever received a student without a life history" (Dewey in Mayhew Papers, undated, p. 13).

Throughout her lifetime, Dewey was an ardent champion of the woman suffrage and feminist movements. Like the rest of her work, her activism here had an educational focus. In 1910–1911, Dewey was vice president of the **National College Equal Suffrage League*** of New York, organized to collect and distribute information about suffrage to college women and alumnae.

In 1911, she boldly invited African American women to her apartment to teach about woman suffrage. This caused a protest from the landlord who did not want African Americans in a social capacity in the building. The newly founded **National Association for the Advancement of Colored People*** joined Dewey in protesting the landlord's stance.

In a February 1915 *New York Times* editorial, Dewey responded to an anti-suffrage writer by comparing his arguments against woman suffrage with those used to keep women from a college education. She challenged that:

Gentlemen then spoke for God, as he does here, to protest against the order of nature. Their so-called arguments are as whimsical and humorous to the modern reader as the hats and clothes of that day are to the modern dressmaker. And we now know that these arguments have about the same relation to the reality of the case of college education for women.

For three years, 1919–1921, Alice and John Dewey traveled to Japan and China where they both lectured and met with government leaders. Alice spoke on topics such as "The Necessity of Education of Chinese Women," "The History of the American Woman's Struggle for Voting Rights," and "The Education of Girls in America." In Tokyo, she met with women who asked about suffrage and the education of girls. She argued that since women were as intelligent and emotionally stable as men, they could be depended upon to vote at least as well as men and that any society that refuses to give girls equal educational opportunities is depriving itself of contributions of one-half its population. When the Deweys were honored with a special dinner by the governor of Hunan province in China, Alice boldly told the governor in an after-dinner speech that his province must adopt coeducation.

Alice Dewey died at her home in New York City of arteriosclerosis in 1927 at age sixty-eight. Her body was cremated.

Bibliography: Alice C. Dewey, "The Place of the Kindergarten," *Elementary School Teacher*, 3 (January 1903): 273–288; Katherine Camp Mayhew and Anna Camp Edwards, *The Dewey School* (1966); Arthur G. Wirth, *John Dewey as Educator* (1966); John Dewey, *The School and Society* (1900, rept. 1990); Robert B. Westbrook, *John Dewey and American Democracy* (1991). Alice Dewey's papers are found with the Katherine Camp Mayhew Papers, Milbank Memorial Library Special Collections, Teachers College, Columbia University, New York City.

Irene Hall

district schools. The term *district school* refers to the type of public school in the United States prior to the **common schools*** of the mid-1800s. Towns and territories were divided first into societies and then districts. Children of school age attended the school within their own district.

In 1655 a court decision in Hartford, Connecticut, required the state to educate its children: Sons were to learn to read and write, daughters to read and sew. By 1657, Massachusetts School Law required reading and writing be taught in the schools. But for the most part, females in New England were excluded from town schools until after the Revolutionary War; they were taught at home to read. In 1779 Virginia passed a school bill that included girls, and in 1789, Boston city schools opened to girls, but from April to October only. In the 1700s, girls were expected to learn to read and to sew and were educated generally only until the age of twelve.

In the early nineteenth century, district schools were organized into winter and summer terms, with winter term beginning the week after Thanksgiving and continuing for twelve, fourteen, or sixteen weeks. The only holiday within the bounds of either term was Independence Day. Winter terms were taught by a man and ran Monday through Saturday. The summer term began the first Monday of May. Mostly younger children came in the summer, as the older boys were working in the fields. There were no books for the youngest students. The summer term was taught by a woman who was addressed as "Marm." Sewing was taught in the summer, and the schools were closed every other Saturday.

No curriculum was prescribed by law but generally included spelling, reading, arithmetic, and writing, as well as geography, history, and grammar.

Both girls and boys attended district schools between the ages of four and sixteen, although most students left at age fifteen, which was the end of schooling for most girls. Boys could then study at an academy or with the local minister to prepare for college.

Discipline in district schools was most often maintained by feruling (beating with a rod). In addition, boys were often made to sit in the girls' seats and girls to sit on the masculine side, causing much embarrassment to all.

Districts were very unequal in facilities, population, teaching, curriculum, and funding. The population of school-age children within each district often ranged from less than 5 students to more than 500, causing inequality in the education of children within the same town. District schools were supported by local taxation or the state. No controls or guidelines for curriculum, teaching credentials, or testing existed. The schools were governed by a local committee or committeeman, whose duty it was to hire a teacher and see that the schoolhouse was kept in repair. Teachers generally boarded around the district. The committeeman did not report to the people or any other central authority, so hiring practices were often suspect, with members of the committeeman's family and friends often receiving employment with no consideration of their teaching credentials.

The district system in Massachusetts was finally abolished in 1882, when the common school movement succeeded in improving public education.

Bibliography: Warren Burton, *The District School as It Was* (1833); Clifton Johnson, *The Country School in New England* (1893); John S. Brubacher, ed., *Henry Barnard on Education* (1931); George Willis, William H. Schubert, Robert V. Bullough Jr., Craig Kridel, and John T. Holton, *The American Curriculum: A Documentary History* (1993).

Joan F. Pengilly

Dodge, Grace Hoadley. Founder of Teachers College, Columbia University, Grace Hoadley Dodge (1856–1914) was a lifetime advocate of education for girls and women. She was born in 1856, daughter of William E. Dodge, a wealthy and prominent businessman and philanthropist, in Manhattan Island. In 1874 Dodge left school and, having rejected traditional "coming out," involved herself instead in volunteer activities. She taught girls' Sunday school classes and organized them into a sewing and health club. She also taught sewing for the Children's Aid Society. Dodge volunteered to teach in the Kitchen Garden, a school that taught household economy to poor girls, and established the Kitchen Garden Association in 1880; its purpose was to promote domestic industrial arts among girls of the laboring classes.

In 1881 Dodge began meeting with girls working at a New York City silk factory, holding discussions on improving their lives. In 1884 she and some of the girls organized the Working Girls' Society, which held classes in health, dressmaking, and machine operation, and continued the discussions, called "practical talks." Topics included health, happiness, and how a working girl should dress; later topics expanded to immigration, organization of labor, and equalization of men's and women's salaries. They fought for respect for their work and compassion for their working conditions. By 1890, membership totaled 2,151 women. Dodge took these messages to **women's clubs,*** churches, **women's colleges,*** and any other place that would invite her. By 1894 there were five associations: New York, Massachusetts, Connecticut, Brooklyn, and Philadelphia. Dodge left the society in 1896 to spend more time pursuing educational endeavors.

In 1884 she founded the Industrial Education Association (IEA) to replace the Kitchen Garden Association, to expand its goals, and to promote industrial education for both boys and girls. Perhaps revealing some prejudices of the era, Dodge made herself vice president but sought a man as president. During this period she also served as the first woman commissioner for the New York City school board and, in spite of opposition from men on the board, worked behind the scenes to institute changes. Worried about propriety, her father insisted that Dodge be accompanied by an older woman; as a result, Mrs. Richard Olney became a commissioner also.

Although Dodge and other members of the IEA were afraid no one would be interested in their classes, when they opened their headquarters, they were mobbed by children who wanted to take sewing, cooking, and manual training after school hours. When philanthropist George Vanderbilt donated $10,000 to the organization, Dodge hired Nicholas Murray Butler, associate professor of philosophy at Columbia University, as president. He served from 1887 to 1891.

Dodge soon became concerned about a lack of competent teachers for industrial education and changed IEA into the New York College for the Training of Teachers in order to focus on teacher preparation. Vanderbilt again donated money to purchase land for the school to move, and Columbia University moved to an adjacent site. Dodge worked tirelessly to keep the new college alive, seeking donations, writing 5,000 to 6,000 letters per year. In 1899 they incorporated as Teachers College and, in 1893, affiliated with Columbia University. For many years Dodge served as treasurer and chairman of the finance committee of the board of trustees.

In 1906 Dodge was elected president of the National Board of the **Young Women's Christian Association*** (YWCA) of the USA and spent much of her later years working with that organization. She also volunteered with the Travelers Aid Society and many other organizations. She died on December 27, 1914, in her family home in Riverdale, New York.

In spite of being a woman in a time that often did not recognize women's real accomplishments, Dodge accomplished much. Perhaps her contributions have been overlooked because she often took a lesser position in order to put a man in a position of prominence. For example, some historians have credited Nicholas Murray Butler as the founder of Teachers College. In fact, he was president, but Grace Dodge was founder. Convinced of the importance of girls and women, she devoted much of her life to their education in a variety of settings, from the shop floor to the classroom. [See also **teacher education**.*]

Bibliography: National Board of the Young Women's Christian Association, *Grace H. Dodge, a Woman of Creative Faith* (1915); Abbie Graham, *Grace H. Dodge: Merchant of Dreams* (1926); Ester Katz, *Grace Hoadley Dodge: Women and the Emerging Metropolis, 1856–1914* (1980); G. H. Dodge, *Grace H. Dodge: Her Life and Work* (1974, 1987).

Louise E. Fleming

E

Early, Sarah Jane Woodson. African American educator, temperance leader, community organizer, and advocate of racial self-help, Sarah Jane Woodson Early (1825–1907) was among the first African American women to complete a college degree and the first to teach at the college level. She was the daughter of Thomas and Jemimma (Riddle) Woodson and reputedly the granddaughter of Thomas Jefferson. Her father was an articulate proponent of black separatism and self-help in early nineteenth-century Ohio, and an activist in the African Methodist Episcopal (AME) Church. He helped found the all-black community of Berlin Crossroads, Ohio in 1830, where Sarah grew up in relative prosperity, surrounded by self-sufficient black farmers.

After completing preparatory study at a manual labor academy, in 1852 Early enrolled in **Oberlin College,*** one of only two colleges open to both women and African Americans in the 1850s. Like many college students of her era, she financed her schooling in part by **teaching*** during vacations. She completed Oberlin's Literary Degree in 1856, at age thirty, and continued teaching and serving as principal in Ohio's black communities. Her educational attainments were far in advance of most teachers, white or black, in midcentury. Her dedication and success as an educator brought an invitation in 1866 to join the faculty of **Wilberforce University,*** Xenia, Ohio, an AME institution.

Her career as the first African American woman faculty member was brief, however. After one year at Wilberforce, she accepted an offer from a Philadelphia **Quaker*** group to become principal of a school of more than 300 African American students in Hillsboro, North Carolina. She remained two or three years, meanwhile meeting Jordon Winston Early, an AME minister, and marrying him in 1868. They moved to Tennessee where Sarah continued to teach and hold principalships in Memphis, Nashville, Edgefield, and Columbia until her retirement in 1887.

Early taught and administered black schools in the North and the South for over three decades. During much of that time she also assumed the often arduous role of wife of a successful black minister, superintending the Sunday schools, raising money, and leading women's groups. She was also active in social reform, particularly temperance. Upon her retirement from education, she moved into leadership in the **temperance movement**.* In 1888 she became superintendent of the Colored Division of the Women's Christian Temperance Union (WCTU), a post she held until 1892. In one year alone her duties required her to travel over 6,000 miles across five southern states, to deliver 130 lectures and hundreds of private talks, and to write extensively on temperance and self-help.

Although there is no record of Early's position on women's **suffrage**,* she believed passionately in the propriety of women's activism and in the urgency of black women organizing for moral reform. She spent most of her life in separate black communities and organizations, and while she worked successfully in predominantly white institutions such as Oberlin and the WCTU, she appeared to have little interest in integration and no faith in white benevolence. Her commitment, imbibed from her father and her childhood experiences in Berlin Crossroads, was to racial self-help and solidarity through education, organization, and reform.

Bibliography: Sarah Woodson Early, *Life and Labors of Jordon W. Early, One of the Pioneers of African Methodism in the West and South* (1894); Ellen N. Lawson, "Sarah Woodson: Public Leader in the South," in Lawson, *The Three Sarahs: Documents of Antebellum Black College Women* (1984). Early's papers have not survived.

Ronald E. Butchart

early childhood education. Early childhood education encompasses all forms of education, educational institutions, and pedagogy for young children before they begin academic instruction in first grade. Preschool programs for children under age six include **kindergartens**,* prekindergartens, **nursery schools**,* child care and day care, parent cooperatives, and play groups. Many of these efforts were instigated, supported, and spread by women, making early childhood education especially significant in the history of women's education.

Though there has always been informal early childhood education, the movement to provide extrafamilial education for young children originated as a response to the political, industrial, intellectual, economic, and domestic revolutions that transformed Western societies in the seventeenth and eighteenth centuries. Since the early nineteenth century successive waves of social and educational reformers have attempted to universalize access to preschools. In 1816 British utopian communitarian Robert Owen started the first infant school, in Scotland. In 1837 German Romantic educator Friedrich Froebel founded the first kindergarten, in Thuringia. In 1913 British socialist Margaret McMillan opened the first nursery school, in a London slum. These movements spread to the United States, where they were taken up by female and male educators and women's education advocates such as **Elizabeth Palmer Peabody**,* Henry Barnard, and others.

The kindergarten was particularly important in the history of women's education because it was one of the most generative, inclusive, and successful of American women's movements. Kindergarten advocates Lucy Wheelock and Elizabeth Harrison founded training schools that became **teacher education*** colleges. Kate Douglas Wiggin, Nora Archibald Smith, and others started charity or "free kindergartens" in urban areas, and kindergarten mothers' meetings and classes reached women from different social class backgrounds. Kindergarten **teaching**,* training, and advocacy became an important career and educational cause for educated women, resulting in the eventual incorporation of kindergarten associations into public school systems.

The nursery school movement was more experimental, pedagogically pluralistic, and scientifically based than the kindergarten. In the early 1920s Caroline Pratt, Harriet Johnson, and **Lucy Sprague Mitchell*** organized the Bureau of Educational Experiments, in New York City, a unique data-gathering agency that included a nursery school, and a training program that became **Bank Street College**.* Female and male parent educators and psychologists such as Abigail Eliot at the Ruggles Street Nursery Training Center in Boston, Edna Noble White at the Merrill-Palmer Institute in Detroit, Helen Thompson Woolley and Lois Meek Stolz at Teachers College, Arnold Gesell at Yale University, and Ethel Puffer Howes at the **Institute for the Coordination of Women's Interests*** at **Smith College*** also developed combined preschool and training programs that included strong research components.

Despite psychological research showing the benefits of preschool and intensive children's welfare advocacy, federal support for early childhood education occurred only during times of perceived national emergency. During the 1930s depression and World War II, the government funded emergency nursery schools and children's centers to employ out-of-work teachers and provide child care for war workers.

Project Head Start was begun in 1965 as part of the War on Poverty. After more than 150 years of preschool organizing efforts, early childhood education in the United States is still a patchwork of public and private programs with access and quality correlated with income. Educated women have played a lead role in founding, running, and staffing preschools, but societal resistance to mothers of young children working outside the home and devaluing the work of female caretakers remain obstacles to extending and funding early childhood education programs. [See also **early childhood education managers**,* **early childhood teacher education**.*]

Bibliography: National Society for the Study of Education, *Twenty-eighth Yearbook: Preschool and Parental Education* (1929); Michael Steven Shapiro, *Child's Garden: The Kindergarten Movement from Froebel to Dewey* (1983); Barbara Beatty, *Preschool Education in America: The Culture of Young Children from the Colonial Era to the Present* (1995).

Barbara Beatty

early childhood education managers. An early childhood education manager is an administrator and/or supervisor of a program that may include children from birth to age eight. This person is responsible for overseeing and coordinating human and material program resources so that goals can be reached with greatest efficiency. **Early childhood education*** is among the first fields where women were able to rise to managerial positions because, historically, work with young children was one of few acceptable professions for women. Directors of early childhood education programs have usually come from **teaching**,* **social work**,* **home economics**,* or nursing, although these baccalaureate degrees rarely provide sufficient foundation for the many responsibilities and tasks they must undertake.

Organizational structure, sponsorship, and funding for early childhood education programs is quite diverse, leading to a variety of managerial formats. In small child care centers, administration and supervision are performed by one person, the program director. In addition, this individual often has teaching responsibilities. In larger organizations, the tasks are performed by several people, possibly at different levels of organizational hierarchy. Programming, planning budgets, personnel direction, parent involvement, and politics and public relations are areas of expertise all deemed necessary for early childhood program managers. Among the administrator's responsibilities are recruitment of children and staff, accreditation and licensure, maintenance of health and safety standards, daily operations, development and implementation of educational policy, program evaluation, communication, and setting the center's "tone." Supervisory tasks include oversight of program content and quality of staff interactions with children and families.

A majority of directors of early education programs are women. They usually are promoted from the "operations" or educational area, with little or no preparation or training for their new responsibilities. Early historical accounts show that there were no schools of administration; therefore, prospective directors of programs for young children learned to teach and manage by apprenticing themselves to prominent early childhood educators (**kindergarten*** or **nursery school*** teacher/directors) or to the teacher training departments of their schools. Upon completion of the training program, they returned to their home community and opened a school based upon what they had studied and practiced. They became at once a teacher of young children, a program manager, and, often, a teacher-trainer. This model of management training for women persisted from the inception of programs for young children through the 1960s. Middle- and upper-class women "of means" became day nursery reformers. They created and maintained nurseries for children from families of limited resources, served as the day nursery managers/administrators (but did not run daily operations), and some became leaders in related local and national organizations, including **Patty Smith Hill*** and Anna Bryan. The fact that women managers were training other women to assume administrative and supervisory roles is unique in the history of women's education. More recently, both men and women have assumed this function.

Much of management training occurred through observation and demonstration; therefore, there are few written records of early childhood management training prior to the 1960s. Notable exceptions are descriptions of the management of federally funded WPA (Works Progress Administration) Nurseries of the 1930s and the Lanham Act Child Care Centers of World War II, chronicled by James L. Hymes, Jr., in his *Living History* book series. Prior to 1965, there were few, if any, formal efforts to guide and train managers of early education programs. Kindergarten teacher training institutions included classroom management and administration, but not program administration, in their coursework. No books on child care management were available. With the advent of Head Start and Title XX Day Care in the 1960s, systematic professional development opportunities for program managers became available through workshops, courses, and written materials.

Since the 1960s, emphasis for early childhood education managers has changed dramatically from a focus on program knowledge to a broad range of fiscal, regulatory, personnel-related, team-building, assessment, and organizational knowledge. A few undergraduate and a greater number of graduate programs include administration and supervision. A few institutions offer master's degrees in early childhood education management. However, the great majority of program directors continue to rely upon workshops, individual courses, and publications for their professional education. The magazine *Child Care Information Exchange* has become a forum for dissemination of both theoretical and practical knowledge.

Approximately fifteen early childhood management texts have been published since 1965. These books provide in-service training for directors with no previous exposure to principles of effective administration and supervision. A mid-1990s movement toward implementation of a credential for directors highlights the paucity of educational opportunities available for those who hold or seek a management position. Such a director's credential would serve dual purposes of recognizing professionalism of effective directors and stimulating directors to improve their performance. Additionally, credentialing directors would increase public respect for the field of early childhood education. Thus, this field that first placed women in managerial roles now seeks broader acknowledgment and acceptance through credentialing, a process in which education can serve as the vehicle for goal achievement.

Bibliography: M. S. Host and P. B. Heller, *Day Care #7: Administration, United States Department of Health, Education and Welfare, Office of Child Development* (1971); A. Pagano, "The Role of the Manager of Early Childhood Programs," in B. Persky and L. H. Golubchick, eds., *Early Childhood Education* (1977); Blythe F. Hinitz, "Managing Child Care Programs: An Historical Perspective," in Persky and Golubchick, *Early Childhood Education*, 2nd ed. (1991); F. O'C. Rust and J. S. Delano, "Supervision and

Administration of Early Childhood Programs,'' in L. R. Williams and D. P. Fromberg, eds., *Encyclopedia of Early Childhood Education* (1992); National Institute for Early Childhood Professional Development, National Association for the Education of Young Children, Symposium Notes, ''Advancing Career Development in the Era of New Federal/State Relationships: New Developments in Director Credentialling,'' *Fifth Annual Conference* (June 6–7, 1996).

Blythe S. F. Hinitz

early childhood teacher education. Early childhood teacher education is the professional field that prepares those who educate and care for children ages zero to eight in schools, center-based programs, and homes. Such programs include two-year, four-year, and five-year undergraduate degree programs, and graduate degree programs in institutions of higher education. Courses, seminars, and workshops under sponsorship of a school, college, university, or organization are also constituents of the **teacher education*** field.

The earliest American teacher education programs for those working with young children were apprenticeships in **kindergartens*** and **nursery schools**.* Master teachers such as **Susan Blow**,* **Patty Smith Hill**,* **Lucy Sprague Mitchell**,* and Abigail Adams Eliot developed teacher training departments to complement their programs for children. From the beginning, ''kindergartners'' (the term used for kindergarten teachers) and nursery school teachers considered themselves professionals whose work required specialized training. From the 1850s on, there were kindergarten training schools that served as tertiary schooling for young women who had graduated from **high school*** or **normal school**.* Kindergarten training institutions had rigorous admission standards and graduation requirements, which often exceeded those of normal schools. Some kindergarten training schools had agreements with nearby universities that permitted students to obtain baccalaureate degrees following two years of further study.

A frequently assumed criterion for entry into kindergarten training was that the candidate be female because early childhood education was one of the few acceptable professions for women during this time. Many prospectuses for kindergarten training institutions opened with a quotation from **Elizabeth Peabody***: ''To be a kindergartner is the perfect development of womanliness—a working [with God] at the very fountain of artistic and intellectual power and moral character. It is, therefore, the highest finish that can be given to a woman's education, to be educated for a Kindergartner'' (prospectus of Mathews Normal Training School, Portland, Oregon). Society frowned upon both women's work and their education; however, ''kindergartening'' was accepted because it was deemed preparation for marriage and childrearing. Parents assumed that upon marriage their daughter would leave **teaching*** to raise her own children. Among the few reasons a woman would return to teaching after marriage were becoming widowed, impoverished, or less frequently, divorced. However, a number of married kindergarten teachers later became supervisors of kindergartens or faculty members of kindergarten normal schools, **seminaries**,* institutes, or training colleges.

Teacher candidates were required to be moral and "of good character." References were sought from the young woman's pastor or principal of the last school she attended; some training programs required a six- to eight-week probationary period for faculty to assess this characteristic. Good health and fitness, refinement and "general culture," and musical ability were other important criteria; native teaching ability, sympathetic attitude toward or love for children, and mental maturity or scholarship were others.

Many of the first heads of kindergarten training institutions were women. However, as early childhood teacher education moved into normal schools, teacher training schools, and colleges and universities, men headed more and more institutions. For example, the Normal College of New York City carries the name of its former president, Thomas Hunter [see **Hunter College***]. An 1878 article in *Harper's New Monthly Magazine* describes the average student day at the Normal College. Nine o'clock morning assembly included a Bible reading and a "quotations" session in which students volunteered personally selected quotations to exercise their memories and inspire self-confidence. Regular recitations followed, consisting of four fifty-minute periods with five-minute intervals.

Preservice teachers studied Latin, German, or French; ancient and modern history; mathematics (algebra and plane geometry); sciences (physics, botany, astronomy, chemistry, zoology, geology, and mineralogy); physiology; music; drawing; penmanship; English composition; rhetoric; and English language and literature. One component of the kindergarten training program was devoted to courses in child study, psychology, or educational psychology; physiology or child hygiene; sociology or social welfare; reading of literature; children's literature and storytelling; oral composition (public speaking); music; physical culture and games or physical training or folk dances; art; ethics; biblical history; and homemaking. One training college required that three theses be written prior to graduation. Another part of the program consisted of courses in principles and philosophy of education; school management or school organization; school law; and training and practical drill in schoolroom management.

The kindergarten-specific portion of the program included principles and methods; curricula; kindergarten Gifts and Occupations and their history; songs and games or the practical study of Froebel's *Mother Plays*; and both kindergarten manual activities, also known as constructive occupations, and industrial or manual arts and handwork. "Great educators" were studied in second- or third-year courses bearing such titles as history of education and Froebelian philosophy.

Practical work was a very important part of the training. Students were required to study program planning, to develop a "program book," and then to study program making or program work. In the great majority of training programs, the morning was spent in such practical work. All required some form of daily classroom contact. On the student's individual program would be found such course titles as: observation and practice in kindergarten, observation and classroom management, and student teaching.

The third-year course prepared the kindergartner to teach at the primary level. Academic content courses included: geography, literature, philosophy of literature, myth study, language, nature study, vocal music, drawing and water color, art history, decorative design, and philosophy of architecture. Among the education courses were: reading, child culture, primary methods, primary curricula, games, grade work, intellectual philosophy, theory of teaching, school economics, and school administration.

Many of these subjects form the core of modern early childhood teacher education programs, which requires a broad foundation in general education along with a major in an academic field. Although new curricula incorporating developmentally appropriate practices, thematic integrated unit teaching, whole language, cooperative education, and technology education are found in current course catalogs, many of the basic ideas build on work of the last century.

Programs that prepare today's early childhood educators are usually found in institutions of higher education. Programs at two-year institutions often have a vocational emphasis. Some holders of associate degrees also become credentialed as Child Development Associates. This national credential verifies demonstrated competencies in thirteen functional areas. Four- and-five-year undergraduate early childhood degree programs prepare teachers of grades kindergarten through four for state licensure, as do initial programs at the graduate level. For this reason, program content is often constrained by state licensing standards and criteria. Master's and doctoral programs prepare early childhood education leaders and policymakers.

Professional organizations also play an important role in early childhood teacher education. The National Association of Early Childhood Teacher Educators, the association of professors of early childhood education and related fields, provides conferences, seminars, publications (including a journal), and a professional network for members. The National Association for the Education of Young Children (NAEYC) and the Association for Childhood Education International (ACEI) include providers and beneficiaries of professional development opportunities. NAEYC sponsors a National Institute for Early Childhood Professional Development, which holds annual leadership conferences and serves as a portfolio review agency for the National Council for Accreditation of Teacher Education.

Women have been in the forefront of the creation and maintenance of a strong early childhood teacher education system for over a century. Women and men working together, relying on principles set down and demonstrated by the first early childhood leaders, continue to broaden and deepen the system that prepares qualified candidates for a variety of professional positions working with young children and their families.

Bibliography: ''The Normal College of New York City,'' *Harper's New Monthly Magazine*, 56 (April 1878): 672–683; Bernard Spodek and O. Saracho, eds., *Early Childhood Teacher Preparation*, Yearbook in Early Childhood Education, vol. 1 (1990); Blythe F.

Hinitz, "The Transmission of Culture through Early Childhood Teacher Education in the United States and England between 1850 and 1990: Examples from Archival and Interview Research" (paper presented at the XVI Conference of the International Standing Conference on the History of Education, Amsterdam, 1994); Hinitz, "Policies and Training Frameworks for Early Childhood Education in the United States: The Child Development Associate and Other Credentialling Frameworks for Paraprofessionals" (paper presented at the Second Warwick International Early Years Conference, Coventry, England, 1996); National Association for the Education of Young Children, *Guidelines for Preparation of Early Childhood Professionals* (1996).

Blythe S. F. Hinitz

euthenics. Euthenics was a reform movement popularized just after the turn of the twentieth century to improve the human condition through bettering the environment. Sometimes confused with eugenics—the effort to enhance mankind through selective genetic breeding—euthenics shared with eugenics a belief in people's improvability. Euthenics, however, sprang from the reform side of **Social Darwinism,** * which believed that environment counted more heavily than heredity in determining human conduct. In women's education, euthenics attracted a particular notoriety through a short-lived effort at **Vassar College** * to connect women's liberal arts education to a science of homemaking.

Ellen Swallow Richards, pioneer of the scientific **home economics** * movement, coined the term *euthenics*. Richards was the first woman to receive a degree from the Massachusetts Institute of Technology (MIT), and she served for many years as its sole female faculty member. Having first studied science at Vassar, Richards furthered her work in chemistry at MIT but found few opportunities to practice as a scientist. Like many early women scientists, she assisted her husband, a young professor at MIT, in his work as a metallurgical engineer. Eventually, when MIT created a laboratory to study sanitation, Richards received a belated appointment and faculty post.

Work in sanitation allowed Richards to pursue her belief that poverty and poor urban conditions harmed people's health and learning opportunities but that these could be remedied through urban reform. She joined and sponsored efforts to improve sanitation, nutrition, housing, and housekeeping and was instrumental in the pioneer group that created the American Home Economics Association in 1908. In 1910, Richards published *Euthenics: The Science of Controllable Environment*, a book that advocated better nutrition, education, and sanitation as keys to the immediate improvement of the human condition.

Home economics followed a varied history in American schools and colleges, often becoming a place where women scientists with strong training were sidetracked into studies of homemaking. Advocates for the power of domestic science in education and women's lives were often frustrated by the lack of understanding of the field's scientific bases. Vassar College, Ellen Richards's alma mater, was more sympathetic to the potential of domestic science in women's education and, through the concerted work of its president Henry Noble MacCracken, created an entire school of euthenics in 1924.

MacCracken had been warring with his board of trustees, and he used the euthenics program to assert his own vision for the college as well as to connect Vassar's liberal arts curriculum to the more practical side of women students' future lives. In this vision, MacCracken was influenced by alumna Julia Lathrop, a strong reform activist who worked with **Jane Addams*** at Chicago's **Hull-House**.* Lathrop's ideas further coincided with those of board member Minnie Blodgett, who contributed $550,000 for Vassar's division of euthenics.

MacCracken and Blodgett believed that euthenics could serve as a rallying point for many of the courses already offered on the Vassar campus, informing them with a new spirit that connected women's education to their home lives. Many faculty members disagreed, seeing the effort as a way to denigrate women's educational opportunities, forcing women back into the confines of the home. The president's vision won out, armed with the firm support of Blodgett's gift. Blodgett Hall of Euthenics was built with ample space for classrooms, demonstration rooms, auditoriums, and laboratories.

Over the next few years, other buildings and functions attached themselves to the euthenics section of campus. A **nursery school*** provided a child care option for local mothers who trained in euthenics; Vassar students learned the details of child development by providing assistance. A physical education building was added, as was a student dormitory. In all, a whole section of the campus projected Vassar's belief in the connection of home and education.

Vassar's focus on euthenics declined after the 1920s, as did smaller experiments with domestic science at other women's colleges throughout the 1920s. Home economics retained a strong popularity, particularly at the land-grant institutions where considerable numbers of female faculty and students focused their energies in the field. However, the particular effort to blend liberal arts, domestic science, and reform efforts that characterized euthenics did not withstand the waning of the **Progressive Era*** by about 1930. The combination of a declining reform movement, new collegiate interest in careers, and the growing force of a collegiate student culture weakened rigid curricular plans like the euthenics program at Vassar. [See also **science education**.*]

Bibliography: Helen Lefkowitz Horowitz, *Alma Mater: Design and Experience in the Women's Colleges from Their Nineteenth-Century Beginnings to the 1930s* (1984); John L. Rury, "Ellen Swallow Richards," in Maxine Schwartz Seller, ed., *Women Educators in the United States, 1820–1993: A Bio-Bibliographical Sourcebook* (1994); Sarah Stage, "Ellen Richards and the Significance of the Home Economics Movement," in Sarah Stage and Virginia B. Vincenti, eds., *Rethinking Home Economics: Women and the History of a Profession* (1997).

Linda Eisenmann

F

---

female literacy. *Female literacy* refers to the reading and writing skills of women. The term denotes not only "head counts" of people with technical and measurable skills but also the uses of literacy in a historical context. Often assessed in comparison with men's literacy, women's literacy nevertheless has a chronology of its own, which follows the evolution of gender roles. Furthermore, the specificity of female literacy concerns the gendered institutions of literacy, from family to school to study clubs and libraries.

Historically, the acquisition of reading skills—and to a lesser extent, writing skills—by American women depended on social attitudes toward educating women. Colonial women's literacy both lagged behind men's and improved at a slower pace. Looking at the mere ability to sign one's name, a majority of colonial women were indeed illiterate. The literacy rate stagnated during the seventeenth century, then rose by the second half of the eighteenth century, narrowing the gender gap by 1790. The relative inertia of female literacy at the beginning of the period, capping at a signature literacy rate of 45 percent of New England women after 1670 (compared to 70 percent for men), was due not only to the frontier environment, which made schooling precarious for both sexes, but also to Puritan belief in women's subservience.

Nonetheless, women's ability to read might have been more widespread than bare signing literacy indicates. During the last twenty years, historians have questioned equating literacy with signing, in part because estate documents (wills, deeds, probate records) overrepresent men and wealthy classes. Moreover, because reading instruction preceded writing instruction, many women could read but not write, and there seemed to have been no stigma attached to a woman's inability to sign. Since reading instruction did not require that the teacher know how to write, colonial children often learned to read from "nonwriting mothers," while others received instruction at **dame schools*** or "reading schools.'' In contrast, writing or penmanship remained for a long time a male teaching preserve, not taught by women.

Although most colonial period data pertain to New England, comparative studies reveal lower literacy rates in colonies more troubled by violence and disorder or affected by the constant influx of immigrants with uneven literacy skills. However, by the eighteenth century, more women in New England and elsewhere were learning better writing skills. Scholars have attributed the rise of women's literacy to several factors: the establishment of more schools early in the eighteenth century; the devotional appeal of the **Great Awakening***; and the midcentury market forces and consumerism that required farmwives to read handwriting and keep accounts. As improved schooling and rising male literacy resulted from the period of economic development and increasing population density between 1720 and 1765, so did the demand for writing skills among women, who often learned to write after leaving school. The ability to read and write did not translate into greater economic opportunities for women as it did for men, but it fostered personal independence among women of the Revolutionary period.

The post-Revolutionary era continued to promote expansion of female literacy. In particular, the ideology of **"Republican motherhood"*** encouraged the education of virtuous mothers, often through new female **academies**.* In turn, signature literacy rates soared to 80 percent for New England women by 1790. The literacy gender gap continued to be wider in rural areas than in commercial centers.

In the nineteenth century all classes of women progressively found avenues to acquire reading and writing instruction, and women's literacy rates closed the gap with men's. The rise during the first half of the nineteenth century has been attributed to improved schooling for native-born white women, but regional differences lingered. Class and rural location converged with gender to result in lower school attendance and higher illiteracy among lower-class southern women, for example. Census records, which first included a literacy question in 1840, indicate that by 1860 northern women narrowed the gender gap with only a 6 percent illiteracy rate (4 percent for northern men). In contrast, southern women trailed both southern men and northern women with an illiteracy rate of 15 percent (11 percent for southern men).

Antebellum moral reforms such as school reform produced better educational attainment and in turn feminized the **teaching*** profession [see **feminization***]. Although operating under the ideology of **separate spheres**,* reformers like **Catharine Beecher*** saw teaching as a nurturing occupation for young single women before following their true vocation as mothers. In the pre–Civil War decades, women came to make up the majority of the teaching force from Massachusetts to the western frontier [see **pioneer women teachers***].

To be sure, the ideology of universal literacy excluded enslaved African Americans, who were forbidden to learn to read and write. Those who did risked harsh punishment, even amputation of a finger. Some slaves, however, fought to gain literacy or learned to read the Bible because white slave owners or missionaries taught them. Historians estimate the literacy rate among former slaves at 5 to 10 percent. The link of literacy with white privilege and freedom explains the drive of African Americans for education and their campaign for free schooling in the post–Civil War era. Also, because of gender restrictions in other professions, a significant number of African American women became teachers during Reconstruction, which incidentally reveals hidden literacy during **slavery**.* The task of the next century was to close the racial literacy gap, reducing the black illiteracy rate that was close to 80 percent in 1870 and 70 percent in 1880 to merely 1.6 percent (including elderly illiterates) by 1979.

Further improvement toward mass literacy was the work of late nineteenth-century women's networks. In the 1890s the first generation of highly educated women created the so-called maternal commonwealth. **Jane Addams**'s* leadership in the **settlement house movement*** contributed to cultural assimilation of poor immigrants in American cities, while **M. Carey Thomas*** crusaded for educational equality through **women's colleges**.* Advanced literacy was also achieved by the **women's study club*** movement, which benefited white middle-class American women. Inspired by Reading Parties in early nineteenth-century Boston and **Margaret Fuller**'s* Conversations on literature and culture, post–Civil War clubwomen met in each other's homes to study literature, art, and history [see **reading circles***].

African American women, too, applied their skills to social action through black **women's clubs*** for elevation of their sex and advancement of the race. The numbers of clubwomen from all class and racial backgrounds were not insignificant. Between 1880 and the mid-1920s, about 2 million women joined clubs for self-improvement and philanthropy. At the same time, the rise of mass-circulation magazines such as *Ladies' Home Journal* confirmed the importance of a female readership in the new consumer economy. In sum, from the beginning to the end of the nineteenth century, expansion of women's "proper sphere" underscores the gendered uses of literacy. Unlike their silent foremothers of early America, literate nineteenth-century women used reading and writing skills to effect social reforms.

Finally, in the last hundred years women have been helped to gain equality in literacy by various institutions of literacy—from schools to libraries to publishing companies. While rudimentary literacy has been almost universal in the twentieth century, different tests have led to distinctions of functional literacy. Coined in the 1930s, *functional literacy* has been measured by educational attainment, moving from fourth grade in World War II to an eighth-grade level in 1960. The 1985 survey of the National Assessment of Educational Progress, which examined three types of literacy—prose, document, and quantitative—concluded that at least 10 million Americans lacked the language and literacy skills of competent fourth graders. More recently, the 1992 National Adult Literacy Survey defined literacy as "using printed and written information to function in society, to achieve one's goals, and to develop one's knowledge and potential.'' In the survey's first report titled ''Adult Literacy in America'' (1993), the Department of Education estimated the adult illiteracy rate at 21 to 23 percent, or 40 to 44 million American adults. It also indicated that 90 million American adults scored in the lowest two levels of a five-point scale, emphasizing that half the adults in the lowest level were living in poverty.

Such disturbing findings on combined adult performance, however, tend to obliterate specific data on female literacy. On the one hand, the late-twentieth-century literacy gender gap favors women, both in functional literacy tests and in school completion. But on the other, there is still a female underclass in contemporary America, for which illiteracy rates are linked with teenage pregnancies and dropout rates. Demographers and historians of education must assess the behavior and educational attainment of young females in recent history, just as they have identified a definite relationship between education and fertility in the nineteenth century. Also, more studies will further distinguish the performance of women in numerical and computer literacy from their great strides heretofore in print literacy.

Bibliography: Theodora Penny Martin, *The Sound of Our Own Voices: Women's Study Clubs, 1860–1910* (1987); E. Jennifer Monaghan, ''Literacy Instruction and Gender in Colonial New England,'' *American Quarterly*, 40 (March 1988): 18–41; Janet Duitsman Cornelius, *''When I Can Read My Title Clear'': Literacy, Slavery, and Religion in the Antebellum South* (1991); Carl F. Kaestle, ed., *Literacy in the United States: Readers and Reading since 1880* (1991); Catherine Hobbs, ed., *Nineteenth-Century Women Learn to Write* (1995).

Isabelle Lehuu

The Feminine Mystique. *The Feminine Mystique* by **Betty Friedan**,* a national best-selling book when it was published in 1963, became a social catalyst for the American women's movement of the 1960s and 1970s. In the late 1950s, Friedan began documenting a strange ''illness'' that she and countless other women were experiencing wherein they seemed to be suffering the same chronic symptoms: lethargy, anxiety, fatigue, and depression. Such symptoms were unusual considering the affluent and comfortable surroundings in which these upper-middle-class women lived. Friedan found that she and the women of her study (fellow alumnae of **Smith College***) had much in common: a college degree, a former career, two or more children, a house in the suburbs, and nothing meaningful to fill their time. These women were well-educated, highly motivated individuals who nonetheless felt that the only socially correct option in life was to resign themselves to roles as housewives and mothers.

Before *The Feminine Mystique*, many women like Friedan had struggled for years with this subtle yet debilitating disease that they were not able to name; *The Feminine Mystique* was the first book to document their unnamable problems of emptiness and lack of fulfillment. These upper-middle-class women spoke of guilt, anxiety, and shame from feeling miserable in lives that were outwardly filled with prosperity and harmony. They spoke of feeling lonely and useless in a life centered around chauffeuring children, giving dinner parties, and lunching at the club. All the glamorizing and advertising of the happy homemaker in mainstream American culture could not make homemaking into a fulfilling occupation for these women. Before *The Feminine Mystique* exposed the prevalence of these problems, women assumed they were completely alone and voiceless in their dissatisfaction.

Although psychologists and popular writers referred to the "trapped housewife" syndrome and "the housewife's fatigue" as symptoms of the "problem that has no name," Betty Friedan certainly had named the problem. *The feminine mystique* was the term she gave to the distorted image of the modern woman and the mentality she maintained during the years following World War II. From her research, Friedan explained that during the war women had been encouraged to enter the labor force, soon discovering financial and social independence. When the war ended, however, and men returned home, women essentially were forced to retire, hand over their jobs to men, and retrace their steps back to the domestic realm.

Such popular publications as *McCall's* and *Redbook* magazines frequently printed articles and fiction extolling the virtues of keeping a clean home, rearing perfect children, and being a dutiful wife. In a society shaken by the dislocations of war, the new mass media seemed to perpetuate women's dependence on husband and children as the way to define and give meaning to life. Friedan analyzed these images of the postwar housewife, contrasting them with those of the prewar and wartime eras when the media portrayed women as courageous heroines and independent workers. In *The Feminine Mystique*, Friedan noted that the influence of Freudian psychology had become so mainstreamed that women feared being accused of penis envy if they even desired to work outside the home. Ironically, though, it was quite likely that their own mothers had worked through the Great Depression and the World War II years with a sense of independence and equality.

The Feminine Mystique was a book of great significance in the vanguard of the 1960s women's movement. Its words struck a deep-rooted chord in a generation of socially tranquilized women and spurred them into raising their voices again in American society. *The Feminine Mystique* became a best-seller by addressing the growing national need for a women's civil rights movement. Friedan herself became a household name, and she was a prominent figure on the lecture circuit as well as a founder of the **National Organization for Women*** in 1966.

Following publication of the book, a collective sigh of relief and recognition was heard among women who had felt stifled educationally, professionally, and socially. Women realized they were not alone in wondering, "Is this all there is?" The book ignited a revolution among women and sent them off to search and listen to those voices of liberation inside themselves that had been squelched for so many years, voices that propelled women to fight for and to demand equality in all facets of American society.

Bibliography: Judith Hole and Ellen Levine, *Rebirth of Feminism* (1971); Pam McAllister, *This River of Courage: Generations of Women's Resistance and Action* (1991); Joan Kennedy Taylor, *Reclaiming the Mainstream* (1992); Elizabeth Fox-Genovese, *Feminism Is Not the Story of My Life* (1996).

Meredith Bouldin Andersen

feminization. The feminization of **teaching***—that is, the transformation of teaching from a predominantly male to predominantly female occupation—was a process set in motion early in the eighteenth century and accomplished by the late nineteenth century throughout the United States. In New England, where women first became the majority of teachers, women held 40 percent of all teaching positions before the Civil War and increased their presence to 80 percent of all teachers by 1880. Feminization, however, meant more than a statistical change: It also included modification of ideas concerning which gender could best teach. Formerly, conceptions of men's superior intellect and godliness mandated that only men could teach effectively. By the mid-nineteenth century, new formulations of the cult of domesticity stipulated that females were the superior instructors.

Current explanations for the feminization of teaching range from those that employ neoclassical economic models of supply and demand to those that use arguments that posit a cultural connection between mothering and teaching. Economic models predominate, stressing demand factors such as the increased need for teachers in the nineteenth century due to school reform, or supply-side factors such as the increased number of educated women from the growth of female **academies**.* But the process is so historically contingent and embedded in other social changes, such as industrialization, that it eludes straightforward applications of neoclassical supply and demand models. More fruitful investigations should search deeper into the historical context, recognizing that a full understanding of feminization depends on a close empirical study of the interplay among many social forces.

Historical analysis makes clear that feminization came about, in part, from the actions of a number of actors. **Horace Mann*** and Henry Barnard perceived female teachers as crucial to school reform and actively attempted to persuade local school committees to hire more women, arguing that women's ''nature'' made them the preferred teachers. **Catharine Beecher,*** advocating the advancement of women, also strove to increase the number of female teachers by employing similar arguments. Nineteenth-century women, themselves, perceiving teaching as a way to lead independent, self-improving lives, sought teaching positions. Significantly, many female teachers did not believe that women's nature especially equipped them for teaching, though such beliefs may have persuaded school committees to hire them.

Feminization occurred while teaching was becoming a profession and had a profound impact upon the outcome: Teaching never developed into a profession that bestowed upon its members the autonomy and control found in the legal and medical professions [see **legal education**,* **medical education***]. Rather, teaching developed characteristics of a women's profession [see **semiprofessions***]. Like nurses and **social workers**,* teachers began to work under the control of bureaucracies, which denied them authority over policy. At the same time, state school officials turned over **teacher education**,* once the responsibility of private female academies, to state-controlled **normal schools**.*

Feminization had other effects on women's education. By arguing that women teachers needed higher education, Catharine Beecher and **Mary Lyon*** raised money for the **Hartford Female Seminary*** and **Mount Holyoke Female Seminary**,* respectively. At the same time, for women attending early female academies and **seminaries**,* teaching furnished an opportunity for employment after graduation when jobs for educated women were scarce. In the first graduating classes of Mount Holyoke, more than 50 percent of the women assumed teaching positions. Teaching also provided funds for women to attend female academies and seminaries; frequently, women worked in **district schools*** between academy sessions to earn money for tuition.

In the nineteenth century, the feminization of teaching had a profound influence on the teaching profession, on female higher education, and on women's employment opportunities. These influences continued into the twentieth century with the persistence of teaching as women's work. School bureaucracies still oversee the work of female teachers, women still predominate in teacher education programs, and schools still remain a major employer of women.

Another aspect of feminization in education, not connected directly to the increase in female teachers, is the perceived feminization that occurred when women's share of collegiate enrollment neared 50 percent early in the twentieth century. Women's entry into higher education had lagged behind men's because of societal pressures against their participation. However, after 1900 women began to attend colleges and universities in much greater numbers; by 1920 women constituted 47.3 percent of collegiate enrollments. Fearing feminization of the campuses, especially of liberal arts courses, many administrators imposed restrictive measures including **quotas*** or changes to the curricula that limited the number of women. Stanford University and the **University of Chicago*** were two of the best-known cases where officials instituted limits on women's participation. Other schools that had been coeducational [see **coeducation***], such as Wesleyan University, closed their doors to women or segregated them into **coordinate colleges**.* Many of these quotas continued formally and informally for decades, raising questions even into the era of **affirmative action*** and **Title IX**.*

Bibliography: Barbara Miller Solomon, *In the Company of Educated Women: A History of Women and Higher Education in America* (1985); Myra Strober and Andrea Lanford, "The Feminization of Public High School Teaching: Cross-sectional Analysis, 1850–

1880,'' *Signs: Journal of Women in Culture and Society*, 11 (1986): 212–235; Richard Altenbaugh, ed., *The Teacher's Voice* (1993); Jo Anne Preston, "Domestic Ideology, School Reformers, and Female Teachers: Teaching Becomes Women's Work in Nineteenth-Century New England," *New England Quarterly*, 66 (1993): 531–551; Preston, "Gender and the Formation of a Profession: The Case of Public School Teaching," in Jerry Jacobs, ed., *Gender Inequality at Work* (1994); Sari Knopp Biklen, *School Work: The Cultural Construction of Teaching* (1995).

Jo Anne Preston

Field Matron Program. The Field Matron Program (1890–1938), an effort that sent women to Indian reservations to train native women in Euro-American homemaking skills including cooking, sewing, cleaning, and child care, was established by the Office of Indian Affairs (OIA, later the **Bureau of Indian Affairs***) in 1890. The OIA was charged with overseeing the education and acculturation of the Indian population of the United States. The premise of the Field Matron Program was that native women's traditional knowledge was useless and must be replaced with "superior" values associated with Euro-American womanhood. Field matrons were also instructed to serve as role models for native girls returning to the reservation after attending off-reservation boarding schools.

Field matrons were directed by the OIA to encourage native women to participate in Christian religious activities. Many of the matrons had worked as missionaries and considered religious teaching central to their role as field matrons.

In order to become a matron, a woman had to be of good moral standing and well educated. She needed to pass a civil service examination that included questions about housekeeping as well as English, U.S. history, and geography. Most matrons were middle-aged and were or had been married, many to local OIA-employed schoolteachers. Most matrons did not have children, which were viewed as a liability by the OIA. If a woman had children, it was felt she should be spending full time as a wife and mother.

Although the majority of women in the Field Matron Program were Euro-American, a small percentage were Native American. Between 1895 and 1927, thirty-four native women served as matrons, while over 400 Euro-American women served. Many of the native field matrons had attended off-reservation boarding schools such as **Carlisle Indian School.*** While the OIA acknowledged that some native women were qualified to serve as field matrons, it rarely permitted a native woman to serve as a matron among her own tribe, believing that a young woman would not have sufficient authority and objectivity to work with her own people.

Bibliography: Rebecca Herring, "The Creation of Indian Farm Women: Field Matrons and Acculturation on the Kiowa-Comanche Reservation, 1895–1906," in John Wunder, ed., *At Home on the Range: Essays on the History of Western Social and Domestic Life* (1985); Martha Knack, "Philene Hall, Bureau of Indian Affairs Field Matron: Planned

Culture Change of Washakie Shoshone Women," *Prologue: Quarterly of the United States National Archives*, 22 (1990): 150–167; Lisa Emmerich, " 'Civilization' and Transculturation: The Field Matron Program and Cross-Cultural Contact," *American Indian Culture and Research Journal*, 15 (1991): 33–48; Emmerich, " 'Right in the Midst of My Own People': Native American Women and the Field Matron Program," *American Indian Quarterly*, 15 (Spring 1991): 201–217.

Jo Ann Woodsum

Fisk University. Fisk University, originally called the Fisk Free Colored School, was two years old during the Tennessee race riots of 1868 in which twelve schoolhouses for black children were burned, a man was whipped for teaching eight boys to read, and one hundred Klansmen rode on horseback through downtown Nashville. Despite the fact that the post–Civil War years "were bitter and fearful ones—a time of intimidation, bigotry, lynchings, and murder—both teachers and students at Fisk were optimistic and students came by the hundreds" (p. 7), according to Fisk historian J. M. Richardson. This enrollment, signifying the passion with which former slaves throughout the South embraced education, was augmented by the Tennessee School Law of 1867, which mandated free, but segregated, elementary education. Although that legislation was denounced by Fisk's founders John Ogden, Edward P. Smith, and Erastus Cravath as "an attempt to pander to wicked prejudices" (Richardson, p. 9), it solidified the university's importance as a training ground for black educators.

From the beginning, coeducational Fisk never lacked applicants; however, low tuition, generous financial aid, and insufficient funding by sponsors (the **American Missionary Association*** and the Freedmen's Bureau) failed to meet expenses. With money and resources perennially in short supply, Fisk students were proactive in generating revenue. The first graduating class reputedly gathered rusty handcuffs from Nashville's former slave market and sold them as scrap metal to purchase textbooks. In 1876, the Fisk Jubilee Singers were founded to help raise money; in their travels through Europe, they introduced the spiritual to the world as a unique African American art form.

From its inception, Fisk was intended to be a first-class liberal arts college rather than a vocational institute. Its mission was to educate what W.E.B. Du Bois called the "talented tenth," or the black elite, for community leadership. By 1873, Fisk offered a rigorous program of Latin and Greek, mathematics, German, French, natural philosophy (physics), history, and political science. Although many graduates entered the professions, a large percentage became teachers; during the 1870s it was estimated that over 10,000 children in every state of the South were taught by Fisk graduates.

In many ways, Fisk is representative of the historically black schools founded after the Civil War. Although Fisk always practiced **coeducation**,* admitting women and men on an equal basis, for many years rules regarding women's conduct were more stringent. For example, women remained in the dining room until men were dismissed; women's lights were shut off at 10 P.M.; and the women's dress code filled three pages of the 1928 Handbook, which stated that "the Fisk girl of today aspires to a high standard of womanliness which includes scholarship, good health, justice and fair play, self-control, a love of beauty, and courtesy to all."

Fisk's reputation as one of the most academically challenging black colleges received empirical support in 1900 when its famous alumnus Du Bois statistically evaluated schools based on entrance requirements and concluded that Fisk was only one or two years behind prestigious New England colleges—a strong accomplishment in that era. In 1913, Fisk administrators organized a conference of top-rated black schools to discuss entrance requirements; from this meeting emerged the Association of Colleges for Negro Youth, the first step toward standardization and quality control in historically black colleges.

In the early twentieth century, social, economic, and political change had a negative impact on black education, and Fisk dealt with typical issues. Up to this point, the black intelligentsia had been groomed in church-sponsored, liberal institutions designed to educate egalitarian leaders who would fight for civil rights. As religious denominations became increasingly unable to support these schools, however, wealthy industrialists began to finance black education. Although they gave some assistance to colleges like Fisk, they favored a socially conservative, vocational curriculum such as that offered by **Tuskegee*** and **Hampton Institutes**.* Booker T. Washington, who endorsed this position, was rewarded by generous support for his institution and the other vocational schools that he favored.

Washington's intellectual opponent, Du Bois, objected to vocationalizing black education, claiming that "to use Fisk for **vocational education*** would be like using a surgeon's knife for chopping wood. . . . The world needs wood but it has axes for cutting it" (Du Bois, p. 28). Similarly, he protested Fisk's refusal to allow fraternities as another blow to black autonomy, maintaining that "fraternities and **sororities*** are offering scholarships and prizes to colored graduates. Fisk University has no right . . . to ban these powerful and influential organizations." Du Bois criticized the administration for disbanding **student government**,* suspending publication of the *Fisk Herald* (the oldest student publication among black colleges), reorganizing the board of trustees along more conservative lines, and forbidding a chapter of his own organization, the **National Association for the Advancement of Colored People**.*

These changes had been made by Fisk presidents seeking to conform to the social agendas of powerful donors who feared that the mass migration of people of color to northern cities and the rise in black nationalism after World War I threatened the industrial status quo. In the end, Du Bois's philosophy prevailed, and "although it suffered financial consequences for a few more years, Fisk adhered to the cause of higher education. . . . [W]hen the balance swung back toward college instruction, the school was in an excellent position to build on an even stronger foundation" (Richardson, p. 61).

Women have made significant contributions to Fisk, distinguishing themselves in education, politics, law, science, religion, literature, and the military. They include **Margaret Murray Washington*** (class of 1889), who married Booker T. Washington and was instrumental both in developing Tuskegee Institute and in persuading Andrew Carnegie to donate a library to her own alma mater; and Hazel O'Leary, Secretary of Energy in the Clinton administration. Also in the political and educational arenas, alumnae include Constance Baker Motley (class of 1944), who became New York's first black female federal judge and state senator, and Althea Brown Ediston (class of 1901), a missionary to Central Africa who compiled a dictionary and grammar for the Bukuba Tribe. Another noted alumna was Du Bois's own daughter, Yolanda, who almost did not graduate due to her father's outspokenly feminist commencement speech in which he complained that "college women are put in uniforms in a day when we reserve uniforms for lackeys, insane asylums, and jails" and that "we base female eligibility for marriage on exotic personal beauty and childlike innocence, and yet pretend to desire brains." Finally, poet Nikki Giovanni, who founded a chapter of the Student Nonviolent Coordinating Committee on campus and was expelled because "her attitudes weren't in accord with a Fisk woman" (Ihle, p. 12), returned to graduate in 1967.

Bibliography: C. S. Johnson, *The Negro College Graduate* (1938); W.E.B. Du Bois, *The Education of Black People: Ten Critiques, 1906–1960* (1973); V. P. Franklin and J. D. Anderson, *New Perspectives on Black Educational History* (1978); J. M. Richardson, *A History of Fisk University, 1865–1946* (1980); J. D. Anderson, *The Education of Blacks in the South, 1860–1935* (1988); E. L. Ihle, *Black Women in Higher Education* (1992).

Cynthia Davis

freedmen's teachers. The American Civil War (1861–1865) resulted in the emancipation of over 4 million African American slaves. While they were technically freed by the Emancipation Proclamation (1863), in fact, tens of thousands had freed themselves earlier, beginning with the earliest days of the war. The former slaves quickly came to be known as the freedmen.

Caught in the terrors and dislocations of warfare, destitute and suffering, the freed people needed immediate relief in the form of clothing, food, and medicine. In the long term, they required protection and the right of self-protection, access to land and economic opportunity, and training for their new economic and political position in postbellum society. In the effort to meet at least some of those pressing needs, thousands of teachers, primarily women, journeyed into the American South to spend anywhere from a few weeks to decades working among the former bondsmen.

The earliest freedmen's teachers were not northerners, however, but southern African Americans, women and men, many of whom had been teaching covertly in the heart of **slavery*** for years. Jane A. Deveaux and Simeon W. Beard in Georgia, George F. T. Cook and John F. Cook in Washington, D.C., Anna Bell Davis and Mary S. Peake in Virginia, among others, continued **teaching**,* more openly, as soon as Union forces occupied their towns or cities. By early 1862, northern teachers, mostly women, began to move into areas secured by the military to provide relief and assistance and to establish schools wherever learners could be brought together.

From the beginning, the African American response to the opportunity for literacy and the other fruits of education was overwhelming. The northern voluntary and missionary organizations sponsoring the teachers could not meet the demand. Classrooms were crowded with students of all ages. Throughout the 1860s, teachers routinely reported classrooms numbering from a few dozen to a hundred or more, ranging in age from five to eighty. Hundreds of young freed adult women and men began teaching their own schools after four or five years of study, to extend the opportunity of education to still more of their people.

The original corps of teachers who went into the South to work among the ex-slaves was predominantly female. Roughly three-quarters of the teachers were women. The race of the teachers was a significant factor, however: White women accounted for four of every five white teachers and remained longer in the freedmen's schools than white men; among northern African American teachers, on the other hand, nearly half were men, and both female and male black teachers remained longer in the South than whites. Remarkably, though African Americans accounted for less than one-twentieth of the northern population, they constituted roughly one-eighth of the northern teachers.

The freedmen's teachers are often characterized as young, affluent, single women. Yet the average freedmen's teacher was over thirty years old when she first made her way across the Mason-Dixon Line; black northern teachers were significantly younger. She was as likely to come from the genteel poor as from the comfortable middle class. Few were wealthy. One-fifth of the women were married; most were experienced educators. Despite their social class standing, the women had achieved a higher level of schooling than was common for their day. Traditional stereotypes of the freedmen's teachers imply that the teachers had the leisure for social dilettantism; the reality suggests a willingness to disrupt established lives and risk economic hardship for a cause.

The work among the freed people was dangerous, isolating, challenging, and poorly remunerated. Southern whites generally opposed the effort to educate African Americans and expressed their antipathy through ostracism, intimidation, and occasional violence. Schools were held in cramped cabins, drafty sheds, abandoned plantation houses, or church sanctuaries, without student desks, adequate books, or ordinary teaching aides such as blackboards and slates. Many teachers taught daytime classes, evening school for working adults, and Sunday school. They also distributed donated clothing, advised the freedmen regarding contracts and domestic arrangements, wrote letters for the illiterate, and cajoled northern friends to donate supplies and money.

The women among the first generation of freedmen's teachers established many of the educational institutions that served southern African Americans for the next century. Laura Towne and Ellen Murray, beginning their work in 1862, launched Penn School on St. Helena Island, South Carolina, and taught there for the next four decades. Caroline Putnam founded the Holley School, Lottsburg, Virginia, in 1868, remaining at the school nearly five decades. Martha Schofield, who began teaching the freed people in 1865, established the Schofield Normal and Industrial School in 1871 in Aiken, South Carolina, where she remained for forty-five years. Lucelia Williams helped create **Hampton*** Normal and Agricultural Institute; after disagreements with Samuel Chapman Armstrong regarding the intellectual capacity and needs of African Americans, she went to Jacksonville, Florida, to found Stanton Normal School. Cornelia Hancock erected the Laing School in Mt. Pleasant, South Carolina, in 1866. Rachel C. Mather founded the Mather School in South Carolina where she labored from 1867 to her death, thirty-six years later. Alida Clark was the driving force in building Southland College in Helena, Arkansas, working there from 1864 to 1887. Sarah A. Dickey had been teaching the freed people for eight years when she founded Mt. Hermon Seminary in Mississippi, patterned after **Mount Holyoke Female Seminary**.* She remained at its head until her death in 1904. Hundreds of other women established schools that were eventually absorbed into the emerging southern school systems. Scores served as principals and occasionally as superintendents. With notable exceptions, when men remained in southern black education, they generally became presidents and professors in the new black colleges; women remained in the less prestigious, but perhaps ultimately more important, work of elementary, secondary, and teacher training schools.

In the first decade of freedmen's education, over 6,000 women and men taught among the freed people. Their intentions varied. Racial solidarity impelled northern African American teachers to the South, but questions of racial justice or the social or civic future of African Americans appear seldom to have motivated white teachers. White teachers most often responded to missionary impulses or a general desire for usefulness. White men occasionally used freedmen's education to achieve political or economic ends. A few of the women teachers may have sought to realize, through teaching in southern black schools, the dangers, valor, and patriotic meaning that men presumably experienced in the war. Many women, black and white, found ample opportunities to exercise leadership and initiative. Whatever their intentions, the freedmen's teachers were courageous and resourceful. They contributed to the transition from slavery to freedom by vastly expanding southern black literacy and laying the foundations for southern public education. [See also **American Missionary Association**,* **female literacy**.*]

Bibliography: Ronald E. Butchart, *Northern Schools, Southern Blacks, and Reconstruction: Freedmen's Education, 1862–1875* (1980); Jacqueline Jones, *Soldiers of Light and Love: Northern Teachers and Georgia Blacks, 1865–1873* (1980); Robert C. Morris, *Reading, 'Riting, and Reconstruction: The Education of Freedmen in the South, 1861–1870* (1981); Butchart, ''Perspectives on Gender, Race, Calling, and Commitment in Nineteenth-Century America: A Collective Biography of the Teachers of the Freedpeople,

1862–1875,'' *Vitae Scholastica*, 13 (Spring 1994): 15–32. See also the American Missionary Association Archives, Amistad Research Center, Tulane University.

Ronald E. Butchart

Friedan, Betty Goldstein. Author and activist Betty Friedan (1921–) is credited with igniting the spark of the modern American women's movement in the 1960s. Through her book *The Feminine Mystique** (1963), Friedan rejected the prevailing ideology that upper-middle-class women were satisfied to abandon education and career for the exclusive roles of housewife and mother. Instead, Friedan exposed and named a debilitating disease that she termed ''the problem with no name,'' calling this ennui ''the feminine mystique.'' In this name, she was referring to the mystery of why the overwhelming majority of middle-class women were sacrificing education and career to become housewives and mothers, only to find themselves dissatisfied and miserable, even while surrounded with material comforts. As her book hit the best-seller list, Friedan herself was thrust into the spotlight, heralded as the leader of this new feminist movement.

Born in Peoria, Illinois, Friedan grew up in an upper-middle-class home where both parents had careers. Like her mother, who was a former editor for the women's page of the Peoria newspaper, Friedan grew up using her journalistic talents and became a labor journalist in New York in 1942 after studying social science and psychology at **Smith College*** and Berkeley. She later lost this job because of her second pregnancy during her marriage to Carl Friedan. Betty Friedan then renounced her life in the working world, consigning herself to a New York suburb chauffeuring children, giving dinner parties, and attending Parent-Teacher Association (PTA) meetings just as the other women in her social circle did.

Intensely dissatisfied with this life, Friedan began documenting facts about the ''trapped housewife'' and ''housewives' fatigue.'' She began writing about the boredom and dissatisfaction she felt and saw in many other women. Through publication of her book, which exposed problems of the modern housewife, she started a revolution across the country among popular writers, psychologists, and women who were also ready to challenge prevailing stereotypes. Her newly found confidence as author of this new feminist bible propelled Friedan to help establish NOW, the **National Organization for Women,*** which advocates educational, social, and political rights for women. Friedan helped found the organization in 1966 and served as its first president until 1970.

Friedan continued the campaign for women's causes through her work in the National Women's Political Caucus in 1971, the International Feminist Congress, and the National Women's Strike for Equality. She was also active in the unsuccessful movement to ratify the Equal Rights Amendment. Friedan has written two other books, *The Second Stage* (1981) and *The Fountain of Age* (1993). *The Second Stage* is seen by many as a reversal of the doctrines she set forth in *The Feminine Mystique*, as she urges women to be less judgmental and more tolerant toward all women and to respect their choices about working outside the home and having children. *The Fountain of Age* is Friedan's perspective on how women age, physically and psychologically.

Friedan's work and dedication to women's causes have been a strong influence on American women in the last half of the twentieth century. Much of what she wrote and campaigned for in the 1960s and 1970s has helped women in the 1980s and 1990s carve a firm place for themselves in the bedrock of American society, in education, in the workplace, and in the political arena.

Bibliography: Judith Hole and Ellen Levine, *Rebirth of Feminism* (1971); Pam McAllister, *This River of Courage: Generations of Women's Resistance and Action* (1991); Joan Kennedy Taylor, *Reclaiming the Mainstream* (1992); Elizabeth Fox-Genovese, *Feminism Is Not the Story of My Life* (1996).

Meredith Bouldin Andersen

Fuller, Margaret. Margaret Fuller (1810–1850) was a prominent intellectual and critic of the mid-1800s, best known for her feminist essay *Woman in the Nineteenth Century* (1845). A driven and dedicated scholar, Fuller critiqued literature, art, and social issues, arguing for the intellectual equality of women. In her time she gained a worldwide reputation as a critic and stunning conversationalist and is acknowledged as one of the first American feminists.

Born on May 23, 1810, to Timothy and Margaret Crane Fuller in Cambridgeport, Massachusetts, Sarah Margaret Fuller was the first child and lived for many years as an only child. Timothy Fuller, a lawyer and politician, gave his daughter an education that would have been considered demanding for most boys of the period, even potentially damaging for girls, as overstimulated intellects were thought to impair girls' inclinations toward domesticity and motherhood. Fuller was an exacting tutor, teaching Margaret Latin, history, literature, and mathematics when he returned from work each day. Fuller's mother was sickly and quiet, spending a great deal of her life bed-ridden, and appears not to have been much involved with her daughter's upbringing. Fuller blamed her overly demanding studies for the anxieties, headaches, and nightmares that plagued her most of her life and that also removed her from the normal society of girls her own age. In 1824, Fuller's attendance at the Misses' Prescott School in Groton, Massachusetts, proved difficult, as her classmates found her intellectual ability and forthrightness off-putting; in 1825 she returned home to stay, finished with the only formal education she would ever receive.

In 1833 the family moved from Cambridge to a farm in Groton, where Fuller became responsible for tutoring her younger brothers and sisters, as well as for the numerous chores that accompanied farm life. She found the farm's isolation difficult after the lively intellectual climate in Boston and found her domestic tasks a poor substitute. When Fuller was twenty-five, her father died of cholera, leaving Margaret with financial responsibility for her mother and nine siblings.

In 1836 her new friend, philosopher and essayist Ralph Waldo Emerson, introduced Fuller to Bronson Alcott, who offered her a teaching job at his school, The Temple School. There she taught German, French, Italian, and Latin; gave private language lessons; and fulfilled numerous other school responsibilities to help support her family. When scandal surrounding Alcott's liberal ideas caused enrollment at his school to decline, Fuller's assistance was no longer needed, and in 1837 she accepted a post at the Greene Street School in Providence, Rhode Island. Her salary there was large, and her workload lighter than at Temple. She was given considerable freedom in this position and accepted the challenge of raising what she deemed a relatively low level of knowledge and intellectual skill in her new students. She taught both boys and girls of all ages and was well loved by her students; her decision to leave in 1839 was met with sadness. Fuller had been working for some time on her translation of *Eckermann's Conversation with Goethe* (1839) and felt that she could not both teach and write; it was time to return to Boston and pursue her career as a writer and thinker.

Fuller realized that women in her time were, for the most part, educated to participate in polite society, for decorative purposes, or for the entertainment of future husbands. Women were never given the chance to utilize and synthesize knowledge; Fuller felt that they had "few inducements to test and classify what they receive" (*Letters*, vol. 2, p. 87). To respond to this lack, in autumn of 1839 she began a series of meetings that she called Conversations, designed to bring women together to discuss intellectual matters. Fuller led the group in discussions of mythology, art, literature, and social issues, demanding that all participate, think, and write. These Conversations gained a great reputation in Boston and were attended by wives and daughters of Harvard professors and other intellectuals, for whom these two-hour meetings were as close to higher education as they would ever come. Fuller provided this well-loved forum for Boston women until 1844.

From 1840 to 1843 Fuller also assumed responsibility for editing the new publication of the New England Transcendentalists, *The Dial*. Though this work was supposed to pay $200 per year, her pay never materialized, while the work was a much greater burden than she had anticipated. Submissions were difficult to obtain, and Fuller was forced to fill in a great deal of text herself. Among these articles was her well-known "The Great Lawsuit," later expanded to her best-known work, *Woman in the Nineteenth Century*. This revolutionary book caused tremendous controversy, touching on such subjects as sex and prostitution but focusing primarily on how rigid gender roles for men and women limit them both. Fuller argued for the equal ability of women and men to pursue education and detailed how lack of education for women is a hardship, restricting their freedom to learn and think. She asserted that women are not made only for love, but for Truth as well, and exhorted them to claim some independence from men. While this book was widely read, discussed, and sometimes praised, Fuller also received much criticism for her radical notions.

Fuller's work on *The Dial* and her first book, *Summer on the Lakes*, caught the attention of Horace Greeley, editor of the *New York Daily-Tribune*. Greeley published Fuller's *Lakes* and offered her a post as a journalist and literary critic, making her the first American female to support herself through this type of writing. While doing journalistic work, Fuller became aware of such social problems as the effects of poverty on women, and her writings began to take an increasingly political slant. In 1846, Fuller traveled to Europe with her friends, the Springs, visiting much of Britain and settling in Italy, all the while writing articles for the *Tribune*. While in Europe she met novelist George Sand, the poet Adam Mickiewicz, political activist Giusseppe Mazzini, and the newly married Elizabeth Barrett and Robert Browning, as well as Fuller's future husband, Giovanni Ossoli, an Italian aristocrat. Through her observations and acquaintances, Fuller became increasingly involved in the rights and needs of the impoverished and disenfranchised, eventually accepting a post overseeing an Italian army hospital and tending the sick during the revolution that began in 1848.

Fuller had a child by Ossoli out of wedlock, scandalizing those of her friends who knew; it is probable the couple married before returning together with their son Angelo to the United States in 1850. The ship on which Fuller, Ossoli, and Angelo rode ran into a sandbar in a storm off Fire Island on July 19. The bodies of Angelo and Ossoli were recovered, as were a few of Fuller's letters, but neither Fuller's body nor the history of the Roman Republic on which she had been working was ever found, though friend Henry David Thoreau searched for both. Shortly after her death, her friends Emerson, William Henry Channing, and James Freeman Clarke completed her *Memoirs*, glossing over her more scandalous actions and downplaying her contributions to intellectual society. Largely through their treatment of her personal life and writings, the significance of her reputation in her lifetime was lost to later generations. Only recently have Fuller's writings been recognized as valid in their own right and her importance as a feminist and critic revivified. An ambitious intellectual and firm believer in women's rights to education, Fuller was a model and forerunner for women who later took up the torch of women's rights.

Bibliography: Julia Ward Howe, *Margaret Fuller* (1883); Mason Wade, *Margaret Fuller, Whetstone of Genius* (1940); Margaret V. Allen, *The Achievement of Margaret Fuller* (1979); Robert N. Hudspeth, ed., *The Letters of Margaret Fuller* (1983); Donna Dickerson, *Margaret Fuller, Writing a Woman's Life* (1993).

J. Susannah Shmurak

G

G. I. Bill. The Servicemen's Readjustment Act of 1944, colloquially known as the G. I. Bill, provided a variety of benefits for veterans of World War II, but the particular title of the act that allowed for subsidized tuition at colleges and universities marks the "G. I. Bill of Rights" as an important event in educational history. Contrary to popular understanding, the motivating concern behind creation of the G. I. Bill was fear of widespread unemployment rather than extension of educational opportunity. A dual significance emerged from implementation of the bill, with unfortunate results for women. First, individuals who had been previously labeled unfit for collegiate study because of age, class, or preparation, when given access to institutions of higher learning, proved their academic capacity to be at least equal to more traditional college students, in direct contradiction to the expectations of educational "experts." Second, as overall enrollments at colleges and universities increased because of veterans' participation, women's position in these institutions slipped, relative to men's. Even as women's participation rose numerically, it declined as a percentage of all students.

As historian Keith Olson details, the bill from its inception was a measure designed to stave off massive unemployment rather than an expression of gratitude to veterans. Less than a year after the United States entered World War II, the federal National Resources Planning Board established a committee to prepare for demobilization of forces at war's end. These plans led to formation of the G. I. Bill, which was supported by the American Legion, the American Council on Education, and the U.S. Congress. Opposition emanated from elite universities, through spokespersons such as James B. Conant, president of Harvard, and Chancellor Robert M. Hutchins, of the **University of Chicago**.* Fearful that the veterans' presence on their campuses would lower academic standards, Conant and Hutchins argued against using their institutions as national warehouses for surplus laborers.

In spite of such protests, response to the education component of the G. I. Bill was tremendous; 1,013,000 veterans enrolled in colleges in the fall semester of 1946, almost doubling the college population in the United States in one term. As colleges opened classrooms to the mostly male veterans, women's percentage of enrollment dropped. By 1947 approximately one out of three college students were women, following their wartime percentage of 40 percent. Since women made up less than 3 percent of the armed services, they did not benefit from the G. I. Bill in large percentages. However, they did use the bill in proportion to their representation in the service: By 1956, 64,728 of the 2,232,000 veterans (2.9 percent) served by the G. I. Bill were women.

Women's access to undergraduate, graduate, and professional schools narrowed as institutions altered their admission patterns to favor veterans. Colleges were not eager to turn away veterans, or the government subsidization of their education, and even **women's colleges*** such as **Vassar*** began to admit males. As a result, women as a percentage of all college graduates decreased, even as the number of women graduates was on the rise. For example, 77,000 women constituted 40 percent of all college graduates in 1940. Their numbers increased to 104,000 in 1950, yet this figure represented just 25 percent of total graduates. Women took 38 percent of all master's degrees awarded in 1940, but only 29 percent in 1950. Women earned 13 percent of the Ph.D.s conferred in 1940, and 10 percent in 1950 [see **graduate education***].

Restricted opportunities for women in graduate and professional school paralleled an increased emphasis on domesticity at undergraduate colleges and universities during the late 1940s and 1950s. Nearly half of the campus veterans were married; some historians suggest that this influence fueled the desire of some undergraduates to find a spouse. In any event, in the face of various societal pressures, increasing numbers of women dropped out of college in the postwar years to marry.

The great lesson of the G. I. Bill is found in its contradiction to class-bound notions of academic ability. Veterans, many of whom would otherwise have been denied access to education, established themselves as highly motivated students and as a group attained higher grade-point averages than nonveterans. The great misfortune is that this lesson came at the expense of women students. As the American College Public Relations Association noted in 1946, the G. I. Bill created a crisis for women by blocking them from their educational heritage.

Bibliography: Keith W. Olson, *The G. I. Bill, the Veterans, and the Colleges* (1974); Susan M. Hartmann, *The Home Front and Beyond: American Women in the 1940s* (1982); Barbara Miller Solomon, *In the Company of Educated Women: A History of Women and Higher Education in America* (1985).

Karen L. Graves

General Federation of Women's Clubs. The General Federation of Women's Clubs (GFWC), a national network of volunteer organizations, was organized in 1890 to unite the many community women's clubs in the United States. Jane Cunningham Croly, who had formed Sorosis, an elite women's culture club in 1868, initiated formation of the GFWC in New York City "to bring into communication with each other the various women's clubs throughout the world, in order that they may compare methods of work and become mutually helpful" (quoted in Blair, p. 95). Charlotte Emerson Brown was the first president (1890–1894), predecessor to what one scholar called a "series of sophisticated presidents" who steered the organization, fostering and encouraging its members to become involved with social, educational, and economic problems in local communities and the whole country (Scott, p. 126).

The ideal clubwoman was described as a woman who "studies family economics and home management, keeps up-to-date on consumer information, and takes part in action to protect her fellow-consumers. She strives to improve the quality of family living, looks to the well-being of her family both young and old, and stresses the spiritual value of religious beliefs" (Wells, p. 11).

This turn-of-the-century "municipal housekeeping" was mainly the purview of the white women who belonged to GFWC-affiliated clubs. In fact, at times in the federation's early history its members objected to the participation and membership of black women's clubs. The occasional black member was admitted to an all-white club, but by and large, the GFWC was a network of white women's clubs. The many black women's clubs were affiliated with the National Association of Colored Women's Clubs, which, among other goals, sought to improve white women's perceptions of blacks. Pervasive racism throughout the United States prevented the two organizations and other local clubs from integrating.

The GFWC was a "three-tiered network of organization and social communication" (Skocpol, p. 329). The first tier was the national organization, which held annual conventions, published a journal, and oversaw various departments, including Art, Civil Service Reform, Education, **Home Economics**,* Public Health, and Industrial and Child Labor. The second tier contained the state organizations, which also held annual conventions. Thousands of clubs then operated at the local level focusing on cultural and civic concerns. The work of the GFWC, an outgrowth of the **women's club movement**,* influenced schools, health reform, and industry standards, took part in and supported cultural events, and established public libraries and scholarships. Affiliated clubs supported conservation and preservation efforts, such as in the Palisades of the Hudson River (1896), reforestation efforts, and supported legislation to create the National Park Service (1916). With its growing emphasis on social reform, the federation attracted such women as **Jane Addams*** and Florence Kelley as speakers to its annual conventions.

At the turn of the twentieth century, the GFWC became increasingly involved in social reform initiatives, wielding its influence through the great number of women affiliated with the organization. Under the second president, Ellen Henrotin (1894–1898), the number of affiliates doubled. Henrotin was a powerful influence who pushed the federation toward the overall goals of the women's movement. For example, in 1908, the GFWC asked Congress to establish a Department of Education and requested creation of a Health Department in 1910. Along with other groups, the federation played key roles in passing legislation, such as that establishing the Pure Food Bureau in 1907 (now the Food and Drug Administration), the Children's Bureau (1912), and the **Women's Bureau*** (1920).

The GFWC changed after **suffrage*** for women was won in 1920. Its membership was no longer drawn from the eclectic collection of women's clubs in the United States but became mainly a group of clubs that focused on self-culture. Not only did its membership rolls suffer, but the quality of leadership deteriorated.

In 1953, at the time of the GFWC's first written history, over 800,000 women in approximately 15,000 clubs in fifty states were members of the GFWC, a stark contrast to the sixty-seven delegates from seventeen states at the original organizational meeting. Through the 1960s, the GFWC was active locally, especially in awarding money to community projects and encouraging the arts through scholarships to music schools and summer music camps. It remains active nationally, supporting the endowment of the John F. Kennedy Center for the Performing Arts in Washington, D.C., establishing a museum at the base of the Statue of Liberty, and supporting the Women's History and Resource Center in its Washington, D.C., headquarters. [See also **Progressive Era**.*]

Bibliography: Mildred White Wells, *Unity in Diversity: The History of the General Federation of Women's Clubs Diamond Jubilee Edition* (1965); Karen J. Blair, *The Clubwoman as Feminist: True Womanhood Redefined, 1868–1914* (1980); Anne Firor Scott, *Natural Allies: Women's Associations in American History* (1991); Theda Skocpol, *Protecting Soldiers and Mothers: The Political Origins of Social Policy in the United States* (1992); Anne Meis Knupfer, *Toward a Tenderer Humanity and a Nobler Womanhood: African American Women's Clubs in Turn-of-the-Century Chicago* (1996).

Christine Woyshner

Gilman, Charlotte Perkins. Charlotte Perkins Gilman (1860–1935), lecturer, author, and recognized intellectual leader of the turn-of-the-century women's movement, was born in Hartford, Connecticut, the last surviving child of Frederick Beecher Perkins and Mary Wescott Perkins. Perkins was the grandson of Connecticut's famous evangelical preacher, Lyman Beecher, and Gilman was extremely proud of her Beecher relatives—**Catharine**,* Henry Ward, Harriet Beecher Stowe, and Isabella Beecher Hooker—whom she considered ''world servers.''

Eight months after his daughter's birth, Perkins left his family to seek employment. Though he enjoyed some success, it was not shared with his family, who moved nineteen times in eighteen years and lived at the mercy of relatives. At thirteen, Gilman's parents divorced. Frederick remained Gilman's initial intellectual mentor, influencing her conception of the nature of society and introducing her to the intellectual debate on **Social Darwinism**.* But with the departure of her husband, Mary Perkins, more than anyone in Gilman's youth, taught her daughter the gender discrepancies within patriarchal society and family structures.

Gilman's education commenced at home, and by fourteen she had but four years of formal schooling in seven different schools. Yet she was a highly driven individual who embarked on a rigorous course of self-education.

At seventeen, Gilman consciously dedicated her life to serving humanity, though she had neither a specific direction nor a definite medium through which to proceed. She supported herself as a Sunday school teacher, commercial artist, and governess yet felt her destiny lay in writing. Her goals and aspirations, however, were directly challenged when Charles Walter Stetson, a promising young artist, proposed. For years she wavered but finally married in May 1884. Their only child, Katherine, was born the following March. Initially happy, within a year Gilman became increasingly depressed, to the point where routine functions were overwhelming. In 1885, she traveled to California without her husband to recover her health and ambition. Upon her return, she fell so low that in 1887 the neurologist S. Weir Mitchell was called to prescribe his famous "rest cure," which nearly drove her mad. To maintain her sanity, Gilman moved to Pasadena with her daughter in 1888. Although they tried to reconcile, Gilman divorced her husband in 1894. Directly after the divorce, Stetson married Grace Ellery Channing, Gilman's closest friend. The three remained very close, and Gilman sent Katherine to Rhode Island to live with the newlyweds, causing quite a scandal on both coasts.

Gilman's experience as wife and mother greatly informed her ideas on society. Her loss of economic, social, and personal independence, compounded by suppression of her intellectual, emotional, and sexual desires and interests due to overwhelming cultural norms and domestic chores, forcefully reaffirmed her early lessons in the gender imbalance of society. Gilman embarked upon another intellectual journey, this time studying works by and about women. She recognized how the social norms of womanhood denied females equality with males and how ill-designed women's education was in preparing girls for the life and duties society prescribed for them.

Gilman educated others through her pen. The initial focus of her brutal attacks on society was the suppression, ignorance, and unequal treatment of women in marriage. Yet it was not until after her nervous breakdown, the move to Pasadena, and the publication of *The Yellow Wallpaper* (1892), her fictitious account of her breakdown, that she truly established herself as an intellectual force. She began her lecturing career, speaking on issues related to women, labor, and transformation of society. Lecturing became a constant aspect of her life and her primary source of income. Her audiences ranged from working-class men to upper-class and middle-class women.

From 1890 to 1896 Gilman lived in Pasadena, San Francisco, and Oakland, California. Between 1896 and 1900 she lived as a nomad, traveling throughout

America and abroad, first staying at **Hull-House*** in Chicago and then with her father in Manhattan. Her interest in socialism grew as she met such Fabian intellectuals as George Bernard Shaw and Sidney and Beatrice Webb. The most influential intellectual relationship she formed at this time was with sociologist Lester Frank Ward, who challenged the competitive bias of Social Darwinism. Ward emphasized people's "conscious ability" to direct social evolution and human nature through education, arguing that society could not advance if only men were elevated.

In 1898 Gilman published *Women and Economics*, using Ward's thesis to expose the destructive sexuo-economic dependency of women and the gender discrepancies of society. A clarion call for women's financial independence, the book became a "feminist manifesto," widely read throughout the United States and Europe. Two years after its publication, Gilman married her cousin, George Houghton Gilman, and moved to Manhattan. With his support, she continued to lecture and write, publishing a half dozen books between 1900 and 1934 and serializing a half dozen more in a monthly magazine, *The Forerunner*, which she wrote, produced, and edited for seven years by herself.

As a social philosopher who never identified herself with any particular movement or ideology, Gilman was able to move laterally across the associations and movements of her day. Until her death, she was involved on a peripheral level with Margaret Sanger's efforts for birth control, with Carrie Chapman Catt on women's **suffrage,*** and with **Jane Addams*** in the Women's Peace Party [see **peace education***]. In 1934, after she was diagnosed with breast cancer, Gilman began her autobiography; in 1935, she committed suicide by ingesting chloroform.

The foundation of Gilman's social vision was evolutionary philosophy. She believed that humankind was involved in a constant yet gradual process of development from the simple to the advanced and that education was the medium of human and social advancement. Primary to her vision was her radical conception of womanhood and her belief that progress depended upon eradicating gender discrepancies within society. The new woman was to be an intelligent, well-informed, well-educated free thinker, economically self-sufficient, socially independent, and politically active. This redefinition was Gilman's chief contribution to American educational thought.

Gilman urged educational institutions to teach social service, not individual attainment. She wanted women prepared for careers in business, law, and medicine. However, she also sought to organize and professionalize the knowledge encapsulated within women's sphere and envisioned professional instruction by women for women in the areas of marriage, motherhood, nutrition, child care, and domestic industry.

Gilman maintained that predominant educational philosophy was too narrow since "masculine traits were defined as *human* traits and female traits were defined as other" (*The Home*, 1903, p. 90). She believed that this imbalance in women's education resonated in the types of knowledge extended to women:

masculine knowledge presented within a masculine culture in a masculine way. In *Women and Economics*, she exposed the educational omission of the domestic disciplines as deleterious to social progress, believing that professionalization of education and childrearing would signify new opportunities for women. In *Herland* (1915), her female utopia, the interests of women, children, and the state are one.

Gilman's life combined vast energy and physical health with periodic yet severe mental depression. She balanced a passion for philosophy with a devotion to practicality. Yet her inability to resolve the duality between work and love, rationality and sensuality, resulted in conflicting theories regarding the capabilities of women and the existence of exclusively "feminine" characteristics.

Gilman remained on the cusp of the modern era. Her vision of women was forward thinking yet tinged by the Victorian belief in specific gender characteristics. Further, she never could shed her Anglo-centric, middle-class bias, so her concerns failed to address fully the problems of the working classes and immigrant populations that she championed.

Bibliography: Mary Hill, *Charlotte Perkins Gilman: The Making of a Radical Feminist, 1860–1898* (1980); Jane Roland Martin, *Reclaiming a Conversation: The Ideal of the Educated Woman* (1985); Maureen Egan, "Evolutionary Theory in the Social Philosophy of Charlotte Perkins Gilman," *Hypatia*, 4 (Spring 1989): 102–119; Deborah De Simone, "Charlotte Perkins Gilman and the Feminization of Education," *Willa*, 4 (1995).

Deborah M. De Simone

Girl Scouts. Girl Scouts of the USA, one of the best-known extracurricular organizations for girls' education and community service, was founded as Girl Guides in England in 1909 when Sir Robert Baden-Powell, founder of Boy Scouts, realized that more than 6,000 girls had registered as Boy Scouts. He believed that girls needed a separate organization more in keeping with cultural expectations for women, focusing on "homemaking and mothercraft" instead of boys' "robust outdoor adventuring." He named the new group Girl Guides after a similar group in India. His sister, Agnes Baden-Powell, became the first leader.

Juliette Gordon Low, a native of Savannah, Georgia, met the Baden-Powells in 1911 and became very interested in Girl Guides. Although living with her husband William in England, she sailed home to Savannah in order to begin a troop. She began with eighteen girls, dividing them into two patrols. Her niece, Daisy Gordon, and a few other women served as leaders.

By 1913 enough interest had grown in Girl Guides to open a national headquarters in Washington, D.C. The organization was renamed Girl Scouts, and the first manual entitled *How Girls Can Help Their Country* was written (rewritten 1916). The number of Girl Scouts continued to increase, and the organization incorporated in 1915. Yearly membership dues were established, and a new headquarters was established in New York City in 1916.

Low traveled extensively to assist troop leaders. She paid all expenses and salaries for leaders; she even sold her own jewelry when her family funds were curtailed during World War I. In 1917 Girl Scouts assisted in the war effort by selling bonds, helping with food production and Red Cross activities, teaching English to soldiers, and many other tasks.

By 1920 Girl Scouts boasted nearly one hundred councils in eleven states and Hawaii, 3,000 troops, and 10,000 members. Each troop was to be self-governed democratically. Membership was open to all incomes, races, and religions, and a special emphasis was made to include girls with physical disabilities. Growth soared throughout the decade; by 1929 there were over 200,000 members. Community service and ''heroic actions'' were emphasized. Camping became an important part of Girl Scouts in order to teach good health and to develop good character.

During the depression years, Girl Scouts again helped their communities. They collected clothing, made quilts and toys, gathered food, and served in hospitals and with visiting nurses. They helped in community programs such as canning projects and serving food in school cafeterias. Girls were not turned away if they could not pay dues, and by 1936, troops needed money for equipment and other needs. Cookie sales were introduced in order to fund troops.

Girl Scouts were characterized by their uniforms and badges. Uniforms varied over time. The first were navy blue, changed to khaki during World War I, and then to brown for Brownies and gray-green for Girl Scouts in the 1920s. They wore skirts and blouses or dresses; some uniforms featured hats. Over the next decades, uniforms changed several times, and pants and vests were incorporated.

Badges became one of the educational aspects of scouting, allowing girls to pursue study in a variety of areas and to demonstrate their proficiency. These areas have always been varied. For example, from 1913 to 1938, girls' badges included horsemanship, economist, electrician, farmer, businesswoman, hospital and home nursing, wood craft, laundress, archer, rambler, observer, rifle shot, swimmer, pioneer, flyer, cook, insect finder, rock finder, tree finder, beekeeper, and automobiling.

During World War II, Girl Scouts served their communities. They worked in food preservation, nutrition, and child care; providing shelter, transportation, and clothing; serving as bicycle couriers; and selling war bonds and stamps. Thousand of girls worked on farms in the Farm Aide Project.

By 1944 there were over 1 million Girl Scouts. During the 1940s the organization made a priority of including girls with disabilities and extending membership to all races and ethnicities. During the 1940s and 1950s camping and conservation were emphasized, and more camps were added to Girl Scout holdings. In the 1950s outreach was aimed at migrant workers, Alaskan Eskimos, girls with disabilities, and military personnel.

In the 1960s badge work emphasized careers, and in the 1970s more girls with disabilities and more minority girls were recruited. Girl Scouts often served less in their communities because more of their mothers worked outside the home, leaving them less available for providing help and transportation. Badge activities diversified to include tours of space flight centers, environmental activities, participating in archaeological digs, coeducational activities, and careers. Many activities were also aimed at reducing gender stereotyping.

In the 1980s and 1990s badges were updated to reflect interests in careers for women but to retain areas such as outdoor activities. Badge activities focused on raising self-esteem and respect for others. Such topics as drugs and child-abuse prevention, low-impact camping and cooking (using less meat), and budgeting were added. By 1988 membership totaled over 3 million, with almost 15 percent minority girls and women.

In the 1990s, Girl Scouts deemphasized troop self-sufficiency. Many activities are planned at council or "neighborhood" levels, such as parties, contests, and learning programs, and troops are expected to participate. This centralization, however, detracts from time troops have to pursue their own education and service projects. Additionally, troops receive a small percentage of the cost of a box of cookies. Therefore, although national dues are inexpensive, troops are often forced to charge extra dues or have girls pay for their own activities, a problem for girls whose parents' incomes are limited.

In spite of these problems, Girl Scouts has continued to evolve into an important educational organization for girls. Although Baden-Powell was limited in his vision for girls, Low provided a good example at the organization's outset in the United States. She believed in the abilities of girls and women and the necessity of an outlet for their education. Early badges included typically feminine occupations, but they also included areas that enhanced women's outlook. Girl Scout leadership has continued to be sensitive to the changing needs of girls and women and to provide opportunities that women perhaps have lacked in other spheres.

In its infancy, Girl Scouts attempted to include girls and women of diverse backgrounds and varied needs. The organization has continued to be inclusive of diversity in income, race, ethnicity, disability, and religion. The messages girls get from Girl Scouts are healthy: to respect oneself, to respect people and cultures, to be a change agent, to conserve nature, to seek careers of their choice, and to help others, especially other girls and women.

Bibliography: Ely List, ed., *Juliette Low and the Girl Scouts* (1960); William Hillcourt, *Baden-Powell: The Two Lives of a Hero* (1964); Ruby L. Radford, *Juliette Low: Girl Scout Founder* (1965); Girl Scouts of the USA, *75 Years of Girl Scouting* (1986); Mary Degenhardt and Judith Kirsch, eds., *Girl Scout Collector's Guide* (1987).

Louise E. Fleming

Girls' Latin School. Girls' Latin School opened in 1877 in Boston after the first women elected to the Boston School Committee used their new political power to guarantee girls a Latin school education. Although their goal of making the prestigious Boston Latin School coeducational failed, the committeewomen did achieve a Latin school for girls. Qualified girls continued to attend a separate Latin school until 1972 when the Boston School Committee implemented an act forbidding sex discrimination in public schools passed by the Massachusetts state legislature a year earlier.

The long drive for secondary education for Boston girls began in 1826 when the first Girls' High School opened. Its unexpected favorable appeal caused the School Committee to close it in 1828, probably because of the expense, and to allow girls to continue in grammar school for an extra year instead. In 1852, the School Committee opened a **normal school*** for girls to supply women assistants to the male masters in primary and grammar schools. By 1854, the school had become Girls' High and Normal School; only in 1872 did the two become separate schools. Although the popular headmaster of Girls' High, Dr. Samuel Eliot, included some college preparatory work, the new school committeewomen were not satisfied with the curriculum.

Abby W. May led the drive of the Boston school committeewomen to allow girls to earn a Latin school education. Her own brothers and the brothers of the two women serving with her in 1877, Lucia Peabody and Lucretia Hale, had all attended Boston Latin School. Three women's organizations also worked to convince the School Committee to admit women to Boston Latin: the Education Committee of the New England Women's Club (chaired by Abby May), the Women's Education Association, and the Massachusetts Society for the University Education of Women, founded originally to address the needs of the new Boston University, which admitted women from its 1869 opening. A leader of the Massachusetts Society was Emily Talbot, mother of **Marion Talbot**,* a Boston University graduate and later the first **dean of women*** at the **University of Chicago**.* The Talbots had experienced difficulty finding a formal college preparatory program for Marion and wanted Boston schools to offer such opportunities to future young women.

In 1877 the Women's Education Association and the Massachusetts Society for the University Education of Women petitioned the Boston School Committee to allow women to prepare for college in the public schools. The Massachusetts Society presented more than a thousand signatures. Although Boston's educational and community leaders rallied to support a Latin school education for girls, concern over **coeducation*** defeated the proposal to admit girls to Boston Latin School itself. Girls were admitted to a Latin school program, but it was separate from boys. Girls' Latin School's beginnings were inauspicious. Classes were held in a few rooms in the Girls' High School, and although Girls' Latin eventually acquired its own building, accommodations were often moved and remained inferior to Boston Latin School throughout the separate history. Girls' Latin did succeed in preparing young women for college. Admission to the school was highly competitive because graduates were virtually assured of acceptance at major colleges and universities.

A 1971 court case demonstrating that the cutoff point for girls on the Latin school entrance examination was higher than for boys proved that Boston practiced sex discrimination by maintaining separate Latin schools. When women were finally admitted to Boston Latin in 1972, the cutoff point was equalized. The two buildings were retained, with the former Girls' Latin School renamed Boston Latin Academy. On the day Boston Latin became coeducational—September 7, 1972—the headmaster protested the end of 488 years of tradition.

Bibliography: Boston School Committee Proceedings (1877); Massachusetts Society for the University Education of Women, *Third Annual Report* (1880); Lucy R. Woods, *History of Girls' High of Boston, 1852–1902* (1904); "The Day English and Latin Went Coed," *Boston Globe* (September 7, 1972); Polly Welts Kaufman, *Boston Women and City School Politics, 1872–1905* (1994).

Polly Welts Kaufman

Godey's Lady's Book. *Godey's Lady's Book* (1830–1898) was the most popular magazine for women in nineteenth-century America. Louis Antoine Godey founded the *Lady's Book* in 1830. His greatest coup was to buy the *American Ladies Magazine and Literary Gazette* from Sarah Josepha Hale in 1836 and to hire her as editor of the combined magazines. Hale edited the magazine with Godey from 1837 to 1877. Godey sold the periodical in 1877. He died in 1878, and Hale died in 1879, although the magazine continued until 1898.

Godey began his magazine in 1830, modeling it after other American and European magazines for women. He clipped articles and copied fashion plates from various other periodicals. Hale, who is credited with writing "Mary Had a Little Lamb" and with promoting Thanksgiving as a national holiday to show off the culinary talents of American women, began her literary career after the death of her husband in 1822. She published a book entitled *Northwood* dealing with the issue of **slavery*** and, with a sister-in-law, published a book of poems. The *American Ladies Magazine* was a platform for women to educate themselves. When economic difficulties forced Hale to sell the magazine to Godey, she took with her an editorial vision that the magazine should focus on American women's concerns. Godey and Hale worked together for almost forty years, bringing to American readers a variety of American literary talent. They published separate editorial columns, although Godey retained the upper hand on editorial content as publisher.

Godey and Hale made two important contributions to the literary culture of the nineteenth century. First, they both believed in securing original contributions and paying authors for their efforts. Hale had begun this practice in 1828 when she founded the *American Ladies Magazine*; Godey announced the same policy in 1836. Their other contribution was to copyright all material. It had been standard practice throughout the nineteenth century for magazines and newspapers to clip articles from other sources, giving credit only to the publication but not paying the author. Although greeted with outrage by other publishers, their practice was eventually adopted by the magazine industry.

Godey's included articles by Ralph Waldo Emerson, Henry Wadsworth Longfellow, Harriet Beecher Stowe, Edgar Allan Poe, and Nathaniel Hawthorne. It printed fiction geared to women's lives, as well as poetry and music. *Godey's* is a primary source for understanding women's fashions in the nineteenth century. Its color plates of women's styles were the source of sewing ideas for American women. Hale objected to the continued inclusion of these plates, but Godey overrode her. Almost 150 women were employed as hand tinters of the plates. The magazine also included plans for building houses and varieties of advice about manners and morals [see **prescriptive literature***]. It chose to ignore the Civil War, holding to an editorial policy that the magazine was an "oasis" from the war. Its circulation figures for 1851 were approximately 63,000; by 1860, there were over 150,000 subscribers.

Bibliography: Sarah Josepha Hale, *Traits of American Life* (1835); Hale, *Woman's Record* (1853); Hale, *Manners; or, Happy Homes and Good Society All the Year Round* (1867); Isabelle Webb Entrikin, "Sarah Josepha Hale and Godey's Lady's Book" (Ph.D. diss., University of Pennsylvania, 1943); Sherbrooke Rogers, *Sarah Josepha Hale: A New England Pioneer, 1788–1879* (1985); Patricia Okker, *Our Sister Editors: Sarah J. Hale and the Tradition of Nineteenth-Century American Women Editors* (1995); Kenneth M. Price and Susan Belasco Smith, eds., *Periodical Literature in Nineteenth-Century America* (1995).

Mary Lee Talbot

Goldman, Emma. Emma Goldman (1869–1940), an anarchist popularly derided in her lifetime with the nickname "Red Emma," spent most of her life trying to educate the public through lectures and writings on her major concerns: government oppression, social justice, and free speech. Of particular importance to women's educational history was her espousal of sexual and economic freedom for women and her role as pioneer in disseminating information on birth control.

Born in the Russian province of Kovno (today Kaunas, Lithuania), Goldman grew up amidst government oppression, strong anti-Semitism, and economic dislocation. Her family moved several times in her father's generally unsuccessful attempts to improve his family's financial conditions. Goldman's limited formal education was overall a painful, unhappy experience, but she later credited a German teacher in Köninsburg, Prussia, with developing her interest in music and literature. Although her formal schooling ended with Goldman's working in a glove factory only six months after the family moved to St. Petersburg, Russia, in 1881, she associated with university students and read widely in Russian populist and nihilist literature. Goldman was also influenced by Judaic ethics, especially belief in community self-help and social justice.

In 1885 Goldman immigrated with a half sister to the United States, settling in Rochester, New York, where she worked in clothing factories. Her experience with the exploitation of workers rapidly made her a critic of capitalism, and the trial and subsequent execution of the Haymarket anarchists for exploding a bomb in Illinois in 1886 spurred her interest in anarchist philosophy.

Following a short-lived, unsuccessful marriage to Jacob Kersner, Goldman moved to New York City in 1889, determined to become involved in the anarchist movement. In 1892 she helped Russian anarchist Alexander Berkman plan an assassination attempt on Henry Clay Frick, manager of the Carnegie-owned steel mills in Homestead, Pennsylvania, then involved in a bitter labor dispute with striking workers. Berkman succeeded only in wounding Frick, however, and was imprisoned for fourteen years. Goldman escaped indictment for her involvement, but she suffered a year's imprisonment in 1893 at Blackwell's Island penitentiary in New York when arrested for inciting to riot. She had urged unemployed workers to steal or take bread by force if necessary for their survival.

In prison Goldman received training as a practical nurse and, following her release, went to Vienna for more training in nursing and midwifery. In addition to her medical work, she began lecture tours in Europe and the United States. A charismatic, powerful speaker, she eventually built a reputation as one of the most accomplished, dynamic women speakers in American history. Goldman's lectures focused on free speech and elimination of prejudice and oppressive government. She was also instrumental in popularizing European drama in the United States with lectures on Ibsen, Shaw, and Strindberg, whom she admired for their social views. Her lectures, delivered to as many as 50,000 persons a year during her most successful tours (1908–1916), were collected in *Anarchism and Other Essays* (1911) and *The Social Significance of the Modern Drama* (1914). Goldman also published her views in *Mother Earth*, the journal she edited with Berkman from 1906 to 1917.

An outspoken critic of the **suffrage*** movement, Goldman was more concerned with what she felt to be the crucial issues for women—sexual and economic freedom. Of particular importance was a woman's right to determine whether or not to bear children. Goldman's lecturing on and distributing information about contraceptives led to her arrest and brief imprisonment in 1916.

Goldman's anticonscription campaign with Berkman during World War I evoked more serious problems—arrest and imprisonment in Jefferson City, Missouri, in 1917 and deportation to Russia two years later. A strong advocate of the Soviet system, Goldman nevertheless became disillusioned and critical over the oppressiveness of the Bolsheviks. She fled from Russia and expressed her reactions in *My Disillusionment in Russia* (1923) and *My Further Disillusionment in Russia* (1924). Goldman spent the remainder of her life in Europe and Canada, trying to maintain financial independence through lectures and writing. Her highly regarded autobiography, *Living My Life* (1931), reflects her philosophical views. She maintained that society should be based on free cooperation of the masses, and she continued to support anarchist causes.

Despite her desire to return to the United States to live, Goldman was permitted only a three-month lecture tour in 1934. While in Canada in 1940 trying to raise money for the anti-Franco revolutionaries in the Spanish Civil War, she suffered a stroke. Following her death three months later on May 14, her body was taken to Chicago for interment near the graves of the Haymarket strikers.

During her lifetime, Emma Goldman evoked strong and varied reactions from the American public. Although detractors regarded her as dangerous and cheered her deportation in 1919, the *Nation* declared in 1922 that her name belonged on any list of the greatest living women. An inspirational and provocative orator, she failed to win many converts to anarchism, but she succeeded in educating the public on crucial social issues and heightening public awareness of feminist issues. In recent years she has become almost a cult figure among feminists who view her as a role model for women seeking emancipation amidst societal pressures.

Bibliography: Alice Wexler, *Emma Goldman: An Intimate Life* (1984); Martha Solomon, *Emma Goldman* (1987); John Chalberg, *Emma Goldman: American Individualist* (1991); Marian J. Morton, *Emma Goldman and the American Left* (1992); Bonnie Haaland, *Emma Goldman: Sexuality and the Impurity of the State* (1993). See also Emma Goldman Papers, New York Public Library Manuscript Collection.

Verbie Lovorn Prevost

graduate education. Graduate education encompasses a variety of postbaccalaureate educational opportunities—especially master's, doctoral, and professional degrees—that provide advanced training for the professions and for research. Graduate-level schooling in the United States became common only toward the end of the nineteenth century and, like early collegiate opportunities, initially barred women. Using a range of strategies from providing their own laboratories to funding professorships, women entered most American graduate schools just after 1900. Their share of Ph.D.s earned grew to 18 percent by 1930 but slipped during the next four decades until rising again significantly starting in the 1970s. By the mid-1990s, women accounted for 38 percent of Ph.D.s earned in the United States (47 percent of degrees earned by U.S. citizens).

The story of women's pursuit of equal graduate education parallels their demand for collegiate training but differs due to the investment symbolized by doctoral or advanced training. A person who commits two years for a master's program or many years for a doctorate is asserting an expectation that she or he will pursue a professional or academic career. Yet in the early years of graduate training, beginning in the 1870s, few clear roads appeared for women to use such advanced schooling.

The doctorate was not required for college **teaching*** until well into the twentieth century. After 1900, the prestigious research-oriented schools expected Ph.D.s from their faculty, but many other institutions retained faculty with only some graduate training. Nor was a professional degree required of nineteenth-century lawyers, physicians, or business managers. Apprenticeship characterized most **legal education*** before the turn of the century; only by 1920 or so had law schools replaced individual training in lawyers' offices. **Medical education*** followed a different route, with a range of opportunities open to women in the 1800s, including some female-only institutions. However, medical schooling was standardized after Abraham Flexner's influential report for the Carnegie Foundation in 1910, resulting in the closure of many women's institutions and less-prestigious medical schools. Business administration connected slowly with graduate training. Only after the 1910s and 1920s did college become a clear advantage for men planning business careers; women's involvement in M.B.A. training occurred much later.

Most women who pursued graduate schooling hoped for lives as scholars, although early teaching options were generally limited to **women's colleges*** and **normal schools***—both institutions serving a female clientele. Economist Susan Carter has shown that women's enrollments may have driven the hiring of women faculty more than previously assumed. Carter observed that the large land-grant and state institutions, often in the Midwest and West, hired female faculty when their programs in **teacher education*** and **home economics*** drew considerable numbers of local women students. Many of the faculty who took these posts had been well trained in the sciences or humanities but were shunted into home economics or pedagogy programs rather than welcomed into the male-dominated arts and sciences curricula.

Carter's observation that women faculty often possessed credentials superior to their actual jobs characterizes much of the history of women's graduate education. Some prestigious institutions opened graduate training to women (including a few like Yale University who continued to bar women from their undergraduate schools) but declined to hire females onto their faculty, encouraging a diaspora of women into a range of institutions across the country. In the sciences, institutions frequently denied women the postdoctoral and laboratory training experiences necessary to qualify them for prestigious posts, limiting them to institutions with lesser facilities. This scattershot hiring pattern doubtless inhibited women's ability to create networks or to build what historian Margaret Rossiter calls "protégée chains" whereby women faculty trained and subsequently placed their own students.

In terms of numbers, graduate education remained a small enterprise before 1900. Men earned the first American doctorates in 1861 from Yale; **Helen Magill*** (later White) was the first woman to earn the Ph.D., completing her degree at Boston University in 1877. Between 1877 and 1900, women earned 229 Ph.D.s in the United States. Four institutions predominated in awarding these early doctorates to women: More than half were earned at Yale, **Chicago**,* Cornell, and New York Universities. Notwithstanding the availability of graduate education for women at some prestigious institutions, several of the most notable research universities continued to exclude females. Johns Hopkins and Clark, the two universities that led graduate education in the early 1900s, joined Harvard in prohibiting women in doctoral programs, at least initially. Harvard created the **Radcliffe*** Graduate School in 1902 to sidestep the issue of granting its degrees to women already pursuing graduate work; Radcliffe would join Columbia and Chicago as the primary producers of women's doctorates in the middle part of the twentieth century.

Harvard's action demonstrates the symbolic difference in allowing women to study in graduate school versus earning a graduate degree. Just as the earliest college students had often been allowed to study before they were permitted to earn a degree, so, too, did women encounter resistance to their earning the Ph.D. Many institutions, like Harvard, might allow a sympathetic professor to teach female students, but jealously guarded the degree itself.

A few hardy American women traveled to European institutions in hopes of both earning degrees and influencing Americans who emulated the German research model. **M. Carey Thomas**,* later president of **Bryn Mawr College**,* studied at Leipzig when Johns Hopkins refused to welcome her. Leipzig, however, would not confer a degree. Generally, American women who studied at the various German universities were sent to Zurich in Switzerland for award of the degree. Eventually, in 1895 and 1896, the German universities at Göttingen and Heidelberg each granted a first Ph.D. to an American woman, Margaret Maltby of **Wellesley College*** and physiologist Ida Hyde, respectively.

Back home, advocates for women's graduate education continued to push on two fronts in what Rossiter calls an "educational guerilla warfare": They continued to apply and study at American universities in hopes of pressuring them to accept women, and they raised money for fellowships to Europe. The **Association of Collegiate Alumnae*** (ACA, later the **American Association of University Women*** [AAUW]) rallied around raising funds for women's fellowships, a program that continues a century later. Spurred by psychologist Christine Ladd-Franklin, the ACA began awarding fellowships to Europe in 1890. At Carey Thomas's instigation, members of the group also formed the Naples Table Association for Promoting Laboratory Research by Women in 1898; this philanthropic support created a table, or site, for women scientists to conduct research at the prestigious Naples Zoological Station.

A combination of such creative fund-raising and networking sustained women in graduate work until the 1920s, when Ph.D. training became a more regular feature of American institutions and the professoriate. Although opportunities remained limited, by the 1920s women could afford to approach doctoral training vocationally. In 1929, **Barnard College*** economist Emilie J. Hutchinson studied 1,025 women who had earned the doctorate between 1877 and 1924. The women's fields of study represented a good balance, with one-third pursuing literature, language, and the arts; one-third the social sciences; and one-third natural sciences and mathematics. At the time of the study, fully 58 percent of these doctors held teaching posts, five-sixths of them in colleges or universities. Another 10 percent held research jobs. Nonetheless, many of the women reported to Hutchinson a dissatisfaction with the occupational segregation and bias they had encountered in academe. Many complained of biases in salary, promotions, fellowships, and research assistantships. In addition, three-quarters of the women had not married, a figure that demonstrates the commitment required of a scholarly career and one that matches the earliest women collegians.

After 1930, three decades of depression, war, and recovery confounded women's efforts to advance in professional and research fields. Although women's absolute numbers grew in graduate education, the greater proportions of men attending suppressed women's chances for significant gains. Historians suggest that women advanced via a territorial strategy, sometimes focusing on a segregated aspect of a field that men left to women, other times filling subordinate roles that did not match their credentials. In academe, for example, the land-grant institutions increasingly hired women faculty after 1930 during the same decades when other institutions—including some women's colleges—sought to "upgrade" their faculties by hiring men. By 1960, following a dismal decade for professional women's progress, only 22 percent of all college faculty were women, and women were earning only 10 percent of all doctorates.

Increased support—legal, financial, and social—appeared in the 1960s and 1970s with the women's movement and **affirmative action**.* Organizations like the AAUW that had long histories of support for women were joined by new groups like the Women's Equity Action League and the **National Organization for Women*** in pushing for equality in educational and professional opportunities. Gradually, financial and fellowship support increased, as did the flexibility for women to study part-time or to return to school after marriage or motherhood [see **continuing education***]. Although equal career opportunities lagged behind the availability of schooling, women made significant gains in all graduate areas. In 1970, women earned just under 40 percent of all master's degrees, only 5 percent of first professional degrees, and 13 percent of doctorates; by 1993–1994, their share of master's degrees reached 54 percent, first professional degrees jumped to 41 percent, and doctorates rose to 38 percent (National Center for Education Statistics).

From the 1890s to the 1990s, graduate education has not been given to women—they have won it. In the last century, women pressured, financed, and strategized to create an entering wedge. Decades later, legal tools complemented these continuing strategies to open the doors that admit women into entry levels of the professions.

Bibliography: Emilie J. Hutchinson, *Women and the Ph.D.* (1929); Susan B. Carter, "Academic Women Revisited: An Empirical Study of Changing Patterns in Women's Employment as College and University Faculty, 1890–1963," *Journal of Social History*, 14 (Summer 1981): 675–699; Margaret Rossiter, *Women Scientists in America: Struggles and Strategies to 1940* (1982); Barbara Miller Solomon, *In the Company of Educated Women: A History of Women and Higher Education in America* (1985); Linda Eisenmann, "The Costs of Partial Support: One Hundred Years of Brown Graduate Women," in Polly Welts Kaufman, ed., *The Search for Equity: Women at Brown University, 1891–1991* (1991); Rossiter, *Women Scientists in America: Before Affirmative Action, 1940–1972* (1995); National Center for Education Statistics, *Digest of Education Statistics* (1996).

Linda Eisenmann

Great Awakening. The Great Awakening is the name given to a series of intensely emotional religious revivals beginning as early as the end of the seventeenth century and building through 1750. The phenomenon, influenced by a variety of religious leaders, occurred in several Christian sects and spread from Georgia to Maine. The revival was the first commonly experienced movement of English-speaking colonists, promoting changes in citizens' role in society. Since conversions of women were numerous, attitudes about their roles in the church, society, and home eventually changed and expanded.

The experience of religious awakening crossed doctrinal and geographic boundaries. In the middle colonies, revival began around 1720, influenced by two Presbyterian Scots, William and Gilbert Tennant. In 1734, the brilliant Yale-educated minister Jonathan Edwards, concerned about the religious state of young people in his Northampton, Massachusetts, Puritan congregation, encouraged them to discard sinful practices and seek evidence of salvation. His preaching, empowered by graphic and frightening metaphors, and then fueled by untimely, unexplained deaths among the congregation, initiated heartfelt repentance and emotional responses to evidences of God's grace. Fiery British Methodist preacher George Whitefield read Edwards's published accounts of the revival in Northampton and responded by journeying to the colonies where he joined other revivalist preachers. Whitefield traveled from Maine to Georgia, preaching several times a day, sometimes to crowds of 20,000.

The common revival experiences centered on an emphasis on the individual's response to God. Language expressing terrible knowledge of personal guilt and an awareness of dreaded separation from God was typical of those affected by the phenomenon. Self-abasement was followed, often at moments of heightened despair, by an experience of God's grace and a sense of forgiveness. The movement's leaders stressed such individual experiences. Conversion was seen as essential to salvation.

The revival ultimately affected views of women's proper roles. Religious leaders such as Edwards and Cotton Mather recognized that the necessary and much-desired experience of God's grace was given indiscriminately to men and women. For the first time, women were permitted greater access to ministry opportunities. Some, like Sarah Osborn, led prayer groups and gave public instruction to women about spiritual growth and doctrine. Other women published accounts of their experience receiving God's grace. Though women's religious interests were promoted over academic interests, the increase in ministries available to women and the recognition of equality in their capacity to respond to God's grace sparked growth in attitudes about women's rights.

Similarly, the emphasis the Great Awakening placed upon the individual provided an important shift in focus. Thousands of recent converts chose new churches that differed in doctrine and flavor from long-established denominations. Theses new congregations often chose ''preachers'' who shared their intense religious experience but who had not been educated at Harvard or Yale.

Finally, institutions of higher education, such as the College of New Jersey, later known as Princeton, were established as alternatives to Harvard and Yale. This shift in focus toward the individual promoted alternatives to established institutions and systems.

Bibliography: Douglas Sloan, *The Great Awakening and American Education, a Documentary History* (1973); Rosemary S. Keller and Rosemary R. Ruether, *Women and Religion in America, Vol. 2: The Colonial and Revolutionary Periods* (1983); Samuel Eliot Morison, *A Concise History of the American Republic* (1983).

Loris C. Nebbia

Grimké, Charlotte Forten. Charlotte Forten Grimké (1837–1914), African American educator, abolitionist, and writer, is best known for her passionate writing on racial oppression and, in the field of education, her mission teaching the freedpeople of South Carolina during the Civil War.

Born a fourth-generation free black on August 17, 1837, in Philadelphia, Forten was the daughter of Robert Bridges and Mary Virginia Woods Forten. Charlotte's grandfather, James Forten, was a prosperous sailmaker whose business successes enabled the family to climb Philadelphia's social ladder during the Jacksonian era. He labored to advance the social and political rights of African Americans—both free and enslaved. As a close ally of William Lloyd Garrison, Forten was an early supporter of Garrison's militant abolitionist newspaper, *The Liberator*. Forten's wife, Charlotte, was active in the Philadelphia Female Anti-Slavery Society, along with her daughters Margaretta, Harriet, and Sarah Louisa. The Forten women were also active in the women's rights movement. Like his sisters and parents, Robert Bridges was an ardent reformer and civil right's advocate. During the Civil War he enlisted in the 43rd United States Colored Infantry, one of the early black regiments in the Union Army. Mary Woods Forten was likewise active in **abolitionism**,* although she died when Charlotte was only three. Charlotte learned her racial commitment from her grandparents, her parents, and her extensive family network.

The term that best characterizes Forten's work is **racial uplift**,* a concept that in the mid-nineteenth century denoted working toward abolishing **slavery**,* organizing educational and other self-help associations, social reform, and political activism. Since liberation of the race was the primary goal, Forten placed great importance on education. She was painfully aware of the racial hostilities that had divided Philadelphia in the antebellum years, and she believed that African Americans encountered racism because whites viewed blacks as innately inferior. This inferiority stemmed presumably from their lack of education. To prepare herself to campaign for the racial advancement of her people, Forten embarked upon a program of rigorous study. Intellectual improvement also served as a source of her own liberation.

Rather than remain in Philadelphia, where the segregationist policies precluded Charlotte from obtaining equal opportunities for education, Robert Forten arranged to have his daughter educated in Salem, Massachusetts, one of the first cities in the North to create racially integrated schools. By 1855 the idea of a **teaching*** career had taken concrete shape in Charlotte's mind, and after grammar school, she enrolled in the Salem **Normal School**,* a preparatory institute for teachers. By the time she graduated, she had obtained a teaching post in Salem. Forten taught on and off in Salem and Philadelphia between 1856 and 1862.

Forten's schooling prompted her interest in the written word. She commenced keeping a journal after her arrival in Salem both to record events and to assist in assessing her intellectual growth. Forten also began writing poetry and essays. Writing provided a nourishing outlet, a way of transferring anger about racial oppression into artistic creativity. Although some of Charlotte's writings reflect the romantic language of the dominant discourse, her voice also mirrored her blackness; Forten's isolation from larger society gave her a perspective on its language and thought. This distance proved beneficial in enabling her to issue social commentaries capturing the essence of the mid-nineteenth-century northern black experience. Forten's texts evoke the conditions of her people: slavery, degradation, isolation, oppression.

Although deeply concerned about racial oppression in northern communities, the cause of the slave stirred her the most. Forten was a member of the Salem Female Anti-Slavery Society and active in the Philadelphia Female Anti-Slavery Society. Working at antislavery fairs and bazaars, distributing abolitionist tracts, and attending lectures gave her immense personal gratification. "I crave antislavery food continually," she confided in her journal (*Journals*, p. 169).

Forten's commitment to her people culminated in her mission teaching the freedpeople on the South Carolina Sea Islands between 1862 and 1864. This chain of isles nestled between Charleston and Savannah had been captured by federal forces in November 1861 as part of the Union strategy to blockade southern ports. Union occupation of the Islands paved the way for an early Reconstruction program in South Carolina. Hired by the Port Royal Relief Committee of Philadelphia, Forten was one of dozens of teachers and missionaries who journeyed to South Carolina to help the Sea Islanders in their transition from slavery to freedom [see **freedmen's teachers***]. By day she taught freedchildren the alphabet, spelling, reading, and writing; by night, she provided lessons for the adults. Forten also made a conscious point to teach her students African American history, especially the struggles of the abolitionist movement. Forten remained on the Islands for eighteen months. Her essay "Life on the Sea Islands" was published in the *Atlantic Monthly* after her return to the North.

Forten's mission in Port Royal paved the way for her future teaching and missionary efforts. Between 1865 and 1871 she worked for the New England Freedmen's Union Commission. Hired as secretary of the Teachers Committee, her work entailed acting as liaison between the teachers of the freedpeople in the South and their northern supporters. She left this position to teach freedchildren at the Shaw Memorial School in Charleston, South Carolina. After a year, Forten moved to Washington, D.C., to teach at the Preparatory High School. In 1878 she married Francis J. Grimké, a former South Carolina slave and half nephew of Sarah and Angelina Grimké, two prominent early women's rights advocates. Francis Grimké served as pastor of the Fifteenth Street Presbyterian Church in Washington. In 1885 he accepted the pastorate at the Laura Street Presbyterian Church in Jacksonville, Florida. The Grimkés remained there for four years, before returning to Washington. Besides her missionary work with her husband, Grimké continued to write essays and poems for publication. She died on July 22, 1914, after a year's illness. Charlotte Forten Grimké's life work in education, reform, and missionary activity is testimony to her deep commitment to extend the goal of equal rights and justice to all African Americans.

Bibliography: Anna Julia Cooper, *Life and Writings of the Grimké Family* (1951); Janice Sumler Lewis, "The Fortens of Philadelphia: An Afro-American Family and Nineteenth-Century Reform" (Ph.D. diss., Georgetown University, 1978); Dorothy Sterling, ed., *We Are Your Sisters: Black Women in the Nineteenth Century* (1984); Brenda Stevenson, ed., *The Journals of Charlotte Forten Grimké* (1988); Janet Rider, "Charlotte Forten and the Port Royal Mission" (master's thesis, Sonoma State University, 1995).

Janet Rider

"grinds." Women college students at the turn of the twentieth century divided themselves into sets or cliques forming a hierarchical scale with serious, studious "grinds" at the bottom and "swells" and "all round girls" at the top. There were four basic types, representing different student subcultures, into which students divided their classmates: Popular swells and all round girls were admired, grinds were considered inoffensive and were tolerated, and "freaks" were beyond endurance. "Digs" were those who fit neither socially nor educationally. The grinds were mild and unassertive and were frequently trampled down by the swells when it came to class presidencies and other activities based on popularity.

Nineteenth-century founders of **women's colleges*** had intended them for the typical students of that era—the serious, hardworking daughters of the middle class who were preparing to teach. Although from the beginning there were some scholarly daughters of the wealthy among the students, by the 1890s colleges attracted a new clientele—the daughters of the wealthy intent on enjoying college life with no thought of a future career. After the turn of the century college-going became much more common, and some students used college preparation for social mobility, while others used it to affirm their hold on social status. Thus, student subcultures developed, separating swells from grinds, depending on background and intentions in college.

Social class divisions at colleges were so great that at **Wellesley College*** the society members thought there might be a need for a club for those digs and nonsociety students from modest backgrounds. A grind was a woman with a modest background combined with a quiet manner and a studious nature. In "Georgia Oberley," a **Vassar College*** short story writer described the grind: "Georgia was the typical grind, pale, worn and nervous. No one knew her. In her Junior year her class were still calling her Miss Oberley." The poor collegian groaned: "I can't stand my life here. I'm not like most of the girls, I don't care for parties, or athletics, or the class, or any of the things they get so excited about. I just want to study." Because she planned to teach, she tried for honors, which was explained away: "You know, outsiders set so much more value on those things than we do." She was such a grind that she "hadn't even a picture on the wall for fear that it would distract her mind" (Gallaher, p. 28). Socially, grinds usually led lonely lives or associated with other grinds. Acceptance into swell society was almost impossible for a grind, although in some unexpected cases it did occur.

One example of a grind who briefly tasted life as a swell and finally ended up being an all round girl was Lydia Waitley, in another Vassar story. Lydia was studious and serious. Confined to what was referred to as a "pest house" during a bout of illness, she was lucky to convalesce with Elizabeth, a college swell. Elizabeth's company and her friendship succeeded in making a swell out of a grind for a while. Elizabeth, on her part, was surprised to find that a grind who had never even owned a visiting card in fact could be a lady in manners and speech. Elizabeth understood that Lydia was craving some fun in college but did not have any friends. She introduced her to the swells over whom she held sway, and Lydia saw for herself how swells played college life. Lydia enjoyed the change but became careless with her money and her time. Consequently, her work suffered, and at the end of the school year, she was behind in three classes and owed the college money. Lydia decided that she must earn the money and make up the subjects by going back to being a grind. "No more fun with anyone. Henceforth she would be numbered among the grinds, the shabby, overworked, worried ones, for there are degrees even in the state of grinds" (Gallaher, p. 210). Her story ends happily, however. Lydia earned the money she owed and made up the work. She developed her own opinions and took an interest in college clubs and activities. By the end of the year, she was elected class president and was considered the "broadest, coolest girl."

In their ambitions for using college to get ahead, grinds were at the lower end of the social scale by which students measured themselves. Although the term *grind* faded away after the 1920s or so, student subcultures have continued to differentiate according to class and background, and other terms and notions took the place of *grind* to describe the quiet, industrious student.

Bibliography: Grace Margaret Gallaher, *Vassar Stories* (1900); Grace Louise Cook, *Wellesley Stories* (1907); Helen Lefkowitz Horowitz, *Alma Mater: Design and Experience in the Women's Colleges from Their Nineteenth-Century Beginnings to the 1930s* (1984); Horowitz, *Campus Life: Undergraduate Cultures from the End of the Eighteenth Century to the Present* (1987); Lynn D. Gordon, *Gender and Higher Education in the Progressive Era* (1990).

Rajeswari Swaminathan

Gruenberg, Sidonie Matzner. Author and director of the Child Study Association of America (CSAA), Sidonie Matzner Gruenberg (1881–1974) is best
known as a leader and publicist in the parent education movement and for her
prominence in the larger field of child study [see **child study movement***]. She
began her career in 1907 when she joined the Federation of Child Study, a
mother's group of Felix Adler's Ethical Culture Society, and remained as director until her retirement in 1950. Gruenberg's contributions lie in her leadership of the CSAA over nearly forty years (including as director 1923–1950),
her body of writing for parents on childrearing and child development, and in
the special form of women's culture she created within the organization.

Matzner, oldest of six children, emigrated from Austria to New York with
her family in 1895. There she grew up within the decidedly reform atmosphere of the Ethical Culture Society, the Workingman's School, and later the
Ethical Culture Normal School. The Society and its educational affiliates were
founded by Felix Adler, a reform Jewish rabbi who broke away from traditional Judaism in 1877 to organize a new society based on a more inclusive,
humanistic creed of justice and ethics. Through the Ethical Culture Society,
Matzner met and married Benjamin Gruenberg, a biology teacher, in 1904;
they had four children.

Gruenberg became interested in the Federation for the Study of Child Nature
shortly after the birth of her first child in 1907. Its precursor, the Society for
the Study of Child Nature, was founded in 1888 as a mother's club of the Ethical
Culture Society of New York. The club began as a **kindergarten***; however,
as the mothers began reading a broad range of ideas relating to children, their
purpose turned more to their own educations. Within three years, the kindergarten was abandoned, and the women reorganized as a **women's study club***
whose primary focus was on learning the newest European and American theories of psychology and child development.

By the time Gruenberg joined the group, the society had expanded to include
several chapters, becoming the Federation for the Study of Child Nature. No
longer a small democratic study club, the new federation leadership was now
separate from the membership, and its focus shifted from self-help to processing
information for others, more like a service organization.

Shortly after joining, Gruenberg began studying the new behavioral sciences
at Teachers College of Columbia University. In 1911 she wrote a column in
The Housekeeper, a popular women's magazine, on children's fears. The successful column immediately became a regular feature where Gruenberg presented topics being discussed in federation study groups, such as children's
imagination, discipline, and adolescence. A collection of her columns was published as a book, *Your Child Today and Tomorrow*, in 1913. In these essays,
Gruenberg exhibited her talent for synthesizing the best sources of child development information and translating them into language parents could understand
and trust. The combination of conventional wisdom and a willingness to exper-

iment with new ideas is representative of Gruenberg's style as a popularizer of new research in the social and behavioral sciences.

In the early years, Gruenberg worked at enlarging membership, reaching more parents, and expanding the public visibility of the federation and its mission. Gruenberg's professional ideas were driven by her progressive, positive view of the sciences and her belief in the power of education to improve the lives of parents and children. She advocated flexible methods of childrearing and expanded roles for women, emphasizing the need for women to pursue meaningful work in addition to domestic responsibilities.

Although Gruenberg had risen to voluntary leadership immediately, it was not until the federation received substantial funding from the Laura Spelman Rockefeller Memorial in 1923 that she was officially named director and received a salary. The federation had grown to sixty-three active chapters and more than 1,500 members; the name was changed to the Child Study Association of America.

Gruenberg practiced a particular style of leadership that empowered mothers to study and educate themselves as well as their children. Her more important contributions were not only promotion of educated parenthood through the CSAA and her writing but also a form of women's culture that she was able to create within the association. Characterized by mutual respect and support, accommodation, and flexibility regarding the special needs of mothers, the CSAA gave women the opportunity to be both mothers and professionals without having to excuse either. Fostering a nontraditional model that would elude many women even decades later, federation workers permitted children to move freely in and out of the building, making the separation between home and work less rigid than would be permitted in a conventional workplace. Indeed, flexible work schedules during the day, and over years, defined this as a female, rather than a male, organization. Rather than putting women's intellectual ability and competence in competition with childrearing, this model supported both. Over many years, Gruenberg and her colleagues allowed themselves to claim the centrality of their families while working full-time.

In the end, under Gruenberg's guidance, the CSAA evinced an unmistakable female culture, but its work did not occupy a **separate sphere**.* Professionally, it was integrated into the larger world of New York urban reform, the Rockefeller network of social science research, and the national community of child development research and educators. Gruenberg herself was consistent in the life she advocated and the life she lived: a balance of family, motherhood, and competent work over time.

Bibliography: Linda Mainiero, ed., *American Women Writers* (1980); Walter I. Trattner, ed., *Biographical Dictionary of Social Welfare History in America* (1985); Roberta Wollons, "Women Educating Women: The Child Study Association as Women's Culture," in Joyce Antler and Sari Biklen, eds., *Changing Education: Women as Radicals and Conservators* (1990). See also the Benjamin and Sidonie Gruenberg collection at the Library of Congress and the CSAA papers at the Social Welfare Archive at the University of Minnesota. Gruenberg's major works include: *Your Child Today and Tomorrow* (1913); *Sons and Daughters* (1916); *We, the Parents* (1939); *The Wonderful Story of How You Were Born* (with Benjamin Gruenberg in 1952, rev. 1970); and *The New Illustrated Encyclopedia of Child Care and Guidance*, 4 vols. (1954, rev. 1967).

Roberta Wollons

H

Haley, Margaret. Margaret Angela Haley (1861–1939) was the leader of the first elementary teachers union and one of the first proponents of women teachers' legal and political rights in the United States. Haley was born in Joliet, Illinois, on November 15, 1861, of working-class Irish immigrants and attended local rural schools in Illinois. At sixteen she was, as she recalled, "catapulted" into teaching by her father's financial troubles, and she taught at a local country school until moving to Chicago in 1880. From 1884 to 1900 Haley taught in an elementary school on the edge of Chicago. While a teacher, she studied progressive child-centered education at Cook County Normal School and at Catholic summer schools for teachers [see **child study movement***].

Haley was an early member of the **Chicago Teachers' Federation,*** organized in 1897 under the leadership of teacher Catharine Goggin to represent elementary school teachers in response to an attack on a newly instituted pension law. Haley quickly rose to district vice president of the federation and left the classroom to investigate the Chicago Board of Education's claim that a shortage of school funds necessitated freezing a promised salary increase for teachers. Haley found that the shortage was due to tax underassessment of a number of Chicago's largest corporations, and she led a successful lawsuit to assess the corporations their full value and assure the salary increase. Her leadership of the tax equity battle gained national attention, drawing support from a wide variety of social and political reformers and inspiring the creation of elementary **teacher unions*** across the country. The fight also spurred teacher membership in the federation so that by 1900 over half of all Chicago elementary school teachers were members of the federation, making it the largest women's union in the country.

As the emerging leader of the federation, Haley molded the group into a powerful force in Chicago politics. She consistently advocated for a stable pension plan and for tenure laws, arguing that the single women who made up most elementary **teaching*** staffs particularly needed job and pension security. To strengthen the federation's authority, she negotiated an unprecedented affiliation with organized labor by joining the predominantly female federation with the industrial Chicago Federation of Labor in 1902. In 1916, the federation became Local 1 of the newly formed American Federation of Teachers.

Haley also fought for women teachers' rights in the National Education Association (NEA), which she accused of being administratively biased, excluding the voices and interests of elementary teachers. In 1901 she became the first woman and first elementary school teacher to speak at a public NEA forum, and she promoted reorganization of NEA elections to facilitate election of candidates who were women classroom teachers. In 1910, she orchestrated the successful election of **Ella Flagg Young*** as first woman president of the NEA. In her notorious 1904 speech before the NEA, "Why Teachers Should Organize," Haley laid out her reform proposals not only for organization of protective unions for teachers but also for an expanded notion of teacher professionalism that included the opportunity to develop progressive pedagogy, improve educational practice, and promote democratic participation of teachers in school administration.

Haley's individual politics took her across a wide spectrum of the American Left. She supported women's **suffrage**,* child labor laws, direct primaries, and tax reform and was a member of the **Women's Trade Union League**.* She lived and worked in a wide circle of women friends and political leaders, including Young, Goggin, and **Jane Addams**.* A self-educated legal scholar and political tactician, Haley was a popular consultant to fledgling teacher organizations and women's groups.

Haley's federation reached its peak of influence between 1909 and 1915 when federation friend Young was Chicago's superintendent. In 1915, a city law prohibiting teachers from joining **labor unions*** forced Haley to withdraw the federation from the Chicago Federation of Labor. In 1916, her longtime colleague Goggin was killed in a traffic accident, leaving Haley alone to fight intensifying political opposition to the federation. Through the antilabor 1920s, the federation declined in power, and Haley's influence faded through the 1930s as a new generation of teacher union leaders joined the American Federation of Teachers. She died on January 5, 1939, at age seventy-seven.

Bibliography: William Hard, "Chicago's Five Maiden Aunts," *American Magazine*, 62 (September 1906): 481–489; Carl Sandburg, "Margaret Haley," *Reedy's Mirror*, 24 (September 1915): 445; Margaret Haley, *Battleground*, ed. Robert Reid (1982); Wayne J. Urban, *Why Teachers Organized* (1982); Marjorie Murphy, *Blackboard Unions: The AFT and the NEA, 1900–1980* (1990). See also papers of the Chicago Teachers' Federation at the Chicago Historical Society.

Kate Rousmaniere

Hampton Institute. Hampton Normal and Agricultural Institute, a privately endowed, coeducational [see **coeducation***], nonsectarian school, was established in April 1868 to meet the educational and spiritual needs of freed slaves living near Hampton Roads, Virginia. The first president and leading force behind the school was Samuel Chapman Armstrong, a former Union officer who commanded African American troops during the Civil War.

After the war, General Oliver Otis Howard, director of the Freedman's Bureau, appointed Armstrong to oversee a ten-county region in eastern Virginia. In 1867, teachers from the **American Missionary Association*** established a small school in Hampton, the Butler School, to provide rudimentary training for recently freed slaves who lived nearby. A short time later, Armstrong pushed for a centrally located school that would produce literate, trained artisans and teachers capable of returning to some of the South's poorest black communities.

Ten years after its establishment, Hampton Institute broadened its mission by welcoming a handful of American Indian students. These students, former prisoners of war, came to the school with their warden, Richard Henry Pratt. Their presence heralded an era of assimilationist policies designed to transform Indian pupils into carbon copies of their Euro-American teachers. Government officials also hoped that eastern boarding schools like Hampton would help make tribal leaders more manageable and cooperative. The Plains wars, it appeared, had been replaced by a different kind of warfare—a battle for the hearts and minds of the next generation of American Indian leaders [see **Bureau of Indian Affairs***].

Hampton's 1,451 American Indian scholars struggled to enter advanced classes. Like their African American classmates, they were exposed to a program structured to train their heads, hands, and hearts. Hampton's academic and **vocational education*** curriculum was designed to cultivate the pupils' industry, perseverance, honesty, and devotion to others. Armstrong fashioned the well-rounded course of study hoping that the Indian and black graduates would become cultural missionaries capable of leading and serving others.

Hampton's faculty paid special attention to the education of Indian women. The first of the 518 female Indian students came to Hampton in November 1878. By 1923, the year Hampton's experimental Indian program ended, 70 (nearly 14 percent) of the Native American women had graduated. Hampton officials worked hard to recruit Indian women but failed to establish an equal ratio of male and female students. Armstrong, disappointed that so few female natives enrolled, complained that it was useless to talk of civilizing a nation without civilizing its women.

Armstrong and his successor, Hollis B. Frissell, devoted considerable attention to the education of young women; they believed that women and men students should receive equal opportunities. Despite such views, female scholars, both Indians and blacks, received a more general education than did their male counterparts. Besides taking the required elementary academic subjects, female students were also expected to master the drudgery of household arts. Many women, however, rejected the tedious chores that failed to prepare them for life after Hampton. Frissell addressed these concerns in 1898 by establishing a Domestic Science department. Besides preparing the female scholars for future careers as teachers of sewing, cooking, and laundering, faculty members also encouraged female Hamptonians to try a variety of manual trades. As a result, the women tended garden plots and participated in the school's "Technical Round," a twice-weekly course that taught students basic carpentry and proper use of everyday tools, skills that unmarried rural teachers and reservation employees put to good use.

Hampton's curriculum for female scholars changed again in 1922 when school officials introduced courses leading to a college degree. In time, administrators gradually dropped elementary and secondary offerings and devoted all of the school's resources to college-level programs.

Hampton's skeptics predicted that American Indians could not be educated. Still others questioned the wisdom of educating Indian youth in a black institution. Perhaps Armstrong hoped to prove his doubters wrong; he may also have agreed to accept Pratt's prisoners of war to bolster Hampton's finances. In either case, the decision changed the way Native Americans were formally educated. Hampton's apparent success led to establishment of **Carlisle Indian School*** in 1879 and a host of other off-reservation boarding schools.

Much of Hampton's growth has occurred since the 1970s. Besides broadening its undergraduate offerings, Hampton achieved university status. In the mid-1990s, female students can pursue graduate degrees in nursing, communication disorders, museum management, biology, science management, business administration, and physics.

Bibliography: Francis G. Peabody, *Education for Life: The Story of Hampton Institute* (1918); Keith L. Schall, ed., *Stony the Road: Chapters in the History of Hampton Institute* (1977); Mary Lou Hultgren and Paulette F. Molin, *To Lead and to Serve: American Indian Education at Hampton Institute, 1878–1923* (1989); David Wallace Adams, *Education for Extinction: American Indians and the Boarding School Experience, 1875–1928* (1995).

Jon L. Brudvig

Hartford Female Seminary. Hartford Female Seminary (1823–1888), a school for girls in Hartford, Connecticut, was founded by **Catharine Beecher**,* a leading nineteenth-century proponent of education for young women. Beecher, who served as principal of the school from its founding until her resignation in 1831 (and again briefly in 1870 and 1871), used the **seminary*** as a proving ground for her educational ideals, especially in training women as teachers and for their domestic roles as mothers of the expanding nation [see **"Republican motherhood"***]. Beecher's ideas were continued by her successors, many of whom were former teachers, pupils, or both. The seminary was one of the first to offer opportunities in higher education to American women, in what historian Joan Hedrick calls "a republican experiment in women's education" (Hedrick, p. 31).

In its heyday, the school boasted over 200 students a term, with a national reputation that drew women from all over the United States and Canada and from American families living abroad.

Women's educational opportunities in the 1820s were limited, and girls' schools were generally considered inferior to boys', providing no set curriculum, no serious courses of study aimed at preparing women beyond "social" skills, and even lacking regular programs or attendance policies [see **common schools***]. Beecher believed that women deserved an equal opportunity in education because of their special place in society: As mothers they were the first and most important teachers, responsible for both moral and intellectual instruction of their families. At Hartford, she established a program of study comparable to those being offered at boys' schools and other modern schools for girls, modeled on the "English" school concept espoused by Benjamin Franklin, aimed at preparation for a practical vocation in the business world.

The school opened in May 1823 with seven students. The first quarters were a single room on the third floor over a harness shop on Main Street, with Catharine aided by her sister Mary and their aunt, Esther Foote. The school was popular, filling a void created by the 1819 closing of Lydia Sigourney's fashionable school for girls. Enrollment increased steadily, requiring a change within a few years to the basement of North Church.

In early 1827 the school was incorporated under the name "Hartford Female Seminary," with eleven trustees, comprising local merchants, ministers, and lawyers. Largely due to Beecher's fund-raising activities, ninety-seven shares of stock (at a par value of $50 each) were subscribed to by fifty-two investors, raising a total of $4,850. This money was used to build a permanent structure for the school at 100 Pratt Street. The new building was planned and designed by Beecher, with assistance by Daniel Wadsworth, a local businessman and friend.

The new academy, which consisted of six recitation rooms, lecture room, and study hall that could accommodate 150 students, was staffed by eight teachers. The school year was divided into two twenty-two-week terms, each term divided into two quarters. The seminary offered a variety of courses for three separate classes, or departments—the Primary, Middle (later called Junior), and Senior. Primary studies were aimed at providing the basics, with remediation as needed, in grammar, arithmetic, composition, and history. Middle studies included work in natural philosophy, algebra, natural history, chemistry, botany, and rhetoric. The final, or senior, year was devoted to geometry, mental and moral philosophy, theology, and analogy.

While the seminary had large numbers of local students, a greater group came from surrounding towns and even out of state. These girls boarded with local families "of good reputation." Tuition varied over the years, from $12 a term in 1831 to $37.50 a term in the late 1860s. Extra charges were made for use of instruments, piano lessons, French and German classes, and instruction in painting, drawing, and singing. Board was separate, ranging from $2.50 to $3.00 a week, with extra charges for fuel and laundry; a few lucky girls had the opportunity to board with the principal, at a cost of $100 per term (1852–1853 catalog). Eventually tuition and board were combined, set at $162.50 per term in 1863–1864, and $500 per year in 1877–1878.

Between 1830 and 1870, enrollments were strong, averaging 160 students per term. An expansion of facilities in 1862 added a gymnasium and studios for both art and music. In the 1860s, a fourth year and a Preparatory Department were added designed to take younger girls and improve remedial offerings. Financing for building additions came from a new subscription of stock, $3,000 raised from the sale of seventy-five newly issued shares. After the Civil War, enrollment declines forced the trustees to borrow money for operating expenses. This trend continued for a number of years, with the 1877–1878 catalog listing only 66 students.

In October 1888, the stockholders voted to sell the building to pay the increasing debts. A sale was arranged to the Good Will Club of Hartford, and $17,000 was received. After settling the institution's debts, between $7,000 and $8,000 remained, which some hoped would be seed money for a new building fund. After brief discussions, the stockholders voted to close the corporation as a legal business and divided up the remaining monies.

Reasons for the seminary's failure and its declining enrollments center around the school's failure to expand into a college curriculum, as had other women's schools like **Smith**,* **Wellesley**,* and **Mount Holyoke**.* Another factor was the post–Civil War shift in educational values, which fueled a marked increase in free public **high schools**.* Locally, competition from Hartford Public High School contributed to the attrition, while nationally the trend resulted in declining enrollments statewide and of out-of-state students. It is ironic that a school that succeeded by being ahead of the curve in the national consciousness would find its demise by failure to keep up.

Bibliography: Catharine Beecher, *An Essay on the Education of Female Teachers* (1835); Beecher, *Educational Reminiscences and Suggestions* (1874); Mary Kingsbury Talcott, ''Historical Sketch of the Seminary,'' in *Hartford Female Seminary Reunion* (1892); Katherine Kish Sklar, *Catharine Beecher: A Study in American Domesticity* (1973); Daniel Walker Howe, *The Political Culture of the American Whigs* (1984); Joan Hedrick, *Harriet Beecher Stowe: A Life* (1994).

Thomas Ratliff

Heterodoxy. Heterodoxy was a feminist club begun with twenty-five women members in 1912 in Greenwich Village, New York City. Marie Jenny Howe, a Unitarian minister and suffragist, founded the organization, demanding only that a member ''not be orthodox in her opinion.'' A number of famous women belonged to this club, including writer **Charlotte Perkins Gilman**,* social investigator Crystal Eastman, psychologist Leta Hollingworth, anthropologist Elsie Clews Parsons, **suffrage*** leader Doris Stevens, and journalist Rheta Childe Dorr.

Howe called a mass meeting on February 17, 1914, at Cooper Union in lower Manhattan to discuss the question, What is feminism? Howe provided her own answer, calling it ''women's effort to break into the human race.'' She urged the assembled group to work for women's entrance into every field of human endeavor.

Heterodoxy met every other Saturday for lunch to discuss topics that included pacifism, birth control, the Russian Revolution, civil rights for African Americans, anarchism, women's education, and free love. The group was concerned with the effects of these developments on women's lives, especially in their opportunities for economic independence and sexual freedom. A number of men, including Max Eastman, Floyd Dell, and George Creel, also addressed the meetings.

Leta Hollingworth and Elsie Clews Parsons offered research to support the notion of men's and women's essential similarity. Hollingworth's study of women's intellectual aptitude and Parsons's cross-cultural investigation of gender roles provided scientific authority for new attitudes about women. Club members believed that feminist ideals could be promoted through education in schools and colleges, the workforce, and labor and socialist organizations.

Members of Heterodoxy included heterosexual, bisexual, and lesbian women who seemed to respect their colleagues' choices. Despite their ''free-willed'' and ''individualistic'' natures, as one member described fellow clubwomen, they supported efforts to develop cooperative solutions to problems faced by professional women, such as housework. Heterodoxy was significant in providing a small, yet influential, group of women a forum to discuss and develop the concept of feminism in a more radical direction than that espoused by mainstream suffrage organizations of the day.

Bibliography: Rheta Childe Dorr, *A Woman of Fifty* (1924); June Sochen, *The New Woman: Feminism in Greenwich Village, 1910–1920* (1972); Judith Schwarz, *The Radical Feminists of Heterodoxy* (1982); Rosalind Rosenberg, *Divided Lives: American Women in the Twentieth Century* (1992).

Margaret Smith Crocco

high schools. By the 1880s high schools had become the dominant institutions for secondary education in the United States. Their proliferation in the latter part of the nineteenth century was a joint function of urbanization and the **common school*** movement. High schools were more adaptive to cities than the **academies*** and **seminaries*** that they eventually displaced. In many districts the high school was held up as the capstone of the local school system, providing a sense of symmetry, academic incentive to students in lower grades, and teachers for the burgeoning elementary schools.

During the nineteenth century the high school's primary objectives were intellectual and moral development of students. Educators in early high schools instituted a classical curriculum that, they believed, would address intellectual and moral development as well as prepare students for college. Not all students were college bound, however. The high school curriculum reflected the influence of the academy as it added courses in advanced mathematics, sciences, modern languages, and history. During the final decades of the nineteenth century, then, the public high school represented a synthesis of the Latin grammar school and the academy.

Educators in the United States committed themselves to the comprehensive high school, rejecting the European model of specialized secondary schools, prior to the turn of the twentieth century. The comprehensive high school, while it denied student segregation by schools, did not ensure equal education for all. A differentiated curriculum accompanied acceptance of comprehensive high schools and, since 1900, has remained a dominant feature of the U.S. public high school. This, perhaps more than any other innovation, altered women's high school experience. The differentiated curriculum was based on the premise that the primary objective of a high school education is to prepare students for specific life roles. One result is that schooling has been strongly connected to work throughout this century. The idea that the first objective of high school study is to develop intellectual capacities of an individual has given way to the notion that schools are to fit students for their life's work and, thereby, serve the interests of the larger society. In a society that perceives women's work as distinct from men's, the assumption follows that women's education should differ. This thinking has determined the trajectory of American women's high school education in the twentieth century.

The English Classical School, the first high school in the United States, was established in Boston in 1821. It followed the common practice of excluding girls from public institutions of secondary education. The Boston High School for Girls opened in 1826. As might be expected, given the success of women's seminaries, students responded enthusiastically to the new opportunities and performed well. Just one year later, however, city officials refused to fund the Boston High School for Girls, arguing that since women's contributions to the public sphere were few, no need for public funding of their secondary education existed. Some cities in the East established separate high schools for girls, but these generally were not equivalent to those for boys; frequently, the girls' schools were **normal schools*** dedicated solely to teacher preparation.

The years following the Civil War marked the beginning of growth for high schools, and the great majority were coeducational. The cost of providing separate schools was too burdensome for most cities. Further, since **coeducation*** was a widespread convention in primary grades, parents and teachers found little problem with extending the practice.

It is difficult to determine precisely the number of nineteenth-century high schools due to two factors. First, poor records were kept, and many often conflict. This may be connected to the second factor, lack of a clear definition for what type of institution would qualify as a high school. Nonetheless, there were an estimated 1,026 high schools in 1870, 6,005 in 1900, and 14,326 by 1920.

Support for public high schools was spurred by an 1874 court case. In *Stuart v. Kalamazoo*, the Michigan Supreme Court ruled that the state constitutional provision for free schools included high schools, and therefore taxation to support public high schools was constitutional. This case inaugurated rapid high school development; however, an expansion in secondary schooling did not occur for all segments of the population. Public high schools for African Americans in the South were virtually nonexistent from 1860 through 1935. While 216 private high schools in the South accepted African American students, there were only 58 public high schools for African American children in all sixteen former slave states as late as 1916. Georgia, Mississippi, South Carolina, Louisiana, and North Carolina provided no four-year public high schools for African Americans; Florida, Maryland, and Delaware had one each.

The numbers of students enrolled in public high schools increased by more than thirty times between 1890 and 1940 as enrollments soared from 202,963 to 6,545,991. Still, for most of these years these numbers represent less than half the school-age population. In 1890 only 6.7 percent of persons age fourteen to seventeen were enrolled in secondary (including private) schools; in 1910, 15.4 percent. The 50 percent mark was reached in 1930, and by 1940, 73.3 percent of school-age children were attending secondary school. The percentages of graduates were much lower. In 1890, 3.5 percent of all seventeen-year-olds had graduated from high school; in 1910, 8.6 percent. Less than one-third of seventeen-year-olds graduated in 1930 (28.8 percent), and as of 1940, 49 percent were high school graduates. The failure of southern states to provide public high schools greatly affected African American students. In 1890 fewer than 1 percent (0.39 percent) of African American children of high school age who lived in southern states attended high school. In 1910 the figure stood at 2.8 percent. Even by 1940, only 22.9 percent of school-age African American children were attending public high schools. The comparison makes the effects of racist school policy clear.

Throughout the nineteenth century the high school maintained small enrollments, and attrition was high. Rural youth had limited access, African Americans virtually none, and immigrant enrollments varied. Working-class children, in general, could not afford the time-cost associated with attendance; even though tuition charges were phased out in the early stages, money lost in time away from work was too great a sacrifice for poor families. George Counts's 1922 study of secondary schools found it a selective institution, primarily serving the middle class.

One characteristic of the high school student population captured the attention of contemporary educators and the general public but has often been overlooked since. From 1870 to 1930 girls constituted the majority of high school students and graduates. In 1900, for instance, 58 percent of public high school students were girls (63 percent of graduates). Girls comprised an even greater percentage of the African American student population; 68 percent of all African American high school students in 1898 and in 1918 were girls. During the nineteenth century girls and boys studied the same subjects, with girls equaling or outperforming boys academically. Near the turn of the century, educators devoted great effort to resolving this "boy problem." The curriculum transformation that resulted had a major impact on the twentieth-century high school.

The mission of the nineteenth-century high school radiated in three directions. From an organizational standpoint, the urban high school was expected to unify the local system of schools and help standardize the elementary curriculum by requiring an entrance examination. Educators hoped that students would be enticed to continue their studies by the possibility of high school matriculation. Preparation for college marked another element of the mission, although few students who entered extended their formal education. Finally, the high school marketed itself as "preparation for life." With the exception of young women preparing to teach, however, any connection to specific job training was tenuous. Rather, the high school credential was perceived as a sign of good conduct and perseverance, highly valued skills in the job market.

Changes in the political economy stemming from urbanization, industrialization, and immigration melded with an ideology of **Social Darwinism*** based on a perception of the world as an evolving organism and new conceptions of humanity based on the emerging science of psychology to create a vastly different educational philosophy. Perceived differences among individuals and groups were stressed by intellectuals who saw the social order based on specialization and unification. On one hand, it was expected that each individual had a particular societal role to play; on the other, reformers believed human progress was dependent on careful orchestration of individual components. Therefore, early in the twentieth century the high school mission shifted; it became a social screen of sorts, a place where students were categorized and prepared accordingly for their economic and social destinies. The differentiated curriculum was pressed into service as the all-purpose mechanism. The implementation of the differentiated curriculum serves as the watershed that distinguishes the distinct educational philosophies undergirding the nineteenth- and twentieth-century high schools.

Historian Edward Krug has asserted that social efficiency was the driving concern in the twentieth-century high school. When it meant preparation for employment, women's schooling was thus limited to training for "women's jobs." When it meant preparation for effective citizenship, women's schooling focused on studies for "municipal, or **social housekeeping**."* Twentieth-century educators clearly sanctioned different educational objectives for the sexes. In most high schools the push for social efficiency did not lead to physical separation of the sexes, but the notion that schooling would prepare girls and boys for different roles did affect patterns of course selection. For example, girls' enrollments in mathematics and science decreased significantly, but they came to dominate others. Given the intensified connection between school and work, and women's entry into clerical jobs during the **Progressive Era**,* **commercial education*** became a sex-stereotyped course. In 1922 girls constituted

63 percent of all high school students in bookkeeping, 76 percent in shorthand, and 70 percent in typing.

The surge toward social efficiency in the early 1900s continued in the 1940s emphasis on life adjustment education. Promoters of this antiintellectual movement argued that the primary goal of high school was social adjustment, and they emphasized a "functional" education for low-income students. Life adjustment educators believed that practical classes would benefit most students who were expected to serve society as home members, workers, and citizens. This phase came under criticism during the Cold War when fear of communism and concerns for social stability took a commanding role in directing public policy. Harvard president James Bryant Conant's studies in the 1950s and 1960s emerged as a leading critique. He expected the differentiated curriculum to track the majority of students into general studies or **vocational education**,* while the "academically talented" would be funneled into college preparatory classes. Unity would be preserved by mixing students together in homerooms and government classes.

Throughout the twentieth century, concerns for social stability and employability, not intellectual development, have directed development of the high school. Vocational education has claimed a larger share of the curriculum. The 1980s reform movement, which declared the United States "at risk" because of poor school performance, appears to be inconversant with this history of the high school. Academic study was deliberately abandoned for many students as part of school policy. David Nasaw has suggested that the high school, as a social panacea, was eclipsed after half a century; today it is merely a staging area for youth on their way to work or higher education. This development had particular consequences for girls. Educational historians describe the high school as one of the most egalitarian public spaces for women in the nineteenth century. However, once the institution took the role of fitting students for a sexist social order, the type of education offered girls changed and a new model was established. The academic legacy of nineteenth-century high school girls has been all but forgotten in the process.

Bibliography: George Counts, *The Selective Character of American Secondary Education* (1922); Edward A. Krug, *The Shaping of the American High School*, 2 vols. (1972); David Nasaw, *Schooled to Order: A Social History of Public Schooling in the United States* (1979); Clarence J. Karier, *The Individual, Society, and Education: A History of American Educational Ideas*, 2nd ed. (1986); James D. Anderson, *The Education of Blacks in the South, 1860–1935* (1988); David Tyack and Elisabeth Hansot, *Learning Together: A History of Coeducation in American Public Schools* (1990); William J. Reese, *The Origins of the American High School* (1995).

Karen L. Graves

Hill, Patty Smith. Patty Smith Hill (1868–1946), pioneer in the Progressive education movement and early childhood teacher educator, devoted her life to child advocacy and community service.

Hill was born and raised at Bellewood Female Seminary, the school for young women founded and headed by her father, Dr. William Wallace Hill, in Anchorage, Kentucky. In the 1860s, Hill was an advocate of independent women, and he encouraged his children (female and male) and his students to prepare for a career. Patty's mother, Martha Jane Smith Hill, was college educated, most unusual for a pre–Civil War woman. The family lived in Missouri, Texas, and Kentucky during Hill's childhood, where her father presided over two colleges before his early death. Alternating periods of prosperity and destitution, as well as love and respect for learning in her family, left a lasting impression on Hill.

Hill received a solid classical education, graduating in 1887 from Louisville Collegiate Institute. She immediately became one of the first five students in Anna E. Bryan's newly organized training department of the Louisville Free Kindergarten Association (LFKA). Following initial training, she was asked by Bryan to head the association's premier **kindergarten**.* Hill continued to develop her interests in play, **child study**,* and creativity. Bryan and Hill sustained their professional development by attending courses and workshops as colleagues. At a lecture by G. Stanley Hall detailing his research in child development, they learned Hall's views regarding the psychological unsoundness and limitations of Froebelianism. Hill integrated the work of several prominent educators with whom she had studied, including Hall, into both her kindergarten program and her display at the 1893 **World's Columbian Exhibition*** in Chicago, one of several expositions to acquaint the general public with the merits of kindergarten.

In 1893 Hill became director of the LFKA and began her twelve years of supervisory stewardship. Her duties included supervising the training school and nine kindergartens, overseeing the nurses and Sunday school training departments, coordinating parents' classes and clubs, and boarding arrangements for nonresident women attending kindergarten training school. Hill's philosophy was one of inclusion, and she aimed the LFKA program at children who came from different conditions due to home environment, race, and the physical, social, and intellectual status of child groups. Children's cleanliness and health concerned the administrator and teachers as much as their play and learning.

Hill's curriculum development initiatives began during her days as a kindergarten teacher in Louisville and continued during her tenure as supervisor and director. Her work bore fruit in the 1923 publication of *A Conduct Curriculum for the Kindergarten and First Grade*, during her time on the faculty of Teachers College, Columbia University, in New York City. The Conduct Curriculum supported the view of character building through training called ''habit formation'' and was based on stimulus-response psychology. A ''habit inventory'' of skills, attitudes, habits, and ideas that teachers could inculcate through classroom activities was developed and utilized at the Horace Mann School of Teachers College. Weber recounts that the incompatibility of elevating a fixed set of habits as goals of the kindergarten program with expounding the concept of individual purpose and psychological continuity of growth (after Dewey's flexible social framework of problem solving) apparently went unrecognized by those closely involved in the experimentation. However, the Conduct Curriculum publication does recognize an important part of Hill's work: the emphasis on the continuity between kindergarten and first grade, in curriculum, methodology, and professional education.

Hill was an early childhood teacher educator [see **early childhood teacher education***] for most of her professional life. She began, as did most female teacher educators of her time, with the model of apprenticeship she herself had followed. In supervising the training department of the LFKA, she offered young women internship teaching positions and provided courses and workshops for teachers already employed by the program. Hill's evolving national reputation led to a 1905 visiting lectureship at Teachers College. She was responsible for presenting a series of lectures on new views of the kindergarten, alternating with **Susan Blow.*** Blow, a well-respected Frobelian twenty-five years her senior, was a lecturer. It is a tribute to Hill's graciousness and charm as well as her capability as a thinker and exponent of the beliefs of the Progressive wing of the kindergarten movement that this lecture series led to a permanent faculty position at the college.

Hill joined, and was influenced by, such notables of education as John Dewey, William Heard Kilpatrick, and Edward Thorndike in the experimental atmosphere at Teachers College. She earned rapid promotions, unusual for a woman, reaching full professor in 1922. Hill was accepted because she fit into a niche defined as women's work. She did not encroach upon men's domain but became even more proficient in her own, and she turned to them for support when the tedious work had been done. In 1910 she became Head of the Department of Nursery School, Kindergarten, and First Grade Education, which she held for thirty years. In 1921 she undertook a second post as Director of the Institute for Child Welfare Research (later known as the Institute for Child Development), with its related **nursery school.*** Her work at Teachers College was focused in three areas: design and implementation of her laboratory kindergarten and nursery schools, and her teacher training program.

Hill was a founding member of the two major early childhood education organizations in the United States. She helped create (1892) the International Kindergarten Union (IKU), now known as the Association for Childhood Education International (ACEI), and served on its Committee of Nineteen for a decade beginning in 1903. Hill authored the report on the liberal position, one of three reports examining different viewpoints about psychology and kindergarten curriculum held by kindergartners (the term for kindergarten professionals) and IKU members of the time. For fifty years Hill served on numerous IKU and ACEI committees, spoke eloquently at national conferences, and wrote for the organization's publications. She served as vice president and president of the IKU. She was founder of the National Association of Nursery Educators, when she called together a group of twenty-five nursery school and parent educators and psychologists in New York City in 1926. The National Association for Nursery Education (NANE) was formally chartered in 1929 and is currently known as the National Association for the Education of Young Children (NAEYC). Hill was a speaker and workshop leader in its early years, but she never held elective office. She was named the first honorary member of NANE in 1931.

Her own publications covered a wide range of topics, including all areas of **early childhood education*** curriculum, application of philosophical principles to practice, experimental research in kindergarten and nursery education, the function of the kindergarten, and education of nursery and kindergarten teachers.

The story of the song "Happy Birthday to You," written by Patty and her sister Mildred, and published in their book *Song Stories for Children* (1899), is a prime example of Patty's humanitarian and organizational commitments. One night in 1935, she attended a Broadway play in which "Happy Birthday" was sung. The Hill sisters were not credited in the program, nor had they given permission for their copyrighted song to be used. Patty won a lawsuit against the show's producer and initially used the money to establish nursery schools and kindergartens for low-income children in New York City housing projects. Hill instructed her heirs to name ACEI the remainder beneficiary of money generated by the song. The final transfer of this gift in 1996 supports and perpetuates both her memory and her extensive and outstanding work in early childhood education and teacher education.

Bibliography: E. Weber, *The Kindergarten: Its Encounter with Educational Thought in America* (1969); A. Snyder and Early Leaders in Childhood Education Committee, *Dauntless Women in Childhood Education 1856–1931* (1972); Dorothy Hewes, "Patty Smith Hill: Pioneer for Young Children," *Young Children*, 31 (May 1976): 297–306; M. A. Fowlkes, "Patty Smith Hill: Pivotal Figure in Childhood Education" (paper presented at the Association for Childhood Education International: One Hundred Years of Kindergarten, 1992). Patty Smith Hill's papers are housed at the Filson Club (historical society), Louisville, Kentucky.

Blythe S. F. Hinitz

Hispanic American women's education. The diverse people who constitute the Hispanic American population include Mexican Americans (representing almost two-thirds), Puerto Ricans, Cuban Americans, and Central and Latin American immigrants. The educational history of Hispanic American women occupies a nebulous position between the few works that examine the history of schooling for Hispanic Americans and the post-1970s flowering of scholarship on the history of women. Consequently, researchers and students studying the history of schooling for Hispanic American women must seek information from widely scattered articles; no single book exists on this subject.

Within the larger experience of Hispanic American children in the United States, Latinas have faced issues universal to all members of this group, namely, discrimination in segregated and inferior schools, a loss of culture and language upon entering the public schools (particularly early twentieth century restrictions against speaking Spanish in schools), and familial obligations that curbed educational opportunities and ambitions.

From the colonial period in the Southwest until the Treaty of Guadalupe Hidalgo in 1848 when Mexico surrendered large portions of territory to the United States, schooling for young women of Hispanic background, mostly the Hispanos of New Mexico and the Mexican Americans of California and Texas, occurred under the auspices of **Catholic teaching orders**.* Upper-class Mexican girls in late nineteenth-century Texas, for example, attended the Ursuline Convent in San Antonio or the Incarnate Word of Brownsville. After annexation, the development of public education in southwestern communities explicitly and subtly curbed educational opportunities by legal means such as the English-language law enacted in Texas only two years after public schools were established (1856). Similarly, in California the Education Code stipulated that Mexican American children be educated in separate schools. In 1947 this ruling was no longer part of the code de jure but remained a de facto situation for many Hispanic children, particularly those in large cities such as Los Angeles.

Hispanic women educated in these discriminatory settings vividly recall the humiliation endured in public school. Born in 1934, Rosa Ramirez Guerrero attended schools in El Paso, Texas. Her teacher verbally and physically injured her for speaking Spanish, saying, "Don't you speak that ugly language, you are an American now, you Mexican child," and would give Rosa a severe paddling. These experiences led Guerrero, who became a high school teacher, to later explain, "That's why I'm so committed to the bilingual program, heart and soul, because I suffered horribly. I wasn't the only one, there were thousands of people who suffered in Arizona, Colorado, New Mexico, Texas, California; they stereotyped us horribly" (Ruiz, pp. 226–227).

Hispanic challenges to unfair practices and conditions in schools have been documented in several works. San Miguel's *"Let All of Them Take Heed": Mexican Americans and the Campaign for Educational Equality in Texas, 1910–1981* was the first book-length study of the history of education in a Chicano community. Subsequent works such as Gilbert Gonzalez's *Chicano Education in the Era of Segregation* (1990), Charles Wollenberg's *All Deliberate Speed: Segregation and Exclusion in California Schools, 1855–1975* (1975), and Judith Rosenberg Raftery's *Land of Fair Promise: Politics and Reform in Los Angeles Schools, 1885–1941* (1992) have included, or focus exclusively on, the struggle for Chicano educational rights. These works and studies of **vocational education*** show that Mexican American girls in the first decades of the twentieth century, similarly to African African girls, were channeled into vocational training classes designed to match their perceived futures as servants, waitresses, or other menial laborers.

While historians are slowly piecing together various aspects of the history of schooling for Hispanics in lower levels of education, such as the experiences of children in publicly supported migrant schools and histories of Puerto Rican and Cuban immigrants, the history of higher education and Latina women also cries out for research. In Padilla's *The Leaning Ivory Tower*, Latina women who have entered academe candidly recount their isolating experiences. In 1996 only 3 percent of U.S. professors identified themselves as of Hispanic origin, and of those, most likely less than half were women. Despite the barriers facing Latinas in higher education, scholars such as historian Vicki Ruiz, sociologist Maxine Baca Zinn, and anthropologist Adelaida Del Castillo have not only provided role models for Latina women but have dedicated their research to issues of importance to the Hispanic American community.

In the public sector, Linda Chavez, author of *Out of El Barrio: Toward a New Politics of Hispanic Assimilation* (1991), worked for the National Education Association, served as a consultant to the U.S. Department of Health, Education and Welfare, and joined the staff of the American Federation of Teachers. In 1983 she was appointed executive director of the U.S. Commission on Civil Rights and in 1996 was president of U.S. English, a private nonprofit organization designed to make English the official national language. Mari-Luci Jaramillo, born in 1928, also used education to rise to positions of influence. Jaramillo first taught elementary school, then joined the faculty of the University of New Mexico. After serving as ambassador to the Honduras under President Jimmy Carter, she returned to academe until 1987 when Educational Testing Services hired Jaramillo first as vice president of its San Francisco Bay area office and in 1992 as assistant vice president for field services. In 1986 she was named corecipient of the Harvard Graduate School of Education's Anne Roe Award honoring influential women educators.

The educational history of Hispanic American women has suffered from neglect in the fields of both American women's history and educational history. As contemporary educators and analysts continue to express alarm at the high rates of **high school*** dropouts among Latino/a youth and low rates of college attendance, exploration of the myriad cultural and historical contexts in which Latina women have experienced schooling will enrich our understanding and policymaking for the twenty-first century.

Bibliography: Maxine Baca Zinn, ''Mexican American Women in the Social Sciences,'' *Signs: Journal of Women in Culture and Society*, 8 (1982): 259–272; Vicki L. Ruiz, ''Oral History and La Mujer: The Rosa Guerrero Story,'' in Ruiz and Susan Tiano, eds., *Women on the U.S.–Mexico Border: Responses to Change* (1987); Guadalupe San Miguel, *''Let All of Them Take Heed'': Mexican Americans and the Campaign for Educational Equality in Texas, 1910–1981* (1987); Diana Telgen and Jim Kamp, eds., *Notable Hispanic American Women* (1993); Ruth F. Zambrana, ''Toward Understanding the Educational Trajectory and Socialization of Latina Women,'' in Lynda Stone, ed., *The Education Feminism Reader* (1994); Raymond V. Padilla, *The Leaning Ivory Tower: Latino Professors in American Universities* (1995).

Victoria-Maria MacDonald

home economics. *Home economics* refers to the theory and practice of homemaking. Home economics emerged as a discipline for study in the late nineteenth century and rather quickly emerged as a "women's profession." Today it is taught in a variety of formal and informal settings from public schools and universities to home extension work, television shows, and how-to literature.

The roots of home economics are found in the domestic science advice of the mid-nineteenth century. With increasing industrialization and the removal of male work from the home, the work of men and women was eventually separated. Developed to justify this separation, the ideology of **separate spheres*** held that men's proper role was to go out into the harsh and impersonal public world to make a living for their families. By contrast, the work of married women was to create a home that was a haven from this cruel world [see **prescriptive literature***].

Not only did industrialization segregate men's and women's spheres of activity, but the development of wage labor encouraged the notion that real work was that which earned cash. In order to elevate the status of women's work, many reformers began to call for the professionalization of homemaking.

To this end, a number of women, **Catharine Beecher*** being the most famous, began to write household instruction manuals, including the classic *Domestic Economy* (1845). These books taught women that their work might be tedious, but it was very important. The housewife made critical decisions about the health and well-being of her family. Household instruction manuals applied science to housekeeping, presenting it as a systematic process requiring specialized knowledge of nutrition, hygiene, and chemistry, among other sciences. Motherhood, too, became a job to be scientifically managed, and advice manuals were full of instruction on how to raise healthy and responsible young citizens.

Although **Charlotte Perkins Gilman**,* author of *Women and Economics* (1898) and *The Home* (1903), and other midcentury reformers advocated schemes for cooperative housekeeping that would have further rationalized homemaking by removing its most odious chores, these plans were offensive to domestic science reformers who believed that the only way to raise the status of women was to raise the status of work they performed in their homes. As a result, domestic science advice served to isolate the individual woman, devaluing communal mutual aid strategies. The development of domestic science advice was part of the mid-nineteenth-century process of privatizing the nuclear family.

Beecher and her peers advocated teaching domestic science in schools. The domestic science movement led to the first organized program of domestic education at **Mount Holyoke Female Seminary*** in Massachusetts in 1837. Other women's schools began offering domestic instruction. In 1862, with the passage of the **Morrill Land-Grant Act*** to fund agricultural colleges, college-level domestic science instruction spread. Reformers believed that women should be educated in domestic science so that they would make efficient and thrifty wives for farmer or businessman husbands.

Gilded Age and **Progressive Era*** reformers saw domestic science as a way to bring order to cities, intervening directly in working-class households by teaching poor urban women how to run decent and clean homes. Reformers also believed that domestic science could play an important role in Americanizing immigrants. By the late nineteenth century, **settlement houses*** and public schools joined colleges and universities in offering domestic science instruction.

The rise of various domestic science programs led to a new group of professionals specializing in domestic science education. Particularly at the university level, home economics provided a new field of professional opportunity for college-educated women who could not otherwise find jobs. Women with degrees in the sciences, unable to find employment in scientific research, often found places in college home economics departments, which were quickly expanding at the turn of the century to accommodate young women students flooding American universities. Seeking to gain the respect of their fellow faculty members, many home economics professors followed the lead of Massachusetts Institute of Technology–trained chemist and home economist Ellen Swallow Richards in seeking to upgrade their curricula as well as the quality of advice being offered by domestic science experts, engaging in research on the scientific bases of nutrition, household sanitation, and childrearing [see **science education***].

In order to organize themselves and confront issues facing their profession, participants in various domestic education programs convened in 1899 at Lake Placid, New York. They began to meet annually, renaming themselves the American Home Economics Association in 1908. College and university programs began to specialize in preparing home economics professionals who would work as home extension agents, public school teachers, and settlement workers. The movement received a real boost with passage of the 1914 **Smith-Lever Act*** to fund **home extension education*** and the 1917 **Smith-Hughes Act*** to fund vocational instruction, including home economics teaching, in public schools.

The twentieth century saw an explosion in household technology, and home economists eagerly encouraged its use. Women's magazines, books, and home economics teachers all taught women to plan their work carefully and to use the new technology to introduce rationality and efficiency into their housework. Unfortunately, the new technology and the teachings of home economists also raised standards for homemaking; new levels of cleanliness were expected in middle-class homes. Moreover, home economists encouraged increased consumption by homemakers. Recognizing the potential in the home economics movement, manufacturers hired home economists to develop new uses for consumer products and to educate homemakers about their use.

Sweeping social changes in the twentieth century have seen many women enter the workforce, forcing home economists to alter their advice. Today the advice of home economists still turns on efficient housekeeping and motherhood, but specific instruction often centers more on such topics as preparing quick meals after work and juggling the demands of motherhood and a full-time job. Home economics instruction is often directed at young men as well as women, with high school home economics teachers offering such courses as ''Bachelor Living'' and ''Family Living.''

Home economists continue to work in diverse settings: as high school and university instructors, as magazine writers, as product developers for manufacturers of consumers products, as home extension agents, and even as television show hosts. Most Americans have been exposed to some level of home economics education.

Bibliography: Bettina Berch, ''Scientific Management in the Home: The Empress's New Clothes,'' *Journal of American Culture*, 3 (Fall 1980): 207–219; Susan Strasser, *Never Done: A History of American Housework* (1982); Ruth Schwartz Cowan, *More Work for Mother: The Ironies of Household Technology from the Open Hearth to the Microwave* (1983); Margaret Rossiter, *Women Scientists in America: Before Affirmative Action, 1940–1972* (1995).

Melissa Walker

home extension education. Home extension education (also known as home demonstration work) is **home economics*** education delivered directly to homemakers by local home economists.

Home extension education grew out of cooking schools for farmers' wives that were held at farmers' institutes sponsored by agricultural colleges during the 1890s. Gradually some farmers' organizations, **Progressive Era*** reformers, and local government officials perceived a need to teach farmwives modern home management practices in order to enlist them in the fight to make the family farm more economically viable and country life more comfortable and attractive. Some counties and farmers' organizations hired trained home economists to provide systematic home economics education to farm women. Seeing the success of this effort, Progressive reformers urged Congress to set up a national system of extension education with agriculturalists teaching farmers improved farming practices and home economists helping rural women adopt more efficient housekeeping methods. In 1914 Congress passed the **Smith-Lever Act**,* which provided matching funds to state and local governments for hiring agricultural and home extension agents.

The Smith-Lever Act established a nationwide system of extension education for farm families. The act also established an Office of Cooperative Education within the U.S. Department of Agriculture that coordinated national extension work and set policy regarding topics for extension education. Using state and local funds in addition to monies provided by the act, counties appointed agriculturalists who provided education to farmers and home economists who worked with farm women.

Home extension agents organized home demonstration clubs, which formed the center of home extension education. Although the agenda for home demonstration work was heavily influenced by the home extension workers and the Office of Cooperative Extension, clubwomen themselves ultimately determined which topics they wanted to learn. Home extension agents learned about new research in home economics from specialists based at the state's land-grant university. They brought this information back to the local level and trained a few farm women to ''demonstrate'' the new techniques to others at home demonstration club meetings. Home extension agents also worked with children enrolled in 4-H clubs. In the South, home extension work was segregated until the 1950s, with black agents serving black women.

Much of the work of home extension agents focused on turning farmwives into educated consumers. Women were also taught improved methods of food preparation and preservation, nutrition and menu planning, sewing techniques, home decorating, and budget management. Home extension work reinforced suburban middle-class notions that women should be homemakers and consumers rather than producers of farm commodities or profits.

As the country's population was transformed from rural to urban, home extension agents shifted their focus to the educational needs of the suburban homemaker. Today, home extension education provides information on topics as diverse as traditional cooking and time management for working mothers. In 1985, the National Extension Homemaker's Council, an organization made up of 30,000 organized home demonstration clubs, boasted over 500,000 women enrolled in home extension work. Millions more women not enrolled in home demonstration clubs received advice from home extension agents on an ad hoc basis.

Bibliography: Eleanor Arnold, ed., *Voices of American Homemakers* (1985); Earl W. Crosby, ''The Struggle for Existence: The Institutionalization of the Black County Agent System,'' *Agricultural History*, 60 (Spring 1986): 123–136; Joan M. Jensen, ''Crossing Ethnic Boundaries in the Southwest: Women's Agricultural Extension Education, 1914–1940,'' *Agricultural History*, 60 (Spring 1986): 169–181; Wayne D. Rasmussen, *Taking the University to the People: Seventy Five Years of Cooperative Extension* (1989).

Melissa Walker

Howard University. Howard University is a private, coeducational, historically black university located in Washington, D.C. Founded in 1867, Howard served a dual mission of educating blacks and other youth in the liberal arts and sciences. In existence for 130 years, the institution has over 70,000 alumni and offers bachelor's, master's, and doctoral degrees as well as professional degrees in law, medicine, pharmacy, dentistry, and divinity. One of the nation's premier black institutions, Howard has been open to women since its founding.

The university was chartered on March 2, 1867, in an era when blacks had new liberties from the Emancipation Proclamation and the Thirteenth Amendment, which abolished **slavery.*** Before the official chartering, two alternative proposals were offered to its presumptive board of trustees. The first, drafted November 1866, was to establish a theological seminary for training black preachers to provide spiritual services to other blacks. The second plan, in December 1866, proposed to establish the Howard Normal and Theological Institute for the Education of Teachers and Preachers. The intent of this proposal was to discourage widespread notions that the formerly enslaved blacks were intellectually inferior to whites. Such racist ideologies were promoted by people and organizations such as John C. Calhoun, Thomas R. Dew, and the American Colonization Society. This latter organization, along with colonization societies in New England and elsewhere, rationalized slavery by claiming that Africans were savages and heathens and should be brought to the new American colonies to be disciplined with civility and Christianity. These ideologues felt it was their God-given duty to indoctrinate such "savages." In this milieu, Howard's trustees responded by creating an institution committed to educating youth in liberal arts and sciences. The trustees accepted the second proposal and elected to change the institution's name to Howard University.

The university was named after Civil War hero and Freedmen's Bureau commissioner General Oliver O. Howard. Howard, who was white, was one of the institution's founders and served as its second president from 1869 to 1873. He is credited with laying the foundation for the university's educational framework and for establishing its physical site through solicited donations and his own personal contributions. Howard University was financially supported by the Freedmen's Bureau until its dissolution in 1873. At that point private contributions, donations, and federal government subsidies sustained Howard.

At Howard's inception, there was no distinction made in admissions based on gender or race. Within a few years, however, Howard became a predominantly black institution. Howard University contributed significantly to the education of black and white women at a time when women's higher education was being debated. The education of blacks was a major focal point of Reconstruction policies, with the Freedmen's Bureau serving as one important vehicle. But the era also considered how to apply the ideals of **"true womanhood"*** to both blacks and whites. True womanhood for whites utilized education as a means to emphasize feminine qualities such as innocence, purity, piety, domesticity, modesty, and submissiveness. True womanhood seemed less pertinent to black women, however, who used education as a means to elevate an oppressed race. This concept was known as **race uplift***: By receiving an education, black women were expected to aid in the economic, social, educational, and cultural development of a great mass of people.

Early in Howard University's history, there were two major schools of thought regarding the education of blacks. Booker T. Washington forwarded the idea that blacks should seek an industrial education, which would allow them to gain economically by providing skills and services from which both blacks and whites could benefit, including domestic service and masonry. Dr. W.E.B. Du Bois challenged Washington's notions by arguing that blacks should receive a liberal arts education so that they could become the "talented tenth"—intellectuals who contribute to and disseminate a body of knowledge. Du Bois saw black teachers, professors, and other professionals as leaders in the campaign toward equality.

Howard University subscribed to the Du Boisian tenet, affording both black and white women the opportunity to teach and learn. Because few women had received college or university education at the time that Howard opened, very few females taught on its faculty. However, its first **dean of women**,* **Lucy Diggs Slowe*** (1922–1937), was instrumental not only in strengthening women's place at Howard, but also in professionalizing the dean's role nationally. Howard University began graduating women with the A.B. degree in 1874; Matilda Adams Nichols was the first recipient. Between 1872 and 1898, nearly twenty-five women received degrees in law, medicine, and pharmacy. A century later, women constitute more than half of Howard's students, studying in all areas of the university. Howard University has supported the careers of thousands of black women professionals. [See also **graduate education**.*]

Bibliography: U.S. Government Printing Office, *Survey of Negro Colleges and Universities* (1929; repr. 1969); Rayford W. Logan, *Howard University: The First Hundred Years 1867–1967* (1969); Ronald E. Butchart, *Northern Schools, Southern Blacks, and Reconstruction: Freedmen's Education, 1862–1875* (1980); Linda M. Perkins, "The Impact of the 'Cult of True Womanhood' on the Education of Black Women," *Journal of Social Issues*, 39 (1983): 17–28.

Adrian K. Haugabrook

Hull-House. Hull-House, founded by **Jane Addams*** and Ellen Gates Starr in Chicago in 1889, was in the vanguard of the worldwide **settlement house movement**.* Originally conceived as an oasis for educated women desiring to live independently in pursuit of their own interests and talents, the institution and its social orientation expanded over time. Less than a decade after its founding on the second floor of a decaying former mansion, Hull-House sprawled over an entire city block—an institution rivaled in size only by the **University of Chicago**.*

The impressive institution grew steadily from its single floor in the former Hull mansion, located at Polk and Halsted Streets approximately a mile and a half from the city center. In 1889, during the second of the European tours that Addams took after completing her degree at the **Rockford Female Seminary*** in Illinois, she had visited London's Toynbee Hall, the original settlement house. Toynbee deposited Oxford graduates in the middle of London's slums in order to serve philanthropic ends at both the physical and intellectual levels. Addams, long in search of her own motivating purpose, felt that in Toynbee Hall she had found her calling. Indeed, many of the early buildings in the Hull-House complex were consciously designed by architect Allen Pond with the gothic architecture of Toynbee in mind.

The interior design of Hull-House as well as its philosophical structure followed the theories of social reformer John Ruskin and the Arts and Crafts movement. Both Ruskin's emphasis on the importance of exposing the masses to the high culture widely assumed to be the exclusive province of the wealthy and his prediction of the devastating social and personal impact of industrialization inspired Addams and influenced the nature of Hull-House projects.

Hull-House served a significant educational function for both the progressive women who lived there as residents and the immigrant community in its environs. In fact, Hull-House joined forces with the University of Chicago to provide the first college extension courses in the city. In addition, residents of Hull-House responded directly to the needs of their immigrant neighbors by offering the city's first citizenship preparation classes.

A firm believer in the importance of exposing members of the working class to cultural benefits enjoyed by the wealthy, Addams turned the parlor of Hull-House into a salon that featured performances by the Hull-House Players. The troupe was so successful by 1912 that they were invited to perform for a six-week run at Dublin's prestigious Abbey Theater.

Equally aware of the more basic needs of her community, Addams offered pragmatic courses at Hull-House with instruction in sewing, home finance management, nutrition, and cooking. Hull-House offered its neighbors ample opportunity to play as well as to study and work—the Boys' Club featured a bowling alley and billiards tables in the basement of the main building, and the property became the site of the first public playground in the city.

The city eventually took over the playground in a process that was to become typical of Hull-House's relationship to the larger society. Addams and her colleagues would develop projects that were then adopted by city government and implemented on a much broader scale. Hull-House residents pioneered investigations into social problems such as truancy, improper sanitation, infant mortality rates, and labor laws. Florence Kelley, a Hull-House resident, became the first Illinois factory inspector; her diligent assaults on the abuses she discovered served as a catalyst for significant labor law reform.

Hull-House became a haven for workers, particularly women, in the early twentieth century. The Hull-House salon, auditorium, and meeting rooms played host to some of the first **labor unions*** organized in Chicago, including the Women Shirt Makers, the Women Cloak Makers, and the Chicago **Women's Trade Union League**.* Though Addams had personal misgivings about women leaving young children behind in order to work, she understood the financial necessity and sought to address child care needs of working women at Hull-House. The creche, or nursery, was the forerunner of the modern day care center, and Hull-House eventually included a **kindergarten*** as well.

In yet another first, Hull-House was the birthplace of the Chicago Arts and Crafts Society in 1897. The society provided classes in woodworking, photography, and metal shop, among other artisan skills. Ellen Starr, Addams's traveling companion from her European wanderings, had returned to England in the 1890s to study bookbinding, which she then brought back to Hull-House, setting up a bookbindery on the premises and offering instruction in traditional processes.

Though its social purpose expanded at a dizzying rate, Hull-House never ceased to serve its initial mission of providing an outlet for the energies of educated, motivated, independent women. By 1929, there were seventy residents including some of the most ambitious and progressive women in the country. Hull-House served as a home both for the educated woman seeking a connection to the larger world outside of the "society" drawing room as well as the woman who had fought her way through still restricted educational channels to join this first generation of professional, educated women. Although Hull-House eventually offered accommodations for married couples (1902), it was first and foremost a community of women. Hull-House residents received the double boon of freedom from marital and maternal commitments and the companionship of intelligent, impassioned, socially motivated women.

The Hull-House complex came full circle by the end of the twentieth century. The University of Illinois at Chicago sprang up on the city block that the institution once dominated, and the original Hull mansion and one adjoining structure are all that remain on the site. These two buildings support the Jane Addams Hull-House Museum. Though its centralized location has been dissolved, Hull-House continues to lend its name to a wide array of social service facilities and programs throughout the city. [See also **Progressive Era**,* **social housekeeping**.*]

Bibliography: Daniel Levine, "Hull House: Institutional Growth," in Daniel Levine, ed., *Jane Addams and the Liberal Tradition* (1971); Helen Lefkowitz Horowitz, "Hull-House as Women's Space," *Chicago History*, 12 (Winter 1983–1984): 40–55; Ira Harkavy and John L. Puckett, "Lessons from Hull House for the Contemporary Urban University," *Social Service Review*, 68 (September 1994): 299–321.

Regina Buccola

Hunt, Harriot. The first woman to successfully practice medicine in the United States, Harriot Kezia Hunt (1805–1875) devoted her entire life to opening medical training for females. The woman referred to as "Mother of the American Woman Physician" began her professional career as a teacher, the only acceptable career path for women of her day. She quickly became disillusioned with **teaching*** and its limited income potential; she longed for a chance to pursue a medical career.

The majority of physicians of this era were trained via apprenticeship, but such opportunities were normally unavailable to females. British "naturalist physician" Richard Mott had forged close personal ties with the Hunt family. Struck by their brilliance, he broke gender traditions and accepted both Harriot and her sister Sarah as pupils in 1833. Upon completing their training in 1835, the sisters began a practice in Boston that grew quickly, treating mostly women and children. Sarah married several years later, leaving Harriot in solo practice.

Ironically, Elizabeth Blackwell, rather than Hunt, is routinely credited with being the first American female physician because she was the first woman accepted to a medical college (Geneva College, New York) in 1847 and to earn a medical degree in 1849. Blackwell's admission to a traditional medical school prompted Hunt to reassess her own career. The need for formal **medical education*** was emerging as the norm in Boston, and Hunt desired the credibility that accompanied the diploma. Encouraged by those familiar with her diagnostic skills, Hunt boldly sought admission to Harvard, the most prestigious of American medical schools, in 1847 at the age of forty-two. Despite the fact that males with lesser credentials were routinely awarded honorary degrees, her application was twice denied.

Although her quest for admission to this most traditional of male bastions earned her the feminist tag that would adhere throughout her career, Hunt's fundamental motivation for application was her desire to obtain the finest medical education. She steadfastly believed it was wrong to exclude females from medicine and was deeply committed to fostering a change in public attitude. As a result, Hunt's actions were perceived as a direct challenge to traditional gender norms and created significant turmoil in both Boston society and its medical community.

Hunt continued in practice for another twenty-five years after Harvard's denials. She believed she could best contribute to the cause by serving as a role model for young women. Her actions catalyzed the fight for female acceptance into the best male colleges, a struggle that continued for years. Although she was never formally accepted to medical college, Harriot Hunt was a pioneer for all women aspiring to careers as physicians. Having served on the faculty of several women's medical colleges, she was awarded an honorary degree in 1853 by New England Female Medical College. Hunt died in Boston in 1875.

Bibliography: Harriot K. Hunt, *Glances and Glimpses: Fifty Years Social, Including Twenty Years Professional Life* (1856); Mary Roth Walsh, *Doctors Wanted, No Women Need Apply* (1977); Jeanne Achterberg, *Woman as Healer* (1991); Eleanor G. Shore and Miles F. Shore, ''Vita: Harriot Kezia Hunt,'' *Harvard Magazine*, 98 (September–October 1995): 55.

Kimberly A. Crooks

Hunter College. Hunter College, founded in 1870 as the first public **high school*** for girls in New York City, was by the 1930s the largest women's college in the United States. Currently part of the public City University of New York, Hunter has trained generations of women as teachers, primarily for the New York City schools. Hunter was also unusual in its openness to women of all racial and ethnic backgrounds: Prior to the 1950s, Hunter enrolled more African American women than any institution not a historically black college. In addition, the school provided an entry to higher education for generations of Eastern European immigrants; at various points in its history, Hunter served a student body that was 80 to 90 percent Jewish. Now coeducational, Hunter offers a full liberal arts and sciences curriculum.

Hunter is second in age only to the City College of New York as a public higher education institution serving New York City students. Founded in 1870 by the city's board of education, Hunter began as a **normal school*** to prepare teachers for the growing demands of the city's public schools. High school was not yet an established institution in the 1870s, nor did an obvious or implicit educational ladder exist leading students from grade school through high school to college. Teachers often had little more training than their students; in fact, most **teacher education*** in New York City consisted of Saturday or summer **teacher institutes.***

Hunter, created as the Female Normal and High School, envisioned more ambitious and intellectual training for female teachers. Spurred by the professional efforts of Thomas Hunter, the admired first president of the institution, the college opened on a plan copying the most advanced teacher training available in the normal schools of the eastern United States. Hunter, who had been lured to the college presidency from his principalship at one of the city's best-regarded boys' schools, established a three-year certificate program for the teen-age students seeking teacher training. The first two years included academic work that, although strong, was not the thoroughly classical curriculum available at the newly opening **Seven Sisters*** **women's colleges.*** Only in the third year did Hunter students focus specifically on pedagogy and practice teaching, assisted by the creation of a model elementary school right on the college campus. In recognition of its focus, the school was renamed the Normal College of the City of New York shortly after classes began in 1870.

Like most fledgling institutions, the Normal College scraped for funds and a permanent building site for its first few years. By 1873, public support and private fund-raising provided the first building on Park Avenue. At the building's dedication, the U.S. Commissioner of Education joined the mayor and the governor in offering speeches and goodwill for the burgeoning institution. The college distinguished itself by choosing students through competitive examinations, thereby creating a student body of well-intentioned teacher candidates. The procedure also reduced the influence of ward bosses and trustees, traditional powerbrokers in appointing teachers for local schools. Thomas Hunter was sending a message that the college saw teacher training as a serious business—a message that sometimes found him at odds with politicians of the city schools and the board of education.

As demand for teachers grew, the board challenged Hunter by creating three new teacher training institutions around the city—all schools that did not have the collegiate ambitions of Hunter. Over time, the Normal College established a four-year curriculum that emphasized academic training plus teacher preparation, while the teacher institutions remained centers for pedagogic training. The Hunter graduating class of 1892 was the first to earn the bachelor's degree.

Hunter himself encouraged nonprejudicial admissions at the college. Historian Linda Perkins notes that Hunter provided an unusual opportunity for black women in New York City and elsewhere throughout the country. In the city, black students still attended segregated elementary schools. Perkins found that fifty-six African American women had attended Hunter by 1890, although their employment opportunities were more limited than white students'. Hunter also launched the teaching careers of a huge number of the daughters of Eastern European Jewish immigrants. These parents were busy establishing themselves financially, and they valued the opportunity to help their daughters enter a respected profession such as **teaching**.* Hunter, with its free tuition, easy access, and vocational orientation, provided excellent opportunities. Compared to the country settings and generally Christian orientations of the Seven Sisters women's colleges, Hunter and its ''subway scholars'' seemed more receptive to working-class families. Stories of students' difficult balancing of school responsibilities with part-time jobs fill Hunter student newspapers and magazines.

Like some other women's colleges, Hunter was slow to open its faculty to women; the initial faculty was all male, supplemented by a group of female assistants and tutors. Thomas Hunter hired Lydia Wadleigh, herself the principal of a well-known girls' school, as ''lady superintendent'' to supervise Normal College student behavior. After the turn of the century, women gradually infiltrated the ''regular'' faculty, but only in 1945 was the first African American woman appointed to the faculty.

Much as the Normal College had been challenged by the creation of public teacher training institutions, it also faced new competition by the opening in 1889 of **Barnard College*** and the New York College for the Training of Teachers (the precursor of Columbia University's prestigious Teachers College). Over time, Hunter—renamed in honor of its first president in 1914—set itself against these collegiate opportunities, forsaking the normal school association of its beginnings. When most of the nation's normal schools gradually shifted into **teachers colleges*** and then, eventually, to state colleges, Hunter committed itself early on to a collegiate format. Its students pursued academic majors first and then focused on pedagogic training. The initial high school component remained, however, in the campus-based Hunter College High School.

Hunter prospered as a tuition-free institution for the young women of the city. By the 1930s, Hunter College was the largest women's college in the United States, with more than 5,000 regular students enrolled and another 15,000 in an array of summer and extension courses. When the original Park Avenue location could no longer hold the growing student population, branch campuses opened in the Bronx (1920), Staten Island (1921), Brooklyn (1926), and Queens (1927). The elegant centerpiece building of a revitalized Park Avenue campus—sometimes referred to as ''the Palace of Park Avenue''—opened with considerable fanfare in 1940.

The 1940s brought a major change in Hunter: the shift to **coeducation*** from the influx of male veterans returning from World War II. Fueled by funding from the **G. I. Bill**,* Hunter, as well as other women's colleges, accommodated male veterans who needed additional vocational training. In September of 1947, the peak semester for veteran enrollment, Hunter served more than 1,100 such men. Unlike most other women's colleges, however, Hunter was changed permanently by the presence of the veterans. This public institution, which had faced questions of both coeducation and merger with the male City College throughout its history, chose to admit men to all its programs.

Throughout the decades, the City University of New York has added other campuses to serve the population throughout the city and its boroughs. Hunter has remained a distinguished part of the larger institution, serving almost 9,000 students by the 1990s and sustaining active **continuing education*** and extension opportunities to working students. The college continues to value diversity in its student population and its programs and values its rich history of access to students of all backgrounds and ambitions.

Bibliography: Samuel White Patterson, *Hunter College: Eighty-five Years of Service* (1955); Katherina Kroo Grunfeld, "Purpose and Ambiguity: The Feminine World of Hunter College, 1869–1945" (Ed.D. diss., Teachers College, Columbia University, 1991); Ruth Jacknow Markowitz, *My Daughter, the Teacher: Jewish Teachers in the New York City Schools* (1993); Linda Perkins, "African-American Women and Hunter College, 1873–1945," in *The Echo: Journal of the Hunter College Archives* [special issue in celebration of the 125th anniversary of Hunter College] (1995).

Linda Eisenmann

hygiene movement. The hygiene movement was a short-lived formal effort on college campuses around the turn of the twentieth century to examine the scientific issues involved in health. Originally started by male physicians, the field soon became "feminized" when many women scientists, physicians, and physiologists were shunted away from teaching pure science into teaching hygiene to college women. There were, however, many women professors and doctors who advocated for this work; Dr. Lillian Welsh of Goucher College, for example, taught hygiene for thirty years and developed her work into a premedical program for women through a department of physiology and hygiene [see **medical education***].

An example from the February 1909 *University Bulletin* of the University of Wisconsin clarifies the personal and public health aspects of a course in general hygiene. The purpose of the course was to include study of "the relation of the mind to health, the care of the nervous system, infectious diseases and antitoxins, the effects of drugs, alcohol, and tobacco, food supplies and their adulteration, exercise and health, water and milk supply, and a series of similar subjects . . . [including] two lectures in this course on air supply and ventilation and on water supply and water purification."

Hygienic training at the turn of the century included physical exercise, nutrition and dietetics, sanitation, personal hygiene, and social hygiene (sex and morals education). In some cases, it also included the study of eugenics (the agencies under social control to improve racial qualities in future generations).

Although health and exercise courses had long been available to young women, in 1882 the **Association of Collegiate Alumnae*** had organized with an initial task of investigating physical education in its member colleges and encouraging the "introduction of a consistent, thorough, and scientific course of physical education for women." Colleges looked to these subjects as important not only for the health of individuals but as good training for young ladies who would one day be wives and mothers.

Unlike the similar field of **home economics**,* hygiene did not flourish over time. By the 1920s, hygiene courses had generally disappeared from colleges, usually replaced by work and specialists in physical education. For a short time, however, the field offered focused work for women professionals.

The significance of hygiene training for women was not only in providing information for their individual lives but also in improving conditions in schools and other social settings while offering opportunities for social work in communities by providing this information to others.

Bibliography: Marion Talbot, *The Education of Women* (1910); Margaret Rossiter, *Women Scientists in America: Struggles and Strategies to 1940* (1982).

Susan Clark Studer

Immigrant Protective League. The Immigrant Protective League (IPL) was established in Chicago in 1908 to assist immigrant women arriving alone in the United States. Contemporary records indicated that 20 percent of women and girls entering the country through Ellis Island and heading for Chicago did not reach their destination. These travelers were often waylaid by cab drivers, railroad workers, and even policemen who directed them to bars, houses of prostitution, and labor camps. The IPL, led by women such as **Jane Addams*** of **Hull-House*** and Grace Abbott, who served as executive secretary of the league for twenty years, sought to welcome newcomers, help them avoid exploitation, and assist them in assimilating into American society.

Although the IPL offered services to male and female immigrants, its leaders, like many female **Progressive Era*** reformers, were particularly concerned with problems women faced in urban, industrial Chicago. A major factor contributing to immigrant women's vulnerability was their inability to read and speak English. The IPL encouraged both single and married women to take advantage of educational opportunities available at **settlement houses**,* churches, night schools, and the **Young Women's Christian Association**.* The IPL advertised in immigrant newspapers the availability of night classes and scheduled special courses for women. The IPL considered education in English especially crucial for mothers so they could help their children remain in school. Immigrant women were suspicious of public schooling, fearing it would be used by the government to induct their husbands into the army. The IPL conducted special outreach to reassure women that education would benefit them. The league's leaders and case workers viewed **female literacy*** as a practical tool to empower immigrant women to make better decisions for themselves and their children.

While the IPL encouraged education for women as a solution to the obstacles they faced, it also believed in education as a tool of assimilation. Yet the IPL differed from other Americanizing forces, such as many state and private agencies, in not considering immigrants inherently inferior. Rather, it asserted that their poverty was caused by their social, economic, and political status as new-comers. The organization believed that immigrants would enhance the quality of American life by stamping it with their own cultures and customs. The league, however, expected immigrants to become fully Americanized and to embrace the country's ideals in place of their European sensibilities.

For immigrant women, assimilation often meant learning the middle-class norms of native-born wives and mothers who remained in the domestic sphere. These norms often differed from their experiences in Europe where many women participated in the economic life of the household. The IPL also urged immigrant women to adopt middle-class Americans' diet and standards of clean-liness. The league investigated infant mortality and advocated education about pregnancy for immigrant women in their own languages to promote the health of mothers and children. Interestingly, female IPL leaders, who were in the vanguard of expanding gender roles in the early twentieth century, championed traditional responsibilities for immigrant women. For these reasons, some his-torians have criticized organizations like the IPL for teaching immigrants that a woman's role was limited to the domestic sphere.

By 1917, the reduction in immigration as a result of World War I and national legislation diminished the need for the IPL's services. It remained active in a variety of guises until it became part of the Traveler's Aid Society in Chicago in 1967.

Bibliography: Henry B. Leonard, "The Immigrants' Protective League of Chicago, 1908–1921," *Illinois State Historical Society Journal*, 66 (Autumn 1973): 271–284; Lela B. Costin, *Two Sisters for Social Justice: A Biography of Grace and Edith Abbott* (1983); John F. McClymer, "Gender and the 'American Way of Life': Women in the Ameri-canization Movement," *Journal of American Ethnic History*, 10 (Spring 1991): 3–20.

Carol Cullen

in loco parentis. *In loco parentis* is a Latin concept meaning "in the place of parents," or charged with a parent's rights, duties, and responsibilities. In loco parentis as a legal concept in education was the result of parental demands for the school system to meet the needs of students that parents no longer could provide or did not desire to provide.

The notion that an instructor stands in loco parentis to his or her students was developed early in English common law. Under the paternalistic educational system of the seventeenth century, students at Oxford and Cambridge Univer-sities were subject to many restrictions and rules. Many of these same policies were found in early American **colonial schooling*** as well, carried into the educational system either by delegation of the parents of schoolchildren or as-sumption by school officials.

During colonial times, school, church, and parental influence were interwoven with a discipline that rewarded hard work. Puritan ideology was severe in its discipline of children, and corporal punishment was liberally applied both at home and at school, accepted as necessary literally to "beat the devil" out of misbehaving children.

Schools, including colleges, possessed authority that had been delegated to them by parents to supervise students in every aspect of education, both in and out of the classroom. In college, students often lived away from home and needed substitutes for parental direction; instructors and school officials served this function.

Throughout the years U.S. courts have ruled that school officials stand in loco parentis to their students in matters of mental training, moral and physical discipline, infliction of corporal punishment, expulsion from school, and demands upon students' time either during or after school hours.

More recently, in a post-1960s environment that is notably more student centered in policy and approach, courts have questioned the validity of the concept in colleges and universities, with a trend toward liberalizing the harshness of discipline and a more tolerant emphasis placed upon services to students.

Bibliography: Herman Edward Harms, "A History of the Concept of in Loco Parentis in American Education" (Ph.D. diss., University of Florida, 1970); Arnold M. Zeagler, "Attitude of Resident Students and Staff of Selected Public Universities in Texas toward In Loco Parentis" (Ph.D. diss., North Texas State University, 1978); Vernon Keith Gilbert, *In Loco Parentis: A Teachers Guide to Educational Administration* (1985).

Gerald L. Willis

Institute for Colored Youth. The Quaker Institute for Colored Youth was an influential school for African Americans begun near Philadelphia in 1839. Over its history, it served African American women and men with a strong preparatory school, **high school**,* evening program, industrial and vocational courses, and a **normal school*** for teacher training. Its principal **Fanny Jackson Coppin*** (1875–1901) made the school a model for meeting the diverse needs of the late nineteenth-century African American population. The Institute eventually became Cheyney State Teachers College.

The Institute was founded by Quaker Richard Humphreys, who, at his death in 1832, provided money for a school to train African Americans in mechanics, trades, and agriculture. In this effort, Humphreys followed the **Quaker*** tradition of advocacy and support for both women and African Americans. Trustees organized the school, originally opened as a residential farm training school, outside Philadelphia in 1839 with five students. The school failed in 1846 due to its demand for manual labor and extended indenture by students. It was reopened by 1849 in the city of Philadelphia. In 1857, an evening school with an apprentice program was established for African American boys. Its success prompted the Quaker managers to develop a day school to serve even younger boys and, for the first time, girls. Boys and girls at least ten years old with some prior schooling received preferential admission. Older students who were capable could enroll in chemistry, Greek, Latin, natural philosophy, and advanced mathematics. The boys department was led by Charles L. Reason; the girls department opened in 1853 under the direction of Grace Mapps.

With its strong curriculum and free tuition, both the boys' and girls' departments expanded, the girls' experiencing more growth. Managers began another building program in 1863 and continued to seek qualified staff. By 1865, the school consisted of two preparatory departments for girls with two separate sections for boys. Separate high school programs were established for the two groups. The high school admitted students by examination only; such strong standards required the best teachers.

The Quakers hired Fanny Jackson Coppin, a well-trained graduate of Rhode Island Normal School and **Oberlin College**.* Coppin proved to be a crucial educator at the Institute. She taught from 1865 to 1875, when she was made principal of the entire institution. Coppin broadened the curriculum and established a normal school program for **teacher education**,* with an innovative field education component.

Industrial education made an impact on the Institute under Coppin's direction. She introduced courses for girls in sewing, cooking, millinery, and business. She also pushed the managers for a stronger industrial education course for men who did not wish to become teachers, businessmen, or clergy. The industrial education department opened in 1889. That year, 500 African American youth were Institute students.

Coppin retired in 1901, passing leadership to Hugh M. Browne, who focused the school's mission on the industrial education model articulated by Booker T. Washington of Alabama's **Tuskegee Institute**.* After Browne's tenure, the institution searched for a relevant mission and purpose. Eventually, it became the Cheyney Training School for Teachers. Under this name, it embraced the mission of founder Humphreys and advanced by its only female leader, Coppin. Cheyney became a state-owned school in 1922 and, as Cheyney State College, part of the Pennsylvania state university system in 1981.

Bibliography: Linda M. Perkins, ''Fanny Jackson Coppin and the Institute for Colored Youth: A Model of Nineteenth Century Black Female Educational and Community Leadership, 1837–1902'' (Ph.D. diss., University of Illinois, 1978); Perkins, ''Heed Life's Demands: The Educational Philosophy of Fanny Jackson Coppin,'' *Journal of Negro Education*, 5 (1982): 183; Elizabeth L. Ihle, ''Free Black Adult Education before the Civil War,'' Reports and bylaws of the Institute for Colored Youth, and the administrative papers of the Richard Humphreys Foundation, are at the Friends Historical Library, Swarthmore College, Pennsylvania.

Imani-Sheila Newsome-McLaughlin

Institute for the Coordination of Women's Interests. The Institute for the Coordination of Women's Interests was a research and demonstration center at **Smith College*** from 1926 to 1931, designed to help college-educated women integrate their intellectual lives with their responsibilities as wives and mothers.

Founded and sustained by feminist reformer Ethel Puffer Howes, a Smith alumna, the institute combined research studies, collegiate courses, and demonstration work for both Smith students and the interested public. Short-lived and not much copied by other **women's colleges**,* the institute declined from a lack of widespread support and from Howes's inability to connect her mission with the educational philosophy of many of Smith's faculty.

Ethel Puffer Howes was an experienced reformer who held a Ph.D. from **Radcliffe College***; studied philosophy in Europe and at Harvard with some of the era's most prominent philosophers; held teaching appointments at Harvard, Smith, and **Wellesley Colleges***; and served as executive secretary of the **National College Equal Suffrage League**.* Married at age thirty-six and a mother in her forties, Howes experienced the difficulties and prejudices facing those who would combine motherhood and professional life. Long involved in **suffrage*** and other reform movements, after 1920 she focused on understanding what real difference the vote would mean for women. In 1922 she wrote two articles for the *Atlantic Monthly* that captured her concerns for modern women. In "Accepting the Universe," she observed that women would never have the same freedom as men to pursue careers because of familial duties and responsibilities. Rather than continuing to chafe at the situation, however, she advocated for "provisions" that would support women in both career and domestic roles. In "Continuity for Women," she advanced her belief that women's higher education should provide a "continuous use" of the powers that it develops. Women should use the skills and ideas they develop through intellectual work, but they should be permitted to go more slowly than men as they must seek an integration of both sides of their lives.

In addition to her theoretical approach, Howes was deeply involved with socialized domestic movements such as community kitchens, communal laundries, and cooperative home service clubs. For *Woman's Home Companion* magazine, she described her visits to such cooperative ventures all around the country, advocating them as a sensible solution to problems facing women of all backgrounds. At the same time, Howes conceived the idea for an institute that would not only support such efforts but also provide a research base for the philosophical underpinnings of her beliefs. She convinced the Laura Spelman Rockefeller Memorial Foundation to provide $36,000 to create such a center at Smith College, her alma mater. Smith provided additional funds and space, and the Institute for Coordination of Women's Interests was launched in 1926.

The purpose of the new institute was to help women "order their lives that their individual powers and interests, developed by education, should not, in the pressure of normal family life, be dulled" (Howes, p. 8). Howes, with her own strong educational background, recognized that the "technique" of cooperative living was insufficient without a "philosophy" to sustain it, and she advanced these as the twin efforts of her new center. Combining the philosophy with the activities made the project an educational concern, in her eyes.

The institute pursued several directions simultaneously. First, it surveyed

Smith alumnae to examine their reasons for working and their experience in combining career and marriage. Generally, the women worked for both "personal and economic" reasons: Women need work for "their own mental health; they are far happier when they have it; and happiest of all when they can do it in partnership with their husbands," the institute concluded (Howes, p. 12). Yet as their colleagues in the 1960s feminist movement would observe, the researchers found that many women approached their concerns as individual problems. What was needed, Howes concluded, was a "coherent social order" that would support women as a group.

Other institute efforts included surveys of household techniques to help women, such as cooperative services for food preparation and child care and demonstrations to help women develop these programs on their own. A nursery school and cooked food supply program served public needs. Researchers planned studies of the various professions, to examine what supports women would need to succeed in each. After studying journalism and architecture, the preliminary results suggested that successful practitioners would require, first, "thorough schooling in all the principles" and second, "at least two years completely foot-free intensive experience." The institute warned that only after two solid years in the field "may you dare marry!" (Howes, p. 14). The final elements of the institute's program included courses for Smith juniors and seniors to discuss vocation and career, as well as public conferences for non-Smith women.

Howes's program waned quickly in the 1930s. Historian Dolores Hayden, who studies the history of domestic feminists, attributes the institute's decline partly to the rise of consumer behavior after World War I that denigrated efforts at cooperative housing and community kitchens. Corporations began advertising for their labor-saving household appliances, all of which could be used by individual women in private homes. Simultaneously, Howes failed to win over women's educators who urged the college-educated woman to eschew work in the home for devotion to career or intellectual life. Howes's approach seemed too mixed for many of these advocates who believed that a full-fledged focus on career was necessary to overcome societal prejudice against women. At a school like Smith that valued its rigorous academic curriculum, Howes's work may have carried too mixed a message. In the end, the Smith faculty ousted the institute for being too nonintellectual.

Although short-lived on the Smith College campus, the Institute for the Coordination of Women's Interests nonetheless highlighted an ongoing concern for collegiate women throughout the twentieth century. Once college women began to marry in larger numbers, starting in the 1920s, the challenge of combining their intellectual development and their societal roles would cycle continuously through decades of war, peace, and feminist activism. [See also **home economics**,* **social housekeeping**.*]

Bibliography: Ethel Puffer Howes, *The Progress of the Institute for the Co-ordination of Women's Interests,''* Report at Alumnae Conference (1928); Dolores Hayden, *The Grand Domestic Revolution: A History of Feminist Designs for American Homes, Neigh-*

borhoods, and Cities (1981); Barbara Miller Solomon, *In the Company of Educated Women: A History of Women and Higher Education in America* (1985).

Linda Eisenmann

Ivy League. As a phrase "Ivy League" has come to refer to selective, elitist, residential, and often ritualistic private higher education in the United States. It also signifies a group of institutions that were not especially hospitable to women students or faculty, at least not until late in the twentieth century. The origins of the term are vigorously disputed. Although it gained currency in the 1930s as a collective for eight old eastern universities (Harvard, Yale, Princeton, Brown, Columbia, Cornell, Dartmouth, and Pennsylvania), claims are made that the term was employed as early as 1900, and then referred not to vines clinging to old buildings but rather to the Roman numeral IV that was used on trophies awarded for athletic competitions between Harvard, Yale, Princeton, and Columbia. The *IV* became *Ivy*.

The phrase has been used increasingly in popular parlance as a description not for the original eight but for a larger group of prestigious private schools, with comparatively recent but selective institutions such as Stanford and Duke included when mentioning Ivy style and panache. With women's institutions, the term sometimes is applied to the so-called **Seven Sister*** colleges: **Radcliffe*** (1879), **Barnard*** (1889), **Bryn Mawr*** (1885), **Smith*** (1875), **Vassar*** (1865), **Mount Holyoke*** (1837), and **Wellesley*** (1875). The *Seven Sisters* term dates to at least 1926, although the concept was already recognized in 1904 when plans for the new library at Mount Holyoke included stained glass with seals of the six other Sisters.

In terms of Ivy education, all eight universities in the original Ivy League eventually became coeducational, although Harvard, Columbia, and Brown first created **coordinate colleges*** (Radcliffe, Barnard, and Pembroke, respectively) as institutions to serve women students while keeping them organizationally and physically separate. Cornell was coeducational almost from its beginning, opening in 1869 and accepting women in 1872; Pennsylvania became coeducational in 1876. But Yale, Dartmouth, and Princeton were resolutely male during the nineteenth century, not accepting women as regular students until 1969 or later. Although women have overcome barriers to admission as students, the Ivy League universities continue to show a woeful record of major faculty appointments of women.

By 1879 half of all colleges in the United States admitted women. But Vassar's purpose was from the very start "to build and endow a college for young women which shall be to them, what Yale and Harvard are to young men." Thus, the Seven Sisters and other elite women's colleges fought not only for acceptance of the idea of higher education for women but for social status, and their early battleground was conservative New England where **coeducation*** dawdled in comparison to the Universities of Iowa (1855) or Wisconsin (1863).

Arguably, then, the Seven Sisters provided the women's Ivy League. There was indeed an effort to propagate ivy as a plant representing women's intellectual growth. At Smith, Ivy Day was celebrated as early as 1902, when classes planted shoots to beautify the campus. A Bryn Mawr alumna praised ''the grand old stone buildings covered with ivy.'' The institutional aspirations of the Seven Sisters and their colleagues such as Sarah Lawrence, Scripps, and Mills Colleges were socially different from the many already existing **seminaries*** and colleges that admitted women.

Whether women or men are concerned, the use of the term *Ivy League* is an acknowledgment that some educational institutions confer more social prestige than do others. Barnard, for example, was considered necessary because City University's already existing **Hunter College*** for women was thought not to confer the cachet or maintain the standards that a certain social class considered part of a university experience. Today's equivalent of the old Ivy League is perhaps the less-known Consortium on Financing in Higher Education, a club of thirty-two institutions that includes the old Ivy League, the Seven Sisters except Vassar, and schools like Amherst, Williams, Swarthmore, and Pomona. The consortium is a low-key association that exchanges information about common problems and was the original participant in a 1990s federal antitrust suit charging price fixing in financial aid.

The struggle to provide elite education for women was a long one and part of the larger campaign to prove their intellectual ability. Whatever one thinks about the snobbery sometimes associated with the Ivy concept, the successful fight to establish Ivy League as an appropriate cachet for women's education as well as men's has answered that objection.

Bibliography: Frederick Rudolph, *The American College and University: A History* (1962, repr. 1990); Catherine Clinton, *The Other Civil War* (1984); Helen Lefkowitz Horowitz, *Alma Mater: Design and Experience in the Women's Colleges from Their Nineteenth-Century Beginnings to the 1930s* (1984); Shirley Marchalonis, *College Girls: A Century in Fiction* (1995).

Paul Rich

J

Jeanes teachers. Established in 1907 by Anna T. Jeanes, a **Quaker***** philanthropist, the mission of the Rural School Fund (otherwise known as the Jeanes
Fund) was to assist the "rural schools of the Southern U.S. Community." Over
the next sixty years, the Jeanes Fund, along with other philanthropies in the
South, helped develop public education for rural blacks into a more organized
and better coordinated program. The fund also provided professional opportunities for hundreds of women to work as teachers.

The Jeanes action plan, later known as the "Henrico Plan," was originated
by Virginia E. Randolph, daughter of ex-slaves, who graduated from **high
school*** and began a **teaching*** career at age sixteen. At her school in Henrico
County, Virginia, Randolph emphasized industrial arts such as cooking, sewing,
and gardening in addition to academic subjects, and her curriculum stressed
values of cleanliness and orderliness. When Jackson Davis, school superintendent of Henrico County, received a Jeanes Fund grant to implement new teaching methods in black schools, he adopted Randolph's model, thereby providing
a template for fund efforts. Randolph made visits to other teachers, helping them
improve their schoolhouses and initiate industrial training. After coming to the
attention of James H. Dillard, the Jeanes Fund's first president, Randolph was
appointed the first Jeanes Supervising Industrial Teacher in 1908. Dillard soon
received requests for similar teachers around the state and beyond. Their salaries
paid by the fund, this group of Jeanes teachers spread throughout Virginia and
into North Carolina, establishing a pattern that was eventually integrated into
southern public education.

The role of the Jeanes teacher more closely resembled that of facilitator than
supervisor. The fund required that she be recognized as a regular employee of
the local school system, responsible to the superintendent and school board. The
work she undertook was determined by the wishes of the superintendent, local
community needs, and her own unique skills. Less than three years after the

program began, 129 Jeanes teachers (all female, and most of them African American) were supported by the fund at a cost of $44,250.

As focal points for their schools, Jeanes teachers provided much of the organization and support for rural schools for southern blacks. Jeanes teachers urged community members of both races to take an interest in school activities and the problems of rural people. They integrated what children learned in books with the nonformal education drawn from their everyday environment. As community activists, they encouraged construction of more and better schools. They occasionally attended Sunday services at local churches to address congregations on school-related matters. They organized improvement leagues and mothers' clubs as a means of ensuring school support, sponsored concerts and other entertainment to raise funds, and helped teachers plan commencement exercises.

Emphasizing a connection between community improvement and the home, the teachers extended their work to the homes of community members by teaching needlework, health care, nutrition, and homemaking skills. A parallel strategy was stimulation of a connection between school and home. For example, the school garden and its products demonstrated how models could be shaped at school to guide students' domestic life at home. Planting school gardens was intended to teach children to grow or manufacture at home many of the products ordinarily purchased from stores. Garden products grown by agriculture students were canned and preserved by those studying domestic arts. Under the supervision of the Jeanes teachers, students made new equipment for the school. Through manual arts training, students learned skills such as changing apple boxes into furniture and pickle jars into vases. Jeanes teachers also assisted other teachers with lesson plan development. As an adaptation of the Jeanes program, some southern schools eliminated traditional textbooks and instituted new courses more closely related to rural life.

By 1936 there were 426 Jeanes teachers operating in fourteen southern states. Forty-five percent had obtained bachelor's degrees, primarily by attending summer courses at **Hampton Institute*** paid for by the Jeanes Fund. The work of the Jeanes teachers joined with that of other programs such as the Slater Fund, which established county training schools, and the General Education Board and others, which provided special agents who traveled throughout the southern states to stimulate interest in better public schools for black children. Together, these improved public schooling for African Americans in the rural South, providing more professional teachers and stronger curricula.

Bibliography: Ambrose Caliver, *Rural Education among Negroes under Jeanes Supervising Teachers* (1933); Arthur D. Wright and Edward E. Redcay, *The Negro Rural School Fund, Inc. Anna T. Jeanes Foundation, 1907–1933* (1933); Henry Allen Bullock, *A History of Negro Education in the South; from 1619 to the Present* (1967); James D. Anderson, *The Education of Blacks in the South, 1860–1935* (1988); Darlene Clark Hine, ed., ''Jeanes Fund and Jeanes Teachers,'' in *Black Women in America: An Historical Encyclopedia*, vol. 1 (1993).

Jayne R. Beilke

Jordan, Barbara. Barbara Charline Jordan (1936–1996) gained national prominence as a congresswoman from Texas, professor of public policy, and keynote speaker at two Democratic National Conventions (1976 and 1992). An African American, Jordan spent her professional life advocating the rights of the poor, black, and disadvantaged. She was born in Houston. Her father, Benjamin, was a Baptist preacher, and her mother, Arlyne, a domestic worker. Jordan received her early education at Houston's Robinson Elementary School and Phyllis Wheatley High School. At Wheatley she discovered her extraordinary talent in debating and graduated in the top 5 percent of her class. Attending Texas Southern University (1952–1956), Jordan excelled, graduating magna cum laude with a double major in history and political science. She then earned her law degree at Boston University in 1959. During the 1959–1960 academic term, Jordan was assistant professor at **Tuskegee Institute*** in Alabama where she taught political science. In 1960 she returned to Houston, where she took her bar examination and set up private practice.

Always interested in public life, in 1965 Jordan was appointed administrative assistant to the county judge of Harris County. The following year, she was elected to the Texas State Senate in 1966, becoming the first black to hold such office since Reconstruction in 1883. She was also the first black state senator to chair the important Labor and Management Relations Committee and the first black to preside over the state senate on March 21, 1967. Jordan received early recognition for her legislative ability when she was named to the Texas Legislative Council as a freshman senator. Five years later, her colleagues unanimously elected her president pro tempore of the senate. She was further distinguished that year by being named Governor for a Day. As a state senator, Jordan sponsored bills that lessened the social and economic burden on the poor. Her most notable achievement was the Workman's Compensation Act, which increased the maximum benefits paid to injured workers.

In 1972, Jordan was elected to the United States Congress representing Houston. During her tenure, Jordan continued her interest in the poor and disenfranchised. She sponsored legislation that strengthened the Voting Rights Act of 1965. She was especially concerned that Hispanics were being denied their civil rights through unfair voter registration practices, noting that many southwestern states, including Texas, required minorities to pass a literacy test [see **female literacy**,* **Hispanic American women's education***].

During the Watergate hearings in 1974, Jordan became an overnight national celebrity because of her positions during the impeachment hearings of President Richard Nixon. Voting for impeachment, Jordan stated, ''My faith in the Constitution is whole, it is complete, it is total. I am not going to sit here and be an idle spectator to the diminution, the subversion, the destruction of the Constitution'' (Jordan and Hearn, pp. 186–187). National audiences soon became familiar with her, when, in 1976, she was asked by presidential candidate Jimmy Carter to be keynote speaker at the Democratic National Convention. Her speaking ability attracted national attention because of her logical presentation, studied use of vocabulary, and distinctive delivery. She again faced the national spotlight when President Bill Clinton asked her to keynote the Democratic convention in 1992.

Amidst continuing honors, Jordan retired from public life in 1978 to become professor of ethics and public policy at the Lyndon Baines Johnson School of Public Affairs at the University of Texas at Austin. During her seventeen-year tenure there, students filled her classes because she inspired them to go out and change the world. As one student said, "I've never met a person who believed so strongly that we can actually change the world, and that gives me confidence that we really can."

Among Jordan's most distinctive awards and recognitions was her 1979 selection by *Redbook* magazine as one of America's women who could become president. This followed recognition by the *Ladies' Home Journal*'s pick of Jordan as Woman of the Year and the Women's National Democratic Club's 1975 Democratic Woman of the Year. In 1996, Jordan passed away in Austin after a lengthy battle with multiple sclerosis.

Bibliography: Barbara Jordan and Shelly Hearn, *Barbara Jordan: A Self Portrait* (1979); Ruthe Winegarten, *Black Texas Women: 150 Years of Trial and Triumph* (1995).

Anna V. Wilson and William E. Segall

K

kindergarten movement. The kindergarten is an educational program for children ages four to six that strives to develop at an early age their social, emotional, and intellectual potential.

The American kindergarten movement originated in the ideas of Friedrich Froebel, a German educator. In 1837, Froebel opened a kindergarten that stressed a curriculum of structured play and handwork rather than reading, writing, and counting. Influenced by the European Romantic movement, he hoped to link spiritual development with forces of emotion, perception, and reason. By playing and working with ''gifts'' such as balls, cubes, and blocks, the child would learn to see abstract patterns of meaning. The gifts were followed by ''occupations,'' such as sewing and stick laying, which would allow children to move to creating their own forms. Songs and games were important to helping achieve aims such as morality and social harmony. Froebel saw a central role for women in the development of kindergartens, believing the new institution would play a role in women's emancipation.

The kindergarten concept was brought to America in the 1850s by German immigrant women. Margarethe Meyer Schurz, born in Hamburg, opened the first American kindergarten in 1856 in Watertown, Wisconsin. However, the association of kindergartens with German immigrants limited the impact of the new pedagogy. The person most responsible for broadening its appeal was **Elizabeth Peabody**.* Froebel's ties to European Romanticism were particularly appealing to Peabody, a member of Boston's Transcendentalist circle. She opened the first English-speaking kindergarten in the United States in 1860. In speeches, correspondence, and writing in the *Kindergarten Messenger*, which she founded in 1873, and the *New England Journal of Education*, Peabody was a major disseminator of kindergarten concepts.

Peabody convinced the Boston School Committee to open an experimental kindergarten in 1870, but lack of interest and funds closed it in 1879. Perhaps foreseeing failure of the publicly funded Boston kindergarten, she helped influence **Pauline Agassiz Shaw*** to open in 1877 the first of what would eventually be over thirty charity kindergartens for poor children in the Boston area. With the opening of charity kindergartens, the movement focused on saving children from the curses of poverty and incorporating immigrant children into mainstream American culture.

As with other social reform movements of the Gilded Age, arguments of the charity kindergarten movement revealed a strain of social control. Some of the middle- and upper-class women who dominated the movement spoke of kindergartens helping to reduce perceived dangers such as crime, vice, and slothfulness among poorer, and most often, immigrant children. An important spokesperson for this view was Louise Taft in Cincinnati, mother of the future president. Still, the major motivation of kindergartners (the name for teachers in the movement) appears to have been a genuine and sympathetic desire to assist in the lives of their young charges.

Women were responsible for extending and transforming the charity kindergarten concept across the continent. Anna Bryan and **Patty Smith Hill*** in Louisville in the late 1880s and early 1890s began to modify the rather rigid Froebelian principles under which most kindergartens operated. A major change was to have children incorporate themes from their everyday lives into kindergarten activities. In San Francisco in the same period, Kate Douglas (Smith) Wiggin, at the private Silver Street kindergarten, helped develop the concept that kindergarten education should be publicly supported as a universal right for all socioeconomic classes. The private charity kindergarten movement would influence not only the future public school kindergartens but the **settlement house movement*** as well, where some of the concerns for young children would be extended to adults.

The first permanent public kindergartens originated in St. Louis with its large German American population. There **Susan Blow*** in 1872 persuaded the school system to allow her to start a kindergarten. Others soon followed. Within eleven years, however, court decisions had restricted kindergarten to five-year-olds, which would eventually become the most common age for kindergarten attendance. The school system also charged parents for children's participation.

In 1888 the Boston School Committee took over Shaw's charity kindergartens, and in the 1890s, other cities such as Chicago and New York began public funding of kindergartens. By World War I, most large school systems and many smaller cities included kindergartens. A notable exception was the South where kindergartens particularly failed to serve African Americans. While the depression saw shrinking numbers of children attending kindergarten, the post–World War II period brought a revival of enrollments. By the late twentieth century, over 80 percent of eligible children attended kindergarten.

The early twentieth century, which had seen the rapid spread and acceptance of public kindergartens, also produced new problems and conflicts. Public control often brought conflict between male-dominated school bureaucracies and women kindergartners. A major source of tension was the desire of school administrators to bring businesslike efficiency and economy to the schools. The most important manifestation of this drive was widespread introduction of double sessions. Women kindergartners' major objection to this change was that it prevented teachers from providing home-visit services to families. Administrators also pressed for kindergartens to prepare children explicitly for success in the higher grades, a goal opposed by kindergarten pioneers. Despite these pressures and modifications, the kindergarten retained in the public school system its particular emphasis on the integrated social, emotional, and intellectual development of the child.

The movement was also divided internally in the early twentieth century by a split between orthodox Froebelians and those influenced by newer trends in the social sciences and philosophy. Susan Blow was the principal defender of the traditional approach, and Patty Smith Hill argued for newer strategies based on the **child study movement**,* pragmatism, and behaviorism. These newer approaches stressed cooperative learning, spontaneity, age-appropriate motor activities, and free play. Both Blow and Hill taught at Teachers College, Columbia University, where conflict centered. Blow's resignation in 1909 marked the ascendancy of Hill's approach, but in actual kindergartens, a variety of approaches was found.

Involvement in the movement led some kindergartners, such as Sarah B. Cooper in San Francisco, to question the concept of a **separate sphere*** for women and to suggest that the movement could be a springboard for extending women's power and influence. Indeed, as early as the 1870s, the fight to gain women the vote in municipal school elections grew in part from a desire to promote kindergartens.

The kindergarten was part of the maternalist strain of women's movements, which stressed women's vital role in protecting the interests of other women and children. The kindergarten movement was overwhelmingly composed of women, and it has proved one of the most successful and enduring educational reforms of post–Civil War America. Perhaps the most important reason for its success was its ability to adapt to pressures and incorporate newer concepts and approaches. The kindergarten also helped transform the higher grades of elementary education, which moved away from some of the rigidities found in nineteenth-century schools. [See also **early childhood education**,* **early childhood teacher education**.*]

Bibliography: Elizabeth Dale Ross, *The Kindergarten Crusade: The Establishment of Preschool Education in the United States* (1976); Michael Steven Shapiro, *Child's Garden: The Kindergarten Movement from Froebel to Dewey* (1983); Larry Cuban, "Why Some Reforms Last: The Case of the Kindergarten," *American Journal of Education*, 100 (February 1992): 166–194; Barbara Beatty, *Preschool Education in America: The Culture of Young Children from the Colonial Era to the Present* (1995).

Thomas A. McMullin

labor colleges. Founded primarily in the first two decades of the twentieth century as an alternative to mainstream higher education, labor colleges offered both training and education to female and male **labor union*** members and trade workers. Growing out of a worldwide workers' education movement, the labor colleges reached their peak in the 1920s. At the beginning of the decade, approximately 60 separate colleges existed; by 1930, about 300. Many programs, however, did not survive beyond the 1930s. Women were significantly involved in the labor colleges as college founders, students, and union supporters.

Ruskin College in England was a model for labor colleges, founded in 1898 as part of, yet separate from, Oxford University. Ruskin offered workers a sophisticated program in public administration, trade unionism, economics, and labor history. A prime goal was to create labor intellectuals from among workers themselves, rather than academics. A Ruskin branch opened in the United States in Trenton, Missouri, in 1901 with a four-year program on a residential campus. Eighty students registered for full-time study, and another 200 studied via correspondence. In addition to funds from British and American trade unionists, the Missouri campus was supported by endowment money from residents of the town of Trenton.

Early in the twentieth century, as organized labor prospered, trade unionists increasingly sought alternatives to the public school system and to traditional colleges and universities. Mainstream education was seen as antilabor and narrow in its approach to workers' issues, creating structures to reproduce rather than challenge the management-labor arrangements of the emerging capitalist state. Although some unions continued to press schools for more open education, much of the organized effort took place at the adult education level. Labor colleges provided one venue; others included union training, party-based training (e.g., communist and socialist), and university-based educational experiments. Unions sponsored education for their members in an array of opportunities, and

female-dominated trades led the way. The **Women's Trade Union League***
(WTUL) and the International Ladies' Garment Workers' Union (ILGWU) offered the most prominent training programs. In addition to local classes and
workshops, the WTUL created the Training School for Women Organizers in
Chicago in 1914 to train union leaders via a year of classroom study and fieldwork. The ILGWU offered short courses in negotiation, bargaining, and arbi-
tration as alternatives to striking (although the leadership was hardly opposed
to strikes when necessary). Classes also focused on health education and housing, offering basics to their members as well as advanced training for leaders.
Fannia Cohn was educational director for the ILGWU and organized and promoted programs from the union's base in New York City.

Some workers' education took place within traditional higher education. The
Bryn Mawr Summer School for Women Workers* used the traditional
women's college* campus during the summers from 1921 to 1938 for short-
term, residential training of union and nonunion women workers. Over time,
these university-based programs would prove most long-lived, although the
workers' education they sponsored transformed into labor education and labor
studies programs rather than maintaining their separate, radical roots in the labor
movement. Bryn Mawr was the most noted program solely for women; the
Universities of California, Syracuse, Harvard, Tufts, and Cincinnati were among
others who responded to workers' education, often through more culture-
oriented programs that did not identify as firmly with the workers' movement.
Extension school programs and adult education received big boosts from these
early efforts.

The autonomous labor colleges differed in size, scope, and support. Some
met once or twice a week as study groups, holding classes in union halls,
schools, libraries, or other public meeting places. Others created campuses with
full-fledged curricula and staffing. Numbers could be small: Some served only
a dozen students, but the larger colleges supported several hundred per year.
The shorter-term efforts were taught by local teachers, union officials, or labor
supporters. Larger programs tapped the same groups for their faculty members
but also relied on a cadre of college professors, journalists, and a labor intelligentsia devoted to these alternative education efforts.

Similar to union-based education, labor colleges had two educational goals,
described by labor historian Clyde Barrow: "One goal was to provide rank and
file workers with the kind of general political education that would assist them
in their mobilization as active citizens of unions, the workplace, and the wider
political community. A second goal was to offer more advanced and specialized
training in the professions and social sciences to adult workers who were expected to remain in the labor movement as public servants of the working class"
(Barrow, 1989, pp. 52–53). Curricula varied but leaned heavily on the social
sciences, including economics, labor history, government, social psychology,
and industrial relations. Management studies provided technical skills in accounting and bookkeeping, as well as wider philosophical study of labor rela-

tions and political science. Likewise, basic language skills included English as a second language for the large number of immigrant workers; advanced communications focused on lecturing, public speaking, debate, and parliamentary procedure.

Brookwood Labor College, founded in 1921 in Katonah, New York, reached the highest prominence among the separate colleges and was sometimes referred to as "labor's Harvard." Helen and William Fincke, both pacifists, had opened a progressive school for working-class children and were instrumental in forming a group of labor leaders and intellectuals who pushed for a college to serve a range of students and union members. Socialist A. J. Muste, executive secretary of the Amalgamated Textile Workers, supported the Finckes in Brookwood's program of **peace education**,* democratic principles, and progressivism. Brookwood offered a full academic program at a tuition of $450 per year, with scholarships regularly offered by many of the dozens of unions (internationals, state federations, central labor unions, and locals) that supported the college. Hundreds of workers attended and graduated from Brookwood until it closed in 1937, pursuing further work as "union organizers, grievance committee workers, clerks, secretaries, business agents, journalists for the labor press, teachers or executives at other labor colleges, as well as socialist and communist party officials" (Barrow, 1990, p. 402).

Although Brookwood may be the best known of the labor colleges, dozens of others existed, some with women as prominent leaders. Commonwealth College founded in 1923 in Mena, Arkansas, was created by William Zeuch and Kate O'Hare, a socialist activist with a national reputation as a labor speaker. The Philadelphia Labor College served hundreds of students per year in the mid-1920s; it was created through the joint efforts of the city's local machinists and electrical unions and the Philadelphia branch of the **Women's Trade Union League**.*

Most of the independent labor colleges closed during the 1930s. Some were eased out of positions of strength when the American Federation of Labor (AFL) took control of the Workers' Education Bureau (WEB), a clearinghouse for information and publicity about the colleges. Over time, AFL centralized control of the WEB, limiting the autonomy of the independent colleges. In addition, by maintaining independence, the labor colleges had limited their sources of long-term support. Usually built on coalitions of unions, parties, and individuals, they led insecure existences, subject to the continuing goodwill of their supporters. Finally, organized labor increasingly accepted support from both the federal government and the traditional universities for different types of labor education programs, siphoning energy and students away from the colleges. For two strong decades, however, these independent alternative institutions served thousands of women and men through workers' education and offered employment for hundreds of labor activists and intellectuals.

Bibliography: Joyce Kornbluh and Mary Frederickson, eds., *Sisterhood and Solidarity: Workers' Education for Women, 1914–1984* (1984); Clyde W. Barrow, "Pedagogy, Politics, and Social Reform: The Philosophy of the Workers Education Movement," *Strat-

egies: A Journal of Theory, Culture, and Politics, 2 (1989): 45–66; Richard J. Altenbaugh, *Education for Struggle: The American Labor Colleges of the 1920s and 1930s* (1990); Barrow, "Counter-Movement within the Labor Movement: Workers' Education and the American Federation of Labor, 1900–1937," *Social Science Journal*, 27 (October 1990): 395–417; Ruth Jacknow Markowitz, "Fannia Mary Cohn," in Maxine Schwartz Seller, ed., *Women Educators in the United States, 1820–1993: A Bio-Bibliographic Sourcebook* (1994).

                                                                    Linda Eisenmann

labor unions. By the 1820s, some northern single women began to work in textile, shoe, and munitions industries as wage laborers. Yet on the whole, wage-earning women's efforts to organize or join unions failed until 1910 when the International Ladies' Garment Workers' Union (ILGWU) successfully negotiated with several New York shops for better wages and working conditions. Official acceptance of all labor unions came later when Congress passed the Wagner Act in 1936. Eventually, national unions like the American Federation of Labor (AFL) and the Congress of Industrial Organizations (CIO) accepted women's membership in their unions.

In 1821 Francis Cabot Lowell opened textile mills in Lowell, Massachusetts, that employed only single women and boarded them at the factory. Early mill workers enjoyed their work and the range of activities provided by the company [see **Lowell Mills*** and *Lowell Offering**]. By 1845, however, conditions had changed considerably as workers experienced wage cuts and speedups. Although the women organized the Female Labor Reform Association (FLRA) with the intent to improve their conditions, manufacturers opted to hire immigrant women workers, predominantly from Ireland, who were believed to be more tractable than native-born women. The FLRA nonetheless represented the earliest attempts of women workers to educate the community about working conditions. From the beginning, these educative efforts distinguished women's labor organizations from men's because women workers sought to educate the public about working conditions and wages, while men tended to use strikes.

Although some male workers in particular crafts like the shoe industry organized small unions, efforts to build a national union began in 1866 with an organization called the National Labor Union (NLU). This union—along with broad goals of banking reform, an end to convict labor, and support of the eight-hour day—endorsed the cause of working women and men, but it campaigned against immigrant labor. In 1879 Terrence Powderly led the Knights of Labor, which, similar to the NLU, supported various social and economic reforms. The Knights welcomed female members and rejected strikes in favor of consumer cooperatives. Among the many organizers, Mother Jones traveled across the country to recruit workers.

By the late 1880s, the American Federation of Labor replaced these broadly based organizations. Led by Samuel Gompers, the AFL focused on specific issues such as wages and working conditions. Refusing to admit women, blacks, and many immigrant workers, Gompers and other AFL leaders stressed "the family wage''—a salary that would allow men to support their wives and daughters without the latter's labor. In 1909, however, women garment workers proved their ability to organize when they struck in New York against poor working conditions and low wages. Not only was the ILGWU successful in gaining membership and gaining better wages; it also obtained the support of the **Women's Trade Union League*** (WTUL), a group that raised funds and publicized the plight of the female shirtwaist maker.

Formed in 1903, the WTUL served as a coalition of working-class and upper-class women in order to improve the organizational efforts of working women and to educate the public and unions. Among the many women who enlisted in the WTUL were Florence Kelley, Rose Schneiderman, and Mary Dreier. Although some shirtwaist workers returned to the same conditions as before the strike, notably in the infamous Triangle Shirtwaist Factory, the WTUL and the ILGWU proved that women could organize and that cross-class alliances among women were possible and productive. Targeting consumer education as a main strategy, the WTUL designed clothing labels that indicated those companies that adhered to WTUL standards of working conditions and wages.

During the early years of the Great Depression, the numbers of unskilled, unorganized workers increased. After the National Labor Relations Act, or Wagner Act, some AFL members like John L. Lewis and Sidney Hillman started the Committee for Industrial Organization, later renamed the Congress of Industrial Organization, which unionized workers in the automobile, coal, and steel industries. Still, like the AFL, the CIO emphasized bread-and-butter issues rather than educating consumers. And when thousands of women worked in the automobile and electrical industries during World War II, the unions failed to win equal pay or seniority rights for women workers. Most women continued to enter gendered professions like nursing and **teaching*** [see **semiprofessions***].

Yet women's salaries during World War II taught many families the valuable economic assistance wives and mothers could provide as wage earners. The numbers of married women in the workforce rose throughout the 1940s, and by 1950, over 50 percent of women workers were married women. As working mothers became a reality of the Cold War era, so did women's and blacks' membership in unions such as the United Auto Workers and other male-dominated unions.

Some female-dominated occupations remained unorganized, depending upon geographic location and type of labor. Teachers, for example, formed cohesive unions in Chicago, Cleveland, New York, and other urban centers, but southern teachers rarely organized [see **teacher unions***]. Many flight attendants organized unions, while department store clerks and waitresses tended to be nonunion. On the whole, northern women workers joined unions more than southern women. Unionization won many workers benefits, better wages, and working conditions. More important, women's struggles to organize the ILGWU educated the public and other workers about the specific problems women workers faced. The WTUL stands as one of the few efforts to educate consumers about poor working conditions and how those conditions could be changed.

Bibliography: Philip S. Foner, *Organized Labor and the Black Worker, 1919–1973* (1974); James R. Green, *The World of the Worker: Labor in Twentieth-Century America* (1980); Nancy Woloch, *Women and the American Experience* (1994).

Ann Short Chirhart

Laney, Lucy Craft. Lucy Craft Laney (1854–1933), African American educator, founded and served as principal of one of the premier secondary institutions in the South, the Haines Normal and Industrial Institute in Augusta, Georgia [see **normal schools***]. Laney was born in Macon, Georgia, the seventh of ten children of David and Louisa Laney. David, a carpenter and minister, purchased both his and his wife's freedom from **slavery**,* but Louisa continued to work for her former owners, the Campbells. The Campbells' daughter recognized the precociousness of Lucy, who had been taught to read and write by her mother, and encouraged her to read widely from the family library. Laney entered Lewis High School (later Ballard-Hudson High School), a private institution for African Americans, when it opened in 1865. After graduating in 1869, she was among the first students admitted to Atlanta University, founded in 1869 by the **American Missionary Association**.* Laney developed a reputation as one of the most intelligent students at Atlanta and was among the first four students to receive degrees in 1873.

After graduation, Laney began her **teaching*** career at Milledgeville, Georgia, and continued at Macon, Savannah, and Augusta during the next ten years. At Augusta she also played a significant role in establishing Georgia's first African American public **high school**.*

In 1883 Laney opened a private school for African American children in Augusta. Although Laney was especially interested in the education of African American females, believing them best capable of **race uplift**,* she also accepted males. Affiliated with the Presbyterian Church, the school grew rapidly to over 200 students in just two years and was chartered by Georgia in 1886. To meet financial needs, Laney traveled to Minneapolis to seek support from the Presbyterian Church in the U.S.A. Although the Board of Missions for Freedmen [see **freedmen's teachers***] offered only moral support, individuals responded with assistance, among them Mrs. F.E.H. Haines of Milwaukee. In honor of her benefactor, Laney named her school the Haines Normal and Industrial Institute. Other benefactors provided funds for buildings, and eventually the Presbyterian board assisted with salaries and maintenance.

With self-sacrifice, hard work, emphasis on a liberal arts curriculum, recruitment of excellent teachers (including **Mary McLeod Bethune***), and maintenance of high academic standards, Laney developed Haines into one of the best secondary schools in the South. Laney's other contributions included opening the first **kindergarten*** in Atlanta, conducting **teacher institutes**,* and establishing a nursing program that later developed into the nursing school at Augusta's University Hospital. She died in her eightieth year of nephritis and hypertension and was buried on the Haines campus.

Haines Institute began to decline during the 1930s depression with decreasing support from both the Presbyterian Church and private contributors and the establishment of public schools. Haines closed in 1949, and the buildings were torn down, but the Lucy C. Laney High School erected on the institute site honors Lucy Craft Laney's lifetime of contributions to educating African Americans.

Bibliography: Sadie Daniel St. Clair, ''Lucy Craft Laney,'' in Patricia E. Sweeney, ed., *Biographies of American Women: An Annotated Bibliography* (1990); Casper LeRoy Jordan, ''Lucy Laney,'' in Jessie Carney Smith, ed., *Notable Black American Women* (1992); June O. Patton, ''Lucy Laney Craft (1834–1933),'' in Darlene Clark Hine, ed., *Black Women in America: An Historical Encyclopedia*, vol. 1 (1993).

Verbie Lovorn Prevost

Larcom, Lucy. Lucy Larcom (1824–1893) was the most famous of the ''mill girls,'' women who became the transient workforce in the 1830s and 1840s for the newly established textile mills in Lowell, Massachusetts [see **Lowell mills***], while pursuing self-improvement and cultural opportunities. Larcom's life as a mill girl was the beginning of a career as a professional writer, teacher, and editor. Larcom personified the mill girl in her sense of independence, love of education, and determination to pursue these while working full-time.

Larcom was born in Beverly, Massachusetts, one of ten children of a sea captain and his wife. The death of her father in 1832 forced Lucy's mother, Lois, to find a way to support her family. In 1835 Lois Larcom became a supervisor of one of the new boardinghouses for unmarried female workers in Lowell. These dormitories were established to provide cheap housing and close supervision for the women. It was crucial they be run by respectable women, since New England families would not allow their daughters to move away from home if they believed there would be any danger to their reputations or health. Because of their importance, the boardinghouses paid relatively well. Soon several Larcom daughters were working in the mills to contribute to family support. Lucy quit school and began working at age eleven at the Lawrence Manufacturing Company as an unskilled laborer, beginning over ten years as an operative, during which she moved up the ranks of jobs. In the cloth room, where jobs had some flexibility and the rooms had more light, Larcom was sometimes able to study during working hours. Although she had quit formal schooling, she was determined to continue her education and participated in many of Lowell's cultural opportunities. She was an avid reader and subscribed to the lending libraries.

In 1840 Lois Larcom returned to Beverly, leaving three of her daughters behind. The three, Lucy, Emeline, and Octavia, began to send money to their mother whenever possible. Their letters show a strong attachment to family and the many demands on their pay. The Larcoms were more dependent on mill wages than many, and this financial uncertainty would be with Lucy the rest of her life. With the departure of the family, the three girls were very dependent on each other for support and encouragement. This was also typical of mill girls, many of whom came to Lowell with an existing network of family and friends, which helped to alleviate homesickness.

Larcom gained prominence through her contributions to the many magazines that sprang up in Lowell. Magazines usually originated in the "improvement circles" that local clergy encouraged the women to form. These small groups met regularly to share members' efforts at writing, sketching, and other artistic activities. Larcom published her first piece when she was thirteen, and her early contributions were to the magazine her sister Emeline helped establish. After that magazine closed, Larcom became a major contributor to the most well known of the magazines, the **Lowell Offering**.* This magazine, with support by the mill owners, reached a larger public than the workers. People such as Charles Dickens read Larcom's and other contributors' work and were very complimentary. Larcom contributed poems and short stories, usually with conventional, sentimental, or spiritual themes such as "Sabbath Bells." Larcom's later recollections of the mills acknowledged the tedium of the work but focused on the many opportunities that Lowell offered for her education.

Larcom left the mills in 1846 when she moved to Alton, Illinois, to be with Emeline. She taught school there for three years and became friends with poet John Greenleaf Whittier. She graduated from Monticello Female Seminary in 1852 and returned to her family in Massachusetts. She continued to write but moved to Norton, Massachusetts, to assume a position as teacher of literature and rhetoric at **Wheaton Seminary**.* In 1862 she left Wheaton and lived independently. She taught once more in 1872 at Bradford Seminary but for the rest of her life earned her living as a writer and editor [see **seminaries**.*]. From 1865 to 1873 she was an editor for a children's magazine, *Our Young Folks*, published in Boston. To earn her living, she also edited several poetry anthologies, including some that appeared under Whittier's name.

Larcom published four volumes of poetry. Although her style has not retained much appeal, her recollections of her youth have a vividness and strength that make them still very readable. She published her remembrances in the November 1881 *Atlantic Monthly* as "Among Lowell Mill-Girls: A Reminiscence." Later, she published a book, *A New England Girlhood* (1890). Both are still helpful in understanding the experience of being part of the first industrial planned community in the United States.

Lucy Larcom died of heart failure at age sixty-nine. Her legacy was her pioneering efforts as a mill girl, and although she never wrote about the feminist or labor struggles of her time, her later career independence foreshadowed generations of women. She symbolized the first group of independent American women who worked and lived outside their homes and communities.

Bibliography: Arthur L. Eno, Jr., *When Cotton Was King: A History of Lowell, Massachusetts* (1976); Philip Foner, ed., *The Factory Girls* (1977); Shirley Marchalonis, *The Worlds of Lucy Larcom, 1824–1893* (1989); Thomas Dublin, *Farm to Factory: Women's Letters, 1830–1860*, 2nd ed. (1993).

Donna J. Schroth

League of Women Voters. The League of Women Voters was conceived as a "non-partisan and non-sectarian" organization, according to Carrie Chapman Catt, president of the **National American Woman Suffrage Association*** (NAWSA), to support women as voting citizens. Catt called for establishment of such a league in 1919, one year prior to ratification of the Nineteenth Amendment for women's **suffrage**,* with three aims in mind: (1) to ensure final enfranchisement of women nationwide; (2) to remove legal discrimination against women in states' constitutions and laws; and (3) to extend the reach of women's influence and that of the United States to the rest of the world.

By the end of 1920, the National League of Women Voters (NLWV) under Maud Wood Park, the first president, had organized chapters in forty-six states. However, its overall membership reached only 200,000, one-tenth that of the largest national suffrage organization, the NAWSA. The NLWV encouraged women to join political parties and get involved directly with the political process. Thus, some women simply bypassed the NLWV and joined the Democratic and Republican Parties, which established separate women's organizations during the 1920s.

Of primary concern to the league was persuading women to vote. In anticipation of passage of the Nineteenth Amendment, citizenship schools were established in various locations across the country by suffrage groups. The NLWV promoted replication of these schools in every town in order to explain government, political process, and voting procedures to women. In subsequent decades, however, only a minority of women exercised the right to vote. In the election of 1920, the addition of women to the electorate reduced the overall turnout rate to under 50 percent. Women did not vote in proportions equal to men until the 1980s; since that time, their voting has declined at a slower pace than men's. As a result, in the 1990s, women constitute the majority of the voting electorate.

The national organization concentrated on a federal legislative agenda of social and political reform. The league organized its chapters into departments to study subjects related to this federal agenda and to lobby for parallel legislation in the states. During the 1920s, the NLWV focused on women's political and legal rights, child and maternal welfare, labor legislation, consumer protection, civil service reform, conservation, and world peace.

In 1920, NLWV leaders arranged for coordination of ten women's groups to achieve these legislative objectives. The Women's Joint Congressional Committee (WJCC) claimed over 10 million members within its constituent organizations. The league encouraged state affiliates to form comparable umbrella groups. Efforts of these coalitions contributed to a number of laws during the

1920s and 1930s, for example, the Sheppard Towner Act for maternal and infant health care.

A stumbling block to achievement of NLWV goals during these years stemmed from differences of opinion over the Equal Rights Amendment (ERA), authored by Alice Paul, leader of the National Women's Party. Paul viewed the Nineteenth Amendment as a steppingstone to broader change in women's social, political, and economic status that could then be achieved only through an equal rights amendment. The NLWV joined forces with the National Consumers League and the **Women's Trade Union League*** to oppose the ERA, arguing that the amendment would destroy "protective legislation" supported by these groups that had established women's special treatment within the labor force, for example, limiting hours women could work and jobs they could hold.

Protective legislation reflected the perception by Congress and some women's organizations of essential differences between men and women. Women were seen as vulnerable, moralistic, and humanitarian; their special status as mothers and potential mothers demanded protection under law. ERA opponents had worked hard to achieve this recognition for working women by state and federal government.

By contrast, ERA proponents wished to erase distinctions between men and women in the eyes of the law. This difference of opinion created a wedge in the women's movement for several decades. Rivalry between the two factions both in the United States and abroad undermined the ability of either group to achieve its goals. Nevertheless, the league did make some gains during these years in social welfare legislation and marriage, divorce, and property rights for women.

Subsequently, the NLWV continued to work for a variety of causes of special interest to women. In the Great Depression, the league opposed initiatives limiting women's right to work and restricting their access to federal relief. In the 1930s and 1940s, however, national energies were diverted from women's rights to other issues. The NLWV continued citizenship efforts, monitoring the electoral process and educating voters concerning issues and candidates.

In the 1950s, the league fought McCarthyism and, in 1954, changed its position on the ERA. Nevertheless, the amendment died once again but resurfaced twenty years later in 1972, following passage of the Civil Rights Act and the Voting Rights Act. League support for the ERA at this time moved the process of adoption along; however, ratification ultimately failed.

During the 1980s and 1990s, league efforts have been directed at health care, campaign finance reform, presidential debates, voter registration, the environment, reproductive rights, and family leave legislation. Chapters now exist in many foreign countries as the league's outreach extends to promoting peace and assisting emerging democracies worldwide. In the United States, the mandate for an informed women's citizenry continues in the league's efforts at organizing and educating women about issues of political, social, and economic concern.

Bibliography: J. Stanley Lemons, *The Woman Citizen: Social Feminism in the 1920s* (1973); Louise Young, *In the Public Interest: The League of Women Voters 1920–1976* (1989); Becky Cain, "Learning from the Suffragists: The League of Women Voters Educates Citizens for Action," *Social Education*, 48 (1995): 290–292; Nancy Neuman, *The League of Women Voters in Perspective: 1920–1995* (1995).

Margaret Smith Crocco

legal education. As three justices of the U.S. Supreme Court wrote in *In re Bradwell* in 1873, the "natural and proper timidity and delicacy which belongs to the female sex evidently unfit[ted]" women for admission to the bar, thus articulating a widespread view that hindered women's opportunities for legal education for many decades. Even after formal barriers to women's practice of law collapsed in the beginning of this century, social and, in some cases, formal bars prevented significant numbers of women from attending law schools, particularly the elite institutions that traditionally trained judges and leaders of the profession. Major changes came only with the 1960s women's movement: After remaining almost flat for nearly a century, the percentage of law graduates who were women increased from 5 percent in 1970 to 30 percent in 1980. While the rate of increase has now slowed, federal statistics show that women now consistently make up more than 40 percent of law school enrollments. In a further sign of progress, women constituted more than 35 percent of law school faculty by 1992, although they remained concentrated at junior levels.

In comparison to **medical education*** or **graduate education*** generally, the entry of women into the legal profession was hindered until recently by two related factors. First, even though more lawyers have always performed office work than have fought in court, the primary image of an attorney was a gladiator, battling for (invariably) his client. Thus, judges, law professors, lawyers, parents, and some women themselves were simply unable to accept the general idea of women lawyers, even when they accepted the few exceptions. Second, unlike medicine or graduate education, there were few, if any, areas of the law that women successfully colonized as "women's work." However, a few outstanding women made substantial accomplishments in pro bono defense and juvenile law.

While Margaret Brent, a cousin of Lord Baltimore who arrived in Maryland in 1638, is considered the first American woman lawyer, she apparently appeared in court only as the executor named under a will. The first American woman admitted by a court of record to represent others in court was Arabella (or Belle) Babb Mansfield, who passed the Iowa bar exam in 1869 and was admitted to practice by that state's supreme court. After graduation from Iowa Wesleyan College, Mansfield had apprenticed with her brother's law firm.

Two months after Mansfield's admission, Myra Bradwell, wife of a Cook County judge and publisher of a legal newspaper, took and passed the Illinois bar exam after studying in her husband's office. But the Illinois Supreme Court refused to admit her to practice, and on appeal, the U.S. Supreme Court held

(*In re Bradwell*, quoted above) that women applicants to the bar had no constitutional right to equal treatment, a decision that meant that each state could set its own rules for permitting or barring woman lawyers.

The first woman to attend an American law school was Lemma Barkaloo, a woman from Brooklyn, New York, who applied to and was accepted into the Law Department at Washington University in St. Louis after having applied to and been rejected by Columbia Law School. Although she received high marks, Barkaloo did not complete the course of study at Washington, instead taking and passing the Missouri bar exam in 1870.

Mansfield, Bradwell, and Barkaloo were not unique in obtaining most, if not all, of their legal education by apprenticeship. In the colonial era, and for some time after, American men trained for the law by apprenticing with a practicing lawyer. As late as 1876, a majority of those seeking to become lawyers proceeded solely through apprenticeships, and not until 1920 did law school replace apprenticeship as the primary portal to the bar. Particularly since many of the pioneer women lawyers were married women seeking to join their husbands' practices, domestic apprenticeship was a common path to women's legal education. Social factors, however, mitigated against single women seeking apprenticeships; thus, the shift to law schools as the primary forum for legal education effectively opened new doors for women seeking legal training.

In 1870 Ada Kepley of Illinois became the first American woman law graduate when she completed a program at Union College of Law, now part of Northwestern University. Before attending law school, Kepley had studied law in her husband's office. Like Bradwell, Kepley was not admitted to the Illinois bar until the legislature enacted a law providing that no person could be precluded from any business or profession, except the military, on the basis of sex.

From about 1870 the number of women attending law schools, particularly in the Midwest, increased steadily. Most midwestern state universities, like Iowa, Michigan, and Wisconsin, had practiced **coeducation*** nearly from the outset, which helped ensure that women seeking admission to the law schools would receive a respectful, if not always welcoming, reception. By 1890, when the national census reported a total of 208 American women lawyers, Iowa had 27 women law graduates and the University of Michigan had graduated more women than any other in the country. It was at Michigan that the Equity Club, the first national association of women lawyers and law students, began in 1887.

Law schools in the East were less ready to admit female students. In Boston, for example, Boston University was for many years the only law school to admit women. Consequently, a number of law schools or legal educational organizations developed specifically for women. In 1908 the Portia Law School, now New England School of Law, was founded in Boston, initially as an evening bar review course for women. In 1919 Portia was empowered to grant degrees, and in 1922, it added a day division. Portia continued to grow, eventually becoming coeducational; by 1948 it had thirty faculty and 450 students. A less successful experiment was Cambridge Law School, founded in 1915 after several **Radcliffe*** seniors failed to persuade Harvard Law to admit women. This elitist institution, which closed after two years, had parallels in other northeast cities where upper-class college women sought to establish new law schools rather than mingle with lower-class women or men of other races who were seeking professional degrees in the schools already open to women. In Washington, D.C., women shut out of the established law schools created Washington College of Law, now part of American University, in 1898. Like Portia, it soon became coeducational, and men eventually outnumbered women law students.

The elite law schools were the last to open their doors to women. Although a drafting oversight in the school's catalog allowed Alice Jordan to register at Yale Law in 1885 and to graduate the next year, Yale did not intentionally admit women law students until 1918. Columbia Law did not admit women until 1926 after Dean Stone, a fierce opponent of women law students, left to become a justice of the U.S. Supreme Court. Harvard Law was among the last bastions of exclusion, not admitting its first women until 1950.

Long after formal barriers to their obtaining legal education vanished, women law students faced pressures not imposed on men. A feeling that each woman in law school was taking a man's place led to strict **quotas**,* demonstrated by the short-lived increases in the number of women law students during both world wars and the Korean War. Women's applications were reviewed separately and often under stricter criteria. Only in 1968 did the percentage of women in law school rise above 5 percent.

Until recently, women's experience in law school was quite different from that of men. Their sex and their different living arrangements effectively barred women from most of the informal study groups that men joined to share notes, prepare for the next day's cases, and build contacts for the future. In class their small numbers ensured special treatment—sometimes patronizing, sometimes hostile. Until the late 1960s, professors at a number of schools held "Ladies Days" at which women were singled out for questioning and occasional humiliation. While, admittedly, law school used to be more brutal for all students, it was unquestionably harder for the few women students.

Societal changes and the sharp increase in the percentage of women law students led to rapid changes in law schools after 1970. Students routinely hissed statements by colleagues or faculty that they deemed patriarchal, and women won both formal and, somewhat later, practical equality in admission, course selection, and access to prestige positions like law reviews and clerkships. Law school curricula slowly began to reflect the interests of the greater number of women students and professors. The first course in Women and the Law was taught at New York University in 1969, and soon other law schools offered similar courses. The 1980s saw the rise of feminist legal studies, in which women's advocates analyzed and challenged received opinion on a wide range of legal topics from a feminist viewpoint.

Bibliography: Lawrence A. Cremin, *American Education: The National Experience*

1783–1876 (1980); Cynthia Fuchs Epstein, *Women in Law* (1981); Barbara Miller Solomon, *In the Company of Educated Women: A History of Women and Higher Education in America* (1985): Karen Berger Morello, *The Invisible Bar: The Woman Lawyer in America from 1638 to the Present* (1986); Virginia G. Drachman, *Female Lawyers and the Origins of Professional Identity in America: The Letters of the Equity Club 1887 to 1890* (1993).

Stephen S. Ostrach

librarianship. Librarianship, long considered a female profession (or even a **semiprofession***) like nursing or **teaching**,* has suffered from the general lack of respect given to other women's professions. Although in the 1990s women constitute 80 percent of the professional librarian workforce, they much less frequently hold positions of authority, and the history of the profession has usually celebrated male leaders like Melvil Dewey rather than the numerous women who opened and staffed community, college, specialized, and public libraries since the late 1800s.

Before the development of the modern public and academic library in the nineteenth century, libraries were organized and staffed mainly by men and served a limited population, such as religious libraries or subscription libraries. The free public library movement would not be widespread until late in the century, and many academic libraries enjoyed limited use. The first woman hired in a public library was in Boston in 1852. Shortly thereafter, women became the majority of the library workforce as librarianship became a safe and cultured career for the educated woman. Male library directors saw women as hardworking, paying attention to detail where males did not. Hiring women also became a major cost-saving measure at a time when demand was rising much faster than available funding, paralleling the **feminization*** of the teaching profession, which also relied on women's cheaper labor for growing numbers of jobs. Male library administrators knew that women would work at lower pay than men and assumed that most women would retire to marry and raise a family. Much later, civil service laws of the 1930s and 1940s in some areas barred married women from working, closing off a major area of career advancement.

As the nineteenth century progressed, librarianship developed a more professional outlook. The American Library Association (ALA) and the *Library Journal* were founded in 1876. While women did not dominate either the association or the journal as their numbers might indicate, Theresa West Elmendorf did become the first female president of the ALA in 1911–1912. In 1970, the Feminist Task Force on Social Responsibilities Roundtable was founded, the beginning of a strong feminist voice for women in the ALA.

The role of women in the field was debated periodically throughout the twentieth century. These discussions often mirrored those of society, as women were encouraged to advance in the workforce during periods of war and discouraged from professional participation afterwards. Within the profession itself, there are a number of divisions by sex. For example, children's librarians are almost all female, are rarely considered for administrative positions, and receive lower pay. The same holds true for many catalogers, especially as their work becomes increasingly automated.

Professional training for librarianship began in 1886, when Dewey founded the School for Library Economy at Columbia College in New York. Training for librarians in formal settings grew rapidly in the United States, with major schools founded at Pratt Institute, Drexel, and Illinois Universities by the beginning of the twentieth century. Education for librarianship included both the baccalaureate and master's levels, although by the 1960s the trend was moving toward a master's degree as an entry-level qualification for many professional positions. In the 1980s, major library schools such as Columbia and Chicago closed, citing the high cost of tuition at these elite institutions and the low entry-level salaries of librarians. As technology developed and computerization of information took firm hold in the 1990s, many schools of library science expanded to include information science as well to survive challenges by university administrations under pressure to restructure their operations. Many librarians today work in nontraditional fields such as database design and organization of Internet resources.

The current public library field lacks a firm requirement for entry-level librarians. Funding shortages often dictate that many small rural libraries are run by volunteers or an interested community member without formal library education. School libraries have suffered a similar fate, with librarians replaced by part-time library workers or parents. Only academic libraries, who have the master's degree established as an entry-level qualification, have avoided this pitfall.

Bibliography: Kathleen M. Heim, ed., *The Status of Women in Librarianship* (1983); Mary Niles Maack, "Gender Issues in Librarianship," in Wayne A. Wiegand and Donald G. Davis, eds., *Encyclopedia of Library History* (1994); Suzanne Hildenbrand, ed., *Reclaiming the American Library Past* (1996).

Catherine Doyle

Litchfield Female Academy. Litchfield Female Academy (1792), one of the earliest women's academies, significantly advanced and shaped educational opportunities for American women at the beginning of the nineteenth century. In the early Republic, such female **academies*** played a role in producing community leaders and leaders of benevolent, charitable, and other voluntary organizations. Until midcentury, through their central role in training teachers and through their own curricular innovations, they also laid foundations for advances in **female literacy**,* development of antebellum female **seminaries*** and **women's colleges**,* and a broad public acceptance of the principle of **coeducation*** in **high schools**,* colleges, and universities.

Sarah Pierce founded Litchfield Female Academy in 1792 in Litchfield, Connecticut, a major commercial, political, cultural, and social center of stately homes and unusually well-educated residents, distinguished for having the nation's first law school. At the time, public-supported education for girls beyond the primary level did not exist in America; small private, coeducational or female schools providing further education were accessible only to the few families able to pay for it.

Although scholars know little about Pierce's earliest education, they do know that in 1776 and 1777 her family sent her to a private, "select" school, extending her education well beyond the primary level. Following her father's death in 1783, her elder brother John sent Sarah to New York to train as a teacher and make appropriate contacts to help with family finances by heading a school. Following John's death, Sarah assumed financial responsibility for the family. At twenty-five, Sarah opened her school in the dining room of her Litchfield home. Prominent men of the town, including Judge Tapping Reeve, founder of the law school, supported education for females and raised $385 in subscription funds to erect a schoolhouse. In 1827, the school was incorporated as "The Litchfield Female Academy." Pierce retained complete pedagogical and administrative authority and took on most of the teaching responsibility, assisted principally by her nephew, John Pierce Brace, a Williams College graduate.

Litchfield is distinguished in the post-Revolutionary period for the large number, as well as the geographic and socioeconomic diversity, of women it educated. Pierce enrolled at least 1,700 students, reaching a peak annual enrollment of 169 in 1816. As one historian noted, "Very few schools in other states achieved comparable enrollments prior to 1830" (Brickley, p. 27). Students from fourteen states and territories, including Canada and the West Indies, ages from six to midtwenties, boarded with village families. They were daughters of landed gentry; the growing professional class of ministers, lawyers, and doctors; prominent settlers of western frontier states; merchants; and traders. Upper-class families desired an adequate education to ready their daughters for social responsibilities among the elite. Middle-class children attended for the "general good" of education. Financially poor but educated families sent their daughters to receive teacher training and to improve their earning power until marriage. Not unlike other academies of this period, some boys also attended Litchfield, at least 125.

In addition to large numbers of students, Litchfield is important for success in designing and implementing an innovative, rigorous curriculum. In the beginning, Litchfield, like other female schools, taught English grammar, history, sacred history, elementary arithmetic, and geography with major emphasis on **ornamental education*** in needlework, art, and music. But Pierce wanted her students to learn leadership for moral and social reform. Curricular design and philosophy both reflected her embrace of **"Republican motherhood"***—the idea that future wives and mothers must be educated not for political but for moral leadership in order to pass on to children the particular moral insights, virtues, and sensibilities of the new nation. To emphasize academics, Pierce used ornamental subjects to reinforce lessons learned in history or geography.

Eventually Pierce enriched the curriculum with higher mathematics, science, rhetoric, and advanced history, geography, and English. However, unlike male academies where this "English" curriculum was for vocational preparation, at Litchfield it prepared women to enter the female sphere of influence with skills in "polite accomplishments" and, critically, for their role as Republican mothers. Thus, English topics addressed proper habits, writing and conversation, the consequences of unfeminine or un-Christian behavior, and moral and spiritual obligation; themes in geography included the supremacy of God's plan for creation of the world's lands and peoples.

In addition to a rigorous academic curriculum, Litchfield influenced the new Republic's conception of the role women could play in public arenas, leading moral reform, charitable, and benevolent activities. Litchfield also participated in the religious revivals of the **Second Great Awakening**.* Pierce, a Congregationalist, believed that conversions—acknowledgment of sinfulness and submission to God's will—were a mark of adulthood and prerequisite to responsibilities of marriage and motherhood. She also believed conversion would lead women to fulfillment as reformers and perfecters of American society through public activities and efforts. Thus, staff lectured on the importance of "doing good," presented historical accounts of benevolent women, and involved students in benevolence work through the school's Benevolent Association. Numerous alumnae later became involved in moral reform work.

Litchfield Academy's greatest impact on women's education was in training teachers and school founders. Pierce trained and hired former students as assistants; in addition, she recognized the role of apprenticeship in training teachers. Women became heads of student divisions, then assistant teachers, but always under supervision. Pierce oversaw their placement in **teaching*** jobs or helped them open their own schools. More than forty alumnae taught in fourteen or more states; fifteen opened their own schools, including Middlebury Female Academy established under Idea Strong in Vermont; Poughkeepsie Female Seminary and Cottage Hill Seminary, founded by Lydia Booth, who also interested her uncle, Matthew Vassar (founder of **Vassar College***) in expanded educational opportunities for women; and Irene Hickox's first female school in Cleveland, Ohio. Other alumnae joined their husbands in running female academies, opened small private schools for young children, and taught in or established female seminaries connected with their husbands' missionary work at home and abroad. **Catharine Beecher**,* the most famous Litchfield alumna who opened **Hartford Female Seminary**,* was influenced by John Pierce Brace's teaching and chose him to replace her in 1832.

By the mid-1820s, new locally established female academies in New York, Ohio, Vermont, and western Massachusetts competed for Litchfield students. Particularly, the new female seminaries of **Emma Willard*** in Troy, New York, and Beecher in Hartford made Litchfield appear old-fashioned. Moreover, Litchfield Village had declined in importance as commerce moved to the Connecticut River Valley, and Harvard and Yale established law schools.

By 1827, Sarah Pierce, sixty years old, in poor health, could no longer run the academy. She applied to Connecticut to incorporate the school under a board of ten trustees elected from a group of subscribers for a new school building and furnishings. The new building, however, did little to increase enrollments. As principal, Brace could not make ends meet and resigned his post to run Hartford Female Seminary. In 1832, the academy closed. In 1882, the school building was purchased and converted to a private home, which still stands in Litchfield.

Bibliography: Emily Noyes Vanderpoel, *Chronicles of a Pioneer School* (1903); Vanderpoel, *More Chronicles of a Pioneer School from 1792 to 1833* (1927); Lynne Templeton Brickley, ''Sarah Pierce's Litchfield Female Academy, 1792–1833'' (Ed.D. diss., Harvard University, 1985); Theodore and Nancy Sizer, Sally Schwager, Lynne Templeton Brickley, and Gylee Krueger, *To Ornament Their Minds: Sarah Pierce's Litchfield Female Academy 1792–1833* (1993).

Mildred G. Carstensen

Lowell mills. The Lowell mills in Lowell, Massachusetts, introduced both a new manufacturing concept and a unique social practice in the 1820s by mechanizing and integrating all the processes of textile production under one roof and by hiring girls and young women to operate the machines in a socially sanctioned environment.

Working women's labor was essential to the early development of this innovative factory system. Several forces converged to make the textile industry attractive to New England women. Rural men did not want to give up their independent working status on their farms, and families preferred to keep the homemaker out of the labor force. Because a single woman was socially defined as a daughter and child, she was economically dependent upon her father, who often had many other children to care for in difficult times. Factory owners knew that these young women would accept lower wages than men. All factors considered, the Lowell mills offered young rural females, whose average age was sixteen, an alternative to farmwork, allowed them to maintain self-respect while gaining self-improvement and independence, and provided them an opportunity to support themselves and their families financially.

The Lowell factory/community system adhered to the belief that individual success resulted from sound moral and mental discipline, enhanced by repetition and regimentation. Clearly a paternalistic system, the mills required females to live in company-built boardinghouses or dormitories, each housing twelve to thirteen girls, supervised by a matron. Church attendance was mandatory, and ''mill girls'' were to observe a strict code of behavior: no immodesty, dishonesty, idleness, intemperance, profanity, dancing, or gaming. All aspects of life were not only regulated but also synchronized to the chime of a time bell.

During their employment, which usually lasted four to six years, working girls focused on two aspects of life: their work and their self-improvement. As they tended the power looms, the one hundred girls in each large room talked to each other and shared personal experiences. Isolated as they were from the larger world, the girls developed great loyalty, often shouldering extra work responsibilities when another employee became ill. As they gained work skills, the girls trained new factory workers for several months, even though they themselves never held formal supervisory positions. Because they considered themselves "family," the girls did not feel exploited as workers.

The factory work entailed about seventy-three hours per week; after that the women attended to their self-development. The *Lowell Offering*,* a monthly literary magazine written by the women, emphasized self-improvement as a vital way to become a lady. During the mill's early days in the 182Cs and 1830s, the women viewed education as a way to refine themselves. They read earnestly and studied literature and foreign languages; attending lectures, morally uplifting organizations, Sabbath School, and church was also popular. Women also recognized that their status as working girls offered them chances to meet eligible young men, and they worked even harder to become ladies, advising each other about proper speech and dress. The early workers often described themselves as pioneers in widening women's experiences. Through their intense interaction, both in the dormitory and in the workplace, the women developed a strong sense of community.

In the 1840s, working conditions changed when the mill owners attempted to reach higher productivity by speeding up the machines and expanding operations. Workers now had to tend three or four looms in an environment where the rules were oppressive and where the increased heat, lint, and noise became intolerable and unhealthy. In a highly competitive business, owners turned to recent immigrant women as the new workforce. Not surprisingly, the women's attention changed from writing articles and poetry for literary magazines to writing factory tracts denouncing company policies. Their new-found independence resulted in rebellion: They protested by organizing reform associations and participating in strikes to fight for their rights. The socialization that had developed from working so closely on the factory aisles created a proud and articulate "band of sisters." Economic forces swept over the Lowell girls' protests, and they found themselves undermined by a new wave of workers—Irish men and women—who were willing to work for bottom wages and who tolerated harsh overwork.

Bibliography: Thomas Dublin, *Women at Work: The Transformation of Work and Community in Lowell, Massachusetts, 1826–1860* (1979); Alice Kessler-Harris, *Out to Work: A History of Wage-Earning Women in the United States* (1982); Brooke Hindle and Steven Lubar, *Engines of Change: The American Industrial Revolution, 1790–1860* (1986); Alan I. Marcus and Howard P. Segal, *Technology in America: A Brief History* (1989); Dublin, ed., *Farm to Factory: Women's Letters, 1830–1860* (1993).

Deborah Elwell Arfken

Lowell Offering. The *Lowell Offering* was the best known of several magazines publishing works by the women who worked in the new textile mills of Lowell, Massachusetts, in the mid-nineteenth century [see **Lowell mills***]. The magazine was a phenomenon of its time for creating the image of women who worked all day in a mill yet still had energy and intellectual interest to pursue cultural activities, an image that did not fit the picture of mill workers presented by European social reformers and union supporters. The publication began as a basis of pride for the workers and the owners but became a source of controversy as conditions in the mills and the women's expectations changed. It began to be seen as an apologist organ for the owners, not as a tool for the women's original purpose of supporting their claims of social status. The *Offering* was the only one of several mill magazines to garner a national and international reputation. At its peak, famous and influential people such as Charles Dickens, Anthony Trollope, and George Sand read it and publicly marveled at its quality, providing wonderful free advertising for the mills and allaying public concerns about work conditions.

The desire of the young mill workers for a cultural life in their free time led to creation of "improvement circles," gatherings strongly supported by local clergy for young women workers to read their poems, short stories, and essays and to learn more about fine arts. One such group, under the aegis of the Second Universalist Church pastor, determined to publish a magazine of the writing of current and former female mill workers [see **reading circles***].

The first efforts of the *Offering* were four small quartos of sixteen pages each, costing six and one-quarter cents per copy. The magazine appeared sporadically between October 1840 and March 1841. Its main function seems to have been to offer a positive picture of both factory life and the workers. The women, the majority of whom came from the rural New England middle class, were very concerned that mill work not reduce their status; the magazine was one way they tried to bolster the picture of themselves as genteel and refined. Most did not see working in mills as their life's work, and they were concerned about being able to find acceptable husbands afterwards. Therefore, many essays and poems idealized the women as selflessly working to support their families, put brothers through college, and pay mortgages on family farms. In addition, there was a strong element of escapism in many stories, with common magazine literary elements of the period such as orphans who triumphed over difficulties.

After the magazine's first issues, two women mill operatives, Harriet Farley and Harriot F. Curtis, took over producing the *Offering*. By 1842 they were full-time employees of the publication. They produced a monthly magazine of thirty-two pages. The magazine was published, with changes in ownership, until December 1845. There were five volumes of the *Lowell Offering*, containing the work of over fifty women. In 1847, Farley attempted to revive the magazine as the *New England Offering* for two more issues, but it never achieved the success of the original.

Beginning in the 1830s, the mill owners began reducing workers' pay, increasing hours, and demanding a speedup of work. The women attempted protest but were not successful. Such struggles were seldom addressed in the *Offering*, and this lack of coverage came under increasing attack by **labor union*** supporters. The strongest attack came in 1845 by Sarah Bagley, a founder of the Female Labor Reform Association, who claimed that she had submitted articles to the *Offering* about these conditions but had been rejected as too controversial. She criticized the magazine's lack of support among current women workers, pointing out that most subscribers were outside of Lowell, and many were mill agents who used them as positive publicity when recruiting young women as mill workers. Although Farley vehemently protested these charges, support for the *Offering* dwindled rapidly and the last magazine appeared in December 1845.

The *Offering* was a unique endeavor. It was entirely produced by mill women, many of them working full-time. Its articles still offer some of the best insights into the life of these early industrial workers and, most important, their social aspirations. However, the magazine also was a priceless publicity tool for mill owners, and the editors accepted financial support from owners. The owners, in turn, used the *Offering* to prove that life in Lowell was a positive, respectable alternative for women. To combat criticism abroad and at home, they sent copies to social leaders and organized tours of Lowell's cultural efforts for presidents and literary figures. There can be no doubt that the owners used the cultural aspirations of the young women to showcase their business and to counter criticism about their venture. And, as conditions changed, the efforts of the magazine to support positive images about the women turned into a tool for covering up increasingly poor working conditions in the mills.

Bibliography: Hannah Josephson, *The Golden Threads: New England's Mill Girls and Magnates* (1949); Harriet Robinson, *Loom and Spindle, or Life among the Early Mill Girls* (1976); Philip Foner, ed., *The Factory Girls* (1977); Thomas Dublin, *Women at Work: The Transformation of Work and Community in Lowell, Massachusetts, 1826–1860* (1979).

Donna J. Schroth

lyceums. The lyceum movement was a nineteenth-century means of adult education and the precursor to most adult education efforts in the United States. The name was taken from the school near Athens where Aristotle taught. The first American lyceum was founded in 1826 in Millbury, Massachusetts, by Josiah Holbrook. Lyceums spread useful knowledge through lectures and debates. Temperance speaker Dio Lewis was on a lyceum circuit tour in the winter of 1873–1874 when he roused women in Fredonia, New York, and Hillsboro, Ohio, to close the saloons through prayer. When these women met at the newly founded Chautauqua Assembly in 1874, they organized the Woman's Christian

Temperance Union [see **temperance movement***]. Lyceums also encouraged the founding of libraries and museums in towns across the United States.

The **Chautauqua movement*** was the most direct descendant of lyceums. Toward the end of the nineteenth and early twentieth centuries, lyceum circuits started to die out. Several people, like James Redpath, picked up the idea of the Chautauqua Assembly and took education and family entertainment to small towns in the Midwest and West. These are the "Chautauquas" that most people remember. These "tent chautauquas" were never formally aligned with the Chautauqua Assembly, and in 1903, a legal settlement mandated use of the small "c" when referring to tent chautauquas. These chautauquas continued to tour until the 1930s depression.

Many cities still have "town hall" lectures that bring in leading speakers and writers to talk about subjects of interest to the general public.

Bibliography: John F. Noffsinger, *Correspondence Schools, Lyceums, Chautauquas* (1926); G. Hartley Gratton, *In Quest of Knowledge* (1954); Gratton, *American Ideas about Adult Education, 1710–1951, Classics in Education Series, no. 2* (1959); Joseph Kett, *The Pursuit of Knowledge under Difficulties: From Self-Improvement to Adult Education in America, 1750–1990* (1994).

Mary Lee Talbot

Lyon, Mary. Mary Lyon (1787–1849) was founder of **Mount Holyoke Female Seminary**,* one of the earliest schools for women's secondary education. Founded in 1837, Mount Holyoke became a college in 1887 and survives today as one of the oldest institutions for women's higher education in the United States. In creating this institution, Lyon fostered greater acceptance of education for women and helped pave the way for the founding of **women's colleges**.*

Born in the western Massachusetts town of Buckland, Lyon came from a family that instilled a lifelong desire to promote religious faith. Raised a Baptist, she joined the Congregational Church in 1822. The **district school*** being far from home, she initially pursued "home study" until old enough to board with relatives or acquaintances who lived nearer to a school. She started **teaching*** in 1814 at seventeen. In 1817, Lyon attended the new Sanderson Academy in Ashfield, Massachusetts, where she earned tuition money by listening to recitations; the following year she spent a term at Amherst Academy (Massachusetts). She continued to alternate periods of studying with periods of teaching for many years, attending in 1821 the Byfield (Massachusetts) Female Seminary, headed by Rev. Joseph Emerson. Lyon was impressed with Emerson's religious ideals and his teaching methods, which emphasized comprehension over memorization.

In 1823, Lyon lived with friends Edward Hitchcock and his wife in Amherst. Hitchcock, professor of chemistry and natural history at all-male Amherst College, instructed her in chemistry. In spring 1824, she also attended Amherst lectures by Amos Eaton, first principal of the new Rensselaer School of Technology, and she spent time in Troy, New York, studying with Eaton, whose laboratory method of teaching science she adopted. Lyon worked another ten years in teaching and administrative posts under **Zilpah Polly Grant Banister*** (another former pupil of Emerson's), first at Adams Academy in Derry, New Hampshire, and later at Banister's Ipswich Academy. In 1824, Lyon opened her own school for girls in Buckland, which flourished until she closed it in 1828 to devote her energies entirely to Ipswich. The 1829 Ipswich catalog shows that Lyon had incorporated Eaton's laboratory methods of teaching into her own. During this period, she often taught at different schools during different terms of the year.

During summer 1833, while traveling to purchase scientific apparatus for Ipswich, Lyon determined to found her own **seminary*** for young middle-class females. Its purpose would be training teachers, missionaries, and wives of missionaries through ''an elevated standard of science, literature and refinement'' governed by ''the spirit of the gospel.'' In the 1835 prospectus for what would become Mount Holyoke, Lyon promised that the school would give the ''same high standard of mental discipline'' available at Ipswich and ''raise among the female part of the community a higher standard of science and literature, of economy and of refinement, of benevolence and religion.'' She also proposed that expenses should remain low enough to suit a middle-class budget.

Leaving Ipswich meant leaving daily work with Banister, who remained Lyon's friend over many years. Lyon left, however, because she doubted that the businessmen-owners of Ipswich would ever support the permanent, endowed school she envisioned. The fund-raising for Mount Holyoke took three years, with Lyon and the founding trustees conducting a door-to-door campaign, generating $27,000 from citizens of ninety-one towns.

Mount Holyoke Female Seminary opened in South Hadley, Massachusetts, in November 1837 with eighty students aged sixteen or older. For nearly twelve years, Lyon was principal as well as teacher of chemistry and religion. Like her teachers Emerson and Eaton, she subscribed to the inductive method, relying on understanding and experimentation rather than on pure rote learning so common at the time. During the first year, Lyon staffed Mount Holyoke with Ipswich faculty whom she had handpicked and trained in her methods. After the first year, she chose new faculty from her own alumnae.

Lyon believed that teachers should help students learn self-discipline and self-discovery, while training them for service to Christ. She held that learning should be sequential and that the seminary should allow for individual progress, while maintaining rigorous academic standards. Teachers were to be both ''moral architects'' and facilitators of learning for students. Lyon treated her teachers as equals and created a cohesion and interdependence among her staff for sharing learning. Faculty and students worked cooperatively, faculty members living and eating in dormitories, promoting a familial bond as well as minimizing expenses.

Lyon oversaw every facet of the seminary's financial and academic policies, designing the course of study, teaching chemistry and religion, and advising students in course placement. By her death in 1849, the curriculum had been sequenced and expanded to a rigorous and balanced course of study. She urged students to experience teaching as a "valuable preparation for influence" because "the teaching of children decides the destiny of the nation." About 80 percent of Lyon's graduates taught for at least six years.

Through her love of science and her pioneering teaching methods, Lyon gave Mount Holyoke a scientific focus that remains to the present [see **science education***]. For Lyon, like many of her era, study of science was inextricably linked to study of religion: Science gave students a wider view of God's works. She held that experimentation in science was more important for females than for males, "as they have a less number of years for the pursuit and as their time must be more occupied with other things." As a teacher of teachers, Lyon was responsible for disseminating Eaton's methods of teaching science throughout nineteenth-century American **academies*** and **high schools**.*

Lyon died in 1849 of erysipelas, a streptococcal infection characterized by acute inflammation of the skin and subcutaneous tissue, which she contracted from a student.

Mary Lyon created Mount Holyoke to provide women an education equally rigorous to that of contemporary men's colleges. She hoped this would give middle-class women an excellent foundation for teaching and missionary work and thus prepare them for self-sufficient lives. The success of Mount Holyoke Seminary led to wider acceptance of women's education and laid a path for the creation of women's colleges.

Bibliography: Edward Hitchcock, *The Power of Christian Benevolence, Illustrated in the Life and Labors of Mary Lyon* (1858); Sarah D. Stow, *History of Mount Holyoke Seminary during Its First Half Century* (1887); Marion Lansing, *Mary Lyon through Her Letters* (1937); Elizabeth Alden Green, *Mary Lyon and Mount Holyoke: Opening the Gates* (1979); Carole B. Shmurak and Bonnie S. Handler, " 'Castle of Science': Mount Holyoke College and the Preparation of Women in Chemistry, 1837–1941," *History of Education Quarterly*, 32 (Fall 1992): 315–342. See also Mount Holyoke College Library Archives for most of Lyon's papers, including *A Missionary Offering*, her only book, and several pamphlets.

Carole B. Shmurak

M

Magill, Helen. Helen Magill (White) (1853–1944) was the first woman to receive a doctorate from an American university. Boston University conferred the Ph.D. in 1877 for Magill's dissertation "Greek Drama." Magill was also the first woman to take and pass the undergraduate honors examination in the Classical Tripos at Cambridge University, England (1881).

The Ph.D. was relatively new in the United States in the years Magill studied. Specialized training for academics had taken hold only during the 1840s and 1850s. Yale Sheffield Scientific School granted the first American Ph.D.s to three men in 1861. In 1876, the year before Magill received her degree, twenty-five institutions awarded a total of 44 doctorates to men. After Magill's accomplishment, no additional women earned doctorates in American universities until 1880. Thereafter, some women obtained the degree every year; the largest number, 38, was awarded in 1898. In total, 228 women received 229 American doctorates during the nineteenth century.

Magill, born on November 28, 1853, in Providence, Rhode Island, was educated at home and at the Public Latin School of Boston. Her father, Edward, principal of the Latin School and later president of Swarthmore College, was a **Quaker*** who supported **coeducation**.*

Magill graduated with the first Swarthmore class in 1873, then worked as a secretary and taught Latin, gymnastics, and Greek. As for marriage, Magill disdained women who simply waited for the right man, believing that self-sufficiency through work and education strengthened the marriage union, which should be based on love and common interests.

Although Magill's parents expected her to marry, they also expected her to continue her education and fostered her scholarly aspirations until that time. When Boston University opened in 1873 as the first university to permit coeducation in all its postcollegiate professional schools, Magill, believing that all-female institutions "segregated women in an unnatural environment and allowed opponents of coeducation to assert that women already had outlets for their educational aspirations'' (Altschuler, p. 32), recognized an ideal opportunity. President William Warren reviewed her Swarthmore credentials and offered her a postgraduate program with her choice of studies and the Ph.D. degree upon completion. Magill rejoiced that she could meet her parents' expectations: She was living proof that coeducation worked.

Magill earned her degree in two years. Living alone, tutoring classics, and socializing only with her best friend Eva Channing, Magill completed a dissertation. Nevertheless, she remained unsure about career prospects because the university lacked a true graduate curriculum. Following graduation, she declined an offer to teach at **Wellesley College**,* disliking its strict rules governing students. Swarthmore had no openings.

Magill decided to attend Cambridge University, which had opened to women in the 1870s, to get a ''first-rate'' education. Cambridge's residential colleges for women offered curricula identical to that offered men, although the university refused to grant women official membership, voting rights, or degrees. Magill prepared for the tripos, the undergraduate honors exam. She also worked successfully to expand educational rights of Cambridge women including admission to exams, official recognition, and the right to receive degrees. Her tutor convinced her that she had the potential to teach Greek and that strong examination results would assure a position, in England if necessary but preferably at Boston University. Unfortunately, Magill was poorly prepared academically and subject to low spirits and ill health. She took the tripos in February 1881; but feeling unfit for the task, she froze during the examination. After four years of study in Europe, she placed only in the middle of her class, eliminating possibilities for teaching in England and reducing prospects in America.

Magill preferred an academic post in a coeducational institution. But of the few women hired as college faculty during this period, only a handful found jobs in coeducational schools. Most women were distributed among institutions that largely educated women—public and private **normal schools*** and prominent **women's colleges*** that recruited faculty from among their graduates. Magill's parents encouraged her to seek a position at **Smith**,* **Vassar**,* or Wellesley. But even at women's colleges, classics professorships were scarce. Furthermore, Magill lacked strong credentials. Her letter of recommendation from Cambridge candidly stated that she had broken down to the point of being unable to write answers on her exams. Thus, over the next nine years, Magill secured only administrative and **teaching*** positions in preparatory schools.

In 1882, Magill organized the coeducational English Classical Academy in Johnstown, Pennsylvania. In 1883, she became principal of Howard Collegiate Institute in Bridgewater, Massachusetts, a program for women preparing for Smith or Wellesley. When problems with trustees and supervision of students forced her to leave these positions, she took a professorship in ancient languages and history at Evelyn College, the newly founded women's **coordinate college*** at Princeton. There, however, Magill taught only small classes to one or two unenthusiastic students. She wrote her parents full of foreboding about her future and returned to Swarthmore in March 1888 with little hope for a university post. Her last position was as a physical geography teacher at a girls' **high school*** in Brooklyn, New York.

In 1890, at age thirty-five, Magill married Andrew Dickson White, retired president of Cornell University. White believed it was a wife's duty "to make her husband content and in return to be 'kept from all care—to be watched over—to be kept happy—to be guarded from fatigue' " (Altschuler, p. 104). White asked Magill to curtail or quit her work at Brooklyn. Her parents, believing that marriage was preferable to spinsterhood, supported White's position. Magill, too, did not advocate work outside the home for herself or other women after marriage.

In 1892, Magill accompanied White to Russia where he served as United States minister. Their daughter, Karin Andreevna White, was born in 1893 in Helsinki. White encouraged Magill to write, but only as his intellectual assistant, doing proofreading and research. He believed a return to the classics might impair Helen's health and interfere with her duties as wife and mother. From 1887 to 1902, White was ambassador to Germany. When they moved to Italy, Magill resumed writing and delivered a series of lectures to Saturday **reading circles*** in Italy and Germany.

Returning to Ithaca in 1904, Magill never resumed her professional career. She wrote, studied Greek at Cornell, danced and read literature with students at Cornell's Sage College for women, prepared a lecture on the early history of the Society of Friends for the Unitarian Church, served as patroness at dances and concerts, and attended Saturday sewing circles. She supported Martha Van Rensselaer in establishing the Department of Domestic Economy and Prudence at Cornell [see **home economics***].

Magill shared her husband's view that cultivation of an elite class would result in a civilization superior to that produced by egalitarian principles. As for her responsibility to the poor and lower classes, she believed that "acts of charity ennobled the philanthropist even if they did not fundamentally change the recipient" (Altschuler, p. 152). Thus, she encouraged student benevolence toward the poor and worked toward public school reform, lobbying for higher teacher salaries and pensions despite little faith that public schools could do more than teach the rudiments of civilization and provide manual training for workers.

Needing close companionship after White's death, Magill eventually built a home in Kittery Point, Maine, next to her sister Beatrice. In 1936, she became incapacitated. Her daughter lived with her until she died just short of her ninety-first birthday. Magill was buried in the antechamber of Sage Chapel at Cornell University. [See also **graduate education**.*]

Bibliography: William Fairfield Warren, *American University Education in the Birth-Year of Boston University* (1913); Walter Crosby Eells, *Earned Doctorates for Women in the Nineteenth Century* (1956); Richard J. Walton, *Swarthmore College: An Informal History* (1986); Geraldine Joncich Clifford, *Lone Voyagers: Academic Women in Co-*

educational Universities, 1870–1937 (1989); Glenn C. Altschuler, *Better Than Second Best: Love and Work in the Life of Helen Magill* (1990). Magill's papers are preserved at the Division of Rare and Manuscript Collections, Cornell University Library.

Mildred G. Carstensen

Mann, Horace. Horace Mann (1796–1859) was a Massachusetts statesman and educational reformer credited with founding the nation's first system of public elementary education. Through a series of twelve annual reports written between 1837 and 1848 while serving as secretary of the Massachusetts Board of Education, Mann was successful in convincing the people of Massachusetts and the nation that competently taught, free public schools were necessary for successful democracy.

Born on the family farm in rural Massachusetts, Mann's early years were marked by poverty, overwork, and poor health. Like most farmers' sons in the era, his formal schooling was limited to one six- to eight-week session each year. Yet his parents instilled in him a thirst for knowledge and confidence to pursue his dreams of college. Mann graduated with honors from Brown University in 1819; following law school, he practiced law from 1823 to 1837. During these years, he gained a reputation as an orator and influential politician while a member of the Massachusetts legislature. After resigning from the board of education, Mann served in the U.S. House of Representatives from 1848 to 1853, filling a vacancy caused by the death of John Quincy Adams. In 1852, Mann was appointed first president of Antioch College, Ohio. The problems of securing financial backing for the fledgling college, exacerbated by bitter controversy among his faculty, took their toll on Mann, never robust in health, leading to his death in 1859.

Mann's efforts to shift from privately supported education to a centralized, public system had contradictory effects on opportunities for girls and women. His plan for feminizing the **teaching*** force encouraged white, middle-class women to become teachers, helping to establish teaching as a valued occupation for women. At the same time, the increasing reliance on female teachers fostered the development of a gendered bureaucracy, where male teachers supervised and controlled work of female teachers. As an instrumental agent in establishing **normal schools*** to train women teachers, Mann offered a persuasive rationale for continuing women's education beyond the elementary level. At Antioch, Mann opened college doors to students interested in obtaining a classical education, irrespective of their sex or race, further broadening women's access to higher education. Yet in both normal schools and Antioch, Mann's firm belief that advanced education for women was necessary solely as preparation for their natural roles as wives, mothers, and teachers failed to challenge Victorian notions limiting the scope of women's education.

Mann and other educators of his day saw public-supported education as the best means of addressing societal changes brought about by industrialization, urbanization, and immigration. Fearing an American reenactment of England's

social unrest and anarchy, Mann believed that the **common school*** would act
as an antidote by developing social harmony and a strong sense of nationalism.
The nation's ability to weather the unprecedented changes in political economy
depended upon universal and common education—universal in being for all
children, whether new or immigrant, rich or poor, male or female, and common
in that all children would receive the same curriculum. Bringing together girls
and boys from various class and religious backgrounds in the same classroom
would develop a common American culture necessary to assimilate immigrants
and prevent political fragmentation.

Putting into practice Mann's belief that all white children should receive the
same basic education meant reconceptualizing both the nature of that education
and the role of the teacher. Rather than advocating a classical education, his
emphasis was on providing an education consonant with the requirements of
republican citizenship. Mann argued that children's moral and civic development
was best placed in the hands of women, who could make the schoolroom an
extension of the home. Mann was suggesting that women were instrumental to
universal education; that women were, in fact, better suited to teach young
children than were men. Mann argued not only that women's gentler nature was
better suited to teaching young children but that by substituting natural affection
for coercion and corporal punishment, female teachers would be able to use the
maternal relationship to shape attitudes and mold behavior [see **"Republican
motherhood"***].

Mann's plans for the common school called for increasing the length of the
school term as well as encouraging regular attendance. Although enrollment
figures indicate that Mann's efforts to coordinate a public school system did not
significantly increase numbers, his attempts at intensification, combined with a
steady increase in immigrants during the 1830s and 1840s, required a substantially increased teaching force. The lack of prestige or remuneration attached to
teaching convinced Mann that an adequate supply of male teachers could not
be recruited, since men had more lucrative opportunities. By using women,
Mann could count on an almost limitless supply of hardworking teachers willing
to work for half to a third of men's salaries. Calling teaching "holy work" and
proclaiming that "the divinely appointed mission of woman is to teach," Mann
cast teaching in terms of a religious calling, entirely congruent with the primary
function of women as wives and mothers. But since a free common school
depended upon limited taxation resources, Mann also knew that unless an affordable cadre of teachers could be supplied, the common school system would
never become a reality. On balance, then, Mann's attempts to open teaching to
women increased job opportunities, but at the same time, by basing their suit-
ability for teaching on gendered characteristics and paying them far less than
what men were paid, the **feminization*** of teaching effectively devalued it as
women's work.

Despite Mann's rhetoric concerning women's ability to discipline, he and
others were concerned with disciplinary problems in schools when young

women tried to control unruly older boys. To address this, graded classrooms were introduced by 1850, where women taught under the supervision of a male head teacher. Discipline and control, of both students and teachers, were entrusted to the male principal or superintendent, thus establishing a two-tiered system of bureaucracy that separated administration from teaching.

Despite the fact that teaching confirmed Victorian ideals of women's role in society, young, white middle-class women in Massachusetts were drawn for several reasons. As industrialization shifted production from home to factory, the labor of young women was less critical to maintaining the family and home. However, women's choices for paid employment were limited to domestic service, work in textile mills and factories, or teaching. Among these, teaching was considered a genteel occupation to fill the years between adolescence and marriage, allowing young women the satisfaction of contributing to the financial support of the family and offering ideal preparation for motherhood. In fact, one of four native-born white women in pre–Civil War Massachusetts was a teacher at some time in her life.

Criticizing conditions in Massachusetts schools, Mann's second report called for establishment of normal schools to provide training for teachers. The first public normal school opened in Lexington in 1839 for women only; subsequent normal schools, although open to men, enrolled primarily women. Although normal schools did provide credentials for women, they were something of a dead-end educationally in the narrow vocationalism of their curriculum and orientation. Normal schools helped legitimize women's education beyond the grammar school level but failed to provide the kind of intellectually vital education available to males in universities and colleges.

In 1853, Mann was named founding president of Antioch College, one of few colleges in the country to admit women in a coeducational setting. Attesting that "the female has every right to a full and complete mental development," Mann initially welcomed the opportunity to educate women and men together. He had always supported opening common schools to children of color but felt he jeopardized the success of the movement by advocating racial mixing. At Antioch, Mann was able to put his beliefs into practice, admitting women and men of all races. Although Mann never questioned women's physical ability to withstand the rigors of an academic curriculum, he expressed increasing concern regarding the propriety of men and women living and studying in close proximity. To the disappointment of many female students, Antioch male administrators and teachers defined what was appropriate for women's education, explaining they did not mean identical education. He was willing to allow women greater access but only after arranging elaborate safeguards to prevent them from being contaminated, either by too close association with men or by more worldly aspects of the curriculum. Called the "Great Experiment" for its allegiance to **coeducation**,* Antioch was one of the early terrains where educators and students alike attempted to determine just what coeducation in higher education would mean.

Throughout his career, Mann's primary concern was with the oppressed and downtrodden. In the Massachusetts legislature, he was instrumental in rescinding the state's debtors' laws and in founding the first mental hospital in North America. Although often in the minority, he spoke for religious freedom and against alcohol. Mann's keen interest in public education convinced him to abandon a promising political career. Mann's work for a tax-supported school system open to all influenced education not only in Massachusetts but throughout the United States as well. About **abolitionism**,* Mann was ambivalent. Although he firmly believed that **slavery*** was a moral abomination that should be eliminated in time, abolitionist demands for immediate freeing of slaves seemed to threaten the concept of private property and thereby the stability of the Republic. After his resignation from the board of education, however, Mann was able to publicly support abolitionism while in the U.S. House, a position that cost him his seat in 1852. Often controversial, Mann was highly respected for his integrity and commitment to the common good.

Mann's work for common schools, women teachers, and normal schools and at Antioch clearly benefited women. Yet Mann's position in educational history is contradictory, since his efforts resulted in both expansion and contraction of educational possibilities for girls and women. At the same time, too narrow a focus on the contemporary outcomes of Mann's reforms in public education obscures the breadth of his vision and lifelong commitment to making education more accessible to all children.

Bibliography: Jonathan Messerli, *Horace Mann: A Biography* (1972); Richard M. Bernard and Maris A. Vinovskis, "The Female School Teacher in Ante-Bellum Massachusetts," *Journal of Social History*, 10 (1977): 332–345; Carl F. Kaestle, *Pillars of the Republic: Common Schools and American Society, 1780–1860* (1983); John Rury and Glenn Harper, "The Trouble with Coeducation: Mann and Women at Antioch, 1853–1860," *History of Education Quarterly*, 26 (Winter 1986): 481–502; S. Alexander Rippa, *Education in a Free Society: An American History* (1988).

Sharon Hobbs

medical education. Medicine has traditionally lagged far behind other fields of higher education in terms of gender equity. The proportion of female medical students has stagnated under 10 percent for most of the twentieth century; sharp increases in the number of women pursuing medical careers are relatively recent. While the ratio is not yet equal, statistics indicate that 42 percent of first-year entrants to U.S. medical schools in 1993–1994 were female. This represents an increase of 22 percent within a twenty-year time span (from 19.7 percent in 1973–1974), more than doubling the number of women opting for careers as physicians.

Focusing on the twentieth century fails to reflect adequately the history of women in medicine. Early in the nation's development, both men and women were involved in the practice of medicine. Such integration was necessary prior to the Revolution due to an absence of formal training sites: There were no medical schools in the country during its first 150 years and very few hospitals. Pioneer women often had no choice but to serve as midwives. Those with a willingness to learn read medical books and improved their skills by repetitive experience and observation. Their services often expanded into general practice for their communities.

As the nation matured, a more established and gender-restricted training system emerged. Young men who wished to become doctors trained via apprenticeships under practicing physicians, rather than in educational institutions, following the custom for most trades. American medical school development mirrored the European system, which limited admission to men. As options for medical training increased in number, popularity, and prestige, women were denied these career opportunities. Women who wished to practice were relegated to midwifery on a subprofessional level, and two distinct practitioner levels evolved.

Historically, the rise and fall of the number of female medical students in the late nineteenth century has been overlooked, resulting in the notion that significant numbers of females in medical education are a twentieth-century occurrence. In fact, female physicians were not uncommon during the late 1800s, and a large increase can be attributed to the rising feminist movement. Many women were midwives, homeopaths, or sectarian practitioners, thought of as "irregular healers." Yet these were the only training opportunities open to females. Once women chose such career paths, they were stereotyped as "quacks" even in the dark ages of medicine.

Concurrently, a number of degree-granting women's and coeducational [see **coeducation***] medical colleges emerged as females were denied apprentice opportunities for training and practice. Nineteen such institutions were founded in the nineteenth century; as these multiplied, the number of women physicians swelled. Examples include New England Female Medical College (1848), Woman's Medical College of Pennsylvania (1861), and the strongest model, Dr. Marie Zakrzewska's New England Hospital for Women and Children (1862). A simultaneous shift in medical training, prompted by Abraham Flexner's highly critical 1910 report on medical education for the Carnegie Corporation, was also occurring, and greater importance was placed on attaining a formal degree.

Boston served as the hotbed of activity for female access to medical education. The city was regarded as the premier center for medical education, serving as headquarters to the most prestigious professional societies. Boston's experience preceded the national struggle. Feminism fostered a polarization of sex roles; men and women alike were threatened by reforms prompted by the women's rights movement. Those who disapproved of coeducational medical education mounted a medical campaign to define women by their reproductive capabilities, pronouncing them unfit to practice because of "menstrual difficulties." Ironically, these detractors were quite supportive of women's roles as

nurses. Proponents publicly demanded female physicians on principle and promoted large fund-raising efforts to create scholarships and support institutions
that provided training for women [see *Sex in Education**].

The first women to break the educational barriers were **Harriot Hunt*** and
Elizabeth Blackwell. Hunt was the first woman to successfully establish a medical practice, beginning in Boston in 1835. Blackwell was the first female accepted to a traditional medical school that restricted access to men, as well as
the first to earn a formal medical degree, from Geneva College in 1847. Yet
rather than opening the doors of traditional schools for other women, Blackwell's acceptance caused significant **backlash*** within the medical community
and Boston society. Hunt, who had been practicing for nearly a dozen years,
applied to Harvard Medical School on two separate occasions, 1847 and 1849.
Hunt's courage in promoting women's freedom to pursue the finest medical
training launched a furious campaign for female access to medical education.
Eventually, her personal quest took on new importance and greater significance,
developing from an individual goal to a group struggle in the feminist movement. The 1848 **Seneca Falls*** Convention further ignited the cause, and the
notion of professional educational opportunities for females surfaced even before
suffrage.*

Ultimately, the walls of Harvard proved too rigid, and the access campaign
shifted from Boston to other cities. Women were admitted to the universities in
Kansas, Michigan, and Rhode Island by 1877. The fight to gain admission to
Harvard waged for most of the century, taking on a new twist in 1881 when
leading figures in the cause offered an endowment of $50,000 to accept women
students. When Harvard declined, the feminists set their sights on another location. Newly founded Johns Hopkins University accepted a similar arrangement
in 1893, but the sum rose to $500,000. The college proclaimed its action as a
new direction for American medical education. Other institutions such as Cornell
then followed the coeducational trend. Feminist leaders proclaimed victory and
universally favored the closing of women's institutions; coeducation was preferred over segregation.

Despite substantial gains for women during the nineteenth century, real equality for the long term was denied. Once women achieved their hard-fought goal
of admission to predominantly male institutions, the erroneous assumption that
female institutions were no longer necessary followed. Women were eager to
enter male medical schools. Seeking the prestige and stature these schools afforded, women abandoned existing female institutions. As a result, women's
hospitals and medical colleges that had developed and flourished in the late
1800s disappeared rapidly. While the mission to break barriers had been won,
a failure to gain any sort of significant institutional control or influence would
hamper the number of women admitted to the profession for decades to come.
For most of the twentieth century, a **quota***-type situation existed, as most
traditional medical schools admitted classes averaging only 5 to 6 percent
women. The medical establishment could no longer be accused of denying qual-

ified women the opportunity for admission, but strict numerical limitations were maintained. [See also **graduate education**.*]

Bibliography: Ester P. Lovejoy, *Women Doctors of the World* (1957); Mary Roth Walsh, *Doctors Wanted, No Women Need Apply* (1977); Ruth Abram, *"Send Us a Lady Physician": Women Doctors in America 1835–1920* (1985); Thomas Neville Bonner, *To the Ends of the Earth: Women's Search for Education in Medicine* (1992).

Kimberly A. Crooks

Mitchell, Lucy Sprague. Lucy Sprague Mitchell (1878–1967) was a progressive educator, author of children's literature, social reformer, and designer of experimental institutions for the education of children. Most notably, in 1916 she founded the Bureau of Educational Experiments (later known as **Bank Street College of Education***). For several decades, the Bureau occupied a prominent place in American schooling for its unusual blending of progressive education, scientific child study techniques, applied research, and humanistic perspectives.

The Bureau also offered professional and personal opportunities to women who, like Mitchell, were struggling to reconcile family and career choices in a formidable era of transition from Victorian culture to early progressivism. Not only were women highly involved in the Bureau's power structure; their life experiences and intellectual autonomy were emphasized in its innovative approach to **teacher education**.*

Mitchell was born into a wealthy, prominent Chicago family on July 2, 1878. She received most of her education at home, then attended **Radcliffe College**,* graduating with honors in 1900. She became the first female faculty member of the University of California at Berkeley, teaching English and poetry as an assistant professor. In 1906 she was appointed Berkeley's first **dean of women**.* In 1912 she married economist Wesley Clair Mitchell, whom she had met at Berkeley; they had four children.

Before her marriage, Lucy Mitchell had worked in New York City for several months, exploring women's career options and apprenticing herself to several New York social workers, including Lillian Wald of the Henry Street Settlement and Florence Kelley [see **settlement house movement***]. Her experiences awakened her to rampant social injustice, including poor living and working conditions of immigrants. They also deepened her conviction that **teaching*** was a calling and that enlightened school practice could contribute to society's betterment. For Mitchell, teaching and social reform were inextricably linked; she decided that teaching children in public schools was the best way to address an immediate need while simultaneously working toward long-term social change.

When Mitchell and her husband came to New York soon after their marriage, she encountered the progressive movement through the cultural and intellectual milieu of Greenwich Village and through courses with John Dewey and Edward Thorndike at Teachers College, Columbia University. She taught at Caroline Pratt's Play School in Greenwich Village, an important progressive site because of its emphasis on active, constructivist learning, intrinsic motivation, experimentalism, art and music, and field trips. Mitchell began to view school as a place planned on the basis of children's growth. To that end, she advocated children's creative self-expression, later applying early twentieth-century expressionist ideas to teaching and learning in the Bureau's laboratory school.

In 1916, Mitchell's wealthy cousin Elizabeth Sprague Coolidge offered to finance an educational project of Mitchell's design. Thus began the most important work of her lifelong career in education. Mitchell, her husband, and their friend Harriet Johnson founded the Bureau of Educational Experiments as a pioneering attempt to promote school reform through scientific study of children. Informed by progressive ideas on the relationship between education and science, Mitchell assembled a staff of psychologists, physicians, teachers, and **social workers*** to bring together the experimental school movement and the scientific education movement. The Bureau combined schooling and research, expression and experience, and art and science, with a research focus on child development applied to children's learning environment. Pratt's Play School became the Bureau's laboratory school. Mitchell also promoted the involvement of her staff in a number of curricular and teaching experiments in New York public schools, thus establishing a pattern of school-college cooperation that other institutions soon replicated.

In 1930 the Bureau began an experimental program for the education of teachers that eventually became one of its primary missions and led to the founding of Bank Street College. The **teacher education*** program soon moved to the forefront of progressive education and became a clearinghouse for child-centered learning. Mitchell and her colleagues conducted unique educational experiments and gathered information from their own staff's observations to develop a body of research on teaching and learning. They created the "developmental-interactionist" perspective, a synthesis of progressive values and developmental educational theories that came to be widely known as the "Bank Street approach" to teacher education.

Mitchell's search for meaningful work and her experiences as a social worker in New York City led to her advocacy of a "curriculum of experience" as the starting point in schooling, both for teachers and their students. Like Dewey, Mitchell sought connections between education and experience. Importantly, however, she broadened her search to incorporate experiences of teachers themselves. Teachers must first know who they are, she asserted, so that they can be more intentional in their teaching. She encouraged teachers to take responsibility: to ask their own questions, inquire into their practices, reflect on their experiences, and develop an experimental attitude through their own valid observations of children's learning.

Mitchell was also an innovator in children's literature, authoring several social studies series and numerous storybooks. In particular, the *Here and Now Storybook* (1921) transformed the field through use of speech, rhythm, and repetitive patterns of children. *Young Geographers* (1940) emphasized the ecological relationship between humans and their environment. At the Bureau, she conducted a writer's laboratory based on her own system of recording children's language and communicating in terms of their sensory impressions.

Mitchell's work with the Bureau of Educational Experiments and the Bank Street College of Education—scientific study, collaborative projects in schools, publications, teacher training, writers' workshops—made a significant impact on **early childhood education*** and on the progressive education movement. Moreover, her role as a successful post-Victorian working wife and mother, her emphasis on reflective practice, her validation of teachers' life experiences, and her insistence that teachers take more responsibility for their teaching choices exemplified what her biographer has called "feminism as life process." Mitchell died in Palo Alto, California, on October 15, 1967. [See also **child study movement**.*]

Bibliography: Lucy Sprague Mitchell, *Two Lives: The Story of Wesley Clair Mitchell and Myself* (1953); Mitchell, "Making Real Teachers," in Charlotte B. Winsor, ed., *On Teachers and Teaching* (1979); Joyce Antler, "Progressive Education and the Scientific Study of the Child: An Analysis of the Bureau of Educational Experiments," *Teachers College Record*, 83 (1982): 559–591; Antler, *Lucy Sprague Mitchell: The Making of a Modern Woman* (1987); William Ayers, "A Teacher's Life More Fully Lived," *Teachers College Record*, 89 (1988): 579–586; Barbara Beatty, *Preschool Education in America: The Culture of Young Children from the Colonial Era to the Present* (1995). See also interviews with Mitchell in the Oral History Interviews Collection, University of California, Berkeley; Biographical Oral History Collection, 1948–1968, Columbia University Libraries; and in the Elizabeth Sprague Coolidge Papers, Library of Congress, Music Division, Washington, D.C.

Elizabeth Anne Yeager

Mitchell, Maria. Maria Mitchell (1818–1889) of Nantucket Island, Massachusetts, the first astronomy professor of **Vassar College**,* is considered the first American woman astronomer. Through her two decades of teaching at Vassar and her staunch support of rigorous education for women, she strengthened science teaching and fostered the careers of numerous women scientists. Maria (pronounced ma-RYE-ah), the third of ten children, was born into the subject— her father William was a respected amateur astronomer. He taught Maria the art of calibrating whalers' chronometers using the stars, and she became his assistant at an early age. At twelve, she counted off seconds for him while he observed a solar eclipse. Mitchell began her education at local private schools, but when her father became a schoolmaster and later founded his own school, Maria became one of his pupils. She finished her last year of school (1835) in Cyril Peirce's school for "young ladies." Of her own abilities, Mitchell remarked, "I was born of only ordinary capacity, but of extraordinary persistency."

At eighteen Mitchell opened her own private school for children ages six and older. By admitting several black children, she had what was possibly the first known integrated school in New England. Her school closed the following year, and she became a librarian at the Nantucket Athenaeum, a post she held for twenty-four years. There she studied famous works on mathematics and celestial mechanics. She continued observing, and on October 1, 1847, discovered a comet that brought her worldwide fame. The King of Denmark had founded a medal in 1831 for discoveries of telescopic comets. Mitchell's father wrote to William Bond of the Harvard College Observatory announcing his daughter's discovery, but the mail did not go out from Nantucket until October 4. Meanwhile, observers in Rome and England immediately reported discovering the comet and were awarded the medal. Letters from Mitchell's father and other astronomers resulted in her being declared the rightful winner one year later.

Thus in 1848 Mitchell was elected the first woman member of the American Academy of Arts and Sciences and received a medal from the Cantons of Switzerland for outstanding service to the sciences. In 1849 she worked as a computer for the U.S. Nautical Almanac office. As the only woman on the computing staff, it seemed obvious to her superiors that she should be given the tables of Venus to work on. She continued various computations for the Almanac until 1868. In 1857 she traveled to Europe and met famous astronomers including John Herschel and Mary Somerville. On her return, Mitchell was presented with a five-inch Alvan Clark refractor by a group of Boston women on behalf of ''the women of America.'' After the death of her mother in 1861, Mitchell and her father moved to Lynn, Massachusetts, to be near one of her sisters.

Mitchell's life changed drastically in 1865 with the opening of Vassar College, one of the country's first **women's colleges**.* Matthew Vassar's goal was to offer women, for the first time, a course of study equivalent to that at the best men's colleges. He sought the finest women scholars as professors, and Mitchell, even without a college education, was his natural choice. She became professor of astronomy and director of the observatory. The college provided a house for her and her father, and they lived and worked together until his death in 1869.

Vassar supplied Mitchell with a twelve-inch refractor, the third largest in the country in 1865; however, the optics were poor quality, and in 1868 Alvan Clark and Sons refigured the telescope. The mounting system limited her research to the planets and their moons, but in 1887, she persuaded the college to rebuild the mount so that comet and asteroid positions and measurements could be done.

Her teaching methods were considered unorthodox. Instead of lecturing, Mitchell stressed small classes and individualized attention. She insisted on learning by observation, not memorization, saying ''nature made woman as observer—the schools and schoolbooks have spoiled her'' (quoted in Wright, p. 141). She ignored the conventional grading system, saying, ''[Y]ou cannot mark a human mind because there is no intellectual unit'' (quoted in Wright,

p. 169). She also refused to take attendance. Routinely, Mitchell took her students to New York City and into the nearby countryside to make astronomical observations, and she led expeditions of students and alumnae to solar eclipses in Iowa and Colorado. A testament to the success of her pedagogy is the fact that four of her students became well-known astronomers: Mary Whitney (her successor at Vassar), Margaretta Palmer, Antonia Maury, and Caroline Furness (Whitney's successor). Also, twenty-five of her students were listed in "Who's Who in America." Failing health forced Mitchell to retire from Vassar on Christmas Day, 1888. Although she was offered a permanent home in the observatory, she returned to Lynn, Massachusetts, where she died from "brain disease" six months later.

A **Quaker*** by birth, Mitchell believed in the message of love and peace but did not like rigid institutionalized religion. Once when a regular chapel service at Vassar threatened to interfere with her observations of Saturn, she wrote to the president of the college asking him to shorten his prayer.

Mitchell was a staunch supporter of women and women's education, stating, "I believe in women even more than I believe in astronomy" (quoted in Wright, p. 190). She argued that "women are needed in scientific work for the very reason that a woman's method is different from that of a man. All her nice perceptions of minute details, all her delicate observation of color, of form, of shape, of change, and her capability of patient routine, would be of immense value in the collection of scientific facts" (quoted in Wright, pp. 12–13). She was a founding member of the Association for the Advancement of Women in 1873 and served as president from 1874 to 1876 and chairperson of the Committee on Science from 1876 to 1888.

Mitchell received honorary degrees from Hanover College (1853), Rutgers University (1870), and Columbia University (1887) and has a lunar crater named in her honor. Her name is also inscribed on the frieze of the Boston Public Library and a bronze bust in the New York University Hall of Fame. But perhaps her greatest legacy is the Maria Mitchell Observatory on Nantucket. After Mitchell's death in 1889, many former students visited her old home there. Family members, friends, and Vassar alumnae founded the Nantucket Maria Mitchell Association in 1902, and an observatory was built in 1908. In the 1950s, Dorrit Hoffleit, then director of the Maria Mitchell Observatory, began a summer research program for women undergraduates. During Hoffleit's twenty-two years at the observatory, over one hundred girls took part in the program and over twenty-five went on to earn Ph.D.s. The program continues but is now coeducational. [See also **science education**.*]

Bibliography: Maria Mitchell, "The Collegiate Education of Girls," in Anna C. Brackett, ed., *Women and the Higher Education* (1893); Helen Wright, *Sweeper in the Sky* (1949); Sally Gregory Kohlstedt, "Maria Mitchell: The Advancement of Women in Science," *New England Quarterly*, 51 (March 1978): 39–63; Deborah Jean Warner, "Women Astronomers," *Natural History*, 88 (1979): 12–26; Pamela E. Mack, "Straying from Their Orbits: Women in Astronomy in America," in G. Kass-Simon and Patricia

Farmes, eds., *Women in Science: Righting the Record* (1990); Dorrit Hoffleit, *The Education of American Women Astronomers before 1960* (1994). Diaries, letters, lectures, and observing notebooks are in the library of the Nantucket Maria Mitchell Association; observing notebooks and correspondence are in the Vassar College Library.

Kristine Larsen

Montessori, Maria. Maria Montessori (1870–1952) was an Italian educator, physician, and early feminist whose system for educating young children has been influential worldwide and has enjoyed a renaissance in the United States over the past few decades. Born in Chiaravalle, Italy, the only child of well-educated, middle-class parents, Maria distinguished herself intellectually at an early age. Against her father's wishes, she entered at thirteen a technical school to study for a career in engineering. Later studies in mathematics, physics, and natural science at the University of Rome convinced her to forego engineering for a career in medicine. She graduated at the top of her class in 1896, the first woman in Italy granted a medical degree [see **medical education***].

Montessori's educational successes with mentally and developmentally disabled children as director of the Orthophrenic Institute in Rome led to her appointment in 1907 as director of the Casa dei Bambini, a new day care center housed in the slums of San Lorenzo. At the institute, Montessori had developed a set of didactic **teaching*** materials that allowed her disabled charges to master skills, to learn to read and write, and for many, to pass the same examinations given in regular primary grades. Convinced that the poor children of San Lorenzo, left alone throughout the day while their parents worked, could benefit from the same approach to education that had been so successful with disabled children, Montessori made the Casa dei Bambini a place where children aged two-and-a-half through seven could learn in a homelike environment.

Eventually Montessori toured the world, addressing issues of children's education and world peace [see **peace education***]. With the dual perspective of social crusader and scientist, Montessori was a tireless advocate for the rights of women and children throughout her life. Proceeds from her popular lectures often went to support public kitchens and shelters for the poor. She was a three-time nominee for the Nobel Peace Prize, and her seven books explicating her philosophy and educational methods have been translated into many languages. Montessori schools are located worldwide.

Montessori's educational work has been described as "a social movement, a philosophy, a theory of development, a curriculum model and a set of methodological strategies" (Loeffler, p. 19). In brief, Montessori's method developed from careful attention to the activities of children. Combining an intuitive and rational understanding of the cognitive growth and development of the young child, Montessori conceived an educational experience designed to facilitate physical, intellectual, and spiritual growth. Based upon observation, Montessori challenged prevailing attitudes that children should be treated as miniature adults. She argued that the child has her own interests, purposes, and needs, and the classroom curriculum and environment should be determined accordingly. Montessori stressed the importance of the developmental stage between three and six in shaping adult potential. During this sensitive period, the child requires freedom to explore the world in time to her own individual rhythms and simultaneously requires stability, predictability, and safe limits. The natural learning cycle of the child moves from observation to participation to repetitive practice to mastery. Montessori's specially developed teaching apparatuses facilitate this progression.

Unlike most classrooms where a dyadic relationship between teacher and students is the norm, the Montessori classroom is built upon a triadic set including teacher, students, and the environment of the classroom. The teacher, or directress (Montessori's preferred term), carefully prepares and controls the physical environment, giving demonstrations on how to use various didactic teaching materials, encouraging children, then allowing them to work uninterrupted on tasks they have chosen. The directress's attitude toward students is one of profound respect and caring. Within this prepared environment, children develop a sense of individual competence and community with their fellow students.

Despite proliferation of Montessori schools and training programs throughout the world, Montessori's impact on American education has been uneven. When she first toured the United States in 1913, she was heralded as a "woman who revolutionized the educational system of the world." A devoted coterie of followers, many of whom had trained with her in Italy, spread her method to nearly one hundred schools by the end of that year. Her work was a central focus at educational conferences throughout the country. Yet by 1916, the Montessori method had slipped into oblivion, not rediscovered again until the late 1950s.

How can the meteoric rise and fall of the Montessori approach be explained? One critic suggests that the facts that Montessori was a woman, a foreigner, and Catholic were all strikes against her in the eyes of American educators. Moreover, her approach to **early childhood education*** was out of step with American educational notions that held that intelligence was fixed, that sensory training was a waste of time, and that the young child's educational experiences should be limited to play and fantasy, not the real-life experiences that Montessori advocated. Early in the century, schooling was viewed primarily as an instrument of social change, not of the child's individual development.

Montessori's credibility in the United States received a death blow from William Heard Kilpatrick, popular educational philosopher at Columbia Teachers College and disciple of John Dewey, who published a condescending attack in 1914, *The Montessori System Examined*. Kilpatrick concluded that Montessori "belongs essentially to the mid-nineteenth century, some fifty years behind the present development of educational theory. . . . Stimulating she is, a contributor to our theory, hardly, if at all" (Chattin-McNichols, p. 30). Kilpatrick's harsh evaluation, combined with Montessori's own proprietary interest in maintaining tight control over training and establishment of Montessori schools, brought a sharp decline in interest in both Montessori and her educational philosophy.

A second wave of American interest in Montessori occurred in the late 1950s and early 1960s. Fueled by parental anxiety resulting from the Soviet Sputnik success in 1957 and by advances in cognitive psychology that created a more hospitable climate for Montessori's conceptions of child development, Montessori schools again began to proliferate. By the early 1990s some one hundred public school districts in the United States included Montessori programs; Montessori-type programs could be found in day care and preschools, magnet schools, bilingual programs, special education, gifted education, Head Start programs, and programs for children of migrant workers.

Renewed interest in Montessori programs has appealed to two quite dissimilar groups. Middle-class parents see the system as a way of giving their children an intellectual head start, leading to early reading, writing, and mathematical competence. In fact, many private Montessori schools serve a relatively homogeneous population. Yet, beginning in the 1960s, Montessori's original work with extremely poor children has made her approach appealing to educators and policymakers looking for the optimum education for "at risk" children. Based on a theory of cultural deprivation, Lyndon Johnson's War on Poverty enlisted the Montessori approach in many Head Start programs; today Montessori strategies are often recommended for teaching children with special needs.

Although it may be too early to call it a third wave, educators such as Jane Roland Martin find much in Montessori's writing that speaks to current needs. Martin sees in Montessori's Casa dei Bambini a model for education that blends public and private, school and home, to provide a safe, supportive, nurturing community often lacking in children's lives. Other educators claim Montessori as an early constructivist because her work highlights "the paths the child follows in the active construction of his individuality" (Loeffler, p. 57).

Many of Montessori's ideas and techniques have become so commonplace in preschool and day care programs that we often forget what a radical departure from established traditions they represented in Montessori's day. Her work continues to be a source of both controversy and enlightenment.

Bibliography: Maria Montessori, *The Montessori Method* (1964); Rita Kramer, *Maria Montessori: A Biography* (1976); John Chattin-McNichols, *The Montessori Controversy* (1992); Margaret Howard Loeffler, ed., *Montessori in Contemporary American Culture* (1992); Jane Roland Martin, *The Schoolhome: Rethinking Schools for Changing Families* (1992).

Sharon Hobbs

moonlight schools. Although the phrase *moonlight school* carries with it two separate definitions, its common denominators are moonlight, emancipation, and women. At the heart of moonlight schools lays the fact that clandestine, secret, or "by moonlight" efforts were made to provide education for individuals, regardless of color, creed, or race, who had been enslaved by illiteracy. Not only did women teach in these schools but, in some cases, did so at great risk to their safety.

Chronologically, the first moonlight schools were connected to clandestine efforts to educate slaves [see **slavery***]. So that slaves might attend, secret school was often held between midnight and 2 A.M., moonlight providing the only illumination for reading instruction or finding the way to school along the path. Diaries and journal entries verify the work of such women as Mary Peake who ran a secret school in the 1850s and 1860s in her home for dozens of African Americans, along with reports of forced closings and punishment for teachers and/or slaves. Receiving clandestine schooling herself, another woman, Milla Granson, held secret classes so that contrabands might learn to ''read and write a legible hand'' by using the light from the fire of pitch-pine splinters fashioned into bundles. In some parts of the South, schools established by the Freedmen's Bureau meant that clandestine efforts to educate slaves could be discontinued [see **freedmen's teachers***].

Years later, a second version of moonlight schools, established in 1911 in the Kentucky mountains, were the educational programs conceived by Cora Stewart Wilson, superintendent of Rowan County Schools [see **county superintendents***]. With hopes of bringing people out of the foothills and mountains for opportunities to learn to read and write or simply expand their knowledge, evening schools were begun on ''moonlight nights'' so the moon might provide light for students to find their way to school. Teachers volunteered their services and literally went door to door to invite people, young and old alike, to attend. The beginnings of the adult evening school movement came through the ingenious efforts of women such as Wilson, Granson, and Peake who saw the value of moonlight to kindle the desire for learning. [See also **female literacy.***]

Bibliography: C. W. Stewart, *Moonlight Schools for the Emancipation of Adult Illiterates* (1922); J. C. Spruill, *Women's Life and Work in the Southern Colonies* (1969); R. C. Morris, *Reading, 'Riting, and Reconstruction* (1980); W. E. Nelms, ''Cora Wilson Stewart and the Crusade against Illiteracy in Kentucky, 1916–1920,'' *Register of the Kentucky Historical Society,* 82 (1984): 151–169.

Andrea Wyman

Moravians. The Moravian church stems from the pre-Reformation Hussite movement of the fifteenth century in Bohemia and Moravia. Following a period of persecution and decline, Moravians underwent a revival in the eighteenth century and began an expansive mission program, which brought them to the American colonies in 1735. In America, Moravians were known for their strong reliance on informal education among women and for their creation of female schools and **academies,*** especially in the mid-Atlantic states.

Although the Moravians' most famous pedagogue was Bishop John Amos Comenius, the educational practices and philosophies of Moravians in America owe much to Count Nicholas Ludwig von Zinzendorf, a Saxon nobleman who headed the eighteenth-century resuscitation of Moravianism. A great lover of children, Zinzendorf especially emphasized the responsibilities of the community and parents in proper childrearing.

For Moravians, education was largely a process of leading children to a close, personal relationship with Jesus. Although they did not deny the doctrine of Original Sin, Moravians represented the early stages of the Romantic movement that viewed childhood as a stage of purity and innocence. In highly romantic terms, Zinzendorf expressed his view that childhood was a distinct and admirable stage of life: "Children are little royal majesties. Baptism is their anointing, and from then on they should be treated as none other than a king by birth."

Moravians also placed special emphasis on motherhood. Describing the Trinity as a family, consisting of a father, mother, and child, Moravians stressed the action of the mother (the Holy Spirit) in leading an individual to Christ. Moravian women were encouraged to reflect on their own important roles as mothers. Believing that a mother's education could not begin too early, Moravians held religious services and group meetings for pregnant and nursing women.

Because of the Moravians' vigilance in segregating the sexes, women learned much about Moravian beliefs from daily interaction with other women. Moravians initially organized their community at Bethlehem, Pennsylvania, by dividing the population into groups, called "choirs," each consisting of individuals similar in age, sex, and marital status. Within these choirs, male leaders ministered to boys and men, while women ministered to girls and women. Moravians did not replicate the choir system in their numerous missions to Native Americans in New York, Connecticut, Pennsylvania, and Ohio; however, even in these missions, white and Indian women were extremely influential in serving as spiritual advisers to other women.

Besides a myriad of informal ways that Moravian women educated other women and inculcated their community's values, Moravians also used formal schooling to further their religious goals. In 1742 Zinzendorf's daughter opened a girls' school at Germantown, Pennsylvania, one of the earliest female boarding institutions in the colonies. After several relocations, this school settled permanently at Bethlehem in 1749 and, after 1785, was opened to non-Moravian girls. Encompassing both elementary and secondary work, the curriculum of the Bethlehem Female Seminary after its 1785 reorganization included the three "r's," grammar, history, geography, astronomy, plain sewing, fine needlework, and music. German was an elective. In the early twentieth century the **seminary*** developed a college program, which merged with its male counterpart in 1953 to form the newly incorporated Moravian College.

Not just in Bethlehem but wherever they established communities, Moravians provided day schools and sometimes boarding schools, seeking basic and sometimes advanced education for both sexes. The Linden Hall Seminary at Lititz, Pennsylvania, began as a Moravian girl's day school in 1764, later developing into a sizable boarding institution. In 1804 the Moravians opened a boarding school for girls at Salem, North Carolina, modeled on the Bethlehem Female Seminary. By the Civil War, the Salem Academy had become an important educational institution in the state.

Bibliography: Mabel Haller, *Early Moravian Education in Pennsylvania* (1953); Madeline M. Allen, "An Historical Study of Moravian Education in North Carolina: The Evolution and Practice of the Moravian Concept of Education as It Applied to Women" (Ph.D. diss., Florida State University, 1971); Beverly Prior Smaby, *The Transformation of Moravian Bethlehem: From Communal Mission to Family Economy* (1988); Gary Steven Kinkel, *Our Dear Mother, the Spirit: An Investigation of Count Zinzendorf's Theology and Praxis* (1990); Les Reker and Martha Reid, eds., *Moravian College, 1742–1992: A Celebration* (1992).

Amy C. Schutt

Morrill Land-Grant Act of 1862. In 1862, Abraham Lincoln signed into law the Morrill Land-Grant Act, which provided for the sale of public lands to provide states with necessary "support and maintenance of at least one college where the leading object shall be, without excluding other scientific and classical studies, and including military tactics, to teach such branches of learning as are related to agriculture and the mechanic arts." This became the impetus for creation and funding of land-grant colleges and universities in the United States. Although not specifically aimed at women, the act benefited women's higher education almost by default, encouraging a new type of university opportunity that enrolled women as students and introduced disciplines of interest to them.

The Morrill Act was proposed in Congress in 1857 by Vermont Senator Justin Morrill. After acrimonious debate where the issues of constitutionality and state's rights versus federalism predominated, the bill barely passed. President James Buchanan, however, vetoed the measure, citing constitutional concerns but more likely fearing the escalation of sectionalism. After secession, Morrill reintroduced the bill; it passed Congress and was signed in 1862.

The Morrill Act is, in many ways, a historical curiosity. While popularly considered a pioneering piece of educational legislation, it was neither pioneering—there were examples of agricultural education prior to 1862, and the idea of using land sales to further education was tried in 1787 with the Northwest Land Ordinance—nor especially educational in intent. In fact, educational arguments and pedagogical considerations were largely absent from congressional debates over the act. Instead, the Morrill Act came to be regarded as important educationally, not because of the educational vision of its sponsor or the debate that ensued but because of the subsequent importance of certain Morrill Act institutions to American higher education.

The Morrill Act kindled a new interest in public higher education as several states eagerly capitalized on the federal largesse. In some states, the land-grant institution became the premier public institution (e.g., the University of Wisconsin). In others, land-grant institutions and another state university both rose to prominence (e.g., land-grant Michigan State University and the University of Michigan). In either case, public higher education grew at a precipitous rate in the late nineteenth and early twentieth centuries. The relatively low cost of public higher education is the basis of the Morrill Act's most enduring legacy—

that of "democratizing" higher education. A public college education was financially accessible to a greater number of students, and the emphasis on practical or even vocationally oriented subjects made state colleges more curricularly relevant to myriad walks of life.

While it is important to note that such democratic idealism existed in the rhetoric of the era and perhaps in the popular imagination, it is equally imperative to recall that reality, typically, fell far short of the ideal. For the most part, social mobility and equality of opportunity in the nineteenth century were limited to native-born, Protestant, white males, who were more than likely of at least middle-class origins. The university participation rate of women and African Americans grew much more slowly. In many cases, entry was granted only after protracted and bitter struggles.

Ironically, however, land-grant institutions and their sister state institutions did play an important role in expanding higher education for women, although such an outcome is surely an unintended legacy. Significantly, state colleges and universities were at the forefront of **coeducation**,* the mode of education chosen by the vast majority of women.

There were early experiments with coeducation before the Morrill Act. In the 1830s **Oberlin College*** was both coeducational and integrated, while Antioch College became coeducational in the 1840s. The University of Wisconsin admitted a few women to a **normal department*** for teacher training in 1851, but the dominant model before the Civil War was clearly single-sex education, with women's options limited to a few early **women's colleges*** and **academies**.*

During the 1870s and 1880s, the chronically cash-strapped, relatively young public institutions recognized the financial benefits of increased student enrollment, even women students. By the later half of the nineteenth century, state institutions also were aware of the acute need for teachers in the expanding public school systems and newly created **high schools**.* Driven by these pragmatic concerns and augmented by arguments regarding equality of opportunity and the rights of all state residents for participation, state institutions, some quite begrudgingly, opened to women. The first such full liberal arts degree conferred on a woman was at Indiana University in 1869.

Another benefit to women was the relative curricular flexibility of these institutions. Having broken with the long-standing tradition of classical education by offering agriculture and the mechanical arts, state universities proved quite receptive to introduction of new disciplines and were unabashed about the careerist orientation of their students. Coeducation and the need for teachers prompted universities to create normal departments to train teachers. Another curricular addition was "domestic" studies, eventually known as **home economics**.* One of the earliest programs was at the University of Iowa in 1871, but several other state universities followed within a decade or two.

The role of home economics in the history of women's education was equivocal. Many educators, both male and female, supported women gaining the practical training it offered; on the other hand, it was viewed by others as a step backward. Different faculties focused on various aspects of the discipline— scientific, social, economic, or domestic—but the steady growth of enrollments across universities demonstrated its popularity. However, home economics became a ghetto of sorts for women academics unable to secure positions in other disciplines. By 1911, over 60 percent of all female professors at coeducational institutions were housed in domestic science.

These two fields—**teacher education*** and home economics—absorbed the majority of female enrollments in the nineteenth century. By 1900, there were 61,000 women in coeducational institutions; 43,000 were enrolled in education departments and 2,000 in home economics. After 1900, women students and educators pushed for courses related to women's interests, heightened by the reformist movements of the **Progressive Era**.* Such included child psychology, marriage and family, **social work**,* settlement work, poverty, and charity. The overall effect was greatly expanded professional opportunities for women upon graduation.

In summary, the Morrill Act of 1862 set into motion a sequence of events that contributed to the education of women primarily because of the type of institution it spurred. These institutions were coeducational, low cost, and less elitist in their curriculum than older private colleges. They were more willing to admit women and therefore provided access for many who did not choose, or could not afford, private single-sex education. An often overlooked outcome is that these institutions also provided access to **graduate education*** and professional education for women that the women's colleges could not. The public sector of higher education played an important role for women, despite the more romantic notions and potential benefits associated with single-sex colleges. As of 1996, the public sector was fully coeducational due to the Supreme Court ruling that dictated that states cannot provide public education that does not offer equal benefits to women.

Bibliography: Edward Danforth Eddy, Jr., *Colleges for Our Land and Time: The Land-Grant Idea in American Education* (1956); Allan Nevins, *The State Universities and Democracy* (1972); George N. Rainsford, *Congress and Higher Education in the Nineteenth Century* (1972); Eldon L. Johnson, "Misconceptions about the Early Land-Grant Colleges," *Journal of Higher Education*, 52 (July–August 1981): 333–351; Barbara Miller Solomon, *In the Company of Educated Women: A History of Women and Higher Education in America* (1985).

Jana Nidiffer

Morrill Land-Grant Act of 1890. The second Morrill Act of 1890, like its predecessor the **Morrill Land-Grant Act of 1862**,* made no specific mention of women's education. However, this follow-up piece of legislation is generally credited with continuing and expanding the benefits to public higher education inspired by the 1862 act. In that sense, the second Morrill Act ensured that gains women made in the public sector in the mid-nineteenth century extended into the twentieth.

The 1890 Morrill Act had three significant outcomes. The act was a financial boon to existing land-grant colleges, providing increased funds for instruction at the same time of rapid increases in student enrollments. In fact, the act more than doubled the federal contribution to land-grant colleges. It further encouraged increased state support and the development of a pattern of regular tax support for state colleges. Second, this act instituted a pattern of federal control in grant giving that continues today, making very specific requirements of state grantees.

The third feature was the guarantee that African Americans would benefit from the act's provisions. By 1890, the South had accepted the provisions of the first land-grant act for white institutions and had established separate, usually inferior, colleges for African Americans without using federal funds. The second Morrill Act stated that funds would be denied to any state or territory "where distinction of race or color is made in the admission of students" and allowed state-supported colleges for African Americans not already designated as land-grant to become so. In this era where the "separate but equal" doctrine of *Plessy v. Ferguson* dominated, however, the federal government stated that it would allow separate facilities, provided that federal funds were divided equitably. Such equity never occurred, but federal funds poured into white southern land-grant institutions nevertheless. Seventeen southern and southwestern states set up separate institutions for African Americans. The second Morrill Act, therefore, has the dubious legacy of perpetuating the separate but equal doctrine that would take another half century to sunder.

A century later, in the mid-1990s, sixty-nine land-grant universities existed. Each of the fifty states has at least one Morrill Act institution. There is also one institution each in the District of Columbia and Puerto Rico. Seventeen states (most of them southern) have two land-grant institutions.

Bibliography: Merle Curti and Vernon Carstensen, *The University of Wisconsin: A History, 1848–1925*, 2 vols. (1949); Allan Nevins, *The State Universities and Democracy* (1972); George N. Rainsford, *Congress and Higher Education in the Nineteenth Century* (1972).

Jana Nidiffer

Mount Holyoke Female Seminary. Mount Holyoke Female Seminary was established in 1837 in South Hadley, Massachusetts, by **Mary Lyon**.* In 1887, it was chartered as Mount Holyoke College and remains one of the oldest institutions for women's higher education in America. Its emphasis on the sciences has helped produce a large number of women scientists over the past century and a half [see **science education***].

In the 1835 Mount Holyoke prospectus, Mary Lyon promised that the school would "raise among the female part of the community a higher standard of

science and literature, of economy and of refinement, of benevolence and religion.'' Lyon envisioned a seminary that would prepare young women to be teachers, missionaries, and wives of missionaries. She proposed that expenses should
remain within the budget of the middle class. Tuition was $60 per year in 1837
and remained so throughout Lyon's tenure; this was less than one-half the tuition
at Amherst College, one of the least expensive men's institutions.

Mount Holyoke opened with eighty students. For nearly twelve years, Lyon
was principal as well as teacher of chemistry and religion. In addition to a
faculty carefully chosen from former colleagues at Ipswich Academy and later
from her own alumnae, Lyon also brought to campus lecturers from New England men's colleges to speak on current literary, scientific, or religious topics.
Lyon's love of science as well as her religious fervor gave the seminary a unique
blend of science and religion that characterized it for many years.

Conscious of the need for regular physical exercise, Lyon included it within
the program. Also significant was systematic study of the Bible. The class day
was structured with specific times for meals, class periods, study hours, and
domestic duties (required of all girls as a teaching aid and to reduce the expense
of hiring domestic help). Each day included ''lessons, sleep, one hour in domestic, calisthenics, music, prayer, needlework, social intercourse, walking and
botanical excursions.'' Oral recitations took place Monday through Thursday,
with written essays on Friday. There were weekly reviews in each subject and
a final review at term's end. Students were encouraged to strive for excellence
and to pursue learning for its self-satisfaction.

Nearly 90 percent of Mount Holyoke students came from families of limited
means from small New England or New York communities. Girls had to be at
least sixteen years old to matriculate, an unusual stipulation for the era. Lyon
made this decision because she wanted students old enough to be self-reliant
and academically prepared to move into more advanced courses, while still
young enough to be malleable and open to new educational ideas. She gave
them opportunities for decisionmaking and impressed upon students a sense of
honor and awareness of personal responsibility.

Throughout Lyon's years at Mount Holyoke, she continually experimented
with educational design. She added courses, redesigned programs, upgraded facilities, and strengthened academic admission requirements. Returning students
were examined on what they retained, until faculty were satisfied that students
were ready to proceed with new course work. Poet Emily Dickinson, who attended Mount Holyoke briefly, reported that she wished never to ''endure the
suspense . . . during those three days again for all the treasures in the world''
(letter to Albiah Root, November 1847).

As the institution's reputation increased, so did applications for admission.
Three years after its founding, the number of students had increased to 113;
three years later, the student body had almost doubled. By 1846, age of admission was raised from sixteen to seventeen because of the maturity needed to
handle a broader curriculum. At the same time, students were advised that they

would be best served by remaining at Mount Holyoke for three consecutive years.

When Lyon died in 1849, Mary Whitman was appointed acting principal for 1849–1850. In 1850, Mary W. Chapin, who had taught at Mount Holyoke for eight years, became head of the school, remaining until 1865. Under Chapin's leadership, entrance requirements and academic standards became stricter. A thorough foundation in mathematics was required for entry. The first few weeks of school were considered probationary, and if a student was deficient in either knowledge or emotional maturity, she was asked to leave. Students advanced according to their own progress, not according to time spent. The seminary curriculum expanded to four years, like other institutions of higher education.

As the school entered the 1860s, the student body increased to 289, with students from many states as well as India, China, Ceylon, and Turkey. Sophia D. Stoddard was principal from 1865 to 1867, followed by Helen M. French (1867–1872) and Julia E. Ward (1872–1883).

By 1876, a new science and art building was completed, equipped with lecture rooms, laboratories, and an art gallery. In 1883, with Elizabeth Blanchard as principal, the seminary began to grapple with shedding its secondary school status in favor of becoming a college. Mount Holyoke was chartered as a college in 1887, and Blanchard's title was changed to president.

At the seminary's semicentennial celebration in 1887, just before it became a college, Lydia Shattuck, a botanist and chemist and one of Mount Holyoke's preeminent scientists, said:

Our non-resident professors give us credit for doing good work in science. One of them recently suggested that in the future as a college we give a special scientific direction to our pursuits. . . . Since, therefore, the instruction of the Seminary has had a scientific trend from the first, without tendency to convert us into agnostics or infidels; since this is a scientific age and we are bound to keep abreast of the times; since every college has its own particular individuality—let us press onward in these lines till we obtain full recognition among the colleges of New England. (Quoted in Carr, p. 159)

Mary Lyon created Mount Holyoke to provide middle-class women with an education equal to that provided by men's colleges. The success of her seminary helped foster the acceptance of women's education and the growth of **women's colleges**.* Lyon's emphasis on the sciences as well as on religion made the seminary and later the college the fountainhead of many of America's women scientists. [See also **academies**,* **seminaries**,* **Seven Sisters**.*]

Bibliography: Sarah D. Stow, *History of Mount Holyoke Seminary during Its First Half Century* (1887); Emma P. Carr, "The Department of Chemistry: Historical Sketch," *Mount Holyoke Alumnae Quarterly*, 2 (October 1918): 159; Arthur Cole, *A Hundred Years of Mount Holyoke College* (1940); David Allmendinger, "Mount Holyoke Students Encounter the Need for Life-Planning, 1837–1850," *History of Education Quarterly*, 19 (1979): 27–47; Elizabeth Alden Green, *Mary Lyon and Mount Holyoke: Opening the Gates* (1979); Carole B. Shmurak and Bonnie S. Handler, " 'Castle of Science': Mount

Holyoke College and the Preparation of Women in Chemistry, 1837–1941,'' *History of Education Quarterly*, 32 (1992): 315–342.

Carole B. Shmurak

Murray, Judith Sargent. Judith Sargent Murray (1751–1820) was a late eighteenth-century writer and feminist theorist who used her pen to advance the rights of women during a period when women had no voice in the governing institutions of society. Along with **Abigail Adams*** and Mercy Otis Warren, Murray questioned women's inferior status in society, arguing that women held as great a stake in the infant nation as men. For over two decades, Murray wrote poems, essays, stories, and plays promoting an active role for the daughters of the Republic. Intrinsic to her calls for the rights of women was educational reform.

Born in Gloucester, Massachusetts, on May 1, 1751, Murray was the daughter of Winthrop and Judith Saunders Sargent. Winthrop was a prosperous merchant who sat as a delegate at the Massachusetts state convention for ratifying the Constitution in 1788. Judith assumed a domestic role and bore eight children, four of whom survived; Judith, Jr., was the eldest. One son, Winthrop, Jr., served with George Washington in the Continental Army during the Revolutionary War. He later became the first governor of the Mississippi territory. Another son, Fitz William, followed his father's footsteps in the maritime business and made a fortune in the Far East and India trade.

Judith Sargent married John Stevens, a sea captain and merchant, in 1769. After the Revolutionary War, Stevens fell heavily into debt. He fled to St. Eustatius in the West Indies in 1786, hoping to force his creditors to accept a compromise; however, Stevens died suddenly thereafter, leaving Judith a poor widow. Two years later she married Rev. John Murray, pastor of the Universalist Church in Gloucester, Massachusetts. Murray had arrived in the colonies from England in 1770 to preach the Universalist message of universal salvation and is considered the founder of the Universalist Church in America. John exerted a powerful influence on Judith, having been her spiritual instructor since 1774. That year, she experienced a profound religious conversion from Calvinism to Universalism, a change that she described as an immediate "emancipation" of her body and soul. Before converting Judith had "sought to *veil* the inconsistencies which obstructed the path of reason" (in *Letters*, p. 31). But after converting, she felt "wrapt [*sic*] in pleasing wonder, at the amazing height of my elevation." Clearly, her conversion acted as a liberating force.

Murray's feminism grew largely out of her faith. Universalist doctrines held that women and men were equal both intellectually and morally. The notion that she was equal in mind and spirit to men and the knowledge of her immortality heightened Murray's awareness of existence as an individual in her own right. The egalitarianism implicit in her faith motivated her to spread the message of Universalism not only to attract converts but also to attempt to elevate women's status in society. Her first published piece was a catechism, *Some Deductions from the System Promulgated in the Page of Divine Revelation* (1782), intended as a guide to parents and instructors. Murray's ideas about women were also shaped by her experiences. As a child, the only education she had received was that provided by a provincial "old woman" along with a "few novels." By contrast, her brother Winthrop received an advanced education and attended Harvard. Judith could hardly help but recognize these disparities. In her adult life, Murray had also endured economic hardship, particularly during her first marriage. She concluded that an inadequate education not only reinforced assumptions in society about women's intellectual inferiority, but it precluded women from access to opportunities outside the domestic realm. To help reform the inequities facing her sex, Murray commenced writing.

Not surprisingly, the education of women was the dominant motif in Murray's writings. She believed that women needed education not only to obtain knowledge but also to train them to make judicious decisions premised on reason. Murray's most important polemic advocating women's education, "On the Equality of the Sexes," was drafted in 1779 and published in 1790. She argued that women were men's intellectual equals, and she urged men to loosen the reins of authority and open up opportunities for the education of women. At this time, she called for education, however, solely to benefit women in the domestic sphere.

Yet by 1798, Murray's feminism had evolved to advocate an active public role for the women of the Republic. In 1798 Murray's three-volume *The Gleaner* was published. This work represented a compilation of her writings published earlier in the decade, including two plays and several dozen new pieces. Styled in the genteel discourse of the period, *The Gleaner* bears witness to Murray's intellectual progression as a feminist theorist. Essays 88–91 are noteworthy, representing a revision of her work "On the Equality of the Sexes." In these essays, Murray called for the economic and political independence of women, proclaiming the "dawning of a new era in female history." She recognized, however, that women could only learn to be independent through extensive cultivation of the mind. Knowledge and learning, then, represented the building blocks for women's complete emancipation.

By the time *The Gleaner* was published, the Murrays had moved to Boston, where John assumed the pastorship of the First Universalist Church. Besides writing, Judith was immersed in the education of her daughter, Julia Maria, during these years. Judith admitted that a primary reason for publishing *The Gleaner* was economic. John had been intermittently ill, and Judith hoped to earn sufficient income to support her daughter, should her needs require it. Judith would be disappointed about the work's potential for economic security, however; it would not go through a second edition. Ten years later, John suffered a paralytic stroke that left him an invalid; Judith cared for him until his death in 1815. She was crucial in preparing for publication his *Letters and Sketches of Sermons* (1812–1813) and his autobiography *Records of the Life of Reverend John Murray* (1816). Judith's preoccupation with family concerns left her little time to devote to her own writing for publication. Julia Maria married Adam Lewis Bingaman of Natchez, Mississippi, in 1812, after his graduation from Harvard.

Judith moved to Mississippi after her husband's death to live with her daughter and near her brother and his family. Murray died at Oak Point, near Natchez, on July 6, 1820. The inscription on her tombstone reads: "Beloved wife of John Murray, and beloved daughter of Winthrop Sargent." Her daughter included in the inscription: "Dear spirit, the monumental stone can never speak thy worth." Social philosopher, writer, Christian feminist, Judith Sargent Murray never wavered from her belief in the equality of the sexes.

Bibliography: Vena Bernadette Field, "Constantia: A Study of the Life and Works of Judith Sargent Murray, 1751–1820" (master's thesis, University of Maine, 1931); Alice S. Rossi, *The Feminist Papers: From Adams to de Beauvoir* (1973); Nina Baym, Introduction, *The Gleaner: A Miscellaneous Production* (1992); Marianne Dunlop, Introduction and transcriptions, *Judith Sargent Murray: Her First 100 Letters* (1995); Kirstin Wilcox, "The Scribblings of a Plain Man and the Temerity of a Woman: Gender and Genre in Judith Sargent Murray's *The Gleaner,*" *Early American Literature*, 30 (1995): 121–144.

Janet Rider

music education. Researchers have identified more than 3,000 women composers since the time of Sappho (seventh century B.C.). On the performance side, women interpreters of "serious" and popular music have become better known than ever, especially since 1880. Yet, beside and behind these composers and performers were innumerable women music teachers and scholars whose contributions, unfortunately, are even less well understood and recognized than those of their performing and composing sisters.

From the 1850s to the 1930s, more than 50 percent of all Americans working in "music and related professions" were women. The census includes as "musicians" everyone from symphony musicians to Broadway choristers to small-town band leaders. By 1940 females constituted 43 percent of musicians and music professionals. By 1993 the figure was 33 percent, mainly due to masculinization of certain high-wage categories in music performance. In the industrialized world, the ratio of males to females in all "professional" categories of musical employment was nearly two to one.

Researchers since 1945 have produced considerable work on these matters, one example being cultural studies of images of women in popular music, especially rock music, since the late 1950s. Another is assessment of the rise of women concert artists and all-women music groups (for example, the New York Women's Symphony Orchestra).

Discovery of women's music and growing acceptance of women composers and performers were outcomes of a half century of social change, of the feminist movement, and of a rising "pluralist" consensus in Europe and North America. Dominant art traditions and male performance traditions were at last open to criticism, even replacement, and there was by the late twentieth century room for women in musical life. The question is, Was the history of women's music analogous to that of women in music education?

Who educated nineteenth-century musical foremothers? Were most nineteenth- and twentieth-century teachers merely women composers and performers forced by economic circumstance to teach for a living? Were there women music teachers who did not aspire to the status of "professional" but instead willingly occupied the social category "woman music teacher," defined and limited by social expectations? And among women who considered themselves professional composers, performers, or impresaria, what did "professional" mean in practical terms?

The vast majority of music teachers in the United States, Canada, and England after 1800 were women. After the rise of mass public education (1845–1885), but particularly after 1900, women occupied well over half of all **teaching*** posts in state-supported and private elementary and secondary schools. Once the social status of teaching stabilized around 1900 and salaries had sunk to generally low levels, the **feminization*** of teaching proceeded at a fast pace. In 1930, 83 percent of U.S. public school teachers were women, 70 percent in 1960, and most taught music at some time in their careers.

Yet if women delivered music education to the masses, it could not be said that they shaped or controlled it. In the United States and Canada, curricula and pedagogy of public music education were in the hands of male civil servants, at least until the 1960s. Where civil servants lacked expertise, university music departments, **normal schools**,* and private conservatories stepped into the breach. These institutions were largely male preserves. Among three of the highest-ranked American university and conservatory music schools, consider faculty numbers in 1945: Indiana University, one female in twelve total professors; Yale University, none in fourteen; Juilliard School of Music, six women of thirty-one.

Even after formation of professional teachers' associations (1880–1920) and organization of national music educators' associations, women did not usually assume leadership roles. The Music Educators' National Conference (founded in 1907 as the Music Supervisors Conference) and its *Music Educators Journal* (1934–) had few women leaders and editors and, until World War II, usually saw music as a device for maintaining morale in difficult times, for popularizing "national[ist] song," and as an indispensable element in "general education."

Reasons for excluding women from leadership roles in music education were in one sense narrowly historical. Collective memory recalled music as a female "accomplishment," appropriate as an adornment, but dangerous if studied or performed to excess. Although the tradition of female education in "the attainments" declined after introduction of mass public instruction, social expectations and practices led most North Americans to see music teaching—public or private—as woman's work. Private music teachers expected most pupils to be girls throughout the nineteenth and twentieth centuries. Public music teachers could expect one-half of their pupils to be boys because public education was universal.

After 1950, just as women began to assume executive offices in professional associations and school systems, the role of music in public curriculum came under prolonged scrutiny. This was not coincidental, as women entered political life in academic and skilled professions after 1950. One effect of this vast sea change was a series of national debates in the United States and Canada on the "right place of music" in community life.

A feminist view notes that few women composers have been trained by women. Clara Schumann (1819–1896) had no women teachers from age five. Amy Beach (1867–1944), an enormously talented American composer, left her mother's tutelage at age eight and studied exclusively with men until she declared musical independence in her late teens. Ethel Smyth (English, 1858–1944), Nadia Boulanger (French, 1887–1979) and Jean Coulthard (Canadian, b. 1908) were all unusual in having acquired significant musical culture at home before leaving as adults to study with well-known men. All these women were themselves successful teachers of men and women composers and performers, this in times when social and financial rewards for women in music were, at best, remote. They were, however, highly exceptional, and their music was not welcomed.

A social/intellectual historian faced with these cases does well to recall material facts of the times. The usual route for women composers and performers was to spend adult life in a succession of occupations, occasionally interrupted by parenthood. Beach was professionally successful and unusual in that respect; Smyth, Boulanger, and Coulthard all came from upper-middle-class families. It is important to remember an overwhelming truth: The great majority of women music educators were either small-time private operators, working from their own homes, or schoolteachers who could teach music only in the limited way possible under mass education. Before about 1940, their incomes were often necessary for family support. At all times, their work offered a modest independence from poverty or from unsympathetic husbands and families.

From 1900 on, North American and European women organized musical societies for themselves, sponsoring concert series and offering scholarships. With the rise of near-universal postsecondary education, and particularly since 1950, three developments suggest that women music educators have acquired a distinctive role in formal and informal educational life. First, overall increase in size of the student body, and since 1965, a vast increase in graduate studies in music, has led many thousand young women to undergraduate and graduate programs in performance and musical theory [see **graduate education***]. In the United States, the federal government's National Foundation on the Arts and the Humanities since 1965 has provided funding and encouragement for graduate studies, advanced composition, new courses and programs of study—all areas with increasing female participation.

Second, in the United States but also elsewhere, legislative provisions for employment equity have compelled universities, colleges, and conservatories to consider seriously women scholars for tenure-track teaching positions.

Finally, a boom in research on women in music and in the performance of women's music has led to new books, periodicals, concert organizations, and special-interest associations. Since 1995, the International Alliance for Women in Music has published a *Journal*, supplemented by *Women and Music: A Journal of Gender and Culture* (1996–). Another American journal, *Women of Note Quarterly* (1993–), raises the profile of American and Canadian women composers and reviews important recording and publishing projects.

The impact of these developments on daily lives of women music teachers and educators is difficult to assess. It is certain, however, that the broader public is increasingly aware of women music educators and the particularities of the musical training of women composers and performers.

Bibliography: Susan C. Cook and Judy S. Tsou, eds., *Cecilia Reclaimed: Feminist Perspectives on Gender and Music* (1994); Sophie Fuller, "Dead White Men in Wigs: Women and Classical Music," in Sarah Cooper, ed., *Girls! Girls! Girls! Essays on Women and Music* (1995).

William Bruneau

National American Woman Suffrage Association. In 1890 the American Woman Suffrage Association and the National Woman Suffrage Association merged to form the National American Woman Suffrage Association (NAWSA)—the woman's organization that would lead the fight for American women's **suffrage*** into the twentieth century. Initially headed by early suffragists Susan B. Anthony and Elizabeth Cady Stanton, NAWSA eventually drew its membership from women's reform groups. After dropping the campaign for a federal amendment for women's suffrage in the 1890s, NAWSA targeted state legislatures for gaining the right to vote. By 1900, with new leaders like Carrie Chapman Catt and Anna Howard Shaw, NAWSA attracted a new generation of women who believed in legislative remedies for social problems and formed a cohesive organization.

Although NAWSA supported state legislation for women's suffrage, most of its efforts focused on educating the public concerning why women should be given the franchise. In brochures, speeches, and publications like its *Women's Journal*, NAWSA stressed women's special qualities like female benevolence that entitled women to vote. Because of women's traditional role in the home, NAWSA argued, they needed to protect interests in children, education, women and children's labor, and health—issues they believed men neglected. NAWSA's new direction—the emphasis on female differences rather than equality—attracted hundreds of members, predominantly from women's reform groups like the **Women's Trade Union League,*** Women's Christian Temperance Union, and the **settlement house movement.*** These groups, accustomed to **Progressive Era*** campaigns for legislative reforms, contributed to NAWSA's attempts to change legislation at the local and state levels by using arguments for female moral superiority. NAWSA's membership expanded from 13,000 members in 1893 to 75,000 by 1910.

Notwithstanding African American women's persistent petitions for admission into NAWSA, leaders like Catt and Shaw tended to ignore them. Hoping to attract a southern white female constituency, NAWSA focused on forming local white organizations and tolerated racist statements from some southern suffragists like Kate Gordon and Laura Clay. As had happened in the campaign for the Fifteenth Amendment in the 1860s, black women were once again slighted [see abolitionism*]. Some NAWSA leaders, including Anna Howard Shaw, promoted women's suffrage to protect native-born women from immigrants and the working class. Indeed, most NAWSA members came from white, middle-class, and urban households. NAWSA nonetheless included many prominent reformers of the late nineteenth and early twentieth centuries like Jane Addams,* Florence Kelley, and Frances Willard.

Unlike the more radical National Woman's Party (NWP), NAWSA supported the United States' entry into World War I. Thousands of women eagerly joined volunteer groups to support the troops. This stance led to an increase in NAWSA's membership to a peak of 2 million in 1919. More important, NAWSA's war efforts persuaded President Woodrow Wilson to endorse women's suffrage. Catt's plan of supporting the war rather than denouncing it like Alice Paul's NWP led to congressional passage of the Nineteenth Amendment. On August 26, 1920, Tennessee ratified the amendment, and women's suffrage became legal nationwide.

Following the suffrage campaign, NAWSA sought to register every available woman to vote. Yet after ratification, NAWSA's membership began to decline. Eventually after 1920, NAWSA reorganized and became the League of Women Voters,* which supported women's reform agendas, protective labor legislation, and educational issues. When the NWP called for the Equal Rights Amendment in 1921, former NAWSA members like Florence Kelley, who had battled for protective women's labor legislation, were outraged. The Equal Rights Amendment failed to pass.

NAWSA represented the combined efforts of most women's reform groups and what they could accomplish when unified. Women publicly demonstrated their skills at organization and education, serving notice to the nation that they could act as agents of change. More than seventy years after the Seneca Falls* Convention, women finally gained political recognition as citizens. The campaign nonetheless preserved many of the class and racist tendencies that began in the early suffrage movement, tendencies that reinforced the perception of feminists as white, middle-class women.

Bibliography: Paula Giddings, *When and Where I Enter: The Impact of Black Women on Race and Sex in America* (1984); Nancy Cott, *The Grounding of Modern Feminism* (1987); Marjorie Spruill Wheeler, *New Women of the New South: The Leaders of the Woman Suffrage Movement in the Southern States* (1993).

Ann Short Chirhart

National Association for the Advancement of Colored People.

The National Association for the Advancement of Colored People (NAACP) was organized in 1909 as an interracial civil rights organization seeking to eliminate all remnants of racial discrimination and segregation from American life and has grown into one of the foremost civil rights groups in both size and influence. At its founding, the NAACP's major objectives included abolishing lynchings, providing equal education for all black children, ensuring voting rights, and securing basic freedoms to procure property of one's choice and to seek public accommodations without discrimination. Through its legal arm, the NAACP Legal Defense Fund, the organization works judicially to uphold constitutional rights for blacks. The NAACP also publishes its own magazine, *The Crisis*. Women have been strong participants in the organization since its founding, and many black women used their experience in the **women's club movement*** to sustain the work of the NAACP over many decades.

Before the NAACP there were several attempts to organize people around the issues of securing, promoting, and protecting the rights of blacks. The National Negro Convention was held in Philadelphia in 1830. In 1849, the State Convention of Colored Citizens of Ohio committed to assisting escaped slaves and pursuing educational rights for all blacks. That organization's belief was that blacks were "entitled to all privileges—moral, mental, political, and social—to which other men attain." Other early organizations included the First California Negro Convention (1855), Young Men's Progressive Association of New Orleans (1878), Convention of Colored Men of Texas (1883), Macon (Georgia) Consultation Convention (1888), and the National Afro-American League (Chicago, 1890).

The precursor to the NAACP was the Niagara Movement, spawned from a scholarly group of twenty-nine black professional men and women, ministers, editors, and teachers from diverse parts of the nation. This group, founded in 1897, was formally known as the American Negro Academy. Among its most prominent founding members were Ida B. Wells, black female journalist, and Dr. W.E.B. Du Bois, scholar and social activist. In 1905, Du Bois dispatched a call for the academy to host a conference for the purpose of "insisting on manhood rights, industrial opportunity, and spiritual freedom" for all blacks. The conference was held in Niagara Falls (on Canada's side because blacks were restricted from American hotels), and the group formed itself as the Niagara Movement. In 1908, the all-black Niagara Movement joined forces with a group of whites who had similar goals and objectives. They met together in 1909 as the National Negro Conference and within a year became the National Association for the Advancement of Colored People.

The NAACP was organized in the midst of extreme racial prejudice. The idea for the group was born from a letter written in 1908 by Mary White Ovington to William English Walling. Ovington was a young **social worker,*** freelance writer, and humanitarian; Walling was a white southern journalist with liberal racial perspectives. Both saw the devastation being caused by racial conflict throughout the North and South, and they responded by calling for a national conference. Their conference included the likes of Du Bois; **Jane Addams,*** founder of **Hull-House***; Professor John Dewey of Columbia University; **abolitionist*** William Lloyd Garrison of Boston; Mary E. Woolley, president of **Mount Holyoke College***; Ida B. Wells Barnett; and others. In total, sixty prominent black and white Americans were involved. Besides this initial leadership, women have also served as fund-raisers, membership chairs, and advisory board members throughout NAACP history. For example, both **Mary McLeod Bethune*** and **Nannie Helen Burroughs*** sat on the national advisory board for decades, and Kathryn Johnson was the first field secretary (1910–1916).

Many NAACP members have served on faculties of colleges and universities around the country. With support of the organization, these faculty members have helped spur social activism on many college campuses. In 1939, for example, female students invited NAACP President Walter White to the **Vassar College*** campus to discuss race relations in the South. After the conference, students confronted Vassar to attract more black females to study on campus.

Since its inception, the NAACP has sought to protect civil rights of black Americans. The organization has continued to define its humanitarian and constitutional principles by pushing the federal courts to oppose segregation laws. One of the most prominent Supreme Court cases argued by the NAACP came in *Brown v. Topeka Board of Education* (1954), the ruling that refuted the "separate but equal" doctrine of *Plessy v. Ferguson* (1896).

Bibliography: Langston Hughes, *Fight for Freedom: The Story of the NAACP* (1962); Harvard Sitkoff, *The Struggle for Black Equality 1954–1980* (1981); Barbara Miller Solomon, *In the Company of Educated Women: A History of Women and Higher Education in America* (1985); Lerone Bennett, Jr., *Before the Mayflower: A History of Black America*, 6th ed. (1988); Denton L. Watson, "Assessing the Role of the NAACP in the Civil Rights Movement," *The Historian*, 55 (Spring 1993): 453–468.

Adrian K. Haugabrook

National Association of College Women. The National Association of College Women (NACW) was founded in 1923 during a period of growing enrollment at black colleges and universities in the United States. Following the philosophy of W. E. B. Du Bois to develop a "talented tenth" of black leaders, the NACW concentrated its programs on women graduates of prestigious **Howard**,* **Fisk**,* **Spelman**,* **Bennett**,* and other colleges. The NACW encouraged women graduates of these institutions to help younger black women continue their education beyond elementary school or technical programs. The NACW affiliated itself with other organizations that shared its goals, including the United Negro College Fund and the Leadership Conference on Civil Rights. Like these groups, the NACW was concerned with specific racial and social problems.

The association's institutional history included significant study of problems women encounter in social and school settings. Accordingly, it has developed programs that encourage girls to succeed at various educational levels. Its "After School What?" program is specifically intended to help young women succeed academically through formal tutoring activities. The program helps girls learn and, at the same time, gives them social experiences with older women who act as models and mentors. In addition, the NACW has encouraged women of all races to continue their educational careers so they will be successful when they enter the professions and society. The association supports the view that education socially empowers women.

One program that reflects the association's philosophy of empowering women in society is "Women of Action: Reaching, Risking and Responding." This program encourages young women to identify their academic talents and develop a personal commitment to improving themselves educationally. It enhances women students' understanding that as they enter new and different occupations and professions, they are becoming role models for women who follow.

The NACW structure includes standing committees in such areas as Literacy Program Development, Political Awareness, and National and International Affairs. The Scholarship Committee administers annual awards and fellowships for women, and the NACW maintains a placement office.

In 1974, the National Association of College Women recognized the need to change its name to reflect a higher education culture that was shifting its academic and research goals to meet the new challenges of a diverse society involved with supranational problems. Since many colleges had assumed the designation "university" to indicate their new missions, the National Association responded by modifying its name to the National Association of University Women.

Headquartered in Washington, D.C., the association by the mid-1990s served 4,000 members divided into five regional and ninety-two local groups. The NAUW's outreach efforts include publishing the *Journal of the National Association of University Women*, as well as an annual *Bulletin*, and an annual convention in Washington, D.C.

Bibliography: David Garrow, *Bearing the Cross: Martin Luther King, Jr., and the Southern Christian Leadership Conference* (1986); Lerone Bennett, Jr., *Before the Mayflower: A History of Black America*, 6th ed. (1988); Taylor Branch, *Parting the Waters: America in the King Years 1954–1963* (1988).

William E. Segall and Anna V. Wilson

National Association of Colored Women. Through the formation of the National Association of Colored Women (NACW), African American women conjoined their social, political, educational, and economic activities to improve the lives of African Americans at the community, regional, state, and national levels. Although African American women had been involved in community uplift activities as early as the late 1700s, it was not until 1895 that they organized nationally to consolidate their efforts. In that year, Josephine St. Pierre Ruffin had convened a meeting of African American women in Boston to protest a slanderous letter written by a southern journalist. Within three days, the National Federation of Afro-American Women was created. Comprising thirty-six **women's clubs*** in twelve states, the organization flourished under the presidency of **Margaret Murray Washington**.* The same year, another African American female organization, the National League of Colored Women, was created under the auspices of **Mary Church Terrell*** in Washington, D.C. In 1896, these two organizations agreed to merge to form the National Association of Colored Women.

The NACW experienced three distinct developmental periods: organization and expansion; the creation of departments; and the formation of state federations. During its fledgling first period, the organization held annual national meetings in which members from various women's clubs reported on their community uplift activities [see **race uplift***]. To consolidate this club work, various departments with corresponding officers were formed. These departments were many, including those devoted to education, children's welfare, female employment, **suffrage**,* and legal and political equality. In the last stage of development, state federations were formed to work collectively on issues important to the entire state. For example, African American women in Alabama lobbied successfully in securing state appropriations for an industrial school for their children.

Congruous with the **General Federation of Women's Clubs**,* the white women's national organization, the NACW's ideology and discourse focused on women's socially appropriate and traditional roles as mothers, homemakers, and wives. However, for African American women who historically had been prevented from practicing motherhood in culturally veritable ways, the NACW's emphases on better home conditions, children's welfare, and mothering bespoke the twinned concerns of family and community life. In referring to the NACW as a "noble army of mothers," Josephine St. Pierre Ruffin inscribed the dual roles of the organization. Not only did the clubwomen perceive themselves as exemplary models of motherhood for poorer African American women, but they also helped uplift their lives through establishment of community facilities as various as missions, **kindergartens**,* settlements, day nurseries, industrial schools, homes for working girls, travelers aid societies, and recreation facilities.

In conjunction with the NACW's motto "Lifting As We Climb," the women's clubs sponsored activities that promoted self-cultivation as well as community improvement. For example, musical recitals, theatrical productions, and literary contests not only provided learning opportunities for the clubwomen; they also raised much-needed monies to maintain community institutions the clubs had founded. One of the most notable examples was the Phyllis Wheatley Club of Chicago, whose philanthropic events like charity balls, theater performances, and musicals sustained the Phyllis Wheatley Home, a home for young working girls new to the city. Following W. E. B. Du Bois's model of "talented tenth" leadership, the clubwomen distinguished themselves from poorer African American women in their club memberships, activities, and middle-class status. Nonetheless, they also joined with all African Americans on issues of suffrage, and discrimination in employment, education, and access to public facilities.

So successful was the NACW as a national organization that by 1914 its membership had increased to 50,000 African American women in over 1,000 clubs and twenty-eight state federations. By 1928, national headquarters were established in Washington, D.C., under the administration of **Mary McLeod Bethune**.* That same year, the organization embarked on the ambitious project of preserving the historical documents and home of Frederick Douglass. The NACW continues today to engage in social uplift through its city, district, state, and national organizations.

Bibliography: Elizabeth Davis, *Lifting as They Climb* (1933); Tullia Hamilton, "The National Association of Colored Women, 1896–1920," (Ph.D. diss., Emory University, 1978); Charles Wesley, *The History of the National Association of Colored Women's Clubs: A Legacy of Service* (1984); Dorothy Salem, *To Better Our World: Black Women in Organized Reform, 1890–1920* (1990); Gerda Lerner, ed., *Black Women in White America* (1992); Anne Meis Knupfer, *Toward a Tenderer Humanity and a Nobler Womanhood: African American Women's Clubs in Turn-of-the-Century Chicago* (1996). See also Mary Church Terrell Papers, Library of Congress and Moorland-Spingarn Center, Howard University, Washington, D.C.

Anne Meis Knupfer

National Association of Deans of Women. Founded in 1916 at Teachers College, Columbia University, the National Association of Deans of Women (NADW), the first professional society for **deans of women*** to attract a national membership, provided a professional network until the demise of the office of dean of women in the 1970s. Although by 1900 more colleges and universities had hired deans of women to supervise the growing number of female students, the profession itself remained remarkably unorganized. Deans of women at various midwestern institutions recognized this problem and founded the first professional societies. In 1903, **Marion Talbot**,* dean of women at the **University of Chicago**,* established the Conference of Deans and Advisors in State Universities, which met biennially and drew membership primarily from public institutions in the Midwest. In addition, a group of deans of women, primarily from eastern institutions, began meeting informally in 1911 at the annual convention of the **Association of Collegiate Alumnae**.*

The moving spirit behind the National Association of Deans of Women was Kathryn Sisson McLean, dean of women at State Teachers College, Chadron, Nebraska. While taking graduate courses during the summer of 1915 at Teachers College, McLean realized that neither professional training nor informal professional organizations such as the Conference of Deans of Women could foster national connections among deans. In 1916, she made the dream of a national association a reality.

Learning that the National Education Association (NEA) would meet in New

York City in the summer of 1916, McLean asked that Teachers College graduate students be allowed to hold an organizational meeting for deans of women. NEA officials agreed, and on July 6, 1916, over 200 persons gathered to hear a variety of speakers, including two of the most prominent women in the profession, Gertrude S. Martin, adviser of women at Cornell University, and Virginia Gildersleeve, dean of **Barnard College**.* Meeting in executive session following the formal addresses, the deans organized the NADW and elected McLean president.

During its early years, the NADW addressed three closely related problems: perception of the office of dean of women, preparation of candidates for the position, and professional connections among practitioners. Most people, including academic professionals, seemed confused about the purpose of the office. Was the dean a glorified housekeeper, or did she have a genuine educational and administrative function? Determined to answer such questions—for the general public and for potential deans—the NADW supported, undertook, and disseminated research concerning the profession, especially through its Committees on Press and Publications and on Research.

The NADW actively circulated research through several publications. In 1923, it established the *Yearbook*, which contained, in addition to officers, committee assignments, and membership lists, papers presented at the annual convention. Nearly 25 percent of these addressed the central issue of perception of the dean of women. NADW also commissioned Ruth Merrill and Helen Bragdon of the Harvard Graduate School of Education to write an analysis of the position. Their work, *The Vocation of the Dean* (1926), was one of the central statements of the profession. In 1938, the association inaugurated the *Journal of the NADW*, a scholarly journal edited by Ruth Strang, faculty member at Teachers College.

Cognizant of public perception of the office and of the great difference in academic training among current practitioners, the NADW sought to identify basic professional standards. In 1928, NADW President Dorothy Stimson, academic dean at Goucher College, appointed a committee, under the leadership of Margaret Morriss, dean of Pembroke College, the women's **coordinate college*** at Brown University, to construct a formal statement of the qualifications necessary for the deanship. The committee advocated not only a bachelor's degree from an accredited college or university but also additional course work in sociology, human physiology, and psychology.

Essential to its success as a national professional organization was establishment of a permanent office and clerical staff. In 1926, NADW hired a part-time membership secretary and established the Headquarters Office, using space provided by the **American Association of University Women**.* Five years later, NADW found a permanent home in the offices of the NEA and hired a permanent membership secretary.

The association held annual conventions, through which deans could foster a national network. Although issues of cost and location prevented many deans from attending, the racial question presented a particularly troubling problem.

A small number of black deans of women, including **Lucy Diggs Slowe**,* dean of women at **Howard University**,* joined NADW; however, they always faced the prevalence of Jim Crow practices at the annual meeting. Although the association seldom held meetings in the South, it found that other cities also remained reluctant, despite formal protests from NADW, to admit black members to convention hotels on the same basis as white members. Although black deans founded their own professional society in response—the **Association of Deans of Women and Advisers to Girls in Negro Schools***—a small number nevertheless retained membership in NADW.

The NADW faced a serious crisis during the Great Depression, when membership decreased drastically. The association survived but held no conventions between 1943 and 1946, in deference to World War II. In the postwar period, the association, in response to the paradoxical growth in the student personnel profession but demise of the office of dean of women, expanded membership to include a wide variety of academic workers.

Between 1920 and 1970, virtually every coeducational [see **coeducation***] institution in the United States employed a dean of women. These institutions differed dramatically, as did the financial fortunes of those who became deans of women. Nevertheless, the National Association of Deans of Women provided for them an essential source of professional identity and community, and its history symbolizes many issues facing women in the profession.

Bibliography: Paula A. Treichler, "Alma Mater's Sorority: Women and the University of Illinois, 1890–1925," in Paula A. Treichler, Cheris Kramarae, and Beth Stafford, eds., *For Alma Mater: Theory and Practice in Feminist Scholarship* (1985); Carolyn Terry Bashaw, "We Who Live 'Off on the Edges': Deans of Women at Southern Coeducational Institutions and Access to the Community of Higher Education, 1907–1960" (Ph.D. diss., University of Georgia, 1992); Jana Nidiffer, "More Than 'A Wise and Pious Matron': The Professionalization of the Position of Dean of Women" (Ed.D. diss., Harvard University, 1994).

Carolyn Terry Bashaw

National College Equal Suffrage League. Organized as an auxiliary to the **National American Woman Suffrage Association*** (NAWSA), the National College Equal Suffrage League worked from 1908 to 1917 to spark political awareness and activism among collegiate women. Responding to a call from **Bryn Mawr College*** president **M. Carey Thomas*** and others, suffrage groups from campuses in fifteen states attended the 1908 NAWSA convention in Buffalo, New York. On October 17, the national College League was formed. Among its first officers and directors were graduates or faculty from Bryn Mawr, **Barnard**,* **Radcliffe**,* and **Smith Colleges*** and the Universities of Wisconsin, California, and **Chicago**.*

The first college suffrage league had been formed in 1900 by two students at Radcliffe, Maud Wood Park and Inez Haynes Gillmore. Prosuffrage students at **Vassar*** formed a league in 1908, but in a decision that shows the controversial nature of **suffrage*** on campuses, the group was forced by a disapproving administration to meet clandestinely until 1915, when a faculty-trustee committee finally permitted the club to declare itself a division of the national league. In 1904, Park began a personal campaign to recruit college women for the cause, beginning in New York State. At the 1906 NAWSA convention in Baltimore, Park was officially appointed to organize college leagues throughout the United States. When the national league was formally recognized, Park became its vice president, a position she held until the league disbanded in 1917.

Banded together in a national organization, local college leagues campaigned for passage of the Nineteenth Amendment. Formed in 1909, the College Equal Suffrage League of Northern California, for example, fought successfully for passage of state suffrage, distributing leaflets, mounting plays, speaking at vaudeville shows, and campaigning by automobile. In the District of Columbia, league members prepared a report on women in history textbooks used in area schools. Nationally, the college league engaged speakers, including suffragist Emmeline Pankhurst and **Jane Addams**,* to address students. Traveling libraries on suffrage topics circulated among colleges, and educational literature was sent by the national office in New York City to students and alumnae.

The Vassar chapter was the first to establish a suffrage school, educating local women about political issues while training them as debaters and speakers. Further south, the Lynchburg branch of the Virginia Equal Suffrage League cooperated with the Randolph-Macon Woman's College League to present classes for suffrage workers, charging twenty-five cents a lesson, a dollar and a half for the entire course. Directed jointly by Elizabeth L. Lewis (president of the Lynchburg league) and Nellie V. Powell (a Randolph-Macon instructor), classes were intended to cover "the questions of the day, political, social, legal, and historical," as well as public speaking. By 1909, secretary Caroline Lexow reported that the college league boasted twenty-four branches in as many states, and twenty-five chapters in as many colleges; theirs was the largest voting delegation at the national suffrage convention except for the state of New York.

"The object of the college women's league," Maud Wood Park explained, was "to bring the question of equal suffrage to college women . . . [and] in short, to make them feel the obligation of opportunity" (quoted in Harper, Vol. 5, p. 171). By January 1917, however, the league faced severe financial hardship. League president M. Carey Thomas again made one of many appeals to the participating colleges, this time to raise funds to meet operating expenses. But in the face of world war, her call went unanswered. At its annual meeting on December 17, the league unanimously voted to disband. With 5,000 members enrolled in over fifty state associations, the league claimed victory because of "this revolution in educated opinion." Its loans and debts (amounting to $6,686) were paid by Thomas.

By mobilizing collegiate women, the league made a valuable contribution to the fight for equal suffrage. As M. Carey Thomas proclaimed, "It is unthinkable that women who have learned to act for themselves in college . . . should not care for the ballot.'' For league members, education encompassed civic as well as academic concerns, paving the way for radical political change.

Bibliography: National American Woman Suffrage Association (NAWSA), Convention Programs (1910–1917); NAWSA, Annual Reports (1912–1917); Lynchburg Equal Suffrage Club (LESC), Annual Reports (1913–1917); LESC, ''School for Suffrage Workers'' (1915); Jane Ellen Harrison, '' 'Homo Sum': Being a Letter to an Anti-Suffragist from an Anthropologist,'' listing league officers and chairs of standing committees; all in the Equal Suffrage League Collection, Library of Virginia; Ida Husted Harper, ed., *The History of Woman Suffrage*, Vol. 5–6 (1922); Lynn D. Gordon, *Gender and Higher Education in the Progressive Era* (1990).

Jennifer Davis McDaid

National Congress of Mothers. Known today as the National Congress of Parents and Teachers, or the PTA (Parent-Teacher Association) the National Congress of Mothers (NCM) was formed in 1897 to unite the scattered and varied mothers' clubs within the **women's club movement*** into a national network. After organizing at the national level, NCM grew from the top down; state branches were formed that encouraged women to organize local mothers' clubs. The NCM supported women's private and public roles as mothers, sought to educate mothers of all races and socioeconomic classes, and promoted child study. In its first charter, the congress listed its aims, including: ''[T]o promote conference among parents upon questions vital to the welfare of their children; . . . to cooperate with educators and legislators to secure the best methods in the physical, moral, and mental training of the young; . . . [and] to uplift and improve the conditions of mothers in all walks of life.''

Alice McLellan Birney, cofounder of the NCM, found initial support among women in the **kindergarten movement**.* She declared that a gathering of mothers, a congress, would raise awareness of the importance of their work and would be an ideal forum through which mothers would learn the latest scientific methods of childrearing. Birney, employing the maternalist rhetoric characteristic of many reformers of the **Progressive Era**,* claimed that her own experience with motherhood prompted her to organize the NCM for parent education. She garnered support from philanthropist and activist Phoebe Apperson Hearst, who helped organize and fund the NCM's first convention. Birney served as NCM president until 1902, and Hearst was vice president during its first year. The two were declared cofounders in 1905, after Birney died.

The first gathering of the NCM was held in Washington, D.C., February 17–19, 1897, and was attended by far more women than anticipated, including many kindergarten teachers and sponsors of the free kindergarten movement. In her welcoming address Birney expressed the main goal: social reform through the mothers of the United States. She cited the ''ignorance of untrained parents'' as responsible for the crimes and ills of society. She suggested establishing mothers' clubs in every community, all of which would be affiliated with the larger national organ, to disseminate the latest in ''child psychology and child development, nutrition and **home economics,*** kindergarten and preschool education, social hygiene and mental hygiene," for the betterment of society (National Congress of Parents and Teachers, p. 146).

Hannah Kent Schoff was named Birney's successor in 1902 and remained president until 1920. Schoff changed the focus of the congress to child welfare activism, including revision and implementation of juvenile court legislation, and emphasized its relationship with the public schools. Her administration saw the NCM grow from eight state branches to thirty-seven. Under Schoff's leadership the National Congress of Mothers began an eponymous magazine in November 1906, which four years later was called *Child-Welfare Magazine.* Succeeding presidents were Katherine Chapin Higgins (1920–1923) and Margaretta Willis Reeve (1923–1928).

Despite the early call by Birney and her colleagues that "no color line [would be] drawn," the congress comprised mostly middle-class white women. Current research on the NCM points to the strong influence of psychologist G. Stanley Hall in shaping the organization: "Elite club mothers saw in Hall's **child study movement*** a way to dignify Anglo-American motherhood" (Ladd-Taylor, p. 47). Hall was supportive and spoke at the first NCM; the congress promoted Hall's research and ideas long after they lost popularity. Hall encouraged the mothers affiliated with the NCM to partake in child study by turning their homes into laboratories and by monitoring their children's physical development. With Hall's influence, the NCM maintained a conservative bent and supported maternalist issues, primarily the view that women belonged in their homes.

Due to encouragement by and widespread publicity of the National Congress of Mothers, thousands of women formed or joined mothers' clubs. It is difficult to assess the congress's impact on women at the local level, although many women certainly learned about parenting through their participation; whether they learned the lessons of child study is unknown. However, many mothers ran clinics, supported child welfare charities, raised funding for playgrounds, and opened libraries.

In 1907 the NCM added a department of parents and teachers "to promote systematic organization of these units," and the change was reflected in the organization's name. In 1924 "Congress of Mothers" was eliminated from the title, resulting in the name that remains today, the National Congress of Parents and Teachers; this change reflected a commitment to parent involvement in public schools. Before the shift in emphasis to parent-teacher interactions, reflected in the name change to PTA, the NCM "played a critical role in the popularization of parent education and child psychology and in the expansion of American public education, health and welfare services . . . in the early twentieth century" (Ladd-Taylor, p. 44).

Bibliography: Martha Sprague Mason, ed., *Parents and Teachers: A Survey of Organized Cooperation of Home, School and Community* (1928); National Congress of Parents and Teachers, *The Parent-Teacher Organization: Its Origins and Development* (1944); Steven L. Schlossman, "Before Home Start: Notes toward a History of Parent Education in America, 1897–1929,'' *Harvard Educational Review*, 46 (1976): 436–467; Molly Ladd-Taylor, *Mother-Work: Women, Child Welfare, and the State, 1890–1930* (1994).

Christine Woyshner

National Council of Negro Women. The National Council of Negro Women (NCNW) was founded by **Mary McLeod Bethune*** in December 1935 to help African American women understand social problems from a national and international perspective. As the NCNW's first president (1935–1949), Bethune observed that African American women's organizations such as the **National Association of Colored Women*** were primarily interested in solving social problems at the community level. The NCNW, she believed, should manage or coordinate significant activities common to individual black **women's clubs*** throughout the United States and abroad. Bethune's philosophy expressed her belief that African American women should have common opinions on social issues, which, in turn, would lead to cooperation among women's groups.

Issues that first concerned the NCNW concentrated on race relations in southern states. Focusing on unfair trials and lynching of blacks by white vigilantes, the organization gained national prominence as an active defender of the Scottsboro Boys, a group of nine black men denied their Fourteenth Amendment rights in a noteworthy Alabama rape case in 1931.

True to Bethune's interest, the NCNW pursued involvement in social issues internationally. Building upon the first overseas chapter established in Liberia in 1951, the NCNW maintained offices in both western and southern Africa. These centers specialized in helping African women improve their lives socially and economically. The NCNW is especially interested in helping rural women equalize their social status with males.

The NCNW has grown in numbers and influence over the past six decades. With international headquarters in Washington, D.C., by the mid-1990s it comprised 240 local groups and thirty-one national organizations and served 40,000 members. During its history, the NCNW has remained loyal to Bethune's original charge: to help develop black women's leadership abilities at local, national, and international levels. To assist, the NCNW administers the Women's Center for Education and Career Advancement in New York City, which focuses on helping minority women succeed in nontraditional careers. The council also maintains a clearinghouse that distributes information on such issues as juvenile justice and public health and highlights the history of women in the civil rights movement. Through various activities, the NCNW continues to foster cooperation among African American women at various economic levels by focusing on social issues common to all. Through all this, it acts as a focal point for women to discuss and become involved in issues that have a direct impact on them and society. The NCNW publishes several magazines such as *Black Woman's Voice* and a quarterly, *Sisters Magazine*, and holds conferences in Washington, D.C.

Bibliography: Olive Burt, *Mary McLeod Bethune* (1970); Milton Meltzer, *Mary McLeod*

Bethune: Voice of Black Hope (1987); Malu Halasa, *Mary McLeod Bethune: Educator* (1989).

                                                                    William E. Segall and Anna V. Wilson

National Organization for Women. The National Organization for Women (NOW), founded in 1966, has become the most vocal, visible, and widely based feminist association in the United States. The organization was a catalyst in activating the women's movement of the 1960s and 1970s, and its vision has remained focused on women's equal rights in education, politics, and the workplace. Although ratification of the Equal Rights Amendment was the organization's original focus, it has litigated, lobbied, and acted on behalf of various women's issues at the national level. NOW was also the first organization to face issues of abortion and a woman's right to control her body. Since 1966, NOW has promoted such issues as child care programs, equal pay for equal work, insurance and pension equity, and the banning of sexual discrimination through the Pregnancy Discrimination Act. NOW traditionally works to improve women's educational and employment opportunities by promoting legislation, as well as lobbying in Washington and around the country.

On October 29, 1966, **Betty Friedan*** became NOW's first president, along with Dr. Kathryn Clarenback as chairman of the board and Richard Graham as treasurer. The choice of Friedan as first president was based on the success of her book, ***The Feminine Mystique**** (1963), which stirred a revolution among upper-middle-class housewives and mothers. Friedan quickly evolved as leader of the modern feminist movement, based on the feminist ideology she advocated in her book. Friedan served as NOW's spokesperson for the four years following its inception, but she resigned in 1970 when endless debate over the group's agenda developed among members. During those formative years, bitter disagreements ensued between liberal feminists (actually considered more conservative) and radical-socialist feminists over such issues as lesbianism and the rejection of motherhood. Liberal feminists favored pragmatic reform and working within established sociopolitical parameters, whereas radical-socialist feminists aligned themselves with Marxist theories, lesbian lifestyles, and deconstruction of the establishment. Friedan considered the radical-socialist group destructive to the group's cohesion, claiming it took a negative stance of "sexual shock-tactics, man-hating, and down with motherhood." The organization held itself together, however, despite the feuds and clashing of personalities, as it maintained democratic membership and a system of decentralized power. Essentially, NOW is a modern version of older feminist organizations at the turn of the century, although some of its rhetoric and confrontational tactics have been more radical and extreme than those of its predecessors.

The Equal Rights Amendment (ERA) was NOW's priority throughout the 1970s, and it was not until the amendment's defeat in 1982 that attention to that issue began to wane within the organization. Increasingly, other concerns such as electoral politics came into focus, leading to a loss of the more radical members and an increase of mainstream feminism. NOW's new focus in the 1980s was twofold: support of the Democratic ticket and the nomination of Geraldine Ferraro as Walter Mondale's running mate in the 1984 presidential election, and prevention of Robert Bork's nomination to the Supreme Court in 1987 because of his history of opposing abortion rights and access to birth control. Soon after the ERA's failure and the unsuccessful Mondale/Ferraro campaign, NOW's membership became split by bitter feuds pertaining to such issues as reproductive choice, achievement of equal pay for women, and increases in educational and career opportunities.

Through all the arguments and emotional issues, NOW has managed to grow and thrive. Membership remains steady and publishes a successful national bimonthly newsletter, *NOW Times*. Local chapters publish monthly newsletters that discuss women's issues, actions, and outcomes. Although NOW has lost a good number of the more radical activists of the 1960s and 1970s, the organization has continued to serve women's needs, and mainstream feminism is a thriving political influence in America. Women's educational and career opportunities have greatly increased, partly as a result of this organization's push for America to recognize and honor the scope of women's issues.

Bibliography: Judith Hole and Ellen Levine, *Rebirth of Feminism* (1971); Sara M. Evans and Barbara J. Nelson, *Wage Justice: Comparable Worth and the Paradox of Technocratic Reform* (1989); William Chafe, *The Paradox of Change: American Women in the Twentieth Century* (1991); Pam McAllister, *This River of Courage: Generations of Women's Resistance and Action* (1991); Elizabeth Fox-Genovese, *Feminism Is Not the Story of My Life* (1996).

Meredith Bouldin Andersen

National Youth Administration. President Franklin D. Roosevelt created the National Youth Administration (NYA) (1936–1943) by executive order on June 26, 1935. The NYA was designed to deal specifically with the problems of young men and women aged eighteen to twenty-five during the Great Depression. NYA advocates cited the failure of the nation's schools in addressing problems facing depression-era youth as justification for a federally funded youth program. In fact, the NYA's primary architects were **social workers*** and youth activists rather than educators. They included Katherine Lenroot of the Labor Department; Eleanor Roosevelt; Works Progress Administration director Harry Hopkins; and his lieutenant, Aubrey Williams, who was chosen to direct the NYA. Another important figure was **Bethune-Cookman College*** president **Mary McLeod Bethune**,* who headed the agency's Division of Negro Affairs. Bethune played a crucial role in increasing African American involvement in the NYA, including creation of a special fund for black graduate students.

By the mid-1930s, youth unemployment was widespread, **high school*** and college dropout rates were rising, and popular fears were growing that depression-era youth represented a ''lost generation.'' The NYA sought to ameliorate these problems through three programs: financial aid to students from

elementary school through college, **vocational education**,* and industrial training. During its first years, the primary NYA goal was to keep as many young
people as possible in school and out of the workforce.

Of the 3.9 million unemployed youth in 1937, 1.5 million, or 38.5 percent,
were female. Although the NYA included women in its programs, it did little
to challenge contemporary stereotypes regarding women's education or their role
in society. Female work projects concentrated on traditional occupations such
as clerical work, health care, **home economics**,* education, nutrition, arts, and
recreation. The prevailing NYA view was that the agency would keep young
women out of the workforce and prepare them for marriage. It was only after
the NYA began to shift focus to defense production training in 1938 that women
were slowly integrated into industrial training projects. By 1943, women made
up about 42 percent of youth involved in defense production training.

In contrast, women outnumbered men in educational aid in all but one of the
NYA's eight years, with their percentage increasing each year. During the 1936–
1937 school year alone, 225,000 women received NYA grants for work-study
aid. By 1943, in part because of World War II, women outnumbered men in
the educational aid program by more than two to one. For many women during
the depression, NYA aid made the difference between staying in school and
dropping out.

The most unique NYA educational program for women was led by Hilda
Worthington Smith, who founded the **Bryn Mawr Summer School for Women
Workers*** in Industry at **Bryn Mawr College*** during the 1920s. Smith organized educational camps for women within the Federal Emergency Relief Administration in 1934; the program was transferred to the NYA in 1935 for its
final two years. The camps, often referred to as the ''she she she,'' were designed to teach female workers about economics, labor problems, and contemporary social conditions in order to heighten social consciousness among women
unlikely to continue their education beyond high school. Some camps also experimented with integrating women from different racial and economic backgrounds; while the majority of NYA programs were segregated, NYA women
tended to accept interracial activities more readily than men. In 1938, the camps
became part of the NYA's resident training program, focusing mainly on vocational training for boys; by then, however, roughly 8,000 women had participated.

The NYA had to defend itself against opponents from 1935 on. Professional
educators resented what they saw as government usurpation of their functions.
Conservatives in Congress attacked the NYA alternately as an American version
of Hitler Youth or as a haven for communists. Though it began as a critique of
American education, the NYA never posed a serious threat to education, nor
did it foster fascism or communism. In fact, its founders strove to make the
NYA a vehicle for inculcating young people with democratic ideals. Though
conservative opposition to the NYA did play a part in its termination, it was

the rising employment opportunities provided by World War II that ultimately made the NYA unnecessary.

The National Youth Administration failed to expand educational opportunities for women, but it did help a large number continue in school. For a small number of working-class women, it also allowed a unique, but limited, opportunity to interact with women of different classes and races. The NYA's effect on the generation of American women who came of age during the depression and war may not be entirely clear, but it cannot be ignored.

Bibliography: Betty Grimes Lindley, *A New Deal for Youth: The Story of the National Youth Administration* (1938); Elaine M. Smith, "Mary McLeod Bethune and the National Youth Administration," in Mabel E. Deutrich and Virginia C. Purdy, eds., *Clio Was a Woman: Studies in the History of American Women* (1980); John A. Salmond, *A Southern Rebel: The Life and Times of Aubrey Willis Williams, 1890–1965* (1983); David Tyack, Robert Lowe, and Elisabeth Hansot, *Public Schools in Hard Times* (1984); Richard A. Reiman, *The New Deal and American Youth: Ideas and Ideals in a Depression Decade* (1992).

Ben Hall

"New Woman." *New Woman* was a term frequently used between 1890 and 1920 to describe the young, college-educated, upper- and middle-class woman who questioned traditional roles of women in society. While the popular media frequently depicted the New Woman as a cigarette-smoking, bicycle-riding, "fast" girl recklessly ignoring her obligations to marry and to mother [see **race suicide***], her freedoms were more apparent than real. Still, many New Women pioneered in business, government, and academe and were original, daring, and influential. Prominent educators, social scientists, reformers, and feminists counted themselves as New Women.

New Woman was a class-based term descriptive of the generation of college-educated women whose unique experience as educated women caused them to feel a special sense of identity and closeness (women of the working class in nontraditional roles were simply called "working girls"). Frequently unmarried, the New Women saw themselves as frank and independent spirits who rode bicycles, golfed, played tennis, and disliked household duties. They wanted to meet men on a basis of "perfect fellowship" and converse freely on "every topic." They shortened their skirts, attended ballroom dances, and admired women such as **Charlotte Perkins Gilman**,* who wrote "The Waste of Private Housekeeping," and Rheta Childs Dorr, the newspaperwoman who asserted that women "wanted to belong to the human race, not the ladies aid society to the human race."

The New Woman had an impact far beyond her actual numbers (in fact, only about 4 percent of the age group attended college in 1920). While some New Women became feminists, socialists, anarchists, and Greenwich Village bohemians, large numbers were joiners, participating in societies and clubs that campaigned for **Progressive Era*** reforms in turn-of-the-century America. Advocates of the New Woman frequently urged that women turn their housekeeping skills to the public good and "clean up" politics, the schools, or the slums [see **social housekeeping***]. New Women were bolstered in their ambitions to change the roles of women by the empirically based "New Psychology" of John Dewey and William James. Women at institutions such as the **University of Chicago*** conducted research on gender that indicated that innate differences between men and women were much smaller than popularly believed, and the New Women used such research to support demands for expanded roles and freedoms.

New Women were active in the **suffrage*** movement, **social work**,* the domestic science movement, **women's clubs**,* and **labor unions**.* The years between 1890 and 1920 forever changed the lives of women as education, suffrage, birth control, and new sexual and social freedoms reached women everywhere in the United States. As the Victorian world of **separate spheres*** for women ended and women began to participate in public life, the educated New Woman played a vitally important actual and symbolic role in the emancipation of American women.

Bibliography: J. Sochen, *Movers and Shakers: American Women Thinkers and Activists 1900–1970* (1973); Rosalind Rosenberg, *Beyond Separate Spheres: Intellectual Roots of Modern Feminism* (1982); Barbara Miller Solomon, *In the Company of Educated Women: A History of Women and Higher Education in America* (1985).

Sharon Clifford

Newman clubs. Newman clubs are organizations established on the campuses of secular colleges and universities by the Roman Catholic Church to attend to the religious education, pastoral care, and apostolic formation of Catholic students. Newman clubs are named in honor of John Henry Cardinal Newman, the nineteenth-century English theologian and scholar whose insights place theology at the heart of the university experience.

The first Newman club was founded in 1893 at the University of Pennsylvania by Timothy Harrington, a graduate medical student, and Father P. J. Garvey, pastor of St. James Church. Newman clubs grew in popularity after the turn of the century as the children of immigrants ventured into the mainstream of American life through higher education but found that most institutions available to them were public and secular. These students discovered the Newman club as they sought spiritual guidance and religious instruction that were not provided to them by the university. The clubs were coeducational [see **coeducation***] and provided leadership opportunities for Catholic students on secular campuses.

The typical modern Newman club offers a variety of activities designed to foster an integration of the religious, social, and intellectual dimensions of life. Spiritual activities include Bible study, spiritual reading, faith sharing, community masses, days of reflection, retreats, and ecumenical prayer gatherings.

Among the social functions sponsored by the club are dinners, community outreach, sporting events, and orientation for new students. Educational activities address contemporary questions and issues, usually based within the context of the Church. [See also **Catholic colleges**,* **Catholic education**.*]

Bibliography: John Whitney Evans, *The Newman Movement: Roman Catholics in American Higher Education, 1883–1971* (1980); George A. Kelly, *Catholic Higher Education: Is It in or out of the Church?* (1992); Philip Gleason, *Contending with Modernity: Catholic Higher Education in the Twentieth Century* (1995).

Joseph E. Weber

normal departments. Created during the third quarter of the nineteenth century, normal departments were short-lived university departments for training elementary teachers, mainly at recently established midwestern state universities. The normal departments' mission ostensibly matched that of the separate **normal schools*** that grew in number during the same period. The departments frequently served as the first place for women students to enter the university.

Brown University in Rhode Island had the first normal department, established in 1850 but suspended in 1854. The University of Indiana had a normal department off and on from 1852 until 1873, and the University of Wisconsin's normal department existed from 1863 until 1866. The Universities of Iowa, Missouri, and Kansas established such departments in 1855, 1868, and 1876, respectively. During the 1890s, the Universities of Utah and Wyoming essentially had normal departments because they housed state normal schools.

Like separate state normal schools, university normal departments offered instruction in pedagogy and classroom management, as well as general or liberal arts courses. Many supported model, or practice, schools. Students often covered general education subjects by taking preparatory or mainstream college courses. During this period, elementary school **teaching*** did not require a college degree; accordingly, normal departments tended to have lower admission standards and less academic rigor than others. They also offered special degrees, such as Bachelor of Pedagogy. Many university administrators, faculty members, and students considered normal departments inferior.

Because the elementary-level teaching force consisted mainly of women by the latter part of the nineteenth century, normal departments served as a back door for female students to enter many midwestern state universities. For the most part, female professors would have to wait longer, as even most normal department professors were men. Wisconsin provides an excellent illustration of the back door at work. Soon after it was established in 1848 with an all-male student body, the university had a normal professor, but general lack of interest and funds delayed establishment of a normal department until the Civil War. The university suffered a decline in enrollment as a result of the war; to bolster numbers, women were admitted—to the normal department—for the first time in 1863. As normal students, these women undergraduates could take advantage of university courses outside the department; some never intended to enter teaching.

In 1868, Wisconsin's normal department was transformed into the Female College in order to segregate women students. Although they would be restricted to the Female College for six years, women students gained a foothold at Wisconsin through the normal department. The story was similar at many other institutions; whether or not normal departments marked the first entrance of female students, they usually resulted in a stronger campus presence for women.

The normal departments' limited spread and short life span were due mainly to prejudices in the university community and the popularity of separate state normal schools. Administrators, faculty members, and male students were often openly hostile toward female students, campaigning against their admission. Another source of prejudice was the perceived inferiority of the normal departments; many feared that normal departments would lower their institutions' status. At the same time, **common school*** advocates were enthusiastic about state normal schools as vehicles for preparing large numbers of teachers required by growing school systems.

Normal schools were well established in the eastern United States by 1850, which explains the paucity of normal departments in that region. For instance, the suspension of Brown's normal department coincided with establishment of a state normal school. This pattern later repeated itself in the Midwest, where state normal schools were established throughout the second half of the nineteenth century.

The few normal departments that withstood the prejudices of the university community and the popularity of normal schools became departments of pedagogy or didactics during the 1870s and 1880s. The University of Iowa listed a professor of pedagogy in 1873, and Kansas and Missouri listed professors of didactics by the mid-1880s. Departments of pedagogy and didactics had different purposes than the earlier normal departments: preparing teachers for **high schools**,* rather than elementary schools, and undertaking a scientific study of education. These were the roots of twentieth-century university schools of education. By 1892, more than thirty universities had chairs of education or didactics, and more than forty others offered instruction in pedagogy in combination with another subject, such as philosophy. While didactics and pedagogy established education as a legitimate field of university study, they also attracted more male students than the normal departments had. Female students had gained a foothold during the era of the normal department; by the end of the nineteenth century, they were a strong presence on university campuses but no longer dominated the university study of education. [See also **teacher education**.*]

Bibliography: G. W. A. Luckey, *The Professional Training of Secondary Teachers in the United States* (1903); Merle Curti and Vernon Carstensen, *The University of Wisconsin: A History* (1949); Geraldine Joncich Clifford, " 'Shaking Dangerous Questions from the Crease': Gender and American Higher Education," *Feminist Issues*, 2 (Fall

1983): 3–62; Irving G. Hendrick, "Teacher Education and Leadership in Major Universities," in John I. Goodlad, Roger Soder, and Kenneth A. Sirotnik, eds., *Places Where Teachers Are Taught* (1990).

Christine A. Ogren

normal schools. Normal schools, from the original French *école normale*, were schools for training teachers that emerged in France and Prussia during the eighteenth and early nineteenth centuries to promote the new science of **teaching**,* or pedagogy. Imported to the United States, the normal school at Lexington, Massachusetts, was the first in America, established in 1839. There were significant differences between the European normals and their new American counterparts. Among those differences, including the role of the federal government, state governments, religion, and teaching methods, was that of the prominent role of women in American education. A little more than a century later, the idea and spirit of the normal schools faded as colleges and universities replaced them in providing American **teacher education**.*

Compulsory schooling laws, child labor reform, and other factors led to increasing school enrollments and attendance through the nineteenth century, and a shortage of teachers followed. In the century's early decades, teachers had received training in private **academies*** and **seminaries*** like **Emma Willard's*** **Troy Female Seminary*** (1821) or **Mary Lyon's*** **Mount Holyoke Female Seminary*** (1837). By midcentury, both the public and elected officials realized that private seminaries and academies could not meet the demand for teachers. Legislators, particularly in Massachusetts and New York, tried to foster growth in existing programs and entice new academies into providing teacher education by offering state subsidies. Facing mounting public advocacy, and with convincing proposals offered by education experts like Willard, **Catharine Beecher**,* Henry Barnard, and **Horace Mann**,* states began establishing their own institutions to train teachers—the normal schools.

Normal schools grew rapidly in popularity in the Northeast, Midwest, and West. With a few exceptions, normals were rarely established in the South, where private tutoring remained common until later in the century. State normal schools were first established in the Northeast, setting the tone for those to follow. Like public **common schools**,* normals were a new kind of American institution. Although counties and some municipalities created normal schools, and some academies and colleges opened **normal departments**,* the state-supported normal school model was most widespread. At century's end, more than one hundred state normal schools existed.

Enrollment in normal schools grew tremendously through the late nineteenth century. By 1874, nearly 30,000 (one-half women) attended normal schools. In the public normals, women were nearly two-thirds of the students. By 1894, normals boasted 100,000 students, 86,000 of them female (Ogren, 1996, pp. 6–7). Normal school founders did not intend for them to compete with academies; in fact, normals were structured to educate students after they completed academy study. Competition did result, however, because academies charged tuition, and many normal schools were free.

Not all attendees at normals either wanted to or did go on to become teachers. Women and men alike saw the normal schools as an opportunity for a free education and took advantage of it. Faced with a choice of attending a university or a normal school, many students chose the normal rather than paying the higher university costs in tuition and time for a degree. Both women and men appreciated the new opportunity, especially as the curricula of the normal schools expanded to include traditional liberal studies, science, and humanities. Eventually, feeling pressure from both colleges and high schools, the normal schools were forced to focus their curricula on pedagogy to attract only students who wanted to become teachers. This shift also marked a point in the debate between a narrow focus on pedagogy and the need for teachers to explore a wider context in arts and sciences.

Recent research on normal schools suggests that previous ideas about the role of the normals might not be correct. Historians have believed that women and men who studied in normals had little impact on the practice of education because they were so few in number and their careers were so short. By these accounts women taught only until they married and left the profession; likewise, men were said to teach only until they found a better job. In fact, new research suggests that women and men who graduated from normals taught longer and had more influential careers than teachers either with no training or with skills only from teacher institutes. Normal graduates often went on to become principal teachers, normal school teachers, and district and state school system administrators. They held enormous influence not only in their own classrooms but also in the shaping of public education through the nineteenth century.

During the early to mid-twentieth century, normal school curricula again expanded to include more than just teaching methods. This change was part of a movement to expand state higher education institutions, enabling them to provide college education to a growing number of **high school*** graduates. Starting at the turn of the century and continuing until the 1950s and 1960s, normal schools were converted into state **teachers colleges*** that offered arts and science degree programs. Some were further expanded to include many professional colleges, degree programs, and graduate studies, changing their names to state colleges. This sequence is typical of most state systems established in the nineteenth century.

The term *normal school* is rarely heard today because most of these schools were either closed or converted into colleges or universities during the rapid expansion of state university systems during the mid-twentieth century. The legacy of the normal schools lives on in the debates in contemporary teacher education programs where the issue of what forms of knowledge are valid for teachers remains contested. [See also **feminization,*** **semiprofessions,*** **women's colleges.***]

Bibliography: American Normal School Association, *American Normal Schools: Their Theory, Their Workings, and Their Results, as Embodied in the Proceedings of the First Annual Convention of the American Normal School Association Held at Trenton, New Jersey August 19 and 20* (1860); Jurgen Herbst, *And Sadly Teach: Teacher Education and Professionalization in American Culture* (1989); John I. Goodlad, Roger Soder, and Kenneth A. Sirotnik, eds., *Places Where Teachers Are Taught* (1990); Christine Ogren, "Where Coeds Were Coeducated: Normal Schools in Wisconsin, 1870–1920," *History of Education Quarterly*, 35 (1995): 1–26; Ogren, "Education for Women in the United States: The State Normal School Experience, 1870–1920" (Ph.D. diss., University of Wisconsin, 1996).

Victor Parente

nursery schools. Originally private institutions for preschool-age children, nursery schools were created in the early twentieth century as a concerted reaction to statistics reflecting children's poor health upon entering school despite their good health at birth. Public nursery schools did not enjoy long-term implementation until recently; many were created during times of great need, such as the Great Depression and World War II, but their funding typically was cut when the need eased. The public nursery school's present-day counterpart, Head Start, began in the early 1960s as a programmatic result of President Lyndon Johnson's "War on Poverty."

Founded mainly by psychologists and **social workers**,* nursery schools emphasized good health as well as education. Their founders believed that education for children was necessary before age five. The nursery school curriculum incorporated activities based on eating, dressing, napping, playing, and **hygiene**.* Nursery schools were created in a climate of behavioristic psychology's support of the move away from mother as child's best teacher to a trained professional assuming that role. For mothers who did not work, nursery school was an important formal, early beginning to the child's education. As one scholar has explained, "The universal theme of the nursery school movement was that all parents, rich and poor, could become better parents through the application of scientific educational principles and the enrollment of their young children in nursery school" (Beatty, p. 136).

Nursery schools were more than just institutions for the very young. Training schools for teachers at the nursery, kindergarten, and primary schools levels were often created at nursery schools. Early founders, like organizers of the **kindergarten movement**,* believed that parent education was integral to success of their programs. Parents were participants in the schools, too, learning about childrearing from teachers. The influence of the **child study movement*** was evident in early nursery schools, where organizers encouraged an emphasis on the social sciences and psychology. One organizer described nursery schools as the "real-life laboratories for the study of growth and development" of children (Eliot, in Hymes, p. 19).

Margaret McMillan organized the first nursery school in England in response to concerns about the poor health of young children. She founded an open-air nursery school in 1913 in industrial Deptford, England; McMillan's curriculum emphasized fresh air and outdoor play. In 1918 the Fisher Act provided monies for establishment of nursery schools throughout England.

McMillan's school influenced organizers in the United States within a short time. A cooperative nursery school was formed at the **University of Chicago*** in 1916. Shortly thereafter, other nursery schools were formed. Harriet Johnson, who had trained as a nurse, opened a school in New York City in 1919 affiliated with **Lucy Sprague Mitchell**'s* Bureau of Educational Experiments (BEE) [see **Bank Street College of Education***]. The BEE nursery school was created primarily to conduct research on children. Social worker Abigail Eliot studied under McMillan in 1921. In 1922, Eliot became director of the Ruggles Street Nursery School in Boston, where the hallmark was Eliot's emphasis on positive treatment of parents. In 1926 an adjoining training school for nursery school teachers was opened, called the Nursery Training Center of Boston. It offered one- to two-year programs in nursery school education for **high school*** and college graduates.

Kindergarten educator and Columbia Teachers College professor **Patty Smith Hill*** visited Ruggles Street in its early days and later established the Manhattanville Day Nursery as an observation center for her students. In Detroit, Edna Noble White, a **home economist**,* opened the Merrill-Palmer Nursery School in 1922. White, unlike Eliot, retained McMillan's emphasis on hygiene and cleanliness. Merrill-Palmer was organized to train young women for motherhood and later expanded to the study of child development. It became a famous training center, cooperating with local colleges and universities.

Women's colleges* also established nursery schools in the 1920s. In 1926 **Vassar College*** had the first, with Mills in California, **Wellesley**,* and **Smith*** following suit shortly thereafter. Ethel Puffer Howes, who started the cooperative nursery school at Smith in 1926, created a program that attempted to research ways of coordinating women's interests with those of their children; it did not meet with success. However, Howes later chaired a committee of the **American Association of University Women*** on "Cooperative Home Service," from which a program at Smith called the **Institute for the Coordination of Women's Interests*** (ICWI) resulted. The ICWI was designed to "find ways of helping well-educated women continue to use their education after marriage and motherhood" (Beatty, p. 162).

Children from diverse backgrounds had access to nursery school education, though overall very few attended. Of the small percentage who attended private nurseries in the 1920s, the majority were middle- and upper-class children. In the 1930s, funding for private nursery schools began to decline. Children from less affluent backgrounds could attend charity nursery schools such as the one connected to **Hull-House*** (the Mary Crane Nursery, 1925). Or they might attend one of the several public nursery schools created on an experimental basis in the 1920s by the women of the **settlement house movement*** and **women's clubs**.* The first was Chicago's Franklin Park Public School Nursery, founded in 1925.

Both private and public nursery schools exist today. Despite the continuing efforts of many advocates, public nursery schools never became connected to public schools the way that kindergartens did. Instead, Head Start, considered the nation's public nursery school, is a social welfare and community action program, not run by the Department of Education. Yet Head Start retains the original goals of nursery schools: nutrition, parental involvement, and early learning. Considered "one of the most popular and successful of federal programs . . . [longitudinal studies of Head Start] have helped create a new groundswell of attention and broad-based public support for preschool education" (Beatty, p. 199). [See also **early childhood education**,* **early childhood teacher education**.*]

Bibliography: James L. Hymes, Jr., "America's First Nursery Schools: An Interview with Abigail A. Eliot," *Early Childhood Education: Living History Interviews*, book 1 (1978): 7–32; Sonya Michel, "Children's Interests/Mothers' Rights: Women, Professionals, and the American Family, 1920–1945" (Ph.D. diss., Brown University, 1986); Barbara Beatty, *Preschool Education in America: The Culture of Young Children from the Colonial Era to the Present* (1995).

Christine Woyshner

O

Oberlin College. When contemporary readers think of Oberlin College, they imagine a model for the small liberal arts college well known for a liberal-thinking faculty, student body, and administration. Historians know the institution best for its lead in providing education for women and African Americans. Since 1837 women have attended an Oberlin practicing **coeducation**,* and the school opened with a commitment to accept students without regard to race. Dozens of influential female educators, especially African Americans, are Oberlin alumnae.

Oberlin Collegiate Institute was incorporated on February 2, 1834. Incorporation of a college in northeast Ohio was the plan of Reverend John J. Shipherd and his associate Philo P. Stewart. Shipherd was pastor of the Presbyterian Church in Elyria, and Stewart, a former missionary among the Cherokees in Mississippi, was living with Shipherd's family. The original plan was to constitute a school surrounded by a Christian community modeled after the life and ideals of German pastor John Frederick Oberlin. In 1835 the board of trustees voted to admit students ''irrespective of color'' and thereby set Oberlin on its path of distinction.

From the beginning the school was to be open to both sexes. Like most nineteenth-century institutions, Oberlin had a Preparatory Department to help students not yet ready for collegiate study. The Collegiate, Theological, and Teacher Departments completed the Institute, and a manual labor system provided students financial support [see **normal departments***]. Oberlin students considered themselves poor, and a long break at midterm allowed them to earn money at such jobs as **teaching*** in order to pay tuition. This practice continued until 1877 when the college adopted a more traditional calendar.

The ambitious first annual report in 1834 spoke of ''the diffusion of useful science, sound morality, and pure religion, among the growing multitudes of the

Mississippi Valley'' and the desire to extend these blessings ''to the destitute millions which over spread the earth.'' Among unique features was a governance structure that gave faculty responsibility for day-to-day operation of the institution.

There is no mention in the earliest accounts of the special program for women known first as the Ladies Course (1836–1874) and then the Literary Course (1875–1894, when it was terminated). Oberlin is known as the nation's first coeducational college; however, it was not until September 1837 that four females enrolled in the collegiate program. To compare, not until the 1870s did women attend Cornell and the Universities of Michigan and Wisconsin, institutions that professed to be coeducational from their start.

Oberlin opened on December 3, 1833, with thirty-four students. Among the forty-four who eventually arrived during that first academic year were twenty-nine men and fifteen women. Most women joined the Preparatory Department, and very little is known of them. In July 1835 a literary society—the Young Ladies' Association of Oberlin Collegiate Institute—was formed, certainly the first for women students anywhere. It allowed graduating females a place to deliver their commencement addresses, since they were not yet permitted to speak in public. A Female Board of Managers was appointed in 1836 to control the female department.

While many women attended classes with men, most were enrolled in the Ladies Course. Their numbers greatly expanded in the antebellum period to over 2,000 women. The women's program of study resembled that of the **seminaries*** formed in the West based upon the **Mount Holyoke Female Seminary*** model of **Mary Lyon.*** Oberlin's neighbor, Western Reserve College, did not adopt coeducation but formed a **coordinate college*** late in the nineteenth century.

Oberlin College (the official name after 1850) attracted notice for its willingness to admit students of all races and to allow students and faculty to be active in **abolitionism.*** Professors Asa Mahan and John Morgan from the Lane Seminary were known abolitionists, as was President Charles Grandison Finney, also a model for religious evangelism. This combination of religious fervor and identification with social causes set the tone for the type of institution that Oberlin remains to this day. Both the **American Missionary Association*** and **Catharine Beecher's* Board of National Popular Education*** found Oberlin an excellent source for recruits.

Except for the large percentage of females, Oberlin's student body resembled other western colleges', with students from the same general areas in New York and neighboring Pennsylvania, Michigan, and Indiana. As Ohio grew, more students came from within the state. Religious spirit was evidenced in letters of application, which expressed students' desire to participate in Oberlin's spirit of reform and moral self-improvement. This Oberlin brand of perfectionism became a lasting legacy.

By the twentieth century, Oberlin had become a traditional liberal arts college offering course work in the arts, sciences, languages, and literature while granting a single degree, the bachelor of arts. From 1864 to 1900 a Scientific Course had been offered, as well as a bachelor of science.

Other twentieth-century changes included the merger of the Graduate School of Theology with Vanderbilt University and its move to Tennessee. In 1903 a bachelor's degree in music was authorized. The Conservatory of Music remains an important part of Oberlin, while the School of Theology has become an important memory.

Twentieth-century students remained active in social causes during the free speech movement, the civil rights movement, the 1960s fight against the military-industrial complex, and concern for the environment. The ideas of Oberlin perfectionism are alive, although now they might be as easily represented by Orthodox Jewish students protesting for a kosher dining room.

Bibliography: Frances J. Hosford, *Father Shipherd's Magna Charta: A Century of Co-education at Oberlin College* (1937); Robert S. Fletcher, *A History of Oberlin College: From Its Foundation through the Civil War*, 2 vols. (1943); Rita S. Saslaw, "Student Societies: Nineteenth Century Establishment" (Ph.D. diss., Case Western Reserve University, 1971).

Rita S. Saslaw

ornamental education. *Ornamental education* refers to a curriculum appropriate for a young gentlewoman in the pre-Revolutionary colonies emphasizing music, dance, needlework, French, and other accomplishments. Tracing development of its ideological underpinnings reveals significant changes in roles and expectations for women in pre- and post-Revolutionary America.

In the early years of the colonies, forging a living from an oftentimes inhospitable land consumed efforts of men and women alike. To suggest that women's time should be spent in ornamental needlework or playing the spinet would have been ridiculous. Whatever education women received was suited to their roles as wives, mothers, and producers of household goods. Education, whether learning to make soap, stitch a dress, or read the Bible, was based on utility. But as the colonies grew and stabilized in the latter part of the eighteenth century, more time could be afforded to culture and refinement. Daughters and wives of wealthy men no longer were required to provide the labor necessary to run a household. Servants or slaves took over care of the house, prepared meals, and tended the young children, freeing wealthy women to attend to their own and their husband's pleasure. As these roles changed, what was deemed a suitable education also changed. Reflecting the role of such women in England, ornamental education, also referred to as "accomplishments," prepared female American aristocrats for their places in society.

In New England, instruction for wealthy young women was generally provided in schools or **academies*** run by women of good character. A typical advertisement was a notice of a Boston academy at the close of the eighteenth century where young women could learn the following: "plain and ornamental needlework, tapestry, embroidery, marking, pattern drawing, wax work, transparent 'filagree,' painting upon glass, Japanning, quill work, featherwork, gold and silver embroidery, imitation of Brussels's lace, shell work, flowers for the head, 'shaded work in colors,' Dresden work, flowering on muslin, making 'furbelow'd scarfs,' quilting, flourishings, turkey work, and spinning" (Woody, p. 150). Since many schools or instructors covered only one type of accomplishment, women often attended a number of schools to obtain the necessary skills. Although many schools included reading, writing, and other academic instruction, their primary purpose was to develop the social graces.

In the pre-Revolutionary South, increased wealth, leisure, and social stability led to a view of women as the ornament or jewel of the house, to be beautifully dressed, coiffured, and behaved. Young southern women on plantations were instructed by tutors well versed in music, dancing, and proper etiquette; in southern cities, instruction in the gentle art of being a lady was provided in schools and academies. An advertisement in the May 1770 *South Carolina Gazette* read: "A Boarding School for the Education of Young Ladies, Will be Opened . . . by Mrs. Duneau, a Gentlewoman come from England, Who has brought up many Ladies of Rank and Distinction . . . Teaching the French and English Languages grammatically—Geography—History—and many instructing Amusements to improve the Mind—with all Sorts of fashionable Needle Work." This ideal closely constrained the education available to young southern women.

At the same time that ornamental education was occupying the time and interest of many wealthy young women, a contradictory ideology of **"Republican motherhood"*** was being advanced by such advocates as Benjamin Rush, **Emma Willard,*** and **Catharine Beecher.*** In the post-Revolutionary excitement to solidify the new nation, Rush argued that girls' education must reflect the needs of the country. In his 1787 address, "Thoughts upon Female Education," Rush argued that "it is incumbent upon us to make ornamental accomplishments yield to principles and knowledge, in the education of our women." He recommended a curriculum including English language and correct spelling, penmanship, figures and bookkeeping, geography, biography, astronomy, natural philosophy, chemistry (for domestic and culinary purposes), vocal music (but not musical instruments, considered too time-consuming), dancing, poetry, and moral essays. The Republican woman's education must be socially useful, training her to be "an agreeable companion for a sensible man," an efficient housekeeper, and an upright mother capable of molding moral standards in her sons.

The new ideology stressed, if not women's intellectual equality with men, their newly recognized position as partners in strengthening the moral fiber of the new nation. The rejection of elitist education for women on grounds that education must be useful rather than simply ornamental marked a positive step in women's access to a more academic education. The female academies of Emma Willard, **Zilpah Polly Grant Banister,*** Catharine Beecher, **Mary Lyon,*** and others gained ground in the 1820s and 1830s. Yet despite a redefinition of the kind of education appropriate for women in the fledgling nation, what remained unchanged was the belief that a woman's education should prepare her for an ideologically circumscribed role in society.

Bibliography: Thomas Woody, *A History of Women's Education in the United States*, Vol. 1 (1929); Nancy F. Cott, *The Bonds of Womanhood: "Woman's Sphere" in New England, 1780–1835* (1977); Linda K. Kerber, *Women of the Republic: Intellect and Ideology in Revolutionary America* (1980); Mary Beth Norton, *Liberty's Daughters: The Revolutionary Experience of American Women, 1750–1800* (1980); Kerber, "Daughters of Columbia: Educating Women for the Republic, 1787–1805," in Linda Kerber and Jane DeHart Mathews, eds., *Women's America: Refocusing the Past* (1982).

Sharon Hobbs

P

Palmer, Alice Freeman. Alice Elvira Freeman Palmer (1855–1902) was a premier figure in women's higher education in the late nineteenth century, eventually becoming a sought-after speaker on women's educational issues. Her most notable position was president of **Wellesley College*** in Massachusetts from 1881 to 1887. She resigned that post to marry Harvard philosopher George Herbert Palmer but remained active in women's education until her death at age forty-seven.

Freeman's childhood was spent in the farming communities of upstate New York. The first of four children, she was born in Colesville near Binghampton and lived with her parents James Warren Freeman, a farmer, and Elizabeth Josephine Higley. In 1861, her father enrolled in medical school [see **medical education***]. Graduating in 1864, he moved the family to Windsor, New York, where young Alice was enrolled in the Windsor Academy in 1865.

A very bright and capable student, she attracted the attention of Thomas Barclay, a Yale theology student teaching part-time to help pay his college expenses. Barclay and Alice were engaged to marry, but Alice broke the engagement two years later to pursue her dream of a college education.

Despite her academic ability and their support of young Alice, the Freemans were not convinced that college was appropriate. Few women attended college in the late nineteenth century (less than 2 percent of the age group), and it was an expensive proposition. Over time, however, Freeman won them over by promising to provide financial assistance for educating her younger brother and sister. In 1872, Freeman and her father made the long trip to Ann Arbor, Michigan, for an interview with James Angell, president of the University of Michigan. Angell was impressed with Freeman, but the admissions committee found her preparation for college study weak. Angell allowed her to return in the fall, and after additional tutoring, she was fully admitted.

Freeman was both a successful student and a very popular figure on campus.

Students and faculty alike found her quite engaging. Although she was one of the few women on campus, she was elected one of four senior class speakers at her graduation in 1876. Often scrambling for funds from term to term, Alice, like many students of the era, supported herself by **teaching*** and tutoring in local schools, even leaving campus in 1874 to serve as principal of a **high school*** in Ottawa, Illinois.

After graduation, her first job was teaching at Lake Geneva Seminary, a struggling private secondary school. Most important, the school offered a free education to Alice's sister Ella. The following summer, Freeman returned to Michigan for a graduate degree in history. Through a recommendation from James Angell to Henry Fowle Durant, founder of Wellesley College, she was offered a teaching position at Wellesley in 1877. She declined the offer to become principal at East Saginaw High School. Her father had suffered several financial setbacks through poor investments, and the higher salary as principal allowed Alice to support her family, whom she moved to a rented house in Saginaw, paid for by Alice and Ella. Freeman stayed in Saginaw for two more years. In June 1879, her younger and favorite sister, Stella, died after a long illness. Wellesley College beckoned again with an increased salary, this time exceeding her principal's pay. Freeman left for Massachusetts.

Henry and Pauline Durant's original conception of Wellesley was to provide a Christian education for young women. Compelled by an evangelical spirit after the loss of their only child several years earlier, the Durants built Wellesley on the site of their country estate, originally intended as an inheritance property for their son. Henry Durant was a trustee at **Mount Holyoke Female Seminary*** and patterned the early vision of his college after that institution.

Immediately popular with students, Freeman quickly impressed her employers as well. Her high energy, dedication, and charismatic personality made her an instant celebrity on campus. Following Henry Durant's death in 1881, Pauline asked Freeman to become president.

While she accepted much of the Durant philosophy, in her new role as president, Freeman began to effect subtle changes in the Wellesley culture in line with her own vision. Convinced that women must know the learned arts and sciences in a changing world, she recruited a more demanding faculty, altered requirements for graduation, and raised admission standards. Freeman was torn between women's duties to domestic responsibilities such as marriage and family, while at the same time she valued academic study and intellectual rigor. She believed women would be called to lead social crusades as well as maintain order in the home, but to do so required a sound college education. Therefore, under President Freeman's view, Wellesley women would be challenged by their studies, yet retain their femininity. To ensure the latter, she instituted a ''cottage'' system, small residences that served as living quarters and gathering places for informal get-togethers and seminars. She encouraged faculty to participate and even moved her own residence to one of the cottages.

One of Freeman's greatest assets as president was superior administrative skills. Through her gentle but persuasive maneuvers, Wellesley became a model of her vision of women's education. By emphasizing the sciences and a more rigorous commitment to the liberal arts, she pushed Wellesley into the vanguard of innovative American institutions of higher education and, in the longer term, insured that Wellesley would remain a leader in women's education [see **science education***].

Freeman's dilemma over women's role as domestic figure and intellectual equal was exacerbated in 1886 when at age thirty-one she met Professor George Herbert Palmer, age forty-four. The attraction was mutual, and after an extended courtship between two ambitious academics, the Wellesley president and the Harvard philosopher were married in Boston in December 1887. Freeman had tendered her resignation as president in fall 1887. From her letters, statements, and deep sorrow, it is clear she would have stayed on at Wellesley, but Palmer insisted she be a wife only. Freeman complied, taking solace in the fulfillment of her other lifelong goal, marriage.

Even after marriage, Freeman maintained a steady and far-reaching influence on higher education for women. She was instrumental in raising money to establish a Harvard Annex for Women, later renamed **Radcliffe College**.* She was a charter member of the **Association of Collegiate Alumnae**,* an influential women's organization that became the **American Association of University Women**.* She also accepted an offer from William Rainey Harper to be **dean of women*** at the **University of Chicago*** when it opened in 1892 but only on a "part-time" basis. She held the position for three years and then resigned to live full-time in Boston.

Alice Freeman Palmer was a very popular speaker on women's education and other topics related to women, education, **women's colleges**,* and issues of the time. Her charisma and engaging demeanor made her well liked, even loved, by many who knew her. While on a trip overseas with her husband and her friend, educator **Lucy Sprague Mitchell**,* Freeman became seriously ill from a congenital intestinal disorder. She lingered and then died in Paris in 1901. Several memorials were held in her honor over the next several years in Ann Arbor, Wellesley, Chicago, and Boston, final testimony to the wide reach of her influence.

Bibliography: George Herbert Palmer, *Alice Freeman Palmer; A Life* (1908); Alice Fleming, *Alice Freeman Palmer: Pioneer College President* (1970); Roberta Frankfort, *Collegiate Women: Domesticity and Career in Turn-of-the-Century America* (1977); Ruth Bordin, *Alice Freeman Palmer: The Evolution of a New Woman* (1993); Patricia Palmieri, *In Adamless Eden: The Community of Women Faculty at Wellesley* (1995).

Robert A. Schwartz

Peabody, Elizabeth Palmer. Educator Elizabeth Palmer Peabody (1804–1894) was at the forefront of the Boston Transcendentalist movement of the mid-nineteenth century; most significantly, she was a leading figure in introducing the **kindergarten*** and kindergarten training school to America. Peabody played a key role in promoting public acceptance of the kindergarten and its large number of female teachers as a legitimate intellectual enterprise and an essential part of childhood education.

Born in Billerica, Massachusetts, on May 16, 1804, Peabody attended her mother's private school and later taught there. She received an eclectic, liberal education both at school and at home, where her parents emphasized cultivation of the intellect through study of literature, art, and philosophy of education. Peabody started a school in Lancaster, Massachusetts, when she was sixteen and later opened another school in Boston. She studied Greek with Ralph Waldo Emerson in 1822. Peabody also worked as secretary to William Ellery Channing, early leader of American Unitarianism, in Boston from 1825 until 1834, when she became assistant to Bronson Alcott at his Temple School in Boston until 1836. Her work with Alcott led to her anonymous 1835 publication *Record of a School*, which described Alcott's unique approach to childhood education.

When she returned to her parents' home in Salem in 1836, Peabody began attending Transcendental Club meetings at Emerson's home. In 1839 she returned to Boston to open her West Street bookshop, which quickly became the center of the Transcendentalist movement, attracting writers, philosophers, Harvard professors, and liberal clergymen. She set up a printing press in the shop's back room and published *The Dial*, organ of the Brook Farm community (1842–1843). She also published some writings of **Margaret Fuller**,* and, because of her strong sentiments on **abolitionism**,* various pamphlets of the Anti-Slavery Society. In addition, Peabody published several works by childhood friend Nathaniel Hawthorne, who married her sister Sophia in 1842.

From about 1844, the focus of Peabody's work was education. After a chance meeting in Boston with the founder of the first American kindergarten and an introduction to the educational ideas of Friedrich Froebel, she founded the first private, English-speaking American kindergarten in Boston in 1860. A lifelong apostle of Froebel, Peabody studied his methods abroad in 1867, lectured on kindergartens in the United States, and wrote about them in the magazine *Kindergarten Messenger* (1873–1875) and *Lectures in the Training Schools for Kindergartens* (1888).

Peabody contributed to women's education by facilitating establishment in Boston of one of a handful of kindergarten training schools. These schools were to prepare young women, equipped with the latest Froebelian knowledge and skills, for positions as kindergarten teachers and nursery governesses. She also promoted kindergarten programs for home use, supporting German trainers who taught young mothers the theories and practices of Froebelian education and childrearing. Froebelian-trained mothers, Peabody assumed, would be best fit to cultivate their children's mental, moral, and physical development.

In 1870, Peabody established in Boston the first public kindergarten system, although funding eventually was discontinued by Boston's School Committee. Later, Boston philanthropist **Pauline Agassiz Shaw*** provided the necessary financial assistance as part of her own drive to promote the public kindergarten movement.

A noted lecturer in history who donated much of her income to educating Native Americans, Peabody published her *Chronological History of the United States* in 1856 and taught history at Alcott's Concord School of Philosophy from 1879 to 1884. She maintained a lifelong friendship with **Horace Mann,*** founder of the American **common school*** movement. Mann married Peabody's sister Mary in 1843. A few of Peabody's articles and memoirs were published in *A Last Evening with Allston* (1886). Peabody died at age eighty-nine in Jamaica Plain, Massachusetts, on January 3, 1894. [See also **early childhood education,*** **early childhood teacher education,*** **nursery schools**.*]

Bibliography: Evelyn Weber, *The Kindergarten: Its Encounter with Educational Thought in America* (1969); Michael Steven Shapiro, "Froebel in America: A Social and Intellectual History of the Kindergarten Movement, 1848–1918" (Ph.D. diss., Brown University, 1980); Bruce A. Ronda, ed., *Letters of Elizabeth Palmer Peabody, American Renaissance Woman* (1984); Katherine H. Sale, "Elizabeth Palmer Peabody: New England Educator," *Journal of Rural and Small Schools*, 3 (1988): 32–35; Barbara Beatty, *Preschool Education in America: The Culture of Young Children from the Colonial Era to the Present* (1995). See Peabody's papers in the Rebecca Kinsman Munroe Collection, Smith College Library, Northampton, Massachusetts. See also the Peabody Sisters Papers, 1835–1880, and Nathaniel Hawthorne Papers, both at University of Virginia Library, Charlottesville; Aubertine Woodward Moore Papers, State Historical Society of Wisconsin Collections; Ralph Waldo Emerson Papers, Houghton Library, Harvard University.

Elizabeth Anne Yeager

peace education. Peace education played a role in the evolution of the political education of women, especially entwined with their struggle for equality in the early days of the **suffrage*** movement. Women s political education, especially related to shared decisionmaking and equal roles in citizenship and governance, began far in advance of their receiving the vote in 1920, motivated also by their dream of a world at peace. Many women, prominent and unknown, played central roles, though the origins and historic records are truly a strand of "hidden history," not generally included in mainstream educational literature.

Peace education has been described as multifaceted and cross-disciplinary, with a myriad of dimensions, including issues of nonviolence, peace, social justice, economic well-being, political participation, conflict resolution, and concern for the environment. It has been identified by Spodek and Brown as an important alternative curriculum in **early childhood education**.*

As early as 1828 with the founding of early peace societies, women envisioned an alternative path, forming their own societies apart from men. Women were often extolled in peace journals as a source of intellectual power and patriotism "capable of training their children to a love of peace and a deep habitual abhorrence of war." These stirrings of separate peace societies for women could also be considered the genesis of the women's equal rights movement. Woman, as first teacher and guide for ethical character, appeared often as a theme in peace society literature and especially in the work of **Horace Mann**,* a founder of the **common school*** movement.

As America entered the 1900s, peace education was influenced by two advocates, both educators from New England: Fannie Fern Andrews and Lucia Ames Mead, who devoted their entire adult lives to writing, lecturing, and inspiring others to join networks for their mission. Through the American School Peace League (1909–1915), which she founded, Andrews attempted to organize America's teachers and schoolchildren, including publication of textbooks for history and citizenship, dissemination of curriculum guides, and promotion of a special holiday, Peace Day (May 18).

Mead, a Boston teacher, author, and lecturer, argued that peace and justice were attainable through a permanent court of international justice. She helped **Jane Addams*** organize the Woman's Peace Party (1915) and sowed the seeds of education for world citizenship and peace education. Mead also headed the Massachusetts Woman's Suffrage Association and was considered one of the most prominent women in the peace movement in the century's early decades.

Political education of women and progress for peace education were both advanced with the founding of the Woman's Peace Party. The platform crafted by Addams, Mead, and Carrie Chapman Catt, among others, created concentric circles for peace education and woman suffrage, involving many of the same women as activists for both causes. Political activism for women meshed with education for peace as a valid method for changing institutional structures. Political activism was viewed as a next step in the evolution of women's political fate, with a pathway envisioned through official government circles and the political power structure. The agenda was first to gain the vote, then, with political power, to secure a world of peace. The platform of the party (predecessor to the present-day Women's International League for Peace and Freedom) gave a prominent place to peace education and the role of women, considered the nurturers and guardians of human life, present and future. Education of youth in ideals of peace and removal of the economic causes of war played prominent roles.

Women involved in advocacy for peace education and social reform were victims of widespread persecution during World War I, accused of unpatriotic links with the so-called Pacifist-Socialist movement. "Red Scare" tactics unfairly branded Addams and Mead, in particular. As a result of these accusations, over the course of several decades peace education became even further removed from the mainstream of education and political life.

Inspiration for women's further activism most likely grew out of their experiences in the civil rights movement, the Vietnam War, and the 1960s antiwar movement, events that transformed countless women's lives as they learned firsthand about advocacy for peace and nonviolence through direct action. Since the 1970s, conflict resolution, as a linchpin in the peace education curriculum, has been the focus of many women educators who believe in its potential for significant change in women's lives and in school environments. Women such as Grace Contrino Abrams and her sister Fran Schmidt, cofounders of the Peace Education Foundation, Priscilla Prutzmann, Children's Creative Response to Conflict Program, and Betty Reardon, Peace Education Program, Teachers College, Columbia University, are recognized as pioneer peace educators. Since the 1980s, others such as Diane Levin and Nancy Carlsson-Paige, Boston early childhood educators, have contributed to the literature on conflict resolution. The feminist perspective in contemporary peace education, especially in the 1980s and 1990s, has been represented by Reardon and Birgit Brock-Utne, among others. Reardon's viewpoint includes ecological concerns as well.

Research on the socialization of women teaching peace studies in higher education reveals that they were sustained by frequent contact with spirituality during childhood. Clearly, these influences, from childhood through adulthood, along with educational, religious, and community experiences, have shaped their sense of social responsibility, the core of citizenship education.

Peace education has played a role in the political education of American women since the mid-nineteenth century. American women may consider this strand of "hidden history" a valuable ally in their progress toward political maturity.

Bibliography: Betty Reardon, *Educating for Global Responsibility: Teacher-Designed Curricula for Peace Education*, K–12 (1988); John Craig, *Lucia Ames Mead (1856–1936) and the American Peace Movement* (1990); Harriet Hyman Alonso, *Peace as a Women's Issue: A History of the U.S. Movement for World Peace and Women's Rights* (1993); B. Spodek and B. C. Brown, "Curriculum Alternatives in Early Childhood Education," in Spodek, ed., *Handbook of Research on the Education of Young Children* (1993); Aline M. Stomfay-Stitz, *Peace Education in America: Sourcebook for Education and Research* (1993); Reardon, *Learning Peace: The Promise of Ecological and Cooperative Education* (1994). Fannie Fern Andrews's papers are in the Schlesinger Library, Radcliffe College, Cambridge, Massachusetts; Lucia Ames Mead's papers are in the Swarthmore College Peace Collection, Swarthmore, Pennsylvania.

Aline M. Stomfay-Stitz

Phelps, Almira Hart. Almira Hart Lincoln Phelps (1793–1884) was, like her famous sister **Emma Hart Willard,*** a noted school administrator, women's educator, and textbook author during a long career spanning the nineteenth century. Phelps was born in Berlin, Connecticut, seventeenth and last child of Lydia and Samuel Hart. She started her formal education at the village school and at sixteen entered **teaching.*** In 1810 her sister Emma invited her to Middlebury, Vermont, where Willard was running a school, and Phelps was put to work studying with a small group of young men enrolled at Middlebury College. Phelps then accepted the invitation of her cousin Nancy Hinsdale, who was running an **academy*** in Pittsfield, Massachusetts, to be an assistant teacher. Simultaneously, Phelps also taught the New Britain winter school, a common practice among women teachers. Her success in these positions led to an offer to take charge of a private school in Berlin and then in Sandy Hill, New York.

Phelps continued this work until she married in 1817; she and husband Simeon Lincoln had three children. When Lincoln and one of their children died in 1823, Phelps sought support and comfort from Willard, who was by this time head of **Troy Female Seminary**,* an institution Willard founded in 1821. Willard was determined to offer Phelps additional educational opportunities and continue to advance her teaching skills. Willard, without funds to hire a permanent science instructor, arranged for Phelps to study with scientist and lecturer Amos Eaton at nearby Rennselear Institute. Phelps learned quickly and soon became both Eaton's "scientific assistant" and head of the Troy science department. In addition, she wrote many science textbooks that were included not only in the Troy curriculum but across the country. In 1829 she published *Familiar Lectures on Botany, or Lincoln's Botany*, as it came to be known. This textbook was a compilation of lectures she had given to students at Troy. To that time, botany had been taught in very few schools. However, within four years of publication of her textbook, 10,000 copies had been sold. In 1835, of the forty-two academies in upstate New York, ten were using Eaton's Manual of Botany and the rest were using Phelps's botany textbook. Her other texts included *Dictionary of Chemistry* (1830), *Botany for Beginners* (1833), *Chemistry for Beginners* (1834), and *Familiar Lectures on Natural Philosophy* (1837) [see **science education***].

The period between 1823 and 1830 was an intellectually charged time for these two sisters at Troy. Willard and Phelps, in tandem, developed a curriculum that combined each of their strengths. Willard's primary roles were chief administrator, historian, poet, politician, and visionary; Phelps was trusted assistant, scientist, novelist, artist, and counselor. Both were prolific authors who supported each other's work.

In 1830 when Willard toured England's schools, she left Phelps in charge of Troy. Phelps successfully proved her administrative skill. When Willard returned in 1831, her sister accepted the marriage proposal of John Phelps and moved to Vermont with him; together they had two children. Phelps continued to produce revisions of her textbooks, write new ones, and help organize members of the Guilford, Vermont, community around educational issues. In 1836 Phelps was asked to lead a female **seminary*** in West Chester, Pennsylvania, which she did with support from her husband. Unfortunately, this institution folded during the Panic of 1837, but Phelps was soon invited to run a school in Rahway, New Jersey, for a short term.

In 1839 Phelps accepted an invitation to lead Patapsco Female Institute in Maryland, and her work there proved to be one of her crowning achievements. She rebuilt the institution on the **Troy Plan**,* including its featured science curriculum, public examinations, and monitorial disciplinary system. Patapsco was soon hailed as the Troy Female Seminary of the South. Her husband served as Patapsco's business administrator until he died in 1849. Phelps then added his financial duties to her own.

In 1856, suffering extreme grief over the death of her oldest daughter in a railroad accident, Phelps retired from Patapsco. She was sixty-three years old, yet remained unusually active for the next twenty-eight years. Phelps spent her time addressing scientific and educational organizations, organizing church missionary work and female associations that raised money for female education, developing position papers and memorials regarding political issues that she submitted to Congress, and revising her textbooks. She also spent considerable time advising her son Charles Phelps, a Harvard Law School graduate who served as U.S. senator from Maryland. Phelps remained close to her sister throughout her life. Phelps died at ninety-one.

Bibliography: Emma Lydia Bolzau, *Almira Hart Lincoln Phelps: Her Life and Work* (1936); Anne Firor Scott, "Almira Lincoln Phelps: The Self-Made Woman in the Nineteenth Century," *Maryland Historical Magazine*, 75 (September 1980): 203–216; Helen Buss Mitchell, "Almira Hart Lincoln Phelps" (Ph.D. diss., University of Maryland, 1990); Thalia M. Mulvihill, "Community in Emma Hart Willard's Educational Thought, 1787–1870" (Ph.D. diss., Syracuse University, 1995).

Thalia M. Mulvihill

pioneer women teachers. Pioneer women living on the nineteenth-century western frontier faced the problem of educating their children. Before the arrival of teachers from the East or opportunities for training indigenous teachers, the only method available was home schooling, using whatever materials could be found. As the frontier became settled, **county superintendents*** qualified local women as teachers through examinations and tried to standardize the length of the school year. **Teacher institutes*** and the new western **normal schools*** gradually replaced informal methods of teacher preparation.

The first women pioneer teachers from the East were sponsored by formal organizations or female **seminaries.*** Between 1835 and 1839, the Ipswich (Massachusetts) Female Seminary trained and sponsored fifty-seven women to teach in Ohio and the Mississippi Valley. **Mount Holyoke*** and **Troy Female Seminaries*** sent their alumnae to teach in the West, often under the care of a minister. Nearly 300 Protestant women taught in missions in the Indian Territory between 1820 and 1860, and religious communities of Catholic women opened schools on the northern Great Plains, in the Mississippi Valley, and in Vancouver, Washington [see **Catholic education***]. As cross-continental transportation improved, such individual women as Olive Pickering, the mother of Jeanette Rankin (elected from Montana as the first woman in the U.S. House of Representatives), left New Hampshire to teach in Montana.

The organization that most consistently sent women teachers to the West before the Civil War was the **Board of National Popular Education,*** which operated between 1846 and 1857. Nearly 600 pioneer women teachers from

New England and New York State journeyed by train, lake, river, canal, stage-coach, and farm wagon to the Mississippi Valley under the board's auspices. A few crossed the Isthmus of Panama to become teachers in California and Oregon. Their six weeks' training in Hartford, Connecticut, was supervised by Nancy Swift, who also corresponded with the teachers from their western posts. Although the National Board teachers were propelled by their goal of bringing education and Protestant evangelical religion to the West, they were also looking for opportunities so lacking in the crowded East. Many said that they were "entirely dependent" upon "their own exertions" for their support; others explained that they were looking for "a wider sphere of influence" (Kaufman, p. 14). The National Board teachers were actually on journeys to new lives; two-thirds never returned to the East but became pioneer settlers.

The percentage of women to men teachers in the western public schools rapidly rose during the nineteenth century. As superintendents lengthened the school term and informal **teacher education*** was replaced by normal school courses and teacher institutes, opportunity costs increased enough to discourage men who saw **teaching*** as a supplementary or temporary position. Unlike the men, young women saw teaching as the only profession open to them, and they were willing to increase their investment in time and money to prepare for these positions. As a result, Iowa, where only 19 percent of the teachers in 1848 were women, had 65 percent women by 1865. By 1870, 56 percent of the teachers in the ten North Central states were women. Although one-room schools were common workplaces for rural women teachers, their success rate was high: Between 1870 and 1900, literacy in Kansas, Iowa, and Nebraska increased to 97 percent [see **female literacy***].

Daughters of the first pioneers took advantage of the new western normal schools. In Colorado, more than 90 percent of the 300 women who graduated from Colorado State Normal School in the decade after 1891 found teaching jobs. Western women teachers in developing communities could aspire to become county superintendents; the first woman elected to that post was Julia Addington in Iowa in 1869. Although nearly half of California's county superintendents were women in 1900, they served in the mountainous northern counties. California women educators continued to find positions as rural supervisors well into the first third of the twentieth century.

Journals, letters, and oral histories of pioneer women teachers open a window into their lives and teaching experiences and conditions. Frontier teacher Fanny Warner introduced blackboards and singing to her Wisconsin students in 1851. When she had a globe sent from her home state of Massachusetts, she found the students had thought the world was "round like a wheel rather than an orange" (Kaufman, p. 29). Warner married in the West and became a settler. The roof in Martha Rogers's one-room log school in Missouri leaked so much when it rained that students had to keep moving to different spots to stay dry.

Pioneer teachers proved that they could adapt to new conditions in the West. Cynthia Bishop, who had worked in the **Lowell mills*** to earn money for her education, taught in the first public schools in Lafayette, Indiana, in 1853. Not allowed to use the Bible in her school because the district hoped to attract Catholic children, she decided to teach the Golden Rule but not explain its source.

In rural America, pioneering conditions, often in the shape of the one-room school, continued well into the twentieth century, and women continued to accept the challenges of pioneer teaching. In 1905 Ethel Waxham, a native of Denver and a recent graduate of **Wellesley College*** in Massachusetts, journeyed to the Wyoming range near the Sweetwater River to teach seven students in a fourteen-by-sixteen-foot log school with a sod roof. As she read *Uncle Tom's Cabin* and *Kidnapped* with her students around the stove, she carried on what became a century of pioneer teaching. [See also **common schools**,* **district schools**.*]

Bibliography: Polly Welts Kaufman, *Women Teachers on the Frontier* (1984); Kathleen Underwood, "The Pace of Their Own Lives: Teacher Training and the Life Course of Western Women," *Pacific Historical Review*, 55 (1986): 513–530; Mary Hurlburt Cordier, *Schoolwomen of the Prairies and Plains: Personal Narratives from Iowa, Kansas, and Nebraska, 1860s to 1920s* (1992); Barbara Love and Frances Love Froidevaux, eds., *Lady's Choice: Ethel Waxham's Journals and Letters, 1905–1910* (1993); Kathleen Weiler, "Women and Rural School Reform: California, 1900–1940," *History of Education Quarterly*, 34 (1994): 26–47.

Polly Welts Kaufman

prescriptive literature. *Prescriptive literature* is the name given to a genre of books and periodicals that set standards for women's behavior and advised them on how to live up to those standards. Over the past two centuries, such literature has promulgated several versions of model female behavior. The cult of "**true womanhood**"* was first explored through advice manuals and periodicals of the early nineteenth century. These manuals set the standards for women's piety, purity, submission, and domesticity—hallmarks of the "true woman." They provided advice on how to dress, how to decorate the home, how to be a good wife and mother, and how to participate in limited community activities. These books promoted the sentimental and emotional aspects of women's nature and downplayed women's intellectual gifts.

True womanhood was only one ideal for women promoted by one set of books and periodicals. Evangelical Protestant women followed another ideal that required them to be "up and doing" as a response to their conversion and as an act of faithfulness. These women set forth an ideal of activity in the community, often in the Sunday school and mission societies, both domestic and foreign [see **Board of Foreign Missions***]. The image of the idle lady was the antithesis of what they believed they were called to do. This religious ideal was centered in the Midwest. Another model or ideal was that of "radical womanhood," centered in the Northeast. Radical women often spoke before mixed gatherings and wrote much of the literature, sometimes called *domestic novels*, published in the nineteenth century. They generally held very liberal religious views, tending toward Unitarianism and liberal Congregationalism.

Another round of prescriptive literature was aimed at unmarried young women. Ministers and doctors tended to write such literature, which urged women to be healthy, physically active, pursue an education so that they could support themselves if need be, and marry wisely. One name for this kind of young woman was the ''All-American Girl.''

Two of the largest issues surrounding these various manuals and periodicals are how much they reflected the actual lives of women and how rigidly these ideals were applied; the second issue is to what extent these ideals were promulgated by men for women and how strongly women participated in establishing and changing the models. The case has been made that true womanhood was a masculine ideal created for women but impossible for them to meet. Other scholars have stressed that ideals like evangelical womanhood were creations of women for women. Change in the ideals of evangelical womanhood and radical womanhood came with changing times, and the literature reflected those changes.

How well these books and articles reflected the lives of real women is a subject of debate. Domestic novels tended to deal with the consequences, always bad, of straying from an ideal. Women were looked upon to provide salvation for men, whose baser instincts and interaction with the world led them away from the truth and beauty embodied in the woman and the home she kept. Later in the nineteenth century, novels began to reflect the lives of women who lived on the frontier or worked as missionaries and showed strong, independent and capable women. Vestiges of the multiplicity of ideals for women's lives can be seen in the twentieth-century debates on feminism and how women actually live their lives and the ideals set forth by feminists, nonfeminists, and womanists. [See also **separate spheres.***]

Bibliography: Ronald Hogeland, ''The Female Appendage: Feminine Lifestyles in America 1820–1860,'' *Civil War History*, 17 (1971): 101–114; Barbara Welter, *Dimity Convictions: The American Woman in the Nineteenth Century* (1976); Ann Douglas, *The Feminization of American Culture* (1977); Ann M. Boylan ''Evangelical Womanhood in the Nineteenth Century: The Role of Women in the Sunday Schools,'' *Feminist Studies*, 4 (October 1978): 62–80; Frances B. Cogan, *All-American Girl: The Ideal of Real Womanhood in Mid-Nineteenth-Century America* (1989).

Mary Lee Talbot

Progressive Era. The Progressive Era refers to the years between 1890 and 1914 (although some women's historians extend it through the 1920s) when a widespread movement for reform affected almost every segment of American society. The 1890s marked the ascendance everywhere in the United States of urban industrial lifeways over traditional small communities and farms as the defining characteristic of American life. The nearly unbelievable expansion of industry reached every corner of America, carried by the railroads into the tiniest hamlets. The cities teemed with immigrants, factories employed millions of Americans in dangerous work, political machines in the large cities dispensed patronage, and vast fortunes were made by the tycoons and robber barons of the day. By 1900, many Americans were convinced that these profound social changes had created intolerable problems and that reformers needed to curb the worst of the excesses. That outlook, called "progressivism," led to a thorough restructuring of American society with the result that, between 1900 and 1930, public bureaucracies assumed responsibility for education, health, child welfare, and public morality.

Progressives were remarkably diverse and sought many different types of reforms. Progressives generally agreed that society could be improved and perfected by direct intervention in social and economic affairs, and most believed that such intervention could be most successfully accomplished by government. Beyond this general agreement, enthusiastic progressive reformers followed widely diverging approaches. Some attacked the business monopolies. "Muckrakers" exposed corrupt practices and abuses in business, government, and unions. Others investigated social problems, such as child labor, prostitution, and slum life. The "Social Gospel" movement attracted evangelical Protestants to the aid and reform of the urban poor. Many progressives devoted themselves to destroying the political machines that dominated city life. Progressives commonly used the image of "cleaning up" to describe their goals.

Women were intimately associated with progressive reform movements. Progressive reformers argued that women possessed the maternal skills needed to "clean up" and heal a corrupt society. Women seemed naturally suited to teach the young, care for the poor, and improve the health of women and children [see **social housekeeping***]. **Women's clubs**,* which had become a powerful force in American civic life, strongly supported progressive goals and especially sought reforms that would help children and women. Women's clubs, both black and white, campaigned for improved sanitation, child labor laws, compulsory schooling, and changed age of consent laws. They also waged a crusade for **temperance**,* believing that alcohol had caused more misery for American women and children than any other social problem.

Progressives looked to the nation's **common schools*** as an ideal vehicle for social reform. Public health issues were an important part of the progressive agenda, and the schools were used to carry out campaigns for better sanitation and nutrition. Women urged that health classes taught in the schools include teaching children the dangers of alcohol abuse. In the South, a regional campaign against hookworm was carried out in the schools. Progressives advocated school consolidation, saying that rural children could be better served by being transported in wagons to consolidated schools rather than to scattered local buildings. The new schools would better prepare children for their new roles in an urbanizing nation by breaking down rural isolation. Progressives campaigned for compulsory education laws, which nearly every state adopted by 1914. The increased enrollments in the common schools created a huge demand for teachers, and hundreds of thousands of young women found jobs in the nation's classrooms. This greatly changed the status of women in American society as well as the nature of the **teaching*** profession [see **feminization***].

Progressivism provided a rationale and a focus for the higher education of American women. The emergence of the college-educated woman during the Progressive Era led to the birth of a new ideal for woman, "educated motherhood," which transformed the public and private duties of women as well as the obligations of the state. Women college graduates attacked the problems that industrialization, urbanization, and immigration had created. The **settlement house movement*** was a concrete symbol of the belief that women's maternal skills, combined with college training, could school the young, train and acculturate the immigrant, and improve the health of women and children.

College women led a revived movement for woman's **suffrage**,* which became one of the greatest achievements of the Progressive Era. Suffragists asserted that the state needed women to participate as voters, because women could best contend with such problems as hunger, poor sanitation, and education. Suffragists and college women argued that female morality could clean up public corruption and that women needed the vote in order to protect the special interests of women and families. Suffragists, joined by child welfare reformers, clubwomen, and working girls, formed a powerful Progressive Era coalition that fought for greater protection for women and children. Male progressives believed women's suffrage would curb male competition and corruption and force the state to assume responsibility for public welfare.

The coalition of women reformers of the Progressive Era made truly remarkable achievements. Women in **labor unions**,* settlement houses, and clubs entered the public arena as the strict separation of sexes into **separate spheres*** crumbled. They fought for and won new laws for pure food, protective legislation regulating wages and hours for working women and children, compulsory schooling laws, public health departments, prison and court reforms (especially in the South where women campaigned against lynching), and statutory laws to protect minor girls. Strangely, the ratification of the Nineteenth Amendment (1920), the greatest triumph of American women during the Progressive Era, also ended the solidarity among diverse groups of women that was responsible for so many other remarkable achievements.

Bibliography: Sheila Rothman, *Woman's Proper Place: A History of Changing Ideals and Practices, 1870 to the Present* (1978); Rosalind Rosenberg, *Beyond Separate Spheres: Intellectual Roots of Modern Feminism* (1982); Sara M. Evans, *Born for Liberty: A History of Women in America* (1989, revised 1997); Ellen Fitzpatrick, *Endless Crusade: Women Social Scientists and Progressive Reform* (1990); Morton Keller, *Regulating a New Society: Public Policy and Social Change in America, 1900–1933* (1994).

Sharon Clifford

Q

Quakers. George Fox founded the Quaker religion, also known as the Society of Friends, in England in 1652. Over time in the United States, the Quakers became known for their support of equal education for people of both genders and all races and creeds. Quaker schools educated women, African Americans, and Native Americans, sometimes in separate settings but often via **coeducation**.* Quaker women also were noteworthy for their strong public involvement in various causes. Social consciousness, radical egalitarianism, and equal educational opportunities were the direct results of the Quaker idea that God lives in all people.

Troubled by the dichotomy between what he heard in church and the way most clergy and laypeople lived their daily lives, the Englishman Fox struggled for his own definition of religion and spirituality. The basic tenets on which Fox built the sect included the beliefs that there was ''that of God in every person,'' that religion and spirituality were the result of personal experiences and beliefs, that God lived in the hearts of the common people, and that education was not necessary to minister the word of God. The ''inner light'' was the tool through which women and men knew God, not through sacraments, education, or a weekly sermon. Quaker tenets were a radical departure from the Puritanism under which Fox and others lived in seventeenth-century England.

Quaker worship services are known as ''meetings,'' where individuals gather silently to reflect on the spirit and nature of God within. If a member feels moved by the spirit of God to speak, he or she will address the congregation. No sermons are delivered by trained ministers. While men and women worshipped separately throughout the seventeenth and eighteenth centuries, both were expected to participate fully in the business of the meeting. Larger regional quarterly and yearly meetings gather to discuss social concerns, but local meetings have the responsibility of determining and responding to the educational needs of their community.

For centuries in England and later in the colonies, education generally was considered necessary for people to read scriptures and understand the ways of God. However, education for this purpose was unnecessary for Quakers since individuals had a direct relationship with God. Fox, then, advocated schools that focused on moral education and encouraged the development of thought in each student. He believed that education should be practical and useful, enabling both men and women to earn a living. Quakers were slow to become involved in higher education because of their emphasis on practical learning. They opened Haverford College in Pennsylvania in 1833 when it became obvious that the Quakers were losing their best students to colleges of other denominations.

Quaker-run schools were meant to provide students with a religious education, as well as one that was practical and useful to the student and society. Quakers believed that children learned through experience and were capable of interpreting the world in their own fashion. By providing what they termed a "guarded religious education," Quaker educators could construct an environment suitable for students' greater personal religious and spiritual understanding. Because Quakers educated their own children, some Society members feared that these guarded religious schools were too limiting, keeping students from truly experiencing the world and coming to their own conclusions about how to live. However, both Quaker and non-Quaker children were educated at these schools, illustrating the fact that restrictive beliefs were not imposed on students. While children were expected to attend a worship service weekly, the point of the Quaker school was not to indoctrinate.

Throughout the nineteenth century, attendance at some schools was initially very low, and it was often difficult to pay teachers enough to stay for more than one year. Students whose parents had the means were charged a modest fee to attend, while children of poor families attended free. Local meetings intended their schools to be self-sufficient, but eventually it became obvious that schools would need financial support of local meetings to succeed. By the close of the nineteenth century, schools were supported by the meetings' funds, and teacher salaries and student attendance increased and stabilized.

In 1826 Margaret Hallowell opened a school for girls as part of the Alexandria Boarding School in Virginia that was run by her husband Benjamin. Girls and boys were educated in the same classroom, with the same curriculum. The extensive program included reading, writing, and mathematics, as well as chemistry and the science of mechanics. Students were kept on rigorous daily schedules that included time for study, physical exercise, and worship. Attendance at Quaker meeting was not required so long as students worshipped somewhere.

Quaker women played an unusual role in society during the eighteenth and nineteenth centuries. At a time when many women were confined to their homes with little meaningful community contact [see **separate spheres***], Quaker women were working to improve the lives of African Americans and Native Americans, the urban poor, and other women. In 1796, Anne Parrish and others established the "Society for the Free Instruction of Female Children," which opened the Aimwell School in Philadelphia in 1807. The school taught poor girls to read and write and to become skilled in math and sewing so they could become self-sufficient. Other notable Quaker women included Lucretia Mott and Elizabeth Cady Stanton, both of whom were active in the women's **suffrage*** movement and fought for equal rights for slaves.

Led by the belief that God lives in all people, Quakers pursued efforts to educate racial and ethnic minorities and, as much as they could, to limit social inequality. Quakers were vehemently opposed to **slavery*** and the oppression of Native Americans and did not permit Society members to own slaves. They were also concerned that few women received an education beyond the elementary grades. Quaker Anthony Benezet opened the African School in Philadelphia in 1770 to a class of twenty-two boys and girls. Children studied reading, writing, and arithmetic to "qualify them for a proper enjoyment of freedom." Benezet also opened the Girls' School in 1754, which became famous for its "literary and moral training." The Female Manual Labor School was opened in Baltimore in 1846 to educate Native American women in domestic skills, while the men were taught agriculture and trade elsewhere.

In the 1990s, Quakers continue to make valuable social and educational contributions. The fifty-six Quaker schools in the United States are all coeducational; 10 to 30 percent of students are of minority status. The emphasis on personal growth and social consciousness is still evident in Quaker schools, and while required weekly attendance at meeting is still common, Quakers educate students to find their "inner light" without a heavy emphasis on religious beliefs.

Bibliography: Thomas Woody, *The History of Women's Education in the United States*, Vol. 1 (1929); William C. Dunlap, *Quaker Education* (1936); Harold Loukes, *Friends and Their Children: A Study in Quaker Education* (1958, 1979); Margaret H. Bacon, *The Quiet Rebels: The Story of the Quakers in America* (1969); Hugh Barbour and J. William Frost, *The Quakers* (1988).

Jennifer J. White

quotas. Quotas were used as a mechanism by American colleges and universities at various times to limit and control the student population by gender, race, or ethnicity. During the last half of the nineteenth century, women had struggled to prove that they were equal both intellectually and physically to the demands and challenges of higher education. In fact, women were quite successful on the coeducational [see **coeducation***] campuses of the **Progressive Era.*** The numbers of female students rose steadily during that time, until by 1920 they constituted 47.3% of American undergraduates. Ninety percent of these students attended coeducational schools. Educators, fearing that women were overrunning America's campuses, tried to curb the numbers of female students. A common response to the possibilities of women's enrollment and their subsequent dominating of liberal arts courses and feminizing higher education was to assign quotas limiting their entrance or to impose higher entrance requirements for women. Between 1902 and 1915, Wesleyan College banned women students, while the City College of New York, Stanford, Cornell, Michigan, and Pennsylvania State Universities adopted quotas for women's admission.

At Penn State, for example, the ratio of women to men undergraduates was set at one female for every two and a half males. At Stanford, in 1904, the alumni set the ratio of women and men at three males to each female student. In 1901, 102 women and 98 men graduated, with women receiving a higher number of awards and honors than men. Worried leaders sought to protect the university from **feminization*** through limiting the numbers of women. Jane Stanford, who controlled institutional policy after her husband's death, ignored the university statute that required "equal advantages in the University to both sexes" and set 500 as the maximum number of women to be enrolled at any one time. This quota was not overturned until 1933.

At Cornell, quotas took the form of dormitory residence. A policy requiring residence for women began in 1884. Yet Sage College, the women's division, could accommodate only 120 women. The policy requiring dormitory residence originated in the economic need to fill Sage rooms but remained in effect long after Sage was filled to capacity. Intended as a device to assure parents that Cornell was safe for their daughters, this policy established an absolute limit on the numbers of women. As the numbers competing for admission continually increased, limits on enrollment were necessary and quotas for both sexes were established. Yet quotas for male applicants were determined by the availability of classroom space, while for women, quotas equaled the number of dormitory spaces plus approved rooms in the town of Ithaca. The phrase "female beds" was used by both administrators and students to describe the determinant of women's admission. Cornell's decision to regulate the lives of female students by insisting on university-approved housing severely limited the numbers of women admitted, caused the rejection of more women than men regardless of ability, and subjected women to more selective admission criteria than were applied to men. Quotas as allotted to each division of the university also became a mechanism for channeling women into fields of study considered appropriate for their sex by a conservative society and university administration.

Quotas were also used either openly or subtly to limit the number of racial and ethnic minorities on campuses. Throughout the 1920s, college enrollments grew steadily. Pembroke College at Brown University, like many others, had a new opportunity to exercise control over who was admitted. Previous admission criteria had been rather relaxed, and most students with diplomas from accredited preparatory or **high schools*** and letters from an official attesting to their upright character were admitted. In the 1920s, Pembroke's admissions office began requiring applicants to fill out formal applications and attend on-campus interviews. Admissions officers took notes on the physical attributes and ethnic backgrounds of prospective students. Remarks like "looks too Italian" or "has obvious Jewish features'' appeared in interviewers' assessments of candidates who were nonetheless admitted. It is therefore difficult to ascertain how stringently these criteria were applied or how often they were used to eliminate candidates. In 1936, admissions forms were changed and asked specifically for the candidate's race, religious affiliation, and nationality. Dormitories, in which there was a perpetual shortage of space until the 1960s, were reserved for white Christian women. An official quota limited the number of Jewish women allowed to reside on campus, although local Jewish "city girls" were accepted without restriction. African American women were also admitted in small numbers. The minutes of the Pembroke Advisory Committee refer to an unofficial policy of accepting no more than one black woman a year as late as 1960. Other institutions used formal and informal quotas in similar ways.

Until the era of **affirmative action*** offered different approaches to student populations, quotas served as a device to restrict the numbers of women, racial, and ethnic minorities in higher education and to direct women into particular curricula and courses that were deemed fit for them.

Bibliography: Charlotte Williams Conable, *Women at Cornell: The Myth of Equal Education* (1977); Harold D. Wechsler, ''An Academic Gresham's Law: Group Repulsion as a Theme in American Higher Education,'' *Teachers College Record*, 82 (1981): 567–588; Barbara Miller Solomon, *In the Company of Educated Women: A History of Women and Higher Education in America* (1985); John Mack Faragher and Florence Howe, eds., *Women and Higher Education in American History* (1988); Lynn D. Gordon, *Gender and Higher Education in the Progressive Era* (1990); Polly Welts Kaufman, *The Search for Equity: Women at Brown University 1891–1991* (1991).

Rajeswari Swaminathan

R

race suicide. *Race suicide* is a term coined early in the twentieth century to express a fear that white, college-educated women were dooming America to its growing population of immigrants by their propensity to eschew marriage and motherhood after college. The term connotes the rise of nativism during the swell of Eastern European immigration between the 1890s and 1920s. It was used as both a reprimand and a scare tactic to encourage white women to think beyond their individualistic needs.

Demographically, educated women consistently had married less and produced fewer children than other American women. The difference was most notable among the earliest generations of college- and **seminary***-trained women. A large study of collegiate graduates in 1915 showed that only 39 percent of those women married; another study at the University of Wisconsin showed only 41 percent married. For the national population of women, the figure stood at over 90 percent marrying at some time in their lives.

Although authors had found that college men also tended to remain single (approximately 24 percent of Yale and Harvard men between 1870 and 1890, for example), the concern was directed at women because of the assumption that women's role should naturally include marriage and motherhood, and because of long-standing ambivalence about women's intended purposes for collegiate training. The particular concern over race suicide abated with the closing of immigration in the 1920s, as well as the increase in college women's interest in marriage and dating during that same decade.

Bibliography: Charles Franklin Emerick, "College Women and Race Suicide," *Political Science Quarterly*, 24 (June 1909): 269–283; Association of Collegiate Alumnae, *A Preliminary Statistical Study of Certain Women College Graduates* (1917); Mary E. Cookingham, "Combining Marriage, Motherhood, and Jobs before World War II: Women College Graduates, 1905–1935," *Journal of Family History*, 9 (Summer 1984): 178–195; Barbara Miller Solomon, *In the Company of Educated Women: A History of Women* *and Higher Education in America* (1985); Patricia Ann Palmieri, *In Adamless Eden: The Community of Women Faculty at Wellesley* (1995).

Linda Eisenmann

race uplift. Although practiced by both African Americans and whites during the late nineteenth and early twentieth centuries, notably in **Progressive Era*** reforms and movements, race uplift as a specific strategy was best articulated by black reformers. From Reconstruction into the 1870s, African American leaders like Alexander Crummell espoused self-help, racial solidarity and pride, and the need for social and economic development. Crummell, while recommending that a black elite guide the masses by teaching them about morals and civilization, proclaimed black women's vital role in this transformation. From the beginning, then, proper morals, education, racial solidarity, and self-help—the key aspects of racial uplift—dominated black discussions about race.

During the 1890s, black leaders borrowed from dominant strands in the ideal and differed on how best to uplift their race. For some historians, two educators, Booker T. Washington and W.E.B. Du Bois, represent a split between blacks regarding racial uplift. Washington, an ex-slave and graduate of **Hampton Institute,*** contended that uplift prioritized the duties of black citizens to educate themselves, follow evangelical Protestant morals, build their economic base, and work as a community to improve their lot. Du Bois, a leading intellectual throughout the twentieth century, advocated the political rights of blacks to **suffrage*** and equality as the means to empower them to improve their social and economic position. To Du Bois, neglecting political rights was tantamount to acquiescence to African Americans' subordinate position.

While Washington and Du Bois clashed in speeches and writings, many African American reformers drew from both positions concerning racial uplift. Southern black female educators like **Lucy Craft Laney,*** **Charlotte Hawkins Brown,*** and **Mary McLeod Bethune*** used industrial training in their classrooms and promoted evangelical Protestant values of sobriety, thrift, hard work, and church attendance. At the same time, they stressed an academic curriculum that included foreign languages, upper-level math courses, black history and literature, and the sciences. They urged students to obtain wage-labor positions and avoid the dependencies of sharecropping and domestic service. While they tended to eschew discussions of political rights, they nonetheless instilled dignity and pride in their students.

Other black women joined organizations such as the Women's Convention of the National Baptist Convention and the **National Association of Colored Women.*** These groups borrowed from the language of racial uplift as they contributed funds to Baptist schools, built community playgrounds, opened **settlement houses*** for women and children, and operated libraries and public health clinics. All of these activities advanced their goal of racial uplift, notably in areas of race solidarity, education, self-help, and racial pride.

By 1910, Washington's aversion to political rights became less palatable to some of his supporters. Even ardent advocates like **Mary Church Terrell*** believed that his public submission to white supremacy and his command over white northern philanthropy like the Julius **Rosenwald Fund*** had become excessive. By the 1940s, the emphasis on political rights and equality prevailed over constructions of duties. Yet at its best, racial uplift instilled pride and dignity in countless blacks during a violent and dismal period in American race relations. Across the South, African Americans claimed their right to an education as they improved their communities, expanded their churches, and assisted those in need. The contributions of black female educators and reform organizations, as Crummell had predicted, demonstrated what their race could accomplish when they combined their efforts and created vital social and economic institutions.

Bibliography: Evelyn Brooks Higginbotham, *Righteous Discontent: The Women's Movement in the Black Baptist Church, 1880–1920* (1993); David Levering Lewis, *W. E. B. Du Bois: Biography of a Race, 1868–1919* (1993); Stephanie J. Shaw, *What a Woman Ought to Be and to Do: Black Professional Women Workers during the Jim Crow Era* (1996).

Ann Short Chirhart

Radcliffe College. Radcliffe College was an early and significant provider of undergraduate and **graduate education*** for women in the United States, both in its role as a separate institution and as a coordinate collegiate partner for women's education at Harvard University. Created in 1879 as the "Harvard Annex" to allow women access to the faculty and resources of Harvard, Radcliffe was a pioneer in the **coordinate college*** relationship unique to some men's and women's universities. Chartered officially as a college in 1894, Radcliffe—one of the prestigious **Seven Sisters*** **women's colleges***—granted its own degrees, which were countersigned by Harvard officials in a compromise relationship to avoid complete **coeducation*** at the nation's oldest university for men. By 1977, Radcliffe and Harvard had renegotiated their relationship to allow women receipt of the Harvard degree (1963), coresidence (1971), and joint admission to both institutions (1975). Radcliffe remains a separately incorporated institution with a mission "to advance society by advancing women" and sustains several prominent libraries and **women's centers*** for research.

Some collegiate opportunities for women existed in the late 1870s when a group of prominent Bostonians began pressuring Harvard College to open its doors to female students. Nationally, coeducational schools like **Oberlin College*** existed; some universities, especially the new state institutions, had accepted coeducation; and women's colleges were beginning to appear with the opening of the first three Seven Sister institutions (**Vassar College**,* 1865; **Wellesley*** and **Smith Colleges**,* 1875). Locally, Boston University had opened as a coeducational institution in 1873. Yet citizens of Boston and Cambridge who valued their connections with Harvard wanted that prestigious opportunity offered to their daughters, nieces, and sisters.

Two influential residents, Arthur and Stella Gilman, a retired banker and teacher, respectively, approached Harvard President Charles William Eliot in 1878 with a plan to allow female students to study informally with Harvard faculty, prepare for the same examinations taken by the men, and receive certificates for their performance. This modest request, a concession to the firm opposition to coeducation that existed on the Cambridge campus, created an option for women students both to receive the benefits of Harvard teaching and to affirm women's intellectual equality. Finding that at least forty-one faculty members were, indeed, interested in supplementing their incomes while offering separate courses to well-prepared female students, Eliot accepted the arrangement.

From 1879 to 1893, women students pursued this informal approach to collegiate training in what was familiarly but never officially called the "Harvard Annex." The teaching consisted of private instruction; students boarded in local homes. Many students took only a few classes, while some pursued an entire collegiate course. The enterprise, although significant, was not obtrusive, in keeping with the mere tolerance that Harvard extended. As historian Helen Horowitz notes, "Annex founders had no wish to offer students anything beyond the intellectual element of college experience" (p. 102). Thus, no dormitory or formal administration developed to imitate collegiate status. By 1883, however, the managers of the Annex made their first move to solidify their undertaking by purchasing a large, stately home known as Fay House to replace the rented quarters used by students. Now, a single building provided library, classroom, and study space, although still no dormitory facilities.

In 1882, the Annex was incorporated as the Society for the Collegiate Instruction of Women; like advocacy groups in other cities, the Society advanced its cause through fund-raising and focused public relations. By 1893, the Society, led by Elizabeth Cary Agassiz (widow of prominent Harvard professor Louis Agassiz) negotiated an arrangement with Harvard that created Radcliffe College as a separate, though related, institution. The President and Fellows of Harvard College served as visitors to Radcliffe, and the Academic Board, composed largely of Harvard professors, was responsible for hiring and approving faculty arrangements. Most important, Radcliffe could now grant degrees instead of mere certificates; Harvard would countersign the diplomas. Although some supporters disapproved of the arrangement as keeping Radcliffe too separate, the decision formalized the relationship and began Radcliffe's role as a separate yet "coordinate" collegiate partner with its own president and board of trustees.

Over the decades, Radcliffe differed from other coordinate colleges in certain ways. Like the Women's College at Brown University, Radcliffe never sustained its own faculty. **Barnard College**,* in its affiliation with Columbia University, did build a faculty of women and men committed to the education of female students. Brown, however, did not grant its own degrees, while Radcliffe maintained that authority. Like all such colleges, however, and like female administrators on coeducational campuses, Radcliffe officials took responsibility for advocating for women's share of intellectual, fiscal, and physical resources. Dependent on Harvard for faculty, Radcliffe nonetheless exercised authority over women's curriculum, housing, and campus life. Throughout its history, the college fought to keep women's issues prominent among Harvard's concerns.

After granting its first Ph.D. in 1902, Radcliffe developed a strong Graduate School that became one of the most important providers of graduate education for women in the United States. By 1954, when a major study of its graduate degree holders was conducted, Radcliffe had granted more than 500 Ph.D.s, with particular strengths in English, biology, economics, and history. Only Columbia and the **University of Chicago*** rivaled Radcliffe's production of women doctorates. The Radcliffe Graduate School closed in 1963 when women were finally admitted to Harvard's Graduate School of Arts and Sciences and first received the Harvard Ph.D.

Changing reactions to coeducation and to women's issues in general prompted the biggest shift in the Radcliffe/Harvard relationship in 1971. Sometimes referred to as a "nonmerger merger," Radcliffe ceded to Harvard responsibility for student admissions, housing, and curriculum, although Radcliffe continued to focus special attention on women students' interests. Since the 1970s, Radcliffe and Harvard have pursued a joint effort in supporting women undergraduates at the university and sustaining its research and educational efforts. In the 1990s, Radcliffe's Graduate Studies Center sustains a prominent publishing course and unique Graduate Consortium in Women's Studies with other local universities. Its Institutes for Advanced Studies include four nationally recognized institutions: the Mary Ingraham Bunting Institute for advanced study by women scholars and artists, the Schlesinger Library on the History of Women in America, the Murray Research Center for social science data, and the Radcliffe Public Policy Institute. In supporting these separate institutions, as well as the overall resources of Harvard University, Radcliffe plays a continuing significant role in enhancing women's educational options.

Bibliography: Radcliffe College, Committee on Graduate Education for Women, *Graduate Education for Women: The Radcliffe Ph.D.* (1956); Dorothy Elia Howells, *A Century to Celebrate: Radcliffe College, 1879–1979* (1978); Helen Lefkowitz Horowitz, *Alma Mater: Design and Experience in the Women's Colleges from Their Nineteenth-Century Beginnings to the 1930s* (1984); Werner Sollors, Caldwell Titcomb, and Thomas A. Underwood, eds., *Blacks at Harvard: A Documentary History of African-American Experience at Harvard and Radcliffe* (1992); Linda Eisenmann, "Befuddling the 'Feminine Mystique': Academic Women and the Creation of the Radcliffe Institute, 1950–1965," *Educational Foundations*, 10, no. 3 (Summer 1996): 5–26.

Linda Eisenmann

reading circles. Reading circles became a popular method of in-service instruction for teachers, most of whom were women, during the late nineteenth and early twentieth centuries. Reading circles were particularly encouraged for inexperienced and poorly trained rural teachers. State and local circles created lists of books from which teachers could choose, based on lists compiled by professional educators, university instructors, state superintendents, or other committees of "expert" educators. Teachers were usually encouraged to meet together to discuss the readings and, when finished, would demonstrate their achievements through an established criterion and receive a certificate or some other recognition.

While the reading circle idea was promoted for improvement of all teachers in all types of schools, its primary focus was the education of rural schoolteachers, predominantly young women with meager training. The *Journal of Education* clarified this emphasis in an 1890 article, stating, "No one would claim that a course of reading, though conducted as carefully as possible, would be equal to a course of study in a **normal school**,* but it would constitute a great advance over the preparation which the common **district school*** now gives to its pupils" (Williams, p. 118).

In 1887, the national commissioner of education estimated that twenty states had organized reading circles. By 1908, the number had risen to thirty-five, with memberships ranging from forty teachers in South Carolina to one hundred in Kansas. In 1925, the U.S. Bureau of Education reported that 50 percent of the nation's teachers had access to "professional improvement" through state and local reading circles. A number of states made such work compulsory for teacher certification.

Reading circle organization varied from state to state and was implemented under the auspices of state boards, state teacher associations, university extension departments, and library commissions and, in some states, directly through state departments of public instruction. States with established reading circles usually chose books of a professional nature for their reading lists in areas such as school administration, psychology, government, and **teaching**.*

In 1914, a National Rural Teachers' Reading Circle was organized at a meeting of the National Education Association. The national plan targeted teachers with a serious interest in professional improvement and self-education. National Reading Circle work was promoted as a kind of "graduate course" for teachers who had advanced beyond state and locally initiated programs. The work, however, was coordinated with state departments of education, and though no teacher was refused entry, it was preferred that participants have an extensive literary background. Established as a two-year course, the National Reading Circle directed participants to complete a total of seventeen books from its recommended reading list, which included Goethe's *Faust*, Homer's *Iliad*, dramas by Shakespeare, professional material by Pestalozzi, Rousseau, Froebel, Dewey, and some works from the most current experts on rural education like Cubberley, Eggleston, and Carney. Upon completing the course, teachers received a National Rural Teachers' Reading Circle Certificate to be signed by the commissioner of education and their state superintendent. [See also **continuing education**,* **teacher education**.*]

Bibliography: D. Lathrop Williams, "The Teachers' Reading Circle in Education," *Journal of Education*, 32 (1890); Department of the Interior, Bureau of Education, *The National Rural Teachers' Reading Circle* (1915); Ellwood Cubberley, *Public School*

Administration (1929); Kate Wofford, *An History of the Status and Training of Elementary Rural Teachers of the United States, 1860–1930* (1935); Dina L. Stephens, ''The Role of County Superintendents in Rural School Reform in Late Nineteenth and Early Twentieth Century Wisconsin'' (Ph.D. diss., University of Wisconsin, 1996).

Dina L. Stephens

reentry programs. Beginning in the 1960s, colleges, universities, vocational schools, and the workplace saw an increase in the numbers of women returning to these areas after years out of the mainstream. These ''reentry women,'' often with families and significant adult responsibilities, were bent on improving their conditions in life and were entering the academic and business worlds for a variety of reasons. As **continuing education*** students, they presented needs previously unencountered by their male counterparts or by younger women with whom they might compete in the classroom or for jobs, thus challenging institutions to create new or more flexible delivery systems and student services. Traditional four-year colleges, as well as community colleges and learning centers, stretched their facilities to meet the needs of this new population. The significance of reentry programs is allowing women in various situations with a variety of needs to have access to educations and careers that previously were difficult to attain with families and other outside responsibilities.

Reentry programs, designed to help women whose skills were out of practice or out of date, were flexibly developed to help women succeed. Where programs originally were designed for the woman encountering an ''empty nest'' with time to pursue an avocation, institutions later had to meet needs of women returning to school to prepare for employment, to become financially self-supporting, to increase their chances of being hired or promoted, and perhaps to raise their self-esteem. Colleges and workplaces soon found that in order to help these women successfully compete, they needed to identify these multiple reasons for women returning to school. They also found that most reentry women needed assistance in some form, whether financial, counseling, self-esteem, or child care. Whether in the workplace or the classroom, the needs of reentry women often centered around child care, including maternity and parental leave benefits and flexible hours. Many women benefited and continue to benefit by the inroads made by their predecessors and those sensitive to their needs.

Bibliography: Helen S. Astin, *Some Action of Her Own: The Adult Woman and Higher Education* (1976); L. H. Lewis, ed., *Addressing the Needs of Returning Women* (1988); K. Circsena and F. Hereth, *Continuing Education: Reentry and the Mature Woman (Annotated Selected References and Resources)* (n.d.).

Susan Clark Studer

''Republican motherhood.'' *Republican motherhood* is a term historians use to describe a post–American Revolution philosophy that called for women to utilize their natural, domestic abilities in meeting the need for civic virtue in the new Republic. Because the revolution incorporated concerns about definitions of citizenship and public life, as well as the individual's relation to the state, the postwar period left many questions about the contributions new citizens would make. For women, a tradition of complete separation from politics complicated these questions and left them to create their own place in the Republic [see **separate spheres***].

Individuals such as **Abigail Adams,*** **Judith Sargent Murray,*** Mercy Otis Warren, and Benjamin Rush, who had reflected on the place of free white women in society, influenced many women to see the postrevolutionary period as a time when they should infuse their domestic domain with political significance. The home could operate as an intersection for private and public concerns, serving as the centerpiece of training and education for future citizens. Women, with their newly discovered political awareness, could contribute directly to the state through their maternal roles. As Republican mothers, they could use their domestic behavior to influence and promote civic interest and participation in their family members, especially their sons and husbands, who would presumably then be better prepared to be virtuous citizens.

Between 1776 and 1820, middle-class white women took the lead in practicing and proliferating Republican motherhood. They educated their children in the ways of good citizenship, looked to earlier female models of confidence and self-reliance, and sought to keep themselves politically aware. Self-improvement and benevolence were emphasized as essential elements in their work of shaping virtue in future citizens. The family received their full energies and attention, as they channeled traditional female traits and interests into a larger political goal.

Political activism via motherhood was in many ways a new, and even revolutionary, idea. It suggested that a complete separation between the female domestic world and the male political world was no longer workable and recognized that an individual's politicization began at an early age, when family was a major influence. It emphasized the need for better-educated women as well as stronger political ties between women and the Republic. Conversely, the conservative nature of this philosophy reinforced a limited view of how far women's political involvement should go, always drawing the boundaries at home's edge. Women's political participation was to be channeled through others, and their citizenship was to be of a nature that did not incorporate complete constituency. The true Republican mother recognized this role as both significant and sufficient.

Nevertheless, the ideology had a far-reaching impact on women's education. In their roles as developers of civic virtue, women recognized the need for improving their own training and learning. While advocates never tried to suggest that women should develop their intellectual abilities above all else, they did emphasize the need for women to use education to become better wives and mothers. Women needed, in the words of Benjamin Rush in his 1787 piece on female education, "a peculiar and suitable education, to concur in instructing their sons in the principles of liberty and government." While clearly indicating that women should be educated in a different manner and with a different goal from men, those advocates were responsible for initial calls for better education for women, which would ultimately result in creation of female **academies,*** **seminaries,*** and, later **women's colleges.***

The ideology behind Republican motherhood provided an important definition for white women citizens in the critical years following the American Revolution when new concepts of Republicanism and citizenship were being tested and developed. Women, who knew firsthand the costs, sacrifices, and disruption inherent in the war years, were not satisfied to accept complete isolation from what subsequently unfolded in the country. Thus, they crafted a way for their political contributions to be accepted and for the state to benefit from their unique role that connected domestic endeavors, politics, and citizenship.

Bibliography: Linda K. Kerber, *Women of the Republic: Intellect and Ideology in Revolutionary America* (1980); Mary Beth Norton, *Liberty's Daughters: The Revolutionary Experience of American Women, 1750–1800* (1980); Sara M. Evans, *Born for Liberty: A History of Women in America* (1989); Kerber, "The Republican Mother," in Kerber and Jane Sherron De Hart, *Women's America: Refocusing the Past*, 4th ed. (1995).

Debbie Cottrell

Rockford Female Seminary. Rockford Female Seminary (later, College) in Rockford, Illinois, was founded in 1847 by the same Presbyterian and Congregational leaders who opened the all-male Beloit College in Wisconsin one year earlier. Like many men's schools, Beloit was modeled after Yale College; the women's **seminary*** emulated **Mount Holyoke Female Seminary.*** The hope of the joint trustees was to spread the intellectual and religious heritage of Puritan New England throughout the frontier. They entrusted this challenge to the first principal, Anna Peck Sill.

Sill, youngest of ten children, was born in Burlington, New York, and raised a Congregationalist. Prior to her appointment as seminary head, Sill participated in the religious revivals of the **Second Great Awakening*** that swept New York in 1831, undergoing a long-awaited conversion experience. She entered Phipps Union Seminary in Albion, New York, in 1837 and continued there as a teacher until 1843. She left to open her own seminary in Warsaw, New York, from which she moved to head Cary Collegiate Institute in Oakfield. Despite having decided that her service to God would be in education, a lingering missionary impulse led her to choose a more "destitute field." If not as a missionary, then, she would establish a school in the "wild Northwest." The call came when she was asked to open the private female seminary in Rockford.

Sill took her models for female education from **Mary Lyon*** and her Mount Holyoke experiment in Massachusetts, from the eastern men's college curriculum offered at Beloit, and from her own intention to reach the poorer classes of women and train them to be missionaries and teachers. To accomplish this ideal, the women of Rockford would combine religious, domestic, and industrial training with classical study.

Consistent with the goals of the trustees, Sill's guiding principles were both religious and intellectual. Moral and religious culture dominated the school, preparing women for Christian service. Rockford students attended daily religious services and Bible classes and read the standard textbooks used at Harvard, Yale, and Beloit: Butler's *Analogy of Natural and Revealed Religion*, Alexander's *Evidences of Christianity*, and Wayland's *Moral Philosophy*. In addition to religious instruction, the Rockford "sems" (as students were called) in the collegiate course studied Latin, mathematics (including algebra and geometry), sciences (including physics, chemistry, botany, geology, and physiology), rhetoric and logic, modern literature, and social sciences. Compared to Beloit, however, Rockford was poorly funded, and the women were expected to clean, peel potatoes, and practice other domestic skills that would provide institutional economies, while at the same time prepare them to serve their families.

For thirty years, Sill dominated students' lives, creating at Rockford a reputation for high educational standards and devoted Christian service. Students were subjected to intense pressure to experience conversion, which could be both humiliating and difficult for those who resisted, as it was for Rockford's best-known graduate, **Jane Addams**.*

Rockford's student population during Sill's tenure was predominantly regional, with young women coming from Illinois, Wisconsin, and Iowa, most traveling no more than one hundred miles from home, and from a mix of social classes. Sill's dedication to reaching poorer women and forging them into an army of missionaries established the early social milieu. Most students initially entered the preparatory department, and the seminary offered financial support to those who could not afford it. Sill, however, did not share the trustees' view of women as "vines wrapped around oaks" but rather saw women as oaks themselves. She urged her graduates to become missionaries, not missionary wives. Throughout the 1870s and 1880s, numerous graduates traveled alone to distant fields of service, established churches, built schools and orphanages, taught religious classes, and performed many duties that were allowed only to men in most American churches. As early as 1865, Sill boasted of a legion of Rockford women bringing Christianity to a dozen foreign countries. Annie Howe, for example, went to Japan with the Congregationalist mission, opening a **kindergarten*** and kindergarten training school there in 1887. Loretta Van Hook went to Persia with the Presbyterian Board in 1875, where she established a girls' school modeled after Rockford. Beyond their evangelical work, many of Rockford's missionaries spread the Mount Holyoke legacy, building long-lasting women's educational institutions in their adopted countries [see **Board of Foreign Missions***].

In 1872, frustrated by low teacher salaries and neglect by the trustees, Sill turned to alumnae to overcome the seminary's poor funding. She appealed to graduates to create an endowment that would bypass dependency on the board, which favored Beloit financially. Alumnae were able to raise a substantial endowment, more than Sill had set as her goal.

In 1880, the annual catalog announced extension of the program to four years and the granting of full college degrees; the institution became Rockford College. Students were awarded the Bachelor of Arts for the first time in 1882. With the exception of instruction in Greek, the Rockford collegiate curriculum was equivalent to Beloit's. It was not until Sill's retirement in 1884, however, that the emphasis on Christian service abated. New leaders, changing social trends in women's education, and pressure from students forced the seminary to enlarge its view of women's sphere and raise academic standards. Throughout this decade, annual enrollments ranged between 175 and 200, with a faculty of eighteen teachers, and the majority of students graduated from the noncollegiate programs. Among the collegiate course graduates, the group profile was much like that of eastern women's college graduates: from the total 215 collegiate course graduates to 1899, almost 40 percent worked full-time throughout their lives, a low 58 percent married, and of those, only 62 percent had children.

Bible study remained in the curriculum until past the turn of the century, and the 1905 catalog announced the addition of a full secretarial course and a department of **home economics**.* By 1909, the preparatory department was dropped entirely. What remained of Rockford's early history was a spirit of affinity with the Christian doctrine of service and the pervasive emphasis on self-reliance. By the mid-1990s, Rockford College continued as a strong liberal arts institution and, like other early **women's colleges*** and Beloit itself, had become coeducational [see **coeducation***].

Bibliography: Jane Addams, *Twenty Years at Hull-House* (repr. 1960); Barbara Miller Solomon, *In the Company of Educated Women: A History of Women and Higher Education in America* (1985). In the Rockford College Archives, see Hazel Paris Cederborg, "Early History of Rockford College" (master's thesis, 1926); Helen L. D. Richardson, "The Beginnings of Rockford Female Seminary" (unpubl. centenary history); Lucy F. Townsend, "The Gender Effect: A Comparison of the Early Curricula of Beloit College and Rockford Female Seminary" (paper, n.d.); Roberta Wollons, "The Impact of Higher Education on Women: The Case of Rockford College, 1870–1920" (unpubl. paper, 1977).

Roberta Wollons

Rosenwald Fund. The Rosenwald Fund began in 1917 through the efforts of philanthropist Julius Rosenwald with the stated purpose of enhancing "the well-being of mankind." Over its incorporated existence (1928–1948), the fund contributed to the development of African Americans in four major areas: education, health, fellowships, and race relations.

Rosenwald, son of a German Jew who found success in the clothing industry, became president of Sears, Roebuck and Company in 1906. In 1910 he began a program of matching funds for construction of YMCA buildings for blacks. He formalized his philanthropic efforts by establishing the Rosenwald Fund with initial capital of 200,000 shares of Sears stock, worth approximately $20 million. When the fund was incorporated in 1928, Edwin Rogers Embree, who had served as a director and vice president of the Rockefeller Foundation, became president and served for the life of the fund.

Rosenwald's interest in black education stemmed from the affinity he felt for the self-help philosophy of Booker T. Washington, one of the country's foremost black educators. Rosenwald served as a trustee and patron of Washington's **Tuskegee Institute*** and supported the **Hampton***-Tuskegee program of industrial training for blacks.

Perhaps the best-known fund initiative was its school-building program. Rosenwald himself initiated the building of schoolhouses for rural blacks in 1914, following the philanthropic precedent set by the Slater and Jeanes funds, other organizations devoted to building opportunities for blacks in the South [see **Jeanes teachers***]. Individual states and counties were required to contribute to the school structure itself and to agree to maintain it as a regular part of the public school system. White citizens were required to contribute money and blacks to make gifts of money, labor, or both. When the school-building program ended in 1932, 4,977 public schoolhouses, 163 shops, and 217 teachers' homes had been built in 883 counties of fifteen southern states at a total cost of $28,408,520.

After 1928 the fund worked to develop four "university centers" for educating black professionals: Washington, D.C. (**Howard University***), Atlanta (Atlanta University; Morehouse, Clark, and **Spelman Colleges***; Gammon Theological Seminary), Nashville (**Fisk University*** and Meharry Medical College), and New Orleans (Straight College and New Orleans University). Other fund educational ventures included provision of books to black and white schools and colleges; institution of a county library demonstration program and branch libraries in schools, churches, and stores; and designation of one white and three black southern colleges (West Georgia College, Tuskegee Institute, Fort Valley State, and Jackson College) as exemplary **teacher education*** institutions. Rosenwald also awarded grants to other black colleges, usually private, to maintain summer institutes for teachers, ministers, and agricultural workers [see **teacher institutes***].

The health and medical services effort included two programs: improvement of facilities and personnel working in health care for blacks, and distribution of medical services to persons of moderate means at affordable costs. The program encouraged advanced training for physicians, nurses, and hospital administrators; salary supplements for black health officers; and cooperation with national research programs in reducing tuberculosis. The fellowship program enabled blacks and white southerners to pursue **graduate education*** and professional training at northern universities or to study abroad. In race relations, the fund supported studies, books, and articles intended to increase the opportunity for blacks to join labor organizations, pursue equal justice under law, and avoid employment discrimination.

The Rosenwald trustees generally followed a broad agenda and used interest income as well as capital to effect their aims. Having expended most of its capital, the fund ended in 1948, following Rosenwald's desire that its resources be used to benefit the current generation, rather than being ruled by "the dead hand of perpetuity." From the construction of schoolhouses to the support of graduate and professional training, the Rosenwald Fund's influence on southern education surpassed that of all other educational philanthropic foundations.

Bibliography: Edwin Rogers Embree and Julia Waxman, *Investment in People: The Story of the Julius Rosenwald Fund* (1949); Henry Allen Bullock, *A History of Negro Education in the South from 1619 to the Present* (1967); James D. Anderson, *The Education of Blacks in the South, 1860–1935* (1988); Jayne R. Beilke, "To Render Better Service: The Role of the Julius Rosenwald Fund Fellowship Program in the Development of Graduate and Professional Educational Opportunities for African-Americans" (Ph.D. diss., Indiana University, 1994).

Jayne R. Beilke

S

---

science education. Increased attention since the 1970s to women's low participation in science obscures the fact that women and girls have pursued science education in significant numbers since the nineteenth century. Recent studies find that more girls than boys studied science at nineteenth-century **academies*** and that nearly 30 percent of doctorates earned by women prior to 1900 were in the sciences. Yet, unquestionably, women's interest in science over the past century has not always produced careers equal to either their talent or their educational attainment. In 1992, for example, women constituted 45 percent of all workers in the United States but only 16 percent of all employed scientists or engineers.

Both historians and contemporary analysts point to problems in, first, the educational process and, then, career building that discourage girls' and women's equal participation with men in science. Historians find a systematic exclusion of women from **graduate education*** and career opportunities that would have allowed full development of their scientific inclinations. Since the 1960s women's movement, contemporary advocates for women have focused on a range of environmental, sociocultural, and personal factors that inhibit participation in science by girls and women.

Science was frequently an amateur endeavor in the nineteenth century, practiced by many without collegiate training and learned through popular pursuits such as **lyceum*** lectures, museum visiting, and textbook reading. Women became particularly avid consumers of popular textbooks, and a genre developed of science books written especially for female readers. Originally imported from England, books like Jane Marcet's *Conversations on Chemistry* (1806) and *Conversations on Natural Philosophy* (1819) provided considerable informal scientific education to curious young women.

Before **common schools*** or **high schools*** were widespread in the United States, academies and female **seminaries*** constituted the most frequent schooling for nineteenth-century boys and girls seeking more than the rudimentary education available in **dame schools**.* Many academies were single sex or divided their offerings by gender, demonstrating the nineteenth-century belief that boys and girls needed different types of training suitable for their supposedly different roles in life [see **separate spheres***]. Much of boys' education centered around the classics, especially the Latin and Greek that were required for college. These languages and their literature represented the epitome of a disciplined, masculine mind. Boys filled out their curriculum with core subjects such as arithmetic, grammar, and writing and newer subjects like French, geography, geometry, and astronomy.

In the early 1800s, a few advocates for female education opened seminaries to provide advanced education for girls and young women. **Emma Hart Willard**,* founder of **Troy Female Seminary*** (New York, 1821) was one of the foremost educators of women in midcentury. Her genius consisted of matching her desire for better-educated women with society's recognized need for better-trained teachers. Willard acknowledged the contemporary belief that women's "natural" talents fit them for the nurturance of young children in the home. However, she extended this vision of mothers as teachers into the classroom, suggesting that educated young women could serve as more suitable, dedicated teachers; the fact that they would work more cheaply than men figured into her calculation as well [see **teaching***].

Troy Female Seminary and several of its contemporaries found in the sciences an equivalent to the discipline provided to boys through study of the classics. Without much higher education open to women, Latin and Greek proved unnecessary. The sciences, however, could help girls learn to make critical observations and pursue logical thought. Natural philosophy (like today's physics), botany, chemistry, and astronomy combined with a steady curriculum in mathematics, modern language, history, geography, and literature to provide the most advanced training available to middle-class girls. Studies of nineteenth-century academy advertisements and catalogs show the sciences as a core part of most female academy curricula and only an add-on for men.

Willard and her sister, **Almira Hart Phelps**,* developed a creative pedagogy to accompany the strong curriculum at Troy and at Patapsco Institute where Phelps later taught. They purchased scientific apparatuses to provide students direct experimentation. Phelps studied a range of scientific fields with Amos Eaton, a professor at the nearby Rensselaer Institute, and brought advanced knowledge and laboratory techniques back to her students. The sisters, already well known as school leaders, expanded their educational influence as textbook writers. Willard published a best-selling geography text; Phelps wrote a successful series of science books, including texts on chemistry, natural philosophy, and botany.

A few women's academies—**Mount Holyoke Female Seminary*** being the best known—converted to **women's colleges*** later in the nineteenth century. By 1865, when **Vassar College*** opened as a collegiate-level women's institution, a new opportunity for advanced training appeared for women. By the turn of the century, the prestigious colleges later known as the **Seven Sisters*** (Mount Holyoke, Vassar, **Wellesley**,* **Smith**,* **Bryn Mawr**,* **Barnard**,* and **Radcliffe***) offered strong liberal arts training for women, and many of the older state universities (especially in the Midwest) had opened their doors to women.

Science education, perhaps encouraged by its strong place in the female academies, always held a high priority at the women's colleges. Because resources were limited, the colleges tended to develop particular specialties rather than provide uniform strength in all scientific fields. Usually dependent on having attracted a good female specialist early on, the schools pushed their strengths: Bryn Mawr in mathematics and geology, Vassar in astronomy and physics (thanks especially to the incomparable astronomer **Maria Mitchell***), Mount Holyoke in chemistry and zoology, and Wellesley in botany and psychology. Of the 400 or so practicing women scientists before 1920, the majority had been trained at the Seven Sister schools and at the universities at Cornell, **Chicago**,* Michigan, and Pennsylvania (see Rossiter, table 1.1, p. 11).

These schools played a vital role by providing the only viable professional jobs for women scientists for many decades. Historian Margaret Rossiter has shown how the professionalization of science late in the nineteenth century pushed women to the margins of the field, first, by excluding women from graduate programs and, second, by forcing them into peripheral job opportunities not matching their training. The Ph.D. became the hallmark of a professional researcher around the turn of the twentieth century but initially was closed to American women. Neither Johns Hopkins nor Clark Universities—both founded on the premier new research model—accepted women into doctoral work. Some schools, notably Yale, Chicago, Pennsylvania, and Brown, agreed to let women into Ph.D. programs but only after women had launched a campaign that included pursuit of doctorates in Europe at the schools most emulated by American universities. Women's philanthropy also influenced educational opportunities. The **Association of Collegiate Alumnae*** (ACA, forerunner of the modern **American Association of University Women***), frustrated by the lack of support for women abroad and in the States, created fellowships for women to study in Europe. Members of the ACA also spurred fund-raising campaigns at individual schools (notably Johns Hopkins), which often resulted in individual women being admitted to graduate programs or employed as professors.

By 1900, American women had earned 229 doctorates; one-half had been awarded by Yale, Chicago, Cornell, and New York Universities, and at least 60 of those Ph.D.s were in the sciences (see Rossiter, table 2.1, p. 36). Employment opportunities, however, were scarce, and the women's colleges provided the single best option for well-trained women scientists. Rossiter's analysis of the women listed in the first three editions of *American Men of Science* (1906, 1910, and 1921) found that most were employed at the Seven Sister colleges; a few worked at Chicago, Illinois, or Berkeley. In the mid-twentieth century, the land-grant institutions became more significant employers of women scientists. However, these institutions practiced a kind of occupational segregation by shunting women trained in chemistry, biology, or physics into the **home economics*** or **teacher education*** divisions. Women's comparative lack of advancement in science appears due to the absence of strong and supportive employment opportunities well into the twentieth century. At the coeducational state institutions, they were waylaid into nonspecialist fields; at the women's colleges, they were often valued more as teachers than scientific researchers. Government and industrial employment tended to follow the same approaches, keeping women at lower levels or shifting them to the margins of the strongest scientific fields.

The post–World War II era provided conflicting experiences for women scientists that initially promised expanded opportunities. During the war, women found unusual opportunities—both as students and faculty—at colleges and universities suffering from a lack of male students and staff. Industry, too, welcomed women to jobs vacated by male soldiers. After the war, however, women's gains quickly evaporated as veterans returned to reclaim their jobs and their places in school. The 1950s, ironically, produced a new call for "scientific womanpower" when the Cold War began to reveal America's technological weaknesses. Government and industrial manpower commissions recognized women as a strong source of trained, educated workers. The national rhetoric, however, never matched the reality of women's employment opportunities. Inflexible graduate programs, nonresponsive job markets, and subtle structural discrimination all operated to keep women's gains minimal well into the 1960s.

The 1960s women's movement and subsequent legal and social supports for women have sparked new advances for women as students and professionals in science. Since the 1970s, gains for women in science have been strong, although some observers worry that advances are leveling off in the 1990s. For example, women's share of the Ph.D.s earned in the life sciences has risen from 25 percent in 1979–1980 to 42 percent in 1993–1994; in the physical sciences, women's share has increased from 12 percent in 1979–1980 to 21 percent in 1993–1994. As scientists, women still predominate in the life sciences: They earned only 11 percent of all engineering Ph.D.s in 1993–1994 and 21 percent of Ph.D.s in mathematics. Furthermore, women's representation on the faculty does not yet match their proportion of earned degrees. In 1992, women constituted only 20 percent of all full-time faculty in the life sciences, and a mere 6 percent of engineering faculty (National Center for Education Statistics, 1996).

Scholars have looked for the circumstances that seem to discourage women and girls in their pursuit of scientific careers. At the college level, two places produce sharp drops in women's participation: the initial college years when women face introductory science courses, and the middle of graduate school as women experience lack of mentors and other supports. Another line of inquiry has centered on both the content and pedagogy of girls' classroom experiences. There observers find many factors that discourage girls, including an emphasis on competition over cooperation, a misinterpretation of the nature of scientific objectivity, a lack of connection between classroom material and girls' experience, absence of women as mentors and role models, and a general lack of encouragement for girls' scientific interests and questions. Scholars such as Evelyn Fox Keller, Ruth Hubbard, and Sandra Harding have developed a feminist critique of science that challenges the belief in science as neutral, objective, and not influenced by the gender of those who practice its craft. Rather, these scholars suggest, science has been affected by a masculine bias toward objectivity, competition, and independence. They ask what differences might appear if intuition, insight, interdependence, and cooperation were stressed in both scientific discovery and in science education.

Since the 1980s, women's groups in the sciences as well as governmental agencies and foundations have focused on understanding and ameliorating the barriers for girls' and women's full participation in science. Curriculum projects, mentoring programs, summer enrichment courses, and speakers bureaus have proliferated as advocates reach out to girls ready for encouragement in scientific careers. The success of these efforts may depend on educators' ability to integrate them into regular classroom experiences so that all girls and boys share the opportunity to discover their scientific inclinations. In the long run, however, as historical research has shown, strong employment opportunities must follow any efforts to increase the educational credentials of women scientists. Without matching opportunities to practice and advance in their careers, science education alone will not produce sustained achievements for women in science.

Bibliography: Margaret Rossiter, *Women Scientists in America: Struggles and Strategies to 1940* (1982); Deborah C. Fort, ed., *A Hand Up: Women Mentoring Women in Science* (1993); Sue V. Rosser, ed., *Teaching the Majority: Breaking the Gender Barrier in Science, Mathematics, and Engineering* (1995); Rossiter, *Women Scientists in America: Before Affirmative Action, 1940–1972* (1995); National Center for Education Statistics, *Digest of Education Statistics* (1996); Kim Tolley, ''Science for Ladies, Classics for Gentlemen: A Comparative Analysis of Scientific Subjects in the Curricula of Boys' and Girls' Secondary Subjects in the United States, 1794–1850,'' *History of Education Quarterly*, 36 (Summer 1996): 129–153.

Linda Eisenmann

Second Great Awakening. *Second Great Awakening* is a term used by historians to describe a grassroots religious revival movement among many Protestant Christians in the United States, including the Congregational, Presbyterian, Methodist, and Baptist churches. Although this was a nationwide phenomenon, which began by 1800 in Kentucky and Tennessee, the movement was centered in the northeastern United States and continued through the first third of the nineteenth century. The movement greatly increased women's participation in formal church activities and in informal ways of spreading knowledge and faith.

Some of the factors that led to the Second Great Awakening were the major economic, social, and political changes that occurred after the American Revolution. These include the development of a national market economy, the result of a shift from agricultural production to expanding commerce and the beginnings of industrialization; new transportation networks and methods of technology; increased geographic mobility and a gradual shift from rural to urban areas; a rapidly growing population; new ideas about personal and national identity; changing gender roles and family structures; and new democratic and republican codes of manners and behavior. Changes also occurred in Protestant religious doctrine, such as a transformation from a carefully reasoned study of theology to a more emotional and experientially based religion, a shift in the structure of religious leadership, a moderate decline in the status of clergy and the authority of religion, and a rise in attendance by women who made up two-thirds of Protestant church membership during this period.

Perhaps counterbalancing these profound changes, the Second Great Awakening offered citizens a renewed sense of unity and collective emotional experience through participation in religious revivals. Although revivals varied in type by location, and were usually segregated by age and gender, the main vehicles were small prayer meetings and group conferences. For example, in frontier towns, prayer meetings often took place in tents, but in urban areas, a series of prayer meetings could be held over a period of several months. Regardless of their format, the goal was the same—to renew the faith of revival participants and convert nonbelievers.

Revivals brought many more women than men to the church and began what has been termed the "**feminization*** of religion." Connecticut clergyman Ebenezer Porter, in his *Letters on Revivals of Religion* (1832), estimated that three of five converts in New England revivals between 1798 and 1826 were women. Historian Nancy Cott suggests that these were primarily young (under thirty years of age) unmarried women who embraced religion for a variety of economic and social reasons. Economic changes, for example, displaced their household work, so that when they turned to paid employment outside the home, their lives were more unsettled and they had less emotional support. Combined with an uncertainty about financial support, separation from family, geographic relocation, and ambiguous prospects for marriage, evangelical Christianity may have offered women strength and purpose that found confirmation among their peers.

Along with a dramatic rise in church attendance by women, a change occurred in the development of a preaching style and doctrine created to accommodate women's concerns. For instance, revival preaching stressed that an individual's action could affect his or her salvation through active repentance and eventual conversion. This represented a clear departure from Calvinist doctrine in which one's ultimate spiritual fate was predetermined. Like others of the era, preachers believed that women were more humane and pious than men and therefore more ready for Christ's message. Accordingly, many clergymen changed their preaching to include plain speech delivered in a more emotional, forceful, and highly individualistic style. In addition, sermons delivered in this tough and direct sytle often focused on strong women in the Bible so that women could relate more directly to the message being delivered.

Evangelical theology encouraged religious activism by maintaining that the daily activities of a church member would attest to the reality of his or her conversion. Characteristically, new converts sought to share their experiences, often by working at revivals or by volunteering with evangelical associations. Although the clergy was almost exclusively male, religious activism among women surged, allowing many women to create powerful public roles for themselves. Depending upon the branch of Christianity, women could lead prayers, conduct revivals, or preach publicly. In addition, they assisted evangelists by planning revival strategies, held prayer vigils in their home, traveled abroad as missionaries, taught in Sunday schools, and were actively involved in an array of benevolent voluntary organizations. These included maternal associations, which stressed the responsibility of Christian mothers, promoted the spread of piety especially among children, and established libraries and journals for the dissemination of literature on childrearing, domesticity, and Christian motherhood. In addition, women were active in voluntary reform societies such as the Home and Foreign Mission Society (1812), American Bible Society (1816), American Tract Society (1826), Female Moral Reform Society (1834), and Woman's Christian Temperance Union (1873), all of which conducted social welfare or moral reform programs throughout the country. Women were encouraged to join voluntary associations not only by their ministers but by authors such as Sarah Hale, editor for half a century of the influential magazine *Godey's Lady's Book*,* and **Catharine Beecher**,* author of the best-selling *Treatise on Domestic Economy* (1841). Beecher's book, for example, devoted an entire chapter to the topic of self-denying benevolence and the ''importance of maintaining a system of associated charities.''

Through participation in the Second Great Awakening, the sacred and secular lives of many American women were transformed, as they were able to assert a moral mission to teach and engage in social reform outside the home. Although women did not play a prominent role in the institutional hierarchy of the church, they nonetheless developed a respected vocation, identity, and community during the early nineteenth century. [See also **Board of Foreign Missions**,* **temperance movement**.*]

Bibliography: Nancy F. Cott, ''Young Women in the Second Great Awakening in New England,'' *Feminist Studies*, 4 (Fall 1975): 15–29; Barbara Welter, ''The Feminization of American Religion: 1800–1860,'' in Barbara Welter, ed., *Dimity Convictions: The American Woman in the Nineteenth Century* (1976); William G. McLoughlin, *Revivals, Awakenings, and Reform: An Essay on Religion and Social Change in America, 1607–1977* (1978); Carroll Smith-Rosenberg, ''The Cross and the Pedestal: Women, Anti-Ritualism, and the Emergence of the American Bourgeoisie,'' in Carroll Smith-Rosenberg, ed., *Disorderly Conduct: Visions of Gender in Victorian America* (1985); Nancy F. Cott, ed., *History of Women in the United States: Historical Articles on Women's Lives and Activities, [No.] 13, Religion* (1993).

Elizabeth K. Eder

seminaries. In antebellum America, **academies*** gave way to seminaries as the most common institutionalized form of higher education for women. Some of the most well-known female seminaries include **Emma Willard**'s* **Troy Female Seminary*** (New York, 1821), **Catharine Beecher**'s* **Hartford Female Seminary*** (Connecticut, 1823), and **Mary Lyon**'s* **Mount Holyoke Female Seminary*** (Massachusetts, 1837). All three schools became models for hundreds of others across the country. Just as men's colleges proliferated in this era, so did female seminaries, for several reasons.

First, education became associated with improving women's abilities within the domestic sphere. The argument that education would benefit a woman's family carried more weight than that women themselves would benefit. Ideal women were considered selfless, existing largely to serve others. At the same time, Americans came to agree that educated mothers raised better citizens.

Second, the religious revival known as the **Second Great Awakening*** that prompted the growth of men's colleges in the antebellum era also affected women's education. As historian Lynn Gordon notes, nineteenth-century evangelical Christianity sanctioned education for women as a means of enhancing and enforcing their spiritual authority in the home and the culture at large. Charles G. Finney, perhaps the best-known antebellum evangelist, approved of higher education for women, believing that it would turn immature girls into "true vehicles of God's grace." Finney wrote that the purpose of education was "training of a band of self-denying, hardy, intelligent, efficient laborers, of both sexes, for the world's enlightenment and regeneration." This moral imperative was part of the rhetoric of several advocates of women's higher education. Evangelicalism assumed women's moral superiority and their propensity for self-denying labor. Thus, women used the language of evangelicalism and the ideology of **separate spheres*** to argue for increased opportunities for higher education.

A third factor leading to the growth of the seminary movement, especially in the North, was economic. The shift of labor from households and farms into shops and factories meant that older children had to earn a living outside the home before they married. Northern women who remained single, through choice or necessity, turned to **teaching*** to support themselves.

The economic need was supported by a fourth factor. Not only did women want to teach, but the demand increased rapidly. The **common school*** movement in the North and West took off rapidly in the antebellum period; at the same time, fewer men entered teaching, especially in the Northeast. The combination of increased numbers of children in school, decreased numbers of male teachers, and the fact that women were paid half as much as men led to a huge demand for female teachers. Seminaries trained many of the women who became teachers, and some seminaries, such as Troy and Mount Holyoke, gained reputations as excellent **teacher education*** institutions.

Most advocates of female education sensed that they had a better chance of winning support if they worked within the realm of separate spheres. Some argued that educated women would make better wives and mothers. Some asserted that women's innate characteristics made them adept at teaching, so that women needed high-quality education to prepare them for this work. Still others saw a need for educated women in the evangelical imperative to Christianize. Other school founders combined these justifications to expand women's education and women's sphere, while not completely challenging ideology.

Throughout the antebellum era, seminaries grew more academically rigorous. Some schools still offered **ornamental education**,* such as music, painting and embroidery, but these offerings became more rare. Troy was the first permanent institution to offer a curriculum similar to that of men's colleges. Professors at nearby men's schools attended the public examinations of Troy's students and were "astonished" at what the "ladies" had learned.

Mount Holyoke was one of the most academically challenging, offering many courses comparable to men's colleges. From 1841 to 1849, Mount Holyoke and Amherst, a nearby college for men, used the same texts for algebra, physiology, physics, astronomy, chemistry, geology, natural history, logic, rhetoric, and moral philosophy.

Troy, Mount Holyoke, and others were a tremendous challenge to the prevailing notion that women had inferior intellectual capabilities. However, the majority of graduates still engaged in "women's work": becoming wives and mothers, caring for the sick, teaching Sunday school, or while single, working as teachers. There were exceptions, of course, and rates of seminary graduates remaining single were higher than rates for nonseminary students. But by and large, graduates tended to conform to societal norms.

The growth of female seminaries reached its peak in the 1850s. In the mid- and late nineteenth century, seminaries and colleges for women both existed, and the difference between them was not always clear. By the 1870s, communities were more interested in supporting colleges than seminaries, although college curricula did not always live up to the standards implied by the name. Conversely, Mount Holyoke did not officially become a college until 1893, even though it had long offered college-level courses.

Seminaries faced competition not only from the new **women's colleges**,* but also from **normal schools**,* (teacher training institutes); from **high schools**,* which were gaining in popularity and prestige, especially among the middle class; and from coeducational [see **coeducation***] colleges. By the turn of the twentieth century, seminaries received charters as colleges, were subsumed into high schools, or closed altogether.

Seminaries proved two important points: that women were capable of academically superior work and that education did not "un-fit" them for their sphere. Accordingly, seminaries paved the way for women's colleges.

Bibliography: Thomas Woody, *A History of Women's Education in the United States* (1929); Barbara Miller Solomon, *In the Company of Educated Women: A History of Women and Higher Education in America* (1985); Anne Firor Scott, "The Ever-Widening Circle: The Diffusion of Feminist Values from the Troy Female Seminary, 1822–1872," in Edward McClellan and William Reese, eds., *The Social History of American Education* (1988); Kathryn Kish Sklar, "The Founding of Mount Holyoke

College," in Sklar and Thomas Dublin, eds., *Women and Power in American History, a Reader, Vol. I: To 1880* (1991).

Margaret A. Nash

semiprofessions. Since the beginning of the twentieth century, the definition of *profession* has perplexed academics. Spokespeople from almost every occupation claim that theirs is a profession, and the term has become increasingly muddied. Controversy has focused on new occupations—often labeled "semiprofessions"—that require a high degree of sophisticated knowledge and skill.

The semiprofessions have encountered a bumpy ride on the road toward acceptance. Occupations such as secondary school **teaching,*** **social work,*** **librarianship,*** and nursing do not have fully established status as professions for a number of reasons. Unlike the older professions—especially law, medicine, and divinity—semiprofessions cannot claim cognitive exclusiveness, for many people have access to their knowledge without specialized, prolonged university education [see **legal education,*** **medical education***]. Nor is there an established body of theory upon which their practice is based; instead, there is precise technical skill. Moreover, there is not a definite client orientation such as that derived from a practice. Because semiprofessionals are often employed in bureaucratic organizations, control over their own work is lacking or dissipated. Without a fully legitimated status, individuals do not seek out semiprofessionals for their expertise. For all these reasons, members of semiprofessions are not homogeneous regarding their knowledge and community orientation. Professions and semiprofessions exhibit clear differences in length of training, goals, autonomy, privileges, status, career commitment, and client relationship.

Semiprofessions and their rise are related to the development of capitalism and even more closely tied to an economy based on public service occupations. Understanding the development of professions is essential to understanding the rise of semiprofessions. Although the newer professions are relatively recent social occurrences, traditional professions have long historical ties with universities and the church. Professions based their identity on esoteric knowledge that members alone possessed and that they shared with others on a client basis only. This knowledge was grounded in theory, usually gained in a university. In the Middle Ages the professions were commonly recognized as law, medicine, and divinity (university teaching was considered part of ministry). Becoming a professional was a "calling," and members took consecrated vows to "profess" their knowledge. The professions' monopoly of scarce resources (knowledge) created restricted membership, social prestige, elite associations, and great personal wealth. Above all, professionals prized their autonomy to practice without interference from outsiders.

With the Industrial Revolution and its accompanying emphasis on specialized knowledge, the array of professions broadened to include the military, dentistry, chemistry and other sciences, and architecture. Concomitantly, national professional associations proliferated in the 1840s and 1850s. Bureaucracy and educational mobility provided further impetus for this change. Soon other professions related to emerging new industries appeared: engineering, accounting, and management.

A major exacerbating difference between professions and semiprofessions is gender membership: Professions have traditionally been dominated by men, semiprofessions by women. Because of this sex segregation, authors in the 1960s and 1970s described the semiprofessions as "handmaidens of a male occupation" (Etzioni, p. 231), dependent on true professions for their knowledge. Furthermore, because semiprofessions were characterized by "a main intrinsic appeal to the heart, not the mind" (Etzioni, p. 203), they were viewed as less rigorous, suitable to women with a discontinuous work commitment. Working with people in a service occupation was deemed derogatory; semiprofessions were seen as extensions of natural feminine sex roles in a culture that devalued women.

Recently, the position of professions and semiprofessions has changed: The autonomy of professions has come under sharp scrutiny, and the attempt of semiprofessions to credential themselves has met with community approval. As semiprofessions seek to legitimate themselves, they copy professional measures: They install gatekeeping methods, require higher educational standards, develop a formal code of ethical practice, control licensing examinations, create specialized organizations and publications, and struggle for autonomy in their work.

It is helpful to think of a continuum, with fully fledged professions and unskilled occupations on opposite ends, and semiprofessions and skilled occupations in the middle. Adopting this concept, one can see that semiprofessions are in the healthy process of transition to the point held by professions. Today, semiprofessions often replace theoretical study of a discipline with acquisition and application of precise and sophisticated technical skill at the same time that they welcome women, blacks, and ethnics who were largely barred from professions until the last several decades. Thus, in many ways, the semiprofessions are appropriately called "emerging" professions.

Bibliography: Howard M. Vollmer and Donald L. Mills, eds., *Professionalization* (1966); Amitai Etzioni, *The Semi-Professions and Their Organization* (1969); Magali Sarfatti Larson, *The Rise of Professionalism* (1977); Eliot Freidson, *Professional Powers* (1986).

Deborah Elwell Arfken

Seneca Falls. Seneca Falls, New York, the location of the first national convention held in 1848 to discuss and promote women's rights, is associated with the beginning of women's struggle for equal rights, including **suffrage**.* Many women had begun to speak out for women's rights after being rebuffed in their efforts to work equally with men in the antebellum reform movements of antislavery and **temperance**.* Two such women, Elizabeth Cady Stanton and Lucretia Mott, were organizers of the Seneca Falls Convention. They had attended the London Anti-Slavery Convention of 1840 and had come away with the desire to hold a convention and form a society to advocate women's rights in the United States. Because of their other duties, including motherhood, this idea was not realized until July 1848. Early that month, Stanton and Mott gathered with friends at a tea party and, in the course of the afternoon, discussed the convention idea. The women selected July 19 and 20 for the meeting and advertised in the local newspaper, not really knowing what step to take next or whether anyone would attend.

When the women turned their attention to planning the convention, they were unsure how to proceed, since women traditionally neither held conventions nor addressed the public. Several planners felt that a general list of resolutions could serve as a beginning point for discussion, and they deliberately modeled their **Declaration of Sentiments*** and Resolutions after the Declaration of Independence, using much the same wording. Their hope was to draw on the political heritage of the American Revolution with its demands for legal, economic, social, and political equality.

The organizers determined a good convention location would be the Wesleyan Chapel, founded in 1843 by separatists on the issue of **slavery**.* Perhaps this church would be receptive to yet another group seeking freedom. None of the women felt comfortable in the role of chairperson as none had ever experienced this responsibility. They also wondered how the public would react to a convention led by women. This problem was resolved when Lucretia Mott's husband, James, agreed to preside. Like many women of their era, these activists felt that male leadership would give necessary credibility to their meeting.

The eighteen resolutions of the Declaration of Sentiments were read, debated, and voted upon over two days. The Declaration enumerated several wrongs and asked for a repeal of laws that discriminated against women. It declared that men monopolized all the profitable professions; in fact, very few women practiced in the ministry, medicine, or law [see **legal education**,* **medical education***]. Men also denied women college admission, and they claimed apostolic authority over women in the church, limiting women's participation in religious activities and promoting a moral double standard. After addressing such grievances, the resolutions called for various corrections based on the belief that woman was man's equal. The conventioners wanted equal treatment under the law and equal opportunities in education, employment, and religious activities. The resolutions ended with a call for the "zealous and untiring efforts of both men and women" in pursuit of equality.

Not surprisingly, the most controversial issue of the convention became the basis for its fame today. Stanton had suggested a resolution that women be given the right to vote, but Lucretia Mott questioned the wisdom of including such an extreme resolution. The group was divided between suffrage supporters and their opponents who were concerned that a resolution so radical might invite ridicule. The impasse was eased when Frederick Douglass, ex-slave and abolitionist [see **abolitionism***], asked to address the convention and, in a stirring speech, argued for adoption. The suffrage plank was passed by a narrow margin. At the close of the convention, eighty-six women and thirty-two men signed the Declaration, making it the nation's first formal statement regarding women's rights. Because of the success of this initial meeting, a follow-up gathering was scheduled for August.

The historic meeting is remembered today in the preservation of the original sites associated with the convention and its major participants. The Wesleyan Chapel, the home of Elizabeth Cady Stanton, the home of Jane Hunt where the convention was planned, and the home of Mary Ann McClintock where the Declaration was written are all restored. These sites make up the Women's Rights National Historic Park. The National Women's Hall of Fame, organized in 1968, was formed to honor and recognize outstanding American women of achievement and to educate and motivate women of the present and future. The Hall of Fame is appropriately located in Seneca Falls, the place where American women began organized efforts to achieve equality with men.

Bibliography: Margaret Hope Bacon, "It Happened at Seneca Falls," in Margaret Hope Bacon, ed., *Valiant Friend: The Life of Lucretia Mott* (1980); Robin Franklin and Tasha Wolf, *Remember the Ladies! A Handbook in American History* (1980); Angela Howard Zophy, ed., *Handbook of American Women's History* (1990); Marjorie Spruill Wheeler, "One Woman, One Vote," *Humanities*, 16 (January–February 1995): 29–34.

Linda Boran

separate spheres. The socially constructed division between public and private lives for men and women in the United States prior to the Civil War is often expressed through the image of a *sphere* of activity, a term that had widespread use in the nineteenth century. Thus, *separate spheres* has most often been used to describe divided realms of activity, with primarily white middle-class women conducting domestic responsibilities in the private realm of the home and men engaging in economic and political activities in the public realm. However, *separate spheres* has several meanings that are often used interchangeably. It has been described as an ideology imposed on women, as a culture created by women, and as a set of boundaries expected to be observed by women.

Although separating the "worlds" of men and women into public versus private spheres is an idea that predates the nineteenth century, it was during this period that the term took currency. Due, in part, to the profound economic, social, and political changes that occurred after the Revolution, including the development of industry and the emergence of a market economy and class society, a new set of ideas about women and their role in society emerged in the United States. The French writer Alexis de Tocqueville noticed these changes and alluded to what he believed were the separate roles of men and women in his account of a visit to the United States in *Democracy in America* (1835).

For many middle-class Americans, the reorganization of labor that accompanied industrialization separated the home from the workplace for the first time. Since women were thought to possess four inherent characteristics that set them apart from men—piety, purity, submissiveness, and domesticity—the "privatization of the home" now made "**true womanhood**"* possible. Women's virtues and responsibilities came to be associated with the newly restricted domestic sphere, and although their economic functions became more limited, women became valued for their role as mothers.

The theme of separate spheres was identified by historians in the late 1960s as central to women's historical experience, and the idea that a separate women's culture existed in the nineteenth century gained currency among historians in the 1970s. Since that time, however, some historians have debated the accuracy of the metaphor and have begun to question whether the two spheres are indeed separate. According to historian Linda Kerber, "separate spheres" has multiple meanings and uses by American historians. Karen V. Hansen, for example, suggests that a third sphere, the social, existed, which allowed for a whole range of activity that saw considerable crossover among men and women. In addition, the term has been used to specify separate spheres of activity for men and women (the so-called public/private dichotomy); to define "women's culture" as distinct from "men's culture"; to explore how spheres were "constructed both for and by women"; as a metaphor to describe complex power relations within a social and economic context; and as a literal space within which women and men operate differently.

Bibliography: Barbara Welter, "The Cult of True Womanhood: 1820–1860," in Michael Gordon, ed., *The American Family in Social-Historical Perspective* (1978); Linda K. Kerber, "Separate Spheres, Female Worlds, Woman's Place: The Rhetoric of Women's History," *Journal of American History*, 75 (June 1988): 9–37; Dorothy O. Helly and Susan M. Reverby, eds., *Gendered Domains: Rethinking Public and Private in Women's History* (1992); Karen V. Hansen, *A Very Social Time: Crafting Community in Antebellum New England* (1994).

Elizabeth K. Eder

settlement house movement. The settlement house movement, conceived in the late 1800s, encouraged predominantly middle-class and college-educated women and men to live together in houses located in urban slums. Originating in Great Britain, the movement endorsed the idea that the materially and educationally privileged should meet the working and lower classes as neighbors by living amongst them. Settlement workers were to interact with their neighbors to learn more about the poor's condition and needs. With that knowledge, settlement workers would initiate programs at settlement houses to benefit their neighbors as well as influencing the government, charitable organizations, schools, and other social agencies to better aid the urban poor.

In Great Britain, most of the movement's intellectual and organizational groundwork as well as the staffing of the original houses, such as Toynbee Hall, was done by men associated with Oxford and Cambridge Universities. Later, women would actively participate in the British movement. Several Americans who played critical roles in the American movement, including **Jane Addams**,* Vida Dutton Scudder, Stanton Coit, and Robert A. Woods, became inspired by the British movement through visits to Toynbee or Oxford in the mid-1880s. From the outset, women played prominent roles in all aspects of the American movement.

Addams, Scudder, Coit, and Woods actively participated in separate efforts that led to establishment of the first four settlement houses in the United States between 1886 and 1892. The American movement expanded rapidly. By 1900, there were 204 settlement houses; by 1916, more than 500. Between 1889 and 1914, three-fifths of all settlement residents were women, and almost nine-tenths had been to college. From the outset, settlement houses tended to be identified as either female or male, depending on which sex dominated the staffing. Women's settlement houses often stressed creating a homey atmosphere that encouraged neighbors to feel comfortable.

In 1889, the first two ''women's'' settlement houses opened in Chicago and New York City. Using funds inherited from her father and solicited from Chicago's prosperous citizens and philanthropic organizations, Jane Addams opened **Hull-House*** in a Chicago slum that year. During its history, a number of talented, socially conscious college-educated women, including Addams, Ellen Gates Starr, Julia Lathrop, and Florence Kelley, used Hull-House as a base for activities aimed at political and social reform. Although Hull-House was never formally associated with any university, most of its workers had attended college.

Although she never resided at a settlement house for any extended period, Scudder was one of the most prolific and effective publicists of the movement. Born into a wealthy Boston family, Scudder graduated from Boston's **Girls' Latin School*** and **Smith College**.* She was introduced to the movement during studies at Oxford in the mid-1880s. After returning to America, she became an English professor at **Wellesley College**.* In 1888, at a meeting with other Smith graduates, Scudder actively participated in discussions that led to the 1889 establishment of a settlement house on Rivington Street in New York City. The next year, Scudder became a founder of the College Settlements Association (CSA), which sponsored the Rivington House settlement along with two additional houses opened in 1892, one in Philadelphia and **Denison House*** in Boston.

Dominated by women, the CSA was formed by alumnae of Smith, **Vassar**,* Wellesley, **Bryn Mawr**,* and **Radcliffe**,* but their board would later include members from nine additional colleges. Colleges obtained membership when their alumnae, students, and faculty bought subscriptions to support the CSA's settlement houses. Their houses were staffed primarily with women from member colleges. At times, students resided in the CSA houses during vacations, and activities were held on campuses to foster support for the houses. Between 1889 and 1894, three-fifths of the CSA's residents had attended college; long-term residents, in particular, tended to be college educated.

Little uniformity existed in the governance and activities of different settlement houses. Some were sponsored by charitable, religious, or educational organizations, such as the **University of Chicago**,* the University of Wisconsin, and the Andover Theological Seminary; others, such as Hull-House, were independent. Many heavily depended on the leadership of their headworkers. Because the movement emphasized serving the needs of neighbors, its neighborhood often determined a house's activities. Frequently, activities were educational and aimed at Americanizing immigrants who lived near the houses. Theme clubs, athletic activities, and self-help and language classes, often aimed at neighborhood women and children, were popular. Some houses, including Denison House and Hull-House, became involved in labor activities, in which they tried to stress amelioration between labor and management to avoid the risk of alienating wealthy donors and the general public.

As time progressed, to the lament of many early proponents, settlement residents tended to become more like professional **social workers*** and less like caring amateurs. Complaints accused residents of being more interested in studying their neighbors than in living with them. When some settlement workers drifted from progressive to radical politics, houses risked losing support from their wealthy donors and the general public. This became critical when, during and after World War I, the movement was accused of being anti-American and communistic. These factors all contributed to the decline in the movement's vitality after 1914.

Although movement proponents and workers often exhibited an attitude of noblesse oblige toward their neighbors, they also became more intimately involved in improving the lives of the working and lower classes than most others of their social class. Because college women played key roles in the movement, it is a striking example of how colleges in the late 1800s produced women who worked to break out of women's restrictive domestic sphere.

Bibliography: Vida Dutton Scudder, *On Journey* (1937); Allen F. Davis, *Spearheads for Reform: The Social Settlements and the Progressive Movement 1890–1914* (1967); John P. Rousmaniere, "Cultural Hybrid in the Slums: The College Woman and the Settlement House, 1889–1894," *American Quarterly*, 21 (Spring 1970): 45–66; Mina Carson, *Settlement Folk: Social Thought and the American Settlement Movement, 1885–1930* (1990).

Maureen A. Reynolds

Seven Sisters. *Seven Sisters* is a term referring to seven women's colleges founded on the east coast of the United States in the nineteenth century: **Barnard**,* **Bryn Mawr**,* **Mount Holyoke**,* **Radcliffe**,* **Smith**,* **Vassar**,* and **Wellesley**.* The college presidents formed the Seven College Conference in 1926, and the more informal term "Seven Sisters" came into general use almost immediately afterwards. Each was founded to provide educational opportunity for women equivalent to that offered at the men-only **Ivy League*** universities. All were decried by critics as radical and superfluous institutions that would encourage women to look beyond their prescribed station in life as wife and mother (an 1895 study revealed that only half of women's college graduates went on to marry). In its earliest days, the conference conveyed a sense of power and authority in representing women in higher education.

The Seven Sisters colleges initially followed the "classical curriculum" established by men's schools in their early years, where students focused on mastery of Greek and Latin, supplemented by mathematics, history, science, and other languages and literatures. A variety of deviations from this classical curriculum made the sisters distinctive and innovative; the **women's colleges*** seem to have been less bound by tradition and the pressure of professional academe than their male counterparts.

Mount Holyoke Female Seminary was founded in 1837 in South Hadley, Massachusetts, by noted educator **Mary Lyon*** for the training of teachers and the inculcation of Christian values; it achieved college status in 1888. It still operates as one of the few all-female institutions of higher education in the United States.

Vassar College opened in 1865 in Poughkeepsie, New York. In its initial brochures, Vassar touted not just its classical curriculum but also its emphasis on natural sciences. It adopted full **coeducation*** (after rejecting an offer to merge with Yale University) in 1970.

Wellesley opened in 1875, with a unique all-female administrative and teaching staff (in contrast, only two of the original nine professors at Vassar were women). Wellesley currently boasts a thorough liberal arts curriculum at what is still an all-female college. It participates in a registration exchange with the now-coeducational Massachusetts Institute of Technology.

Funded by the bequest of Sophia Smith, Smith College in Northampton, Massachusetts, also opened in 1875. Its self-proclaimed mission was to preserve students' "womanliness" as it provided collegiate education; the initial curriculum emphasized literature and the arts more than the other sisters. Smith's early contribution to female college life was its cottage system, where students lived in small groups in individual buildings, supervised by one or two older women, rather than in one large dormitory (the standard layout at the older colleges). Smith had 14 students and three faculty members when it opened; by 1910, the college served 2,000 students, making it the largest of the Seven Sisters at that time. Today Smith is still all-women, though it participates (with Mount Holyoke) in a consortium exchange of class registration with four other nearby schools.

Barnard and Radcliffe Colleges both were founded as what became known as **coordinate colleges**,* created in close connection to their related men's schools, Columbia and Harvard Universities. In 1878, young women in Cambridge began paying Harvard professors for instruction similar to that offered in Harvard classrooms. The "Annex," as it was known, was endowed as Radcliffe College in 1894. In 1889 in New York City, the trustees of Columbia agreed to a similar arrangement for the first group of students at what became Barnard; Columbia professors taught Barnard women the same courses with the same exams as those at Columbia, although in much reduced circumstances, in terms of library and laboratory facilities. By 1896, both Radcliffe and Barnard had begun building their own campuses; with curricula still based in that of the men's schools, they developed separate, relatively autonomous identities. Barnard hired its own faculty members as well. Both schools flourished as cosmopolitan, urban centers of women's collegiate education in the first half of the twentieth century. Today, Barnard and Radcliffe exist as nominally separate entities connected to the larger university structures of Columbia and Harvard.

Finally, Bryn Mawr opened as a **Quaker***** college for women in Bryn Mawr, Pennsylvania, in 1885. It was distinguished among the sisters for rigid adherence to the classical curriculum and its absolute admissions system (no students were admitted who could not already read Greek and Latin). Bryn Mawr also offered limited **graduate education**.***** Bryn Mawr has recently curtailed its graduate offerings and fostered a relationship with nearby (formerly all-male) Haverford College; its strongest departments continue to be Greek and Latin.

One secondary effect of the founding of the Seven Sisters Colleges was the creation of a host of schools for girls expressly for training future students of the colleges. Usually founded and staffed by Seven Sisters graduates, these schools, like the Baldwin School outside Philadelphia and the Bryn Mawr School in Baltimore, provided the beginnings of an "old girl" network among secondary and college alumnae.

Such a network continues to exist in some form, though the Seven Sisters are now largely coeducational or involved in reciprocal relationships with coeducational schools. In fact, the term *Seven Siblings* has been adopted informally to recognize the diverse arrangements. The Seven College Conference continues to host an occasional sports tournament, but the sense of solidarity that characterized the conference in 1926 has largely dissipated. The Sisters that are still all-female have discovered a new popularity in the 1990s in the wake of numerous studies (most notably the 1992 **American Association of University Women**'s***** "How Schools Shortchange Girls") showing that women who attend single-sex educational institutions succeed at consistently higher rates than those who attend coeducational institutions.

Bibliography: Elaine Kendall, *Peculiar Institutions: An Informal History of the Seven Sisters Colleges* (1975); Helen Lefkowitz Horowitz, *Alma Mater: Design and Experience in the Women's Colleges from Their Nineteenth-Century Beginnings to the 1930s* (1984); Maria Newman, "Women's Colleges Find a New Popularity," *New York Times* (January 15, 1994); Martha Brant, "Far Beyond White Gloves and Teas," *Newsweek* (April 25, 1994).

Mary Dockray-Miller

Sex in Education. In 1873, **Edward H. Clarke**,* physician and former faculty member of Harvard University Medical School, published *Sex in Education; or, A Fair Chance for the Girls* in which he charged that higher education endangered women's capacity to produce healthy children. This work precipitated the major controversy in the history of women's struggle for access to higher education. Clarke graduated from Harvard College in 1841 and five years later completed medical training at the University of Pennsylvania [see **medical education***]. Upon graduation, he traveled extensively in Europe before returning to Boston to begin practice as a physician. Between 1855 and 1872, he served at Harvard, conducting and publishing research concerning diseases of the ear.

Boston-area advocates of women's higher education counted Clarke among their ranks. Within this context, in October 1872, the New England Woman's Club invited him to address the group concerning the higher education of women. Here the controversy began. Clarke astonished the group when he decried expansion of higher education for women, maintaining that it seriously undermined their health.

The following year, Clarke published an expanded version of that speech in a slender volume, *Sex in Education; or, A Fair Chance for the Girls*. Here he argued that higher education threatened the health of adolescent women, whose essential function was reproduction of the race. During this crucial time in their lives, the nervous and reproductive systems of young women develop simultaneously; adequate rest is essential for proper development. If adolescent women pursue higher education in the same unremitting manner as their male counterparts, Clarke argued, they could permanently damage their ability to bear healthy children. Excessive study and lack of proper rest could precipitate mental and physical breakdowns in women. Clarke did not deny women access to higher education. However, he argued that it should be at a less competitive pace than men's. Without such a change, he contended that a dramatic increase in the number of college-educated women might intensify the contemporary problem of **race suicide**.* Clarke concluded that women should not divert either their mental or physical energy from their essential task of reproduction.

Although *Sex in Education* was but one component in a continuing controversy concerning the propriety of higher education for women, it appeared within a particularly propitious context in the late nineteenth-century United States. The debate over the value of higher education had intensified after the Civil War for a number of reasons. First, women attended land-grant institutions, particularly in the Midwest, in greater numbers during the war, earning degrees and proving their worth [see **Morrill Land-Grant Act of 1862***]. Second, as a consequence of the number of men killed in the war, fewer women married and, hence, needed to be economically independent. Third, even after the war, the number of women attending colleges and universities increased dramatically. Fourth, the quality of many women's institutions improved substantially, discarding older **seminary*** trappings and appropriating instead the rigor of men's colleges.

Most important, however, Clarke's work appeared at the same time many people, both in Great Britain and the United States, enthusiastically embraced the ideas of Charles Darwin and Herbert Spencer. Darwin maintained that men and women reflected divergent forms of evolution, arguing in *Descent of Man* (1871) even more strongly for the marked differences between women and men. Thus, Clarke contended that he based his conclusions not on some innate sense of cultural propriety but on the discoveries of science.

Sex in Education generated some of the most intense debate in the struggle for women's access to higher education, and the publishers reprinted it seventeen times. Response included not only discussion and newspaper articles but also several scholarly rejoinders, including Annie Howes's *Health Statistics of Women College Graduates: Report of the Special Committee of the Association of Collegiate Alumnae* (1885) and Mary Putnam Jacobi's *The Question of Rest during Menstruation* (1876). Edward Clarke, however, did not live to participate fully in the debate. Clarke died in Boston in 1877.

Bibliography: Rosalind Rosenberg, *Beyond Separate Spheres: Intellectual Roots of Modern Feminism* (1982); Barbara Miller Solomon, *In the Company of Educated Women: A History of Women and Higher Education in America* (1985); Sue Zschoche, "Dr. Clarke Revisited: Science, True Womanhood, and Female Collegiate Education," *History of Education Quarterly*, 29 (Winter, 1989): 545–569; David Anderson Douglas, "Edward Clarke's 'Sex in Education': A Study of Rhetorical Form" (Ph.D. diss., Pennsylvania State University, 1992).

Carolyn Terry Bashaw

"sex repulsion." *Sex repulsion* was a term popularized between 1900 and 1910 by observers of both the **feminization*** of the **teaching*** profession and the liberal arts departments at coeducational universities [see **coeducation***]. These men explained the "flight" of young men into other professions as the result of the entry of women, when, in fact, this phenomenon resulted from massive social change in an industrializing economy.

In the teaching profession, longer school terms and increased educational requirements for teachers occurred at the same time that the expanded economy offered young men other job opportunities. School boards, anxious to economize on salaries as compulsory schooling laws increased the demand on the public schools, hired young women in huge numbers. Articles in the popular press lamented the departure of men from the teaching profession. Charles Eliot, president of Harvard University, called the hiring of women an "unwise economy," and other writers on the phenomenon of sex repulsion warned that the influence of women teachers would make American boys unmanly.

In higher education, professors of liberal arts and classics blamed sex repulsion for the departure of young men from their classes, when, in fact, many men preferred practical training that would lead to lucrative careers in the booming economy. Classics professors were especially dismayed at the large numbers of women students enrolled in their classes. Women students were not considered an asset for professors interested in attracting male students, and the programs in which large numbers of women enrolled were greatly devalued by university administrators. [See also **quotas**.*]

Bibliography: Mary Kelley, ed., *Woman's Place: Female Identity and Vocation in American History* (1979); Barbara Miller Solomon, *In the Company of Educated Women: A History of Women and Higher Education in America* (1985); Geraldine Jonçich Clifford, "Man/Woman/Teacher: Gender, Family, and Career in American Educational History," in Donald Warren, ed., *American Teachers: Histories of a Profession at Work* (1989).

Sharon Clifford

sexual harassment. Sexual harassment is a form of sex discrimination that generally involves the connection of job or school opportunities to one's willingness to participate in sexual acts with a person of authority (such as a professor or a supervisor). Sexual harassment can also be an antagonistic atmosphere created through means of sexual insults, innuendos, displayed pornographic materials, and other activities. Such conduct is illegal in three relational contexts: superior/subordinate, coworker/coworker, and teacher/student. Sexual harassment can affect both men and women; however, women are the predominant victims of harassment.

While the public has been particularly attuned to sexual harassment in the 1990s, this problem plagued serfs, indentured servants, and slaves centuries ago and working women during the Industrial Revolution.

Most scholars attribute sexual harassment to several gender stigmas that have existed for centuries. For example, in the Victorian era, women were viewed as pure, sexless beings who should not initiate sex or talk about it. Thus, males must continually push females into sex if they wanted to satisfy their own uncontrollable libido. Yet women who worked outside the home or who were from lower social classes were deemed immoral beings with insatiable sexual desires. The two stigmas encouraged sexual harassment in two ways: first, by suggesting that most women must be continually pursued and pressured for sex; and second, by suggesting that working women would not mind being harassed for sex. Reviews of mid-nineteenth century criminal records reveal that blaming the victim was often a successful legal defense of rape or harassment on the job, even when the rape victim was a thirteen-year-old child and the rapist, her employer.

A century later, the Civil Rights Act of 1964 outlined provisions against sexual discrimination in employment. In 1972, Congress passed the Education Act Amendments, which prohibited sex discrimination at schools and universities that receive any federal funding. But it was not until 1976, in *Williams v. Saxbe*, that sexual harassment was established by a court as an act of sexual job discrimination. In 1977, the first suit of sexual harassment was filed under **Title**

IX of the Education Amendments of 1972* in *Alexander v. Yale University*. This case was later dismissed because the student had graduated.

In the early 1980s, the Equal Employment Opportunity Commission (EEOC) published guidelines on sexual harassment. While the guidelines are not legally binding, many courts, including the U.S. Supreme Court (in *Meritor Savings Bank v. Vinson*) have used them to resolve issues in sexual harassment cases. The EEOC guidelines define sexual harassment as "unwelcomed sexual advances, requests for sexual favors, and other verbal or physical conduct of a sexual nature" when (1) submission to such conduct is made either explicitly or implicitly a term or condition of an individual's employment; (2) submission to or rejection of such conduct by an individual is used as the basis for employment decisions affecting such individual; and (3) such conduct has the purpose or effect of unreasonably interfering with an individual's work performance or creating an intimidating, hostile or offensive working environment.

In determining whether the alleged conduct constitutes sexual harassment, the EEOC looks at the record as a whole and the totality of the circumstances. Specifically, the EEOC reviews the nature and frequency of the advances and the context in which they are made.

From the guidelines, the courts have established two definitions of sexual harassment: quid pro quo and hostile environment. Quid pro quo ("this for that") occurs when a supervisor or someone in authority demands sexual favors from a subordinate in exchange for job benefits such as hiring, promotion, job retention, or training. A hostile environment, created by a supervisor, coworkers, or even nonemployees (such as customers) involves verbal conduct (sexual innuendo, jokes, and sexually derogatory remarks), physical touching, and graphic displays of sexually oriented materials. This form of sexual harassment does not have to result in the loss of a promotion or job; however, victims must prove that the totality of the acts has created a hostile work environment that interferes with their job performance.

Until 1991, most hostile environment claims were governed by the "reasonable man" standard. This standard held that when abusive actions or situations were reviewed by the court, the actions should be viewed in context of how a reasonable man (literally, a male) would react. In 1991, the reasonable man standard was substantially changed to the reasonable woman standard. In three separate cases, the courts agreed that women and men react differently. For example, sexual advances are often viewed as flattering by most males, while the same advances offend many women.

In 1993, the U.S. Supreme Court gave further support to the reasonable woman standard in *Harris v. Forklift Systems, Inc*. The Court ruled that a victim of sexual harassment does not have to prove severe psychological harm when making a claim. Before this ruling, claimants of a hostile environment case had to demonstrate that they suffered harm to the point of psychological devastation.

The Civil Rights Act of 1991 instituted the right to claim punitive and compensatory damages in sexual discrimination claims. Punitive damages are awarded to the plaintiff to punish the defendant; compensatory damages are awarded for the financial or psychological harm the plaintiff has suffered. Earlier, victims could collect only back-pay awards. Many believe this act will encourage companies and schools to enforce sexual harassment policies to avoid huge legal expenses.

Accordingly, the EEOC revised its sexual harassment guidelines in 1993. The agency expanded the definition of sexually harassing conduct to include, but not be limited to, the following: epithets; slurs; negative stereotyping; or threatening, intimidating, or hostile acts that relate to gender; and written or graphic material that denigrates or shows hostility or aversion toward an individual or group because of gender that is placed on walls, bulletin boards, or elsewhere on the employer's premises or circulated in the workplace.

Perhaps no other sexual harassment claim produced more public attention or awareness about sexual harassment than the 1992 congressional hearings on Clarence Thomas's appointment to the U.S. Supreme Court. Before a national audience, law professor Anita Hill charged Thomas with sexual harassment when he was her supervisor. This watershed event caused more women to become involved in government as well as prompting more favorable rulings in sexual harassment case law; in many ways, the hearings presented a televised workshop. The EEOC has witnessed a dramatic increase in claims since the hearings. Additionally, monetary settlements of claims nearly doubled between 1992 and 1993.

Until the 1992 Supreme Court decision in *Franklin v. Gwinnett County* that found schools liable for monetary damages in sexual harassment cases, little attention was paid to this abusive behavior in the schools, particularly to the damage that a hostile environment can cause to students' self-esteem and academic progress. In the early 1990s, however, two major surveys documented the extent of sexual harassment in schools. Louis Harris and the **American Association of University Women*** (AAUW) conducted a poll of 1,600 students in grades eight through eleven and discovered that 85 percent of girls and 76 percent of boys reported being sexually harassed. Furthermore, the poll documented that girls "find it hard to study in such an environment, participate less in class, drop out of extracurricular activities, and dread going to school" (American Association of University Women, "Fact Sheet").

The **Wellesley College*** Center for Research on Women and the NOW (**National Organization for Women***) Legal Defense and Education Fund collaborated in a major study of sexual harassment in schools published in *Seventeen* magazine. Over 4,200 girls in grades two through twelve participated. The findings revealed that harassment "happens in all kinds of schools, to all kind of girls," finding few differences for racial or ethnic background.

Increased awareness of sexual harassment has caused schools and companies to review their policies to minimize legal liability. Most legal advisers recommend the following procedures: establish a written policy prohibiting harassment; communicate the policy and train employees/students in what constitutes harassment; establish an effective grievance/complaint procedure; investigate all claims quickly; take remedial action to correct past harassment; make sure the complainant does not experience **backlash***; and follow up to prevent the continuance of harassment. Aggressive education and continual training are seen as having the best potential to reduce harassment within an organization.

Bibliography: Susan L. Webb, *Step Forward: Sexual Harassment in the Workplace* (1992); American Association of University Women, "Fact Sheet" (June 1993); Robert O. Riggs, Patricia H. Murrell, and Joanne C. Cutting, *Sexual Harassment in Higher Education: From Conflict to Community*, ASHE-ERIC Higher Education Reports, no. 2 (1993); Nan Stein, Nancy L. Marshall, and Linda R. Tropp, *Secrets in Public: Sexual Harassment in Our Schools. A Report on the Results of a* Seventeen *Magazine Survey* (1993); Kerry Segrave, *The Sexual Harassment of Women, 1600 to 1993* (1994); Luis Gomez-Mejia, David Balkin, and Robert Cardy, eds., *Managing Human Resources* (1995).

Brenda Lamb and Deborah Elwell Arfken

Shaw, Pauline Agassiz. Pauline Agassiz Shaw (1841–1917) was a nineteenth-century philanthropist and educator instrumental in promoting the public kindergarten and day nursery movements in the United States. Both movements addressed the social problem of women's uncompensated labor in the care of young children. Furthermore, the day nursery program provided young mothers with a progressive educational setting where they could learn more about parenting and acquire basic job skills.

Shaw was born in Neuchatel, Switzerland, on February 8, 1841. After her mother's death in 1848, she lived with her grandmother in Switzerland until 1850, when she joined her father, noted naturalist Louis Agassiz, in Cambridge, Massachusetts. She received her education primarily in a private girls' school run by her stepmother in the Agassiz home, as well as in the company of her father's academic friends. She married Quincy Adams Shaw in 1860; they had five children.

Shaw's concern for the education of her own children led to her interest in practical training for young people and her establishment of a small private school in Boston. After learning about the Froebelian **kindergarten movement*** that had begun flowering in the United States, and with encouragement from **Elizabeth Palmer Peabody**,* she opened two private kindergartens in Jamaica Plain and Brookline, Massachusetts, in 1877. Later, she started a kindergarten associated with her own private school, as well as a kindergarten training academy. Her efforts were influential: These programs stimulated mothers' meetings, parenting classes and clubs, and day nurseries.

When the Boston School Committee discontinued support for Peabody's public kindergarten system in 1879, Shaw lent her considerable financial backing to maintaining these schools while continuing to administer her own. She eventually financed over thirty free kindergartens. Moreover, she trained young women to supervise and manage the free kindergarten program. Her efforts provided a much-needed stimulus to the kindergarten movement, and by 1887, her success convinced the school committee to reassume financial responsibility for a number of the schools.

Shaw's kindergartens were also the locus of some of the first **child study movement*** experiments in the United States. She facilitated G. Stanley Hall's surveys of children's preschool knowledge by paying several of her teachers to assist him in full-time data collection. Ultimately, his research provided support for valuing kindergarten education.

Shaw's pioneering work in the day nursery movement made her a prominent figure in the education of young mothers. By 1880, she was supervising eight day nurseries and instructing mothers in nursing, **hygiene**,* and **temperance**.* She also conducted classes for women and girls in sewing and mending.

Shaw typically used her immense wealth to finance educational and social service experiments that she believed bettered the human condition. One of her favorite causes was adult citizenship education, which she addressed through endowment of several neighborhood houses that taught citizenship to adult laborers. Another was women's **suffrage**,* which she supported as founder and president of the Boston Equal Suffrage Association for Good Government. Shaw died in Boston on February 10, 1917. [See also **early childhood education**,* **early childhood teacher education**,* **nursery schools**.*]

Bibliography: Evelyn Weber, *The Kindergarten: Its Encounter with Educational Thought in America* (1969); Barbara Beatty, *Preschool Education in America: The Culture of Young Children from the Colonial Era to the Present* (1995). See also Nichols-Shurtleff Family Papers, 1780–1953, and Alexander Family Papers, 1809–1902, Radcliffe College, Schlesinger Library, Cambridge, Massachusetts; Maud Wood Park Papers, Library of Congress, Manuscript Division, Washington, D.C.; and George Robert White Papers, Massachusetts Historical Society Library, Boston.

Elizabeth Anne Yeager

slavery. Slavery in the United States lasted from 1619 to 1865. After capture in their native countries, African men and women were brought to other countries, including the United States, to provide free labor. It is believed that the first U.S. slaves were indentured servants who labored for a number of years to "earn back" their freedom. Although slavery is most commonly associated with the South, it is important to remember that slavery existed in the northern states until abolished in 1800. Most northern women slaves worked on small farms, raising dairy and cattle or vegetables, and working in homes as domestic servants. The situation for southern slaves was far different. Southern slaves provided a much-needed agricultural workforce for large plantations, and during the nineteenth century, the slave population, located solely in the South, grew significantly. In 1800 there were 893,602 slaves and 108,435 free blacks in the United States. In 1860, the last recorded census before slavery was abolished, there were 3,953,760 slaves and only 488,070 free blacks. Although there are records of a few of these free black women attending female **academies*** in the South, slaves were denied by law opportunity for an education.

Slave men and women were treated as property by white slaveowners. Slaves labored from early morning until night and were constantly threatened with whippings and other physical abuse. In the South, both men and women worked the fields raising lucrative cotton and tobacco crops as well as rice and corn on multiacre plantations. Women field slaves were expected to produce as much as many men. Women domestic servants were responsible for care of the house, the slaveowner's children, and food preparation. Both domestic and agricultural slaves performed back breaking manual labor under the threat of severe punishment.

Although both men and women slaves were subjected to inhuman conditions, women slaves carried an extra burden because they were responsible for their own families at the end of the day. Although slave women were expected to fulfill a woman's "traditional" role as mother, the family unit was not stable; families were broken up when slaveowners sold family members. Although it was rare that children were sold away from parents, it was more common that men were sold to other plantations. As a result, slave women were primary caregivers for their children. Women slaves were not only exploited for their skills as laborers but also for their ability to reproduce. In many cases, women slaves were impregnated, against their will, by the slaveowner himself. Since the status of the mother determined the status of the child, these biracial children were also slaves.

All slaves and many free blacks were denied the opportunity for education. It was, in fact, illegal for slaves to learn to read and write, and illegal for whites to teach them. Keeping slaves in ignorance guaranteed slaveowners complete control. The punishment for a slave knowing how to read or write was not only a whipping; often a finger was amputated or the face branded. These punishments were meted out in public as a reminder to other slaves of the price of literacy. However, the violence with which whites reacted to slave literacy served only to encourage the desire for these basic skills. The power of literacy was not lost on slaves. With the ability to read, slaves might find out what was happening in the world beyond them, and with the ability to write, they might be able to write their way to freedom.

Some slaves were successful in their quest for literacy. Although slaves kept their abilities hidden from masters, they shared their skills with fellow slaves. Clandestine **moonlight schools*** were held at night by candlelight. Often, schooling happened on Sundays with letters drawn in the dirt, easily erased if the slaveowner were to pass by. Sometimes slave children learned from the master's children by watching them do their schoolwork or making a game of reading or writing. In some cases, slave children accompanied the master's children to school, carrying books and meals, and stood outside the schoolhouse window. These and other methods allowed some slaves to learn to read and write. Despite the threat of punishment and the lack of formal schools, about 4 to 5 percent of slaves had learned to read by 1860. In contrast, about 17 percent of southern white women were literate by 1860, often through attendance at female academies. The rate of white women's illiteracy in the South was four times that of the North [see **female literacy***].

The end of the Civil War brought great changes to the South. After the war, the Freedmen's Bureau was established by the Department of War to aid in rebuilding the South and to help blacks make the transition from slavery to freedom. With financial help from the **American Missionary Association*** and various religious organizations, the Freedmen's Bureau was able to establish a number of public schools in the South. These schools were open to both whites and blacks; however, since whites refused to be educated alongside blacks, the schools were primarily black. Some southern states refused to allow freedmen's schools to be established. In other places, schools were burned. The **freedmen's teachers*** were mostly New Englanders and were viewed with a mixture of awe and suspicion by blacks and deep contempt by whites. In fact, the teachers were often threatened by southern whites. A small percentage of the teachers were black, graduates of colleges like **Oberlin*** or **high schools*** in northern cities.

Finances were a serious consideration as well. Although the schools were funded in part by the government and private organizations, those who attended were expected to contribute. In some cases, teachers "boarded around"[see **boarding around***] with families and were paid with vegetables or livestock. In addition, as committed as black adults were to having their children learn, they often could not afford the loss of children's labor and wages. The night programs established by some schools were heavily attended, primarily by women. However, there were many families where no one was able to attend school. Although freedom made education an option, it did not guarantee access for blacks.

Bibliography: James McPherson, *The Abolitionist Legacy* (1976); Thomas Webber, *Deep Like the Rivers* (1978); Jacqueline Jones, *Labor of Love, Labor of Sorrow* (1986); Darlene Clark Hine, ed., *Black Women in America: An Historical Encyclopedia* (1993); Patricia Morton, ed., *Discovering the Women in Slavery* (1996).

Cally L. Waite

Slowe, Lucy Diggs. Dean of Women at **Howard University*** (1922–1937), Lucy Diggs Slowe (1885–1937) was the most significant force in the higher education of African American women in the United States in the early twentieth century. Born in Berryville, Virginia, on July 4, 1885, Slowe was the youngest of seven children of Fanny Porter Slowe and Henry Slowe. Having lost both parents by the time she was six, Slowe subsequently lived with Martha Slowe Price, her paternal aunt, in Lexington, Virginia. Seven years later, they moved to Baltimore, Maryland, so that the children might have a better education; Slowe graduated as salutatorian from Baltimore Colored High School in 1904. With the aid of a scholarship, she matriculated at Howard University, where she enjoyed both academic and extracurricular success. She was a founder and officer of Alpha Kappa Alpha, the first **African American sorority*** for women in the United States.

For eleven years following her graduation from Howard, Slowe taught English at Baltimore Colored High School (1908–1915) and at Armstrong High School in Washington, D.C. (1915–1919). She also earned an M.A. in English from Columbia University in 1915. When the city of Washington opened Shaw Junior High School in 1919, the first such institution for African Americans in the District, Slowe became its first principal. At Shaw, she established an integrated in-service course for junior high school teachers, under the auspices of Columbia University.

Slowe embarked upon the most significant phase of her career in 1922, when she became the first **dean of women*** at Howard. Like many other pioneers in this profession, she simultaneously held an academic appointment, as professor of English and education. Despite the segregated nature of the profession, Slowe, like Esther Lloyd-Jones and Sarah Sturtevant, founders of the influential training program at Columbia's Teachers College, considered it essential to upgrade the dean's role from matron to trained professional, equal to any male administrator.

Slowe considered her primary duty as dean of women to be construction of a women's community where students could develop their full range of talents. Determined that women students have access to cultural opportunities, Slowe in 1929 established a Cultural Series, emphasizing Western high culture. She maintained that the many regulations pertinent to women students actually inhibited development of their leadership skills and personal responsibility. Better, she believed, for an institution to indicate confidence in its students, particularly women [see **student government***].

Like other professional women of her generation, Slowe devoted her considerable organizational skills to enhancing professional connections among educated African American women. In 1923, she was a founder and first president of the **National Association of College Women*** (NACW), an organization for African American alumnae of accredited colleges and universities. Six years later, as chair of NACW's Standards Committee, Slowe convened a meeting of advisers of girls and deans of women in African American institutions of secondary and higher education, to form the Conference (later **Association) of Deans of Women and Advisers to Girls in Negro Schools**,* under the auspices of the NACW. In 1935, the conference became an independent organization and elected Slowe president. Slowe also helped create the **National Council of Negro Women*** in 1935, serving as its first president.

Slowe was anxious that African American deans of women communicate with their white counterparts. One of the few African American women members of the **National Association of Deans of Women*** (NADW), Slowe forthrightly protested that group's apparent unwillingness or inability to locate its annual convention in cities whose hotels would allow all members to participate or to

protest the actions of establishments that refused to welcome conference participants regardless of color.

At Howard, despite the respect and affection of her students and professional
colleagues, Slowe encountered sustained opposition concerning funding, administrative authority, domestic arrangements, and job security from Mordecai W.
Johnson, who in 1926 became the university's first African American president.
Johnson repeatedly refused to increase either Slowe's salary or her budget. Furthermore, he sought to undermine her authority in a dispute concerning a male
faculty member accused by a woman student of using questionable language in
the classroom. Slowe's initial attempt to question the faculty member ended
with his disparaging her moral character and the extent of her campus power.
Initially, Johnson supported the faculty member. Following Slowe's threat to
resign, however, he presented the case to the trustees, who granted the man a
leave of absence at half salary.

Determined to assert authority over Slowe, Johnson demanded that she either
live on campus or resign. This was a particularly poignant and bitter point of
contention for Slowe, as it was for deans of women across racial lines. On most
campuses, virtually all male faculty members and administrators—single or married—lived off campus, as did those few married women faculty members or
administrators. However, on most campuses, the dean of women and a cadre of
single women faculty members lived in dormitories to supervise women students. Consequently, those women worked long hours, with minimal privacy or
respite from observation. Slowe cherished her off-campus home, which she
shared with Mary Burrill, a playwright and teacher at the prestigious Dunbar
High School in Washington, D.C. Furthermore, Slowe had made her home the
center of the Howard women's community.

With her own strength of character and widespread support of Howard alumnae and various African American women reformers, Slowe maintained her
domestic arrangement. She did so, however, at a price. The unremitting conflict
with Johnson continued until her untimely death from kidney disease on October
21, 1937.

As a woman active in the progressive tradition, Lucy Slowe made signal
contributions both to the profession of dean of women and to the higher education of African American women. Through her work as a founder and officer
of the Conference of Deans of Women, she sought, like her white counterparts
in the NADW, to establish a professional network, to improve training, and to
enhance the professional status of deans of women. Through her initiatives on
behalf of women, both on and off campus, Slowe fostered personal connections
and social action among African American college graduates and professional
women.

Bibliography: Karen Anderson, "Brickbats and Roses: Lucy Diggs Slowe," in Geraldine Jonçich Clifford, ed., *Lone Voyagers: Academic Women in Coeducational Institutions, 1870–1937* (1989); Linda M. Perkins, "Lucy Diggs Slowe," in Jessie Carney

Smith, ed., *Notable Black American Women* (1992); Kathleen Thompson, "Lucy Diggs Slowe," in Darlene Clark Hine, ed., *Black Women in America: An Historical Encyclopedia* (1993).

Carolyn Terry Bashaw

smashing. *Smashing* refers to a version of same-sex romantic friendships among college women of the late nineteenth century characterized by rituals of declaring love and courting. Young women professed open crushes on each other, fell in love, and courted. Initially viewed as innocent activity, smashing was recast as unnatural in the new twentieth-century vision of sexuality, and it disappeared by World War I.

American culture in the nineteenth century encouraged girls and young women to form powerful and emotionally satisfying friendship networks with one another. Middle-class white society rigidly enforced sex role separation and permitted little fraternization between the genders. Yet friendships among women were deemed socially natural, even ideal, as sources of support and companionship. These friendships, often in groups called a "bunch" or "coterie," continued well after marriage, frequently until death. Within this larger friendship network, however, some women formed intense and exclusive emotional relationships that paralleled heterosexual courtship and love. Historian Lillian Faderman has illustrated that these "romantic friendships" have a long tradition, dating at least as far back as the Renaissance.

When an increasing number of young women began attending college during the nineteenth century, a particular version of romantic friendships appeared on campuses. Women expressed their affection through writing love poems and letters, sending flowers, and exchanging gifts.

The all-female enclaves created within coeducational [see **coeducation***] universities and at the **women's colleges*** were both conducive to women's romantic friendships. In large part, women students, most of whom came from similar backgrounds, lived in a world isolated from men and that championed women's values. At single-sex colleges especially, smashing was even encouraged through all-female social events and dances, as well as student observations of faculty members living in long-term romantic friendships. Frances Willard commented on smashing as early as the 1850s at North Western Female Academy, but the practice is typically associated with the later part of the nineteenth century when college attendance among women rose dramatically. An 1873 letter to the *Yale Courant* described smashing at **Vassar College*** without a hint that the relationships were in any way troubling to the campus or the larger community. Jeannette Marks, the companion of Mary Woolley (president of Mount Holyoke College, 1901–1937), described women's colleges as "hot beds of sentimental friendships."

For many students, smashing was merely part of a rite of passage of college life, and they subsequently entered heterosexual relationships. For others, living with another woman in a romantic friendship, often called a **Boston marriage,*** became a life pattern. Both Boston marriages and smashing were fundamentally emotional relationships, yet evidence does indicate that, for some women at least, there was also an explicitly sexual component. It was not until the turn of the century, however, that society began to look askance at such pairings. Faderman argues that the work of sexologists, Sigmund Freud preeminent among them, was influential in recasting romantic friendships as homosexual and therefore deviant. Colleges, responding to criticisms that their graduates were not marrying and producing children in sufficient numbers, took pains to curb smashing and other reminders of romantic friendships. In 1911, Jeannette Marks published "A Girl's Student Days and After," warning of the dangers of such activity. By the eve of World War I, the transformation was nearly complete, and for the most part, vestiges of smashing and its accompanying rituals disappeared. What had been viewed as innocent and sentimental just a few decades earlier became thought of as unnatural and aberrant.

Bibliography: Nancy Sahli, "Smashing," *Chrysalis*, 8 (Summer 1979): 17–27; Lillian Faderman, *Surpassing the Love of Men: Romantic Friendship and Love between Women from the Renaissance to the Present* (1981); Faderman, *Odd Girls and Twilight Lovers: A History of Lesbian Life in the Twentieth Century* (1991).

Jana Nidiffer

Smith College. Smith College in Northampton, Massachusetts, is chronologically the fourth of the prestigious eastern **women's colleges*** known as the **Seven Sisters,*** founded in 1875 through the bequest of $400,000 by Sophia Smith. Although it began as a small institution, Smith was the largest of the women's colleges by 1900, competing with Harvard and Yale in its student population of nearly 2,000. Smith pioneered for women's colleges a "cottage system" of student residences that copied the more autonomous living arrangements provided for male collegians rather than the earlier **seminary*** model in which all women lived in one main building, under the watchful eye of female professors and supervisors. Even with the 1960s push for **coeducation*** and the proximity of nearby Amherst College, Smith has remained steadfastly a women's college, sustaining itself as one of the most prestigious liberal arts colleges for women in the country.

Sophia Smith of Hatfield, Massachusetts, was an unmarried woman who had depended on her brother and sister for financial and personal support. After the death of both her siblings, Smith inherited a great deal of family money, yet had no particular charity in mind as its recipient. Her pastor, John Morton Greene, agreed to guide Smith's consideration for her legacy and supported the idea of a local women's college. Greene had tutored at Amherst, and his wife had graduated from **Mary Lyon**'s* **Mount Holyoke Female Seminary,*** two connections that made Greene knowledgeable and opinionated about the best sort of higher education for women.

Although Mount Holyoke served as a model for many women's institutions,

Greene and the Amherst professors who joined him in his plan imagined a different type of institution that would provide, in their thinking, a stronger intellectual challenge than Lyon's evangelical focus. One possibility, of course, would have been coeducation at Amherst. This idea received little support and, in fact, most likely pushed the Amherst group into creating a strong college for women at Smith. It also encouraged their choice of a first president—Laurenus Clark Seelye, a minister and brother of noted Amherst professor Julius Seelye. Clark Seelye shared with the Amherst faculty a commitment to the value of the liberal arts, whether for men or women. In an era when college education for women was still challenged and even ridiculed and feared, Seelye supported a separate educational setting for women where they could study together and develop both mind and spirit in line with classical training.

The cottage system of student residences eventually produced a strong collegiate culture among the women, but it was originally designed to place them under closer, familial scrutiny. Seelye and others observed that a strong undergraduate life was developing on all campuses, although it was of particular concern at the women's institutions. Mount Holyoke and **Vassar*** had adopted a seminary model in organizing student life: The teachers served as personal guides over students' lives, acting as matrons living in the single large dormitory and taking responsibility for student supervision. Smith, in its effort to emulate a male institution and declare its strength, had already decided to support male presidents and a faculty of both men and women. Since men teachers would obviously not be appropriate for matronly supervision, Smith needed a familial atmosphere where women were guided not only by their teachers but also by the influences of townspeople leading regular, Christian family lives.

Both the cottage system of residences and the placement of Smith buildings close to Northampton emphasized the college's connection with its local environment. Seelye also determined that Smith should have neither chapel nor library; the women were expected to worship and study in Northampton, thereby enhancing their connection to the town. Before too long, the burden of collegiate needs forced the creation of both chapel and library buildings as well as numerous additional residences and classroom halls.

Smith opened in 1875 with 14 well-prepared students. Unlike most of the women's colleges, Smith determined not to create a preparatory department to boost the skills of entering students. Preparatory departments recognized both the uneven academic offerings available to young women in the nineteenth century, as well as the value of tuition revenue to support the collegiate enterprise. Smith, however, succeeded even without this addition. By 1885, more than 200 students attended; by 1920, when college attendance was surging around the country, Smith housed 1,980 students, making it the largest college for women in the country. President Seelye found another way to bolster enrollments, however. He created two schools within Smith, one for art and one for music—both aesthetic areas that Seelye felt of primary importance to refined collegiate women.

The cottage system and its family focus did not succeed in the long term, as Smith quickly outgrew a familial model. Rather, the autonomy of the separate cottages combined with the size of the student population to foster an active, vibrant student culture that remained Smith's hallmark over time. The earliest male presidents had long and significant tenures, prompting historian Helen Lefkowitz Horowitz to remark that the presidents' ''patriarchal presence meant that women faculty remained relatively weaker at Smith than at its sister women's colleges'' (Horowitz, p. 213). Women, especially alumnae, played a role on the college's board of trustees as early as 1889. After 1941, the chair of the board was always female. Nevertheless, male presidents dominated the institution until 1975 when historian Jill Ker Conway became the first female president of Smith.

Always a strong partner among the Seven Sisters, Smith has produced hundreds of notable alumnae. Dozens from every era of the college's history provided reminiscences of life at Smith and the college's influence on them in a 1975 collection, *College: A Smith Mosaic*. Some of the most well known, each of whom wrote for the *Mosaic*, include Ada Comstock, class of 1897, first **dean of women*** at the University of Minnesota and president of **Radcliffe College**,* 1923–43; chef and television personality Julia Child, 1934; author, feminist activist, and co-founder of the **National Organization for Women*** Betty Friedan,* 1942, whose visit to her Smith reunion catalyzed her challenges to *The Feminine Mystique**; Nancy Davis Reagan, 1943, wife of the former president; and feminist, author, and co-founder of *Ms.* magazine Gloria Steinem, 1956.

In the 1990s, Smith continues its tradition of rigorous liberal arts training for women in a setting committed to single-sex education. It honors its historical role in women's education through the Sophia Smith Collection, a nationally significant archival collection in women's history.

Bibliography: Elizabeth Deering Hanscom and Helen French Greene, *Sophia Smith and the Beginnings of Smith College* (1925); Thomas C. Mendenhall, *Chance and Change in Smith College's First Century* (1976); Helen Lefkowitz Horowitz, *Alma Mater: Design and Experience in the Women's Colleges from Their Nineteenth-Century Beginnings to the 1930s* (1984); Barbara Miller Solomon, *In the Company of Educated Women: A History of Women and Higher Education in America* (1985).

Linda Eisenmann

Smith-Hughes Act. The Smith-Hughes Act, also known as the Vocational Education Act, was signed into law by President Woodrow Wilson on February 23, 1917. It established **vocational education*** programs in the public schools by providing funds for agricultural, industrial, and home economics course work. The act had a mixed benefit for women: On one hand, it opened **home economics*** and some vocational programs to girls, but on the other, it often limited women's horizons to traditional home economics settings.

The act, which confirmed the acceptance of vocational education as a necessary part of schooling, was legislated ''for the purpose of cooperating with the States'' in paying ''the salaries of teachers, supervisors and directors of agricultural subjects . . . teachers of trade, home economics and industrial subjects and in the preparation of teachers.'' Its provisions included the stipulation for ongoing financial appropriations with minimal allotments, allocation of funds based on population, and instructional requirements for and public supervision of classes and schools in specific areas of employment training. The act provided for all-day, part-time, and evening classes in home economics as well as other specified subjects.

The Smith-Hughes Act, introduced by Senator Hoke Smith and Representative Dudley Hughes, both of Georgia, seemed to confirm an educational trend of the era of including vocational education in the curriculum, accelerating and standardizing the process for its acceptance with educational reform moving away from traditional schooling and toward a socially efficient curriculum. The act was designed to encourage schools to better prepare students for the tasks of later life. This, coupled with economic growth of the country and the need for skilled workers in an industrialized nation, determined that the bill would easily pass. With America's impending entry into World War I, President Wilson and the American people viewed vocational education and the passage of this bill as an integral part of the national preparedness plan.

The act significantly narrowed the gap between education and federal involvement and was considered a milestone in the development of federal aid to the states for education. All subsequently legislated aid to further vocational education was based on the provisions of this act.

As required by the act, a Federal Board of Vocational Education was created that included the Secretaries of Agriculture, Labor, and Commerce, the U.S. Commissioner of Education, and three citizens representing manufacturing and commerce, agriculture, and labor to be appointed by the president with the advice and consent of the Senate. To receive benefits, each state was required to designate a state board charged with developing a plan indicating how funds were to be used in that state and reporting annually to the federal board. Interestingly, although the federal board certainly made decisions concerning the education of females, no women were appointed to this early board.

Unlike previous legislation, the Smith-Hughes Act appropriated funds continually and permanently without requiring yearly appeals to Congress. The act required that state and local communities provide necessary physical plants and equipment, that at least one-half of instructional time be devoted ''to practical work on a useful basis or production basis,'' and that vocational education teachers be required to have at least four years of college work in their specialties.

Though not a part of the original act, home economics was added during a final phase shortly before voting took place. The Commission on Vocational Education, grappling with whether to include home economics, finally decided that while some young women would benefit from advanced education in specialized fields leading to careers, all girls could benefit from domestic training. Thus, although legislated to train young people for employment outside the home, the act, with inclusion of home economics, clearly trained young women for "careers" in their own future homes.

Although the act was lauded for recognizing vocational education's place in education, it was also criticized by some educators, including John Dewey, who warned "of making the school an adjunct to manufacture and commerce" with the added "danger that vocational education will be interpreted in theory and practice as trade education: as a means of securing technical efficiency." Dewey warned that vocational education could become "an instrument of perpetuating unchanged the existing industrial order of society, instead of operating as a means of its transformation" (Dewey, p. 316).

For young women, the act, in seeking to provide a vocation where they previously had no training, ultimately provided legislation that has been seen by some to relegate females to traditional roles in the home and family. Although some schools did provide a home economics model that trained girls for employment outside the home, throughout the century it became increasingly clear that most home economics training was preparation for the girl's future occupation as homemaker in her own home. In many schools, home economics was the only vocational area open to women.

In further critiques, some educators have pointed out that vocational education not only separates men from women in the public schools; it also tends to promote a curriculum segregated from academic classes, contributing to the isolation of vocational education from other subjects in the comprehensive **high school*** program. The additional requirements of state boards of vocational education that are separate from general boards of education result in further segregation of vocational education from mainstream schools operations. This creates further problems when utilized, as some educationists believe, as a tracking device to limit certain students to vocational programs.

Though originally a boon to women's education, and a recognition of the necessity of making opportunities available for girls, vocational education can arguably be perceived as a separating device that supports and encourages traditional feminine roles for women. [See also **commercial education**.*]

Bibliography: John Dewey, *Democracy and Education* (1916, reprinted 1966); Gladys A. Branegan, *Home Economics Teacher Training under the Smith-Hughes Act 1917–1927* (1929); Herbert M. Kliebard, *The Struggle for the American Curriculum 1893–1958* (1987); Lawrence A. Cremin, *American Education: The Metropolitan Experience, 1876–1980* (1988); John L. Rury, *Education and Women's Work: Female Schooling and the Division of Labor in Urban America, 1870–1930* (1991).

Susan Clark Studer

Smith-Lever Act. The Smith-Lever Act, signed into law by President Woodrow Wilson in 1914, provided for the dissemination of practical information to farmers and homemakers by establishing extension programs organized through the cooperation of land-grant colleges, various states, and the federal government.

The act appropriated funds made available to states "in order to aid in diffusing among the people of the United States useful and practical information on subjects relating to agriculture and **home economics**,* and to encourage the application of the same." For women in education, the Smith-Lever Act recognized the importance of women's role both in the university and in the home by providing information through home economics courses enhancing the lives of those living in rural areas and providing new vistas of opportunity for women.

The Smith-Lever Act provided dollar-matching federal funds to the states for farm and home demonstration work and was, in essence, an extension of the first and second **Morrill Land-Grant Acts of 1862 and 1890**.* The Morrill Act of 1862 had awarded public lands to the states to establish colleges (the "land-grant colleges") "for the benefit of agriculture and the mechanic arts," and the 1890 act had provided for agricultural work to be conducted in cooperation with the Department of Agriculture.

The Smith-Lever Act, originally prepared jointly by the Land Grant College Association Executive Committee and the Extension Committee, was submitted to Congress in 1911 by Representative Ashbury Lever of South Carolina. The act originally passed the House but subsequently failed in the Senate. The following year it was revived in the Senate by Senator Hoke Smith from Georgia who coauthored the **Smith-Hughes Act*** in 1917. The bill passed the Senate the second time as the Smith-Lever Act, and a conference version was signed by President Wilson in May 1914.

The act enabled and financially supported aspects of home economics benefiting both the profession (dominated by women) and people living in rural areas who did not have access to agricultural educational facilities. It provided for extensions as an adjunct to the experimental stations (colleges) and came at a period when Americans, preparing for war, looked to the extensions for knowledge that would benefit them both at home and abroad. Home extension subjects included technical, scientific, and business methods, sanitation practices, and economic, social, and moral subjects. While providing for teacher salaries and dissemination of information, the act stated that no money was to be used for the purchase, erection, preservation, or repair of any building or land [see **home extension education***].

The Smith-Lever Act was "permanently appropriated," that is, it provided ongoing federal funds to state agricultural colleges and required matching funds from states. The act was available to any state that submitted plans falling within its statutes and limitations. As a result, a new partnership among states, land-grant campuses, and the federal government evolved. As such, this enactment represented the first organized attempt to educate adults for better home living and the first record of definite legislation related to the home.

According to the act, extension work would "consist of the giving of instruction and practical demonstrations in agriculture and home economics to persons not attending or resident in said colleges." Extensions would provide "information on said subjects through field demonstrations, publications and otherwise.''

By using cooperative extension work and practical home demonstrations, the act provided innovative scientific findings in agriculture and home economics from the college to the farm. Through the extension, trained home economists were called upon to demonstrate food conservation techniques and safe health practices and to serve as dietitians at home and abroad. Because of the act's new focus on the importance of the role of the extension instructors in the lives and homes of those they served, home economists increasingly participated in conferences, and women benefited from this new public role. In 1915, for example, two home economists, Henrietta Calvin and Carrie A. Langford, were added to the U.S. Bureau of Education, and in 1919, home economists participated in a presidential Food Administration Conference.

In addition to the significance of scientific agricultural information being imparted to those who could most benefit, the Smith-Lever Act strengthened the role of the farmer by recognizing the farm family's importance during a time when farmers were experiencing problems brought on by industrialization and environmental elements. By providing farmers a pipeline for information, a new basis of political power developed in the American Farm Bureau Association, a powerful national speaker that would be significant, especially during the New Deal.

Women benefited from the act as professional home economists, teachers, and recipients of services. Home economists benefited, for example, by gaining recognition as experts in information, resulting in their inclusion in government efforts. The bill provided opportunities for women to teach in areas where previous importance was not recognized.

Although one might argue that supporting an act that encouraged a traditional female role was detrimental for women, providing information to them in their rural situations actually lightened the load of the farmwife and formally recognized her importance in home and family.

Bibliography: Hazel T. Craig, *The History of Home Economics* (1945); Lawrence A. Cremin, *American Education: The Metropolitan Experience, 1876–1980* (1988).

Susan Clark Studer

Social Darwinism. *Social Darwinism* is a term that invokes the theory of evolution or the writings of Charles Darwin in discussing social policy. The term first emerged in the 1870s, in applying to social developments the concepts of natural selection, the struggle for existence, and the survival of the fittest found in the works of Darwin and Herbert Spencer. The notion implies that struggle and selection within the animal world are also elements of change and progress within human society. It was associated with conservativism and a desire to maintain the status quo, as well as a belief in laissez-faire economics and ''rugged individualism.'' The essence of Social Darwinism concerns whether society should attempt to preserve its weakest members through legal and humanitarian means and whether such actions will prevent the progress of the human race.

In *Origin of Species* (1859) Darwin argued that species varied in nature as well as in captivity and that the struggle for existence preserved the strong and eliminated the weak. The process of natural selection determined favorable variations; through genetic transmission of those variations, a new species would eventually evolve. In discussing the development of human intellect in *The Descent of Man* (1871), Darwin argued that males' higher metabolic rate caused them to vary more and have more attributes when facing forces of natural selection than females; males were stronger and more intelligent because they faced natural selection forces. Motherhood compounded the problem for females by making them dependent upon males. Thus, women were somewhat removed from the full process of evolution and, therefore, one step behind men. Women's brains were underdeveloped (proven by differences in weight) and more attuned to lower levels of cognition. Human beings and the universe, then, were subject to biological determinism and directed by constant struggle and strife in unknown directions.

Various interpretations of Darwinism appeared within ethics, politics, religion, society, and the sciences. The most influential was the British philosopher Herbert Spencer. Concerned with escalating problems in England's urban centers, in *Principles of Biology* (1866), Spencer applied Darwin's biological concept of natural selection to social principles. He believed the competitive struggle for existence in society insured human progress and termed it ''the survival of the fittest.'' Inheritance was central, for it guaranteed the transmission of favorable characteristics to future generations. In *Man vs. the State* (1884) Spencer argued that competition and the individual were the key elements of progress. Government intervention on behalf of the needy was wasteful and harmful to the natural process of evolution. Society was best regulated by the natural process of competition: Democracy and human progress were insured by laissez-faire policies. Banking regulations, poor laws, and compulsory public education could not rid society of its ills. These views were the bedrock of Social Darwinism, as popularized in America by William Graham Sumner in *What Social Classes Owe to Each Other* (1884).

By the 1880s and 1890s, mounting concern for the social cost of industrialization led to organized response to social problems and to increasing criticism of Spencer. Disillusioned by crime, financial panics, class conflict, and other mounting social and economic problems, ''reform Darwinists'' and ''progressive reformers'' rejected Spencer's view that evolution proceeded efficiently. Writers such as Henry George and Edward Bellamy argued that evolution supported cooperation and group solidarity over individualism and that people must intervene in the evolutionary process in order to protect themselves from the devastating impact of competitive struggle. Led by Lester Frank Ward, the reform Darwinists used evolutionary theory to argue that humankind must be an active participant in the evolutionary process by directing human progress through the use of the mind. Reform Darwinists demanded increased government regulation and new efforts of societal welfare and social control, and they helped generate progressive reforms at the turn of the century.

In *Dynamic Sociology* (1883), Ward published a major rebuttal of Spencer, arguing that attention to humankind's milieu would uplift the poor and "inferior" until biological and sociological equality existed for all. If nature progressed through survival of the fittest, then humans progressed through protection of the weakest. Collectivism, not individualism, was society's natural process, and this required rule by intelligence. Further, unchecked natural evolution exacerbated social problems by polarizing the sexes, which limited women's physical and mental development and, thus, their stabilizing force upon society. Through education women could be restored to equal importance and the race could continue to progress. Education, thus, was the "great panacea," the active force in evolution, the cornerstone of social progress, and the remedy for social misery.

The feminist **Charlotte Perkins Gilman*** in *Women and Economics* (1898) popularized Ward's concerns regarding polarization of the sexes. Throughout the course of evolution, she argued, females had been subjugated by economic dependency, resulting in a masculinized society in which competition and adventure overwhelmed cooperation and nurturance. Both Ward and Gilman considered these developments a necessary stage in the evolutionary process but one that was complete. The continuation of female subjugation would only retard human progress. According to Gilman, men's failure to share in the development of what were considered female characteristics was as harmful as women's failure to share in male qualities. The way to achieve this balance was through **feminization*** of society, requiring the end of women's economic dependence, extension of all special and political rights to women, and feminization of the philosophy, methodology, and demographics of higher education.

The issue of higher education was most controversial, since both the "social" and "reform" Darwinists used the theory of evolution to support their conflicting opinions. Social Darwinists viewed the stratification of the sexes into distinct spheres as a hallmark of civilization and argued that such differences should be cultivated, not abolished. Opening higher education to women would have disastrous effects on society: The middle class would fail to reproduce itself and would commit **race suicide***—allowing itself to be outnumbered by uneducated immigrants.

Reform Darwinists and feminists agreed that evolution had produced serious differences in the physical and mental characteristics of the sexes. However, they argued that women were by no means inferior; their mental strength was simply found in different areas. Female uniqueness and special qualities resulting from evolution justified higher education for women. Education would not turn women into men but could infuse men's strength with women's tact and sympathetic insights. In this way, society could check unbridled male aggression, rationalism, individualism, and competition. The reform Darwinists and feminists not only justified entrance of women into higher education but questioned traditional educational philosophy and methodology—a critique begun by Gilman in the 1890s and continued by feminist educational theorists throughout the twentieth century. [See also **Progressive Era**.*]

Bibliography: Janice Law Trecker, "Sex, Science, and Education," *American Quarterly,* 26 (1974): 352–366; Stephanie A. Shields, "The Variability Hypothesis: The History of a Biological Model of Sex Differences in Intelligence," *Signs,* 7 (1982): 769–797; Cynthia Eagle Russett, *Sexual Science: The Victorian Construction of Womanhood* (1989); Carl Degler, *In Search of Human Nature: The Decline and Revival of Darwinism in American Social Thought* (1991); Robin Gilmore, *The Victorian Period: The Intellectual and Cultural Context, 1870–1890* (1993).

Deborah M. De Simone

social feminism. *Social feminism* is a term used to denote the reform endeavors of women in the **Progressive Era*** (roughly 1890–1920). These activities are also referred to by modern historians as **social housekeeping**,* "municipal housekeeping," or "domestic feminism." In response to changing social and economic conditions wrought by urbanization and industrialization, middle- and upper-class women sought to inject what they considered women's distinctive qualities into the public realm. They argued that women's traditional roles as mothers made them best suited to shape social policy regarding children, health, and education, among other issues. The Progressive Era saw the growth of numerous women's organizations dedicated to investigating and ameliorating problems of the poor, immigrants, children, and working women. Although most social feminists were white, Protestant, and middle class, there was a significant black **women's club movement*** that addressed many of the same issues. Some social feminists applied their ideology to female **suffrage**.* However, rather than demanding the vote based on gender equality, they claimed the franchise was necessary to interject their inherent moral and maternal attributes into the political arena.

Social feminists were deeply concerned with education on all levels. During the Progressive Era, public schools were controlled by male administrators and school boards. Women made up most of the **teaching*** force, but curriculum and management decisions were made by men who were often partisan politicians in patronage positions. Hundreds of organizations like the **Women's Educational and Industrial Union*** were formed across the country in cities like Boston, Buffalo, and Topeka around the turn of the century. They launched campaigns to wrest control of public schools from ward bosses by calling for centralized citywide administration of schools. Women also successfully agitated for the right to vote for school board members and to serve as such in several cities, winning this privilege before receiving the general vote.

Clubwomen, in particular, promoted a variety of reforms that resulted in expansion of the social responsibilities of neighborhood schools. They argued that changes in urban and industrial areas had reduced parental control over children's lives, and thus the state had the duty to ensure that schools assume a nurturing capacity. Reformist women expressed particular concern for offspring of immigrants and working parents. Here, the women's class bias showed as they espoused state intervention into the family life of the poor while not sharing their experiences.

Social feminists promoted experimental programs in schools and sought to implement them by pressuring ward leaders and forming alliances with teachers. They pushed for an end to corporal punishment and rote memorization. They advocated for a new pedagogy that emphasized the individual child and taught innovative subjects like manual training, domestic science, and nature study [see **child study movement***]. Their proposals ranged from **kindergarten*** classes to adjustable desks for students. Clubwomen were the creators, funders, and administrators of vacation schools for urban children during the summer months as an alternative to life on the streets. Social feminists also joined in coalitions with working-class parents to bring playgrounds to city children.

Social feminists brought energy and innovation to education in urban America. Using the political avenues open to them as well as moral suasion, they successfully convinced city government to take over many of the programs they supported through their volunteer efforts. Upon municipal assumption of women's initiatives, however, their experimental and reform aspects usually declined.

Higher education in the Progressive Era reflected the impact of social feminists as well as trained a generation of them. At the **Seven Sisters*** colleges and some coeducational [see **coeducation***] schools, women received an education that linked the curriculum to the world. Off-campus political and reform activities partnered with collegiate efforts in order to prepare young women for leadership roles in social service. The first generation of college women who graduated from 1860 to 1890, such as Edith Abbott, Katherine Bement Davis, and Frances Kellor, became activists and social scientists who provided leadership in laying a scientific foundation for understanding industrialization's damaging effects on the poor and the powerless. They served as mentors and role models for the second generation who received their degrees prior to 1920. The higher education of women was resisted by many men in academe who feared **feminization*** of education, but colleges nonetheless provided a space where young women could learn the philosophy and tools of progressive social reform movements.

The legacy of the early twentieth century social feminists is seen in the continuing dialogue about the role and responsibilities of schools in the lives of children, particularly the disadvantaged. The social service components, such as school lunches and parent-teacher organizations [see **National Congress of Mothers***], invented and demanded by these women have become part of the mission of modern schools. Their grassroots activism and alliances with neighborhood coalitions foreshadowed present-day struggles over centralization and local control.

Bibliography: William J. Reese, *Power and the Promise of School Reform: Grass-Roots Movements during the Progressive Era* (1986); Sara M. Evans, *Born for Liberty: A History of Women in America* (1989, revised 1997); Ellen Fitzpatrick, *Endless Crusade: Women Social Scientists and Progressive Reform* (1990); Lynn D. Gordon, *Gender and Higher Education in the Progressive Era* (1990); Anne Meis Knupfer, *Toward a Tenderer Humanity and a Nobler Womanhood: African American Women's Clubs in Turn-of-the-Century Chicago* (1996).

Carol Cullen

social housekeeping. *Social housekeeping* is a term used to describe the widespread involvement of women between 1890 and 1930 in reform activities in the United States. Sometimes labeled ''municipal housekeeping,'' ''public motherhood,'' or **social feminism**,* this movement was a broad-based response to conditions arising from urbanization, industrialization, and immigration during the **Progressive Era**,* a period of nationwide attention to reform. These mostly middle-class women extended the reach of their maternal mission into the public domain in an effort to ameliorate problems apparently associated with these changes. Women's involvement in largely single-sex organizations with a reformist character achieved a scale unprecedented in the country's long history of women's benevolent efforts.

Among groups founded during the Progressive Era that tackled social problems at municipal, state, and national levels were the Women's Christian Temperance Union, the National Consumers League, the National Association of Colored Women's Clubs, the **General Federation of Women's Clubs**,* the **Women's Trade Union League**,* and the **settlement house movement**.* **Suffrage**,* groups like the **National American Woman Suffrage Association**,* and its statewide affiliates also grew in membership and influence. While much overlap existed between suffrage organizations and those involved in social housekeeping, the latter groups emphasized use of social science to battle social ills rather than advocacy for women's rights. Nevertheless, many social housekeeping groups gradually moved to support women's right to vote because they came to recognize its importance in achieving their aims.

The Women's Christian Temperance Union (WCTU) became the largest organization in the United States during this period, with numerous state and local chapters dedicated to the **temperance movement***goal of stamping out the evils of alcohol and its effects on families. The General Federation of Women's Clubs (GFWC) was established in 1890, evolving from its initial identity as a set of literary and self-improvement societies into a national effort for women's education and engagement with social issues. The Women's Trade Union League, founded in New York in 1903, was not a **labor union***but an organization of middle- and upper-class women who wished to organize working women and thus improve their status and conditions of work. By the turn of the century the WCTU reported 800,000 members, and GFWC nearly 1 million. Among their many objectives were demands for pure food and drug laws; the establishment of **kindergartens**,* libraries, and playgrounds; conservation of the environment; protective legislation for working women; and child labor laws.

The most famous representative of the social housekeeping movement is **Jane Addams**,* best known as the founder, along with Ellen Starr, of **Hull-House**,* a settlement in Chicago, in 1889. Settlement houses functioned as social service agencies for newly arrived immigrant populations in urban areas. Many women associated with Hull-House went on to establish other settlement houses and create new vehicles for reform. Florence Kelley and Julia Lathrop helped establish the National Child Labor Committee in 1904. Kelley was also a founding member of the **National Association for the Advancement of Colored People*** in 1909 and the Women's International League for Peace and Freedom in 1919. In 1912, Lathrop was named by President William Howard Taft as first director of the Children's Bureau, a federal commission established because of efforts by Kelley, Lathrop, and other women.

Lathrop's assumption of a government position suggests the close association of social housekeepers with municipal, state, and federal governments. A fundamental goal of the movement was convincing government of the need to adopt a sense of public responsibility for social welfare. Countless women lobbied political leaders to endorse creation of government commissions to assume oversight of health, labor, safety, educational, and recreational needs of communities. As a result, women increasingly were seen and viewed themselves as public players. Because this new function largely represented an extension of the maternal role into the public domain, many mainstream women gradually were won over to woman suffrage [see **Women's Bureau***].

The significance of social housekeeping to the history of women's education is at least twofold. First, organizations like Hull-House offered the opportunity to educated women like Addams and Lillian Wald, founder of the Henry Street Settlement in New York City, to put their educations to practical use. As the number of women attending college increased, many graduates looked for an opportunity to engage in meaningful activity that would apply their education to social problems. The development of social science seemed to promise the opportunity for genuine improvement in social conditions. Progressives in many fields used the new learning to introduce changed approaches to law, education, philosophy, and politics.

Second, for women who did not attend college, organizations such as the **women's clubs*** provided a form of compensatory education. As these groups moved beyond their initial orientation as **women's study clubs*** and self-improvement societies, they invited speakers to address pressing social issues in an effort to stimulate reflection and discussion of these topics. In effect, the social housekeeping movement functioned as a form of advanced education for women that merged new modes of thought with practical efforts to correct social problems.

In the end, social housekeeping was moderately successful in affecting civic life. At local and state levels, for example, measures were passed for meat and milk inspection, playgrounds, libraries, and conservation. At the national level, several examples can be cited. The 1908 Supreme Court decision in *Muller v. Oregon* established protective legislation for women workers due to efforts of women labor advocates. Child labor laws were passed in 1918 and 1922, but the Supreme Court often struck down this and other social welfare legislation. Nevertheless, several states passed child labor laws that endured court tests. Finally, the Sheppard Towner Act of 1920 briefly provided public health nurses for infant and maternal protection until its defeat in 1927.

While historians have generally considered 1920 the end to Progressivism nationwide, women's historians have emphasized its continuation into the 1930s via efforts to use maternalist rhetoric to establish a welfare state. Social housekeeping helped create new vehicles for women's education on social and political issues and an informed constituency for public policy. In so doing, these organizations contributed to women's self-definition as a cohort with identifiable interests and a legitimate public role. Once suffrage was achieved in 1920, many social housekeepers moved into political parties to work more directly for their causes. Nevertheless, continued resistance to such involvement by some men and women significantly inhibited the impact of the vote.

Bibliography: Karen J. Blair, *The Clubwoman as Feminist: True Womanhood Redefined, 1868–1914* (1980); Nancy Woloch, *Women and the American Experience* (1984); Anne Firor Scott, *Natural Allies: Women's Associations in American History* (1991); Seth Koven and Sonya Michel, eds., *Mothers of a New World: Maternalist Politics and the Origins of Welfare States* (1993); Linda K. Kerber, Alice Kessler-Harris, and Kathryn Kish Sklar, eds., *U.S. History as Women's History: New Feminist Essays* (1995).

Margaret Smith Crocco

social work. The term *social work* came to refer to a profession early in the twentieth century, yet only in 1929 did the federal census remove it from the category of **semiprofessions*** that included fortune tellers. The professionalization project within social work generated ongoing internal debates about proper ways to secure legitimation.

Among the most formidable obstacles to professional advancement was social work's historical association with nineteenth-century women's reform and religious work. Throughout the antebellum period, the widespread conviction of women's unique responsibility and "natural" abilities for disseminating virtue and morality was used by women to increase their freedom outside the home and their participation in a wide range of benevolent and evangelical activities. Primarily as untrained volunteers known as "friendly visitors" to the poor, women were involved in a broad spectrum of reform movements including industrial schools, rescue homes, moral reform societies, and missionary activities [see **Board of Foreign Missions***].

However, leaders of the scientific charity organization movement (COS), organized in response to social anxieties about disorder in the late nineteenth century, criticized womanly voluntary ministrations as sentimental and indiscriminate. To elevate the prestige of charity and reform work, COS experts attempted to defeminize benevolence by questioning ideologies of women's special fitness for charity work; they also supplanted notions of woman's moral superiority with the authority of experts trained in scientific charity methods.

The nineteenth-century ideology of women's unique fitness for benevolence was never totally eclipsed, however. According to the federal census in 1930, 70 percent of the nation's 20,000 social workers were women. Although some women assumed leadership positions in national professional associations and social work education, males predominated as agency-level administrators, with women typically confined to direct service.

Zilpha Drew Smith, founder of the Boston Charity Organization Society, asserted that the chief mechanism for educating friendly visitors was "life itself" as well as training in informal, agency-based apprenticeships. Such on-the-job training was initially considered adequate to eradicate the friendly visitor model and to redefine it as a skilled professional relationship based on investigation, diagnosis, and treatment. Soon, however, agency-based, in-service training programs were judged too narrow to advance professional expertise.

Systematic professional education was championed by Mary Richmond, director of the Baltimore Charity Organization Society, who argued in 1897 for a school of applied philanthropy emphasizing a broad scientific knowledge base and generic skills. In keeping with the historical emphasis on apprenticeship, however, Richmond also advocated that a high proportion of trainees' time be spent in agency-supervised fieldwork, a requirement that survives today. Richmond's vision was realized in the first professional training institute, the New York School of Philanthropy, established in 1898 and soon followed by the Chicago School of Civics and Philanthropy and the Boston School for Social Workers. After serving on the faculty at New York, Richmond became director of the Charity Organization Department of the Russell Sage Foundation and was responsible for organizing nationwide summer institutes to disseminate principles of scientific charity. Her 1917 book *Social Diagnosis* became the bible of social work practice, unifying many of its disparate specialties under the rubric "social casework," a diagnostic and treatment process that provided the template for early social work practice (excluding settlement work) and is the forerunner of direct practice today.

Another pathway to professionalization was the increased attention given to establishing schools of social work, especially collegiate schools. By 1919, seventeen schools had been established, most postbaccalaureate, although three undergraduate programs began at midwestern state universities. Many college-trained social work leaders advocated the benefits of university affiliation and

graduate education,* although this issue divided early educators. **Sophonisba Breckinridge*** and Edith Abbott, both college graduates with advanced degrees, pushed for university affiliation to replace part-time institutes and certificate programs. Arguing that full-time graduate training would increase prestige, they were responsible for reorganizing the Chicago School of Social Administration with Abbott as first dean. The increased emphasis on graduate education, however, was met with resistance from many quarters, including working-class students, and most likely eliminated many persons, especially women of color, from professional training.

A survey of 1,258 social workers in 1921 found that only 40 percent of the women were college graduates, and only 7 percent had one full year of training. Despite this gap, the American Association of Social Workers (AASW), established in 1921, further restricted membership in 1932 to graduates of accredited graduate schools. Not until 1968 were graduates of accredited undergraduate programs allowed membership.

The emergent professional identity acquired through formal education and the resultant waning of volunteerism were also nourished by the expansion of specialized professional associations within social work. Unified by a commitment to casework, social workers were increasingly found in hospitals, psychiatric clinics, and schools, where they often were forced to navigate hostile interprofessional relationships with psychiatrists, educators, and physicians seeking to relegate them to junior status.

Ida Cannon, a founder of medical social work who served as director of social services at Massachusetts General Hospital, founded and presided over the American Association of Medical Social Workers. Helping to establish psychiatric social work, Mary Jarrett organized a social service department at Boston Psychopathic Hospital in 1913, and in 1918 she developed a training course in psychiatric social work that led to the founding of the **Smith College*** of Social Work. Jarrett also developed the American Association of Psychiatric Social Workers and became Smith's first associate director [see **medical education***].

Visiting teachers, forerunners of modern school social work, constituted another strand of casework practice that, in part, originated from **settlement house*** reformers. The National Association of Visiting Teachers was established in 1916 and met alternately with the National Education Association and the National Conference on Social Work.

In addition to casework, social group work, stemming from settlement houses, **Young Women's Christian Associations**,* and community and recreation centers, was increasingly accepted as part of professional practice. The American Association of Group Work was organized in 1936 and, under the leadership of Grace Coyle, gained legitimacy within social work education.

In the 1930s, massive federal involvement led to the expansion of public welfare services. At the same time that a huge influx of new workers who had not been university trained entered social work, the AASW raised standards for membership. Also during the 1930s, the Rank and File Movement, composed primarily of public relief workers, provided a challenge to elite university models by its identification with **labor unions**.* The 1940s witnessed another battle in social work over professional recognition of undergraduate programs, while the 1950s brought increased organizational cohesion with establishment of the Council of Social Work Education in 1952, a single accrediting and policymaking body for both undergraduate and graduate education, and the National Association of Social Work in 1955, which brought together several distinct organizations.

Today, women numerically predominate as social workers and as students and clients of social work. However, their proportion decreases as deans and full professors despite passage of an **affirmative action*** policy on women students, faculty, and curricular content.

Bibliography: Leslie Leighninger, *Social Work: Search for an Identity* (1987); Lori Ginzberg, *Women and the Work of Benevolence: Morality, Politics, and Class in the Nineteenth Century U.S.* (1990); Robyn Muncy, *Creating a Female Dominion in American Reform, 1890–1935* (1991); Regina Kunzel, *Fallen Women and Problem Girls: Unmarried Mothers and the Professionalization of Social Work* (1993); Karen W. Tice, *Tales of Wayward Girls and Immoral Women: Social Case Records and the Construction of Professional Knowledge* (forthcoming, 1998).

Karen W. Tice

sororities. Sororities, clubs of women often but not always drawing their support from colleges and universities and using Greek letters for identification and in their ceremonies, trace their origins to the establishment of Phi Beta Kappa at William and Mary College in Virginia in 1776. Early fraternities were exclusively male, drawing much of their ritual from Freemasonry, to which some members belonged. In the nineteenth century, sororities were founded to provide women similar experiences to those offered by male fraternities, and in fact, women's sororities gave female members the opportunity to exercise leadership in ways not usually available in the classroom.

The so-called social Greeks and honorary Greeks eventually went their separate ways. The student-led social Greeks emphasized residential facilities and became part of American folklore with their initiation high jinks. The honorary Greeks, retaining high levels of faculty participation, recognized scholarly qualifications.

As numbers of women students increased, pressures grew to admit them to organizations that male students took for granted. One of the first women members of Phi Beta Kappa was Emily Francis Fairchild of **Oberlin College**'s* class of 1844, but she was elected into the Oberlin chapter only in 1907. The University of Vermont chapter elected Ellen Hamilton and Lida Mason in 1875, evidently the first women anywhere to be selected. Wesleyan's Phi Delta Kappa admitted women in 1876 and Cornell in 1882, although a Cornell male member complained, ''It seems to me in the first place absurd to admit women to a Fraternity, and, secondly, that the whole tradition and character of the concern make it exclusively a male affair.'' **Vassar*** was the first **women's college*** to have its own Phi Beta Kappa chapter, in 1899.

The National Panhellenic Conference for sororities was founded in 1902, seven years before the male National Interfraternity Conference. Problems associated with fraternities, such as hazing and substance abuse, have generally been less a problem in sororities, although some colleges banned sororities out of concern for their supposedly divisive effect on the student body. Brown University did so in 1911, and Swarthmore in 1934. In the history of women's education, sororities hold a shared legacy of enhancing leadership opportunities but also of allowing social and racial divisions. [See also **African American sororities,*** **student government**.*]

Bibliography: Helen Lefkowitz Horowitz, *Campus Life: Undergraduate Cultures from the End of the Eighteenth Century to the Present* (1987); Richard Nelson Current, *Phi Beta Kappa in American Life: The First Two Hundred Years* (1990); Jack L. Anson and Robert F. Merchesani, Jr., *Baird's Manual of American College Fraternities* (1991); Paul Rich and Guillermo De Los Reyes, ''The Origins of Phi Beta Delta,'' *Phi Beta Delta International Review* (1996).

Paul Rich

Southall, Maycie K. An active, dedicated, and influential pioneer in **early childhood education*** and in the supervision of instruction, Maycie Katherine Southall (1895–1992) stands as a premier educator in the South and the nation. In addition to a thirty-five-year **teaching*** career at George Peabody College for Teachers in Tennessee, Southall also exerted influence in national and international organizations including UNESCO (United Nations Educational, Scientific and Cultural Organization), the Association for Childhood Education International (ACEI), and the service-oriented Delta Kappa Gamma.

Ninth of ten children, Southall was born on July 7, 1895, to William Albert Southall, Jr., and Mary Louise Delk at the family home, Vine Hill, in Maury County, Tennessee. She completed her basic education in Tennessee schools at age fifteen. On a visit to her sister in Georgia, she was offered, and accepted, a teaching position in a one-teacher school. Although she turned only sixteen during her first week there, the school prospered under her guidance.

In 1912, she began to take courses at Middle Tennessee **Normal School*** (later Middle Tennessee State University) between terms of teaching in Georgia and Tennessee. In 1918, as a student, she began her longtime association with George Peabody College for Teachers. She earned her B.S. degree in 1920 and hoped to become a mathematics teacher. However, because such a position was not considered appropriate for women, she instead accepted the position of county supervisor of fifty-one rural schools in Pitt County, North Carolina [see **county superintendents***]. After four years, Southall became North Carolina's State Supervisor of Elementary Instruction, a post she held from 1924 to 1928. During summers, she enrolled in courses at Peabody and received her M.A. in 1926.

While Southall worked toward a Ph.D. from Peabody, she also took courses at Teachers College–Columbia University and the **University of Chicago**,* where she studied with nationally famed professors William Heard Kilpatrick and Edward L. Thorndike. In 1929, Southall was only the fifth woman to receive a doctorate from Peabody, the preeminent graduate school of education in the South. Southall immediately began teaching at her alma mater in its department of elementary education and continued teaching and supervising doctoral students until retirement in 1964.

As a professor, Southall retained and always conveyed a genuine concern for her students, just as she had as a schoolteacher. She was described as a mentor who exerted a "quiet expectancy" and who emphasized the practical importance of research. Her former students remember her as a "relentless worker" (Brown, pp. 84, 79) who "was interested in ideas, not statistics, in what counted, not how it was counted" (Davis, 1979, p. 2). Her own list of memberships was substantial, including founding and charter member status in many organizations.

One in which she was quite active was Delta Kappa Gamma, a society for key women educators founded at the University of Texas in 1929. She was attracted to Delta Kappa Gamma because it offered women educators, then too often marginalized in general-purpose groups, opportunities for personal association, growth, and leadership. In 1935, Southall became the first president of Xi State, the Tennessee chapter. She worked successfully with other leaders to expand the society in Tennessee. After serving as state president for three years, she was elected for a two-year term (1938–1940) as national president. She continued to work for expansion of Delta Kappa Gamma, and by 1980 the society enrolled more than 150,000 members. In 1941, she received the society's highest honor, the Achievement Award.

Other organizations in which Southall played leadership roles included the ACEI, the **American Association of University Women** (AAUW), the National Education Association (NEA), and the U.S. Commission for UNESCO. Among her major honors was election to the Laureate Chapter of Kappa Delta Pi.

To further her lifelong goal of enhancing educational opportunities for children everywhere, Southall was attracted to ACEI. She served as Tennessee state president (1931–1932) and national president (1946–1948). The group added "International" to its name during Southall's term as president.

Southall also held leadership positions in ASCD, created in 1943 by the merger of the Department of Supervisors and Directors of Instruction of the NEA and the Society for Curriculum Study. Southall was a prominent opponent of the merger, agreeing with others that a variety of groups should exist especially for women educators. Nevertheless, when the merger was complete, Southall, with characteristic commitment, served actively in many capacities, including four terms on the Executive Committee of the Board of Directors.

For UNESCO, Southall was a member of the Executive Committee of the

U.S. Commission and served as Educational Consultant to the Sixth General UNESCO Conference. She described her work as representing "the U.S. Office of Education in securing UNESCO Aid to the education of all children vs. just those handicapped by W[orld] W[ar] II."

When she retired from teaching, Southall continued her educational leadership. A longtime advocate of public school **kindergartens**,* she influenced legislation to increase their numbers in Tennessee. She also founded the Children's International Intercultural Center in Nashville, served on national committees, and gave numerous speeches locally and across the nation. Her efforts were recognized when the mayor of Nashville named October 16, 1977, "Maycie Katherine Southall Day."

Throughout life Southall remained oriented toward the future. In youth, she turned down suitors, as was often then expected of career women teachers. In making these choices, she believed she was better able to work from within the educational community. In 1940, she was instrumental in Tennessee legislation that enabled married women to teach in the state's schools.

With a career spanning schoolteaching, serving pre- and in-service teachers, supervision, and filled with local and national involvement in educational issues and professional associations, Maycie Southall exemplified both dedication and loyalty. She steadfastly believed that a "lasting peace among nations can best be brought about through the education of children" (Brown, p. 274). Southall died on February 22, 1992.

Bibliography: Maycie K. Southall [personal data sheet], Oral History in Education Collection, University of Texas at Austin (1977); O. L. Davis, Jr., "Symbol of a Shift from Status to Function: Formation of the Association for Supervision and Curriculum Development," *Educational Leadership*, 35 (1978): 609–614; Davis [letter to Louise Brown], Oral History in Education Collection, University of Texas at Austin (1979); D. L. Brown, *Maycie Katherine Southall: Her Life and Contributions to Education* (1981).

Jennifer Deets and O. L. Davis, Jr.

Spelman College. Spelman College, the oldest liberal arts school for African American women in the United States, began in 1880 when the Woman's American Baptist Home Mission Society (WABHMS) of New England commissioned Sophia B. Packard to survey slaves' conditions in the post-Reconstruction South. Joined by her friend and coteacher Harriet E. Giles, the two white missionaries felt "called" to start a school for black women to help "uplift" the Negro race. In April 1881, they met with Rev. Frank Quarles, pastor of Friendship Baptist Church in Atlanta. Quarles introduced Packard and Giles to a group of local black ministers, encouraging them to spread the word about the opening of Atlanta Baptist Female Seminary for Negroes, begun in the basement of Friendship Baptist Church in 1881.

In 1882 John D. Rockefeller began a longtime pattern of philanthropy to black education with his first gift of $250 to the school's building fund, which enabled a move into the "barracks," several surplus buildings that had been occupied by Union soldiers. In 1884 the school's name was changed to Spelman Seminary in honor of Mr. and Mrs. Harvey Buel Spelman, the parents of Laura Spelman (Mrs. John D. Rockefeller).

Packard and Giles resisted attempts by the American Baptist Home Mission Society to introduce **coeducation*** at Spelman by joining it with Atlanta Baptist Seminary. In 1884, a successful fund-raising campaign by WABHMS combined with donations from the Rockefeller family, Northern Baptists and Georgia Black Baptists, allowed Spelman to remain a separate school for girls.

In 1886 Spelman opened the first training school for black nurses in the United States. It added the Missionary Training Department in 1891, sending black missionaries to Africa as well as training Africans for Christian missions in their native land. Stories of these missionaries provided models for the African Americans and Africans in Alice Walker's (Spelman, 1961–1963) Pulitzer Prize–winning novel *The Color Purple*. Packard and Giles placed Spelman's curricular emphasis on training teachers, missionaries, and **social workers*** rather than offering a classical liberal arts curriculum. By 1900 the main campus academic buildings and dormitories had been built with Rockefeller funds, including MacVicar Hospital, added as a practice school for the nurses' training program and a hospital for black women. Rockefeller money improved faculty salaries and affected the curriculum. From 1900 to 1920, influenced by the educational policies of Rockefeller's General Education Board, the Spelman curriculum emphasized "practical" or industrial courses related to nursing, **home economics**,* and **teacher education**.* Teaching majors were able to do practice teaching at demonstration schools on campus. Extension courses provided vocational-technical training to the community.

In 1897, Spelman annexed a collegiate department through the auspices of Atlanta Baptist College/Morehouse. These coeducational classes, taught by Atlanta Baptist/Morehouse faculty, gave Spelman women the first opportunity to work toward a liberal arts baccalaureate degree as rigorous as men's. Included in the curriculum were sociology and history courses related to African Americans developed by W. E. B. Du Bois. Spelman granted its first collegiate degrees in 1901.

Spelman's relationship to Morehouse ended in 1924, when Spelman became an independent college and began to develop a full liberal arts curriculum. In 1927 both Spelman College and Spelman High School became charter members of the Association of Georgia Negro Colleges and Secondary Schools. But by 1930, under the leadership of President Florence Matilda Read, the high school and the Nurses Training Department and Elementary School were discontinued. The college progressed in a new direction, adding courses in the humanities, fine arts, social sciences, and natural sciences. Indicative of its growth, Spelman received an "A" rating from the white Southern Association of Colleges and Secondary Schools in 1932.

Black professors became more representative during the 1920s and 1930s; by

1937, Spelman had twice as many black teachers as white. The first black president was Albert E. Manley (1953–1976). In 1987, after considerable advocacy by students and faculty, a black woman was named president. On April 5, 1987, Johnetta Betsch Cole (Robinson) was appointed as seventh president and first black woman president of Spelman.

Bibliography: Florence Read, *The Story of Spelman College* (1961); Beverly Guy-Sheftall and Jo Moore Stewart, *Spelman: A Centennial Celebration, 1881–1991* (1981); Florence Fleming Corley, "Higher Education for Southern Women: Four Church Related Women's Colleges in Georgia: Agnes Scott, Shorter, Spelman, and Wesleyan, 1900–1920" (Ph.D. diss., Georgia State University, 1985).

Jayne R. Beilke

Stone, Lucy. Lucy Stone (1818–1893), one of the great women suffragists of the nineteenth century, was the first woman from Massachusetts to obtain a college degree, the first woman to lecture full-time for women's rights, and the first known to keep her own name after marriage.

Born in West Brookfield, Massachusetts, on August 13, 1818, Stone grew up resenting the preferences shown to males at home, school, and church. She rejected the view that the husband and father ruled his family by divine right, and she suspected that biblical passages quoted to emphasize women's inferiority were inaccurate; she wanted to study Greek and Hebrew to translate the passages for herself.

As a child, Stone attended a one-room **district school**.* Quite early she determined that she wanted to attend college, an opportunity not yet formally open to women in the United States. Her father regarded her desire as foolish, yet she joined her brothers at private tutorials to prepare them for college. She earned money for books by gathering nuts and berries. At sixteen Stone began **teaching*** school, although she resented being paid less than half the salary of male teachers, a common practice of the era. Despite meager earnings, she saved enough to study for short terms at various select schools becoming available for women, including **Mount Holyoke Female Seminary**,* Quaboag Seminary, and Wilbraham Academy, all in Massachusetts. Stone resolved to attend **Oberlin College*** in Ohio, which had opened its program to women in 1837, and she began studying for the entrance exams while continuing to teach to earn money. By 1843, she had saved enough that, with assistance of loans from a brother and sister, she enrolled at Oberlin. She also worked at Oberlin doing housework and teaching and eventually even received some financial support from her father, now impressed by her persistence. She received a B.A. with honors in 1847.

Stone had hoped to gain experience in public speaking at Oberlin, but women were not allowed to participate. She and a few friends resorted to practicing in secret. She gave her first public address on August 1, 1846, at an antislavery society meeting in Oberlin. Despite strong objections from her family, she determined to become a public lecturer and, following graduation, accepted a position as lecturer for the American Anti-Slavery Society in Massachusetts. Her reputation as a speaker spread quickly, and large crowds gathered in schoolhouses, churches, or outdoors. When she began including women's rights in her talks, the Society objected, fearing a confusion of the two issues. Stone then devoted her weekends to speaking against **slavery*** for pay and during the week lectured on women's rights for free. She soon discovered, however, that she could charge a small fee and still attract an audience.

In May 1850 Stone met with eight other women to form the first national organization for women's rights. They held their first convention in Worcester, Massachusetts, in October with over a thousand participants. Though less known today than the **Seneca Falls*** Convention of 1848, this first truly national convention was widely covered by the press, including full coverage in the *New York Tribune*. The newspaper's account of Stone's address on inequalities in the law for married women led Susan B. Anthony to join the women's movement, and reports overseas influenced John Stuart Mill to write ''The Enfranchisement of Women.''

When Stone married noted abolitionist Henry Brown Blackwell in 1855, they signed a marital agreement expressing their belief in equality in marriage and protesting the legal status of women. Stone, with her husband's support, retained her own name, the first woman in the United States to do so. A daughter, Alice Stone Blackwell, was born in 1857. Minor accidents to Alice when she was left in the care of a nursemaid caused Stone to give up her speaking tours until after the Civil War. She did, however, continue work both on **abolitionism*** and women's rights, and she drew attention to women's plight of taxation without representation by refusing to pay taxes and allowed some household goods to be sold at public auction.

In May 1863 Stone presided at the meeting that led to organization of the Women's Loyal National League, a group that collected more than 100,000 signatures supporting emancipation through ratification of the Thirteenth Amendment. She also worked with state and regional **suffrage*** organizations, helping found the New England Woman Suffrage Association in 1868.

By the end of the 1860s, arguments about the Fourteenth and Fifteenth Amendments (providing equal protection and enfranchisement of black males) split the women's movement into two groups. The National Woman Suffrage Association (NWSA), founded in 1869 by Elizabeth Cady Stanton and Susan B. Anthony, objected to the Fifteenth Amendment if it did not include women. Stone helped organize the rival American Woman Suffrage Association (AWSA) and became chair of its executive committee. The AWSA, more socially moderate than NWSA, resolved to support blacks' rights but fight later for women's suffrage. In 1870 Stone raised funds and founded the *Woman's Journal*, the longest lived of all suffrage publications (1870–1931, with name changes). She served on the editorial staff until her death. In 1890 NWSA and AWSA merged into the **National American Woman Suffrage Association**.* Stone headed the executive committee, and Stanton was president.

Physical problems, especially voice failure, made speaking to large crowds difficult for Stone during the last few years of her life, but she was able to end her career with a speech at the **World's Columbian Exposition*** in Chicago just a few months before her death in 1893. Although her role has not been as widely acknowledged as that of some other suffragists, Stone was a major player in the movement for women's suffrage and for legal equality for women.

Bibliography: E. R. Hays, *Morning Star: A Biography of Lucy Stone, 1818–1893* (1961); Leslie Wheeler, ed., *Loving Warriors: Selected Letters by Lucy Stone and Henry B. Blackwell, 1853–1893* (1981); Carol Lasser and Marlene Deahl Merrill, eds., *Friends and Sisters: Letters between Lucy Stone and Antoinette Brown Blackwell, 1846–93* (1987); Andrea Moore Kerr, *Lucy Stone: Speaking Out for Equality* (1992). Stone's papers are in the Blackwell Family Papers at the Library of Congress and the Schlesinger Library at Radcliffe College, Cambridge, Massachusetts.

Verbie Lovorn Prevost

student government. Student government organizations, which gave undergraduates greater authority in regulating their own conduct and overseeing various aspects of student life, developed on American college campuses in the last decades of the nineteenth century. The increasing popularity of athletics and fraternities during this period, coinciding with arrival on campus of a new generation of professors more interested in pursuing research than in serving **in loco parentis**,* prompted faculty and administrators to shift a greater share of the burden of discipline onto students. By the first decades of the twentieth century, various forms of student self-government had become widespread, reflecting the **Progressive Era*** emphasis on values of democratic citizenship and service to society. Leadership roles within such organizations represented one of the highest honors of undergraduate life. Within the peer-oriented collegiate culture that emerged on campuses during the interwar years [see **"grinds"***], participation in student government along with fraternity membership, contribution to the student newspaper, and athletic prowess all constituted the path to social acceptability, status, and power.

For women at coeducational institutions, however, this path was usually blocked [see **coeducation***]. Like the university as a whole from the late nineteenth through early twentieth centuries, student government organizations, along with most other undergraduate activities, were essentially male preserves. In some cases, females were excluded from student government entirely. More often, they could be members and even hold certain less important offices, including positions reserved especially for women. Only rarely, however, were females allowed to attain leadership. This was particularly the case after 1920, as enrollments expanded and collegiate culture became increasingly masculinized. Instead, women at coeducational institutions tended to form parallel organizations, including women's student government associations. These addressed women's concerns, provided women with a separate power base, and gave them authority over specific female-related areas, while ceding control over general campus issues to men.

Among coeducational institutions, the exception to this pattern may have been at the less-prestigious **normal schools*** and junior colleges, where differences in purpose and status, combined with substantial female enrollments, helped create a more gender-neutral environment, at least before 1920. After that, in many areas including student life, normal schools and junior colleges increasingly emulated the university model.

The true exception to male-run student government occurred at **women's colleges**.* There, female students took part in numerous extracurricular activities, but without restrictive gender stereotypes. Student government represented one of many arenas in which women at single-sex schools participated fully, including taking leadership roles usually reserved for men. In so doing, members of student government at women's colleges often challenged accepted conventions of feminine behavior, a pattern that in many cases continued after graduation. [See also **sororities**,* **women's athletics**.*]

Bibliography: Frederick Rudolph, *The American College and University: A History* (1962); Helen Lefkowitz Horowitz, *Alma Mater: Design and Experience in the Women's Colleges from Their Nineteenth-Century Beginnings to the 1930s* (1984); Horowitz, *Campus Life: Undergraduate Cultures from the End of the Eighteenth Century to the Present* (1987); Lynn D. Gordon, *Gender and Higher Education in the Progressive Era* (1990); Christine Ogren, "Where Coeds Were Coeducated: Normal Schools in Wisconsin, 1870–1920," *History of Education Quarterly*, 35 (Spring 1995): 1–26.

Sarah V. Barnes

suffrage. The suffrage movement in the United States, which began in earnest with the **Seneca Falls*** Convention in 1848 and continued until the Nineteenth Amendment was passed in August 1920, reflected the desire of women to break out of their separate, domestic sphere; to establish themselves as free-thinking, independent beings; and to secure practical social goals by legislation. Women began lobbying for the vote as early as 1647, when Margaret Brent unsuccessfully petitioned the Maryland Assembly. Early voices cried out for reform in a wilderness where power and privilege were almost entirely male; nevertheless, the suffrage movement, through both education and activism, slowly brought about change in American society. The debate between those who advocated the democratic ideology of self-government and those who adhered to established views concerning the proper role of women was conducted in homes, on street corners, and in legislative chambers for over seventy years.

The woman suffrage movement had its origins in the Northeast, along with many other antebellum reforms. Early feminists like Lucretia Mott and **Lucy Stone*** demanded sweeping changes in women's legal, educational, and economic status; many were prompted to speak out for women's rights when their efforts to participate equally with men in the abolition [see **abolitionism***] and **temperance movements*** proved initially unsuccessful. In July 1848, 300 people (40 of them men) met in Seneca Falls, New York, to discuss the social, civil, and religious rights of women. Led by Elizabeth Cady Stanton and Mott, the group adopted a **Declaration of Sentiments*** modeled on the Declaration of Independence. The most radical of the resolutions was a formal demand for the vote. In the dozen years after Seneca Falls, a social movement took shape centered on the demands formulated there. After the Civil War, numerous women's organizations were formed to undertake scholastic study, civic reform, and charitable work, as well as to fight for the vote.

Two woman suffrage organizations were formed in 1869. The National Woman Suffrage Association (NWSA), headed by Stanton and Susan B. Anthony, opposed the Fifteenth Amendment (which extended voting rights to all men), called for a separate federal amendment to enfranchise women, and worked for women's rights. The rival American Woman Suffrage Association (AWSA), led by Lucy Stone, her husband Henry Blackwell, Julia Ward Howe, and others, endorsed the Fifteenth Amendment and, unlike NWSA, concentrated solely on developing support for woman suffrage on the state level through constitutional reform. After two decades of rivalry, the movement reunited in 1890 with the formation of the **National American Woman Suffrage Association*** (NAWSA) under the leadership of Stanton. While continuing to demand a federal amendment, NAWSA leaders agreed that they must build a broad base of support by conducting campaigns in the states. With the efforts of suffragists joined, NAWSA worked successfully to widen its influence through the press, public speaking, legislative lobbies, and congressional hearings.

In fighting for the franchise, suffragists argued that the vote, while it could be used as a tool for change, was equally important as a "plain recognition of an equal humanity." As citizens, taxpayers, and "intelligent, rational beings," women maintained that they deserved to vote. Women likewise had special concern for progressive reforms that were largely dismissed by male legislators but could be well addressed by an educated female electorate. In a radical assertion reminiscent of eighteenth-century notions of **"Republican motherhood,"*** suffragists staunchly maintained that women needed to be good citizens in order to be good mothers. When antisuffragists argued that men were natural-born leaders, intellectually superior to their female helpmates, suffragists countered with the assertion that women could add valuable insight and energy to problems largely ignored by politicians, including education, health reform, and child labor. For suffragists, political activity held the promise for the creation of a truly democratic society.

Between 1896 and 1910, no new states were won for woman suffrage. However, beginning with the leadership of Carrie Chapman Catt (1900–1904), NAWSA underwent a period of rebuilding, reaching out to **women's club*** members, college students, and graduates in an increasingly education-oriented campaign for the vote. NAWSA distributed literature to schools and libraries, sponsored debates, and encouraged members to visit national headquarters in New York City, with its "large light room for study and research; a complete stock of suffrage literature and supplies; [and] a traveling picture gallery of eminent suffragists." The **National College Equal Suffrage League*** was organized as a NAWSA auxiliary in 1908. Local suffrage leagues formed teachers' sections, mobilizing both educators and mothers to fight. For teachers, the vote was seen as a means to improve schools, safeguard the welfare of pupils, and prepare themselves to "train the citizens of the future [with] practical, first-hand knowledge of government" ("Teachers Need the Vote"). Mothers were motivated to obtain equal educational opportunity for their daughters.

With the advent of the progressive movement at the turn of the century, woman suffrage received increased support from those interested in assuring the purity of food and drugs, regulating child labor, and improving public health. Women enlisted in increasing numbers in the suffrage movement once it became apparent that "benevolent enterprise" and lobbying alone could not bring about reform. By 1910, however, the movement had lost much of its urgency. Impatient with the state-by-state approach, Alice Paul (chair of NAWSA's Congressional Committee) and Lucy Burns (vice chair) formed the Congressional Union for Woman Suffrage in 1913 to fight exclusively for a federal amendment. After a rift developed between the Congressional Union and NAWSA over the bold tactics Paul borrowed from militant British suffragists, the Union established itself as an independent organization in 1914. Two years later, Paul organized the National Woman's Party (NWP).

Sparked by progressive reform and world war, the suffrage movement was revitalized, and its focus shifted to the national level. In 1915, Catt resumed the presidency of NAWSA and put in motion her "Winning Plan," launching a vigorous campaign to win a federal amendment. Faced with NWP picketers in front of the White House and considerable pressure from NAWSA, President Woodrow Wilson came out in favor of a suffrage amendment in 1918. The Nineteenth Amendment passed Congress the following year and was submitted to the states in June 1919. Ratified by the thirty-sixth state, Tennessee, on August 18, 1920, the Nineteenth Amendment was added to the Constitution on August 26, in time for the national election.

Bibliography: "Teachers Need the Vote! Reasons Why Teachers Should Work for Woman Suffrage," Teachers' Section, New York State Woman Suffrage Party (n.d.), in the Equal Suffrage League Collection, The Library of Virginia; Elizabeth Cady Stanton, Susan B. Anthony, Matilda Joslyn Gage, et al., eds., *History of Woman Suffrage*, 6 vols. (1881–1922); Aileen S. Kraditor, *The Ideas of the Woman Suffrage Movement, 1890–1920* (1965, repr. 1981); Anne Firor Scott and Andrew M. Scott, *One Half the People: The Fight for Woman Suffrage* (1975); Marjorie Spruill Wheeler, *One Woman, One Vote: A Short History and Guide to the Woman Suffrage Movement in the United States* (1995).

Jennifer Davis McDaid

surplus daughters. "Surplus daughters" is a concept used by historian David F. Allmendinger to describe the opportunity for schooling afforded to some nineteenth-century girls whose labor was not needed at home and who did not find competition from their brothers for family resources. Allmendinger developed the term in a study describing women attending **Mount Holyoke Female Seminary*** from 1837 to 1850. These women came primarily from New England farm communities where land was becoming a scarce commodity, and goods once produced by women's labor on the farms, most notably textiles, had moved to factories with the rise of industrialization. While some young farm women went to work in the factories, such as the **Lowell mills*** in Massachusetts, much of this labor was taken up by new immigrants. Young men from the farms were heading west in search of their fortunes.

Simultaneous with these changes in the mid-nineteenth century, the **common school*** movement—a call for schooling for all young children—resulted in a rapid rise in the number of schools, providing an alternative for young women who were needed as teachers, not only because they could be paid less than men but because with other opportunities available to them, male teachers were in short supply. Most women in **seminaries**,* **academies**,* and colleges before the Civil War could justify their interest in education as preparation for **teaching**,* one of few careers open to women.

However, not all of these learned daughters seem to have been surplus labor. Most students came not from New England but from western New York and the Midwest, where many women came from thriving farm areas where land was plentiful and their labor was still important. In New York, a dairy state, this meant churning butter and making cheese, work not yet industrialized. Textile production did not have the importance to farm families in these regions that it had in New England, but even here industrialization greatly reduced the farm production of cloth, freeing young women from spinning and weaving, and providing them an opportunity to go to school.

Allmendinger looked at families sending daughters to Mount Holyoke before the Civil War and found "serious imbalances in the sex ratios of children in 40 percent of the reconstituted Holyoke families; these families had surpluses of two or more daughters." Because of this, he argued that the daughters had less competition from their brothers for the family's resources. However, he failed to take into account that since all the families had at least one daughter, his sample was already skewed. A study in western New York based on the families with daughters who were old enough to attend college living in three towns with colleges that admitted women found no such surplus of daughters. In fact, the families were remarkably similar with the important exception of wealth. That is, families sending daughters (approximately half in each town) simply had greater resources. It may well be that the common school rhetoric for schools to train all children and the stress of higher education as preparation for life rather than a particular career influenced families and their daughters to seek higher learning.

For many, education was closely allied to religion, and young women sought to become teachers with a missionary zeal. In her study on the founding of Mount Holyoke, Kathryn Kish Sklar noted the economic changes that played a role in parents' desire to educate their daughters, but she also noted the role evangelical religion played. Women teachers were seen as instruments of God, using their influence to reform the world, an influence second only to that of ministers. Demographic changes, industrialization, evangelical religion, and rhetoric about the importance of education all combined to bring women, primarily women from rural families of middling wealth, into higher education—first in seminaries and academies, then colleges—in the period before the Civil War.

Bibliography: David F. Allmendinger, Jr., "Mount Holyoke Students Encounter the Need for Life-Planning, 1837–1850," *History of Education Quarterly*, 19 (Spring 1979): 27–46; Kathryn Kish Sklar, "The Founding of Mount Holyoke College," in Carol Ruth Berkin and Mary Beth Norton, eds., *Women of America: A History* (1979); Patricia A. Palmieri, "From Republican Motherhood to Race Suicide," in Carol Lasser, ed., *Educating Men and Women Together: Coeducation in a Changing World* (1987); Kathryn M. Kerns, "Antebellum Higher Education for Women in Western New York State" (Ph.D. diss., University of Pennsylvania, 1993).

Kathryn M. Kerns

T

Taba, Hilda. Hilda Taba (1902–1967), a woman of strong leadership and astute scholarship, was a twentieth-century pioneer in curriculum development who contributed conspicuously to major developments in American education. Although her accomplishments were varied and numerous, her collaborators are often better known. Having studied under William Heard Kilpatrick and John Dewey, Taba's educational theories and practices derived from progressive educational philosophy. Taba contributed several important ideas to the curriculum field, many of which remain at the forefront of curriculum discourse and practice.

Born in Estonia, Taba came to the United States in 1926 as a European Fellow at **Bryn Mawr College**,* where she earned her master's degree. She continued graduate work with a doctorate in educational administration at Teachers College, Columbia University, the center of progressive educational thought in the 1920s and 1930s. There she clearly was influenced by the work not only of Dewey and Kilpatrick but also of renowned scholars such as Harold Rugg, George S. Counts, Edward L. Thorndike, and L. Thomas Hopkins. Her dissertation, "The Dynamics of Education" (1932), provided a comprehensive portrayal of progressive educational thought as well as an analysis of factors that contribute to curriculum development. In 1933, she received a fellowship to pursue postdoctoral work at Syracuse University, and she also began a position as German teacher and curriculum director at the prestigious Dalton School in New York City [see **Dalton Plan***].

Taba's work at Dalton provided her with the opportunity to meet and, eventually, to work with Ralph W. Tyler, research director of the Progressive Education Association's noted Eight-Year Study. An ambitious attempt to excite curriculum reform, the study, with Carnegie Foundation support, enrolled thirty **high schools*** (one later withdrew) and thousands of students. During the study, colleges suspended other entrance requirements for the study's schools. Consequently, these students were able to pursue an experimental curriculum plan. The study evaluation compared students who experienced experimental curricula with students who followed traditional college-entrance programs, in hopes that high school curricula might be improved and reformed. Its most prominent finding was that experimental school graduates succeeded as well in college as did graduates of traditional college preparatory programs.

As Dalton's curriculum director, Taba drafted proposals to create an integrated curriculum. Initially, she developed a plan in which the problems of human thought and life served as central organizing themes. Adroit at understanding human relations, Taba realized that the plan's success depended upon teacher support and expressed hope that integrated thinking would develop for both student and teachers. Clearly impressed with Taba's work, Tyler invited her in 1935 to become an associate on the evaluation staff of the Eight-Year Study then based at Ohio State University.

Her staff work catapulted Taba into national prominence as an educational researcher and consultant for social studies teachers. As part of developing evaluation instruments, Taba helped the faculties of the thirty experimental schools to formulate objectives to facilitate student learning. Later, she directed the Committee on Social Sensitivity, which constructed special tests. In order to facilitate the work of the Eight-Year Study, Taba established in-service **teacher education*** workshops that brought together teachers from the thirty schools to share ideas, discuss curriculum, and practical problems. Ultimately, this effort enabled Taba to experiment with many ideas that would reappear in her thinking over time. These included integration of the curriculum around significant problems and issues, development of democratic attitudes, and approaches to curriculum development as an ongoing dynamic process.

After her work on the Eight-Year Study, Taba continued to contribute to curriculum development nationally. In 1945, she became codirector of the Intergroup Education Project as well as assistant professor of education at the **University of Chicago**.* Initially, the project sought to change attitudes and behavioral patterns toward members of racial and ethnic minority groups. As the project progressed, its goals broadened to include the dynamics of human relations between groups such as students, parents, siblings, and teachers. It assisted teachers, administrators, and community leaders and attracted much favorable publicity. Participating teachers worked in groups and did much of the actual curriculum development. Taba assisted the teachers with important ideas about the sequence of curriculum development activities and ways to organize content and learning experiences. Another unique aspect of the project was Taba's insistence that teachers conduct classroom-based research and gather data about their students in order to determine the adequacy of the curriculum. Taba and others called this ''action research''; it reflected much of Dewey's thinking about the process for managing a problem. Taba coedited the Sixteenth Yearbook of the National Council for the Social Studies, which focused on intergroup education.

In fall 1951, Taba became professor of education at San Francisco State College. For sixteen years until her death, Taba conducted there some of her most significant practical and theoretical work in curriculum development. Especially fruitful was her longtime relationship with elementary teachers in Contra Costa County schools. These efforts focused on social studies curriculum and continued for two years after she died. In its later stages, it became known as the "Taba Curriculum Development Project." A special aspect focused on the development of student thinking in elementary social studies. With support from the U.S. Office of Education, Taba and teacher colleagues developed an innovative elementary social studies curriculum. Ultimately published, it set standards for such programs. In the midst of this work, Taba published her most widely acclaimed book, *Curriculum Development: Theory and Practice* (1962), considered a classic in the curriculum field.

Hilda Taba contributed uniquely to the field of curriculum development. She authored, coauthored, or edited over seventy books, journal articles, chapters, and conference reports. Taba also conducted important teacher workshops across the nation. She was at the forefront of educational research, particularly with her work in the Eight-Year Study and the Taba Curriculum Development Project and in action research. Most important, she was a remarkable teacher.

Bibliography: Hilda Taba, "General Techniques of Curriculum Planning," *American Education in the Post War Period* (1945); Taba, *School Culture* (1955); M. M. Isham, "Hilda Taba: Pioneer in Curriculum Development" (Ph.D. diss., University of Texas at Austin, 1984); H. M. Kliebard, *The Struggle for the American Curriculum: 1893–1958* (1987); J. R. Fraenkel, "The Evolution of the Taba Curriculum Development Project," *The Social Studies*, 85 (1994): 149–159.

Chara Haeussler Bohan and O. L. Davis, Jr.

Talbot, Marion. Educator Marion Talbot (1858–1948) furthered women's education as a cofounder, with her mother Emily Talbot, of the **Association of Collegiate Alumnae*** (ACA, 1881) and as a pioneer in the field of domestic science. Her most lasting contributions, however, resulted from her tenure at the **University of Chicago*** from 1892 to 1925 as **dean of women**.* There, she helped the struggling young profession grow, offered an intellectual rationale for the work of deans, initiated their first professional meetings, and became an expert on the subject of women's education in coeducational [see **coeducation***] settings.

Talbot was raised in Boston amid economic comfort and influential people such as Julia Ward Howe and Louisa May Alcott. Her father, Israel Tisdale Talbot, was passionate about health reform and homeopathic medicine and became the first dean of Boston University's medical school in 1873. Marion's mother was also a committed health reformer, but the cause she held most dear was expanding women's educational opportunities.

Emily Talbot had an enormous influence on her daughter. Frustrated by the paucity of her own schooling, Talbot wanted a better education for her daughters

Marion and Edith. She provided them home tutoring and even a stint in Europe to learn German and French. Talbot finally secured a place for her daughter in Boston University in 1876, but Marion had considerable academic difficulty compared to the young men better prepared in **academies**.* In 1877, after Marion had already begun college, Emily Talbot succeeded in convincing city officials to open Boston **Girls' Latin School*** so others would not suffer in college as Marion had.

Marion Talbot graduated from Boston University with a B.A. in 1880, after which, like many early women collegians, she felt aimless and uncertain, cut off from her girlhood friends. As Marion commented in her autobiography *More Than Lore* (1925), "[T]he satisfactions obtained in the pursuit of truth make other searches seem trivial in the comparison, and the use of one's mind becomes not only fascinating, but a compelling task."

Emily Talbot sympathized with Marion's malaise. Together with Massachusetts Institute of Technology (MIT) professor Ellen Richards, they organized the first meeting of the ACA in autumn 1881. The ACA was an important organization for Marion, supplying her with a much needed circle of women who shared an interest in intellectual fulfillment and professional accomplishment. Further, the ACA became an organizational base for her own maturing interests in women's education; she served as its secretary for the first fourteen years. The ACA also provided a model of collective action to which she would return when organizing deans of women in 1903. During her years as dean, Marion served as ACA president (1895–1897) and remained connected to the organization until her death. Urged by Marion in 1912, the ACA changed its criteria for accrediting institutions and demanded, among other things, that an approved college or university have a dean of women. In 1921, the ACA became the **American Association of University Women**.* Later, in 1931, Talbot coauthored a history of its founding and accomplishments with another important dean of women, Lois Mathews Rosenberry.

Talbot's passion to find socially useful work led her to resume academic study. After earning a master's degree from Boston University, she enrolled at MIT in 1884, studied with Ellen Richards, and graduated in 1888 with a bachelor of science degree in sanitary (later domestic) science. Talbot was appointed instructor of domestic science at **Wellesley College*** in 1890 at the behest of its president, **Alice Freeman Palmer**.*

Palmer was University of Chicago President William Rainey Harper's top choice for his first dean. She agreed, upon two conditions. Because her Harvard professor husband, George Herbert Palmer, was unwilling to leave Boston, Alice would only work in Chicago twelve weeks a year. She also demanded that Marion Talbot be appointed her deputy. Talbot's title was dean of undergraduate women and assistant professor of sanitary science.

During the **Progressive Era**,* Chicago provided an exciting environment for women, both on campus and off, and Talbot worked to coordinate the two communities. Women were well represented as both undergraduate and graduate

students, and the vital Chicago reform community including **Jane Addams**'s*
Hull-House* provided professional opportunities for graduates. From the beginning, Talbot considered all the women of the university community as her
constituency, although only officially responsible for undergraduates. An un-
compromising advocate for women, she presented the findings of her regular
surveys of women in her annual reports to the president. She emphasized the
accomplishments of female professors, undergraduates, and graduate students to
illustrate that women's presence did not lower any standards.

Talbot also wrote of difficulties and losses for women at Chicago, and she
rarely missed the opportunity to remind Harper that women needed additional
university funds and support. Her most pitched battle began in 1900 when the
university administration proposed the segregation of instruction for men and
women in the Junior college (freshman and sophomore years). Such **backlash***
was strong at the turn of the century. She galvanized the opposition because
separate classrooms threatened her lifelong crusade to establish the intellectual
equality of the sexes. The faculty voted to approve Harper's plan in summer
1902, but it never became fully operational, apparently dying of atrophy.

Talbot did succeed, however, in fostering a women's community through the
creation of the Women's Union in 1901, which was not unlike a contemporary
women's center.* She banned **sororities**,* fearing they exacerbated social class
distinctions. She wanted women to become independent thinkers; however, in
matters of social propriety, she was often strict.

Talbot's opposition to segregated classrooms and simultaneous support of the
Women's Union reflected her philosophy of women's education and served as
the intellectual foundation of the work of deans of women. She believed that
women were as capable of intellectual thought as men and therefore entitled to
equivalent educational opportunities. As she stated unequivocally in her book
The Education of Women, "[W]omen have proved their ability to enter every
realm of knowledge. . . . Unhampered by traditions of sex, women will naturally
and without comment seek the intellectual goal which they think good and fit."
Yet she never completely let go of all the vestiges of Victorian notions of
propriety and **separate spheres**,* other than intellectual. Therefore, women
needed a separate and distinct social environment. In this view, she was an
intellectual bridge between the older view that feminine uniqueness implied
intellectual limitations.

Talbot had a faculty career of some note. Albion Small invited her to join
the editorial board of the newly created *American Journal of Sociology* in 1895.
In 1904, she was appointed head of a new department of household administration. She used her position as department head to secure the appointments of
talented protégées including **Sophonisba Breckinridge**,* a lifelong friend on
whose behalf she battled for years for higher pay and recognition. She took part
in the Lake Placid Conferences, under the leadership of Ellen Richards, that led
to the development of the American Home Economics Association in 1908 and
published her 1912 book *The Modern Household*.

It was, however, her dual role of administrator/faculty member that provided the core of her experience at Chicago. Although the two roles were quite fused in her mind, it was primarily her deanship that made her a visible figure. Already a dean for a decade by 1902, she began pouring energy into building the profession. In addition to articulating a purpose for women's education that laid the intellectual foundations for the work of deans, she was also the catalyst for the first professional meetings.

Talbot organized the first meeting of midwestern deans in November 1903 at Northwestern University. The purpose of the meeting, which became a regular biennial conference, was to share information, discuss policy and practice, and assist each other in coping with the stress of the job. These conferences produced a sense of direction and identity for the young profession and a professional literature upon which future deans built.

Because of her central role in founding the conferences, Talbot was regarded as the "expert" to whom new deans turned and with whom experienced deans shared professional advice. As Ada Comstock, who became dean of women at the University of Minnesota in 1906, recalled many years later upon Talbot's death, "The rapid spread of higher education for women was due in an appreciable degree to Marion Talbot's insistence on standards of achievement and proper arrangements in coeducational institutions for the life and work of women students" (in Haddock, pp. 345–346).

When Talbot retired from the university in 1925 at age sixty-seven, President Charles "Max" Mason did not appoint a successor; the record is not clear on why Mason made this decision. Instead, he divided her duties among several committees. Yet Talbot was given lofty praise indeed when it was noted that she was esteemed as highly by women students as the famous coach Alonzo Stagg was by men. In retirement, she twice served as president of Constantinople Women's College in Turkey, 1927–1928 and 1931–1932. She published her autobiography *More Than Lore* (1925) and other articles on women's education. She died in Chicago at the age of ninety.

Bibliography: Marion Talbot and Lois Kimball Mathews Rosenberry, *The History of the American Association of University Women* (1931); Ruth Haddock, "A Study of Five Deans of Women" (Ph.D. diss., Syracuse University, 1952); Richard Storr, "Marion Talbot," in Edward T. James, Janet Wilson James, and Paul S. Boyer, eds., *Notable American Women, 1607–1950* (1971); Rosalind Rosenberg, *Beyond Separate Spheres: Intellectual Roots of Modern Feminism* (1982); Ellen Fitzpatrick, "For the 'Women of the University': Marion Talbot, 1858–1948," in Geraldine Jonçich Clifford, ed., *Lone Voyagers: Academic Women in Coeducational Institutions, 1870–1937* (1989); Jana Nidiffer, "More Than a 'Wise and Pious Matron': The Professionalization of Deans of Women, 1892–1916" (Ed.D. diss., Harvard University, 1994).

Jana Nidiffer

teacher education. The idea of teaching people how to teach others, or teacher education, emerged in America during the nineteenth century. Earlier, teachers were generally not explicitly trained, and taught students out of their own homes. By the late twentieth century teacher education had expanded to include preparation of primary through collegiate **teaching*** in both public and private institutions.

Early in the nineteenth century, parents and teachers alike assumed that children could be taught by any person with more education than the children themselves. Classes were often a collection of students of varying ages and abilities. Low teacher and student ratios were common, as there was a sufficient workforce of young women and men who took the opportunity to teach before moving to other occupations or getting married. Most men left teaching for other jobs, but women had fewer opportunities.

Most communities relied on teachers who graduated from one of the many **academies*** or **seminaries*** that in the early nineteenth century served an academic function similar to contemporary middle schools or **high schools**.* Curricula and purpose varied in these institutions. They provided training for teachers, offered technical or vocational skills, or prepared students for university study. They were usually founded and run by one or a few experienced teachers, both women and men. **Emma Willard**,* for example, founded **Troy Female Seminary*** in 1821 to provide a source of income after her husband had financial difficulties. Schools like hers were run by individuals; others were operated by groups of teachers, towns, or counties or sometimes financed by state governments. Yet most academies and seminaries were neither public nor private. Funding was provided from a combination of sources, but most costs were covered by student tuition. Admission was largely based on previous education and ability to pay tuition; occasionally, schools administered entrance examinations. Gender was also a criterion for admission. Some schools like Troy and **Mount Holyoke Female Seminary*** were single sex, while others admitted both women and men.

Students in seminaries and academies did not always have a clear trade or career in mind. Some were economically privileged and not pressured to finish school to get jobs. Other students who needed to support themselves or their families usually began work as soon as they acquired enough schooling to get a job. Teaching was often the only option for educated women who did not want to do manual labor.

With growing numbers of students attending grammar schools and similar, but less dramatic, growth in secondary schools, the demand for teachers increased throughout the nineteenth century. Academies and seminaries alone could provide neither adequate numbers nor sufficiently trained teachers. To increase the number of trained teachers, many states fostered teacher education programs through state grants, but few academies or seminaries took advantage. The few that did offered free tuition. But with a future prospect of poor pay in teaching, few women or their families could afford an academy or seminary education. As a result, many teachers taught without much training and relied on sporadic **teacher institutes*** to upgrade their skills.

Since academies could not enroll or graduate enough teachers to meet demand, state legislators began to consult experts like Emma Willard, **Catharine Beecher**,* Henry Barnard, **Horace Mann**,* and others for guidance in developing statewide systems of teacher education. Their efforts created the **normal school**,* a type of teacher training institution imported from Western Europe. Some normal schools, such as Oswego Normal, were incorporated into state systems. Others were founded on charters granted to communities with endorsement and support from the state.

As the number of normal schools expanded between 1840 and 1900, more teacher education moved out of the hands of local schoolteachers and into the hands of normal school, college, and university faculty. Professionalization began to influence the field, with growth of groups like the American Normal School Association. Gender differentiation also increased. The Normal School Association, for example, was almost entirely composed of men. Early in the movement, faculty were primarily women, but the balance shifted quickly. Women were marginalized as purveyors of knowledge about how to teach teachers despite the fact that women's academies and seminaries had pioneered and developed the idea of an explicit teacher education curriculum [see **feminization***].

The curricula of teacher education programs varied from practical and vocational to theoretical and has swayed between these two extremes over subsequent decades. The science of teaching, or pedagogy, starting with Rousseau and Pestalozzi and continuing with John Dewey and others, brought the issues of education, teacher education, and democracy together for debate in the public forum. That debate and its professional discourse have often been dominated by men from the end of the nineteenth century to well into the twentieth. Representation of women in teacher education still does not match the gender representation of education students in most universities and colleges or in the elementary schools.

In the late twentieth century, teacher educators and practitioners find they have decreasing control over their curricula. Because of their lack of autonomy over professional standards and comparatively low pay, teachers are still undervalued in comparison to other professions. [See also **common schools**,* **early childhood teacher education**,* **normal departments**,* **semiprofessions**,* **teachers colleges**,* **women's colleges**.*]

Bibliography: American Normal School Association, *American Normal Schools: Their Theory, Their Workings, and Their Results, as Embodied in the Proceedings of the First Annual Convention of the American Normal School Association Held at Trenton, New Jersey August 19 and 20* (1860); Donald Warren, ed., *American Teachers: Histories of a Profession at Work* (1989); Iram Siraj-Blatchford, ed., *Race, Gender and the Education of Teachers* (1993); Sari Knopp Biklen, *School Work: Gender and the Cultural Construction of Teaching* (1995).

Victor Parente

teacher institutes. Teacher institutes, also known as "traveling teachers' **seminaries**,"* "temporary **normal schools**,"* and "schools of teachers," became one of the most widespread methods of training **common school*** teachers in the nineteenth and early twentieth centuries. Institutes generally comprised in-service teachers who met to receive instruction and inspiration to promote their overall improvement. Institutes were particularly relevant to the education of women, given that by 1900, 74 percent of all teachers in the United States were women [see **teaching***].

Historians disagree about the specific origins of teacher institutes. Some see them as distinctly American enterprises; however, others have argued that institutes predated normal schools in Switzerland, France, and parts of Germany. Most historians credit Henry Barnard with the first effort at organizing teachers for institution-type instruction in Connecticut in 1839. However, J. S. Dennan, school superintendent of Tompkins County, New York, is said to have held in 1843 the first two-week meeting of teachers that specifically bore the title "institute." Regardless of the movement's exact genesis, Barnard was a prominent advocate of institutes as a method of **teacher education**.*

The institute concept took root quickly and spread throughout most of the United States. Institute meetings, once begun, were typically held annually and were organized in many states by local school superintendents. Teacher institutes gained great popularity in the Midwest, where growing concern over inadequately trained rural teachers set the stage for institutes with a particular focus on rural education [see **pioneer women teachers***].

The length and scope of teacher institutes varied from state to state, and even county to county. Lasting anywhere from one day to six weeks, institutes were held either in an impromptu fashion or as formal, well-organized gatherings. By the late nineteenth century, most educational leaders championed institute work, and it had become a significant method of teacher training. Normal school educators generally supported teacher institutes either as a supplement to institutional training or as a way to reach the many teachers with limited access to formal education.

Many states legislated compulsory attendance at institutes, particularly for rural teachers. Eighteen states required attendance by 1900, and ten more within a year. Many states with voluntary institute participation offered inducements for teacher involvement, such as reimbursed travel expenses, salary bonuses, and/or points added to certification exam scores.

Early teacher institutes resembled religious revivals, endeavoring to "awaken" the spirit of both teachers and communities in support of education. As institute instruction became increasingly bureaucratized and tied to the growing educational systems within the states, they functioned in a more official capacity. Professional and academic instruction often focused on the prescribed course of study for common schools or the preparation of teachers for certification exams. Lecturing was most common, particularly during the early years. However, as institute popularity grew, proponents increasingly called for more active participation of teachers.

Eventually, the rise in teacher certification requirements combined with the advancement of supervision and further development of summer schools and normal schools provided options for teacher training that surpassed the capabilities of institutes, even in rural areas. This led to a shift in function for teacher institutes, from academic instruction to emphasis on professionalism and promotion of educational systems. Despite their growing obsolescence, many supporters continued to promote institutes, and the movement died slowly. As late as 1933, twenty-six states still held regular teacher institutes.

Bibliography: Kate V. Wofford, *A History of the Status and Training of Elementary Rural Teachers of the United States, 1860–1930* (1935); Willard S. Elsbree, *The American Teacher; Evolution of a Profession in a Democracy* (1939); Frederick M. Binder, *The Age of the Common School, 1830–1865* (1974); Paul H. Mattingly, *The Classless Profession: American Schoolmen in the Nineteenth Century* (1975); Dina L. Stephens, "The Role of County Superintendents in Rural School Reform in Late Nineteenth and Early Twentieth Century Wisconsin" (Ph.D. diss., University of Wisconsin, 1996).

Dina L. Stephens

teacher unions. During the **Progressive Era*** (roughly 1890–1920), white-collar teacher unions worked toward gaining salary increases, tenure, pensions, and improved working conditions for their members. Unions were comprised primarily of female elementary teachers in urban centers of the Midwest and the East Coast, and they brought white-collar unionism to American women. The unions and their sometimes militant feminist leaders brought issues concerning women teachers to the attention of the male-dominated educational establishment. The gendered division of labor, inequalities of pay scales, and women teachers' participation in school decisionmaking were issues highlighted by the teacher union movement in the first twenty years of the twentieth century.

By 1870, the sizable majority of elementary teachers were women. When their salaries did not keep pace with the cost of living during the severe 1890s depression, teachers began to demand a living wage and economic security. The success of the **Chicago Teachers' Federation*** (CTF) in fighting corporate tax-dodgers and winning a pay increase inspired teachers across the country to organize. Other teacher unions, such as the Interborough Association of Women Teachers (IAWT) (New York City), were single-issue organizations. In 1911 after five years of lobbying, Grace Strachan and the IAWT convinced the state legislature to ensure equal pay for equal work. Historian Wayne Urban suggests that teachers, whether in Atlanta, New York, or Chicago, were primarily concerned with their economic conditions and looked toward unions as a way to lobby school boards for pay increases and other benefits. Teachers were less often drawn to unionism from a belief in unionist ideology than as a pragmatic way to reach their economic goals. Union leaders such as **Margaret Haley*** and Catherine Goggin of the CTF were more inclined than rank-and-file members to be radical and support other progressive reforms like woman **suffrage**,* child labor laws, and municipal ownership of utilities. In their leadership roles, they often allied their unions with other **labor unions*** and civic associations.

Female teacher unionism highlights the divide between women classroom teachers and male administrators. Women teachers in large cities labored in crowded classrooms under the paternalistic and sometimes authoritarian supervision of a male administrator. With the growth of school bureaucracy and the centralization of authority, the gap between teachers and administrators widened: Teachers were relegated to the bottom of an occupational hierarchy, barely one step above students. In fighting administrative reforms, teacher unions were trying to maintain school systems that rewarded teachers for their ties to the local community rather than to the emerging profession. Administrators desired, and ultimately won, a merit system of pay raises and a career ladder based on advanced education as the way to enhance the profession. Teachers and teacher unions, on the other hand, valued experience over education, single pay scales, and seniority—all things that imply a craft-oriented mentality. Teachers believed that the professional image of education would be enhanced by increasing the economic benefits to teachers.

This divide illustrates differences in ideas about professionalization. Administrators saw merit pay and autonomy for educational experts as the way toward professionalization; teachers saw it as coming from economic benefits. In 1904, Haley, in her capacity as president of the National Federation of Teachers (a short-lived national organization founded by Haley, Goggin, and the Chicago teachers), delivered an address at the National Education Association's (NEA) conference that encouraged teachers to unionize. In "Why Teachers Should Organize," Haley argued that through unionization and organization for self-protection teachers would ensure a democratic and effective education for students and avoid the tendency toward "factoryizing education."

Yet Haley's radical position and alignment with trade unionist ideology were not popular with rank-and-file members of CTF or other unions. Teachers were hesitant to affiliate with labor, although many teacher unions did so. In 1902, a San Antonio, Texas, teachers union affiliated with the American Federation of Labor (AFL), and in the same year, CTF's teachers affiliated with the Chicago Federation of Labor. The America Federation of Teachers, founded in 1916, also affiliated with the AFL, but the alliance was tenuous at best. Some professionals in education argued that unionism was inappropriate for teachers because it was antithetical to professional aims, because they feared the loss of status in the community for teachers, or because they did not equate manual and mental labor. Others fought teacher unionism on the grounds that a teachers' strike would be a strike against the government. Most teachers did not favor strikes and were concerned that affiliation would necessitate them, although this did not prove to be the case. Teacher unions typically voted to affiliate with labor for a pragmatic reason: Before the passage of women's suffrage in 1920, male labor unions provided a voting bloc to support teacher-friendly candidates and policies at the state and local levels.

The need for a national teacher organization outside NEA was believed imperative by teacher union leaders because NEA was male, administrator dominated, and did not respond to classroom teachers' issues. Haley's 1904 speech was an effort to promote both local and national teacher unions. Local unions had emerged by this time in Atlanta, Milwaukee, Boston, New York, and other cities. Yet a national organization had not taken hold. Haley's National Federation of Teachers was disbanded in 1905 after an earlier organization founded by CTF died in 1899.

The NEA had commissioned reports on teacher salaries, but many women union leaders did not find these attentive to the gender discrepancy in pay scales, wherein women grade school teachers earned less than male teachers and high school teachers. Many school boards, like New York City's, argued that men had families to support and needed incentives to enter teaching, ignoring the financial responsibilities of many women teachers. The IAWT's Strachan argued that women should receive equal pay for equal work. Such issues drove women into unions, and when the NEA ignored such pressing concerns, women showed their dissatisfaction by attending the 1910 NEA conference in force and electing **Ella Flagg Young*** as its first woman president. Always pragmatic, female teachers then allied with administrators to wrest further control from NEA's old guard of college presidents and direct its concern to practical issues. By 1913, women had established an NEA Department of Classroom Teachers.

Although NEA made some concessions, teacher leaders still desired a national union. It finally appeared in 1916 as the American Federation of Teachers (AFT), founded by eight unions, the majority Chicago teachers. Yet, from the beginning, the AFT chose to ignore the feminist model of leadership provided by Haley, Goggin, and Young by electing a man, Charles Stillman, as first president. AFT membership grew rapidly between 1916 and 1920, climbing to 10,000. During the first half of the century, AFT was more radical than NEA, supporting academic freedom and members with socialist ties. The AFT's voice, *American Teacher*, was edited by Henry Linville, whose socialist ideas were too radical for many teachers across the country. When society's mood became more conservative and antiunion sentiment spread after World War I, AFT membership declined. At the same time, NEA began a campaign to enlist more teachers, and its membership soared to 150,000 by 1925.

By the 1920s, the era of strong female-dominated teacher unions was over. Female teachers had challenged local school boards and male administrators, as well as national organizations. Teachers did win salary increases, pensions, tenure, and limited voices in school decisionmaking. Yet centralization of school systems continued, and administrators gained more authority. Even in NEA where teachers had won temporary control, they lost ground. NEA changed its bylaws in 1920 so that female-dominated locals could no longer pack meeting sites and elect their own candidates. The character of female teachers also began to change. By the 1920s, a new generation of female teachers entered the classroom, sharing the idea of professionalism supported by male administrators, not the craft-oriented approach of feminist unionists like Haley. Young teachers wanted to join the administration, and the merit system and other progressive reforms favored their education over the experience of older female teachers. In general, the ideology of professionalism and antiunion sentiment that made AFT membership decline were obstacles to further women teacher unionism after 1920.

Bibliography: William Edward Eaton, *The American Federation of Teachers, 1916– 1961: A History of the Movement* (1975); Robert E. Doherty, ''Tempest on the Hudson: The Struggle for 'Equal Pay for Equal Work' in the New York City Public Schools, 1907–1911,'' *History of Education Quarterly,* 19 (Winter 1979): 413–434; Wayne J. Urban, *Why Teachers Organized* (1982); Donald Warren, ed., *American Teachers: Histories of a Profession at Work* (1989); Marjorie Murphy, *Blackboard Unions: The AFT and the NEA, 1900–1980* (1990).

Laurie Moses Hines

teachers colleges. Teachers colleges were state-run collegiate institutions that focused on preparing women and men for elementary and secondary **teaching**.* Most teachers colleges began as **normal schools*** in the nineteenth century, became teachers colleges during the first half of the twentieth century, and later became state colleges or regional universities. Coeducational [see **coeducation***], they usually served more women than men.

The first teachers college in the United States was established in 1887 as the New York College for the Training of Teachers and renamed Teachers College in its 1892 charter. Officially a part of private Columbia University by 1893 and an institution strictly for **graduate education*** by the mid-1920s, Teachers College shared only its name with the state institutions that proliferated after 1900. Concerned primarily with educational research, Teachers College exemplified the university department of education rather than the separate state teachers college.

Several factors contributed to the transition of normal schools to teachers colleges. Foremost was the rise of the **high school*** by the late nineteenth century: Increasing numbers of teacher trainees were high school graduates, and the increasing numbers of secondary schools now needed well-trained teachers. Several states began to require college-degree certification standards for high school teachers, while new accrediting associations for colleges and high schools set higher standards for teacher training institutions. Concerns about training adequate numbers of high school teachers made education officials in many states more receptive to local citizens' desires to improve the status of normal schools. While a few state normals had begun granting bachelor's degrees in the late nineteenth century, by the 1910s, they began to adopt the name ''teachers college'' to signal the beginning of a four-year collegiate program.

In 1909, Iowa State Normal School in Cedar Falls became Iowa State Teachers College, and two years later Greeley, Colorado's State Normal School became the State Teachers College. During the three decades that followed, the rise of state teachers colleges was a nationwide phenomenon. Forty-six institutions called themselves teachers colleges by 1920, and 146 by 1933; the numbers continued to grow into the early 1940s. In the West, Midwest, and South, the majority of state normal schools became state teachers colleges during the 1920s (California and Nebraska in 1921; Virginia in 1925). In the East, where normal schools were more likely to have left high school teacher training to the older colleges, just a few state normals became teachers colleges during the 1920s, and most waited until the 1930s or even the 1940s (Massachusetts in 1932, Maryland in 1935, Vermont in 1947). A few institutions, generally founded after 1920, were established as state teachers colleges; an example is Henderson State Teachers College in Arkansas.

Like the normal schools out of which they grew, teachers colleges were usually coeducational, with more female than male students. Also like the normals, teachers college faculties included many women, although the numbers of female professors shrank gradually as the colleges replaced retiring faculty members with holders of Ph.D.s. The large female presence and the teacher training mission enabled women to take part in campus intellectual and social life unencumbered by many of the obstacles that faced women at other types of colleges.

With lower tuition rates than private colleges and many state universities, teachers colleges tended to attract students from the lower middle class, many of whom were the first in their families to attend college. A large percentage held part-time jobs. The proliferation of teachers colleges thus enabled large numbers of women, who might not otherwise have done so, to earn collegiate degrees. These women, as well as male students, tended to be hardworking and serious. Many took part enthusiastically in intercollegiate athletics, social organizations, and other campus activities, but they were also intent on earning useful degrees.

The degrees most commonly offered were Bachelor of Education, Bachelor of Science in Education, and Bachelor of Arts in Education, in a variety of four-year programs geared toward different teaching positions. **Kindergarten*** and elementary courses prepared teachers for the lower schools, while **home economics**,* industrial arts, and secondary subject courses prepared teachers for specific disciplines. Many teachers colleges had practice schools, where students gained experience teaching actual classes. Although they initially focused on educating teachers, some teachers colleges also had liberal arts programs or junior college departments. A few teachers colleges offered master's programs in education before 1920, and more than thirty offered them by 1940.

By the 1940s, state teachers colleges increasingly took on the functions of all-purpose collegiate institutions. They expanded their liberal arts offerings and added courses such as business and nursing. After World War II, the **G. I. Bill*** and the space race with the Soviet Union fueled this trend and significantly altered the teachers college atmosphere by greatly augmenting the male campus presence. At the teachers colleges, female students found themselves in the minority in classrooms and campus activities. Concurrently, the space race focused attention on the sciences and engineering. Teachers colleges invested resources in these areas, which were dominated by men; female students were relegated to the background, and the numbers of women on the faculty continued to shrink. Beginning in the 1940s, and throughout the 1950s and 1960s, teachers colleges became state colleges, the final step toward becoming general-purpose institutions. California's state teachers colleges became state colleges in 1935, Wisconsin's in 1951, and Massachusetts' throughout the 1960s. The state colleges in California, Wisconsin, and many other states later became state universities. As the teachers colleges disappeared, women faced new challenges at the new state colleges. [See also **normal departments,* teacher education**.*]

Bibliography: Charles A. Harper, *A Century of Public Teacher Education: The Story of the State Teachers Colleges as They Evolved from the Normal Schools* (1939); E. Alden Dunham, *Colleges of the Forgotten Americans: A Profile of State Colleges and Regional Universities* (1969); William R. Johnson, "Teachers and Teacher Training in the Twentieth Century," in Donald Warren, ed., *American Teachers: Histories of a Profession at Work* (1989); Richard Altenbaugh and Kathleen Underwood, "The Evolution of Normal Schools," in John I. Goodlad, Roger Soder, and Kenneth A. Sirotnik, eds., *Places Where Teachers Are Taught* (1990); Christine A. Ogren, "Education for Women in the United States: The State Normal School Experience, 1870–1920" (Ph.D. diss., University of Wisconsin, 1996).

Christine A. Ogren

teaching. Women's contributions as teachers in the formal educational systems of the Western world have received relatively little attention in the history and sociology of education. Recently, however, a number of scholars from a variety of fields have attempted to redress this imbalance by bringing the concept of gender to the forefront in studies of teaching as a profession. Within the broader topic of gender and teaching, scholars have focused their research in a number of categories, including the ideology of teaching, employment patterns, career and work rewards, teacher preparation, professionalization, the quality of teachers' work lives, and biographies of women teachers.

Since the mid-1970s, landmark texts by scholars seeking to illuminate the relationship between gender and education have appeared, including: Roberta Frankfort, *Collegiate Women: Domesticity and Career in Turn-of-the-Century America* (1977); Mary Beth Norton, *Liberty's Daughters: The Revolutionary Experience of American Women, 1750–1800* (1980); Gail P. Kelly and Carolyn M. Elliott, *Women's Education in the Third World: Comparative Perspectives* (1982); Nancy Hoffman, *Women's "True" Profession* (1982); Stephen Walker and Len Barton, *Gender, Class and Education* (1983); Elizabeth Fenema and M. Jane Ayer, *Women and Education* (1984); Polly Welts Kaufman, *Women Teachers on the Frontier* (1984); Barbara Miller Solomon, *In the Company of Educated Women: A History of Women and Higher Education in America* (1985); Patricia A. Schmuck, *Women Educators: Employees of Schools in Western Countries* (1987); Madeline R. Grumet, *Bitter Milk: Women and Teaching* (1988); and John L. Rury, *Education and Women's Work: Female Schooling and the Division of Labor in Urban America, 1870–1930* (1991).

A number of scholars have examined the influence of ideology on women's participation in formal education because cultural beliefs about acceptable gender roles historically have played a key part in defining the range of socially acceptable employment opportunities available to women. During various periods, women from all parts of the world have been excluded from the teaching profession because teaching was not considered a suitable role for women. Yet in *Women of the Republic: Intellect and Ideology in Revolutionary America* (1980), Linda K. Kerber argues that in the United States the ideal of **"Republican motherhood"*** provided the first rationale to support women's role as mothers and teachers capable of raising virtuous citizens for the new nation. A second impetus arose with the renewed religious fervor of the **Second Great Awakening*** that swept much of the country from the late 1790s to the 1850s, a phenomenon described in *Women in American Religion* (1978) by Janet Wilson James. These religious revivals increased women's public role in the church and provided another justification for their rudimentary education.

In studying employment patterns of teachers, some scholars have analyzed the social and cultural impact of women's entry into the teaching force. The **feminization*** of teaching was occurring to varying degrees in North America and Europe. During industrialization, so many new employment opportunities emerged for men that schools could no longer attract enough male teachers to fill classrooms. In contrast, women faced restricted employment options and were willing to work for lower salaries than their male counterparts. The resulting shortages of male teachers provided the opportunity for an increasing proportion of women to fill primary and, to a lesser extent, secondary classrooms. By the 1890s in the United States, women comprised 65 percent of the nation's teachers. The proportion of women teachers increased steadily thereafter, until reaching its historically highest point in 1921–1922, when 87 percent of elementary and 64 percent of secondary teachers were women.

In examining the career and work rewards available to women during different periods, feminist scholars have highlighted instances of cultural **backlash*** and discrimination that served to restrict women's employment opportunities to the schoolroom. However, others argue that women's career opportunities have been restricted by other factors as well. For instance, in *Schoolteacher: A Sociological Study* (1975), Dan C. Lortie demonstrates that women's career opportunities in education also have been limited to some extent by the fact that most women do not stay long in the profession. Historically, teaching has been for women a convenient means of financial support prior to marriage. Nevertheless, Geraldine Jonçich Clifford (1995) notes that more women began to pursue additional schooling in the nineteenth century as more attractive schools and more progressive communities began to ask more of their teachers. Women teachers began to use their earnings as **common school*** teachers to purchase further schooling for themselves at **academies*** or female **seminaries**,* thus increasing their chances of securing a better-paid position in a more attractive community. Additionally, the appearance of **normal schools*** for teacher training, and the later rise of coeducational [see **coeducation***] colleges and universities open to women, afforded some ambitious women the opportunity to teach in higher education.

The preparation of women teachers is another important area where scholars have begun to devote attention. In the United States, the first documented school for training teachers was opened by Samuel Hall in Concord, Vermont, in 1823. In 1860, only 11 normal schools existed nationwide, a figure that jumped to 166 by 1898. In many cases, the proliferation and growth of small colleges and universities were also fueled by the increasing numbers of young women who enrolled in these institutions to receive the training necessary for teaching. The feminization of teaching also had an important impact on the status of graduate schools of education in the United States. In *Ed School* (1988), Geraldine Jonçich Clifford and James W. Guthrie note that the preponderance of women in teacher preparation programs, coupled with the low social status and lack of economic power of teaching in general society, deprived graduate schools of education of the money and resources available to higher-status professional schools such as business or law.

The movement to professionalize one occupation after another, beginning in the late nineteenth century and continuing throughout the first half of the twentieth, gradually replaced the independent teacher training institution with the professional department or school of education in the college or university. Professionalization provided some opportunities to women as low-paid lecturers or assistants in newly opened departments of education, but it also created formidable new barriers. New professional associations often required advanced degrees or publications for entry to membership, making it easier to deny women, whose access to **graduate education*** historically lagged that of men. In science, this development has been documented by Margaret Rossiter, *Women Scientists in America: Struggles and Strategies to 1940* (1982). During the early twentieth century, professional science educators erected similar barriers against women schoolteachers and faculty members, as shown by Tolley (1996) [see **science education***]. Issues of professionalization are discussed by Linda Eisenmann (1996).

Although the subjective experience of female teachers in the classroom has been absent from much of educational history, recent scholarship has begun to explore the nuances of teachers' own experiences and perceptions of their work. For instance, Kate Rousmaniere (1994) notes that for women teachers in early twentieth-century America the conflicting pressures of gender roles and the demands of the occupation created a complicated work context, resulting in contradictory relationships between women teachers and students, relationships characterized by nurturance and discipline and by emotional connections and authoritarian regulation.

Recently, some feminist scholars have attempted to provide insights into the life histories of women teachers in an effort to counter the one-dimensional and uniformly apolitical female teachers depicted by many male researchers who have studied their lives. For example, in *I Answer with My Life* (1993), Kathleen Casey investigates the life histories of Catholic women religious teachers, secular Jewish women teachers, and African American teachers, aiming to provide the reader a more thorough understanding of the gender, race, class, and religious dynamics that position teachers in complex ways [see **Catholic teaching orders***]. Geraldine Jonçich Clifford examines the careers of seven women pioneers in coeducational institutions of higher learning in *Lone Voyagers: Academic Women in Coeducational Institutions, 1870–1937* (1989).

Bringing gender to the forefront as a category of analysis in the study of teaching has broadened our understanding of the complex intersections between gender and the social status of teachers. A few recent works, such as Casey's, have also explored the relationship between gender, race, class, and religion within the profession of teaching. Nevertheless, the topic of women in teaching continues to afford the interested scholar a vast range of relatively unexplored territory. [See also **early childhood teacher education**,* **normal departments**,* **semiprofessions**,* **teacher education**,* **teachers colleges**,* **women's colleges**.*]

Bibliography: Nancy Hoffman, *Woman's "True" Profession: Voices from the History of Teaching* (1981); Kate Rousmaniere, "Losing Patience and Staying Professional: Women Teachers and the Problem of Classroom Discipline in New York City Schools in the 1920s," *History of Education Quarterly*, 34 (Spring 1994): 49–68; Geraldine Jonçich Clifford, *"Equally in View": The University of California, Its Women, and the Schools* (1995); Linda Eisenmann, "Women, Higher Education, and Professionalization: Clarifying the View," *Harvard Educational Review*, 66 (Winter 1996): 858–873; Kimberley Tolley, "The Science Education of American Girls, 1784–1932" (Ed.D. diss., University of California, Berkeley, 1996).

Kimberley Tolley

temperance movement. During the late nineteenth and the early part of the twentieth century, the temperance movement in the United States was an important moral movement aimed at promoting, by both persuasion and law, abstinence from alcoholic beverages. While moderate drinking was generally accepted in the United States during the eighteenth century, by the early 1800s reformers became increasingly concerned about excesses in the consumption of alcohol. As early as 1826, with the founding of the American Temperance Society, reformers began pledge drives aimed at signing up individuals who would vow to abstain from any further alcohol consumption.

The Women's Christian Temperance Union (WCTU), founded in 1874 by Frances Willard, was a powerful and influential organization that sought to ban the sale of alcoholic beverages nationwide. Elected in 1891 to lead the World WCTU, Willard also sought to reform working conditions in industry and promoted women's **suffrage**.* Another temperance advocate, Carry Nation, began crusading against liquor in Kansas in 1892. She lectured passionately against the consumption of liquor, and she was known for smashing bottles and chairs in the saloons of Kansas. Refused recognition by the WCTU, Nation eventually took to the vaudeville circuit in order to publicize the temperance cause.

The Prohibition Party (1869) and the Anti-Saloon League (1895) were both very active in applying political pressure to the temperance cause along with the WCTU. But it was not until World War I, with the imminent need to conserve grain, that the federal government took serious notice. In 1917, Congress passed the Eighteenth Amendment, which was ratified in January 1919. The amendment was enforced and defined by Congress in the Volstead Act (1919), which was passed over President Woodrow Wilson's veto. The Eighteenth Amendment, prohibiting the ''manufacture, sale, or transportation of intoxicating liquors'' and their importation and exportation, proved unenforceable and was repealed by the Twenty-first Amendment, ratified in 1933.

The influential role of women in the temperance movement both in America and Europe allowed many an unusual opportunity for public speaking and public influence, including not just the national leaders but also the many women who exercised authority at state and local levels. Thus, the temperance movement can be viewed as a way of informally educating women not only about the moral issues of alcohol consumption but also about possibilities for their own proactive and political involvement, paving the way for work in future social movements.

Bibliography: Susanna Barrows and Robin Room, *Drinking: Behavior and Belief in Modern History* (1991); Linda Clemmons, *Toward Equality: Women in the Temperance Movement* (1991); Sheila Rowbotham, *Women in Movement: Feminism and Social Action* (1992).

Gerald L. Willis

Terrell, Mary Church. Mary Church Terrell (1863–1954), educator and **women's club*** activist, was a pioneer in the struggle against racism and sexism, devoting her life to achieving and sustaining educational equity for women. She was born in Memphis, Tennessee, to an affluent African American family. Although her father, one of the first black millionaires in the South, expected her to live the life of a sheltered Victorian lady, Mary Church received a bachelor's degree from **Oberlin College**,* completing the challenging classical curriculum ordinarily pursued by men rather than the ladies course, and accepted a **teaching*** position at **Wilberforce University*** in Ohio. Two years later she moved to Washington, D.C., where she taught Latin at the prominent African American M Street High School (later renamed Dunbar High), and eventually married the principal, Robert H. Terrell, a graduate of Harvard University. She received a master's degree from Oberlin and also studied in England, Belgium, Switzerland, and Germany.

After her marriage, Terrell, with encouragement from her husband, rejected a conventional life of privilege and leisure and instead labored to advance and promote **female literacy**,* **early childhood education**,* women's **suffrage**,*

racial uplift,* and international peace [see **peace education***]. Her many volunteer activities in cultural, political, and educational organizations demonstrated her strong commitment to service learning, or education through service on behalf of others. Following this philosophy, Terrell chose the women's club movement as her vehicle for social activism, and she became sought after on the **Chautauqua*** circuit. She spoke and wrote extensively in an effort to document and record the achievements of African American women, a subject that she felt was ignored by the mainstream American press.

In 1892 Terrell joined Josephine Bruce, **Charlotte Forten Grimké**,* Fannie B. Williams, and other prominent black women in organizing the Colored Women's League of the District of Columbia. Two months after passage of *Plessy v. Ferguson* (the 1896 Supreme Court decision that upheld separate but equal facilities), Terrell, along with Josephine St. Pierre Ruffin of Boston and **Margaret Murray Washington**,* wife of Booker T. Washington, founded the **National Association of Colored Women*** (NACW). Terrell described the organization as "an association for industrial and educational purposes" and maintained that black women should be "a unit in all matters pertaining to the education and elevation of our race." The goals of the NACW were to train, elevate, and educate young women of the poorer classes and to provide leadership opportunities for middle-class black women, much as the church provided such opportunities for African American men.

The self-help and education projects that Terrell sponsored included a women's night school for English literature and modern languages (she taught German), a free **kindergarten*** and kindergarten teacher training course, a day nursery for working mothers, a mother's club fostering parenting skills, charitable homes for young girls and elderly women, and the promotion of **home economics*** and domestic science courses.

Like other contemporary black educators, Terrell was expected to take a position on the philosophical debate between the era's two prominent black leaders, W. E. B. Du Bois and Booker T. Washington, which centered around the degree to which black people should accommodate the white establishment and pursue **vocational education*** (Washington's position) or demand access to liberal arts degrees and professions (Du Bois's view). Terrell seems not to have been dominated by either man, and while she defended vocational training in 1904, saying, "[W]ith so few vocations open to the Negro, with labor organizations increasingly hostile, and given the Black agricultural community, vocational instruction is best suited to people's needs," she also spoke publicly in support of the more militant goals of Du Bois's **National Association for the Advancement of Colored People*** (NAACP) of which she became a charter member in 1901.

In fact, Terrell became increasingly outspoken in later years: Her work for women's suffrage contributed to ratification of the Nineteenth Amendment in 1920; she led a delegation to the United Nations in the 1940s to free Rosa Ingram, a black sharecropper accused of killing a white man who had assaulted her; she fought and changed the racially exclusionary policies of the **American**

Association of University Women* (AAUW); and at age ninety, she success-fully challenged, both on the picket line and in court, the segregation of public facilities in Washington, D.C.

Terrell died in 1954, two months after the Supreme Court school desegre-gation decision in *Brown v. Board of Education* struck down *Plessy v. Ferguson.* She is buried in the cemetery of the Lincoln Temple Congregational Church that she and her husband had helped establish.

Bibliography: S. Hurley, "Mary Church Terrell: Genteel Militant," in L. Litwack and A. Meier, *Black Leaders of the Nineteenth Century* (1988); B. W. Jones, *Quest for Equality: The Life and Writings of Mary Eliza Church Terrell* (1990); D.C. Hine, *Black Women in America: An Historical Encyclopedia* (1993).

Cynthia Davis

Thomas, M. Carey. Martha Carey Thomas (1857–1935) was the first dean and second president of **Bryn Mawr College*** in Bryn Mawr, Pennsylvania, and one of the defining forces and advocates for women's education in the United States at the turn of the century.

Thomas was born and raised in the **Quaker*** community near Baltimore, Maryland. Resistant to rather than shaped by Quaker religiosity, Thomas nev-ertheless took full advantage of the Quaker belief that girls should be well educated. After attending various **seminaries*** and tutorial situations in her hometown, Thomas departed, with mixed parental blessing, for Cornell Univer-sity; she earned her B.A. in 1877 after two years. After graduation, she attempted to continue her studies at Johns Hopkins, with an eye on a professorship at what would become Bryn Mawr College, then just a topic of conversation in educated Quaker circles.

However, Johns Hopkins, like most colleges of the era, did not admit women, either as undergraduate or graduate students. Thomas applied and was admitted as a graduate student who could seek professors' advice and take the final exams but not attend classes. She withdrew in October 1878 after a difficult year of trying to study for exams for which she received uneven preparation (some professors simply refused to meet with her). After much negotiation with her parents, she managed to go to Europe for three years of graduate study, earning a summa cum laude Ph.D. from the University of Zurich in 1882 [see **graduate education***]. Her doctoral thesis was a philological examination of the texts in a fourteenth century English manuscript ("Sir Gawain and the Green Knight, Pearl, Patience, and Cleanness").

Upon her return to the States, Thomas was appointed dean and professor of English at Bryn Mawr College, which opened in 1885. Her experiences at sem-inaries, at Cornell and Johns Hopkins, and in Europe had given her very definite ideas of what qualities made a good college; she campaigned from the first for a rigorous institution that would liberate scholarship for women. Thomas resisted all efforts from the trustees to make Bryn Mawr into a docile, conservative, female version of Haverford College, the men's Quaker institution in the next town. She hired professors based on the quality of their scholarship and research; much early **teaching*** at Bryn Mawr was conducted by associates and instructors. Thomas toured the previously founded **Seven Sisters*** and learned from them about building, housekeeping, administration, and collegiate structure. In addition to organizing the college in these early years, Thomas taught English literature and gave talks in chapel during which she espoused her philosophy promoting women, their education, and their intellectual equality with men; it is in one of these chapel talks that Thomas supposedly made the apocryphal statement, "Only our failures marry" when she meant to say, "Our failures only marry."

Thomas was appointed president of Bryn Mawr in 1893 after a long political struggle with the conservative Quaker board of trustees. As Bryn Mawr gained its reputation as the most scholarly and most European of the American **women's colleges**,* Thomas focused on expansive building projects, soliciting major gifts from alumnae donors as well as philanthropists like John D. Rockefeller. When she retired in 1922, Thomas's public interests included women's **suffrage*** (Susan B. Anthony spoke at Bryn Mawr), a trusteeship at Cornell, and involvement in a number of women's political causes.

Outside of Bryn Mawr, Thomas's most significant contributions to women's education were her roles in founding the Bryn Mawr School and the Johns Hopkins Medical School, both in Baltimore. Thomas helped to found and sat on the board of the Bryn Mawr School, a girls' institution that trained young women to pass the difficult Bryn Mawr College entrance exams. She also assisted her friend Mary Garrett in the logistics and planning of making a foundation-sized gift to Hopkins for its medical school; the gift was contingent upon the admission of women students to the medical school of the university that had not allowed Thomas in its classrooms thirty years earlier [see **medical education***].

Thomas's personal life could be characterized as that of the "spinster," a term that belied the varied lives of many powerful and active women at the turn of the century. She actually engaged in two long and intimate friendships with women that spanned her adult life. Mamie Gwinn was her companion in Europe and in her early days at Bryn Mawr; later in life, Thomas shared her residence at Bryn Mawr, the Deanery, with the same Mary Garrett who provided the foundation gift to Hopkins Medical (and many donations to Bryn Mawr College). Thomas was Garrett's main beneficiary; after Garrett's death and Thomas's retirement, Thomas used her inheritance to travel the world in luxury. Thomas died of old age and arteriosclerosis on December 2, 1935, in Pennsylvania; her ashes are buried in the cloister of Thomas Library at Bryn Mawr College.

Bibliography: Cornelia Meigs, *What Makes a College?: A History of Bryn Mawr* (1956); Patricia Hochschild LaBalme, ed., *A Century Recalled: Essays in Honor of Bryn Mawr*

College (1987); Helen Lefkowitz Horowitz, *The Power and Passion of M. Carey Thomas* (1994).

Mary Dockray-Miller

Title VII of the Civil Rights Act. Title VII of the Civil Rights Act prohibits employment practices that discriminate against individuals on the basis of race, color, religion, sex, or national origin. The original 1964 law exempted educational institutions from sex discrimination claims by employees who performed work connected with the educational activities of such institutions. In 1972, the Congress amended Title VII to remove the exemption with the admonishment that discrimination in education, especially in higher education, was as pervasive as in any other employment area. Title VII sex discrimination claims in education have arisen from hiring, promotion, and compensation practices, as well as other conditions of employment such as pregnancy policies. Significant differences between employment practices in higher education and those in primary and secondary education may explain why the most prominent issues at these two educational levels have tended to differ.

Legal procedures play crucial roles in the determination of any Title VII sex discrimination claim. Plaintiffs must allege that they were discriminated against because employment requirements or conditions either had disparate impact on or resulted in disparate treatment of one sex, usually female. Disparate impact claims allege that facially neutral employment requirements, such as diploma or licensing requirements, effectively restrict job opportunities for one sex. Plaintiffs must establish a prima facie case of discrimination by showing that they belong to a protected class and that a particular employment policy or practice disadvantages their class. Critically, claimants do not have to prove intentional discrimination. Once a prima facie case has been established, defendant employers must show that there is a necessary business reason for the policy or practice and that there are no less discriminatory alternatives. If a defendant successfully rebuts the plaintiff's prima facie case, the plaintiff must then show that the professed business reason was only a pretext for discrimination.

Although it has been difficult to win claims against educational institutions under the disparate impact theory, the disparate treatment theory has been even more difficult to prove. Significantly, most Title VII sex discrimination claims allege disparate treatment, not impact. Disparate treatment claims must prove that the employer intentionally discriminated against the plaintiff because of sex. Once the plaintiff establishes the prima facie case required in disparate impact cases, the defendant only needs to claim some legitimate nondiscriminatory reason without proving it was actually motivated by that reason. The plaintiff must then prove that the defendant's reason was not the actual one, but only a mere pretext for discrimination. Supreme Court decisions in the 1980s tended to treat disparate impact cases more similarly to disparate treatment cases by interpreting the evidentiary provisions of Title VII so that plaintiffs in both types of cases had to prove intentional discrimination.

Even after Title VII was amended in 1972 with its reference to discrimination in higher education, federal judges continued to interfere only reluctantly with hiring, promotion, and tenure decisions in higher education. Because these decisions tend to be decentralized, it can be difficult to pinpoint where discrimination occurred or who actually discriminated against a claimant. Judicial deference has been given to hiring, promotion, and tenure decisions because of their inherently subjective nature and because of support for the principle of academic freedom. A plaintiff frequently could provide statistical evidence that suggested her institution was practicing sex discrimination, but she had little individual information on the disputed decision in her case. In 1990, a Supreme Court ruling clearly established that a plaintiff was entitled to see her confidential file compiled by the institution to make its employment decision. A 1991 amendment to Title VII that allows juries, in addition to judges, to decide sex discrimination claims may undermine the judicial deference that has traditionally hindered plaintiffs in these discrimination cases in higher education.

In the late 1970s and early 1980s, several successful sex discrimination cases against colleges and universities were pursued despite the difficulties facing plaintiffs. *Kunda v. Muhlenberg College* (1980) held that the college was guilty of sex discrimination for denying tenure and promotion in the physical education program to Connie Rae Kunda because she lacked a master's degree. Kunda proved that males had recently been tenured and promoted in that department without degrees and that other male colleagues had been counseled about the need to obtain their master's degree without her being similarly counseled. This was the first case in which a court ordered tenure for a Title VII violation.

Mecklenberg v. Montana State University, higher education's first successful class action sex discrimination case, arose in the mid-1970s. At Montana State's Bozeman campus, female faculty with comparable educational backgrounds and in comparable positions of responsibility were paid significantly less than males. Women were also underrepresented in university governance. Furthermore, the university had no clear or uniform policies for making or reviewing hiring, promotion, or salary decisions. An unusually sympathetic judge ordered Montana State to review salary when so requested by an individual faculty member, to increase female participation in university governance, and to systematize employment practices.

Factual circumstances like those in *Kunda* and *Mecklenberg* are less likely to occur now. Because colleges and universities are more aware of their vulnerability to sex or other discrimination charges, employment decisions have become more standardized and bureaucratic. Also, faculty and administrators involved in these decisions are more cognizant of the need to avoid the appearance of discrimination. One result of these changes may be a decrease in sex discrimination. However, it probably also makes sex discrimination more difficult to prove because decisionmakers are more careful about what they say and do, while their decisionmaking may continue to be discriminatory. Although the percentage of faculty that is female has grown, during the 1980s and early 1990s women earned doctorates at higher rates than they were hired for faculty positions. This suggests that women might not be obtaining faculty positions at a rate consistent with their proportion of the applicant pool and that sex discrimination continues.

Title VII sex discrimination claims seem less likely to arise in elementary and secondary education. Public school teachers are paid on a set salary schedule based on teachers' seniority and educational qualifications that does not allow for the severe variations in salary found among faculty in higher education. Also, hiring and tenure decisions are neither as complex nor as secretive at lower educational levels. However, the secondary education practice of coupling teaching and coaching positions has provoked sex discrimination claims. In the early 1980s, a female biology teacher successfully argued, using the easier-to-prove disparate impact theory, that she had been sexually discriminated against by an Arizona school district that tied a biology position to a varsity football coaching position.

Pregnant teachers successfully litigated sex discrimination claims under Title VII. Many school districts required all pregnant teachers to go on unpaid leave at set times before their due dates until set times after their deliveries. These periods were sometimes four to five months before due dates and as many as six months after deliveries. In 1974, the Supreme Court ruled that school districts could not have pregnancy rules that arbitrarily applied to all pregnant teachers and were not rationally related to their interest in maintaining continuity of instruction. School districts may now have reasonable rules for continuity of instruction and physical competence, such as requirements that teachers submit timely written notice of the date they intend to begin or end their maternity leave, that maternity leaves start at the beginning of the semester that delivery is expected, or that teachers provide medical certificates of fitness to continue or return to teaching. The Pregnancy Disability Bill of 1979 amended Title VII to provide that pregnancy-related disabilities receive the same insurance coverage and sick-leave benefits as other disabilities.

Title VII is one avenue for females to pursue sex discrimination claims against educational institutions. As with other civil rights laws, its promise has perhaps exceeded its results. Claims are difficult to win and enforce, while being expensive and time-consuming to pursue. Nonetheless, Title VII provided previously absent protection for women employed by educational institutions.

Bibliography: Louis Fischer, David Schimmel, and Cynthia Kelly, *Teachers and the Law*, 2nd ed. (1987); George R. LaNoue and Barbara A. Lee, *Academics in Court: The Consequences of Faculty Discrimination* (1987); Susan Gluck Mezey, *In Pursuit of Equality: Women, Public Policy, and the Federal Courts* (1992); Robert C. O'Reilly and Edward T. Green, *School Law for the 1990s: A Handbook* (1992); Martha S. West, ''Gender Bias in Academic Robes: The Law's Failure to Protect Women Faculty,'' *Temple Law Review*, 67 (Spring 1994): 67–178.

Maureen A. Reynolds

Title IX of the Education Amendments of 1972. Title IX of the Education Amendments of 1972 is the first American law to counter sex discrimination in federally funded educational institutions. It holds that "no person . . . shall, on the basis of sex, be excluded from participation in, be denied the benefits of, or be subjected to discrimination under any education program or activity receiving Federal financial assistance."

Title IX was inspired by the 1954 *Brown v. Board of Education* landmark discrimination case that gave new insight into the importance of equality in education. Title IX was patterned after Title VI of the Civil Rights Act of 1964, which prohibits discrimination in all federally assisted programs on the basis of race, color, and national origin. Congresswoman Edith Green, a former schoolteacher who retired from Congress in 1974, was largely responsible for creating Title IX. Title IX is narrower than Title VI in that it covers only federally assisted education programs, whereas Title VI covers all federally assisted programs. Title IX is broader than Title VI in covering both students and employees, whereas Title VI does not cover employees in certain areas.

In 1984, the Supreme Court decision in *Grove City College v. Bell* was a blow to the advancement of women's causes, as it restricted Title IX to cover only those specific programs and activities funded directly with federal money. As a result, discrimination in many activities and programs was no longer prohibited by Title IX because they did not receive direct federal funds. However, coalitions of women's groups successfully pushed for renewed legislative protection. On March 22, 1988, Congress enacted the Civil Rights Restoration Act of 1987 over President Ronald Reagan's veto. This overturned the Supreme Court's earlier decision and restored Title IX coverage so that it once again applies to the entire institution regardless of where federal funds are utilized.

Title IX has been interpreted to cover all activities and programs of educational institutions and all educational programs of those institutions whose primary mission is not education. The act covers virtually all areas within institutions such as recruiting, admissions, counseling, financial aid, health care, employment, insurance, and extracurricular activities.

Institutions that are exempt from Title IX requirements include those operated by religious groups, when the regulations are inconsistent with their religious beliefs, and the military and merchant marine training schools. Also exempt are youth organizations like the Boy Scouts, Camp Fire Girls, the Young Men's Christian Association (YMCA), the **Young Women's Christian Association*** (YWCA), the Boys State, the Girls State, and membership practices of university-based social **sororities*** and fraternities.

In admissions, some schools are exempt from coverage, for example, private undergraduate institutions, preschools, elementary and secondary schools (other than vocational schools), and single-sex public undergraduate institutions. They are, however, obliged to treat students in a nondiscriminatory manner in all areas other than admissions.

Both Title IX and Title VI are enforced in the same manner, primarily by the Office of Civil Rights of the Department of Education. The department can conduct compliance reviews of institutions and school districts without specific complaints. Besides this, all government agencies have Title IX enforcement responsibilities. If Title IX conflicts with state or local laws, the principle of the federal law holds.

Institutions may not discriminate on the basis of sex in providing housing facilities. Different rules for housing each sex, such as requiring women to live on campus while allowing men to live off campus, are violations of Title IX. Courses and other educational activities cannot be provided separately on the basis of sex, nor can institutions discriminate on the basis of sex in financial aid provisions or in counseling students or guiding parents.

Title IX applies to full-time and part-time employees including student employees and those participating in work-study, cooperative education, assistantships, and internships. For example, giving women students in these positions primarily clerical duties while giving men more substantive work is a violation of Title IX.

Title IX specifies that all educational institutions receiving federal funds must take some action to comply with the law. These actions include designating at least one employee who is responsible for coordinating efforts to comply with Title IX regulations and who would investigate any Title IX complaint; notifying all students and employees of the appointment of the person responsible for compliance of Title IX; adopting and publishing grievance procedures; and notifying students, employees, and applicants of the institution's nondiscriminatory policy and Title IX obligations.

In athletics, federally funded educational institutions are obliged to comply with Title IX in three major areas. First is financial aid, where the total money available for scholarships must be divided equally among men and women in proportion to the numbers of male and female athletes. Second, in equipment and supplies, coaching and academic tutoring, locker rooms, training facilities, and publicity and support services, males and females should receive equivalent treatment, benefits, and opportunities. Third is meeting the interests and abilities of male and female students; according to Title IX regulations, the athletic interests and abilities of male and female students must be equally effectively accommodated. Athletic programs have especially embraced Title IX since it provides for equal treatment of males and females. This resulted in a fourfold increase in the ten years following the legislation's passage in the number of college women participating in **women's athletics**.*

Bibliography: National Advisory Council on Women's Educational Programs, *Title IX: The Half Full, Half Empty Glass* (1974); U.S. Department of Health Education, and Welfare, *Why Title IX?* (1977); Frank D. Aquila, *Title IX: Implications for the Education of Women* (1981); Rosemary C. Salomone, *Equal Education under Law* (1986); Mariam

Chamberlain, ed., *Women in Academe: Progress and Prospects* (1988); Bernice Sandler, *The Restoration of Title IX: Implications for Higher Education* (1989).

Rajeswari Swaminathan

Troy Female Seminary. Troy Female Seminary, an early institution for young women renowned for its demanding curriculum and belief in women's intellectual capacities, was founded by **Emma Hart Willard*** in 1821 when she accepted the invitation of the Troy, New York, Common Council to move her school there from Waterford, New York. Willard accepted because she was confident that the council would convince the state legislature to grant public tax monies to female education, one of Willard's long-standing goals. The seminary was designed on ideas Willard put forth in her *Plan for Improving Female Education* (1819) where she relied on what she called "public guardianship" as the guiding principle under which the state legislature and local residents would establish a permanent relationship with the seminary. After many disappointments over the lack of public funding, Willard produced another document in an effort to influence public policy. Her *Memoir* (1833), written first as a private communication to the seminary's board of trustees and then later publicly shared, explored "public guardianship" as a combination of public financial support and what Willard called a "spirit of education."

The curriculum at Troy Female Seminary forged new educational opportunities for women by offering science, history, mathematics, and pedagogical training rather than the domestic or **ornamental education*** usually offered at girls' institutions. For example, Amos Eaton, noted popular lecturer and scientist at Troy's Rennselear Institute, a college for men (later named Rennselear Polytechnic Institute), lectured occasionally at the seminary and often invited Willard's students to his labs at Rennselear [see **science education***]. In 1834 Eaton offered an experimental course for women on the men's campus. In an advertisement for the course and with propriety in mind, Eaton announced that the women would be supervised by a female teacher as he instructed them, and the students would be required to pay only half the fees usually charged. In 1823 **Almira Hart Phelps**,* Willard's sister, studied directly under Eaton and was soon hired by Willard as head of the seminary's science department. Later, Phelps wrote many science textbooks that were used at the seminary and became the best-selling science textbooks across the country in boys' **academies*** as well as female **seminaries*** and eventually the **common schools**.*

Willard, too, wrote textbooks for the seminary that became best-selling history textbooks for nearly fifty years in academies, seminaries, and common schools. She first coauthored a geography text with William Chauncey Woodbridge in 1822. In the preface, Willard explained her methods for teaching geography based on Pestalozzi's pedagogical ideas of moving from the familiar to the new while focusing on experiential learning. She developed intricate visual depictions of concepts and was hailed for new pedagogical advances.

She also believed that including history in the curriculum for women was essential to stimulating patriotism, explaining the horrors of war, and reinforcing the importance of education for men and women and for America's survival. In this heavily Christian era, history was also used to show how God's plan was unfolding and what responsibilities each person had toward building God's kingdom on earth. History lessons at Troy were a means to pass on culture, knowledge, and informed responsibility to the next generations. Through her teaching and her textbooks, Willard assisted young people in gaining a sense of place and time as it related to them as individuals and as members of a national community. History lessons, for Willard, also served to make the community aspect of the Republic visible and tangible for women.

The Troy curriculum as a whole was comparable to the best men's colleges of the time, including the expectation of public examinations for women students. Willard called together the most notable educators from nearby colleges, local clergy, seminary trustees, and others to examine students in all subjects. She continued to emphasize the necessity of such preparation for future teachers in the Republic.

Between 1821 and 1871 Troy educated more than 12,000 young women. At least 3,500 alumnae from that period responded to the call of a fellow alumna for life history data by way of an extensive survey. From this collection, historian Anne Firor Scott later reported several interesting findings: Some 146 Troy graduates went on to be founder or administrator of a school; 733 never married; the married alumnae had an average of 3.4 children. Only 515 graduates worked for pay before marriage, and 166 worked after marriage. Nearly a thousand (845) graduates joined one or more voluntary associations, and 24 created a nonschool institution. These statistics suggest the tremendous impact Troy had on the life course of women. The seminary and its graduates under the direction of Emma Hart Willard stand as premier examples of the struggles and successes in the early history of women's education in the United States. [See also **teaching**.*]

Bibliography: Emma Hart Willard, *An Address to the Public; Particularly to the Members of the Legislature of New York, Proposing a Plan for Improving Female Education* (1819); A. W. Fairbanks, ed., *Emma Willard and Her Pupils, or Fifty Years of the Troy Female Seminary, 1822–72* (1898); Anne Firor Scott, "The Ever-Widening Circle: The Diffusion of Feminist Values from the Troy Female Seminary, 1822–72," *History of Education Quarterly*, 19 (Spring 1979): 3–26; Thalia M. Mulvihill, "Community in Emma Hart Willard's Educational Thought, 1787–1870" (Ph.D. diss., Syracuse University, 1995).

Thalia M. Mulvihill

Troy Plan. The "Troy Plan," published in 1819 by educator **Emma Hart Willard**,* provided one of the nation's earliest detailed, rational arguments for why women needed to be educated in the new Republic and specific ideas for how to achieve that education. Appearing in the document *An Address to the Public; Particularly to the Members of the Legislature of New York, Proposing* *a Plan for Improving Female Education* (1819) was Willard's unusual argument for use of state tax monies to support female education. Revealing her concern for the pressures felt by school founders, Willard wrote, "Preceptresses of female institutions are [now] dependent on their pupils for support and are consequently liable to become victims of their caprice." Willard claimed that her proposed financial arrangement would hold teachers accountable to the state and thereby eliminate opening of schools by anyone merely wanting to make money. Rather, Willard saw her proposed female **seminary*** as an institution to ensure the credentials of those engaging in educating children of the young Republic. Relying on an argument that historians would later call **"Republican motherhood,"*** Willard insisted it was the state's duty to provide for the present and future prosperity of the country; that this prosperity depended on the character of citizens; that character was formed by mothers; and that only thoroughly educated mothers were equipped to ensure the future of the Republic. Unlike others of her era, Willard believed that the state's role in female education ought to be one of regulation, including certification, sanctioning, and financial support.

In her 1819 *Plan* Willard outlined the curriculum she believed should be the basis for boarding schools for young women. In an era of strong religious feeling, she advocated for instruction in religion and morality, including study of the evidences of Christianity and moral philosophy. She added literary studies including philosophy of the mind, natural philosophy, botany, chemistry, zoology, history and geography. All were complemented with domestic science including healthy exercise and study of physiology. **Ornamental education*** was also important: drawing, painting, elegant penmanship, music, and dance. However, Willard noted that she regarded study of needlework a waste of school time.

In 1818 Amos Eaton, well-known popularizer of science, founded the Troy Lyceum of Natural History, which was widely attended by the community, including Emma Willard [see **lyceums***]. Willard was so excited by what she learned there that she went to work at once incorporating information from Eaton's lectures into **science education*** at the Waterford Academy. After Willard agreed to move her school to Troy in 1821, she was asked by the Common Council to temporarily use the lyceum building while they secured a permanent school building. The school remained there for six months, during which Willard took the opportunity to work more closely with Eaton. Together they developed lessons that later comprised the science curriculum at Troy.

Willard's *Plan* indicated both how representative of her time she was and how wisely she combined the discourses of two dominant political ideologies as she argued for improved conditions for female education. Willard constructed the notion of public authority for education as belonging primarily to women. She saw no separation between woman's role as mother charged with the moral development and well-being of her own children and that of teacher responsible for the moral and intellectual development of other people's children. Motherhood and **teaching*** were both activities in service to God and country. Mothers and teachers were entrusted with shaping young people into qualified citizens. Women derived their public authority, in Willard's view, from this unique combination of roles, bestowed on them by their creator. Although not all women became teachers in a formal sense, they all had responsibility for educating children.

In 1829, Willard wrote an addendum to the *Plan* simply called "Notes on the Plan of Female Education," in which she stated that while disappointed at lack of support by the state, the corporation and the individual inhabitants of Troy had greatly assisted her educational efforts. Although Willard's *Plan* was unable to secure full state funding for female education, it nonetheless remained for fifty years a very influential document on the form and function of educational institutions for young women. Historian Anne Firor Scott reported that 200 schools can be identified as spawns of the "Troy Plan." From 1820 through the 1870s female seminaries and **academies*** developing all across the country and abroad referred to the Troy Plan as their basic blueprint for founding educational institutions and heralded Emma Hart Willard as the architect.

Bibliography: Anne Firor Scott, "The Ever-Widening Circle: The Diffusion of Feminist Values from the Troy Female Seminary, 1822–72," *History of Education Quarterly*, 19 (Spring 1979): 3–26; Nancy Beadie, "Emma Willard's Idea Put to the Test: The Consequences of State Support of Female Education in New York, 1819–67," *History of Education Quarterly*, 33 (Winter 1993): 543–562; Thalia M. Mulvihill, "Community in Emma Hart Willard's Educational Thought, 1787–1870" (Ph.D. diss., Syracuse University, 1995).

Thalia M. Mulvihill

"true womanhood." *True womanhood* is a term found in popular literature from 1820 to 1860 to define a "lady" in American society. The concept is based on the idea of female distinctiveness and the separation of men and women into particular spheres of influence. The ideology was directed at women of the middle or higher classes who worked within the home and were financially dependent on their husbands, yet its impact was felt by working-class and nonwhite women as well. The definition expanded during the Civil War era and into the first quarter of the twentieth century. Though the term became obsolete, many characteristics of true womanhood from the first half of the nineteenth century are reflected in modern images of womanhood.

True womanhood emerged in reaction to the many changes confronting America in the early 1800s. The proliferation of new religious denominations resulting from the **Second Great Awakening*** challenged the cultural hegemony of established Protestant religions; the introduction of universal white male **suffrage*** shook the more established segments of American society; and industrialization changed the nature of work, as many economically productive women found themselves either excluded from the economy or limited by the type of work available to them. With industrialization came urbanization, and many men worked outside the home. Mass immigration added to the growing tension within the cities; yet immigration also meant a steady supply of cheap female domestic labor, which middle-class housewives utilized to enjoy some degree of leisure time. The Civil War increased the sense of social disruption, even as the loss of men created a need for more economically independent women. As society struggled for stability, the desire to clearly delineate the roles of men and women became acute.

True womanhood rested upon "four cardinal virtues": piety, purity, submissiveness, and domesticity. The keystone was piety, considered women's natural predisposition. Their pious nature was a beacon for the godless and sinful world, so women became the exemplars of a righteous and enlightened society. Purity was a moral imperative for the true woman. Upon her wedding night, a lady relinquished all legal and social standing to become the complete dependent of her husband. Submission was a particularly female trait, since men were by nature dominant creatures, the leaders and shapers of society, and women his obedient servants. Domesticity, a cult in its own right, declared that in the home women were to perform their virtuous duties of bringing man back to God and reforming society by raising just children.

While in many ways the tenets of true womanhood were intended to limit and confine women, they actually increased women's authority and enabled them to extend their sphere of influence beyond the home. Piety increased women's power, for while men ruled with laws, women ruled with moral suasion. Domesticity increased women's authority in childrearing: America looked toward its mothers to produce, rear, and educate its future leaders.

The "true woman" was not the first to be seen in this lofty light. At the end of the Revolution, the ideology of **"Republican motherhood"*** had also emphasized the mother's role in nurturing future leaders. **Judith Sargent Murray*** supported development of schools to provide young women with literacy, verbal, and cognitive skills needed to function in an increasingly print-oriented society.

At midcentury it was common for girls of all social classes to spend some months, perhaps a year or longer, attending school. Many middle-class girls were sent to boarding school for a year or more to be educated, weaned from their homes, trained in the social graces, and duly prepared for marriage. The **academies*** that they entered were extremely diverse. Some were day schools, some boarding schools; some were open to all, some to a select few. Though difficult to generalize, all academies provided instruction in reading, writing, and arithmetic, and many provided the opportunity to study history, mathematics, languages, and the sciences. Yet the social graces were also important, with **ornamental education*** in music, painting, needlework, and embroidery.

Formal instruction for women changed with establishment of female **seminaries**,* throughout the northern, southern, and western regions. These institutions differed from academies in that their purpose was primarily to develop a young woman's religious character, as well as her reading, writing, artistic, and domestic skills. While the seminary focus was on moral development, the utilitarian or domestic aspects of a young lady's education were also highly regarded.

The ideology of true womanhood enabled women not only to elevate the domestic arts but also to feminize teaching and professionalize **teacher education**.* **Catharine Beecher**,* for example, recognized piety as the central role of the **common school*** movement and advocated for a trained corps of female teachers. Since the care and education of children fell within women's **separate sphere**,* women were naturally the most fit to be teachers. The **feminization*** of teaching offered women not only the opportunity of a more intellectually rigorous education but a vocation that required some level of autonomy and self-sufficiency.

Higher education on a par with liberal arts training received by males was a greater struggle, but extension of women's sphere through the feminization of teaching justified expansion of higher education to women. New collegiate opportunities for women profoundly redefined womanhood by challenging the Victorian belief that men's and women's social roles were rooted in biology.

The informal education of women was influenced deeply by the combination of their moral superiority and evangelicalism, a combination that enabled the true woman to extend her sphere of influence into society. Though popular and **prescriptive literature*** continued to place women in the home, during the 1830s and 1840s women actively joined social movements. For example, through their efforts as abolitionists [see **abolitionism***], women learned the political skills of lecturing, fund-raising, petitioning, organizing, and **consciousness-raising*** on the local and national levels. The suffrage movement incorporated and later triumphed when it began to rely on the true womanhood thesis of female superiority. Who better to vote against corrupt politicians and to work for legislation to improve the sanitation, living conditions, and moral fiber of our society than the true woman?

Though women's supposed moral superiority was a clear argument toward the end of the nineteenth century, the impact of the cult of domesticity was also evident. Since the true woman's place was in the home, such issues as cleanliness, childrearing, and health fell within the female domain. Consequently, women argued that public policies addressing these issues must also be within their purview, and they fought to participate in creating government policies that directly or indirectly affected the lives of women and children.

The privilege to serve and the responsibility to vote required a very different education than that offered to ladies at seminaries. Economics, political science, environmental science, and sociology were some of the areas women needed in order to participate in the new roles they had created for themselves.

The cult of domesticity also helped women extend their influence into the professional world of work. **Teaching*** had already been recognized as a profession for the true woman, but women also pushed to enter and professionalize nursing. By the end of the Civil War, over 3,000 women had made nursing their profession, and tens of thousands more had served as volunteers. Dr. Elizabeth

Blackwell and Dorothea Dix were instrumental in establishing training centers in the North to educate women in medicine, **hygiene**,* and related skills [see **medical education***].

While true womanhood inadvertently helped women break the boundaries of their sphere, it also helped society form opinions about women that have lasted well into the twentieth century. The residual effects of true womanhood are still evident in men's and women's different experience of education, women's disproportionate representation in nursing, child care, and education, and beliefs about women's emotional characteristics.

Bibliography: Barbara Welter, "The Cult of True Womanhood: 1820–1860," *American Quarterly*, 18 (1966): 151–174; Sue Zschoche, "Dr. Clarke Revisited: Science, True Womanhood, and Female Collegiate Education," *History of Education Quarterly*, 29 (1989): 545–569; Cynthia Eagle Russett, *Sexual Science: The Victorian Construction of Womanhood* (1991); Carol Smart, *Regulating Womanhood: Historical Essays on Marriage, Motherhood, and Sexuality* (1992); Gillian Pascal and Roger Cox, "Education and Domesticity," *Gender and Education*, 5 (1993).

Deborah M. De Simone

Tuskegee Institute. Tuskegee Institute, best known as the site for Booker T. Washington's philosophy of industrial education for African Americans, was founded in 1880 when the Alabama state legislature set aside an appropriation for educating African Americans in Macon County. Washington opened the doors of Tuskegee **Normal School*** for the education of African American teachers on July 4, 1881, to thirty men and women from surrounding counties. The school's mission reflected his strong belief that industrial education was the route to African American self-respect and economic independence.

In the late nineteenth century, many believed that African American education should consist of an exposure to the liberal arts. Yet Washington stressed the value of skilled labor and hard work. He accentuated the need for decency and fair play by encouraging his female and male students to "cast down your bucket where you are and create a better life through hard work and education" (Washington, 1895, p. 148). He and his followers thought that African Americans best became self-sufficient with marketable skills. This accommodationist philosophy, which did not challenge whites for equal economic power, attracted funding from the nation's leading philanthropists, including the Peabody, Slater, **Rosenwald**,* Carnegie, and Rockefeller funds. This funding gave Washington a great deal of power within the African American community.

The Tuskegee curriculum, based on an earlier model at **Hampton Institute**,* combined teacher training with hard manual labor. Supporters believed that traditional liberal arts only created false hope among African American students and should be eliminated from **teacher education*** programs. Thus, women students learned to sew, cook, scrub, and plow. While the prospective teachers never expected to enter these occupations, they were expected to learn the habits and values associated with them. As teachers, they would pass along these values to their students.

Critics of Tuskegee's curriculum attacked the training as a means of reproducing a segregated society in which African Americans could expect very little upward mobility. Henry Bullock offered a critical review:

The industrial curriculum to which many Negro children were exposed, supposedly designed to meet their needs, reflected the life that accompanied their status at the time. They had always farmed. The curriculum aimed to make better farmers. Negro women had a virtual monopoly on laundering, and Negro men had worked largely as mechanics. The industrial curriculum was designed to change this only in so far that Negroes were trained to perform these services better. (Bullock, p. 88)

Proponents of Tuskegee justified the curriculum from a very different perspective. As one supporter said, "[T]he girl in the laundry does not make soap by rote but by principle; and the girl in the dressmaking shop does not cut out her pattern by luck or guess or instinct or rule of thumb, but by geometry" (Bruce, p. 7). Tuskegee was not training farmers, laundry women, or dressmakers but teachers; the teachers learned academic skills accepted by occupations. Tuskegee was a training ground neither for liberal arts nor for industrial education but was a school designed to "train a corps of teachers with a particular social philosophy relevant to the political and economic reconstruction of the South" (Anderson, p. 77).

Booker T. Washington died in 1915. By then, the state of African American education had declined, paralleling the worsening state of civil rights throughout the South. By Washington's death, however, Tuskegee's foundation as a leader in education had been laid. The school at the time had a worth of $2 million and an enrollment of 1,500 students.

As the status of African American education evolved during the gains of the civil rights era of the 1950s and 1960s, so did the status of education at Tuskegee Institute. In 1985, the institute became Tuskegee University. By 1995, the endowment boasted an excess of $40 million, and the school had an enrollment of more than 3,000, with plans to create Ph.D. programs by the turn of the century.

Bibliography: Booker T. Washington, *Address to the Cotton States Exposition* (1895); Washington, *Up from Slavery: An Autobiography* (1902); R. C. Bruce, *Address in New Old South Church, Boston* (1904); Louis R. Harlan, *Separate and Unequal: Public School Campaigns and Racism in the Southern Seaboard States* (1958); Henry Bullock, *History of Negro Education in the South from 1619 to the Present* (1967); James D. Anderson, *The Education of Blacks in the South, 1860–1935* (1988); Wayne Urban, *American Education: A History* (1996).

Charles E. Jenks

U

University of Chicago. The University of Chicago, site of many advances and challenges in women's higher education, was founded in 1892 in the developing city of Chicago, Illinois. The university was the intersection of a vision for a premier academic institution by two men, William Rainey Harper and John D. Rockefeller. Over time, the vision was more than fulfilled as the University of Chicago became one of the most prestigious institutions of higher education in the United States.

William Rainey Harper was the first president of the new university. Harper had ready access to huge sums of Rockefeller wealth (close to $35 million by 1919) to build college buildings, hire a prestigious faculty, and recruit the best students. While Rockefeller saw Chicago as a college created in the image of the Baptist religion and providing educational opportunity to the rapidly growing Midwest, Harper saw it as an opportunity to build an institution primarily dedicated to **graduate education*** and research equal to any on the East Coast.

Harper's oversight of the new university knew no limits. He personally oversaw as much of the design and direction as he possibly could. Harper's megalomania also extended to hiring faculty. He made frequent visits to many of the top institutions in the Northeast, literally recruiting faculty away from institutions such as Cornell, Harvard, Yale, and others with unparalleled promises of large salaries, spacious offices, and research opportunities. With the assurance of the Rockefeller fortune as collateral, Harper was very successful but incurred the wrath of numerous college presidents who accused him, quite accurately, of raiding their campuses of their best faculty. In fact, among Harper's first faculty were nine former college presidents.

One of Harper's recruits was **Alice Freeman Palmer**,* the very popular and successful former president of **Wellesley College*** in Massachusetts. Chicago was to include **coeducation** from its inception, and Harper was determined to have a significant, national figure in women's education as its first **dean of**

women.* Palmer had resigned her position in 1887 to marry Harvard philosopher George Herbert Palmer. Harper successfully lobbied Alice Palmer to the dean's job, but he could not convince George to leave Cambridge. As a compromise, Harper drew up a contract that required Alice to be in Chicago only part of the year so she could maintain her domestic commitments in Boston. Harper also agreed to hire **Marion Talbot**,* Palmer's good friend and longtime associate, as assistant dean. In an important step not always available to later deans, both women also carried academic rank: Palmer was professor of history, and Talbot, assistant professor of household sanitation [see **home economics***].

When the university opened in 1892, the number of women who enrolled surprised many. The numbers of women eager for a Chicago education was close to that of men, and the early population was nearly equal. Palmer and Talbot worked hard to create a hospitable environment for the female students, converting a small hotel near campus, the Beatrice, into the first residence for women while residence halls on campus were constructed. Palmer was eager to recreate the feel of the "cottage system" she had introduced at Wellesley— small, intimate settings that allowed women to "escape" the rigors of academic life.

Palmer left the University of Chicago after three years, and Talbot was made dean of women. Despite the fact that Chicago had been coeducational since it opened its doors, a simmering controversy toward the women students boiled over shortly after the turn of the century, signaling a sort of **backlash*** that appeared on many campuses. Male students and faculty complained bitterly to President Harper that the large numbers of women on campus were diminishing the academic and intellectual rigor of the institution. In fact, however, the women were winning many of the academic awards and honors instead of men. In general, they were better students and more dedicated to their courses than many men, for whom the "gentleman's C" attitude toward grades often prevailed.

Initially Harper resisted these complaints of **feminization**,* but by 1903, he capitulated. Creating a **coordinate college*** or expelling all of the women was out of the question, so the faculty senate did the next best thing. They arranged for coordinate courses that would split men from women. Classes were taught separately, with male students given a lecture, dismissed, and then the same lecture repeated to the female students enrolled in the course. This arrangement, despite the logistical and time complications, continued for several years. Finally in 1907 the system collapsed under the weight of its own folly.

Despite these early stumbles, the University of Chicago flourished. Over the next several decades, the university increased its stature as a premier academic institution, a football powerhouse, and one of the outstanding research institutions in the United States. From a women's perspective, Marion Talbot staunchly defended women's rights on campus until her retirement in 1925. Other notable women on the faculty at Chicago during its first twenty-five years included

Sophonisba Breckinridge* and sisters Edith and Grace Abbott, all influential in the new field of **social work**,* in which Chicago was preeminent.

Over the decades, the University of Chicago has enjoyed a solid reputation for intellectual and academic excellence, boasting a large number of Nobel laureates on the faculty and graduating top students. The university is committed to excellence in graduate study in a variety of fields in addition to a solid core of undergraduate programs. In a final repudiation of the early gender segregation, Hannah Holborn Grey became the tenth president of the University of Chicago in 1978, at the time one of the most prestigious presidencies ever held by a woman.

Bibliography: Thomas Wakefield Goodspeed, *The Story of the University of Chicago* (1925); Marion Talbot, *More Than Lore: Reminiscences of Marion Talbot* (1925); Laurence R. Veysey, *The Emergence of the American University* (1965); University of Chicago Publications Office, *In One Spirit: A Retrospective View of the University of Chicago on the Occasion of Its Centennial* (1991).

Robert A. Schwartz

V

Van Kleeck, Mary. Mary Abby Van Kleeck (1883–1972), industrial researcher and social reformer, devoted much of her career to the economic advancement of women. Her research on women in industry educated legislators and the public about conditions under which women labored and resulted in adoption of national standards for women's employment. She advanced the cause of women's education through her tireless advocacy of social reform and improved employment opportunities and conditions for women.

Youngest of four children, Van Kleeck was born in Glenham, New York, on June 26, 1883. Her father, Robert Boyd van Kleeck, was an Episcopal minister. Her mother, Eliza Mayer, was the daughter of a founder of the Baltimore and Ohio Railroad, and it was her money that supported the family. After Reverend van Kleeck's death in 1892, the family moved to Flushing, New York, where Mary made her debut and graduated from Flushing High School in 1900. She enrolled at **Smith College**,* where she earned high marks and was inducted into several honorary societies, graduating in 1904. In her final year, she was president of the Smith College Association for Christian Work (SCACW), the same year the SCACW brought reformer and activist **Jane Addams*** to campus.

After graduation, Van Kleeck briefly contemplated a **teaching*** career, but at the urging of Smith Trustee Helen Rand Thayer, she applied for the jointly sponsored Smith College Alumnae and College Settlement Associations postgraduate fellowship. She won the award and in 1905, at age twenty-one, went to work for the College **Settlement House*** in New York City's Lower East Side.

Van Kleeck's fellowship marked the beginning of her long and distinguished career as a social researcher. Her early work focused on the overtime of working girls in New York factories and child labor in tenements. Her work gained her recognition and financial support from the Russell Sage Foundation, a philanthropic organization dedicated to social reform. In 1908, funded by Sage, Van Kleeck directed the Industrial Investigation Department of the Alliance Employment Bureau, an organization that placed women and girls in factory and office jobs in the city. In 1910, the Sage Foundation formally absorbed Van Kleeck's department and renamed it the Committee on Women's Work. Van Kleeck remained with the foundation until her retirement in 1948.

Between 1910 and 1917, Van Kleeck directed major studies of women in industry and authored or coauthored books on each: *Artificial Flower Makers* (1913), *Women in the Bookbinding Trades* (1913), *Working Girls in Evening Schools* (1915), and *A Seasonal Industry: Wages in the Millinery Trade* (1917). Her studies, which revealed poor conditions and highlighted the need for regulation and minimum wage guarantees, led to protective legislation for women workers. Van Kleeck's findings suggested that the problems of working women were related to broader industrial and social conditions. When the Sage Foundation established the Department of Industrial Studies in 1916, Van Kleeck was named director.

Van Kleeck's contributions to industrial reform were not limited to her foundation work. From 1914 to 1917, she taught courses on industrial conditions and industrial research at the New York School of Philanthropy, and some of her students collaborated in her research. Van Kleeck also worked for labor reform for women on the national level. On leave from Sage in 1918–1919, she directed the women's branch of the industrial service section of the army's Ordnance Department. The standards she advocated for employment of women in war industries were adopted by the War Labor Policies Board, where she served from 1918 to 1919. In July 1918 Van Kleeck was asked to head the Department of Labor's Women in Industry Service, later known as the U.S. **Women's Bureau**.* During her brief tenure, she set national standards for women's employment and established rigorous research techniques that discouraged challenges to the bureau's policy recommendations. Van Kleeck educated the public through popular exhibits and rallied other organizations to support improvements in women's working conditions. Like many reformers of the **Progressive Era**,* she opposed the Equal Rights Amendment, fearing it would undo the protective legislation she had worked so hard to implement for women.

Van Kleeck worked actively to influence the new field of **social work**.* through her role as a Smith College trustee from 1922 to 1930. She was active in reviewing the Smith College Training School of Social Work, and as part of a three-member subcommittee, she recommended changes in admissions, administration, and fieldwork requirements. She also lectured there during the 1920s. At the national level, she was instrumental in organizing the American Association of Social Workers and served on many of its committees.

Later in her career, Van Kleeck became increasingly interested in global labor issues, and she grew more radical and outspoken in her views on social change.

She advocated the socialization of U.S. industry and natural resources, believing that a collective economy, based on the principles of scientific management, was the best means to prevent poverty and raise the standard of living.

Van Kleeck's ties with international labor organizations, her views on changing the economic and political structure of American society, and her sympathies with Soviet socialism led to a run-in with the McCarthy Committee, which investigated suspected communist involvement among many reformers and activists in the 1950s. In 1953 she testified in a closed hearing before the Senate's Permanent Subcommittee on Investigation but was not recalled. The impact on her professional life seems minimal, although she was temporarily denied a passport renewal four years later.

Van Kleeck continued to research and write throughout her life, on issues ranging from social adjustment to atomic energy. To each social problem she brought her commitment to rigorous scientific inquiry. "Doubtless the desire to make the world a better place to live in has been the driving force in back of my work," she told a reporter in 1926. "And yet this feeling has had to meet the statistical test. My emotional feelings at all times are held in check until I am able to apply this measurement." Van Kleeck was renowned for her intelligence, her insistence on unbiased information, her detached professionalism, and her total dedication to her work. She died of a heart attack in Kingston, New York, at eighty-nine.

Bibliography: Mary Anderson and Mary Winslow, *Women at Work* (1951); Eleanor Midham Lewis, "Mary Van Kleeck," in Barbara Sicherman and Carol Hurd Green, eds., *Notable American Women: The Modern Period* (1980); Guy Alchon, "Mary Van Kleeck and Social-Economic Planning," *Journal of Policy History*, 3 (1991): 1–23. See also Van Kleeck's papers in the Sophia Smith Collection, Women's History Archives, Smith College; material on her work with the Russell Sage Foundation is at the Archives of Labor and Urban Affairs, Wayne State University.

Kimberley Dolphin

Vassar College. Vassar College was founded as the first accredited **women's college*** in the United States in 1865 in Poughkeepsie, New York, by brewer Matthew Vassar, who hoped to use his wealth to build a lasting monument. As the first of the **Seven Sisters*** Colleges, Vassar embarked upon what was largely an experiment in teaching women the collegiate curriculum of the all-male **Ivy League*** schools. Opponents of the college argued, among other notions, that intellectual study would draw blood away from female students' reproductive organs, thus incapacitating them for their natural roles as wives and mothers [see *Sex in Education**]. Nevertheless, Vassar and Milo Jewett (the first president) continued their plans; the college opened its doors to 353 students.

Vassar offered the "classical curriculum" that focused on Greek and Latin, augmented by mathematics, history, sciences, and other languages. The college especially touted its renowned professor of astronomy, **Maria Mitchell**,* who was the first professional female astronomer in the world (Mitchell discovered a comet in 1847) [see **science education***]. Unfortunately, many of the young women initially admitted to Vassar were not qualified for its level of study, and until 1888 Vassar, like many other schools, operated a preparatory department to prepare students for collegiate-level work.

Vassar boasts a tradition of distinguished teachers with unorthodox teaching methods; Mitchell took a group of her students to Iowa by train in order to observe a total solar eclipse. Other notable faculty include drama professor Hallie Flanagan Davis, whose theater productions drew audiences from across the state in the 1920s, and history professor Lucy Maynard Salmon, who resisted conservatizing efforts of the trustees in the 1910s, helped reorganize the faculty along democratic lines, and served as adviser to Vassar's **suffrage*** organization. Salmon was noted for the way she conducted her classes: as scholarly conversations, using the Socratic method, rather than traditional lectures.

Other Vassar curricular innovations included mandatory private conferences with professors and cooperative **teaching*** between literature and composition classes. While we cannot always determine what happened in classrooms over one hundred years ago, the Vassar catalogs indicate that faculty collaborated to teach complementary classes that developed different skills while focusing on the same subject matter—an exceptional practice in the nineteenth century.

A major development at Vassar that influenced curriculum at all women's schools was establishment of the "**euthenics**"* department in 1924 in response to a large monetary donation. Euthenics was defined as merging of studies of the private and public realms. Its advocates called it a progressive application of science to traditional women's duties; its detractors claimed that euthenics glossed over an enforced return of women to the home. Four new buildings—a classroom building, nursery school, dormitory, and gym—provided the locations for students to engage in scientific study of child care and health. Today these buildings house the departments of anthropology and psychology; the **nursery school*** offers day care for faculty and local community children while providing subjects for psychology studies.

Vassar in the twentieth century has carried a reputation for political activism; in addition to suffrage work, Vassar students, faculty, and alumnae were active in the formation of the **League of Women Voters**,* designed to educate women about their newly acquired voting rights. During World War I, a group of students designated themselves "farmerettes" and worked the Vassar farm while male farmworkers served in the military. The bulk of the class of 1945 chose to accelerate its college program and graduate a year early to serve the country more readily; the class of "44/45," as it is known, still has reunions separate from those of 1944 and 1945. World War II also brought the first group of men to attend Vassar; veterans on the **G. I. Bill*** were on campus from 1942 to 1945.

That short-lived coeducational experience did not prepare Vassar for the upheavals of the 1960s, when enrollments declined, and agitation around the country affected the traditionally political Vassar campus as well. A merger with Yale University was proffered but refused; the Yale terms would have included a complete move to New Haven and loss of seniority and leadership positions for Vassar administrators and faculty. Vassar's trustees decided to make a complete change to **coeducation*** rather than merge with an existing men's school or continue operation as a shrinking women's college. In 1970, full-time undergraduate men were admitted to Vassar. In 1994–1995, the student body (2,219 students) was 38 percent male. English continues to be the most popular major at this "political" school where issues of cultural diversity, environmental policy, and social responsibility continue the tradition of political involvement begun by the early century suffragists.

Bibliography: Constance D. Ellis, ed., *The Magnificent Enterprise: A Chronicle of Vassar College* (1961); Elaine Kendall, *Peculiar Institutions: An Informal History of the Seven Sisters Colleges* (1975); Helen Lefkowitz Horowitz, *Alma Mater: Design and Experience in the Women's Colleges from Their Nineteenth-Century Beginnings to the 1930s* (1984).

Mary Dockray-Miller

venture schools. Venture schools of the colonial era were characterized by market supply and demand. They offered whatever subjects people would pay to attend, at times when people were available for classes. Advertisements for such schools indicate that some opened as early as 5:00 A.M. and closed as late as 9:00 P.M. and that the schoolmasters and -mistresses frequently were willing to negotiate meeting times of courses. Managers and teachers of these institutions sought financial gain by making education practical and convenient for the public. Venture schools wed education to commerce, social mobility, and self-improvement.

Venture schools existed throughout the colonial era but were most prevalent in the latter half of the eighteenth century. Rural venture schools were closely associated with traditional instruction, with elementary reading, writing, arithmetic, and Christian catechesis, as well as more advanced classical instruction in Latin, Greek, and Hebrew. But venture schools were predominantly located in commercial centers, especially in northern and southern cities such as Boston, New York, Philadelphia, Williamsburg, and Charleston. Urban venture schools offered elementary and advanced classical instruction, but they also offered numerous other technical courses including surveying, navigation, astronomy, geography, geometry, trigonometry, penmanship, accounting, and mapmaking. On the whole, venture schools were most notable for their variety.

For women, venture schools provided considerable opportunities for cultural refinement and limited opportunities for **vocational education*** and advanced classical instruction. Cultural refinement consisted of **ornamental education*** in painting, drawing, French, vocal and instrumental music, dance, and horseback riding. Vocational instruction included needlepoint, midwifery, sewing and mending, penmanship, spinning of wool and flax, accounting, and millinery. Some women successfully applied these lessons outside the home. They produced goods and services for the market; they managed general stores, taverns, and printing offices; and they taught school. Colonial venture schools were the forerunners of female **academies*** and **seminaries**.*

Venture schools exemplified the inequality of **colonial schooling*** opportunities. Their tuition inhibited participation, and their course offerings frequently differed according to gender. Even so, they provided women a taste of advanced learning and allowed a few to stretch the boundaries of their sphere of influence [see **separate spheres***].

Bibliography: Thomas Woody, *A History of Women's Education in the United States*, Vol. 1 (1929); Edgar Knight, ed., *A Documentary History of Education in the South before 1860*, Vol. 2 (1949); Lawrence Cremin, *American Education: The Colonial Experience, 1607–1783* (1970); Sheldon Cohen, *A History of Colonial Education, 1607–1776* (1974); Joseph Kett, *The Pursuit of Knowledge under Difficulties: From Self-Improvement to Adult Education in America, 1750–1990* (1994).

Benjamin D. Burks

vocational education. Vocational education developed in the United States as part of a curricular transformation that fundamentally transformed public schools in the early years of the twentieth century. *Vocational education* has been confused with *manual training, industrial training, trade education*, and *career education* throughout its history; at times the terms are appropriately interchanged, but each has a distinctive meaning. In a broad sense, *vocational education* refers to schooling designed to prepare students for paid or unpaid labor.

Vocational education was introduced in American **high schools*** as a vehicle for solving the "boy problem" (boys' low attendance rate) and was touted as especially appropriate for working-class children who, according to educators, rejected the traditional academic curriculum. Vocational education was the clearest manifestation of the growing nexus between school and work that accompanied the expansion of the high school during the **Progressive Era**.* Most vocational education programs were either designed as gender specific or resulted in gender-specific courses. That is, vocational education led to a distinction in girls' and boys' schooling that challenged the essence of **coeducation*** even if it did not eliminate the practice. In addition, vocational education fueled a division among women workers of different social classes. As historian Jane Bernard Powers has pointed out, women defined the vocational education movement for women, one of the first instances on the national level where women had a hand in shaping their own educational programs. Thus, when Congress passed the **Smith-Hughes Act*** in 1917, which provided federal assistance for vocational education, **home economics*** was included with agricultural and trade education as programs marked for funding of teacher training and salaries.

The origins of vocational education in the United States can be traced to the introduction of manual training in elementary schools late in the nineteenth century. Handwork involving cooking, sewing, and the use of tools was promoted to strengthen mental powers and encourage good habits. In the twentieth century, manual training was introduced in upper grades for boys; domestic science was generally added later for girls. Manual training was initially conceived as a supplement to intellectual training and considered an important part of each student's education.

Before the turn of the century, however, industrial training replaced manual training as the preferred incarnation of vocational education. Those who supported industrial training shared two basic assumptions: They accepted the inevitability of industrial progress, and they believed that the welfare of the larger society was bound to needs of industry. Thus, vocational education was transformed from a supplement to training with specific ties to the economic sector. Schools promoted "industrial intelligence" to fit students for work in the industrial hierarchy by teaching such worker characteristics as loyalty, punctuality, obedience to authority, and a high tolerance of boredom. This diverged from the early objectives of manual training by replacing academic learning rather than supplementing it. Also, schools differentiated the high school curriculum to provide a hierarchy of workers, thus separating students.

In addition to manual training programs in elementary school, vocational training in **settlement houses*** preceded implementation in public high schools. College students led classes in cultural education and vocations to help "Americanize" immigrants. Vocational education was also tested on African American and Native American students at **Hampton Institute*** in Virginia prior to its introduction in urban high schools. Vocational education entered the high school as part of the differentiated curriculum around the turn of the century in response to demands for social efficiency. Vocational education was the vehicle through which educators hoped to assimilate immigrant children, ease class conflict in the working class, and restore healthy family life—all by strengthening the bond between schooling and work.

Proponents of vocational education were a diverse lot. Employers supported it because it provided free training. Further, by adjusting students to the organizational structure of the workplace, vocational education was one means of quelling labor unrest. Labor unionists supported vocational education after some initial resistance. By 1910 many **labor union*** members came to believe that vocational education would help fit students for work and might enable workers to climb the mythical job ladder. Social reformers supported it with the hope of alleviating poverty by preparing students for a place in the industrial order. Educators supported vocational education for a number of reasons. Some argued that it would stabilize society by providing "equal educational opportunity" for students to prepare for their specific social roles. Others were convinced that vocational education would stem the tide of dropouts. Parents and students who supported vocational education often saw it as a means for upward social mobility.

Women who supported vocational education for females generally were aligned with one of two positions. Members of the National **Women's Trade Union League**,* the **Women's Educational and Industrial Union**,* and the

Sub-committee on Industrial Education for Women in the National Society for the Promotion of Industrial Education supported trade education for women. They presented an egalitarian argument that working women should have equal access to skilled trades. Members of the American Home Economics Association, the **General Federation of Women's Clubs**,* and the **National Congress of Mothers*** supported home economics as women's component of vocational education. Their position was grounded in the belief that women possessed natural abilities that enabled them to take a leading role in public reform. These women contended that the social fabric of the nation, as well as the welfare of each family, depended upon women's ability to perform domestic duties. Ironically, **commercial education**,* the most successful component of vocational education for women as measured by student enrollment, received little support in this public debate.

The Smith-Hughes Act did not include funding for commercial education, yet those enrollments grew at a rapid pace in the early decades of the twentieth century, a phenomenon that illustrated strong ties developing between school and work in the Progressive Era. Enrollments in commercial education were highest in the Northeast, where students could most expect to find office work upon graduation. Over time, however, clerical work became specialized, routinized, and cut off from routes to advancement. This decline in status paralleled the **feminization*** of the occupation; women preferred clerical jobs because they paid more than factory jobs, and the environment was cleaner and healthier. Students were eager to take the commercial course in high school to prepare for office occupations. In 1928 one out of six high school students was enrolled in commercial education courses. In spite of this success, commercial education remained on the outskirts of the vocational education movement, appealing primarily to middle-class girls and, therefore, not fitting the agenda of targeting working-class students. It also did little to alleviate the "boy problem." Commercial education did not come under the vocational education rubric and was denied federal funding until 1963.

Home economics, which was initially promoted as the women's counterpart to industrial education for men, drew support both from those who characterized it as a vocation and from those who perceived domestic science as the last defense of civilization. The argument that a woman's "true" vocation was care of her family and home extended back at least to **Catharine Beecher*** in the 1830s, but twentieth-century conservative feminists noted that industrialization and urbanization altered society in such a way to make domestic chores more complex. Thus, educators stressed the importance of training young women in home economics as a vocation. Others underscored a particular view of the family as the cornerstone of the modern social order and fought for home economics in the schools to counter the perceived ill effect of women in paid labor. Home economics also "Americanized" immigrants. The "vocation" contingent also failed to address a problematic element in their argument: Women were expected to take on a vocation for which there was no remuneration.

Although home economics gained structural and financial support from Smith-Hughes, it did not enjoy the success of commercial education programs. Enrollments were highest in the South, where the rural economy was more closely aligned with domestic work.

Industrial training for girls was, by most accounts, a failure. Women were limited to a narrow range of jobs, most unskilled labor. It simply made no sense to spend time in school studying what one could learn on the job. The few schools that attempted to incorporate industrial training for girls were usually separate institutions. Industrial training programs were often confused with home economics due to the fact that factory work open to women, in the garment trades, for instance, generally reflected an extension of women's traditional work.

Vocational education became entrenched in the high school curriculum shortly after its introduction. In 1906, about 20 percent of the total public high school population enrolled in vocational courses, even higher for urban schools. Most programs were located in comprehensive, coeducational high schools. This pattern continued throughout the twentieth century. Students in vocational courses took less academic work, and their study of mathematics, English, science, and history often differed from their peers. Critics of vocational education point to both theoretical and practical problems. Vocational education has reflected a class bias and has emphasized training rather than education. Further, it fails to meets its own objectives: Studies indicate that programs do not adequately prepare students for the workplace, they reduce the likelihood of graduates attending even one year of college, and they have not been shown to affect the dropout rate. In the 1970s, career education, a movement that emphasized job preparation in schooling for all students, attempted to address these criticisms. It was a short-lived experiment, as the 1980s brought a revival of traditional vocational education. During the 1980s the vocational education budget in schools amounted to almost $9 billion; the federal government contributed roughly 10 percent. Federal funding of vocational education was increased by 59 percent with passage of the Carl D. Perkins Vocational and Applied Technological Education Act of 1990.

The vocational education movement had a great impact on women's education: It led to de facto gender segregation in the public high school curriculum. Although a 1976 amendment to the Vocational Education Act banned sex-segregated vocational schools and required that all vocational education courses be integrated, sex segregation remains high. In addition, vocational education has preserved the existing sexual division of labor. In comprehensive high schools today, girls continue to enroll in vocational education courses with the lowest wage opportunities. Further, as historian John Rury has demonstrated, vocational education reproduced a social division of labor within the female workforce. The high school credential that boosted job opportunities for some blocked advancement for girls who could not, for whatever reasons, attend high school. Via development of home economics courses, vocational education sanctioned training for unpaid labor. Historians also note that vocational education contributed to the dilution of science courses for girls and precipitated a drop in girls' participation in mathematics and science [see **science education***]. In summary, by focusing on predicted roles in the economic sector, the vocational education movement allowed schooling for girls to be constrained by the perception of "women's place" in society.

Bibliography: Paul C. Violas, *The Training of the Urban Working Class: A History of Twentieth Century American Education* (1978); David Tyack and Elisabeth Hansot, *Learning Together: A History of Coeducation in American Public Schools* (1990); John L. Rury, *Education and Women's Work: Female Schooling and the Division of Labor in Urban America, 1870–1930* (1991); Jane Bernard Powers, *The "Girl Question" in Education: Vocational Education for Young Women in the Progressive Era* (1992).

Karen L. Graves

W

Washington, Margaret Murray. Although perhaps most known as the wife of educator Booker T. Washington, Margaret Murray Washington's (1865–1925) leadership in the African American **women's club movement*** and her contributions as teacher and principal at **Tuskegee Institute*** establish her as one of the most influential African American female educators of her time.

Washington was born on March 9, 1865, in Macon, Mississippi, into a family of nine brothers and sisters. Following her father's death when she was only seven, she lived with a **Quaker*** family, who encouraged her to finish school and study to become a teacher. At fourteen, she enrolled in the preparatory school of **Fisk University*** as a working student. Upon completion of preparatory and college course work, Washington received a B.A. in 1889. The same year she was hired as an English teacher at Booker T. Washington's renowned Tuskegee Institute in Alabama; one year later, she became **dean of women*** and director of the Department of Domestic Sciences at the institute, where she supervised courses in dressmaking, cooking, millinery work, laundering, and mattress making. She was also a member of the Executive Committee, which managed the school's affairs during Booker T. Washington's frequent fund-raising and speaking tours. Upon her marriage to Booker T. Washington in 1902, she assumed an even greater role in the school, assisting her husband in speechwriting as well as fund-raising. Her affiliation with Fisk, for example, prompted corporate philanthropist Andrew Carnegie to donate money to that university.

In addition to her activities at Tuskegee, Margaret Murray Washington was deeply involved in community and **race uplift**,* primarily through the African American women's club movement. In 1895, she founded the Tuskegee Woman's Club, composed of female teachers and the wives of male institute teachers. Under Washington's presidency, a group of thirteen women held meetings twice a month in which they pursued self-educative activities such as literary and musical programs, community uplift work [see **women's study clubs***]. Their most notable effort was establishment of a mothers' club for African American women from the local countryside. Washington herself had noticed that most of the rural women who accompanied their husbands to town on Saturday had little to do. Accordingly, she and the clubwomen rented a second-floor hall of a grocery store, where club members discussed child care, **hygiene**,* **temperance**,* and the importance of home life. Beginning with 6 women, that club grew to over 300 members by 1904. Alongside the mothers' group, clubs and educational activities for young children were organized. Through Washington's leadership, the Tuskegee Club founded "social purity clubs" for young girls, boys' clubs, a **kindergarten**,* and a plantation settlement where literacy, agriculture, and domestic classes were taught.

Washington's club involvement, though, was national as well as local. In 1895, Washington was vice president and then president of the National Federation of Afro-American Women, which merged the following year with the **National Association of Colored Women*** (NACW). Immediately, she was elected secretary of the executive board and volunteered as editor of the organization's official publication "Notes" (later "National Notes"). It was not until 1914, however, that she was elected president of the NACW.

Washington's club work also occurred on the state level. Under her presidency, the Southern Federation of Colored Women's Clubs organized kindergartens throughout the region. From 1919 until her death in 1925, she was president of the Alabama State Federation, which established a reform school for African American boys and the Rescue Home for Girls at Mt. Meigs. In 1920, she, along with other African American southern club leaders, participated in the Commission on Inter-racial Cooperation, a white organization created to bring African American and white clubwomen together. Although short-lived, this organization prompted the creation of more schools for African American children.

Perhaps Washington's most ambitious dream was founding the International Council of Women of the Darker Races in 1922. Comprising representatives from Africa, the West Indies, Ceylon, and national organizations in the United States, the group studied the conditions of "women of the darker race." Education was emphasized through dissemination of information, through promotion of cultural awareness and pride, and through participation in social and economic welfare for women. The organization ended with her years later, when Washington died in her sleep at her home in Tuskegee.

Bibliography: Margaret Murray Washington, "The Advancement of Colored Women," *Colored American Magazine*, 6 (April 1905): 183–189; Jennie B. Moton, "Margaret Murray Washington," in Hallie Quinn Brown, ed., *Homespun Heroines and Other Women of Distinction* (1926); Washington, "Club Life among Negro Women," in *Progress of a Race* (1969); Wilma King Hunter, "Three Women at Tuskegee: 1885–1922: The Wives of Booker T. Washington," *Journal of Ethnic Studies*, 4 (September 1976):

76–89; Cynthia Neverdon-Morton, *Afro-American Women of the South and the Advancement of the Race, 1895–1925* (1989). See also Margaret Murray Washington Papers, Frissell Library, Tuskegee, Alabama.

Anne Meis Knupfer

Wellesley College. Henry Fowle and Pauline Adeline Cazenove Durant received a charter to create Wellesley Female Seminary in 1870. The Durants desired to create a college for women that would imitate **Mount Holyoke Female Seminary*** in its emphasis on Christian education, while at the same time provide the most beautiful facility in the world for women's education. Located on several hundred acres on the Durant family estate in suburban Boston, the new institution was given the name Wellesley in honor of an old family name. The town, West Needham, later took the name of the college.

Several factors motivated the Durants. As a trustee of Mount Holyoke, Henry Durant was actively involved in women's education and interested in its development. A lawyer and businessman who had accumulated a comfortable financial status, Durant had later become a minister and was concerned with spreading Christian teachings. After the deaths of both their children, the Durants determined in 1867 to utilize their financial resources to create a **women's college.*** Both Mount Holyoke and **Vassar College*** proved beneficial as the Durants drew on the former for internal curricular models and the latter for external design influences.

To the Durants, women were different from men but were not frail creatures who had to be pampered. Henry believed his school could serve as an experiment in women's education, where a community of women would learn to develop socially and physically while advancing their intellectual pursuits. He also wanted high academic standards. The Wellesley curriculum included traditional studies in Greek, Latin, and philosophy, as well as newer trends in modern languages, English literature, and the sciences. The school temporarily operated a preparatory program to ensure that entering students were ready for the challenging college-level curriculum. The college officially opened on September 8, 1875, with just over 300 students.

The original trustees included five individuals who had served on the board of Mount Holyoke. Henry Durant also placed his wife on the board and within a few years added other women. In a unique move, Durant determined to hire only women as teachers and administrators at Wellesley. He recruited professors from Mount Holyoke, **Oberlin**,* Vassar, and the University of Michigan, as well as from some **high schools*** of good repute. In some cases, Durant would pay for teachers to complete their college degrees after joining the Wellesley faculty. The first president was Ada Howard, a Mount Holyoke graduate. Although she held the presidency from the school's opening until 1881, during her tenure Henry Durant clearly remained the dominant figure. The second president, **Alice Freeman** (later **Palmer**),* was able to have a more direct influence. A graduate of the University of Michigan, she accepted the presidency in 1881 at age twenty-six and quickly indicated her desire to see the college reach new academic levels. She promoted curricular changes, favored a lessening of religious emphasis, and encouraged trustees to be more open-minded in their approach to running Wellesley. Her efforts to make Wellesley a strong liberal arts college continued after she left the presidency upon her marriage to George Herbert Palmer in 1887, as she remained closely involved as a trustee.

Numerous well-known women have associations with Wellesley. Later presidents included Mildred McAfee Horton, who commanded the WAVES (Women Appointed for Voluntary Emergency Service) during World War II, and Nannerl Keohane and Diana Chapman Walsh, both nationally known educators and administrators in the 1980s and 1990s. The faculty has included economists Edith Abbot and Emily Balch, literary critic Vida Dutton Scudder, and poet Katharine Lee Bates. Wellesley has also produced many well-known graduates, including sociologist **Sophonisba Breckinridge**,* politician Molly Dewson, first lady Hillary Rodham Clinton, and U.S. Secretary of State Madeleine Korbel Albright.

By the mid-1990s, Wellesley College continued to maintain its place as a prestigious liberal arts college and a leader in educating women. The college had grown to a student body of approximately 2,200 and a faculty of 300 teaching some 900 courses. Contemporary developments include creation of the Wellesley College Center for Research on Women [see **women's centers***], participation with other New England colleges in the Twelve College Exchange Program as well as in other exchanges around the country, advancement of study abroad programs, and emphasis on a multicultural approach to education. **Women's athletics**,* a mainstay since the first women's college crew team began at Wellesley in 1876, have remained strong. An alumnae network of over 30,000 women has contributed directly to the college's stability and success.

Bibliography: Florence Converse, *Wellesley College: A Chronicle of the Years 1875–1938* (1939); Helen Lefkowitz Horowitz, *Alma Mater: Design and Experience in the Women's Colleges from Their Nineteenth-Century Beginnings to the 1930s* (1984); Ruth Bordin, *Alice Freeman Palmer: The Evolution of a New Woman* (1993); Patricia Ann Palmieri, *In Adamless Eden: The Community of Women Faculty at Wellesley* (1995).

Debbie Cottrell

Wheaton College. Wheaton College in Norton, Massachusetts, was the oldest institution of higher education for women in the United States until 1988, when it admitted its first coeducational class. The school was founded as Wheaton Female Seminary in 1834 by Judge Laban Wheaton at the urging of his daughter-in-law, Eliza Baylies Chapin Wheaton. They were assisted by noted educator **Mary Lyon**,* until she left to found her own seminary, **Mount Holyoke**,* in 1837. In 1912, Wheaton was incorporated as Wheaton College.

Wheaton's development as a **women's college*** must be understood within the context of women's education in the nineteenth and twentieth centuries. In

the early years, Wheaton Female Seminary was similar to the other **seminaries***
for women and was part of a larger movement for women's education initiated
by reformers such as Mary Lyon, **Emma Willard**,* **Catharine Beecher**,* and
Zilpah Polly Grant Banister.* It reflected changes described by historian Patricia Palmieri, who suggests three periods in the history: the Romantic Era
(1820–1860), also the time of **"Republican motherhood"***; the Reform Era
(1860–1890), defined by the opening of women's colleges and emergence of
profound debates about women's higher education; and the **Progressive Era***
(1890–1920), which saw the first college women enter the professions, as well
as a conservative reaction and **backlash**.* Within this context, women's access
to higher education, first in women's colleges and later in coeducational institutions, evolved historically in relation to changing and liberalized conceptions
of their roles, as well as to conservative reactions. Wheaton's location between
Providence and Boston and its relatively affluent student body made it an attractive alternative to the **Seven Sisters*** colleges. By the early 1960s, Wheaton
(incorporated as a college in 1912), in line with the post–World War II expansion of higher education, doubled its enrollment to 1,200 women.

In the late 1960s and early 1970s, as the **Ivy League*** colleges and a number
of women's colleges became coeducational, Wheaton began to consider its future as a women's college. With many women now electing to attend coeducational schools, and with many now viewing women's colleges as quaint
anachronisms, Wheaton began to have considerable difficulty attracting high-
quality female applicants. In the early 1970s, the faculty voted to consider becoming a coeducational institution; however, the administration decided not to
make the change. In the 1970s, Alice F. Emerson became Wheaton's first
woman president, and under her leadership the college moved, first, to
strengthen its position as a women's college and, second, to become a coeducational institution eventually.

In 1980, as part of the influence of feminism, Wheaton began a four-year
"balanced curriculum project." This curricular innovation energized the Wheaton faculty in an institutional effort to infuse gender issues into all facets of the
curriculum and campus life. Faculty and administration made a concerted effort
to change the institution from a college without men to a women's college; that
is, an explicit mission to provide women a feminist curriculum. For the next
four years, they worked arduously toward the creation of a gender-balanced
curriculum, the culmination being a conference and the publication of its proceedings as a model of women's education (see Spanier et al.). As the college
celebrated its sesquicentennial, it seemed to have defined its place as committed
to the serious and distinctive education of women.

However, in January 1987, faced with ongoing enrollment problems and a
continuing decline in the quality of its applicant pool, President Emerson announced a decision by the board of trustees to consider becoming a coeducational college. Emerson announced that the college community would explore

options in spring 1987 and make a final decision by the end of the term for implementation in fall 1988. Faculty, students, and alumnae were dismayed, shocked, and in some cases, outraged. They felt betrayed, both because they felt they were not sufficiently consulted and because they had worked so hard to develop the balanced curriculum project in order to preserve Wheaton as a women's college. The alumnae, especially recent graduates, felt that they had been misled by the sesquicentennial fund-raising drive, which clearly celebrated Wheaton as a women's college. Yet President Emerson and the board maintained that **coeducation*** was the most reasonable course of action if the college was not only to survive but to flourish.

By the end of the spring 1987 semester, the trustees voted to change Wheaton to a coeducational college by the following fall. A group of alumnae intervened by filing legal action aimed at preventing the college from using the money raised in the sesquicentennial drive for a coeducational college and attempted to prevent Wheaton from changing its charter. In spring 1988, the college reached an out-of-court settlement, which allowed alumnae to ask for refunds of their gifts and permitted Wheaton to proceed with coeducation; approximately $150,000 of a $25 million campaign was refunded.

In fall 1988, Wheaton College, after 154 years as an institution for women, admitted its first coeducational class. In the first years, both faculty and women students who had come to Wheaton because it was a women's college expressed concern and, at times, hostility. The faculty, despite its feeling of betrayal, committed itself to translate the balanced curriculum into a "differently coeducational curriculum." In addition, the administration, faculty, and office of student life committed to creating a gender-balanced institution both inside and outside the classroom. Thus, Wheaton College determined to maintain its historical commitment to the education of women in a coeducational environment, and the college began to develop a program committed to gender equity for both men and women. At the 1992 inauguration of President Dale Marshall, the trustees urged her to "heed the proud history of Wheaton College recognizing the promise of the future in the strengths of the past." Consistent with this vision, male students at the 1991 graduation of the last all-women's class presented the graduates with buttons proclaiming "The legacy will not be lost."

Approaching the twenty-first century, Wheaton is an institution still grappling with the effects of coeducation and how to ensure that its "differently coeducational" philosophy, curriculum, and pedagogy are maintained. Although the conflicts over coeducation are largely gone, Wheaton College is seeking to institutionalize its special philosophy of coeducation by balancing its existence as a coeducational college with its past as a women's college. Beginning in 1980 with the balanced curriculum project, the decision to become coeducational in 1987, and the transition from a women's college to a coeducational institution, Wheaton provides an important case study of higher educational change and the education of both women and men.

Bibliography: Louise Boas, *Women's Education Begins: The Rise of Women's Colleges* (1935); B. Spanier, A. Bloom, and D. Boroviak, *Toward a Balanced Curriculum* (1984); P. C. Helmreich, *Wheaton College, 1834–1912: The Seminary Years* (1985); Patricia A. Palmieri, "From Republican Motherhood to Race Suicide: Arguments on the Higher Education of Women in the United States, 1820–1920," in Carole Lasser, ed., *Educating Men and Women Together: Coeducation in a Changing World* (1987); Rosalind Rosenberg, "The Limits of Access: The History of Coeducation in America," in John Mack Faragher and Florence Howe, eds., *Women and Higher Education in American History* (1988).

Susan F. Semel and Alan R. Sadovnik

Whiting, Sarah Frances. Sarah Frances Whiting (1846–1927), first professor of physics at **Wellesley College*** and first woman to join the New England Meteorological Society, made a lasting mark on the education of women for nearly forty years and established the first physics laboratory for women as well as the astronomical observatory at Wellesley. Whiting became interested in physics as a child by helping her schoolteacher father Joel Whiting prepare his class demonstrations. He tutored Sarah in Greek, Latin, math, and physics. She graduated from Ingham University in 1864 and taught math and classics there before teaching at the Brooklyn Heights Seminary from 1865 to 1876.

Whiting was picked by founder Henry Durant to be the first physics professor at Wellesley College in 1875. Durant was impressed by the work of E. C. Pickering, who had established the first student physics laboratory in the United States. He persuaded Pickering to allow Whiting to visit the lab at the Massachusetts Institute of Technology (MIT) and learn about the equipment and procedures. Thus, Whiting commuted to Boston four days a week for her first two years at Wellesley. After ordering all the necessary equipment herself, Whiting set up the country's second undergraduate physics laboratory in an organ loft. Whiting incorporated the latest advances into her laboratory at every chance and, upon hearing of Roentgen's discovery of X rays, immediately built her own apparatus and became the first person to produce X-ray photographs in the United States.

In 1879 Whiting began teaching astronomy. She devised daytime lab exercises to get around the vagaries of New England weather and the lack of equipment, leading to her publication of *Daytime and Evening Exercises in Astronomy* (1912). She became a leader in astronomy education, publishing numerous articles on astronomy pedagogy, especially laboratory exercises and practices. In 1898 Whiting heard of a twelve-inch Clark telescope for sale at half price ($3,000). At a dinner party, she persuaded Wellesley trustee Mrs. John Whitin to fund an observatory and purchase the telescope. The Whitin Observatory opened in 1900.

Whiting was especially fascinated by spectroscopy and instilled this in her most famous student, Annie Jump Cannon, who later gained fame at the Harvard College Observatory for classifying the spectra of over 350,000 stars and devising the Harvard Spectral Classification system. The first woman invited to join the New England Meteorological Society, Whiting set up a weather station so her students could contribute data to the U.S. Weather Bureau.

Whiting was a very religious woman and had engraved over the hearth-fire in the observatory house the closing words of the *Paradiso*: "Love rules the sun in heaven, and all the stars." She retired from physics in 1912, having served under the first six Wellesley presidents, but stayed on as director of the observatory and chair of the Astronomy Department until 1916. She was awarded an honorary degree from Tufts University in 1905 and was one of the first women members of the American Physical Society and American Association for the Advancement of Science. [See also **science education**.*]

Bibliography: Annie J. Cannon, "Sarah Frances Whiting," *Science*, 66 (November 4, 1927); Cannon, "Sarah Frances Whiting," *Popular Astronomy*, 35 (December 1927): 539–545; Janet B. Guernsey and Sabrina Farm, "The Lady Wanted to Purchase a Wheatstone Bridge: Sarah Frances Whiting and Her Successor," in Barbara Lotze, ed., *Making Contributions: An Historical Overview of Women's Role in Physics* (1983); Gladys A. Anslow, "Sarah Frances Whiting," in Edward T. James, Paul S. Boyer, and Janet Wilson James, eds., *Notable American Women, 1607–1950*, Vol. 3 (1971); Dorritt Hoffleit, *The Education of American Woman Astronomers before 1960* (1994). See also Whiting's unpublished works in Wellesley College Archives.

Kristine Larsen

Wilberforce University. Wilberforce University, officially created in 1863 from the merger of two institutions, has provided higher education to African Americans since before the Civil War. Originally, both the African Methodist Episcopal (AME) Church and the Methodist Episcopal (ME) Church desired to establish an educational institution for African Americans in Ohio. In 1844, the AME Church established Union Seminary just west of Columbus. Union taught courses for black students in literature, science, agriculture, mechanical arts, and ministry. In 1856, the Methodist Episcopal Church of Cincinnati endorsed establishment of the Ohio African University in Tawawa Springs, the present site of Wilberforce. The goal of the ME Church was to encourage the "Elevation of Colored People."

During the Civil War, both schools experienced economic hardships that eventually led to the closing of Ohio African University. In earlier years, the school had boasted an enrollment of more than 200; however, by 1862, the student population had dwindled, and the school lost financial support. Bishop Daniel P. Payne of the AME Church offered to purchase the institution by covering its $10,000 debt. One year later, in 1863, Payne merged the two institutions—Ohio African University and Union Seminary—and reopened them as Wilberforce University. As the university's first president, Payne advocated four governing principles: (1) a broad preparatory and collegiate curriculum that emphasized religious training; (2) a code of conduct for faculty and students that encouraged strict discipline and religious piety; (3) a diverse faculty, staff, and student body; and (4) an ecumenical board of trustees to prohibit sectarianism.

Wilberforce became "a pioneer institution for the higher education of the Negro race" (McGinnis, p. 75). Its principles prohibited both racial and sexual discrimination in admissions and in hiring, a goal that encouraged the active participation of women—both black and white—in its development and growth. Women such as Maria L. Shorter, who donated the first $1,000 toward the debt owed by the AME Church, and Esther Maltby, a white missionary who ran the school while male officials were away raising money to rebuild after the school was destroyed by fire, supported the institution's early years. Later, as students, professors, administrators (for example, Sarah Beirce Scarborough, head of the combined Normal and Industrial Arts Department), and presidents (Yvonne Walker-Taylor in the 1980s), women were essential for the development and growth of the university.

In 1887, the Ohio legislature linked Wilberforce, a private sectarian institution, to the state. This bond, initiated by Wilberforce's president and faculty, provided financial support for the struggling school and black votes for white politicians. In the arrangement, Wilberforce provided buildings and **teacher education*** resources, while the state financed a "Combined Normal and Industrial Department," offering courses in **vocational education*** and teacher training. The department was directed by a separate board of trustees and controlled by the public. On the Wilberforce side, the AME Church continued to govern affairs and offered courses in the liberal arts. This union continued over several decades amidst the ebb and flow of political turmoil.

However, in May 1941, what appeared to be a minor name change in the state-controlled **normal department*** caused major concern for the Wilberforce community. The General Assembly changed the Combined Normal and Industrial Department at Wilberforce to the College of Education and Industrial Arts at Wilberforce. The change suggested that the two institutions were more equally structured, and no longer was the state-supported side a mere entity of Wilberforce University. The tension between the two units initially affected the candidacy of Charles Wesley, then a strong contender for the university's presidency. Wesley wrote a letter decrying the "partisan politics" and "clash of personalities" that threatened the smooth operation of the arrangement. After issuing a written list of conditions, Wesley agreed to assume the presidency and, in fact, became one of Wilberforce's most respected leaders. Ironically, he was later accused of causing the split between the two institutions. Wesley had suggested at a commencement exercise that faculty, students, and trustees help him develop a state-supported college of education.

In 1947, the struggle intensified with court battles, name changes, and the need of politicians to control the university, leading to a final split between the state-supported and church-controlled Wilberforce University. The split led to two separate institutions—Central State University and Wilberforce.

In the mid-1990s, the two continue to function as separate institutions with a sister relationship. The student bodies are primarily African American. They share a history that encourages both men and women to work for the betterment of their race and to build a community that supports human equality.

Bibliography: Hallie Q. Brown, *Pen Pictures of Pioneers of Wilberforce* (1937); F. A. McGinnis, *A History and an Interpretation of Wilberforce University* (1941); Lathardus Coggins, *Central State University: The First One Hundred Years, 1887–1987* (1987); Charlotte Harris, "Women of Wilberforce: An Afrocentric Feminist Angle of Vision" (Ph.D. diss., University of Cincinnati, 1995).

Vanessa Allen-Brown

Willard, Emma Hart. Emma Hart Willard (1787–1870) was one of the first and most prominent advocates of women's education in the early Republican era, known both as founder of **Troy Female Seminary*** and author of many nationally used textbooks. Willard was born in Berlin, Connecticut, the sixteenth child of Lydia and Samuel Hart. She began her career as an educator in the wake of the new Republic, a time heavily laden with discourse about how and why a democratic community should be formed and maintained in the new United States. By 1804 Willard was **teaching*** in a village school, and in 1807, she ran a female academy in Middlebury, Vermont, where she met and married John Willard, a local physician.

In 1819 she published a very influential document, *An Address to the Public; Particularly the Members of the Legislature of New York, Proposing a Plan for Improving Female Education.* More detailed than any such previous appeal, Willard's plan provided a thorough, rational argument for why women needed to be educated in the Republic, as well as specific ideas. Part of this *Plan* was Willard's bold argument for use of state tax monies to support female education. She claimed this arrangement would hold teachers accountable to the state and eliminate creation of schools by anyone just wanting to make money. Willard saw her proposed female seminary as an institution that would ensure the proper credentials of those charged with educating children. In a wide-ranging set of arguments, she insisted that it was the government's duty to provide for the present and future prosperity of the country; that this prosperity depended on the character of citizens; that character was formed by mothers; and thus, that only thoroughly educated mothers were equipped to ensure the future. Willard believed that the state's role with regard to female education should be one of regulation, including the responsibilities of certification, sanctioning, and financial support. Later historians have called similar arguments an appeal to **"Republican motherhood."***

In her *Plan*, Willard also outlined the curriculum she believed should be the basis for any sound boarding school for women. She claimed that young women needed instruction in religion and morality, including moral philosophy. Under the heading of literary studies, Willard included work in philosophy of the mind, natural philosophy, botany, chemistry, zoology, history, and geography [see **sci-**

ence education*]. All this was complemented with domestic science, including healthy exercise and study of physiology [see **home economics***]. The arts, including drawing, painting, elegant penmanship, music, and dance, were categorized under **ornamental education**,* but Willard was quick to point out that she regarded study of needlework a waste of school time. She believed that if women were excluded from education, they could not fulfill their God-given talents of teaching and mothering.

By 1821 Willard was actively engaged in designing an educational community whose center was Troy Female Seminary, a boarding and day school for young women that she founded in Troy, New York. Because of Willard's success in implementing her *Plan*, many educators across the country and abroad modeled their educational institutions on Troy, making these views widely known as the **Troy Plan**.* An important part of Willard's innovation was her ability to actualize her proposed curriculum. With the help of Amos Eaton, well-known popularizer of science, and later, her sister **Almira Hart Lincoln Phelps**,* Willard offered instruction in botany, chemistry, and zoology at a level seldom seen in girls' schools.

Willard also authored textbooks in geography, world history, and American history that she used with Troy students. These soon became standard texts for many **seminaries**,* **academies**,* and eventually the **common schools**.* David Van Tassell claims that American history became a recognized school subject in the 1820s and that between 1820 and 1850 history textbooks were a main information source for Americans. Thus, Willard's textbooks, read by many adults in their homes and by students in school, influenced many Americans' views about their nation's history.

In the mid-1840s a conflict developed over the abridged edition of Willard's textbook *Abridged History of the United States; or Republic of America*, a conflict that impacted not only curriculum content but also the common practices by which school districts selected texts. At this time Marcius Willson, a teacher from New Jersey, became a competing textbook author. He joined forces with his publisher to launch an attack to unseat Willard as the premier author. In March 1845, as Willson was marketing his new American history textbook, he prepared in pamphlet form, and then widely distributed, a report to the New Jersey Society of Teachers and Friends of Education entitled "A Critical Review of American Common School Histories." Although he critiqued several texts, Willson paid particular attention to Willard's books, as his toughest competition. In a very public pamphlet war, Willard went head-to-head with Willson, effectively refuting his claims of plagiarism and factual errors. In the aftermath, her texts continued to sell in large quantities.

Throughout her career, Willard spent considerable time writing and speaking on the relationship between the public and education, including the proper role of parents. After a series of legislative sessions failed to accept the responsibility she called "public guardianship" and did not make female education a permanent institution in the Republic, Willard took her appeal directly to the people. She organized parents, church groups, and other town residents on behalf of education. In the 1840s Willard was named the first female **county super-intendent*** of schools in Kensington, Connecticut. There she formed female associations and charged them to work closely with teachers, assisting them with tasks including selection of textbooks. In so doing, Willard was certifying the women of the community to be partners with teachers in developing curriculum, administrative organizational structures, and virtually all matters involving the school. These associations established themselves as important groups exerting an influence on selecting and maintaining curriculum.

In 1837 Willard organized the Willard Association for the Mutual Improvement of Female Teachers, a professional organization of teachers who were graduates. This group sought advice from one another through a round-robin style of correspondence regarding, among other issues, pedagogical matters, adjusting to a new community as a single woman, developing relationships with parents, and securing needed supplies and materials. It was important to Willard to stay in close touch with her graduates and to hear their experiences as teachers. She often would write lengthy pieces of advice to association members, all hungry for her guidance.

Through her organizational efforts, Willard kept alive public discussions about the functions of female education and the importance of professionally trained teachers. Willard also helped citizens across the country understand that their educational mission played an important role in strengthening the country and ensuring the Republic's permanency. Willard involved people in the larger national and international movement for improved female education. Her ideas on the need for communities to assume authority to construct and maintain their own educational systems developed from ideas initially put forth in the eighteenth century, but Willard contributed significantly to the interpretation of that goal by subsequent generations of Americans.

Emma Willard was a significant educational power broker of her time. She struggled to build a consensus among political, social, and educational ideas that often appeared to compete with one another. Willard's pedagogical advances helped change commonly held notions about women's capacities for learning and, in the process, helped reshape the social order.

Bibliography: Anne Firor Scott, ''The Ever-Widening Circle: The Diffusion of Feminist Values from the Troy Female Seminary, 1822–72,'' *History of Education Quarterly*, 19 (Spring 1979): 3–25; Nina Baym, ''Women and the Republic: Emma Willard's Rhetoric of History,'' *American Quarterly*, 43 (March 1991): 1–23; Thalia M. Mulvihill, ''Community in Emma Hart Willard's Educational Thought, 1787–1870'' (Ph.D. diss., Syracuse University, 1995).

Thalia M. Mulvihill

women college presidents. Women college presidents have increased in number from 148 to over 450 during the last quarter of the twentieth century. The growth of acceptance of females in leadership positions in higher education is a reflection of society's growing acceptance of women in nontraditional roles. Customarily, American universities and colleges have chosen male, white, middle-class presidents. Even women's colleges were initially headed by men; only **Wellesley College*** opened in 1875 with a female president. One hundred years later, more than half of the **Seven Sisters*** colleges still had male presidents. Not until 1978 did all seven have females as chief executives.

The history of female heads of institutions of higher education can be considered to commence with the first woman appointed head of a **normal school**.* In 1861, Anna Callender Brackett was appointed principal of the St. Louis Normal School in Missouri, a female institution. Brackett, who believed the purpose of education for girls was to make them levelheaded, left in 1872 in a school board dispute over the number and quality of students.

In 1871 Frances Elizabeth Caroline Willard became the country's first female college president when she was appointed head of Evanston College for Ladies in Illinois. This also was a female institution, with an all-female faculty and board of trustees. When the college became the Women's College of Northwestern University in 1873, Willard served as its dean for one year.

In 1872 Julia Ann Sears, a graduate of Bridgewater Normal School in Massachusetts, became the first female to head a public coeducational [see **coeducation***] institution when she was appointed principal of Mankato State Normal School (now University) in Minnesota. Mankato was a public institution with a coeducational student body and faculty but was ruled by all-male local and state boards. After one year as principal, Sears was replaced by a man with no **teaching*** or normal school experience. The students and citizens of the town revolted in what is known as the ''Sears Rebellion'' but to no avail. Sears went on to Peabody Normal College (now Peabody College of Education of Vanderbilt University) in Nashville, Tennessee, where she had a brilliant thirty-two-year career as head of mathematics, training over 10,000 teachers for the South. One hundred years later, Mankato State hired its second woman president, Margaret Preska.

Between 1865 and 1904, there were only twenty-eight female presidents of female institutions, which were mostly still headed by male presidents. At **Bryn Mawr College**,* President **M. Carey Thomas*** encouraged women to become scholars. Holding office from 1894 until her retirement in 1922, Thomas was a moving force in treating faculty and students alike, whether male or female. Thomas, a renowned leader in women's education, was the first woman, and the first non-European, to receive a Ph.D. from the University of Zurich [see **graduate education***]. Her educational standards at Bryn Mawr were designed to be as rigorous as those in all-male schools; she made Bryn Mawr's admission requirements the same as Harvard's and developed the first graduate school at a major **women's college**.* Other noteworthy women presidents of this era included **Mary Lyon*** of **Mount Holyoke Female Seminary**,* Anna P. Sill of **Rockford Female Seminary**,* Elizabeth Cary Agassiz of **Radcliffe College**,*

Alice Freeman Palmer* of Wellesley (who at age twenty-six was one of the youngest female presidents), and **Mary McLeod Bethune*** of **Bethune-Cookman College**.*

By the early twentieth century a few more females were appointed to the presidential office. Most, like their male counterparts, held office until retirement. A few examples include Rita Bolt, appointed president of Lyndon Normal School in Vermont, a public institution, in 1927. Bolt held this position until retirement twenty-eight years later. In 1930 Mary Elizabeth Branch became the first African American female college president when she was appointed to head Tillotson College (now Huston-Tillotson College) in Texas, a position she held for fourteen years. In 1946 Ruth Haas became president of Danbury State College in Connecticut, serving twenty-nine years until retirement. Some women, however, did encounter political problems such as Sears experienced. For instance, Kate Galt Zaneis was appointed president of Southeastern Oklahoma Teachers College by the governor in 1935, but political problems resulted in her dismissal after only two years.

Rosemary Park became the first female president to be twice named a college president. In 1947 she headed Connecticut College for Women, a position she held until 1962 when she became president of **Barnard College**.* Nannerl Keohane became the first woman president of a major research university when she was appointed president of Duke University in 1993, after leading Wellesley College. That same year Judith Rodin was appointed president of the University of Pennsylvania, the first woman to head an **Ivy League*** institution.

As the number of women college presidents grew throughout the twentieth century, researchers addressed the increase of the nation's female leaders, including the conflicts in roles between being a woman and a college president, and worked to provide historical studies and profiles of female presidents. From 1974 to 1992 twenty-one doctoral dissertations on female academic presidents were written.

By 1975, when the Office of Women in Higher Education of the American Council on Education began collecting numbers on women presidents, 148 women held the presidential office in American higher education institutions; 16 of these headed public colleges and universities. By the 1990s there were over 450 women college presidents, with about 60 percent of all new female presidents in 1993 entering the public sector. At the end of the twentieth century, over 15 percent of all academic presidents in the United States were women. Of these women college presidents, 16 percent were women of color.

Bibliography: Barbara Miller Solomon, *In the Company of Educated Women: A History of Women in Higher Education in America* (1985); C. L. T. McGill, *Women College Presidents as Leaders of Educational Reform, 1880–1910* (1989); J. A. Sturnick, J. E. Milley, and C. A. Tisinger, *Women at the Helm: Pathfinding Presidents at State Colleges and Universities* (1991); Judith G. Touchton, Donna Shavlik, and Lynne Davis, *Women in Presidencies: A Descriptive Study of Women College and University Presidents* (1993);

Joan F. Pengilly, "The First Female President of a Coeducational Public Institution of Higher Education: An Historical Examination of the Presidential Tenure of Julia Ann Sears, 1872–1873" (Ph.D. diss., University of Akron, 1995). See also data from American Council on Education, Office of Women in Higher Education, Washington, D.C.

Joan F. Pengilly

women's athletics. Women participating in athletic and sporting events has a history that goes back to the first palace period in the Minoan civilization of ancient Crete (2000–1700 B.C.). Bull vaulting, in which the participant grabbed a charging bull's horn and performed a front handspring off its back, was a sport popular among young aristocratic men and women. In ancient Greece, young women participated in hunting events and drove chariots. During the Middle Ages noblewomen participated in leisure and cultural activities: chess and other board games, several varieties of ball games, storytelling, singing, playing musical instruments, and dancing.

English feminist Mary Wollstonecraft wrote in *A Vindication of the Rights of Women* (1792), "I wish to persuade women to endeavor to acquire strength of both mind and body ... a character as a human being." While their participation in sporting and athletic events was far less than men of the era, women of the eighteenth and nineteenth centuries did engage in athletic pursuits. Rowing, skating, shooting, riding, and hunting were popular pastimes with occasional female participants.

In eighteenth-century North America, Native American women were active participants in sporting and athletic events such as dancing, foot-racing, ball games, and lacrosse, although women rarely competed against men. African American slave women danced, played games, and ran races. White middle-class women engaged in fishing, dancing, sailing, skating, and sleigh riding, while dancing was the most popular form of recreation among women of the privileged classes.

Prior to the late eighteenth century, women enjoyed participation, albeit limited, in leisure activities as befitted their social class. Toward the end of the 1700s, the cult of domesticity that emerged as a cultural value—women taking on the roles of caregiver, nurturer, and passive supporter of the family unit—essentially made participating in physical activities and sporting events taboo among certain segments of society.

Soon, however, the cult of domesticity began taking its toll physically on women; women's fragility, poor health, and lack of energy became a concern. Most experts agreed that increased physical activity was needed for women to improve their collective physical condition. The advent of this movement could be seen most clearly in women's education, which began to include physical activities and athletics. **Catharine Beecher***** lectured on the value of physical exercise for women and founded two female **seminaries***** that emphasized daily exercise. Her book *Physiology and Calisthenics for Schools and Families* (1856) became a very popular textbook for women's health and **hygiene***** classes in seminaries and colleges around the country. **Emma Hart Willard**,* who founded the **Troy Female Seminary*** in 1821, developed, with her sister **Almira Hart Phelps**,* a daily curriculum that included calisthenics, dancing, riding, and walking.

Women could be found engaging in activities such as horseback riding, bowling, rowing, canoeing, yachting, ice and rollerskating, and particularly bicycling, an activity that came from England in the 1870s and became quite popular in America during the next two decades. The popularity of bicycling among women changed women's leisure fashion, leading to the loosening of corsets and the dividing of heavy skirts into knickerbockers and bloomers. Women were literally becoming freer to engage in sport and exercise. Archery, croquet, golf, and tennis, along with the popular bicycle, were embraced by women and men alike.

During the middle and latter parts of the nineteenth century, gymnastics and exercise became very popular in American schools for both men and women, although there were many who still felt that women's physical pursuits should be severely limited. Gymnasiums were constructed both in schools and communities and were very popular. Physical education classes became the norm in schools nationwide.

It was through these programs of physical education that women's athletics emerged. In the 1890s, basketball was the most popular and fastest-growing team sport. Female physical educators, who directed the early women's athletic and sports programs in higher education, developed vastly different ideals for their programs than their male counterparts. Restricted competition, a feminist approach to individual and team sports, and participation for all—not just a few outstanding athletes as in men's sports—were early virtues that evolved and changed over time as women's athletic programs grew in size and popularity.

The national Committee on Women's Athletics (CWA) was led by the female physical education establishment and focused on team sports and gymnastics in collegiate programs. The CWA shied away from other women's sports that were gaining in popularity outside higher education, such as track and field, which was overseen by the male-dominated Amateur Athletic Union (AAU). As elite female college athletes began to explore opportunities such as track and field outside the collegiate domain, the CWA made efforts to further distance itself from the AAU. The goal of the CWA was to control women's physical education and athletics on all college campuses and direct women away from varsity and Olympic endeavors, keeping with the earlier ideals of women's athletics, believing that participation in sport was more important than competition.

As the AAU gained in status and power, being recognized by the United States Olympic Committee as the governing body of American amateur sport, conflict arose between the CWA and the AAU, with the latter seeking control over women's athletics as well as men's. Time and time again, the CWA refused to affiliate with the AAU, which was quickly becoming an organization with great power in the decisionmaking and governance of sport. In the end, the

AAU won out, moving more of women's athletic programs out of education and into the public sector. Additionally, the AAU remained male dominated.

World War II perpetuated the importance of a strong and healthy nation. Increased levels of competition in women's sports became valued among female competitors due to several factors: an increasing number of female physical educators who encouraged competition; the influential role of the AAU; and popular culture, which emphasized healthy competition.

The old CWA, known during the 1940s as the National Section on Women's Athletics, adopted a more accepting attitude toward rigorous competition; its dominion remained women's athletic programs in higher education, while the AAU continued to oversee amateur sport. The Division for Girls and Women's Sports (1952) created the Commission on Intercollegiate Athletics for Women (CIAW) in 1967, which oversaw major tournaments and national championships for women. From the start, CIAW met conflict from the National Collegiate Athletic Association (NCAA, formed in 1906), which did not see the need for separate men's and women's national championships. The CIAW became the Association for Intercollegiate Athletics for Women in 1971–1972.

The influential **Title IX of the Education Amendments of 1972*** was implemented in large part due to the growth in girls' high school athletics and the power struggles in collegiate athletics. Title IX brought a dramatic increase in competitive opportunities and support for female athletes. However, another consequence of Title IX has been the reduced number of women in athletic administrative positions, as separate male and female athletic departments in **high schools*** and colleges across the nation were often merged into one program, more frequently headed by men than women. With continued consolidation, the NCAA became increasingly powerful, overseeing virtually all aspects of collegiate sports, and is the most powerful organization in amateur sport today.

Nevertheless, opportunities for women in sports continue to improve greatly, while gains in popularity and respect from both collegiate institutions and the general public further advance the status of women as participants and administrators in sports and athletics.

Bibliography: Susan Birrell and Cheryl L. Cole, *Women, Sport, and Culture* (1994); Margaret D. Costa and Sharon R. Guthrie, *Women and Sport* (1994).

Gerald L. Willis

Women's Bureau. The Women's Bureau, as part of the U.S. Department of Labor, is a federal agency developed to serve the interests and promote the welfare of American women. The bureau was originally established in 1918 as the "Woman-in-Industry Service," directed by **Mary Van Kleeck**.* It was made a permanent bureau by congressional act on June 5, 1920. The first director, Mary Anderson, took office in 1920 and continued through 1944. The bureau's original purpose was to "formulate standards and policies which shall promote the welfare of wage-earning women, improve their working conditions, increase their efficiency, and advance their opportunities for profitable employment.''

Although the purpose of the Women's Bureau is not to administer laws, its significance for women has been twofold: first, for its support of labor legislation as a means of ensuring and safeguarding good working conditions and other standards for women in the labor force [see **labor unions***]; and second, for its role as an information agency known for research and dissemination of information to policymaking agencies and to women in the workforce. Throughout the century the bureau has helped formulate policies and programs and has continued to analyze long-term trends in women's employment.

The bureau has issued several important documents. *Women's Occupations through Seven Decades* (1947) traced the occupational progress of women from 1870 to 1940, and *Women in Higher-Level Positions* (1950) reported the extent to which higher-level jobs were open to women, qualifications demanded, and factors favoring or deterring women's advancement. The bureau has also studied wages and working conditions and compiled reports on maternity benefits, industrial injuries, state minimum wage laws, and the legal status of women in the United States. According to a 1965 bureau pamphlet, the ''scope of its concerns includes the status of women as homemakers, volunteers, and citizens, as well as wage earners . . . that every woman in America has the opportunity to make full use of her capacities, *that there may be no waste of womanpower*'' (emphasis in original).

The bureau also sees its role as watching how wages, hours, working conditions, and other labor standards affect women. It is concerned with the educational and vocational guidance and counseling needs of women, the special problems of disadvantaged women and girls, the poor, the civil and political rights of women, women's property, and children and their civil rights.

In December 1961, President John Kennedy appointed the **Commission on the Status of Women*** to examine the needs and changing position of American women and to make recommendations to eliminate barriers to their full participation in economic, social, civil, and political affairs. The bureau fully supported the commission's work, offering staff assistance as well as statistics and advice. The commission's *American Women* report was presented to Kennedy in October 1963 with the intent of increasing awareness of women's capabilities. On November 1, 1963, the Interdepartmental Committee and the Citizen's Advisory Council on the Status of Women were established. During the mid-1960s, the Women's Bureau helped organize the State Governors' Commissions on the Status of Women in forty-five states.

Other related developments of the 1960s were a publicly announced talent search for qualified women to fill government posts at the policy level and a policy by the Civil Service Commission that required justification of any request that specified male or female candidates for job vacancies. Two legislative accomplishments benefited women during this period: the Equal Pay Act of 1963, which prohibited discrimination in pay on the basis of a worker's sex; and **Title VII of the Civil Rights Act*** of 1964, which applied to all phases of employment and prohibited discrimination due to race, color, religion, sex, or national origin.

In the 1970s and beyond, the significance of the Women's Bureau continued to be to examine issues of equal pay and discrimination; to ensure that equal opportunities exist for women in employment, training, and promotion; and to advocate that qualified women get top leadership posts both in and out of government. It serves as a clearinghouse of ideas, information, advocacy, and conferences.

Bibliography: U.S. Department of Labor/Women's Bureau, *The Women's Bureau: Its Functions and Services* (1965).

Susan Clark Studer

women's centers. Women's centers, which are campus or community-based organizations providing services to women, first appeared in the late 1960s and early 1970s as women activists on and off campus demanded that more attention be given to the unique problems of women. The first women's center reportedly opened in Missoula, Montana, followed by the New Haven Women's Liberation Center. Campus-based women's centers opened as women pressured educational institutions to recognize the needs of women students, who have historically been treated very differently from men, at all educational levels. Ironically, the centers began to appear just as the **dean of women*** post on college campuses was being eliminated and replaced by the all-purpose dean of students, leaving many women without an advocate in a male-dominated campus hierarchy.

By the mid-1990s, approximately 1,000 women's centers existed, half located on college campuses. While there is no single model for women's centers, certain programs and services are widely provided, such as assistance for displaced homemakers, self-defense classes, self-esteem and mentoring programs, and assistance with women's health issues. Campus-based women's centers are most common in the Northeast, the Midwest, and the West and tend to be found on campuses of state universities with large residential student populations. Unfortunately, women's centers are much less frequently found at community colleges, although women's needs there may be even more pressing. The National Association of Women's Centers at Miami University in Oxford, Ohio, a national clearinghouse, has observed a recent upsurge of interest in such centers and notes that new centers have opened in every area of the country since 1993.

Center funding and organization vary widely. Campuses providing institutional support and salaried directors are in the minority. Instead, many institutions have women's centers staffed by students and dependent on **student government*** funding, which can create great uncertainty for continuity of programs and personnel. Some institutions have only a ''women's desk.'' Finally, there are student-run centers funded and staffed by feminist groups. These centers come and go based on perceived needs. For example, a rash of crimes against women on campus may lead to opening a center that offers escort services and self-defense training. The marginality of many of these centers has meant that they expend a great deal of effort in raising funds to stay open, rather than in developing programs. The centers often must perform a complicated juggling act to survive. If a center is very active, it may be perceived by administrators as "too radical," while one that pursues a more conservative agenda may be perceived by campus women as lacking credibility.

Research on the needs of women students clearly indicates the potential value of campus-based women's centers. Women consistently report that administrators and faculty appear indifferent and "chilly" to women students [see **chilly classroom climate***]. Women students have particular concerns about physical safety and health issues. In the early days of women's centers, students needed assistance with such issues as birth control and abortion. In the 1990s, they request information and assistance with a wide range of issues such as sexually transmitted diseases, chemical dependency, eating disorders, and abusive relationships. Campus women also seek assistance with career awareness, establishing mentoring relationships, and learning career skills. Finally, large numbers of **reentry programs*** have been created for women who have family and work responsibilities and feel a lack of institutional support for their needs.

Women's centers can respond to these diverse needs and populations, ensuring that women receive a range of services. Programs that will empower women and lead to a heightened awareness of their condition are very popular, running the gamut of films, discussion groups, brown-bag lunches, and guest speakers. Support groups, mentoring groups, and counseling are common, as are workshops addressing self-defense, assertiveness, health, job interview training, and home and car maintenance. Women's centers have proved that they can fill a valuable role on college campuses, and their recent resurgence promises a more supportive environment for all women students.

Bibliography: B. M. Clevenger, "The Mission, Organization, Funding, Programming, and Clientele of Campus-Based, Administratively Organized Women's Centers" (Ph.D. diss., University of Virginia, 1987); K. H. Brooks, "The Women's Center: The New Dean of Women?" *Initiatives*, 51 (1988): 17–21; E. V. Calkins, "Women's Centers in the '90s" (paper presented at the annual meeting of the American Educational Research Association, Atlanta, GA, 1993).

Sharon Clifford

women's club movement. The women's club movement, most active in the United States from about 1870 until the 1920s, fostered women's involvement in community activities through membership in local organizations. While the formation of women's clubs followed no linear progression through stages of development, women ultimately found club work a means to both education and social change. Clubs were organized around a variety of activities and for different reasons; religious as well as secular organizations abounded. Women's groups reached a point of prominence and heightened activism at the turn of the twentieth century, affecting national legislation and creating community institutions.

Historians cite the onset of industrialization that separated work from the home as the major impetus to women's forming societies, clubs, and organizations. As a result of their increasingly isolated domesticity [see **separate spheres***], women sought friendship, edification, and activism through organizations geared toward a variety of goals. In the early nineteenth century, women formed organizations for charitable purposes; these benevolent societies were predecessors to the many women's clubs founded after the Civil War and Reconstruction, which reached their peak membership in the last two decades of the nineteenth century.

African American women were among the first to organize. As one historian notes, "Even more than their white counterparts, black women found voluntary associations to be practically their only avenue to social and educational reform" (Scott, p. 53). Many black women's clubs were thriving in northern cities by the 1830s. These organizations functioned differently from white women's as black women joined to aid one another and for self-education. With most schools closed to them, these women often had to rely on self-education, and some of their first clubs were literary societies. Early on, the black women's club movement "focused on raising the cultural, intellectual, and educational status of black women" (Hine, p. 121). Faced with different societal expectations than white women, "black women emphasized the home as the vital center of reform, and taught gentility as a counter to racial stereotypes, particularly those that labeled all black women as immoral" (Scott, p. 147).

Beginning in the 1870s, many middle-class women formed clubs for self-culture, or **women's study clubs**,* "where women listened to invited lecturers or—more important—themselves gave reports and engaged discussions about books and intellectual topics" (Skocpol, p. 328). As they progressed, women's clubs became more interested in moving beyond self-culture and into their communities. One early example is the Women's Christian Temperance Union (WCTU) [see **temperance movement***]. Started in 1873 and lasting for nearly thirty years, the WCTU, in addition to spreading a social gospel on abstinence, "fought against prostitution, campaigned for female wardens and police matrons, . . . and ran day nurseries for working mothers" (Skocpol, p. 327). In 1890 the **General Federation of Women's Clubs*** (GFWC) formed to unite the increasingly varied groups. The GFWC increased communication among its many state and local affiliates and was active in club work into the 1960s.

The women's club movement reached its peak in 1893, when women from around the country gathered at the **World's Columbian Exposition**.* Women, through club connections, played a large role in orchestrating the event, and the fair "provided an extraordinary opportunity [for women] to see themselves brought together in panoramic display" (Scott, p. 128).

While clubs existed for every woman, regardless of religion, race, or social standing, few were racially integrated. Those that were appeared as antilynching groups in the first few decades of the twentieth century. Such organizations as the Association of Southern Women for the Prevention of Lynching emphasized interracial relations, and the Philadelphia Female Antislavery Society maintained a racially integrated set of members and leaders.

The variety of clubs was vast. Some formed on the basis of ethnicity and professional status, such as working girls' societies designed to provide boardinghouses, classes to improve job options, and other services to support the lives of the increasing numbers of female factory and shop workers. Women formed clubs in the interests of **suffrage**,* self-education, **abolitionism**,* charity, and civic affairs. Through club work, women created community institutions, including orphan asylums, employment bureaus, and libraries. In the later nineteenth century, and into the twentieth, some women's clubs influenced legislation that affected women and children. Yet, despite these variances in membership, locale, and mission, women's clubs were surprisingly similar organizationally. Each had a constitution, rules on membership, dues, and finances. Also, ''[t]he most striking continuity of all was that most of them clung—at least in their public statements—to the notion of woman as moral being whose special public responsibility was to bring the principles of the well-run Christian home into community life'' (Scott, p. 81).

Club work played a key role in women's education. Though many clubs perpetuated the belief in women's traditional roles, the club experience gave women the knowledge and confidence to organize, administer, and implement change. As women gathered, they became conscious of themselves as an efficacious group, a kind of early feminist **consciousness-raising**.* Often clubwomen saw themselves as members of a larger group of women distinguished by race, class, or culture. Clubs offered women ''a chance to establish an identity independent of husbands and a chance to exercise competence or achieve ambition'' (Scott, p. 27).

In addition to self-education, women's clubs, both black and white, were active in schools and viewed education of children as a central aspect of their work. They read and discussed Friedrich Froebel and John Dewey, supplied the funding for playgrounds and **kindergartens**,* and established educational programs for adults and children.

The rich and diverse collection of women's clubs waned after women won the vote. Although women have remained active in club work throughout American history, historians suggest that the women's movement of the 1960s hastened the demise of women's clubs.

Bibliography: Karen J. Blair, *The Clubwoman as Feminist: True Womanhood Redefined, 1868–1914* (1980); Lynda F. Dickson, ''Toward a Broader Angle Vision in Uncovering Women's History: Black Women's Clubs Revisited,'' in Darlene Clark Hine, ed., *Black Women's History: Theory and Practice* (1990); Anne Firor Scott, *Natural Allies: Women's Associations in American History* (1991); Theda Skocpol, *Protecting Soldiers and Mothers: The Political Origins of Social Policy in the United States* (1992); Stephanie J. Shaw, "Black Club Women and the Creation of the National Association of Colored Women," in Darlene Clark Hine, Wilma King, and Linda Reed, eds., *"We Specialize in the Wholly Impossible": A Reader in Black Women's History* (1995).

Christine Woyshner

women's colleges. Women's colleges in the United States trace their origins to the founding of **academies*** for female students in the late eighteenth century. These institutions, which provided limited educational opportunities yet also represented the first serious effort at women's formal education, were created to prepare women as teachers for new and expanding schools. Academies also directly provided an avenue for women to increase their knowledge and prepare for their roles as wives and mothers in the new Republic [see **"Republican motherhood"***].

Promoters and founders of female academies believed that women were entitled to a serious education. At the same time, they tended to promote learning as an acceptable avenue for females without suggesting changes in traditional roles for women. Thus, adherence to Christian womanhood and preparation for a place within the accepted **separate sphere*** of women's influence were encouraged in early female academies. The **Young Ladies' Academy of Philadelphia**,* founded in 1787, and Sarah Pierce's **Litchfield Female Academy**,* Connecticut, founded in 1791, were two of the more prominent women's schools in the post-Revolutionary period.

By the early nineteenth century, these institutions increasingly emphasized preparation for **teaching*** and were commonly referred to as **seminaries**.* Women frequently founded and ran these schools, including **Emma Willard*** (**Troy Female Seminary**,* founded 1821), **Catharine Beecher*** (**Hartford Female Seminary**,* 1828), **Zilpah Polly Grant Banister*** (Ipswich Seminary, 1828), and **Mary Lyon*** (**Mount Holyoke Female Seminary**,* 1837). Seminary founders often faced a myriad of problems. Most academies offered only a three-year program of study, which generally did not consist of college-level work. Because of financial constraints and a prevailing sense that women's education was not essential, it was common for students to attend only intermittently and to leave without completing the course of study. A need for students made it hard for seminaries to enforce strict admissions standards; thus, it was not unusual for students to range in age from twelve to sixteen. Female seminaries also found themselves facing differing demands from parents, communities, and faculty regarding the most appropriate curriculum for young women.

Still, these seminaries often developed innovative curricula and teaching programs and frequently created programs of study on a par with men's. Over time, their offerings more clearly paralleled formal **high school*** and collegiate courses. In this way, they created the foundation and established the patterns that would lead to the creation of women's colleges.

Because of the transitions that many academies and seminaries experienced before becoming colleges, many institutions claim to be the first women's college in this country. Salem College in North Carolina, which began as Salem Academy in 1772, considers its early founding as an *academy* to give it this distinction. Georgia Female College, chartered as a *college* in 1836 (and later renamed Wesleyan College), considers its early founding date as a college to make it the oldest. Mount Holyoke College, which began as a seminary in 1837, considers itself older than many women's colleges that were founded in the 1870s and 1880s, even though it did not convert to a college until 1888.

Mount Holyoke, **Vassar*** (1865), **Wellesley*** (1875), **Smith*** (1875), **Radcliffe*** (founded as an annex to Harvard University in 1879), **Bryn Mawr*** (1884), and **Barnard Colleges*** (founded 1889 as a **coordinate college*** to Columbia University) dominated the concept of women's colleges in this country for many years. Known collectively as the **Seven Sisters**,* these institutions shared prestige, elitism, and rigorous curricula, as well as a parallel to the seven male **Ivy League*** schools. All located between Boston and Philadelphia, they became known for providing unique opportunities for female faculty and administrators while at the same time producing well-known women leaders in a variety of fields. They also served as models for other women's colleges and provided leadership, often fighting on the front lines against critics who suggested that educating a woman extensively was damaging to her mental and physical well-being as well as threatening to society at large [see *Sex in Education**].

Because critics of women's education frequently suggested that females were not strong enough to pursue higher education, women's colleges paid careful attention to exercise and good health. Exercise and sports were a routine part of women's colleges from their earliest days, with team sports such as basketball, crew, and field hockey emphasized along with individual pursuits such as walking and calisthenics [see **women's athletics***].

Women's colleges grew and spread for many reasons in the nineteenth century. They provided opportunities for women who wanted more education and were denied it at most other colleges. Some women's colleges were founded because of the desire to replicate an earlier women's college in a new region, such as Mills College in California, which patterned itself after Mount Holyoke. Just before 1900, the Catholic Church founded several women's **Catholic colleges*** in the Midwest in an attempt to serve religious needs while meeting the demands of women who sought serious educational opportunities. **Spelman College*** in Georgia (1882) developed to provide higher education to former female slaves; **Bennett College*** in North Carolina has also had a long history as a black women's college.

In the twentieth century, women's colleges continued to open, although at a slower pace as higher education became available to women in state colleges and universities and other previously male-only institutions. This trend would have a dramatic impact throughout the twentieth century on the number of women's colleges in existence [see **Morrill Land-Grant Act of 1862***]. By 1960, nearly 300 women's colleges remained in the United States, but by 1996, that number had dropped to 82. The largest decline in women's colleges came in the early 1970s, when many women's colleges either closed or became co-educational [see **coeducation***]. Public women's colleges, such as Mississippi University for Women and Texas Woman's University, have become coeducational in the wake of legal challenges to their tax-supported status.

Contemporary women's colleges face the challenge of promoting single-sex education in a society that has generally moved away from such separatist approaches. Nevertheless, their long history as institutions that offer unique opportunities to women as well as highly reputable academic programs has allowed women's colleges to continue to hold a place in American higher education and to find their enrollments increasing in recent years. Studies indicating that women's college graduates are more likely to pursue **graduate education*** have added to the perception that these institutions continue to meet a valid need.

Slightly more than half of women's colleges today exist in the Northeast, while less than 5 percent are on the West Coast. About half of all women's colleges have a religious affiliation, the other half being private, independent colleges. Some 80 percent of women's colleges have female presidents [see **women college presidents***]. Another common characteristic of women's colleges is an extremely active and loyal alumnae base. That base includes a high number of women of achievement, including anthropologist Ruth Benedict (Vassar), aviator Amelia Earhart (Smith), novelist Mary McCarthy (Vassar), actress Katherine Hepburn (Bryn Mawr), feminist Gloria Steinem (Smith), and first lady Hillary Rodham Clinton (Wellesley).

Bibliography: Elizabeth Alden Green, *Mary Lyon and Mount Holyoke: Opening the Gates* (1979); Helen Lefkowitz Horowitz, *Alma Mater: Design and Experience in the Women's Colleges from Their Nineteenth-Century Beginnings to the 1930s* (1984); Barbara Miller Solomon, *In the Company of Educated Women: A History of Women and Higher Education in America* (1985); Joe Anne Adler, *Women's Colleges* (1994); Patricia Ann Palmieri, *In Adamless Eden: The Community of Women Faculty at Wellesley* (1995).

Debbie Cottrell

Women's Educational and Industrial Union. The Women's Educational and Industrial Union (WEIU), a still-extant educational organization that provides vocational instruction for women of wide socioeconomic backgrounds, was formed in Boston in June 1877 by seven women members of a discussion group that met each Sunday afternoon in the home of Dr. Harriet Clisby. The purpose of the new organization was, in Clisby's words, to "minister to and help women socially, educationally and industrially" and to "lead women to recognize their individual talents and encourage them to exercise those talents." From the beginning, the WEIU was aimed at both a wide spectrum of women and a variety of needs. Thus, it began by not only doing traditional "charity work" such as visiting the poor but also operating a reading room and lounge for working women and consignment shops for both food and handcrafted goods. Quickly, though, it came to emphasize educational, lobbying, and vocational activities.

The WEIU always offered instructional courses, but in its first ten years courses were mainly on literary subjects. Beginning in 1888, however, the WEIU began to concentrate on **vocational education**.* It began by offering sewing classes, and by 1891, these courses provided sufficient training for women to become dressmakers or milliners. In 1895, the WEIU formally opened a training school in dressmaking and millinery and quickly attracted over 300 students. Building on this foundation, the WEIU began offering other vocational courses.

In 1897, the organization created a school for housekeeping that not only trained women to be domestic servants but also offered courses to teach upper- and middle-class women to oversee their own homes and servants. In 1902, in a move that demonstrated the WEIU's connections to women's collegiate education, the school became the Home Economics Department of a new Boston **women's college**,* Simmons College.

Beginning in 1905, the WEIU also began offering training in salesmanship to better prepare women who wanted to work in the new department stores. This training, carried out with several Boston stores, proved so popular that in 1909 a course for teachers of salesmanship was started in cooperation with Simmons. These courses appeared in the Simmons catalog under the Department of Education, and the teachers received an appointment at Simmons. Eventually they became the core of one of the Simmons schools, known as the Prince School of Salesmanship. The connection with Simmons was further strengthened when Mary Schenck Woolman was given concurrent appointments as president of the WEIU and head of the Simmons College Household Economics Department in 1911 [see **commercial education***].

The WEIU research committee, formed in 1905, also had connections to women's education. This department carried out studies of industrial and social conditions, using fellowships financed by **Wellesley**,* Tufts, and **Radcliffe*** Colleges and the **General Federation of Women's Clubs**.* The WEIU and various government agencies published much of the fellows' work, until the research committee was ended in 1932.

The WEIU also operated an Appointment Bureau that helped college women find careers in areas outside **teaching**.* The bureau staff prepared studies of various vocations open to women, gave presentations at colleges, and held conferences with individual students. For a time, the bureau even took charge of vocational guidance at Wellesley College. Beginning in 1913, the bureau began holding conferences on women's employment opportunities. It also operated placement services, including placements for teachers, **home economics*** majors, and secretaries.

The WEIU remains in existence and continues to carry out many of the same activities, including a consignment shop.

Bibliography: Sarah Deutsch, "Learning to Talk More Like a Man: Boston Women's Class-Bridging Organizations, 1870–1940," *American Historical Review*, 97 (April 1992): 379–404; Margaret C. Dollar, "The Beginnings of Vocational Guidance for

College Women: The Women's Educational and Industrial Union, the Association of Collegiate Alumnae, and Women's Colleges'' (Ed.D. diss., Harvard University, 1992). Records of the Women's Educational and Industrial Union, 1877–1980, are in the Schlesinger Library, Radcliffe College, Cambridge, Massachusetts.

John F. Potter

Women's Educational Equity Act. The Women's Educational Equity Act (WEEA) provides financial assistance to colleges and universities, state agencies, and other eligible institutions for specific efforts to ensure gender equity in American education and to comply with **Title IX of the Education Amendments of 1972.*** Originally part of the Special Projects Act of the Education Amendments of 1974, WEEA was reauthorized as a separate program in 1978, amended in 1984 and 1988, and reauthorized for five years in 1994. Under the 1974 legislation, WEEA recipients were to receive grants and contracts to develop and evaluate curricula, textbooks, and other educational materials; to produce model training programs for educational personnel; to support research and development as well as guidance and counseling activities; to develop educational activities to increase opportunities for adult women; and to expand and improve educational programs and activities for women in **vocational education,*** career education, physical education, and educational administration.

Although subsequent acts continued to aim at achieving gender equity in education, WEEA's activities and priorities have changed. The initial act created the Advisory Council on Women's Educational Programs, which was eliminated in 1988, to oversee sex equity legislation and make policy recommendations. WEEA's amendments and reauthorizations emphasized supporting projects for women and girls suffering from multiple discriminations due to race, ethnicity, disabilities, and age. The most recent 1994 reauthorization stressed, among other things, problems related to **sexual harassment,*** inequities in mathematics and science courses [see **science education***], and pregnant and parenting teenagers. The Secretary of Education annually selects one or more WEEA priorities for funding.

Since its inception, WEEA never received the funding anticipated by the original legislation. Consequently, its scope and impact have been significantly less than intended. WEEA's initial funding was $6.3 million; its highest funding, in 1981, was $10 million. Funding decreased dramatically afterward. In 1992, its $500,000 appropriation funded only the WEEA Publishing Center, which since 1977 has provided technical assistance to grantees while their products are in the development stage. Additionally, the center markets and sells WEEA-funded products such as training modules, program manuals, and audiovisual materials. Lack of funding makes WEEA grants one of the most difficult to win, with awards to only seven in every hundred applicants. Its consistently inadequate funding may make WEEA a symbolic gesture toward, rather than a meaningful vehicle for, improving gender equity in American education.

Bibliography: U.S. Department of Education, *Women's Educational Equity Act Pro-*

gram: *Report of Activities 1988–1992* (1992); Nelly P. Stromquist, "Sex-Equity Legislation in Education: The State as Promoter of Women's Rights," *Review of Educational Research* (Winter 1993).

Maureen A. Reynolds

women's studies. "Women's studies" is both an educational movement and an academic field that began in institutions of higher education in the late 1960s. In placing women at the center of academic inquiry, new courses, programs, and the National Women's Studies Association (founded 1978) were inspired by a vision of a world free from sexism and other forms of bias or oppression. According to scholar Marilyn Boxer, women's studies "challenged its practitioners to think beyond the boundaries of traditional sex roles, of traditional disciplines, and of established institutions" (Boxer, p. 662). A wealth of literature has been published on the theory and practice of women's studies by its leading practitioners, notably Florence Howe, Catherine Stimpson, Johnnella Butler, and Beverly Guy-Sheftall.

Some, but not all, of the first courses in women's studies were created by faculty and students associated with the 1960s student and civil rights movements. A ten-course curriculum at San Diego State University became, in 1970, the first officially recognized women's studies program in the nation. Howe and others founded the Feminist Press and the *Women's Studies Newsletter* (later *Women's Studies Quarterly*) soon after. Fifteen years later, more than 300 programs and departments at colleges and universities in the United States offered majors, minors, and certificates in the field. Typical women's studies programs include a broad array of courses, such as Women in Society, Social History of Women, African American Women Writers, Theories of Feminism, Science and Gender, Women and the Law, Sexism and Racism, Issues in Women's Health, Interdisciplinary Research, and Internships. Interdisciplinary in its original conception, women's studies programs offer courses taught from both single- and multidisciplinary perspectives. Although programs are developed to their greatest extent in the United States and Great Britain, there are courses, programs, and research institutes on women and gender in many countries.

Women's studies, along with ethnic studies, had a significant impact on approaches to teaching and scholarship in the liberal arts by the 1990s. In the curriculum, women's studies educators have advocated a redefinition and expansion of general education to eliminate bias and incorporate gender as a category of analysis. In teaching, the experiences and perspectives of women students in all their diversity are integrated into discussions on course topics. "Feminist pedagogy" has expanded this idea, urging that students are the best authorities on their own experience and that they can construct knowledge out of their own understandings. And finally, there has been a flowering of new, critical, feminist approaches in scholarship. Dozens of women's studies-related journals flourish; most academic and trade publishers now offer a women's studies line of books.

Two related societal developments are thought to have generated and sustained these changes. First, the women's liberation movement for equality has transformed educational institutions and practices, just as it has challenged traditional views of the family, the workplace, and other social institutions. The presence of more women faculty and administrators committed to educational equity—a result of **affirmative action*** in hiring and promotion—has supported the innovations. Second, by the 1980s women had become the majority of students in higher education. As more women entered the labor force, they began to attend college in greater numbers to enhance their employment prospects or change careers. The proportion of adult women students over age twenty-five grew dramatically. As a consequence, many women's studies programs offer majors with an applied component to orient women toward careers in the professions of human service advocacy, health care, law, journalism, and **teaching**.* Feminist educators conclude, therefore, that the development of women's studies is the most recent chapter in the 200-year story of women's struggle for meaningful educational opportunities.

A rationale for a distinct African American women's studies was presented in the early stages. Dialogues about racial and cultural "difference" initiated by women of color and lesbians have characterized work in the field for two decades. Newer, global perspectives in women's studies also have helped reconceptualize Eurocentric feminist thought to incorporate various "feminisms."

In the 1990s women's studies programs flourished in spite of some antifeminist **backlash*** against "political correctness" supported by conservative and right-wing foundations. Advocates of women's studies increasingly recognize that they must work in alliance with other interdisciplinary programs to preserve the educational changes of three decades and to inform positively public policy research on women and families. Guy-Sheftall, a prominent women's studies scholar, summarizes: "One of the most urgent challenges for the American academy . . . is to respond to issues of diversity by making the old and new scholarship on people of color and women central, not peripheral, to the curriculum" (Guy-Sheftall, p. 28). [See also **legal education**,* **medical education**,* **science education**,* **women's centers**.*]

Bibliography: Marilyn J. Boxer, "For and About Women: The Theory and Practice of Women's Studies in the United States," *SIGNS*, 7 (1982): 661–695; Gloria T. Hull, Patricia Bell Scott, and Barbara Smith, eds., *All the Women Are White, All the Blacks Are Men, But Some of Us Are Brave* (1982); Caryn McTighe Musil, *The Courage to Question: Women's Studies and Student Learning*, Association of American Colleges (1992); Liza Fiol-Matta and Mariam K. Chamberlain, eds., *Women of Color and the Multicultural Curriculum: Transforming the College Classroom* (1994); Beverly Guy-Sheftall, *Women's Studies: A Retrospective* (A Report to the Ford Foundation) (1995); Elaine Hedges and Dorothy O. Helly, eds., "Anniversary Issue—Looking Back, Moving Forward: 25 Years of Women's Studies History," *Women's Studies Quarterly*, 25, nos. 1 and 2 (Spring/Summer 1997): 1–459. The 1997 Anniversary Issue of *Women's Studies*

Quarterly also contains a complete listing of women's studies programs in the United States.

Ann Froines

women's study clubs. Although forerunners may be traced to Anne Hutchinson's discussion of colonial sermons with a group of women parishioners and to women's reading groups in the early nineteenth century, women's study clubs began in earnest after the Civil War and flourished across America from 1880 to 1900. Meeting in their homes, small groups of white, middle-aged, middle-class women gathered twice a month for several hours to pursue serious study of literature, art, French, music, astronomy, philosophy, geography, and history. Eschewing such controversial topics as religion and politics—and especially women's **suffrage***—these women attempted to provide for themselves an education denied them by formal institutions of the day.

Although a few club members had attended female **academies**,* most had ended their formal education in grammar school; **high schools*** open to girls were rare, and college opportunities for women were virtually nonexistent. Moreover, a woman who pursued higher education ran the risk of being labeled ''strong-minded'' or a ''bluestocking,'' and club members were conservative Victorian women whose first responsibility was to their families. Still, the tenets of **''true womanhood''*** demanded a cultured wife and an educated mother, and quiet afternoon study clubs provided an acceptable means to that end. In addition, study clubs offered women an arena to pursue engagement with the world beyond their homes, as well as a haven of stability in a world rapidly changing by industrialization, immigration, and institutional expansion.

Club methods of operation were simple. As a group, members decided their course of study over the year's meetings from September to June. Programs of the earliest clubs were often desultory, wandering from Greek art at one session to the French Revolution at the next, and were always dependent on the limited number of reference books and ''texts'' available in pre–public library days. Gradually study became more focused and systematic, with a year devoted to one topic, such as Shakespeare's tragedies or the history of painting. Some club names proclaimed their study principle, such as the Ruskin Art Club of Los Angeles and the Castilian Club of Boston. Others, such as The Mustard Seed and Over-the-Teacups, were more circumspect.

Clubwomen took their work seriously. Comparisons of their study clubs to colleges lace the writings of club members: ''What college life is to the young woman, club life is to the woman of riper years,'' wrote one president. Meetings were governed by parliamentary procedure, and offices were rotated through the membership so that each woman could gain experience in ''public'' speaking. After a brief business meeting, the ''lesson'' proceeded with several women reading papers on topics a program committee had assigned. Each paper was subjected to the comments of an elected ''critic,'' who pointed out errors in pronunciation, grammar, and delivery. Every member was expected to participate in some way at each meeting, and many clubs levied fines if a member came unprepared.

Although a few clubs relied on commercial study guides or occasional male lecturers, almost all were devoted to self- and mutual education. Members prided themselves on their own work, which, if not decidedly original, was born of painstaking effort and often practiced before mirrors at home. Competition played no part in club culture; instead, cooperation, encouragement, and delight in each other's achievements comprised the club ethos. Meeting in familiar domestic settings, where they were, indeed, experts, these amateur scholars could take intellectual risks. Private as their efforts were, however, study clubs were seen by some as subversive of home and family. "Clubbers" were criticized in print for "straying from their sphere," pursuing nothing but "culturine," and becoming "aggressive, meddlesome, and angular" (in other words, unfeminine).

While the comparison of their clubs to colleges presumed too much in strictly academic terms, the company of women did not. As did undergraduates, clubwomen adopted club songs, mottoes ("Knowledge rare, we seek and share"), colors, flowers, pledges, and pins. Lifetime membership was common, and traditions developed quickly, for example, a Remembrance Day in memorial to bygone members. Women, who had become increasingly isolated in their homes as migration reduced the extended family and as the focus of their husbands' and children's lives turned more to the outside world, embraced the sorority and potential they found in study clubs. Although most clubs carefully disassociated themselves from "the woman question," stirrings of emancipation were in the air.

For practical reasons, membership in study clubs was generally set at twenty. Beyond that number a public meeting place need be sought (and there were few in which women felt comfortable) and participation, limited. Though locally small, on a national scale club membership numbered around 1 million by the early 1900s, and by 1906, 5,000 clubs had joined the **General Federation of Women's Clubs,*** a figure representing perhaps only 5 to 10 percent of clubs in existence. Despite their ubiquitous presence and the remarkable similarity of their purpose and operation, study clubs remained autonomous and unaffiliated until 1890. To celebrate its twenty-first anniversary in 1889, Sorosis, a New York City club founded by newspaper columnist Jane Croly, invited representatives of all other **women's clubs*** of which it had knowledge (only ninety-seven) to talk about their work. Out of the meeting grew the General Federation, and simultaneously, the movement began to change.

As more colleges opened their doors to women and as women began to take a more active and confident stance in community life, study through books no longer satisfied the interests of an increasing number of women. New "department clubs," with unlimited membership, now offered women a variety of "work" from which to choose: To the inevitable literature department were added departments for current events, schools, local government, and reform. Women moved quickly from education for self to education for service, from the study of Shakespeare's stage to life's stage, from philosophy to philanthropy.

Entering the women's club movement at this point and at a time in American history of increasing racial segregation and discrimination, clubs founded by black women were most often department clubs with a dual purpose: to define themselves as educated women and as black women. Thus, they combined literary study with work for betterment of the race. Club mottoes stressing **race uplift*** such as "Rowing, Not Drifting" and "Lifting as We Climb" inspired black women's clubs to take a more direct role in service to their local black communities, especially in educational matters, and they were active in the establishment of trade schools, night schools, **kindergartens**,* and libraries for blacks.

Although white and black department clubs were the wave of the future, the small study club devoted solely to women's self-education remained on the scene to become a permanent part of American informal lifelong education. The "Light Seekers," as Jane Croly called study clubs, had raised the educational aspirations and intellectual self-confidence of American women. "Thought once awakened does not slumber," proclaimed the Tourist Club of West Union, Iowa, and succeeding generations of women who joined study clubs were increasingly college educated and looked to their clubs not for validation but for further food for inquiring minds and for the respectful interchange and the courage that comes from a sorority of scholars. [See also **Heterodoxy**,* **reading circles**,* **sororities**.*]

Bibliography: Jane C. Croly, *The History of the Woman's Club Movement* (1898); Karen J. Blair, *The Clubwoman as Feminist: True Womanhood Redefined, 1868–1914* (1980); Anne F. Scott, *Making the Invisible Woman Visible* (1984); Theodora Penny Martin, *The Sound of Our Own Voices* (1987); Darlene Clark Hine, ed., *Black Women in American History: From Colonial Times through the Nineteenth Century* (1990).

Theodora Penny Martin

Women's Trade Union League. The Women's Trade Union League (WTUL), organized as both a national organization and local branches, was founded in 1903 as "a unique attempt at cross-class cooperation, its membership and leadership composed jointly of women workers and wealthy reformers" (Ware, p. 48). The WTUL was not itself a separate **labor union*** but rather a private organization encouraging unionization of women workers as well as support for their concerns in all work settings. Over several decades, the WTUL followed a three-pronged strategy to support working women: unionization, legislation, and education. It trained hundreds of women, supported unionization of thousands, and engaged actively in most of the labor issues of the 1910s and 1920s.

The idea for the WTUL grew at a convention of the American Federation of

Labor (AFL) in Boston in 1903. Although the WTUL was affiliated with the AFL and relations between the two organizations seemed cordial, the AFL was, in fact, not a strong supporter of working women, blacks, or immigrants. Thus, the WTUL followed its own approach in support of working women. The original founders were primarily women, including Mary Kenney, Leonora O'Reilly, Mary McDowell, and **Jane Addams*** and Lillian Wald, the latter two active in the **settlement house movement**.*

Composed of both women workers and middle-class reformers, the WTUL believed in the importance of conveying sound data and information to the public as the best way to win support for their causes. The league made its first important contribution by supporting women shirtwaist makers in the first general strike among women garment workers in 1909–1910 in Philadelphia and New York City. Workers at several factories including New York's Triangle Shirt-Waist Company (which would become the site of a notorious factory fire two years later) suffered difficult conditions yet found insufficient support for a widespread strike. With aid from the New York and national WTUL, thousands of women were encouraged to join the garment workers' unions and strike for improved working conditions. The WTUL used this first experience to grow into its role of union supporter, information provider, women's advocate, and fund-raiser. Although the ultimate strike settlement was somewhat disappointing, the case had been made that women factory workers could, indeed, be unionized, and the WTUL had found its strength.

Through its first two decades, the WTUL continued to push for unionization and was involved in most of the country's prominent efforts to unionize women or support women on strike. Simultaneously, the league pushed for labor legislation, seeking protection for women in various industries, clarified working hours, and better wage rates. Much of this involved a public education effort, spurred by women like Addams, Wald, and other **Progressive Era*** reformers who sponsored and conducted comprehensive studies of women workers and their conditions.

The third major area of WTUL effort was education. Like the International Ladies' Garment Workers' Union (ILGWU) and others, the WTUL created its own training programs for women workers. Workers' education in the 1910s and 1920s had several outlets and forms. Some programs were party sponsored by the socialists and communists. Others were offered in **labor colleges**,* autonomous institutions that might offer just a few classes in a shop hall or public library, or create a full-fledged course in social science at a residential campus. As many as 300 such labor colleges existed by 1930. A few traditional colleges and universities also shared workers' training, with programs like the **Bryn Mawr Summer School for Women Workers*** offering a summer's curriculum in economics, political science, labor relations, and English. The WTUL was a consistent strong supporter of the Bryn Mawr program.

A considerable amount of workers' education, however, was offered in union-based programs. Local WTUL branches provided various educational programs to motivate women as union workers and organizers, offering an array of classes on parliamentary procedure, public speaking, letter writing, and lecturing. However, the league's grandest educational venture was its Training School for Women Organizers, created in Chicago in 1914. The school offered a year's residential training in organizing through a combination of academic study and fieldwork. On the academic side, students pursued labor history, industrial relations, labor legislation, trade agreements, and communication skills. In the fieldwork and internship component, they focused on administrative issues related to union organizing. Students received full scholarships from their unions. Although the school did train considerable numbers of women organizers, it was not a long-term success, suffering from lack of consistent funding, a dearth of sufficiently challenging fieldwork, the difficulties of matching academic work with the students' skills and needs, and perhaps, some league leaders' patronizing attitude toward the effort. Within a few years, the full-year course had been reduced to six months.

Funding was a constant problem for the WTUL; some years there was not enough money to hold a national convention. Another issue was the balance of working women and middle-class reformers among the leadership. The league's first three presidents were wealthy women who supported the cause of women workers; Margaret Dreier Robins was a woman of considerable means, and Ellen Henrotin had been president of the **General Federation of Women's Clubs**.* Only in 1921 did the WTUL choose its first president from among the working women membership, Maud Swartz of the typographers' union.

Like other voluntary organizations, the WTUL suffered from lack of energy and membership in the depression decade of the 1930s. At one point, the league could afford only one full-time union organizer, and its national budget was under $20,000. Its legacy, however, remained not only in the hundreds of women it trained and the thousands of women it organized. The Women's Trade Union League also provided a training ground for many of the influential women who would support President Franklin Roosevelt's New Deal, and it educated the American public about issues for working women.

Bibliography: Ellen Condliffe Lagemann, *A Generation of Women: Education in the Lives of Progressive Reformers* (1979); Susan Ware, *Holding Their Own: American Women in the 1930s* (1982); Joyce Kornbluh and Mary Frederickson, eds., *Sisterhood and Solidarity: Workers' Education for Women, 1914–1984* (1984); Robin Miller Jacoby, *The British and American Women's Trade Union Leagues, 1890–1925: A Case Study of Feminism and Class* (1994); Eleanor Flexner and Ellen Fitzpatrick, *A Century of Struggle: The Woman's Rights Movement in the United States* (enlarged ed., 1996).

Linda Eisenmann

Woody, Thomas. Walter Thomas Woody (1891–1960) was author of *A History of Women's Education in the United States* (1929), a two-volume history that is still a standard reference for historians of the early years of education for American women. Woody was raised by a **Quaker*** farm family in Indiana, and his early schooling took place in a one-room school in Walnut Grove. After graduating from Indiana University in 1913, Woody taught German in the Warsaw, Indiana, **high school**.* He then went to Columbia University Teachers College, where he earned his doctorate in 1918, specializing in history of education. After completing his dissertation, Woody worked for the Young Men's Christian Association (YMCA) as a relief worker in Russia and France, seeing the Russian Revolution firsthand. Upon his return to the United States, Woody began teaching at the University of Pennsylvania, where he remained until his death of cancer in 1960. A productive scholar, Woody wrote eight books and over 200 articles during his career; the best known and his greatest achievement is *A History of Women's Education in the United States*.

Woody began work on the history in 1919, inspired by his relationship with Willystine Goodsell, author of *The Education of Women, Its Social Background and Problems* (1923). As Woody studied the early years of American schooling, he saw the need for a complete history of women's education. He researched and wrote the book between 1921 and 1927, then spent considerable time finding a publisher. The book was eventually accepted by the Science Press in Lancaster, Pennsylvania. It sold well and was reprinted in 1966 and 1973 by Octagon Books.

Woody's was the first major effort to trace the role of women in American education, and the history was a massive accomplishment. Extensively researched, this heavily documented book has over 4,000 bibliographic entries. Wide-ranging and well-written, the history discusses the roles of women throughout American history.

Woody believed that schools are the outgrowth of larger social forces and analyzed the impact of social, economic, and political developments on the education of American women. He observed that "looking back over the past three hundred years, it is clear . . . that though political emancipation is the first great symbol of women's victory, their intellectual emancipation, because of its priority and fundamental character, was of vaster significance." He argued that the growth of educational opportunity for American women was due to the rise of industrialization and consequent social change as women left the home for work in other fields, especially the new factories. He also asserted that as the United States industrialized, a population of "surplus" (unmarried) women [see **surplus daughters***] who needed training in order to support themselves increased the demand and acceptability of education for women. Aware of the complexities of the historical process, Woody saw the shifting of women's sphere from hearth to outside world as a critically important event [see **separate spheres***]. Woody believed that the demand for women's **suffrage*** was the natural result of increased educational opportunity and that the new freedoms for women would ultimately lead to larger social benefits for all Americans.

Woody maintained his interest in women's education throughout his life. He believed that one could understand a great deal about a society by observing its treatment of women, and he wrote on women in societies as diverse as ancient

Greece and revolutionary Russia. In a 1938 article, Woody noted that women in the United States had advanced as authoritarian religion declined, political liberalism grew, and industrialization led to development of a massive middle class. Woody was a progressive educator and supporter of democracy and liberalism who believed that schools could be creative forces within a society; he maintained friendships with such educators as John Dewey, with whom he made a second trip to Russia in 1928.

Besides his own writing, Woody accumulated a large educational history collection, which today is housed in the Penniman Library at the University of Pennsylvania.

Bibliography: T. F. McHugh, "Thomas Woody: Teacher, Scholar, Humanist" (Ph.D. diss., University of Pennsylvania, 1973); J. Brickman and W. W. White, eds., *The Thomas Woody Collection of the Penniman Library of Education* (1974).

Sharon Clifford

World's Columbian Exposition. The World's Columbian Exposition, held in Chicago in 1893, was a world's fair that attracted more than 27 million people to its technological, cultural, and industrial exhibits. In addition to several buildings featuring electricity, transportation, horticulture, and fine arts, the Woman's Building—one of the most popular—showcased the artistic, social, educational, and literary interests of a broad spectrum of feminine thought, aspiration, and accomplishment. Through its exhibits and continuing lecture series, the Woman's Building exposed Americans to aspects of life for the active **"New Woman"*** of the coming century and highlighted women's activism and reform work that would increase throughout the **Progressive Era*** (1890–1930).

The Woman's Building served as a focal point for a series of lectures by and about prominent American women, including Susan B. Anthony, Julia Ward Howe, and May Wright Sewall. The written record of these daily lectures was compiled by the Board of Lady Managers, led by prominent Chicagoan Bertha Palmer, edited by Mary Eagle, and published in 1894 as an official record. These presentations were primarily educational, delivered by women from several professions, including lawyers, physicians, educators, religious leaders, and social reformers. Topics were designed to benefit women, such as the "economic and financial independence of woman (as financier and investor) . . . encouragement of home industries, and effective voting" (Eagle, Index to Subjects).

Several themes can be discerned in the work of the women's exhibition: (1) the value of women's networking; (2) a foreshadowing of technology as a liberating force for women in their creative and occupational lives; (3) a showcase for women's artistic, literary, and professional accomplishments; and (4) a platform for the political and social awakening that foreshadowed liberating events, such as **suffrage*** and women's growing role in peace activism.

The first theme—networking—can be seen in the record of the addresses, along with biographical data on the daily platform of speakers. These represented viewpoints by women from thirty different states and countries, designed to "provide for communion and interchange of thought between women engaged in the same and diverse lines of work" (Eagle, Introduction).

The second theme—foreshadowing the role of technology—received attention from a futuristic kitchen furnished "with all modern conveniences and labor saving devices," offered by Ellen Swallow Richards, a founder of modern **home economics**.* In fact, the National Household Economics Association was created at the Exposition, a joining of the first and second themes.

The third theme was a recognition that not only the objects but also the activities of the Woman's Building were consciously designed as a showcase. The physical location, architecture, and interior design were all conducive to networking as well as for exhibiting women's achievements. The building was designed by Sophia Hayden of Boston, whose design was considered quite original. Located near the main gates, it had balconies, a roof garden, both land and water entrances, a gallery, an assembly hall, and reading, writing, and committee rooms. Women's literary accomplishments were highlighted in a library of books by female authors. The design of the Woman's Building reflected women's needs, interpreted in their own terms. There was a model hospital where female physicians and nurses cared for women and children. The **kindergarten*** room ensured that fair-goers' children would receive good care.

The fourth theme echoed the political and civic awakening of women at this early stage of the Progressive Era. In the next few decades, women would storm the political arena, crafting a National Convention of the Woman Suffrage Association (1909); form the Woman's Peace Party (1915), with **Jane Addams*** and Carrie Chapman Catt as leaders; and in 1920 win the right to vote. An embryonic political awareness was apparent in several of the addresses: "Woman in an Ideal Government," "Woman, the Inciter to Reform," "Women: Citizens and People?" and "Legal Condition of Women."

This final theme also included a plea for international peace. An address by Kansas lawyer Mary Elizabeth Lease boldly challenged the "horrible inconsistency between religious belief and action." She stated: "The mothers of this nation . . . shall no longer rear their sons to be slain. . . . If men cannot get along without the shedding of blood, . . . let them . . . turn . . . affairs over to the mothers, who will temper their justice with love and enthrone mercy" (Lease, in Eagle, p. 413).

Sentiments for women's enhanced civic role were echoed in the World's Columbian Exposition as seeds of advocacy were nurtured for women's rights, social reform, education, enfranchisement, and advocacy for children—all efforts that women would pursue in the activism and reform of the Progressive Era. [See also **peace education**,* **social housekeeping**.*]

Bibliography: Annie Curd, "Woman's Work at the Columbia Exposition: The Woman's Building," *Good Housekeeping* (January 1893); John J. Finn, *Official Guide to the World's Columbian Exposition* (1893); Mary Kavanaugh Oldham Eagle, ed., *The Con-*

gress of Women (1894); David F. Burg, *Chicago's White City of 1893* (1976); Stanley Applebaum, *The Chicago World's Fair of 1893* (1980). The Chicago Public Library has a special collection of papers, guidebooks, and memorabilia related to the Exposition.

Aline M. Stomfay-Stitz

Y

Yezierska, Anzia. A novelist and short story writer, Anzia Yezierska (ca. 1890–1970) is widely acclaimed for her role in the development of Jewish American immigrant literature and feminism. Her writings focus on the struggle of the female to gain autonomy both within her own family and in larger American society. Following the pattern of Yezierska's own experience, her protagonists fight to become Americanized and to break through religious rules and social and economic barriers to create a self-determined life.

Daughter of an impoverished Talmudic scholar, Yezierska was born in Plinsk in Russian Poland and immigrated in the 1890s with her parents to New York. Quite early, she determined that the way to become like other Americans was through education, and she sought ways to learn whenever possible. When lack of both finances and family support made formal schooling unavailable to her, Yezierska, according to her own accounts, used money she earned at various menial tasks to pay a janitor's child to teach her English. Clashes with her father led Yezierska to leave home for the Clara de Hirsch Home for Working Girls. She attended night school to improve her English and eventually received a scholarship that allowed her to attend Columbia University Teachers College from 1901 to 1905 and gain certification to teach domestic science.

Yezierska's first marriage ended in annulment after only a few months, and in her subsequent marriage to Arnold Levitas in 1911, she insisted on a religious ceremony only, not a legally binding civil one. The marriage produced a daughter, Louise, in 1912. After only a few years of marriage, Yezierska found domestic life oppressive and left Levitas. Soon thereafter, unable to support herself and a child, she left her daughter in his care.

Although she was not well suited for **teaching**,* disliking both the profession itself and her subject, Yezierska determined to pursue a teaching career because it was acceptable for women. Finding herself in the unsatisfactory position of substitute teacher, however, she went to educator John Dewey in 1917 to enlist his support, hoping to secure accreditation to advance to a full-time teacher. Dewey, with whom Yezierska became romantically linked for a short period, was not impressed with Yezierska's potential as a teacher, but he allowed her to audit his seminar in social and political philosophy. When he saw some of her writings, Dewey encouraged Yezierska to give up teaching and pursue writing, centering on her immigrant experiences.

Yezierska had already published one story, and following Dewey's advice, she began to concentrate more on her writing. She experienced almost immediate success. Her short story "The Fat of the Land" was selected as the best short story of 1919, and a collection of stories, *Hungry Hearts*, published in 1920, was widely praised. When it failed to sell, however, Yezierska went to see Frank Crane, a leading newspaper columnist, and provided him with an embellished story of her life. Crane's subsequent column established the myth of Yezierska as the ignorant sweatshop worker suddenly transformed into a writer. The results were increased book sales, $10,000 for the movie rights to *Hungry Hearts*, and the overnight transformation of Yezierska into a celebrity.

Hungry Hearts, as well as subsequent story collections and novels, centers primarily on the female immigrant's attempts to gain independence and acceptance in American society. Although some Jewish critics were angered by her use of broken English for her immigrant speakers and complained that she was ridiculing her people, others credited her with realism and with effectively capturing immigrant speech patterns. Yezierska's best work is her autobiographical novel *Bread Givers* (1925), whose subtitle *A Struggle between a Father of the Old World and a Daughter of the New* emphasizes its theme.

Yezierska's fame was short-lived, and during the rest of her life she frequently struggled for economic survival. The WPA Writers Project provided assistance through the depression years. She continued to write—novels, stories, essays, reviews, and her critically acclaimed autobiography *Red Ribbon on a White Horse* (1950). Her basic theme remained the struggle of the female to achieve independence, though in later years she intertwined it with the problems of aging. Her best works capture the ambiguities of the immigrant experience in America: the desire to assimilate and the fear of loss of culture and past; the close-knit community of the ghetto and its hunger, dirt, and poverty; the pull toward economic success and anxiety about the pitfalls of materialism. Her protagonists often escape the ghetto through education, become Americanized, only to find themselves suspended between two worlds—the warm, colorful, vitally alive but economically restrictive ghetto and the economically successful but sterile, repressed uptown. Even when financially comfortable, they are never able to eliminate feelings of alienation.

Almost forgotten in her lifetime, Yezierska was rediscovered only a few years after her death in 1970. Her works were reprinted, and critics began examining and praising them. Yezierska is now viewed as a pioneer spokesperson for the female immigrant experience in America, for the outsider struggling to carve out a place in an alien society. In both her life and her writings, she highlighted the difficulties and possibilities of achieving self-determination that confront females from a patriarchal culture.

Bibliography: Carol B. Schoen, *Anzia Yezierska* (1982); Louise Levitas Henriksen, *Anzia Yezierska: A Writer's Life* (1988); Thomas J. Ferraro, " 'Working Ourselves Up' in America: Anzia Yezierska's *Bread Givers,*" *South Atlantic Quarterly*, 89 (Summer 1990): 547–581; Wendy Zierler, "The Rebirth of Anzia Yezierska," *Judaism*, 42 (Fall 1993): 414–422. See also papers in the Boston University Library.

Verbie Lovorn Prevost

Young, Ella Flagg. Ella Flagg Young (1845–1918), superintendent of schools in Chicago, 1909–1915, was the first woman to head the school system of a major city in the United States and the first woman to serve as president of the National Education Association (1910–1911). Born in Buffalo, New York, on January 15, 1845, Young was the second daughter and youngest child of Jane Reed Flagg and Theodore Flagg, Presbyterians of Scottish ancestry. In 1858, the family moved to Chicago where she attended **high school*** and subsequently Chicago **Normal School**,* graduating in 1862. The seemingly ordinary young woman then embarked on a fifty-six-year career of exceptional instructional and administrative service to the city of Chicago.

Flagg initially taught in the Primary Department of Chicago's Foster School. She assumed her first administrative post in 1863 as head assistant at the Brown School. Two years later, Flagg became principal of the Practice School of the Chicago Normal School. In 1868, she married a merchant, William Young; his death the following year reinforced Ella Flagg Young's determination to pursue a public career.

For the next eighteen years, Young held a variety of **teaching*** and administrative positions in Chicago schools, including teacher at Chicago Normal School, 1872–1876; principal of Scammon School, 1876–1879, and of Skinner School, 1879–1887. Throughout this period, she developed a distinct philosophy of the role of teacher and school in a democratic society. She concluded that to be effective instruments of change both in the lives of students and in the operation of schools, teachers needed better education and greater participation in administrative decisions.

In 1887, Young became assistant superintendent of Chicago schools, a position she held for twelve years. During her tenure, she sought to implement her educational philosophy of teacher empowerment. Anxious to enhance teachers' own education, she invited authorities such as John Dewey and William James to address public school faculties. Determined that teachers also have some voice in forming school policy, she organized teachers councils, which assisted in principals' administrative decisionmaking.

In 1895, at age fifty-five, Young entered graduate school at the **University of Chicago*** and continued her course work while serving as assistant superintendent. Four years later, she left the public schools and accepted an offer from the university to become associate professor of pedagogy. John Dewey directed Young's doctoral dissertation, *Isolation in Education* (1900), which the university published as the first volume of its *Contributions to Education* series. Based on her experience as teacher and administrator, Young outlined her educational philosophy that school systems operate most smoothly if democratic decisionmaking defines school practice.

Upon graduation, she remained on the faculty, promoted to professor. Young's varied responsibilities included supervisor of instruction at Dewey's Laboratory School and editor of both *The Elementary School Teacher* and *Educational Bi-Monthly*. She also found time to publish two additional books, *Ethics in the Schools* and *Some Types of Modern Educational Theory*, both in 1902.

Following Dewey's departure from Chicago in 1905, Young also left to become principal of Chicago Normal School. Four years later, she accepted the superintendency of Chicago schools, becoming the first woman to head a major U.S. public school system. Furthermore, her salary of $10,000 was identical to that of her male predecessor.

Determined that ''democracy in education'' be the hallmark of her administration, Young instituted curricular, administrative, and fiscal reforms. To prepare students more fully for participation in a democratic, industrial society, she introduced both physical and **vocational education*** courses. Not only did she continue to foster teachers councils (one of the strongest such efforts in the nation), she also obtained higher salaries for the teaching force.

As superintendent, Young enjoyed unique national visibility among public educators. Her women colleagues, who composed a substantial membership of the National Education Association (NEA), were anxious that she head that organization. With nationwide support from women teachers and the **Chicago Teachers' Federation**,* Young became in 1910 the first woman president of the NEA.

As the first woman to hold such powerful offices in a city that epitomized the rough-and-tumble politics of the Gilded Age, Young attracted both fervent support and fevered opposition. Chicago was a center for women's activism, featuring the Chicago Woman's Club, the Chicago Teachers' Federation, and **Hull-House**,* not to mention the community of women faculty and administrators at the university.

Young elicited their unwavering loyalty in 1913 when, following a serious disagreement with the board of education over several issues, including teacher rights and textbook selection, she resigned. She soon agreed to return, assuming that a majority of the board would vote her a new term of office at its December meeting. Failing to achieve the necessary majority, Young again resigned. Determined that she continue as superintendent, **Jane Addams*** and other supporters organized a meeting of approximately 2,000 women to protest the board's action. Following the resignation of several members, the board reinstated Young, who remained in office until the end of 1915.

In 1917, Young became chair of the wartime Women's Liberty Loan Committee, for which she traveled extensively. As a consequence of overwork, she contracted influenza and pneumonia and died on October 26, 1918. Chicago recognized her exceptional service by lowering flags to half-mast.

Ella Flagg Young's career reflects the Progressive tradition evident in women activists both in Chicago and across the United States. Convinced of the power of institutions such as public schools to implement reform in a democratic society, she worked to expand not only curricular options for students but also educational and management opportunities for faculty. Young's greatest contribution to women's education remains her own remarkable career, which stands as testament to the ability of women to assume positions of substantial professional responsibility.

Bibliography: Judy Suratt, "Ella Flagg Young," in Edward T. James, Janet Wilson James, and Paul S. Boyer, eds., *Notable American Women* (1971); Joan K. Smith, *Ella Flagg Young: Portrait of a Leader* (1979); Carolyn Terry Bashaw, "Ella Flagg Young and Her Relationship to the Cult of Efficiency," *Educational Theory*, 36 (Fall 1986): 363–373.

Carolyn Terry Bashaw

Young Ladies' Academy of Philadelphia. A Philadelphia teacher named John Poor, about whom little else is known, opened a school for girls in 1780. It became the Young Ladies' Academy of Philadelphia in 1787, one of the most well-known examples of a female **academy*** in the early national period. When incorporated under Pennsylvania law in 1792, it became the first incorporated American institution for female education. The school was an immediate success, enrolling one hundred students in 1787. The all-male trustees were prominent Philadelphia doctors, lawyers, and ministers, many of whom had achieved national recognition. Benjamin Rush had served in the Continental Congress, and Jared Ingersoll had sat in the Constitutional Convention. Four were also trustees of the University of Pennsylvania, where four others taught. The school was decidedly nondenominational, and ministers on the board represented a range of Protestant sects.

Rush is one of the most famous trustees, and historians largely have based the ideology of **"Republican motherhood"*** on his speeches. Although the need to educate women to raise good male citizens was part of Rush's philosophy, trustees of the Young Ladies' Academy voiced other reasons: Women needed skills to help their husbands or fathers run businesses, buy or sell advantageously, cast up accounts, and govern their husbands' estates if widowed. Influenced by the Enlightenment, the trustees also advocated education for its sheer pleasure, as well as for enriching women's minds and increasing their understanding of God.

The women studied reading, writing, arithmetic, grammar, composition, rhetoric, and geography. The curriculum mirrored that of the Academy of Philadelphia for boys, which Benjamin Franklin helped establish in 1749. Not only was the curriculum similar, but both academies encouraged competition among students, a strategy referred to as *emulation*. Each half year the Young Ladies' Academy held public examinations and awarded prizes for best performance in each subject. At the close of this event, a trustee and one or more students gave speeches. Trustees delightedly described the competition in combative terms: "You have nobly contended for the prize with very formidable and determined opponents, who disputed the ground with you, inch by inch, with praiseworthy perseverance and undaunted fortitude" (Rise and Progress, p. 34). In both course work and teaching style, instructors, all male, treated girls and boys in these gender-segregated academies very much the same.

Initially, students were daughters of elite Philadelphia merchants and public figures, but by 1794, there were more German and Scotch-Irish students from less wealthy families. It is possible that these middle-class families viewed education as a way to prepare daughters for future economic self-sufficiency, probably as teachers.

Students at the Young Ladies' Academy also seem to have been influenced by the great eighteenth-century proponent of women's rights, Mary Wollstonecraft, whose "Vindication of the Rights of Woman" was published in 1792. Two years later, an academy student named Priscilla Mason gave a valedictory address in which she criticized men who "denied us the means of knowledge, and then reproached us for the want of it." She further chided men for closing doors to places women might put their knowledge to use, including roles in the church, legal profession [see **legal education***], and government.

The Young Ladies' Academy represents strains of contradictory thought in female education of its period. Some saw the school's purpose as preparing young women for domestic roles as wives and mothers. Others saw a need to educate women for tasks they might need to perform if single, whether widowed or never married. By the 1790s some saw the **teaching*** profession as a respectable option for women, presaging the huge influx of women as teachers in the antebellum era. At least a few students saw education as their right and called out clearly for an end to discrimination based on sex.

Bibliography: *Rise and Progress of the Young Ladies' Academy of Philadelphia: Containing an Account of a Number of Public Examinations & Commencements; The Charter and Bye-laws; Likewise, A Number of Orations Delivered by the Young Ladies, and Several by the Trustees of Said Institution* (1794); J. A. Neal, *An Essay on the Education and Genius of the Female Sex to Which Is Added an Account of the Commencement of the Young Ladies' Academy of Philadelphia* (1795); Thomas Woody, *A History of Women's Education in the United States* (1929); Ann D. Gordon, "The Young Ladies Academy of Philadelphia," in Carol Ruth Berkin and Mary Beth Norton, eds., *Women of America: A History* (1979); Margaret A. Nash, "Rethinking Republican Motherhood: Benjamin Rush and the Young Ladies' Academy of Philadelphia," *Journal of the Early Republic*, 17 (1997): 171–191.

Margaret A. Nash

Young Women's Christian Association. The Young Women's Christian Association (YWCA) was founded in England in 1855 and organized in the United

States in 1858 by women devoted to helping other women and girls adjust to urban life created by the Industrial Revolution. Its purpose was to help young women who were "dependent on their own exertions for support to achieve their ideals of personal and social living that came out of Christian commitment." The YWCA attempted to meet the social, physical, intellectual, and spiritual needs of young Protestant women.

Today the mission is to create opportunities for women's growth, leadership, and power, and the YWCA serves more than 2 million women and their families. While nondenominational, the YWCA came from a strongly Protestant evangelical tradition; today its work transcends religious faith. A great source of YWCA leaders came from the college and university YWCAs, founded in 1873. These university groups believed in freedom of inquiry and expression regarding Christian religion. While focusing on young women, YWCAs tried to meet the educational and recreational needs of teenage girls and boys. It also provided programs for young wives. One of the strongest missions of the YWCA was creating safe residences for young women working in the city. Today, there are approximately 450 residences in the United States and 50 in Canada.

The World YWCA was founded in 1894 with headquarters in Geneva, Switzerland. The strong emphasis on its international character led the American YWCA in 1894 to send secretaries, who operated like missionaries, overseas. These women concentrated on work with women, especially in education and health. While independent of the denominational mission boards, they took advantage of many services the denominations could provide, without being tied to male-dominated boards.

In the United States the YWCA was instrumental in founding Traveler's Aid, the National Federation of Business and Professional Women's Clubs, day nurseries, women's exchanges, and in 1941, the United Service Organizations (USO). In recent years the YWCA has been active in antiracism activities. In 1944, the YWCA began to make recommendations about the interracial practices of the organization. In 1946 the Interracial Charter was adopted, its goal being "integration of Negro women and girls 'in the main stream of Association life.' "

Today, the purpose of the YWCA is "to build a fellowship of women and girls devoted to the task of realizing in our common life those ideals of personal and social living to which we are committed by our faith as Christians. In this endeavor we seek to understand Jesus, to share his love for all people, and to grow in the knowledge and love of God" (Hiller and Sabiston, p. 179). The YWCA holds a triennial convention that elects its national board of 120 women. The YWCA insignia, an inverted triangle, emphasizes the growth of the body, mind, and spirit. The YWCA and YMCA (Young Men's Christian Association) are completely independent of each other.

The organization maintains national headquarters in New York City. Its archives contain over 10,000 books, pamphlets, and other source materials on women's concerns. The YWCA also maintains an advocacy office in Washington, D.C., and a national leadership development training center in Phoenix, Arizona. [See also **student government**.*]

Bibliography: M. S. Sims, *The Natural History of a Social Institution—The YWCA* (1936); Sims, *The YWCA: An Unfolding Purpose* (1950); Margaret Hiller and Dorothy Sabiston, *Toward Better Race Relations* (1949); Nancy Boyd, *Emissaries: The Overseas Work of the American YWCA 1895–1970* (1986).

Mary Lee Talbot

Appendix: Timeline of Women's Educational History in the United States

1675	Literacy rate in New England, based on ability to sign documents, is approximately 45 percent for women, 70 percent for men; little formal schooling exists.
1700–1750	The Great Awakening, a period of intense religious revivalism, opens opportunities for women's involvement in established churches.
1770s–1800	Ideology of ''Republican motherhood'' urges education for women to better prepare their sons as informed citizens.
1776	Abigail Adams admonishes her husband John to ''remember the ladies'' in crafting laws to support women's needs in the new Republic.
1790	Judith Sargent Murray publishes ''On the Equality of the Sexes,'' arguing that women are men's intellectual equals and deserving of educational opportunity.
1790	New England women's literacy advances to approximately 80 percent, nearly closing the ''gender gap.''
1792	Sarah Pierce opens Litchfield Female Academy in Connecticut, one of the earliest women's schools; women's academies and seminaries will grow throughout the mid-nineteenth century.
1800–1830	Second Great Awakening increases women's participation in formal and informal church activities and in early social reform movements.
1820–1860	Ideology of ''true womanhood'' encourages white women to be pure, pious, domestic, and submissive.
1821	Emma Willard founds Troy Female Seminary, an important training school for women teachers.
1824	Bureau of Indian Affairs founded; later creates system of day and boarding schools to assimilate Native Americans.
1826	Short-lived Boston High School for Girls opens; not until 1852 does Boston create a permanent high school for girls.

1831	Female Literary Association of Philadelphia formed by free black women for self-education; one of country's earliest study clubs.
1833	Oberlin College founded as nation's first collegiate institution to accept women and black students.
1833	Prudence Crandall of Connecticut, facing open hostility, opens Canterbury Female Seminary to black women students; school eventually forced to close.
1837	Mary Lyon founds influential Mount Holyoke Female Seminary, later College, attracting middle-class girls.
1837	Horace Mann named first Massachusetts Secretary of Education, giving push to common school movement and the opening of teaching opportunities to women.
1839	First public U.S. normal school opens in Lexington, Massachusetts, providing new avenue for training women teachers.
1847–1857	Board of National Popular Education trains single women as teachers for new schools in the West; Catharine Beecher is first recruiting agent.
1848	Seneca Falls Convention issues Declaration of Sentiments, giving force to American women's rights movement.
1848	Astronomer Maria Mitchell, later professor at Vassar College, becomes first woman elected to American Academy of Arts and Sciences.
1860–1880	Kindergarten movement grows in United States through efforts of Elizabeth Peabody, Pauline Agassiz Shaw, and Susan Blow in Boston and St. Louis.
1862	Morrill Land-Grant Act passed, paving way for coeducational public universities.
1863	Emancipation Proclamation ends slavery and, with it, prohibitions on educating blacks.
1865	Vassar College founded in New York, first of the influential "Seven Sisters" women's institutions to open as a college.
1867	Howard University opens in Washington, D.C., for black women and men.
1873	Dr. Edward Clarke publishes *Sex in Education*, challenging women's physical ability to withstand higher education.
1874	Chautauqua movement begins, providing reading clubs and correspondence courses as a means of popular adult education.
1875	Young Women's Christian Association (YWCA), formed nine years earlier, boasts twenty-eight associations; among first to establish training schools for women workers.
1877	Helen Magill, at Boston University, is first woman to earn a Ph.D. in the United States.

1880	Spelman Seminary opens; later, Spelman College will become a premier black women's college.
1880	Women are 80 percent of elementary schoolteachers nationwide.
1881	Association of Collegiate Alumnae formed as first national organization of female college graduates; will sponsor numerous studies of women students.
1884	Catholic bishops issue decree that every parish open a parochial school; by 1910, more than 6 percent of country's entire school population is in Catholic schools.
1889	Jane Addams founds Hull-House, prominent settlement house that uses education to bridge gap between rich and poor.
1890	Field Matron Program begins sending women to Indian reservations to teach domestic skills and child care.
1897	Catherine Goggin and Margaret Haley create Chicago Teachers' Federation, one of first teacher unions to advocate for benefits for elementary teachers.
1897	National Congress of Mothers founded as forerunner of Parent-Teacher Association (PTA).
1901	Margaret Haley is first woman to address a public forum of the National Education Association.
1903	University of Chicago segregates women from its previously coeducational undergraduate program, signaling a backlash against women students.
1908	Alpha Kappa Alpha, first black women's sorority, opens at Howard University.
1909	Ella Flagg Young of Chicago becomes first woman superintendent of a major U.S. school system.
1910	Women are 39 percent of collegiate undergraduates and 20 percent of college faculty.
1913	Girl Scouts opens first U.S. headquarters in Washington, D.C.
1917	Smith-Hughes Act provides federal money for vocational education, including home economics.
1919	League of Women Voters established; will become major informal educational vehicle.
1920	Women's suffrage achieved.
1935	National Youth Administration created to serve young people with financial aid and dropout prevention programs; black educator Mary McLeod Bethune heads Division of Negro Affairs.
1940	Seventy-three percent of school-age population is in high school; girls represent more than half.
1944	G. I. Bill passes, providing educational benefits to World War II veterans; women use about 3 percent of the benefits.

1945   Harvard Medical School accepts its first female student.

1950s   Women as percentage of college students, of graduates, and of faculty drops due to postwar influx of men and resurgent ideology of women's domestic role.

1954   *Brown v. Board of Education* Supreme Court decision declares segregated schools illegal; ironically, integration displaces many African American teachers and school leaders.

1961   President John Kennedy creates Commission on the Status of Women.

1963   Betty Friedan publishes *The Feminine Mystique*, catalyzing new women's movement.

1966   National Organization for Women founded as most widely based U.S. feminist organization.

1970   Several male institutions, as well as established women's colleges, become coeducational.

1972   Title IX passed to counter sex discrimination in federally funded education programs.

1974   Women's Educational Equity Act provides financial assistance for efforts to ensure gender equity.

1980   Women become the majority of all college students, at 51 percent.

1996   Supreme Court rules that Virginia Military Institute must become coeducational, denying argument that it should have special single-sex status.

Selected Bibliography

REFERENCE BOOKS

Bataille, Gretchen M., and Kathleen M. Sands, eds. *American Indian Women: A Guide to Research*. New York: Garland, 1991.

Hine, Darlene Clark, ed. *Black Women in America: An Historical Encyclopedia*. 2 vols. Brooklyn, NY: Carlson, 1993.

James, Edward T., Janet Wilson James, and Paul S. Boyer, eds. *Notable American Women, 1607–1950*. 3 vols. Cambridge, MA: Belknap Press, 1971.

Jones-Wilson, Faustine C., Charles A. Asbury, Margo Okazawa-Rey, D. Kamili Anderson, Sylvia M. Jacobs, and Michael Fultz, eds. *Encyclopedia of African-American Education*. Westport, CT: Greenwood Press, 1996.

Kelly, Gail P., ed. *International Handbook of Women's Education*. New York: Greenwood Press, 1989.

Salem, Dorothy C., ed. *African-American Women: A Biographical Dictionary*. New York: Garland, 1993.

Seller, Maxine Schwartz, ed. *Women Educators in the United States, 1820–1993: A Bio-Bibliographic Sourcebook*. Westport, CT: Greenwood Press, 1994.

Sicherman, Barbara, and Carol Hurd Green, eds. *Notable American Women: The Modern Period*. Cambridge, MA: Belknap Press, 1980.

Smith, Jessie Carney, ed. *Notable Black American Women*. Detroit: Gale, 1992.

Telgen, Diane, and Jim Kamp, eds. *Notable Hispanic American Women*. Detroit: Gale, 1993.

Wyman, Andrea. *Rural Women Teachers in the United States: A Sourcebook*. Metuchen, NJ: Scarecrow Press, 1996.

Zophy, Angela Howard, and Frances Kavenik, eds. *Handbook of American Women's History*. New York: Garland, 1990.

SECONDARY SOURCES

Adams, David Wallace. *Education for Extinction: American Indians and the Boarding School Experience, 1875–1928*. Lawrence: University Press of Kansas, 1995.

Anderson, James D. *The Education of Blacks in the South, 1860–1935*. Chapel Hill: University of North Carolina Press, 1988.

Astin, Helen S. *Some Action of Her Own: The Adult Woman and Higher Education*. Lexington, MA: Lexington Books, 1976.

Beatty, Barbara. *Preschool Education in America: The Culture of Young Children from the Colonial Era to the Present*. New Haven: Yale University Press, 1995.

Birrell, Susan, and Cheryl L. Cole. *Women, Sport, and Culture*. Champaign, IL: Human Kinetics, 1994.

Blair, Karen J. *The Clubwoman as Feminist: True Womanhood Redefined, 1868–1914*. New York: Holmes & Meier Publishers, 1980.

Bonner, Thomas Neville. *To the Ends of the Earth: Women's Search for Education in Medicine*. Cambridge, MA: Harvard University Press, 1992.

Bowker, Ardy. *Sisters in the Blood: The Education of Women in Native America*. Bozeman: Center for Bilingual/Multicultural Education, Montana State University, 1993.

Butchart, Ronald E. *Northern Schools, Southern Blacks, and Reconstruction: Freedmen's Education, 1862–1875*. Westport, CT: Greenwood Press, 1980.

Chafe, William. *The Paradox of Change: American Women in the Twentieth Century*. New York: Oxford University Press, 1991.

Clifford, Geraldine Jonçich. " 'Shaking Dangerous Questions from the Crease': Gender and American Higher Education." *Feminist Issues*, 2 (Fall 1983): 3–62.

Cornelius, Janet Duitsman. *"When I Can Read My Title Clear": Literacy, Slavery, and Religion in the Antebellum South*. Columbia: University of South Carolina Press, 1991.

Cott, Nancy. *The Grounding of Modern Feminism*. New Haven: Yale University Press, 1987.

Eisenmann, Linda. "Reconsidering a Classic: Assessing the History of Women's Higher Education a Dozen Years after Barbara Solomon." *Harvard Educational Review*, 67 (Winter 1997): 689–717.

Evans, Sara. *Born for Liberty: A History of Women in America*. New York: Simon and Schuster, 1989, revised edition, 1997.

Faragher, John Mack, and Florence Howe, eds. *Women and Higher Education in American History*. New York: Norton, 1988.

Goodlad, John I., Roger Soder, and Kenneth A. Sirotnik, eds. *Places Where Teachers Are Taught*. San Francisco: Jossey-Bass, 1990.

Gordon, Lynn D. *Gender and Higher Education in the Progressive Era*. New Haven: Yale University Press, 1990.

Hobbs, Catherine, ed. *Nineteenth-Century Women Learn to Write*. Charlottesville: University Press of Virginia, 1995.

Hole, Judith, and Ellen Levine. *Rebirth of Feminism*. New York: Quadrangle Books, 1971.

Horowitz, Helen Lefkowitz. *Alma Mater: Design and Experience in the Women's Colleges from Their Nineteenth-Century Beginnings to the 1930s*. New York: Knopf, 1984.

———. *Campus Life: Undergraduate Cultures from the End of the Eighteenth Century to the Present*. New York: Knopf, 1987.

Kaestle, Carl F., ed. *Literacy in the United States: Readers and Reading since 1880*. New Haven: Yale University Press, 1991.

Kerber, Linda K. *Women of the Republic: Intellect and Ideology in Revolutionary America*. New York: Norton, 1980.

——. "Separate Spheres, Female Worlds, Woman's Place: The Rhetoric of Women's History." *Journal of American History*, 75 (June 1988): 9–37.

Knupfer, Anne Meis. *Toward a Tenderer Humanity and a Nobler Womanhood: African American Women's Clubs in Turn-of-the-Century Chicago*. New York: New York University Press, 1996.

Kornbluh, Joyce, and Mary Frederickson, eds. *Sisterhood and Solidarity: Workers' Education for Women, 1914–1984*. Philadelphia: Temple University Press, 1984.

Lasser, Carol, ed. *Educating Men and Women Together: Coeducation in a Changing World*. Urbana: University of Illinois Press, 1987.

Martin, Jane Roland. *Reclaiming a Conversation: The Ideal of the Educated Woman*. New Haven: Yale University Press, 1985.

Murphy, Marjorie. *Blackboard Unions: The AFT and the NEA, 1900–1980*. Ithaca, NY: Cornell University Press, 1990.

Oates, Mary J., ed. *Higher Education for Catholic Women: An Historical Anthology*. New York: Garland, 1987.

Pearson, Carol S., Donna L. Shavlik, and Judith G. Touchton. *Educating the Majority: Women Challenge Tradition in Higher Education*. New York: American Council on Education/Macmillan, 1989.

Powers, Jane Bernard. *The "Girl Question" in Education: Vocational Education for Young Women in the Progressive Era*. London: Falmer Press, 1992.

Reese, William J. *The Origins of the American High School*. New Haven: Yale University Press, 1995.

Rosenberg, Rosalind. *Beyond Separate Spheres: Intellectual Roots of Modern Feminism*. New Haven: Yale University Press, 1982.

Rossiter, Margaret. *Women Scientists in America: Struggles and Strategies to 1940*. Baltimore: Johns Hopkins University Press, 1982.

——. *Women Scientists in America: Before Affirmative Action, 1940–1972*. Baltimore: Johns Hopkins University Press, 1995.

Rury, John L. *Education and Women's Work: Female Schooling and the Division of Labor in Urban America, 1870–1930*. Albany: State University of New York Press, 1991.

Salem, Dorothy. *To Better Our World: Black Women in Organized Reform, 1890–1920*. Brooklyn, NY: Garland, 1990.

Scott, Anne Firor. *Natural Allies: Women's Associations in American History*. Urbana: University of Illinois Press, 1991.

Solomon, Barbara Miller. *In the Company of Educated Women: A History of Women and Higher Education in America*. New Haven: Yale University Press, 1985.

Touchton, Judith G., Donna Shavlik, and Lynne Davis. *Women in Presidencies: A Descriptive Study of Women College and University Presidents*. Washington, D.C.: American Council on Education, Office of Women in Higher Education, 1993.

Tyack, David, and Elisabeth Hansot. *Learning Together: A History of Coeducation in American Public Schools*. New Haven: Yale University Press, 1990.

Urban, Wayne J. *Why Teachers Organized*. Detroit: Wayne State University Press, 1982.

Walch, Timothy. *Parish School: American Catholic Parochial Education from Colonial Times to the Present*. New York: Crossroad, 1996.

Warren, Donald, ed. *American Teachers: Histories of a Profession at Work*. New York: Macmillan, 1989.

Woody, Thomas. *A History of Women's Education in the United States*. 2 vols. New York: Science Press, 1929. Reprint, New York: Octagon Books, 1974.

Index

Page numbers in **bold type** refer to main entries in the dictionary.

About the Editor and Contributors

LINDA EISENMANN is Assistant Professor of Education at the University of Massachusetts, Boston, where she teaches the history of higher education and the history of urban schooling in the doctoral program. Previously, she was Assistant Director of the Bunting Institute of Radcliffe College, a multidisciplinary research center for women. She has published on the relationship between higher education and professionalization, the history of teacher education, and the history of women in higher education, including her review article "Reconsidering a Classic: Assessing the History of Women's Higher Education a Dozen Years after Barbara Solomon" in the *Harvard Educational Review* special issue on women (Winter 1997). She is an Associate Editor for Education of *American National Biography* and holds a doctorate in the history of education from Harvard University. Her next project studies the recent history of academic women, especially the effects of philanthropy and institutional efforts at gender equity.

VANESSA ALLEN-BROWN is Assistant Professor of Educational Foundations at the University of Cincinnati, Cincinnati, Ohio. Her research areas include history, philosophy, politics, and liberation theology.

MEREDITH BOULDIN ANDERSEN holds degrees in English and English education from the University of Tennessee, Chattanooga. A high school teacher of American literature, she also writes stories, essays, and poetry.

DEBORAH ELWELL ARFKEN is Professor in the School of Social and Community Services and Assistant Provost for Graduate Studies at the University of Tennessee, Chattanooga.

SARAH V. BARNES of Dallas, Texas, holds the Ph.D. in comparative history from Northwestern University, Evanston, Illinois. Her work examines the history of higher education in England and America.

CAROLYN TERRY BASHAW is Associate Professor of History at Le Moyne College, Syracuse, New York. She has published widely concerning women leaders in higher education.

NIKOLA BAUMGARTEN is an independent scholar in London, Ontario, whose current research is nineteenth-century education, immigration, social, and women's history.

BARBARA BEATTY is Associate Professor of Education at Wellesley College, Wellesley, Massachusetts. She studies the history of childhood and is preparing a book on the history of teacher education.

JAYNE R. BEILKE is Assistant Professor at Ball State University, Muncie, Indiana. Her research interests include educational philanthropy and black educational history.

CHARA HAEUSSLER BOHAN, a doctoral candidate in curriculum studies at the University of Texas, Austin, studies historical thinking and curriculum history.

LINDA BORAN recently completed master's work in English at the University of Tennessee, Chattanooga. She teaches high school English in Tennessee.

JON L. BRUDVIG is Assistant Professor at the University of Mary, Bismarck, North Dakota. He received his Ph.D. from the College of William and Mary.

WILLIAM BRUNEAU teaches in the Department of Educational Studies, University of British Columbia, Vancouver. He studies the history of universities and is completing a biography of Canadian composer Jean Coulthard.

REGINA BUCCOLA teaches in the English and Women's Studies Departments at the University of Illinois, Chicago, where she is a Ph.D. candidate in English literature.

BENJAMIN D. BURKS is a doctoral candidate at the University of Virginia, Charlottesville, and campus minister at James Madison University, Harrisburg.

RONALD E. BUTCHART has written extensively on the history of African American education and the history of classroom practices. He directs the Education Program at the University of Washington, Tacoma.

PATRICK F. CALLAHAN is Assistant Dean for Library Technical Services at St. John's University, Jamaica, New York, and a doctoral candidate in American history at the University of Cincinnati.

MILDRED G. CARSTENSEN is a doctoral candidate at Harvard Graduate School of Education, Cambridge, Massachusetts. Her dissertation studies career transitions of arts and sciences deans in research universities.

JOAN CENEDELLA, formerly Dean of Children's Programs at Bank Street College of Education in New York City, is an independent scholar in Northampton, Massachusetts, with research interests in early twentieth-century experimental schools.

ANN SHORT CHIRHART recently completed her doctorate at Emory University, Atlanta, Georgia. She holds a postdoctoral fellowship at the Smithsonian Institution's National Museum of American History in Washington, D.C.

DELRINA M. CLARIN, H. M., is former Coordinator of Continuing Education at John Carroll University, Cleveland, Ohio. Sister Delrina has worked extensively in religious education.

SHARON CLIFFORD, who teaches history at Miami-Dade Community College, Miami, Florida, works on the history of normal schools and southern women's education.

CAROL K. COBURN, Associate Professor and Chair, Humanities Department, Avila College, Kansas City, Missouri, is preparing a book on the Sisters of St. Joseph of Carondelet.

DEBBIE COTTRELL is Assistant Professor of History and Assistant Dean of Faculty at Cottey College, Nevada, Missouri. She has written a biography of educator Annie Webb Blanton.

MARGARET SMITH CROCCO is Assistant Professor in Social Studies at Teachers College, Columbia University, New York City. Her research includes women's history and the effects of school restructuring on teaching social studies.

KIMBERLY A. CROOKS is Assistant Dean, School of Medicine and Biomedical Sciences, State University of New York at Buffalo School of Medicine and Biomedical Sciences. She holds a doctorate in higher education.

CAROL CULLEN holds an M.A. in American Studies and is a Ph.D. candidate in American History at Clark University, Worcester, Massachusetts.

CYNTHIA DAVIS is Associate Dean of Arts and Sciences, Barry University, Miami, Florida. Her research includes African American culture and literature, educational planning, and distance education.

MATTHEW D. DAVIS, a doctoral student in educational policy and planning at the University of Texas, Austin, researches curriculum policy history.

O. L. DAVIS, JR., is Professor of Curriculum and Instruction at the University of Texas, Austin. His research focuses on American school curricula during World Wars I and II.

DEBORAH M. DE SIMONE is Coordinator of the undergraduate programs in Secondary and Elementary Education at the College of Staten Island, Staten Island, New York. She teaches in Education and Women's Studies.

JENNIFER DEETS, a doctoral candidate in curriculum studies at the University of Texas, Austin, focuses on the roles of language in the curriculum.

MARY DOCKRAY-MILLER teaches English at Boston College's College of Advanced Studies, which serves part-time adult students. She is writing a book on motherhood in Anglo-Saxon England.

KIMBERLEY DOLPHIN is a doctoral candidate at Harvard Graduate School of Education, Cambridge, Massachusetts, studying the academic lives of women professors.

CATHERINE DOYLE is Interim University Librarian at Christopher Newport University, Newport News, Virginia. Her research interests include use of educational technology in libraries.

ELIZABETH K. EDER is a Ph.D. candidate in Comparative and History of Education at the University of Maryland, College Park. Her dissertation examines women who taught in Japan in the nineteenth century and the United States.

R.A.R. EDWARDS holds a doctorate in American history from the University of Rochester, Rochester, New York. Her dissertation is "Words Made Flesh: Nineteenth-Century Deaf Education and the Growth of Deaf Culture."

LOUISE E. FLEMING is Associate Professor at Ashland University, Ashland, Ohio, where she teaches Philosophy of Education and Inquiry. Her research interests include history of education and life writing.

ANN FROINES teaches about women's education, activism, and policy issues in the Women's Studies Program at the University of Massachusetts, Boston.

KAREN L. GRAVES is Assistant Professor of Education at Denison University, Granville, Ohio. Her research centers on the history of American secondary schooling and girls' education.

BEN HALL is a doctoral candidate at the College of William and Mary, Williamsburg, Virginia. His research examines Mary McLeod Bethune's tenure in Washington, D.C.

IRENE HALL is Associate Director of Kids in Business, a creative learning program for urban youth in Bloomfield, New Jersey. A doctoral candidate at Harvard Graduate School of Education, Cambridge, Massachusetts, she is writing a biography of Alice Dewey.

ADRIAN K. HAUGABROOK is Assistant Dean of Student Services and Multicultural Affairs at Framingham State College, Framingham, Massachusetts. His research interests include diversity, organizational culture, and change in higher education.

LAURIE MOSES HINES is a doctoral candidate in History of Education and American Studies at Indiana University, Bloomington, Indiana. Her research includes teachers and education in the Cold War era.

BLYTHE S. F. HINITZ is Associate Professor of Early Childhood/Elementary Education at the College of New Jersey, Trenton, and author of *Teaching Social Studies to the Young Child.*

SHARON HOBBS is Assistant Professor in Educational Foundations at Montana State University, Billings. Her research focuses on building bridges between educational philosophy and public education.

BAIRD JARMAN is a Ph.D. candidate in History of Art at Yale University, New Haven, Connecticut, concentrating in eighteenth- and nineteenth-century American painting.

CHARLES E. JENKS teaches in Behavioral Sciences and Education at Pennsylvania State University, Harrisburg. His research interest is school desegregation.

POLLY WELTS KAUFMAN teaches history at the University of Southern Maine, Portland. Her most recent book is *National Parks and the Woman's Voice: A History.*

KATHRYN M. KERNS is Reference Librarian/Feminist Studies and Library

Instruction Coordinator, Stanford University, Stanford, California. Her research concerns the history of gender in American higher education.

ANNE MEIS KNUPFER, author of *Toward a Tenderer Humanity and a Nobler Womanhood: African American Women's Clubs in Turn-of-the-Century Chicago*, teaches history and sociology of education at Purdue University, West Lafayette, Indiana.

BRENDA LAMB received an M.S. in Industrial/Organizational Psychology from the University of Tennessee, Chattanooga. She is case manager at a law firm in Cleveland, Tennessee.

KRISTINE LARSEN teaches astronomy at Central Connecticut State University, New Britain, including a course on Women's Contributions to Stellar and Galactic Astronomy.

ISABELLE LEHUU teaches in the Department of History at the University of Quebec, Montreal.

VICTORIA-MARIA MACDONALD is Assistant Professor at Florida State University, Tallahassee. Her research investigates the history of southern culture and the origins of Hispanic American education.

THEODORA PENNY MARTIN is Associate Professor of Education at Bowdoin College, Brunswick, Maine, and author of *The Sound of Our Own Voices: Women's Study Clubs, 1860–1910*.

JENNIFER DAVIS MCDAID is a staff member in the Archives Branch of the Library of Virginia, Richmond. She received her M.A. in history from the College of William and Mary, Williamsburg, Virginia.

THOMAS A. MCMULLIN teaches at the University of Massachusetts, Boston, where he specializes in American urban history.

BRENDA WILLIAMS MERCOMES is Assistant Dean in Faculty and Instruction at Massasoit Community College, Brockton, Massachusetts. She is a doctoral candidate in higher education administration.

THALIA M. MULVIHILL is Assistant Professor of Foundations and Higher Education at Ball State University, Muncie, Indiana. Her work explores issues of gender, community, and education.

MARGARET A. NASH is a doctoral candidate at the University of Wisconsin, Madison, where her research includes women's education in the early Republic.

LORIS C. NEBBIA, a writer educated at St. John's College, Annapolis, Maryland, and the University of Maryland, College Park, teaches English in an Annapolis, Maryland, high school.

IMANI-SHEILA NEWSOME-MCLAUGHLIN is a Dean and Professor at Boston University School of Theology. Her research includes the influence of African Americans in educational leadership.

JANA NIDIFFER is Assistant Professor of Education at the University of Michigan, Ann Arbor. Her research interests include the history of women in higher education and social policy.

CHRISTINE A. OGREN, Assistant Professor of Social Foundations of Education at the University of South Florida, Tampa, researches the experiences of female students at state normal schools.

STEPHEN S. OSTRACH is an Associate Justice of the Massachusetts District Court and coeditor of *Practice and Procedure before the Single Justice*. He is a graduate of Harvard Law School, Cambridge, Massachusetts.

VICTOR PARENTE is a doctoral student in Philosophy, History, and Sociology of Education at Syracuse University, Syracuse, New York. He studies the history of normal schools.

JOAN F. PENGILLY holds the Ed.D. from the University of Akron, Akron, Ohio. Her current work is historical research in teacher supervision and nineteenth-century teacher education.

JOHN F. POTTER is completing a Ph.D. in History at Clark University, Worcester, Massachusetts, and holds an M.A. from the University of Massachusetts, Boston.

JO ANNE PRESTON is Assistant Professor of Sociology at Brandeis University, Waltham, Massachusetts.

VERBIE LOVORN PREVOST is Katherine Pryor Professor of English and Director of English Graduate Studies at the University of Tennessee, Chattanooga.

THOMAS RATLIFF teaches history and education at Central Connecticut State University, New Britain, where he received a master's degree in Early American History.

MAUREEN A. REYNOLDS is completing her doctorate in the history of education at Indiana University, Bloomington. She also holds a law degree.

PAUL RICH is titular Professor of International Relations and History at the University of the Americas, Puebla, Mexico, and Fellow, Hoover Institution on War, Revolution, and Peace, Stanford University, Stanford, California.

JANET RIDER is currently working toward her Ph.D. in History at the University of Connecticut, Storrs. Previously, she was a freelance writer and photographer.

KATE ROUSMANIERE is Assistant Professor of Educational Leadership at Miami University, Miami, Ohio. She is author of *City Teachers: Teaching in New York City Schools in the 1920s*.

ALAN R. SADOVNIK is Professor of Education and Director of Academic Programs at Adelphi University, Garden City, New York. His publications include *Equity and Excellence in Higher Education*.

RITA S. SASLAW is Professor and Interim Dean, College of Education, University of Akron, Akron, Ohio. Her research specializes in women's higher educational history.

DONNA J. SCHROTH is Associate Dean of Graduate Studies at Emerson College, Boston, Massachusetts. She studies higher education, especially technology and student support services.

AMY C. SCHUTT, who holds a doctorate in history of education from Indiana University, Bloomington, teaches at Colgate University, Hamilton, New York.

ROBERT A. SCHWARTZ is Assistant Professor in Educational Leadership and Policies, University of South Carolina, Columbia. His research concerns higher education, women's issues, and history of education.

WILLIAM E. SEGALL is Professor of Educational Studies at Oklahoma State University, Stillwater. His research explores diversity and teaching in a pluralistic society.

SUSAN F. SEMEL is Assistant Professor of Education at Hofstra University, Hempstead, New York. Her publications include *The Dalton School* and *Exploring Education*, on the foundations of education.

CAROLE B. SHMURAK teaches secondary education at Central Connecticut State University, New Britain. Her research includes female adolescents' development of career goals, single-sex education, and history of women in science.

J. SUSANNAH SHMURAK teaches at the writing centers of St. Joseph College, West Hartford, Connecticut, and the University of Hartford, West Hartford. Her research interests include women in eighteenth- and nineteenth-century novels.

DINA L. STEPHENS is completing her doctorate in Educational Policy Studies at the University of Wisconsin, Madison, where she studies the history of rural teachers.

ALINE M. STOMFAY-STITZ is Visiting Faculty in Curriculum and Instruction at the University of North Florida, Jacksonville. In addition to research in peace, she serves as a peer mediator in schools.

SUSAN CLARK STUDER is Associate Professor of Education at California Baptist College, Riverside. Her research interests include the philosophy, history, and sociology of education.

RAJESWARI SWAMINATHAN teaches higher education in the Department of Education at Colgate University, Hamilton, New York.

MARY LEE TALBOT is Director of Continuing Education and Special Events at Pittsburgh Theological Seminary. Her dissertation examined the Chautauqua movement.

KAREN W. TICE is Assistant Professor of Educational Policy Studies at the University of Kentucky, Lexington. She studies gender and education in social welfare history.

KIMBERLEY TOLLEY is Assistant Professor of Education at California's College of Notre Dame, Belmont. Her research includes history of education and history of science.

CALLY L. WAITE is Postdoctoral Fellow in History of Education at Teachers College, Columbia University, New York City, where her research focuses on African American education in the nineteenth century.

MELISSA WALKER is Assistant Professor of History at Converse College, Spartanburg, South Carolina. She completed her Ph.D. in American and Women's History at Clark University, Worcester, Massachusetts.

NINA DE ANGELI WALLS, Consultant Historian, holds the Ph.D. from the

University of Delaware, Newark. She is preparing a book on vocational art education for women, 1848–1930.

JOSEPH E. WEBER is Technical Services Librarian and Assistant Professor of Library Science at Christopher Newport University, Newport News, Virginia. He holds both the M.S.L.S. and M.A.

JENNIFER J. WHITE is a doctoral candidate at the University of Virginia, Charlottesville. She studies educational history, policy, and legal aspects of higher education.

GERALD L. WILLIS is a sociologist teaching at Salve Regina University in Newport, Rhode Island, and a doctoral candidate at the University of Massachusetts, Boston.

ANNA V. WILSON is Assistant Professor in Curriculum and Instruction at North Carolina State, Raleigh. After an earlier career in sociology, she recently completed a second Ph.D. in social foundations of education.

ROBERTA WOLLONS teaches in the Department of History and Philosophy at Indiana University Northwest, Gary. She specializes in the history of childhood.

JO ANN WOODSUM teaches American Studies at the University of California, Santa Cruz, and studies native gender systems, legal constructions of Indian identity, and contemporary Native American art.

CHRISTINE WOYSHNER is a doctoral candidate at Harvard Graduate School of Education, Cambridge, Massachusetts. Her interests include teacher education and history of education.

ANDREA WYMAN is Associate Professor of Education at Waynesburg College, Waynesburg, Pennsylvania. She writes and illustrates in women's educational history, children's literature, and the Amish.

ELIZABETH ANNE YEAGER teaches social studies education at the University of Florida, Gainesville. Her research includes a biography of prominent curriculum and childhood educator Alice Miel.

ISBN 0-313-29323-6

90000>

9 780313 293238

HARDCOVER BAR CODE